Managing Innovation, Design and Creativity

Managing Innovation, Design and Creativity

Second edition

Bettina von Stamm

John Wiley & Sons, Ltd

Other Wiley Editorial Offices

John Wiley & Sons Inc., 111 River Street, Hoboken, NJ 07030, USA

Jossey-Bass, 989 Market Street, San Francisco, CA 94103-1741, USA

Wiley-VCH Verlag GmbH, Boschstr. 12, D-69469 Weinheim, Germany

John Wiley & Sons Australia Ltd, 42 McDougall Street, Milton, Queensland 4064, Australia

John Wiley & Sons (Asia) Pte Ltd, 2 Clementi Loop #02-01, Jin Xing Distripark, Singapore 129809

John Wiley & Sons Canada Ltd, 6045 Freemont Blvd, Mississauga, Ontario, L5R 4J3, Canada

Wiley also publishes its books in a variety of electronic formats. Some content that appears in print may not be available in electronic books.

Library of Congress Cataloging-in-Publication Data

Von Stamm, Bettina.
  Managing innovation, design and creativity / Bettina von Stamm. – 2nd ed.
      p. cm.
  Includes bibliographical references and index.
  ISBN 978-0-470-51066-7
1. Technological innovations. 2. Creative ability in business.
3. Technological innovations – Management. 4. Creative ability in
business – Case studies. I. Title.
  HD45.V65 2008
  658.5'14 – dc22

                                    2007042785

British Library Cataloguing in Publication Data

A catalogue record for this book is available from the British Library

ISBN 978-0-470-51066-7 (pbk)

Typeset in 9.5/13pt Gill Sans Light by Laserwords Private Limited, Chennai, India

Contents

Introduction

If you say 'innovation and creativity are vital to growth', nine out of ten people agree with the statement. But when you ask if people know how to practise and inspire creativity in their day to day life, nine out of ten people say no.

Kris Murrin, co-founder of ?WhatIf!, *newdesign*, September 2001

'Innovation', 'creativity' and 'design' are surely amongst the most frequently used – and abused – words in business today, not least because excelling in these areas is widely acknowledged to be associated with business success. But while most managers agree that innovation and creativity are essential to assuring long-term success, many struggle with realising it in their businesses, and translating it into everyday reality. It has been four years since the first publication of this book, and while clearly some progress has been made – and existing chapters have been changed to reflect the latest insights and thinking – even fairly recent surveys indicate that significant dissatisfaction with results prevails (see for example Box I.I).[1]

Box I.1   Results from a Boston Consulting Group Survey, March 2005

- 87% believe innovation essential to success
- 74% of senior executives report increased spending on innovation
- 51% dissatisfied with innovation results

This is still partly due to the variety of meanings associated with these terms (even though companies at the leading edge have understood that innovation is about more than just R&D and products), partly due to a gap in current business education where subjects are generally taught in clearly defined and distinctive disciplines. However, if innovation, design and creativity are to play to their full potential, they cannot be taught in such a segregated way. Innovation, design and creativity are disciplines that span across boundaries, and need to be understood in an integrated manner. Some universities, such as the Joseph L. Rotman School in Toronto or the Danish University of Learning have started to develop courses that are integrative and boundary spanning.

Creating an innovative organisation requires more than understanding the design of an efficient new product development process, more than how to write innovation into a company's strategy document and more than maintaining an active research and development department. Innovation, design and creativity need to permeate every aspect of an organisation. It is of the utmost importance to be aware that creating a more innovative organisation is much more about changing one's frame of mind than it is about a changing the company's processes

---

[1] For some achievements since 2003 and some remaining challenges please see Appendix B. Latest challenges are outlined in Chapter 31.

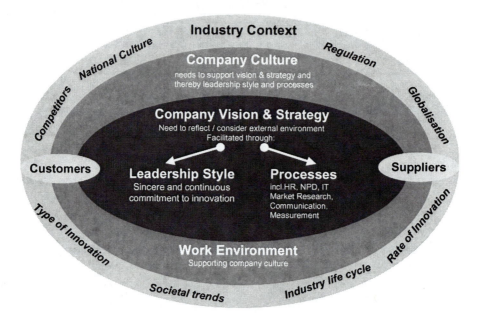

Figure I.1   The BvS innovation framework.

or vision statement. Innovation, design and creativity have to do with curiosity, a taste for experimentation, a dissatisfaction with the status quo and the desire to continuously improve things.

Figure I.1 introduces a framework for a holistic approach to innovation. There are five key areas in organisations that need to be aligned to the innovation ambition:

- Strategy and vision – without an ambitious view of where the company wants to be in the future it is difficult, if not impossible, to develop and select meaningful concepts.

- An organisation's leadership style needs to support and encourage innovation; without sincere and continuous commitment to developing an environment that encourages experimentation, exploration and collaboration and in which failure is tolerated it will be impossible for innovation to survive; this kind of leadership should be visible at all levels, but without this kind of leadership from the top you may as well not start.

- Processes are enablers and can support a culture of innovation; however, if used as a means of control they are more likely to become obstacles.

- Company culture is critically driven by leadership behaviour and supported by the tools and offerings of the HR department (unless HR is purely administrative); challenging of the status quo, prototyping, collaboration, experimentation and learning from failure are signs of an innovation culture.

- The physical work environment can play a role in supporting behaviours that are likely to lead to innovation, e.g. collaboration, chance encounters between people who normally don't meet, etc., changes in the work environment can also be used to signal the sincerity and permanence of change.

- No organisation operates in a vacuum; the 'outside' is important in two ways: first, it is about understanding the wider context in which the organisation operates and secondly, linkages with external constituencies (customers, suppliers and beyond) are becoming increasingly important.

To help understand the various components that make for an innovative organisation, and the mindset that is required to facilitate it, this book combines a set of 12 case studies with chapters on issues relevant to innovation such as strategy and vision, teams, prototyping and the built environment. The aim of this book is to provide managers and students with insights that help them create sustainably innovative organisations – rather than understand how to create a 'one-off' innovative product or service. The insights will help readers to appreciate and understand how their organisation can gain the most from innovation, design and creativity, and more importantly how to translate these buzzwords into action and fill them with life. For the ihavemoved, Black & Decker Quattro and Roche-Saquinavir case studies, a Part B is available online: www.wileyeurope.com/college/von stamm

The writing of the first 10 case studies published in the first edition of this book was sponsored by the British Design Council for which I am most grateful. Two more have been added to reflect the most recent developments in the field of innovation:

- Is the time ripe for a new business paradigm – trust versus control?
- Is disruptive innovation within a large company possible or an oxymoron?

The insights presented in this book are based on the author's own three rounds of research into innovation best practice and future challenges (2001, 2003, 2006) as well as her work with world-class organisations and insights from existing literature. The companies that have partaken in the innovation best practice are listed in Box I.2.

Box I.2   Companies that have participated in one or more rounds of the author's research into 'Innovation Best Practice & Future Challenges'

Abbey National	EDS	The Post Office Research
Allied Domecq	FedEx	Group
AstraZeneca	GKN	Pearl Assurance
AxaSunLife	GlaxoSmithKline	Rabobank
BASF	ICI Paints	Reckitt Benckiser
BBC	Integral	Roche Consumer Health
The Boots Company	LloydsTSB	Royal Mail
BP	Magic Hour Media	Scottish Newcastle
British Airways	Marks & Spencer	Smith & Nephew
BT	Masterfood	Shell
Cadbury Schweppes	The Met Office	Twinings
Cancer Research UK	Microsoft	Unilever
Cargill	Nestlé	Visteon
Castle Cement	Novonordisk	Vodaphone
Centrica	Orange	Wiley
ConceptLabs	Ordnance Survey	Wrigley
Diageo		

The 12 case studies are:

1.   The BBC's *Walking with Dinosaurs* – selling and delivering an innovative television series.

2.   ihavemoved.com – financing and strategy development for an internet company.

3.   Black & Decker's 'Quattro' – design selection and development of a multi-purpose power tool.

4.   The Lotus Elise – innovating through prototypes and collaboration.

5.   Dumfries Recycling's 'Plaswood' – understanding context and constraints for developing 'green' products.

6.   'Saquinavir' by Roche – understanding industry context.

7.   GKN's Light Composite Disc Joint – radical innovation in large organisations.

8.   The Bank of Scotland's 'Shared Appreciation Mortgage' – defining meaning of success and failure and dealing with multiple audiences.

9.   John McAslan & Partners – how to use the built environment to support company culture.

10.   The TTP Group – an example of a company with an innovation culture.

11.   Unilever – disruptive innovation in large organisations?

12.   SAM Headhunting – a new business model?

Supplementary chapters explore a number of subject areas that are pertinent to understanding innovation, creativity and design:

- What are innovation, creativity and design?
- How to organise for the development of new products.
- What are the implications of globalisation?
- Strategy – emergent or planned?
- What role do brands play in innovation?
- How to approach market research.
- What is it about teams?
- What role do prototypes play?
- Why and how to collaborate for innovation?
- What are the effects of industry and cultural context?
- What role do knowledge management and internal networks play?
- Green design – clean environment or clean conscious?
- What to do about intellectual property.
- What is the role of venture capitalists and business angels?
- How to infuse innovation.

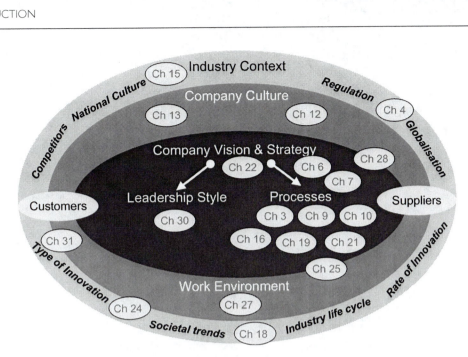

Figure I.2 The chapters in the BvS innovation framework.

- How to innovate in the service industry.
- Success or failure – a question of definition?
- What is architecture's contribution to a company's culture?
- How and when to use external consultants.
- What are the characteristics of an innovative organisation?
- Latest developments in the field of innovation.

Figure I.2 shows how the chapters relate to the Innovation Framework.

The book can be used as a reader by managers who are interested in getting a better grasp of innovation as well as a core text for business education in the management of innovation. Matrices that set out how and in what context the cases can be used are shown in Appendix A.

Acknowledgements

In innovation it is not the processes and structures which make things possible, but people. So, too, has this book been enabled at all levels by the people around me. Be they individuals in the organisations that helped me shape insights and knowledge, be it the members of the Innovation Leadership Forum companies who share their insights and learnings openly and allow me to keep asking questions around innovation. And, of course, perhaps most importantly, those who help keep my private life organised and balanced so I have my head free for things such as this book: my husband Rod Dunlop Brown and my two wonderful boys, Robert and Tobias, and my best friend and PA (Personal Accelerator) Christine von Allwörden.

And not to forget the team at Wiley – Steve Hardman and Emma Cooper, as well as Tessa Hanford, Anitha Rajarathnam, Richard Davey Claire Jardine and Anneli Anderson who were just there, not too pushy but gently reminding, and always available with advice and a quick response.

What are innovation, creativity and design?

This chapter provides an introduction to innovation, design and creativity. It sets out the meaning of these words in the context of this book, how they fit together, and introduces some useful frameworks for the subjects.

INNOVATION

New opinions are always suspected and usually opposed, without any other reason but because they are not already common.

John Locke

Innovation, just as many other things in management and life, means different things to different people. What does innovation mean in the context of this book?

Often 'creativity' and 'innovation' are used interchangeably. However, there are fundamental differences. In fact, creativity is an essential building block for innovation. This is reflected in the now widely accepted definition of innovation equalling creativity plus (successful) implementation. Creativity alone, to come up with ideas, is not enough. In order to reap the benefits one needs to do something with it. History tells many tales of great inventors who were not able to reap the benefits of their labour, think of the x-ray scanner, invented by EMI but made a commercial success by General Electric, VCRs which had been invented by Ampex/Sony but were successfully commercialised by Matsushita, or the vacuum cleaner, invented by a Mr Spengler but commercialised by Hoover. Why might that be? Let's take a closer look at the two components of innovation, creativity and implementation.

Implementation – putting ideas into practice – is made up of three aspects: idea selection, development and commercialisation, and of course creativity is needed here too. What do organisations need to achieve implementation? They need processes, procedures and structures that allow the timely and effective execution of projects; implementation is about team effort. But even companies that have all the right processes, procedures and structures in place are often unable to be innovative.

> "Whilst *Jurassic Park* is hugely regarded by the industry and is considered to be a benchmark in this kind of animation, we established very early on that *Walking with Dinosaurs* would be made in the style of a wildlife documentary, with the viewer watching the dinosaurs going about their normal activities in their natural habitat."

Taking a closer look at creativity might help to explain why that might be. If implementation is putting an idea into practice, creativity is coming up with the idea in the first place. Creativity is an essential part of innovation – it is the point of departure. One of the big concerns for many companies is therefore how to generate more and better ideas – how to become more creative. Consider a few things about creativity:

- As opposed to commonly held opinion, creativity – the act of coming up with an idea–is an inherently individual act. It is the development of an idea and its implementation where the team is needed.

- Creativity has little to do with the 'flash of inspiration out of the blue'. To quote John Hunt, Visiting Professor for Organisational Behaviour at London Business School, "Creativity is not something where someone who has never worked in that field suddenly gets this marvellous idea. Creativity is relating a concept to a particular body of knowledge. The existing body of knowledge is as vital as the novel idea and really creative people spend years and years acquiring and refining their knowledge base – be it music, mathematics, arts, sculpture or design."[1]

- There is often some debate as to whether creativity is for the selected few or everyone. Fortunately more and more people realise that everyone can be creative, just the type and level of creativity vary. Let me share a comment from a large US-based company that participated in the latest round of innovation best practice research (von Stamm, 2006) on how they used an invitation for ideas from everyone in the organisation to kick-start their innovation efforts. "What we learned from the inventory [of ideas] is the following, (1) the more people you invite the better the output, and the higher the achievements; (2) when we looked at where the best, most powerful ideas had come from we could not find any link to either a particular geographical area, nor to a particular level within the organisation's hierarchy, nor to one particular function. There were no hot spots for 'good ideas'. The ideas were rather distributed across all dimensions. The 'winners' had only one thing in common: they were all quite exceptional. So we were pleased we asked everyone, otherwise we would have missed out on some fantastic opportunities."

So while certain people are more creative on their own accord than others, creativity can be stimulated and supported through training, and by creating the right work environment and atmosphere. In her research Harvard Business School Professor Theresa Amabile identified certain characteristics that support creativity in the workplace (see Figure 1.1).

Amabile identified five environmental components that affect creativity:

- Encouragement of creativity (which encompasses open information flow and support for new ideas at all levels of the organisation, from top management, through immediate supervisors, to work groups).
- Autonomy or freedom (autonomy in the day-to-day conduct of work; a sense of individual ownership of and control over work).
- Resources (the materials, information and general resources available for work).
- Pressures (including both positive challenge and negative workload pressure).
- Organisational impediments to creativity (including conservatism and internal strife).

---

[1] Interview for the Innovation Exchange, 1999.

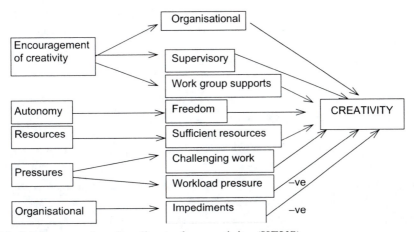

Figure 1.1   Model for assessing the climate for creativity (KEYS).
Source: Amabile, T.M. *et al.* (1996). Assessing the work environment for creativity. *Academy of Management Journal*, **39**, 1154–84.

The components fall into two categories: they are either stimulants to creativity (tapped by scales assessing organisational and supervisory encouragement, work group support, sufficient resources and challenging work), or obstacles to creativity (tapped by scales assessing organisational impediments and workload pressure).

However, creativity cannot be ordered, it relies much more on intrinsic motivation, on people being enthusiastic, inspired and knowledgeable. You cannot tell people to be more creative and innovative, you have to *inspire* them to be so.

Finally, companies tend to require hard facts but creativity and innovation are often based on intuition. And, by the way, as early as the mid-1980s authors such as Peters and Waterman (*In Search of Excellence*) suggested that the modern American manager's overdependence on analytic thought and quantitative analysis was a principal cause for the loss of its worldwide pre-eminence (as reflected in stagnating productivity, ageing and obsolete machinery, and inferior but more expensive products).

So, implementation is about being organised and about using the methodological and systematic approach of a 'hare brain' (see Box 1.1). It needs to be structured and cannot be left to chance. Time is of the essence – you need to be fast. Creativity is less straightforward than implementation, it is not about a new process or establishing a new structure. To be creative people have to think differently. To be innovative people have to behave differently. And to be successful organisations have to employ people that think and behave differently. This is why I often define innovation as 'a frame of mind'. Creativity is about being different, thinking laterally, making new connections. It is about allowing the 'tortoise mind' to work. Creativity can be encouraged, not forced. Time is of the essence too but in as much as creativity cannot be rushed, you need to allow it. Organisations that want to embrace innovation therefore need to find ways of reconciling the tension that lies in the juxtaposition of creativity and implementation.

To clarify, during the creative process intuition and thought are required – as they are for the implementation, analysis and action. However, each of the stages requires different skills and is successful under different conditions.

This has been expressed in the model of 'cycling worlds' by creativity consultants Synectics, whereby I would read what they call the 'innovation cycle' to be the creative process and what they call the 'operational cycle' to be the implementation cycle (see Figure 1.2).

Box 1.1   Summary extracts from Claxton's *Hare Brain, Tortoise Mind*

In his book *Hare Brain, Tortoise Mind* (1997) Guy Claxton makes some interesting observations about the way we think that are relevant to understanding creativity and innovation. The first concerns different modes of responding to a situation. Whereas most of the other models aim to put people in boxes, Claxton goes a step back and suggests that we all are capable of two different ways of responding to a situation. The second explains how people's unconscious exerts an influence in the classification of a new situation.

Modes of response

Claxton describes three different modes of how people respond to a situation. The first is spontaneous and immediate. The person does not think consciously about the situation and a possible response. Claxton classifies such a response as 'instinct'. An example would be removing your hand when it is put accidentally on a hot hob. No one would think whether the sensation is pleasant or not, the hand would be removed as quickly as possible. Instinctive reactions can generally be observed when reacting to a threat where there might not be sufficient time to assess the situation.

The second mode is based on 'conscious, deliberate, purposeful thinking'. Claxton calls this the 'D-mode' or the 'hare mode'.[1] The following is an extract from the traits he has identified for the D-mode:

- D-mode is much more interested in finding answers and solutions than in examining the question.
- D-mode treats perception as unproblematic.
- D-mode values explanation over observation.
- D-mode seeks and prefers clarity, and neither likes nor values confusion.
- D-mode relies on language that appears to be literal and explicit.
- D-mode works with concepts and generalisations.

It seems that one could replace 'D-mode' with 'management'...

However, traits of the D-mode are important and necessary for completing a task: a preference for structure, the ability to plan and organise, to be in control. Structuring and planning help keeping within a set time frame. Hence, the D-mode is efficient and effective when the problem is clear-cut and when there is one possible, straightforward solution. The D-mode is less appropriate when the situation is intricate, ill-defined or complex – and it seems that most product development tasks fall into the latter category, rather than into the former.

If a task is complex and fuzzy Claxton suggests that a third mode of response, the 'tortoise mode', is more likely to yield satisfactory results. This mode of responding is slower, less conscious and less 'provable'. Here a person is more concerned with understanding the questions than with providing an answer fast. This might just be exactly what I suggest organisations need to do in order to improve their new product development. The process of processing the information is less conscious and people often feel that the answer has come 'out of the blue' and Claxton argues that there is a significant advantage in allowing the process of 'slow thinking' when assessing a situation. However, today people are often not 'allowed' to let 'things sink in'. The emphasis, particularly in new product development, is on speed. Claxton remarks on this particular aspect by pointing out that 'time pressure increases the likelihood to rely on existing habits and knowledge'.

This first insight from Claxton's book provided a better understanding of different modes of thinking. It helps to appreciate different approaches – and speeds – of finding solutions. The second insight from Claxton's book I would like to refer to here concerns how we classify new situations as it might help to shed some light on what feeds our habits and assumptions.

Assessing situations

Claxton's work provides insight into how we come to rely on habits and assumptions. Assessments are often based on familiar seeming patterns, the accuracy of which was not questioned. New patterns are fitted to match known patterns rather than being acknowledged as being different. With the benefit of hindsight, it seems obvious that people have been relying on past experience, on the seemingly obvious. This is related to the issue of prior knowledge. An established mindset, or a dominant logic, can prevent us from seeing things as they are but make us see them as we think they should be.

According to Claxton this is because our mind tends to recognise patterns without us being consciously aware of it. This can lead to something being identified as a familiar pattern while, upon closer investigation, it is not.[2] Therefore one has to be aware of the 'pattern recognition process' which happens in what Claxton calls the 'undermind'. An awareness of this process can help to keep an open mind when approaching a new problem. Once an initial assessment of the problem has been made, it should then be asked whether it actually can be taken at face value or whether there are hidden layers of complexity which need to be understood and acknowledged.

However, again human nature does not seem in favour of revising a once made assessment, as Claxton points out, "What seems to happen is that we build up an intuitive picture of the situation as we go along, and it takes work to 'dismantle' the picture and start again." So if later information seems to be at odds with the picture so far, we may unconsciously decide to reinterpret the dissonant information, rather than radically reorganise the picture. And the more we feel under pressure, the less likely we are to make the investment of 'starting from scratch'.

The last observation is particularly relevant in new product development. To illustrate how our mind responds to seemingly similar tasks I would like to cite from Claxton's book where he relates an experiment, undertaken by Abraham and Edith Luchins in the 1950s.

They [the Luchins] set puzzles of the following sort. 'Imagine that you are standing beside a lake, and that you are given three empty jars of different sizes. The first jar holds 17 pints of water; the second holds 37 pints; and the third jar holds 6 pints. Your job is to see whether, using these three jars, you can measure out exactly 8 pints.' After some thought (which may, to start with, be quite logical), most people are able to end up with 8 pints in the largest jar. Then they are set another problem of the same type, except this time the jars hold respectively 31, 61 and 4 pints, and the target is to get 22 pints. And then another, with jars holding 10, 39 and 4 pints where the target is 21 pints. You will find that the same strategy will work for all three problems. But now comes the critical shift. You are next given jars of capacity 23, 39 and 3 pints, and asked to make 20 pints. If you have stopped thinking, and are now applying your new-found rule mindlessly, you will solve the problem – but you will not spot that there is now a much simpler solution. The problem looks the same but this particular one admits of two solutions, one of which is more elegant and economical than the other.

Notes: [1] 'D' stands for default because he feels that that is the mode we use normally. [2] Please refer to Claxton's book for examples and research supporting his proposition.

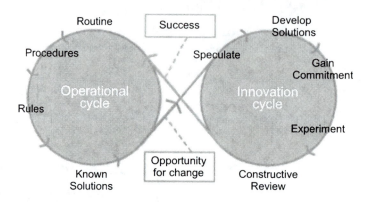

Figure 1.2 Cycling worlds.

So, it is important to acknowledge that an organisation needs both: innovation and operation, and successful innovative organisations seem to manage to balance the tension between the two cycles without compromising either.

However, the verdict is still out on whether large organisations can be good at both continuous improvements and radical or even discontinuous innovation. There is a strong argument that incremental (or continuous) innovation and radical innovation are two different beasts that require different structures, processes and systems and I will come back to that in a little more detail in Chapter 21. Proponents of this view are Tushman and O'Reilly (1997, 2004) who argue that "The same organisation cannot successfully pursue various types of innovation. There are at least two types of innovation, and companies would be well advised to divide their organisations into two to pursue each type of innovation separately. The first type of innovation is incremental and should be practised by the portion of the organisation that is focused on execution. The second type of innovation is architectural or discontinuous, and should be attempted by a separate part of the organisation entirely dedicated to that more ambitious type of innovation. In the Ambidextrous Organisation model, the role of top management is to bring together both components of the organisation into a common vision of the firm and to put in place the management process that balances both agendas."

While there is generally agreement on the components of innovation, that is creativity and implementation, there is often disagreement about what deserves the title 'innovation'. Today it seems to be fashionable to call everything 'innovation', from the redesign of packaging to the introduction of hydrogen-powered cars, basically everything that used to be called 'new product development' in the past. The literature is full of attempts to categorise different levels and types of innovation. One of the more useful and meaningful categorisations are the four categories suggested by Olson *et al.* (1995):

- New-to-the-world products (products that are new both to the company developing them and to the marketplace using them).
- Line extensions (products that are new to the marketplace but not to the company).
- Me-too products (those that are new to the company but not to the marketplace).
- Product modifications (existing products that have been simply modified, i.e. they are new neither to the company nor to the marketplace).

They are more meaningful than for example 'incremental and radical' as this always bears the question, from whose perspective? However, it is important to understand varying degrees of innovativeness from an organisation's perspective as different types of innovation need different conditions, processes and structures if they are to flourish. We will come back to that in Chapters 3 and 31.

As early as 1942 Schumpeter made some observations regarding different types of innovations, which he referred to as 'discontinuities'. The two types of discontinuity he identified are, first, a competence-destroying discontinuity, which renders obsolete the expertise required to master the technology that it replaces; and second, a competence-enhancing discontinuity, which builds on existing know-how embodied in the technology that it replaces.

'Competency-destroying innovation' – today more commonly referred to as 'disruptive innovation' – has gained much more attention over the past few years, not least driven by the work of Clayton Christensen of Harvard Business School. For a discourse and more insights around discontinuous innovation please refer to Chapter 31. A brief explanation of differences and definitions of different types of innovation is given in Box 1.2.

Box 1.2   Disruptive, discontinuous, radical or incremental?

Christensen (1997) comments on disruptive innovation: "A technology, product or process that creeps up from below an existing business and threatens to displace it. Typically the disrupter offers lower performance and less functionality at a much lower price. The product or process is good enough for a meaningful number of customers – indeed, some don't need the older version's higher functionality and welcome the disruption's simplicity. And gradually, the new product or process improves to the point where it displaces the incumbent." Walsh and Kirchhoff (2000) build on this by saying: "Disruptive technologies generate discontinuous innovations that require users/adopters to significantly change their behaviour in order to use the innovation." I quite like the way Linton and Walsh (2002) put it, "disruptive technologies are discontinuous, but discontinuous technologies are not necessarily disruptive". In their review of terminology around innovation Phillips and Nokes (2003) describe implications of discontinuous technologies as follows: "For incumbents, a discontinuous technology becomes a disruptive one when they are unprepared and surprised by the emergence of an emerging discontinuous technology, or lack the necessary experience to cope, requiring the necessary competencies and skills to either exploit or counteract this technology." This is supported by Tripsas (1997) and Rothaermel (2002) who reveal incumbents' survival is more likely if they have the necessary complementary assets required to commercialise the technology.

Phillips and Nokes (2003) give some examples of disruptive and discontinuous innovations:

Disruptive innovation	Discontinuous innovations
Sony v. Microsoft – Playstation v. X-box	GE's digital X-ray
Kodak v. HP, Canon & Sony – digital imaging	GM's hybrid vehicle
Retail stockbrokers – E*Trade and Charles Schwab	Otis bi-directional elevator
Palm Pilot v. Apple's Newton (handheld computer)	Optical fibres (Corning)
Dell disrupted Compaq which disrupted Digital Equipment	Nutrasweet (Searle, now Monsanto)

About radical innovation Leifer *et al.* (2000) say a radical innovation is something "with the potential to produce one or more of the following:

- an entirely new set of performance features
- improvements in known performance features
- improvements in known performance features of five times or greater
- a significant (30% or greater) reduction in cost".

Incremental innovation finally refers to small changes and adjustments to existing products, services or processes.

While building on Schumpeter, more recent literature, with minor variations, refers to four types of innovation. They are architectural innovation, market niche innovation, regular innovation and revolutionary innovation (Abernathy & Clark, 1985; Tidd, 1993).

- **Architectural innovation** – innovation of this sort defines the basic configuration of product and process and establishes the technical and marketing agendas that will guide subsequent development.

- **Market niche innovation** – innovation of this sort opens new market opportunities through the use of existing technology, the effect on production and technical systems being to conserve and strengthen established designs.

- **Regular innovation** – innovation of this sort involves change that builds on established technical and production competence and that is applied to existing markets and customers. The effect of these changes is to entrench existing skills and resources.

- **Revolutionary innovation** – innovation of this sort disrupts and renders established technical and production competence obsolete, yet is applied to existing markets and customers.

The categories of innovation seem closely related to the categories of design devised by Morley and Pugh (1987) and Slusher and Ebert (1992). Heany's (1983) categories of innovation (style change, product-line extension, product improvement, new product, start-up business, major innovation) are also similar to the different product categories introduced earlier. Heany provides a checklist for the categorisation of innovations, based on six different categories, which is shown in the Table 1.1.

Looking at Abernathy and Clark's definitions of innovation one could equate their first three categories with a competence-enhancing discontinuity and the fourth category, revolutionary innovation, with Schumpeter's a competence-destroying discontinuity.

A common categorisation of innovation is to differentiate between: (a) product innovation, the things an organisation offers and (b) process innovation, the ways in which they are created and delivered (e.g. Tidd *et al.*, 2001). Combining levels of innovation with different categories we arrive at what I refer to as the 'innovation-scape' (see Box 1.3).

Table 1.1 Degrees of Innovation

Is the market for product established?	Is the business already serving the market?	Do customers know functions and features?	What is the design effort?		Then innovation is a
			Product	Process	
Yes	Yes	Yes	Minor	Nil	Style change
Yes	Yes	Yes	Minor	Minor	Product-line extension
Yes	Yes	Yes	Significant	Minor	Product improvement
Yes	Yes	Yes	Major	Major	New product
Yes	No	Yes	Major	Major	Start-up business
No	No	No	Major	Major	Major innovation

Source: Reproduced from Heany, D.F. (1983). Degrees of product innovation. *Journal of Business Strategy*, 3–14.

Box 1.3   Levels and categories of innovation

Discontinuous	Cars instead of horses	Internet banking	Pilkington's floating glass	Internet
Radical	Hydrogen powered cars	A new kind of mortgage	Gas-filled thermo glass panes	Online sales & distribution of computers
Incremental	New car model	Different mortgage feature	Differently coloured glass	Selling in business parks instead of town centres
	Product	Service	Process	Business Model

Source: Based on Tidd, J., Bessant, J. & Pavitt, K. (2001). *Managing Innovation; Integrating Technological, Market and Organisational Change.* Chichester, UK: John Wiley & Sons, Ltd.

I have taken the liberty to provide examples, and added 'Business model' though it could be argued that some of this would be covered under 'Process'.[2] As mentioned earlier, most organisations still focus on the bottom left corner: incremental product innovation. Here competition can generally come in quite easily and copy. To create a more sustainable competitive advantage an organisation can do two things: first to move towards the top right corner, but secondly to innovate a number of the fields of the innovation-scape. Apple's iPod is an example hereof. The iPod combines innovation of product – the iPod itself, service and process – the downloading of music, as well as

---

[2]In his book *All the Right Moves* (1999), Costas Markides expands on how to pursue innovation at the strategic level (business model innovation).

the business model – how money is made out of it. Such a systemic innovation is much harder for any competitor to copy, giving the innovator a much longer lead to recoup the investment.

However, most of these categorisations tend to focus on the outcome, that is the product or service, but say little about the process, and the context which is necessary to enable innovation. An approach that focuses too strongly on process is not likely to succeed in creating a continuously innovative organisation. To achieve that, existing behaviours, beliefs and mental frameworks need to be understood and shifted. It is often our expertise and experience – the things that we know to be right and work – that prevent us from coming up with something truly new. Processes can support this shift, but on their own will not achieve it. That is why I define innovation as a frame of mind. Innovation is the art of making new connections, and continuously challenging the status quo – without changing things for change's sake.

CREATIVITY

The uncreative mind can spot wrong answers, but it takes a very creative mind to spot wrong questions.
Anthony Jay

In the previous section we have already talked about some characteristics of creativity. In this section we take a brief look at the origins of creativity, what kind of characteristics tend to be associated with creative people, the creative process, and some tools and techniques that encourage creativity.

In her article 'Making Sense of Creativity' Jane Henry (1991) summarises different views on the origin of creativity, identifying five sources:

- **Grace** – this is the view that creativity comes through divine inspiration, it is something that comes to us, or not, something magic which is out of our control; it is this view that believes 'you either have it or you don't', and companies subscribing to this particular view could only enhance their creativity by hiring people who are graced with divine inspiration.

- **Accident** – with this view creativity arises by serendipitous good fortune and various scientific discoveries have been attributed to this kind of creativity (e.g. Penicillin) – a view that is not particularly helpful to organisations striving to become more creative!

- **Association** – under this theory creativity occurs through the application of procedures from one area to another. Lateral thinking and brainstorming are methods supporting this approach to creativity. Henry points out that we often miss such opportunities, quoting Sigmund Freud's insight that a side effect of cocaine is numbing of the mouth without realising the resulting potential as dental anaesthetic as an example. Following this view companies would provide training for their staff with the aim to improve levels of creativity.

- **Cognitive** – here the belief is that creativity is nothing special but that it relies on normal cognitive process such as recognition, reasoning and understanding. In this view the role of 'application' is crucial, and examples given are the wide range of different filaments Edison used before coming up with a functioning light bulb. The emphasis here is on hard work and productivity, and proponents of this theory such as Weisburg (1986) point out that 10 years of intense preparation tend to be necessary to lead to a creative act. As Henry puts it, "The logic of the cognitive position is that deep thinking about an area over a long period leaves the discoverer informed enough to notice anomalies that might be significant." Companies might like this view best – just make people work harder and the result will be creative solutions. However, the research by Amabile (1988, 1989) suggests that while a challenge is conducive to creativity, demanding too much can be counterproductive. This approach also works only if the problem has been clearly identified and it is about finding the solution. This approach is less likely to result in identifying the right questions so it could be argued that the cognitive approach is about implementation, not creativity.

- **Personality** – here creativity is seen as a particular human ability, an intrinsic part of life and growth and Henry points out, "Viewing creativity as a natural talent directs attention towards removing mental barriers to creativity to allow an innate spontaneity to flourish." Given this explanation I would find the title 'skill' much more appropriate for this view than 'personality' as the latter seems to suggest that creativity is something that we are born with.

To a certain degree the different views as to what lies at the origin of creativity are also time dependent. For example, the view that creativity is based on 'grace' has dominated human thinking until the beginning of the early nineteenth century. Only since the late nineteenth, early twentieth century have people begun to entertain the thought that creativity could be encouraged and trained. It probably started in 1880 when the American psychologist William James declared, "The only difference between a muddle-head and a genius is that between extracting wrong characters and right ones. In other words, a muddle-headed person is a genius spoiled in the making."

The other four origins of creativity make some assumption that creativity is not just something that happens to us, but that it is something that can be encouraged and perhaps even trained. But even when accepting that creativity can be learned, there are some people who are just more creative than others, and much research has been undertaken to identify what their characteristics are. The report *The Creative Age*, published in 1999, by the government think-tank Demos (Seltzer & Bentley, 1999) has a rather short list:

- Creative people have the ability to formulate new problems rather than depending on others to define them.
- They have the ability to transfer what they learn across different contexts.

When looking at great innovations you will find that particularly the latter, transferring insights from one context into another, is of great importance. Think for example about Henry Ford's production line. To come up with his revolutionary production line Henry Ford 'borrowed' from a wide variety of industries such as meat packaging, grain storage, sewing machines, bicycle construction and even brewing.

Persistence . . . .

Charles Goodyear, discoverer and inventor of vulcanised rubber, as well as Chester Carlson, inventor of electrostatic copying, the Xerox process, xerography, worked for over 30 years trying to create a solution.

To move from being a creative person to being an innovative person additional qualities that are required would include being persistent and being willing to take risk. To make things happen you often have to overcome high levels of resistance – often for no other reason than that your path has not been trodden before, as emphasised in John Locke's introductory quote to this chapter.

The most extensive list of habits of creative people I have found has been developed in 1990 Robert Alan Black (1990).[3] While it is titled '32 traits of Creative People' I would rather credit innovative people with these characteristics: some of these characteristics are not necessarily important to come up with ideas; however, they are essential for their implementation (see Box 1.4).

Box 1.4   32 traits of creative people

 1. Sensitive
 2. Not motivated by money
 3. Sense of destiny (believe that you have a special mission or purpose in life you plan or hope to fulfil)
 4. Adaptable
 5. Tolerant of ambiguity (accept multiple answers or causes to a single problem or challenge)
 6. Observant
 7. Perceive world differently
 8. See possibilities
 9. Question asker
10. Can synthesize (see the big picture) correctly, often intuitively
11. Able to fanaticise
12. Flexible (willing to try things in many different ways)
13. Fluent (produce lots of ideas or possibilities when working on a challenge or simply choosing a restaurant to go to)
14. Imaginative
15. Intuitive
16. Original
17. Ingenious
18. Energetic
19. Sense of humour
20. Self-actualising (focus on developing yourself to the best you can be and to discover your specific unique talents)
21. Self-disciplined
22. Self-knowledgeable
23. Specific interests
24. Divergent thinker (looks at things in many different ways at the same time)
25. Curious
26. Open-ended (don't fix on a single idea, keep looking for many different ideas or ways to do things)
27. Independent
28. Severely critical
29. Non-conforming
30. Confident
31. Risk taker
32. Persistent

Source: Black, A. (1990). 32 traits of creative people. http://www.cre8ng.com/newsletter/news02.html Reproduced by permission of A. Black

---

The fact that it might be quite difficult to find all these characteristics in one person makes teamwork such an important aspect of innovation.

---

[3] See http://www.cre8ng.com/newsletter/news02.html.

I would like to conclude the exploration of traits of creative people with a final list, mainly because I like the fact that it highlights one of the underlying reasons for the difficulties that companies have in the realisation of innovation: their paradoxical nature. When exploring the questions in their research

- What kind of people are creative? And,
- What kind of traits lead to creativity?

Csikszentmihalyi came to the following conclusions:[4] "There may be certain neurological physiologies that predispose you to one or another type of creativity, but it doesn't seem to take a particular talent or genius to be very creative." He continues, "However, we do find typically creative individuals have curiosity and interest, and also a certain blend of characteristics often thought of as opposites":

- Divergent and convergent thinking – can think 'outside the box' while also being good at synthesising a number of ideas into a single concept.

- Energy and idleness – high levels of energy, even at a great age (though they may have been sickly as children) but at the same time almost all of them are sometimes seen as being lazy as they don't let themselves be pushed, or keep routines (this is related to incubation, and they feel guilty about it, but they also feel that it's necessary).

- Introversion and extroversion – often being caught up in themselves but also being interested in a wide range of things, interacting with others and seeking stimulation.

- Masculine and feminine – creative people tend to be psychologically androgenous (men who are shy, less aggressive, sensitive women who are feminine but also dominant).

- Passionate and detached – highly intrinsically motivated, loving what they do but at the same time able to stand back, especially when it comes to evaluation.

- Rebellious and traditional – confronting and challenging the existing but at the same time building on the past. As Isaac Newton pointed out: "If I can see farther than other men, it is because I stand on the shoulders of giants."

These lists can be used as starting points for designing training and development programmes for managers who want to improve their employees' creativity (and innovativeness).

De Pree (2001) makes suggestions for how to manage creative people. The first point he makes is that leaders should be open towards creative people and acknowledge the contribution they can make. He further suggest that it might be a good idea to protect such people from bureaucracy and legalism and help protect great ideas from being watered down – certainly a problem mentioned in interviews conducted with members of the Innovation Exchange (von Stamm, 2001). De Pree quotes Peter Drucker as saying, "When you have a real innovation, don't compromise." However, at the same time he emphasises that this does not mean giving creative people carte

---

[4]Extracted from Student Colloquium: Problem Finding and the Creative Process, Dr Mihaly Csikszentmihalyi, Thursday, 11 November 1999. Notes by Anne K. Gay; see http://www.eng.uwaterloo.ca/~ akgay/creative.html

blanche. He points out that, "Creative people, like the rest of us, need constraints", and continues, "One of the most striking characteristics of the creative person I know is their ability to renew themselves through constraints."

This is why it is so important that people are not just told: give us your ideas. Their contribution can be much more relevant and effective if they are asked to contribute solutions or suggestions to a particular problem or scenario. For example, the challenge could be, 'How can we improve our products and services to show our customers we really care?', or 'How can we put men on the moon?'.

Once people realised that creativity might not just be a god-given but that it could be taught, research into the creativity process started. In 1926 Wallas summarised his own and other people's research into the creativity process in the book *The Art of Thought*, concluding that there were the following four steps:

1.   **Preparation** – identification and definition of an issue or problem, based on observation and study.

2.   **Incubation** – this often involves laying the issue aside for a time, what was seen to be the 'magic' bit at the time and which in Claxton's terms would be associated with the tortoise mind resulting in Wallas's step 3.

3.   **Illumination** – the moment when a new solution or concept is finally emerging, often associated with 'the flash of inspiration, out of nowhere' but more likely a result of the ability to make a new connection between extensive and varied bodies of knowledge.

4.   **Verification** – checking out the applicability and appropriateness of the solution for the originally observed problem.

Comparing the various models of the creative process that have developed since Paul E. Plsek (1996) has drawn the following conclusions:

•   The creative process involves purposeful analysis, imaginative idea generation, and critical evaluation – the total creative process is a balance of imagination and analysis.

•   Older models tend to imply that creative ideas result from subconscious processes, largely outside the control of the thinker. Modern models tend to imply purposeful generation of new ideas, under the direct control of the thinker.

•   The total creative process requires a drive to action and the implementation of ideas. We must do more than simply imagine new things, we must work to make them concrete realities.

Again it is obvious that creativity and innovation have been used interchangeably which I believe contributes to the confusion that exists around creativity and innovation, and the problems that exist in establishing an innovative organisation.

Finally, without going into too much detail, I would like to provide you with an overview of some key creativity tools and techniques that are commonly used (see Table 1.2). Remember, these techniques should enable people to look at situations or problems from different perspectives so that novel and better solutions can be produced. As Einstein said, "A problem cannot be solved with the mindset that created it."

Table 1.2 The most common techniques to encourage creative thinking

The technique	The essence
Alex Osborn **Brainstorming** (1930s)	...is "a conference technique by which a group attempts to find a solution for a specific problem by amassing all the ideas spontaneously by its members" • No criticism of ideas • Go for large quantities of ideas • Build on each other's ideas • Encourage wild and exaggerated ideas Where to find out more: http://www.brainstorming.co.uk
Genrich Altshuller's **TRIZ** (1940s)	...has been developed analysing 2.5 million patents, leading to insights into how engineering problems have been solved. Altshuller identified the following patterns: **Patterns of evolution** Approaches to solving problems follow similar patterns over time; using this principle solutions from other areas can be transferred to the problem area in question **Innovative principles** Altshuller identified 40 distinct groups of solutions which he translated into 40 innovative principles **Contradictions** Altshuller patents often contain solutions for what seem to be a contradiction. **Resources** Unlike our normal view of a resource, in TRIZ resources are the things that are currently *not* being used. Look what is currently there but latent! **Ideality** Start with what the ideal solution (maximum benefit at zero cost with zero harmful effects) would be and get as close to it as possible Where to find out more: http://www.aitriz.org/ http://en.wikipedia.org/wiki/TRIZ
Osborn & Parner's **Creative Problem Solving** (1950s)	1. Mess finding (objective finding) 2. Fact finding 3. Problem finding 4. Idea finding 5. Solution finding (idea evaluation) 6. Acceptance finding (idea implementation) Where to find out more: http://members.optusnet.com.au/~charles57/Creative/Brain/cps.htm
Tony Buzan's **Mind Mapping** (1960s)	... a diagram used to represent words, ideas, tasks or other items linked to and arranged radially around a central key word or idea; used to generate, visualise, structure and classify ideas. Connections are presented in a nonlinear graphical manner. Related concepts: semantic network and cognitive map. Where to find out more: http://www.buzan.com.au (the originator's website), also http://www.mind-mapping.co.uk
De Bono's **Lateral Thinking** (1960s)	... is about reasoning that is not immediately obvious and is not following traditional linear logic. Where to find out more: http://www.indigobusiness.co.uk

Table 1.2 *(Continued)*

The technique	The essence
De Bono's **Six Thinking Hats** (1980s)	To help take a different perspective and avoid a standard way of thinking this approach asks team members to consider a problem from a particular perspective. The six differently coloured hats signify: **White Hat:** Data focus; looking at past trend and extrapolating from historical data **Red Hat:** Using intuition, gut reaction, and emotion; also imagining other people's emotional reaction **Black Hat:** Focus on negative points and what could go wrong **Yellow Hat:** Think only positively and about the advantages **Green Hat:** Freewheeling way of thinking – be creative **Blue Hat:** Stands for process control, generally to be worn by the chair Where to find out more: http://www.indigobusiness.co.uk

DESIGN

Good design is about looking at everyday things with new eyes and working out how they can be made better. It is about challenging existing technology.

James Dyson, *Ford Magazine*, summer 1999

In this last section I take a closer look at what design actually means, explore different approaches companies take towards design, and suggest why it might be worth considering design and designers in the context of innovation and creativity. It is interesting to note that an interest in design in the context of innovation has increased significantly since the publication of the first edition of this book. At least in the US, the magazines *Business Week* and *Fast Company* have made design one of their major topics, reporting regularly on companies such as design and innovation consultancy IDEO and Procter & Gamble (P&G), which has made a conscious effort to bring design and designers into the heart of the organisation. As P&G's CEO A.G. Lafley explained in 2005 in a *Fast Company* article, "I want P&G to become the number-one consumer-design company in the world, so we need to be able to make it part of our strategy. We need to make it part of our innovation process." Adds Claudia Kotchka, P&G's Vice President for Design Innovation and Strategy,[5] "Designers at Procter & Gamble historically were called at the end of the project for superficial decoration. Design thinking puts designers and several other critical personas together at the inception of the project. The power of design is leveraged at the beginning and all through the development."

A brief overview of the history of design as well as an introduction to different categories of design can be found in Appendix C.

---

[5] http://www.innovativeye.com/front-end-of-innovation/2006/5/24/claudia-kotchka-design-evangelist-procter-gamble-company.html

Looking up the word 'design' in any dictionary provides a long list of entries. The *Concise Oxford Dictionary* offers 11 different meanings and in the *British Encyclopaedia* we find 33 different entries. In addition to a wide range of options of what 'design' refers to, there is also potential for further confusion due to national differences. Even though 'design' is a word used in many countries, its meaning varies. For example, according to the German dictionary, it only means to 'sketch' or 'pattern'.

In the context of innovation three relevant interpretations of design can be found:

- Design is the tangible outcome, i.e. the end product of design such as cameras, cars, etc.
- Design is a creative activity.
- Design is the process by which information is transformed into a tangible outcome.

It seems that the last, design as process, is the most commonly used, and it is how I understand the word. For me design is the act of conscious decision making so I would vary the definition slightly and add the word 'conscious'. So my definition reads:

The three meanings of design can also be found in the British Standard BS 7000, A Guide to Managing Product Design. The Standard refers to design as a verb (to generate information from which a required product can become reality), as a noun (a set of instructions necessary to construct a product), and as a process. Three different types of design process are distinguished:

1. Conceptual Design – the process in which concepts are generated with a view to fulfilling the objective.

2. Embodiment Design – the process in which a structured development of the preferred concept is carried out.

3. Detail Design – the process in which the precise shape, dimension and tolerances are specified, the material selection is confirmed and the method of manufacture is considered for every individual part of the product.

- **Design** is the conscious decision-making process by which information (an idea) is transformed into an outcome, be it tangible (product) or intangible (service).

Design is about doing things consciously, and not because they have always been done in a certain way, it is about comparing alternatives to select the best possible solution, it is about exploring and experimenting. And exploring and experimentation are at the core of innovation.

Whereas earlier literature on the subject has looked at design primarily from a designer's perspective, more recent books on design and design management invariably make a stronger link to new product development (e.g. Oakley, 1984; Pilditch, 1987; Walsh *et al.*, 1992; Bruce & Biemans, 1995). This is correlated with the growing awareness of the importance of design for a company's success and a call for a wider use of designers in the new product development process (see example of P&G above). For example, research by the British Design Council (2002) found that 75% of small and medium-sized businesses (50–249 employees) declared that design was 'integral' or 'significant' to them, up from 54% in the previous year. As early as the mid-1980s Kotler and Rath (1984) heralded the coming of design as necessary organisational competence, declaring in their article 'Design, a Powerful but Neglected Strategic Tool' that "Design is a potent strategic tool that companies can use to gain a sustainable competitive advantage yet most companies neglect design as a strategic tool. What they don't realise is that good design can enhance products, environment, communications, and corporate identity."

The British Design Council has set up a 'Design Index', which tracks the financial performance of the 63 most design-led companies in the UK since 1993. Whether a bull or a bear market, design-led companies have outperformed the FTSE 100 and FTSE All Share index by more than 200%. I believe that it is the increased emphasis on innovation that has finally led companies to take note of this.

However, there is often still some confusion around the boundaries between design management, new product development and innovation. A contributor to the confusion around design is that, while it is commonly understood that design is undertaken by designers, research has revealed that a significant part of design or decisions influencing design are not made by designers but by other people in the organisation such as engineers, programmers and managers (Hales, 1986; Norman, 1988). These non-designers who have such a significant impact on the design outcome without being aware of it have been titled 'silent designers' (Gorb & Dumas 1987).

Another reason is the differences between designers and managers on a number of issues, and a widespread belief that designers – or creative people in general – cannot be managed. However, David Walker (1990) quotes from a letter of Geoffrey Constable, Head of Industrial Division, Design Council of 17 March 1987 in which Constable states, "It is important to argue that design must be managed and can be managed. There is considerable misunderstanding on both points. Some

> **Evolution of 'design'**
>
> In the traditional understanding, 'design' is often associated with a person who is involved in both the design and production of an object. This concept began to change with the outset of the Industrial Revolution, which initiated the division of work and the need for specialisation. Resulting from this, two strands of design evolved, 'design as art' and 'design as engineering', each with a different meaning and different emphasis in education. Part and consequence of the development into specialisation was the separation of industrial and engineering design about which Ivor Owen (1990), a former Director of the Design Council, says, "I strongly believe that the schism between engineering design and industrial design has been one of the most damaging issues in manufacturing industry imaginable." Sir William Barlow (1988), a former Chairman of the Design Council, asserts this by pointing out that almost every product requires an appropriate balance of both.

managers believe that design is something outside normal business practice and does not benefit from being managed but due to creativity and other uncertainties is regrettably unmanageable. In fact design has to be managed just as much as anything else and the uncertainties that are involved are no more serious or disruptive than the uncertainties inherent in any other task within industry that has to be managed, for example, commissioning a new factory or exploiting a new market."

Walker blames the educational gap. Whereas managers' education and training tend to focus on analytical studies such as accounting and finance, designers are educated and trained to deal with projects that involve unfamiliar concepts, are predominantly visual rather than verbal, involve fuzzy problems and high levels of ambiguity, and assessments which are "variously, subjective, personal, emotional and outside quantification". He comes to the conclusions that "The divergence between managers and designers can be detected in personality traits, in habits of thought and work, as well as in educational background." A comparison between managers and designers is shown in Table 1.3.

While people with different professional backgrounds often have differing value systems that can lead to mis-understandings and conflict, bringing people with different perspectives and ways of thinking together is essential for

Table 1.3 Differences between designers and managers

Characteristics	Managers	Designers
Aims	Long term	Short term
	Profits/return	Product/service
	Survival Growth	quality
	Organizational	Reform
	durability	Prestige
		Career building
Focus	People Systems	Things
		Environment
Education	Accountancy	Crafts Art Visual
	Engineering	Geometric
	Verbal Numerical	
Thinking styles	Serialist Linear	Holist Lateral
	Analysis	Synthesis
	Problem oriented	Solution led
Behaviour	Pessimistic	Optimistic
	Adaptive	Innovative
Culture	Conformity	Diversity
	Cautious	Experimental

Source: Reproduced from Walker, D. (1990). Managers and designers: two tribes at war? In M. Oakley (ed.), *Design Management: A Handbook of Issues and Methods*. Oxford: Blackwell.

innovation. Too often habits and what has worked for us in the past drives our decisions and behaviours. That is why you need people who think differently and challenge the way things are done. As journalist and writer Walter Lipman once said, "If all think alike no one thinks very much." That is why cross-functional teams play a key role in innovation. However, just putting together a cross-functional team and expecting it to work is to set them up for failure. The differences tend to be implicit and mutual understanding is often wrongly assumed. Eliciting the differences in thinking, preferences and even meaning of words is essential for successful collaboration.

Bringing in a facilitator who is equally at home in the different cultures can be necessary until individuals have come to develop an appreciation of the contributions of the 'others'. For example, Claudia Kotchka of Procter & Gamble, mentioned earlier, very much describes her role as that of a 'translator'. In a *Fast Company* article this is described as follows (Reingold, 2005b), "Like a simultaneous translator, Kotchka must express the language of design in a way that people steeped in sales, finance, or research can understand. At the same time, she needs to keep her designers motivated and clear on the fact that an idea that doesn't increase sales is meaningless in a place like P&G."

Teams and tools for understanding different team roles are discussed in more detail in Chapter 10.

Whether or not design actually contributes to the success of a product and a company's performance is critically influenced by management's attitude towards it (Hart & Service, 1988; Hart et al., 1989). In order to provide managers with insights into the implications of different approaches to the management of design Dumas and Mintzberg (1991) have described five different ways and an evaluation of each option (see Table 1.4). In their view the fifth style, infusion, is the one most likely to lead to the most successful and comprehensive employment of design. However, while the suggested categories give a description of what has been found in companies and are

Table 1.4 Styles of design management

Style	Critique
1. Design champion	Whether patron, crusader, team or consultant, may not be a sufficient condition for the full realisation of design in an organisation, but he/she/it may constitute a necessary first step
2. Design policy	Fine as long as it clarifies the beliefs that already exist in a company; by itself a design policy is of little consequence
3. Design programme	Sometimes causes a specific change in an organisation and even has a lasting effect when that change serves as a model for other initiatives. But these follow-up initiatives must be implemented and that is commonly considered to require the next approach
4. Design as a function	For the vast majority of companies, the influence of design is as likely to be measured by the performance of marketing or production as by its own independent efforts
5. Design as infusion	The permeation of design throughout the organisation. Infusion is informal; the ultimate intention is to have everyone concerned with design (silent design)

Source: Based on Dumas, A. & Mintzberg, H. (1991). Managing the form, function, and fit of design. *Design Management Journal*, **2**, 26–31.

important for understanding different levels of commitment of a company to design, the article does not give any indications as to how or what to do to achieve a particular level of design awareness, nor does it help a company choose the approach to design management most suitable for their situation.

The categories devised by Dumas and Mintzberg are not dissimilar to a differentiation between different levels of understanding of design given by Fairhead (1988) (Figure 1.3).

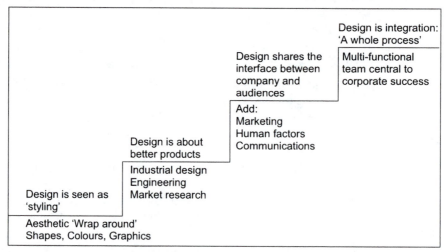

Figure 1.3 Design – The world is growing.
Source: Fairhead, J. (1988). *Design for Corporate Culture: How to Build a Design and Innovation Culture*. National Economic Development Office. Reproduced by permission of HMSO.

Table 1.5 Efficiency versus innovation

Type A: Focus on cost and efficiency	Type B: Focus on support for innovation
Attention to detail	Bigger picture
Present	Future oriented
Clarity and certainty	Accepting of (initial) ambiguity
Predictability	Uncertainty
Numbers driven	Visual, concept driven
Tight control	Autonomy
Repetition	Experimentation
Standards and procedures	Open-mindedness and flexibility
Failure = disaster	Failure = learning
Rational	Emotional
Preserving the status quo	Challenging the status quo

So, we have already heard that design is an important strategic tool, but why think about it particularly in the context of innovation? I have already mentioned the benefit of bringing together people with different mindsets – and the difficulties associated with it. I would like to elaborate on this a bit more. Think about the mindset that will be dominant in many organisations today; it is a mindset that has been formed and influenced by years and years of cost cutting, downsizing and the search for ever-increasing efficiencies and epitomised by the trend to shorter reporting periods. The people who have risen through the ranks of an organisation are most likely those who have excelled in the above. Asking these people, who are good at cost cutting and paying attention to detail, to approve projects that are characterised by high levels of uncertainty – both in the process as well as the outcome – almost feels like asking the impossible. Table 1.5 contrasts characteristics that are advantageous to: (a) driving out cost and being efficient and (b) creating an environment that is conducive to innovation. People who are extremely good at one are not likely to be good at the other – or in fact even value it. Both mindsets are essential to a long-term successful organisation.

Box 1.5 Creative traits and designers

1. Sensitive
2. Not motivated by money
3. **Sense of destiny**
4. Adaptable
5. **Tolerant of ambiguity**
6. **Observant**
7. **Perceive world differently**
8. **See possibilities**
9. **Question asker**
10. **Can synthesise**
11. **Able to fanaticise**
12. **Flexible**
13. **Fluent**
14. **Imaginative**
15. **Intuitive**
16. **Original**
17. **Ingenious**
18. **Energetic**
19. Sense of humour
20. Self-actualising
21. Self-disciplined
22. Self-knowledgeable
23. **Specific interests**
24. **Divergent thinker**
25. **Curious**
26. **Open-ended**
27. **Independent**
28. **Severely critical**
29. **Non-conforming**
30. **Confident**
31. **Risk taker**
32. **Persistent**

I believe that while senior executives have bought into the concept of innovation with their mind, but not with their heart. The rationale for innovation is increasingly difficult to ignore, the figures of successful innovators speak for themselves. But the praxis of innovation, the experimentation, the uncertainty, the 'fuzziness' that characterises innovation – at least at the outset – is very uncomfortable territory for a Type A person.

To change the mindset of leaders and of organisations takes time – anyone engaged in change management is aware of that. One way to accelerate the process might be to bring people on board who already have an innovation-conducive mindset, that is designers. By their inclination, by their personal preferences, and by their training designers have a mindset that thrives on exploration, on challenging the status quo, on developing new solutions. Look at the 32 traits of creative (innovative) people and consider what we have heard about innovation (Box 1.5).

I have highlighted the traits that are often associated with designers too and we find that they share many characteristics of creative people (perhaps not surprising as the design profession is considered to be part of the 'creative industry'). This does not mean that innovation should be left to the designers, only that designers might have an important contribution to make to the innovation process, and that they might be valuable members of innovation teams. Even though the link between skills and abilities of members of the creative industries and the skills and abilities required for innovation seems quite obvious, not many organisations seem to employ it to their benefit. As the UK Government White Paper on Competitiveness (1995) states, "The effective use of design is fundamental to the creation of innovative products, processes and services. Good design can significantly add value to products, lead to growth in sales and enable both the exploitation of new markets and the consolidation of existing ones." It continues, "The benefits of good design can be seen as:

- Processes improved by gradual innovation
- Redesign of existing products in response to user needs, new markets and competitor products
- Development of new products by anticipating new market opportunities."

One final comment on design, in the context of innovation it is the 'design thinking' that is critical. Tim Brown, CEO of IDEO has once described it as, "Design thinking is a human centered approach to problem solving. It is a process built from People (inspiration gained by looking & listening to them), Prototyping (ideating quickly to make things real), and Stories (getting things implemented by selling compelling narratives not 'concepts')." So, design thinking has four principal components:

- **Customer focus and intimacy** – really understanding what the customer wants – not to be confused with what he says he wants or what is suggested he should want (see also Chapter 9 on market research).
- **Experimentation** – the exploration of different solutions and possibilities before narrowing down on one of a few possible solutions (see also Chapter 30).
- **Prototyping** – expressing the concept in three dimensions to enable discussion, understanding and exploration of different possibilities (see Chapter 12 for further discussion on prototypes).
- **Emotional connectedness** – the end result is appealing to its user/consumer at the emotional level, creating the 'I want one of those' effect.

The case study presented in Chapter 2 gives an illustration of the interplay of innovation, creativity and design in a 'real-world' situation.

READING SUGGESTIONS

On innovation

Tidd, J., Bessant, J. & Pavitt, K. (2005). *Managing Innovation: Integrating Technological, Market and Organisational Change*, 3rd edition. Chichester, UK: John Wiley & Sons, Ltd.

Comment: A very comprehensive overview of issues around innovation, slightly biased towards technology

Kelley, T. (2001). *The Art of Innovation.* New York: HarperCollins Business.

Comment: Sharing stories and insights from innovation consultancy IDEO.

On creativity

Henry, J. (ed.) (2001). *Creative Management*, 2nd edition. London: Sage.

Comment: A good collection of articles around creativity, authors include Theresa Amabile, Henry Mintzberg, Daniel Goleman, Michael Kirton, Charles Handy and Rosabeth Moss Kanter.

Denton, K.D. & Denton, R.A. (1999). *The Toolbox for the Mind.* Milwaukee, WI: Quality Press.

Comment: Described on amazon.com as "Fresh, innovative approaches to on-the-job creativity utilize physics, history, biology, and chaos theory to help readers find new organisational structures for improved processes and products. Tips include how to design work areas for maximum creativity, and strategies for implementing innovative ideas."

On design

Best, K. (2006). *Design Management: Managing Design Strategy, Process and Implementation.* New York: AVA Publishing.

Comment: Provides insights on planning and implementing design management practices, supported by examples of successful practice.

Borja de Mozota, B. (2003). *Design Management: Using Design to Build Brand Value and Corporate Innovation.* London: Allworth Press.

Comment: Built on research into how international companies manage design, the book brings practical examples together with a theoretical framework.

Cooper, R. & Press, M. (1995). *The Design Agenda: A Guide to Successful Design Management.* Chichester, UK: John Wiley & Sons, Ltd.

Comment: Nothing earth shattering but a good introduction to design and its place in business.

SOME USEFUL WEBSITES

On innovation

www.innovationleadershipforum.org

Comment: Provides tips and information on innovation (useful websites, organisations, articles).

www.thinksmart.com

Comment: The website of the US-based Innovation Network, a rich source of articles, book recommendations, a great tool for understanding innovation called Innovation DNA and much more.

www.fastcompany.com

Comment: The website of the magazine with the same title, loads of interesting articles on and around innovation, well worth a visit.

http://www.businessweek.com/innovate/index.html

Comment: Business Week has now a section dedicated to design and innovation; good case studies and other information.

http://www.managing-innovation.com/innovation/cda/index.php

Comment: The website accompanying the book by Tidd *et al.* with more case studies, tools and exercises.

www.innovation.gov.uk

Comment: The UK's government website set up with the aim of helping organisations become more innovative, much of it is still under development; it also offers an electronic version of the Design Council's (www.designcouncil.org) tool for the assessment of an organisation's innovativeness (click on 'managing successful innovation').

On creativity

http://creativeideas.20m.com/articles.htm#General

Comment: Website with lots of links to interesting articles and other information relevant to creativity and also innovation.

On design

www.designcouncil.org

Comment: The Design Council are becoming increasingly involved in design's role in innovation, and innovation more generally. They have developed a number of tools, and also provide a wide range of case studies and stories on their website.

www.dmi.org

Comment: This is the website of the Design Management Institute, some aspects of the website are only available to DMI members.

www.nextd.org

Comment: A website that is an online journal, mainly interviews around design, design management and design thinking.

2 Innovation = creativity + commercialisation

CASE STUDY 1: BBC'S WALKING WITH DINOSAURS[1]

How it all started

I wanted people to think that dinosaurs were real animals – not monsters. The only other place you'd see really good digital images of dinosaurs was in Jurassic Park. Our idea was to create a 'David Attenborough' on the prehistoric world.

Tim Haines, Series Producer

Tim had been fascinated by dinosaurs almost all his life and recalls, "There was a footprint in the Tunbridge Wells Museum which I saw when I was five and I have been interested in dinosaurs ever since." Over the years, many films have attempted to depict dinosaurs – often with rather comical results. However, the arrival of computer-aided animation opened up new possibilities, first demonstrated in the highly successful Hollywood movie *Jurassic Park*. Dinosaurs had been a neglected subject for television-makers and no one had attempted to use the same techniques for the small screen.

Introduction to Dinosaurs

- Dinosaur – from the Greek words *deinos* meaning terrible and *saurus* meaning lizard.

- Coined by British scientist Richard Owen who founded the Natural History Museum.

- The first dinosaur fossils were actually identified as belonging to an extinct reptile in 1824.

- The oldest, or earliest, dinosaurs found so far are prosauropods from the Late Triassic around 130 million years ago. These were found in 1999 in Madagascar. The animals are thought to be quite closely related to the great sauropods such as *Apatosaurus* which evolved much later.

- At 70 tonnes the Brachiosaurus is the heaviest dinosaur, equivalent to 14 elephants.

---

[1] The case has been prepared by Dr Bettina von Stamm as a basis for class discussion rather than to illustrate either effective or ineffective handling of a management situation.

- The longest dinosaur is the Diplodocus at 45 m, equivalent to five London double-decker buses.

- The biggest carnivore is a marine reptile called Liopleurodon, it weighed about 150 tonnes, was 25 m long and had a mouth 3 m wide.

- The largest flying animal is the Ornithocheirus with a wingspan of 12 m and a weight of (only) 100 kg.

- The torosaurus (horned dinosaur) has the largest skull: 2.6 m long.

- In *Jurassic Park*, a company lawyer is eaten by a Tyrannosaurus. Scientists have worked out that it would need 238 average sized lawyers a year to keep it going.

- A sauropod's stomach could hold up to half a tonne and had large stones inside it – gastroliths – to help grind down and digest the food.

- A single Diplodocus produced about 1 tonne of dung per day.

Tim has a degree in zoology, specialising in entomology but went into medical journalism after graduation. From there he moved into radio and TV always specialising in science, medicine and the environment. He was just about to start a new series on 'Ice Mummies', but before that he had a couple of weeks to think of new ideas and he knew that the BBC was looking to create a landmark series. Having seen *Jurassic Park* he felt that there was a level of reality to

> "Like anyone who sat watching *Jurassic Park* or who has studied dinosaurs has asked themselves what they were really like, I thought, I'd love to see them alive. They are tremendous evocative creatures, quite unlike anything we have seen before."
>
> Tim Haines

dinosaurs that was not reflected in past or current television programmes. The technology had so much potential yet there was a gap in the market for documentary approaches. He wanted to create a programme that could offer the same quality of special effects that had been used in films such as *Jurassic Park*, but with his programme he wanted to recreate, as far as possible, a true representation of the period – environment, flora and fauna and so forth. His aim was to produce a documentary-like film that would make dinosaurs look like real animals. "I came up with the idea of doing it as a natural history programme because that's how we are used to seeing real animals, but I wanted to make it with top-level graphics."

Having identified his objective his challenge was twofold: (a) he had to consider what kind of money would be required to realise his idea – and whether it would be realistic and (b) he had to identify some people who could actually make such a film happen. Further considerations were target audiences, viewing time, film length and, very important for the costing of the film, how much time per show of animated film he would be looking for.

Selling the idea – phase I

The first step for Tim was to raise money for a pilot. With the programme idea being unusual and very innovative, he felt that in order to raise the money necessary to make the programme it was essential to be able to show people what he had in mind.

Securing some finance was one thing but equally, if not more important, was to find a company who could realise the animation. Initially he contacted the people who had been involved in making *Jurassic Park* but they quoted a production cost of $10,000/sec. With that level of cost for animation they would end up with 3–5 minutes of animation per 30-minute programme. This was not what Tim had in mind and it clearly indicated that they were not really interested. It seemed that people in the US were generally more interested in film work and not TV so the work would have to be done in the UK.

After generating a short list of companies who might be able to do the computer animations, he invited proposals from four companies. The responses from the first three were rather disappointing: company A's suggestion was so poor that it was not worth taking any further; company B could not be bothered to respond; and company C had changed its focus, which meant it was no longer

> "I started ringing around and I whittled it down quite quickly; there are only a handful of people who would be comfortable and capable of trying to realise this and I went round and saw several of them."

suitable. This left company D. The company called Framestore, founded in 1986, specialised in visual effects and computer animation for commercials, feature films, television dramas, video games, promotional graphics and title sequences.

On 8 August 1996, while still filming for the Ice Mummies documentary, Tim Haines went to meet with Mike Milne, Computer Animation Director of Framestore, and a few of his colleagues. Mike remembers, "In a lot of meetings we are asked to do things that are just impossible. Initially the one with Tim seemed to be one of those. It seemed that what Tim was asking for was a *Jurassic Park* for a TV documentary budget, but he was not presumptuous, as a

> Framestore won an unprecedented three consecutive Primetime Emmy awards in the late 1990s for visual effects (*Gulliver's Travels*, *The Odyssey* and *Merlin*) and since then added a further five Emmys including one in 2000 for 'Outstanding Animated Programme' for *Walking with Dinosaurs*.

first step he was asking us whether we had the technical expertise to do it and how much it would actually cost – but even at that point the other people in the meeting still felt it was not quite realistic . . ."

However, Tim had got his timing right, Mike was fascinated by the idea and had also reached a point in his career where he was interested in moving on from the commercials he had been doing for the past few years. He felt that Tim's series was something different, a piece to get his teeth into – and also something that was more meaningful. He liked the idea of a documentary, and, "Working with researchers and scientists who all had a great aim in life – and were pursuing it for not too much money." He knew he would desperately try to make it work. It also helped that Tim had a reputation for good documentaries and had worked with Horizon/BBC2. And finally, Tim pointed out that it would not have to be highly detailed shots. They agreed that Mike should create a short piece of animation to illustrate how he would realise the task.

When Tim went back to look at Mike's first pictures a couple of months later he was impressed. Mike, who had spent time in the London Zoo and the London's Natural History Museum thinking about the project, had also looked at some animal documentaries and realised that the level of detail was often not that great, it was often fast moving and even a bit blurred. So Mike took a misty shot of a rhinoceros and put some very simple dinosaur silhouette figures on top and then composited it in, so the actual amount of animation was quite limited. The detail of the animal was almost nonexistent and the compositing with all that mist around was fairly simple – but the picture at the end was utterly convincing. Tim knew they were thinking on the same wavelength when they met again on the 17 October. He recalls, "The lesson was, don't throw in 500 animators and all the skin designers in the world realising something on which you can see every scale on its body, if you don't need to. It's just as evocative to see an animal in the mist walking towards you." That's how the cooperation started.

The very basic and short video Mike had produced was a great help in raising money for the pilot. Tim's boss bought into the idea straight away and BBC Worldwide was quite interested too. This meant that Tim was able to raise £100,000, which would be enough to produce a 2–3 minute pilot. Mike did not waste any time and while Tim was seeking to raise the money he started planning for the pilot.

But not only did Mike start working proactively, Tim also ensured that the project would move forward in his own time too. While on holiday in Cyprus over Christmas 1996 Tim shot some background footage for the pilot. In January 1997 Mike and his colleague, Andrew Daffy (now Head of Commercials at Framestore), started working on the pilot. It took about 12 weeks to complete and looking back at his diary Mike commented, "I worked 60 days straight without a day's break during that three-month period." The results were impressive, better than Tim had anticipated both in terms of animated time produced and visual effectiveness. "But", Mike says four and a half years later, "while it was great at the time now we would hate anyone to see it."

Once the pilot was done Mike had to sit down and work out the budget. He remembers, "The costing for the project was based on scaling up the pilot, i.e. cost and timing for the 5-minute pilot times 6 = 30 minutes for each programme and again multiplied by 6 for the series; 6 times 2 animators would be needed plus technical staff and admin, etc." This was quite different from how a project would normally be costed within the industry. Work in the industry would normally be based on a 'rate card', which is generally available in all meeting rooms. It means a project is costed based on hourly rates for both people and equipment – but this would have pushed the budget far beyond its limits. So Mike went to see the financial director and together they worked out how to do it another way. One decision was to recruit college graduates rather than experienced animators, another was to get second-hand equipment. However, compromising quality of equipment was not an option for compositing. They realised that they did not have the required number of machines for compositing available but new machines would have cost £800,000 apiece, which was out of the question. So they decided to make do with the machines available but to run them around the clock, staffed with junior staff. As Mike recalls, "We basically treated the project like a start-up." The original idea had been to hire a warehouse for 18 months to bring the team together but eventually it proved more workable to use a floor in the building where Framestore was located.

The proposal they finally came up with was based on cost plus a small profit – and that was exactly how they presented it to the BBC, being entirely open about cost and profit. Tim ended up with a total cost for the series of £6.2 million, including all shooting, location, puppets, sculptures, music, expenses for travel and so on.

Selling the idea – phase II

The budget the BBC is willing to commit to any programme depends on the broadcasting slot and the target audience for the programme. It also depends on the type of programme, for example, a soap opera can be made for much less than £1 million an hour – Tim needed about twice that for his series. A project of this financial scope was new ground for the BBC. However, the BBC was always looking for innovative and new programmes and Tim was convinced, "If we could produce the programme how we imagined it, then it would not only be very novel but also likely to attract a wide audience. The programme was not aimed at dinosaur buffs but whole families who could sit down together and watch it. This was something which the BBC was very keen to encourage."

Armed with the pilot and budget requirements Tim set about securing funding for the series. As Tim had anticipated, the pilot made all the difference. Alix Tidmarsh, Global Intellectual Property Director, BBC Worldwide, remembers, "It enabled people to understand what was in Tim's head and what they would get for their money." Or in Tim's words, "When we showed the pilot to people they immediately understood what we were planning to do – and bought into it."

Within the BBC fund raising did not prove too difficult. It was decided to take the idea forward because it seemed simple and achievable, and, nothing like that had been done on television before. Between them BBC Broadcasting and BBC Worldwide contributed £3.5 million. In total Tim ended up with six investors, besides the two departments of the BBC, ProSieben of Germany, TV Asahi of Japan, France 3 and the Discovery Channel (US) put up money for the programme. While the level of funding was unusually high for the BBC, it still meant that they would not be able to afford more than £1 million per show – not an overly generous budget for a programme that would rely almost exclusively on computer animation.

The development and its challenges

While the fact that they had been able to gain support from television companies around the world was a great success, it also had its downside as it meant that Tim would have to please six masters. The issues were not so much about content, that was clearly the domain of the producer, but different countries had different requirements in other respects, particularly with regards to programme length. This caused big discussions about the format of the series, that is how long each programme should be and how many parts the series would have. For example, the BBC would develop 30-minute programmes, commercial stations would be looking for 50 minutes of production plus 10 minutes for advertising. In the end there was no common format but individual countries would follow what was most appropriate for their environment: in the UK the series was scheduled to run in six 30-minute sessions, the US planned to broadcast a three-hour session with scientists' comments in between and Japan planned to incorporate its own work too. However, in the end all changes had to be approved by the BBC and individual countries were not allowed to alter the creative content of the product. It was Tim's responsibility to negotiate and give his final approval – although, as Alix pointed out, "One has to realise that it can be very difficult if not impossible to control, in the end it becomes a matter of trust and relationships, and it is very important that everyone gets on board early and buys into the idea at the outset."

As the team wanted to make sure that the dinosaur world came alive with as much realism and accuracy as possible, they set about the challenge to making something that was scientifically rigorous as well as being dramatic and entertaining. This meant that important preparatory work had to be done before they could start:

- the right locations had to be found
- dinosaurs to be featured in the series had to be identified, and
- the time periods covered in individual programmes had to be agreed.

This meant consulting with experts in the field. As Tim recalls, "We spent a year and a half designing the storyboards. In the process we consulted over 100 palaeontologists, their area of expertise varying from dinosaur footprints to dinosaur movement to dinosaur dung, all to ensure the programmes would be informed by the latest scientific thinking. In addition, we had a dedicated palaeontologist working with us in that time and a further seven who acted as scientific advisors – each series had its own specialist." Before Mike and his team could go to work, Tim arranged for several of the world's leading palaeontologists to visit Framestore to give staff a two-day intensive course.

As well as the palaeontologists, there were the palaeobotanists and palaeoentomologists and palaeoclimatologists and geologists, etc. What the team was not quite prepared for was that the palaeontologists would all disagree with each other, there did not seem to be one single truth. In the end it was about making the best possible judgement given the information available. The discussions and debates throughout the cooperation were not only educational for the BBC team. The scientific community generally does not have the kind of money available for television work, so scientists would otherwise not have been able to spend the amount of money and time on investigating a particular aspect of dinosaurs, for example how dinosaurs might have moved. It was in the interest of both parties to work together to generate the best knowledge possible because in the end it was all about testing theories that could never be proved. In addition to seeking scientists' advice the team drew on the BBC's natural history library, making cuts of every animal documentary they found to give the animators stimulating ideas about how animals might move.

All the creatures that the team 'created' had to give a realistic impression of scale. Tim comments, "The scale is a very difficult thing if you don't have a human there, you can't tell specific sizes. Since we couldn't put humans in, we tried very hard to get that moment of 'wow, isn't he big!' through the way we designed the shots. Using low camera work and wide angles we tried to achieve a sense of their enormity."

Walking with Dinosaurs took over three years to produce, with 18 months spent on research and two years on production. Asked how long it took to shoot a typical scene producer, Jasper James, answered, "In terms of person-hours, the programmes took 75,000 times longer to make than to watch – the animation was the slow bit not the filming – a 5-minute scene takes about four days to shoot."

Locations and dinosaurs

Location was the first big challenge for the desire to make the film as realistic as possible. Finding the right locations for the filming was not as simple as it may seem. Tim explains, "There was no grass in the dinosaurs' world and no birds (at least, none until the very end of the dinosaurs' reign), so finding places where the pictures looked right and weren't disturbed by today's local wildlife was rather tricky." Joanna Wright, a colleague of Tim's, travelled the globe twice for about three months to find suitable film locations where prehistoric plants had survived and there was no grass, flower or deciduous trees. They ended up with locations as diverse as New Zealand, Australia, Bahamas, New Caledonia, Chile, California and Tasmania.

Over a period of 14 months they filmed in these locations for a total of 27 weeks. Jasper James, recalls, "We were on location about one month at a time, very long hours, hard work, sometimes wonderful, sometimes horrible – nearly always uncomfortable, but the places were beautiful." The plan was to shoot between 10 and 12 set-ups a day but the schedule had to be flexible to allow for incidents. For example, on one occasion in Tasmania they had three days of heavy rain mixed with snow, and were unable to film a single frame. However, on one of their best single day's shooting they covered 26 set-ups. The film crew averaged 10 people; in comparison a miniseries can have a crew of up to 100 strong.

Choosing the dinosaurs was simpler. While it was a long process in as much as it required the gathering and sorting of a great deal of information, they basically went for the ones that were best researched. They made sure that there was a very large fossil site underlying each programme. As Tim pointed out, "There is so little to go on from the fossil record that we need as much help as possible!" See Appendix 2.1 for a list of the stars of the show.

> **How do you know what vegetation was around at the time of the dinosaurs?**
>
> Plants get fossilised just like animals do, although those without hard woody parts tend to get preserved less frequently. Also we have fossilised dung – called coprolites – which tell us not only what plants were around but what the animals were eating! The pollen from plants, though, is often fossilised. This may sound strange, but many millions of pollen grains are produced by plants, and they also have a relatively tough coating, so they do fossilise quite well. It is possible to tell apart pollen grains from different plants (though not always possible to identify which plants it came from), so they can be very useful in telling what species were around when – and where.

Attention to detail

Whatever was decided on, the team tried to stick to what they could reasonably predict rather than speculating wildly. They wanted to avoid any uncertain aspects. Although, as Tim points out, "Of course the simple fact that dinosaurs don't exist any more meant that the production team faced a number of challenges! The research was straightforward enough but we encountered a huge range of conflicting scientific opinions. So, a consensus had to be reached based on the theories with the most evidence to support them." Fortunately, many palaeontologists were happy to help because the programmes would be the first time their research would be brought to life. *Jurassic Park* had certainly been spectacular but it had not been an accurate portrayal of dinosaur life.

With regards to details on individual dinosaurs, stature and size were probably the easiest to answer. Fossilised bones gave a lot of clues as to where muscles would have attached and how big each animal would have been. Other aspects were not as clear-cut, for example speed and motion of dinosaurs, as well as skin colour and behaviours. For all aspects the team sought best advice and then made the best possible decision on the knowledge gathered. For example, as to how they determined at what speed a certain dinosaur would travel researcher Alex Freeman explained, "It was difficult, but not impossible, to estimate the speeds of dinosaurs from their trackways. By measuring the spacing between the feet it should be possible to calculate the running or walking speed – if only we knew the length of the legs. It is rare that we can identify footprints as belonging to a particular dinosaur, but it is possible to estimate roughly the length of the legs of the dinosaur from the size of its feet! Therefore we can make a good guess at the speeds of different dinosaurs."

Detailing the skin was another difficult issue. Initially they tried to use photographs for the skin – but that did not work. However, in some cases they were lucky and some dinosaur skin imprints had been found which showed exactly what some dinosaurs' skin had been like. But there was no direct evidence of any dinosaur's colour, so they had to make guesses using modern animals' colours as a guide. They were also lucky in finding an expert during their recruitment process; a chap called Daren Horley rang up and asked whether they had someone to do the skin for the dinosaurs. He explained that he was a commercial artist but that he had learned everything one possibly could about dinosaurs and their skin. The BBC had originally employed a graphic designer but the first dinosaur that had come to Framestore had not been too realistic, so when Mike showed Tim a dinosaur painted by Darren he got the job. Daren painted highly detailed skin in Photoshop, which was then pasted onto the models.

Just like the colour, sounds were very difficult to speculate about, as Tim explains, "A little brown bird can make an extraordinary set of sounds. In the end, we created sounds that seemed to fit the size and shape of the body."

Theory into praxis

In preparation for the project Framestore decided to hire people rather than put them on time contracts as was often done in the industry. Mike believed that after the making of *Walking with Dinosaurs* this kind of business would take off. He strongly believed this business had a future – he just knew it would be big. However, one problem was to get the right people. For computer-generated imaging there were not many skilled people in the UK. Unlike in the US, at the time no one in the UK offered proper training in that area. Mike points out, "Computer animation is an animation job, not a computer job." Not being able to rely on conventional avenues of recruitment he approached two people from a games company he had come across in an animation software user group. Although the games industry was generally not too well regarded in the industry, these people tended to be quite skilled at animation, work fast and know what they were doing. And, as Mike recalls, "They were desperate to get out and get into something more meaningful. And", he adds, "these two turned out to be our secret weapon." He ended up with a team of about 30, made up of 15 computer animation staff, including nine animators, three technical support staff, one skin designer, two part-time programmers, a team of six to eight worked on the compositing aspects, putting the images together, with the remaining seven to nine working on production and administration.

The project was set up in a completely isolated unit – one reason was to get away from 'infection'. People tended to work on a number of projects and there was always one going wrong, Mike did not want the bad tension to affect the team. Instead he wanted all people to be 100% committed to the project, own it, feel responsible for its success and for solving problems. He wanted people to feel part of a family, of 'being in it together'. He deliberately wanted to create an atmosphere of 'us and them' in the organisation – which was very much against what people at Framestore were used to. He highlighted another reason, "If people work on more than one project and come up against a problem that is tricky, they move onto another project and solve all easier problems first. People tend to postpone working on the most difficult tasks – at least working on the less difficult tasks gives people the sense that they achieve something. If there is only one project to work on, you cannot avoid working on the tricky problems." Mike also decided to emulate American working conditions and divide tasks up among his team according to individual skills. Normal practice in computer graphics across Europe was for staff to become generalists. Framestore decided that to meet the BBC's deadline and produce the highest quality work, the team should make the maximum use of individual skill and over the course of the project each team member became a specialist in their own area.

Walking with Dinosaurs was produced using a combination of CGI (computer-generated images) and 'animatronics'. CGI means that the images come out of the computer rather than being externally generated and then manipulated by the computer. 'Animatronics' – animated models – were used for many of the close-up shots. While computer graphics were good, animatronics were better for long distance shots. Animatronics were more realistic in close-up work, such as a dinosaur eating or drinking. Mike estimated that about 80% of the series had been done in CGI, the remaining 20% using animatronics (made by a UK-based company called Crawley Creatures). An animatronic model could take between two weeks to two months to make. The result was 20 minutes of animation per 30-minute session, in *Jurassic Park* in comparison there were about 7–8 minutes for the entire film.

Tim drew up storyboards thinking he might have to accept that his ideas could not be realised. "I had an ideal that I wanted to aim for but I was always prepared to forget things and try to find another way round things. But Mike Milne and Framestore have this foolish 'can do' policy, so they threw themselves at everything we asked them to do and, as time passed, in fact the reverse happened. They would say, 'You know how the script says that this dinosaur does this? Well, why don't we have him walk right into the camera?' so the whole thing fed off itself and as you are riding the crest of the wave, things just get better and better. None of us was complacent, we were all perfectionists saying, 'no, we can do better' and 'no, let's try that again' and that's fundamental." Mike's praise was equal, "Tim proved to be very flexible, he was willing to change the brief/story if the way he initially proposed was too difficult or too expensive to do."

But the biggest challenge remained how to make something unreal look real. To get an idea about dinosaur movement and behaviour much time was spent studying existing natural history documentaries. Framestore realised that a range of techniques would be needed to make the film look as realistic as possible. Tim explained, "The majority of shots in a documentary have a moving camera, either hand-held, panning or tilting. These we had to create without the assistance of motion control or repeatable memory heads, this was especially difficult for several interaction plates that needed to match seamlessly. We also gathered technical information for every shot which would be used later for creating lighting."

> "Whilst *Jurassic Park* is hugely regarded by the industry and is considered to be a benchmark in this kind of animation, we established very early on that *Walking with Dinosaurs* would be made in the style of a wildlife documentary, with the viewer watching the dinosaurs going about their normal activities in their natural habitat."

The making of dinosaurs

The BBC commissioned three sculptors to produce highly detailed scale models of each of the dinosaurs, based on their skeletons and the most up-to-date research. These were then scanned using Soho Cyberscan, Framestore's state-of-the-art scanning system, specially developed for the project, and which, by using a laser scanner on a robot arm, could build up an incredibly detailed and accurate image. A major challenge was preserving the skin detail of the dinosaur models without overloading the database – a challenge met by a breakthrough in programming made by team member Andy Lomas. A crude version of each character was generated to allow animators to track movements and check positions without overloading the system with too much data. Only towards the end of the process was minute detail, such as skin colour and texture, put back into the image. "One of the fundamental needs for animators are systems that operate with enough speed to enable them to animate intuitively," explains Mike Milne, "SoftImage does not allow animators to switch between simple and complex images swiftly, so another of our team members, Alex Parkinson, built a system that could."

Daren Horley, responsible for designing the dinosaurs' skin, looked at different species in detail, and found himself facing a dilemma. "Ken Carpenter, a palaeontologist from the University of Colorado, was kind enough to leave me some casts of skin impressions from a Stegosaurus. The thing that struck me was the small size of the scales, on a large animal they would be all but invisible at a distance. I discovered that to make the scale texture show up at TV resolution I had to make them reasonably large; it became an informed compromise between what was scientifically accurate and what looked right. The BBC suggested a look that utilised a lot of colour, but I felt that we might risk a toy-like appearance and favoured a muted colour palette."

Bringing the dinosaurs to life

Putting dinosaurs into a background was not an issue, that was something Framestore did all the time but the question was, how to get life-like creatures with life-like movements? A first idea was to use real animals and transfer their movements to the dinosaurs, that was what Mike had done for the pilot (rhinos, elephants) but Mike felt that if only they could get the movements right they would not have to worry too much about the rest. The problem was that there were not many animals around they could use. The right people at the right time helped overcome this issue. Mike remembers, "We were very lucky. The two people I recruited from the games industry were absolutely brilliant, they could not only make movement look just right, they were also very fast doing so. Had we not found them it could have been a big problem."

How long on average did it take to make a fully rendered computer generated (CG) dinosaur?

On average: two weeks to build the CG model from the scanned maquette, two weeks to paint the textures, three to four weeks to animate the basic walks, runs, etc., another four to six weeks to animate all the shots, about three weeks for the computer to render all the frames, and then a couple of weeks to combine the images with the live-action backgrounds.

But even the animation of the animals was only part of the equation. The computer-generated dinosaurs needed to be placed onto live action backgrounds – and they needed to interact with the environment. So it was decided to film various bushes, trees, plants, driftwood and rocks against a portable bluescreen. Using a bluescreen would allow the placing of individual elements together or add aspects into a scene without encountering problems with the background. The BBC crew also scaled trees and tweaked branches with string to simulate a dinosaur's shoulder brushing against it, and threw stones into streams to create splashes where the dinosaur's feet would tread. In the studio dust clouds, splashes, water sprays, drips, etc., were also filmed against a bluescreen backdrop. All camera angles and lenses had to be measured meticulously to make sure that the dinosaur animation matched the movement in the background plates. Lighting references had to be taken (using high-tech equipment such as footballs) to ensure a perfect match for compositing.

Footage was loosely cut together, crude block animations were then placed onto the background plates to give a sense of timing, followed by the modelling and animation. Subtle effects such as reflections in water and shadows were then added and the grading matched between each shot. Once this had been completed the most detailed images of the dinosaurs were composited onto the background plates, using Infemo and Henry, and bluescreen layers were added. Simulations of hand-held camera effects such as pans and tilts were added towards the end of the process, along with other effects such as motion blur to lend realism to the shots. (For more details on the stages of the animation process refer to Appendix 2.2.)

If I only had time . . .

They created a word 'blockmatic' – block-out animation. Mike explains, "It meant you had to decide two things. First, how many creatures are in the picture and second, how fast they are going to move, no more. Setting up the entire episode like that helps the producer to get a feel for the whole flow and it does not require a great creative genius to achieve that. That completed Tim would then decide what actions he would want the dinosaurs to do in each scene. The advantage of breaking it down into such steps is that they are non-threatening and achievable." Mike adds, "and, at any time you have got something you can deliver".

"When working in the creative industry", Mike comments, "it is essential to know when to stop." Creative people tend to want to refine and refine and refine. During the

> ## Computers and software behind the dinosaurs
>
> Framestore used SoftImage, a specialised animation software, costing about £10,000, for all modelling, animation and rendering. The combining of images with live action was done on special machines called "Henry" and "Inferno" which cost nearly half a million pounds. In terms of hardware they used Silicon Graphics Octanes for the animation, dual Pentium IIs for the rendering. The Octanes were not all that powerful – about 200 MHz with 256 MB RAM but they had special graphics boards for really fast previewing. The rendering machines had twin 700 MHz processors with 1 GB RAM.

making of *Walking with Dinosaurs* Mike took the shots out from the previous day first thing the next morning and put them onto the computer. That way he knew exactly what/how much had been done. He would make the decision when something was finished, which members of the team might have argued with, saying that they would want to spend more time on a particular scene but he had the final say. In his view it was preferable to be able to deliver than refine the product endlessly. He explains, "One has to set limits in one's own mind as to what it is people get out of the documentary rather than getting it 100% right." Another way to manage a huge task was to break down the creative tasks into manageable chunks. "But", he emphasises, "you need to do it all in parallel, so at any time there is a finished product and you can see it all at the same level [of quality], then elevate it to the next level, etc."

However, seven months into the project they had still not a single episode completed. Framestore's Managing Director was getting really worried. Mike on the other hand felt that the learning from the first episode would enable them to do the rest much faster later on. They were also developing a set of behaviours that could be used in all scenes. About one-sixth to one-tenth of the scenes would be special and more detailed but going over the same ground again and again was kept to a minimum.

When they were just about one year into the project Mike decided to call a crisis meeting, he felt they had a serious decision to make. They had lost too much time in the beginning and were now running out of time. Mike went to the team and suggested they hire more people to get the work done. This would mean that the profit would get blown out of the window but at least they would be able to deliver on time. The team though did not agree with this. Mike remembers, "They just said, 'no way, not a good idea'. But the good thing was that a few days later they came back with a counter suggestion: the existing team should split in two and just get on with it. Their argument was that they would have to spend so much time training the newcomers they might as well do it themselves. Splitting the existing team in two meant that they could work on the two most straightforward episodes simultaneously." Though the arithmetic seemed a bit strange, it worked, though Mike admits that the quality for one of the two suffered a bit. However, on the upside, the episode for which quality was slightly compromised was set under water where the scenery was so beautiful that it did not need such high quality to have a positive impact on the viewer.

Working with BBC Global Brand Management

In the late 1990s the BBC decided to respond to an increasingly globalised marketplace of television and entertainment. In 1998, about halfway through the development of *Walking with Dinosaurs*, the BBC set up the Global Marketing and Brand Development Department (GMBD) to coordinate and manage products that would sell across media and globally. Part of the responsibility of the new department was to create and ensure brand consistency across the range of products developed in association with a programme.

The new department was part of BBC Worldwide, the commercial arm of the BBC whose responsibility it was to maximise revenues from BBC properties (programmes, brands) so as to generate cash to be reinvested into quality BBC programming. As part of BBC Worldwide, GMBD's remit was to coordinate and raise investment for new projects, liaise with production to develop ancillary products appropriate to the brand, and position those products effectively in the marketplace thereby generating revenues for BBC Worldwide and the BBC.

GMBD played an essential part in realising new productions. First and foremost, BBC Worldwide would acquire the rights from the BBC in return for its investment. Secondly, it would cooperate with production to develop a brand proposition in keeping with television and translate this into brand and style guides[2] – this process aided the crystallisation of a unique selling proposition of a production. Prior to the setting up of GMBD such decisions would have been left to the discretion of the producer. Thirdly, GMBD tended to take a strategic perspective on the development of BBC properties. It would look to identify opportunities across new media, new channels and routes to market.

Throughout programme development the team in BBC Worldwide would also make sure that producers are aware of the commercial necessities. For example, in countries such as Japan, the use of a presenter can cause problems. The Japanese audience would not have responded positively to a British presenter and would require their own. A similar reaction could be expected in France where the issue has more to do with the French perception that the presenter format 'talks down' to the audience. While many producers are aware of commercial necessities when developing programme content and structure, there can be a conflict between commercial and creative interests. And while this may not be explicitly expressed Tim comments, "BBC Worldwide would rarely directly object to any project by a producer but whether they thought it was worth it or not would be reflected in the money they were willing to put up. In the end getting a film off the ground means ensuring that everyone's needs are met." Paul Clarke, Head of Factual Global Marketing, BBC Worldwide, adds, "Collaboration at all levels is the only way to ensure successful acquisition of funds for new programming and ensuring that the brand is marketed effectively."

In the process of programme development there are two main points of contact between commercial and production: tagging meetings and the development of the concept for a production.

If and when required, commercial would call tagging meetings. During these meetings producers present treatments (synopses of what the programme or series is about plus initial budgeting) and GMBD assess them as to their

---

[2] See Appendix 2.3 for an excerpt from the *Brand Guide for Walking with Dinosaurs*.

commercial value and tags those it is interested in. Evaluation criteria would include whether the programme would be likely to be transferable into more than four countries, whether it would have potential to be exploited through a range of media, for example video, book, merchandise, and whether it would have some permanence in the marketplace, that is promises to be a series rather than a one-off. As Paul explains, "To effectively market a title such as *Walking with Dinosaurs* requires significant marketing investment and therefore you need to sustain brands for the long term rather than launch new titles every quarter."

Before the setting up of the GMBD department much of the interaction between commercial and production tended to rely on personal contacts and initiative. Now there were four main kinds of meetings between GMBD and production:

1. *Commercial hours meetings*: ensuring an understanding between production, GMBD and BBC public service of the demand and supply of science, natural history and history, arts and documentaries programming. Insights from the meeting would direct the allocation of investment.

2. *Editorial meetings* between production and GMBD: allowing GMBD to preview up and coming titles and sharing ideas with production.

3. *Title launch meetings*: GMBD would align production with stills/specific requirements to facilitate cross-media exploitation; it would also allow production to update GMBD on latest changes to programme treatment.

4. *Title review meetings*: ongoing and ad-hoc as necessary.

Once a treatment had been selected and budgets have been signed-off an initial development meeting would be held between commercial and production to discuss the latest treatment, as this could change during the first phase, as well as identify stills requirements. It was important to do this early on as production used to work on these aspects towards the end but, as the production of books could have lead-times of 18 months or more, programme and related products would not be available at the same time. Early agreement on ancillary products was important for another reason: different media have different demands on the quality of images. For example, pictures for the book need a higher resolution than those for the film, which meant that additional money would be needed. It was further important to agree to time-lines, particularly as people in production would not always be aware of ancillary product time-lines, which often varied widely from those for television production.

Finally, GMBD would engage in the brand development and positioning. Generally this would involve the following:

*   An outline on how to position the programme.
*   Developing a brand guide.
*   Developing marketing plans.

Effective positioning development would rely on close cooperation between production and GMBD. By necessity this had to be an iterative process given that the ideas would initially be primarily in the producer's head and could change, especially in the early stages. The visual identity would be developed out of the brand positioning and marketing plans would be developed in collaboration with BBC public service marketing media format teams (publishing, video, DVD etc.) and applied to international markets.

For *Walking with Dinosaurs* the process was slightly different as GMBD did not exist when the series went into production. Alix remembers, "The *Walking with Dinosaurs* series was started before we came into being. Half the auxiliary products had already been initiated and we were not too happy with the consistency – or lack of it – across the products." However, in many ways the series was seen as a test case for the new approach signifying a shift from programmes primarily driven by production to programmes developed in close cooperation with GMBD. It was a first not only in its scope of international outlook but also in terms of developing merchandise for a factual – rather than fictional – programme.

The results

Initially it was quite difficult to get licensees to understand the difference between *Jurassic Park* and *Walking with Dinosaurs*. The difference was not in the animation but in the fact that *Walking with Dinosaurs* was aiming to be a documentary whereas *Jurassic Park* was made up beginning to end. In addition, *Walking with Dinosaurs* would not have used human beings in their film or anything else that would not have been consistent with the world in those days.

Still there was some criticism from some palaeontologists. Though Tim Haines pointed out, "90% of the palaeontologists I talked to are delighted and anyone who is involved in museums or institutions that thrive on public interest are also delighted. It is interesting to look at some of the criticisms from the Natural History Museum which has used *Walking with Dinosaurs* in its advertising campaign to get people to attend. Dismissing the series as invalid, because it's based on speculations betrays a deep-seated elitism."

It was felt that there would have been room for improvement. Transmission in the UK was October 1999 – a lot of the products only came out about 12–18 months later. Another issue with the product was, one cannot trademark the 'truth'. Had production been aware of this they could have 'personalised' the dinosaurs, for example a broken tooth, a scar, which would have helped to brand merchandise. Had they been able to liaise with Tim earlier they could have alerted him to that fact and individual dinosaurs would have been more trademarkable. As a consequence BBC Worldwide has now developed a philosophy guide that clarifies unique selling points. In addition there is a brand guide as well as a style guide that outlines how to use the logo.

Despite these issues the series has gone from strength to strength and the results are impressive:

- In September 1999, even before the first broadcast the series had generated more than £1.3 million in television pre-sales.

- The series has been the nineteenth most popular programme ever at the BBC and it has done incredibly well because it is not linked to any particular culture, the words can be translated into any language.

- In the US it broke all records; it was the highest non-sports cable programme; in spring 2000 over 40 million people in the US watched all or some of the programme on the Discovery Channel.

- December 2000: the series had a total retail marketing value approaching £35 million and has generated more than £1.7 million in programme sales with TV deals in 22 countries. BBC Worldwide hold all publishing rights to the series, advance orders and sales of the video and books alone have already been made to the value of £1.25 million.

- By mid-2001 the series had been licensed to over 50 countries.

- By mid-2001 Tim's book had sales in the UK in excess of 700,000 and about the same number of the children's book were sold; the book had also been number 1 in the *Sunday Times* Hardback 'General' category for two weeks.

All in all, the programme has made a turnover of more than £25 million and won several awards (see Appendix 2.4). Tim explains the success as follows, "TV is there to entertain. Also to educate but that is not the primary objective. On TV you want to give people relaxation and *Walking with Dinosaurs* is both highly entertaining and highly educational." He also points out that, "The first programme was even better than the pilot in that it was even more realistic. This was just as well as expectations had been raised through the excellent pilot. As a producer you have a problem, you want people to be excited about a programme but the more fuss people make about a programme the more the pressure is on for the producer to meet or exceed expectations."

> "*Walking with Dinosaurs* is the first major example of global brand marketing in the factual area and is, with all ancillary marketing products, pointed to become one of BBC Worldwide's top earners. It has already broken audience records for ABC in Australia and has been a massive hit in Germany for Pro7 – it is a worldwide phenomenon."
> BBC Worldwide Chief Executive Rupert Gavi

Questions

1. What are the possible mechanisms for ensuring both creativity and commercial realism?

2. What are the considerations in innovating for a global market?

3. Drawing on both your own experience and the case study, what does it take to make an innovative project happen? [What are aspects of innovative projects (a) generally, (b) in this case? How were they addressed?]

4. What are the considerations for developing a global brand?

APPENDIX 2.1: MEET THE DINOSAURS

Starring in each of the series:

1. 'New Blood' – 220 million years ago
    — Coelophysis – meaning hollow form (because of his thin bones) dinosaur; carnivore, meat and fish eating, cannibalistic scavenger
    — Placerias – mammal-like reptile; herbivore
    — Cynodont – meaning dog-toothed; half mammal, half reptile; omnivore
    — Postosuchus – archosaur; carnivore
    — Peteinosaurus – early pterosaur; insectivore

2.   'A Time of Titans' – 152 million years ago
      —   Diplodocus – meaning double-beamed lizard; dinosaur; herbivore
      —   Allosaurus – meaning different lizard; dinosaur; carnivore
      —   Stegosaurus – meaning covered lizard; dinosaur, herbivore
      —   Anurognathus – meaning without tail and jaw; pterosaur; insectivore
      —   Orchitholestes – meaning bird robber; dinosaur; carnivore

3.   'Cruel Sea' – 149 million years ago
      —   Ophthalmosaurus – meaning eye lizard; ichtyosaur; carnivore
      —   Liopleurodon – plesiosaur; carnivore
      —   Rhamphorhynchus – meaning beak snout; pterosaur; carnivore
      —   Eustreptospondylus – meaning well-reversed vertebrae; carnivore
      —   Cryptoclidus – meaning hidden collar bone; plesiosaur; carnivore
      —   Hybodus shark – cartilaginous fish; carnivore

4.   'Giant of the Skies' – 127 million years ago
      —   Polacanthus – meaning many spined; dinosaur; herbivore
      —   Orithocheirus – meaning bird hand; pterosaur
      —   Tapejara – meaning old being; pterosaur; carnivore
      —   Iguanodon – meaning iguana tooth; herbovore
      —   Utahraptor – meaning robber from Utah; dinosaur; carnivore

5.   'Spirits of the Ice Forest' – 106 million years ago
      —   Leaellynasaura – named after daughter of palaeontologist; dinosaur; herbivore
      —   Dwarf Allosaur – meaning strange lizard; dinosaur; carnivore
      —   Muttaburrasaurus – named after a township in Australia; dinosaur; herbivore
      —   Koolasuchus; named after a palaeontologist; amphibian; carnivore

6.   'Death of a Dynasty' – 149 million years ago
      —   Anatotitan – meaning giant duck; dinosaur; herbivore
      —   Torosaurus – meaning bull lizard; dinosaur; herbivore
      —   Ankylosaurus – meaning fused or stiff lizard; dinosaur; herbivore
      —   Tyrannosaurus – meaning tyrant lizard; dinosaur; carnivore

APPENDIX 2.2: STAGES OF THE ANIMATION PROCESS

(Adapted from Framestore's website: http://www.framestore.co.uk)

1. Digitising/Scanning

All dinosaur models in this series began life as a physical maquette. These are high detail, scale models sculpted in clay, from which a resin cast is made, which are used directly for scanning and building the computer graphic models. Upon receipt of the finished maquettes, the digitising process begins. This is represented by three key stages.

(a)   Preparing the maquette for scanning; which entails cleaning and then covering the model with a diffuse and optically opaque white paint.

(b)   Scanning, with an in-house high resolution laser scanner.

(c)   Data cleanup and creating a range of digital models at different resolutions for animation and rendering.

In cooperation with Soho-CyberScan Framestore developed a suite of software tools, to faithfully capture the three-dimensional form and texture detail represented in the original physical maquettes. Once scanned, the model data is initially just a very large cloud of over six million three-dimensional points. At this stage the data is too dense, it has to be reduced to about one million points and linked into a polygonal lattice. A refined form is created using even fewer polygonal facets, however, still maintaining the level of detail seen in the original model. Finally, a low resolution version is made for animation purposes, this enables us to see creature movement playback in real-time.

2. Modelling

When the project started there were originally 24 dinosaurs to be modelled. By the time the last episode was complete this number had grown to 40. New creatures were introduced as the series evolved, and extra model detail was called for in some sequences.

Animation model

Upon receiving the high and low resolution polygonal models from the laser scanner, it was adjusted to the correct scale and orientation, so as to match the camera and scene data for each shot. A simple animation model is built from the low resolution scanned data. This is generally made from a series of cylindrical components.

Patch model

By carefully observing the form 'flow lines' running over the high resolution scanned data, an efficient implicit surface model is built using up to 88 patches.

Fully textured model in neutral position

Finally capturing the fine surface detail seen in the original maquettes involved combining advanced proprietary computer modelling techniques, with the more traditional skills of an illustrator.

3. Skin design

The process of painting the dinosaur skins began with the creation of colour designs which were sent to the BBC directors for approval. In designing dinosaur skin various factors had to be taken into account – habitat, possible lifestyle, whether the dinosaur was a carnivore or a herbivore and body size. The size of an animal has a bearing on its colouration; large animals tend to have dull skin colours (like elephants or rhinos), with bright colours and patterns reserved for smaller, tropical animals such as parrots or lizards. As colour pigment does not fossilise, there is no historical evidence of dinosaur skin colour; however, there is evidence that dinosaurs had scaly reptilian skin. Once the designs were approved, the skins were ready to be painted. The first step was to paint a black and white (or greyscale) image, called a 'bump map', that the computer interprets as bumps in the surface. This creates shadows and highlights, giving the illusion of a rough textured skin.

Next a 'colour map' was painted containing all the skin colour and pattern information. These were then applied to the model. As the maps were two-dimensional images projected onto a three-dimensional model, it was necessary to paint multiple maps to cover the entire surface of the dinosaur. These were combined into one seamless map.

4. Animation

Computer animation is a technique for creating the illusion of movement and life, using computer-generated characters, or in this case photo-realistic dinosaurs. The process is divided into two main parts, primary and secondary animation. Primary animation involves the main articulation and motion of a creature. Secondary animation is all the other movement, such as flesh and muscle movement.

(a)   After the model has been built a 'skeleton' is constructed, which will be used for animating all the movements of the dinosaur.

(b)   Onto this skeleton an interactive model is built, a low detail representation of the very complicated complete model. This is done so the animator can quickly and easily manipulate the dinosaur. The creature can then be animated by moving and rotating different 'bones' or joints. Now that the skeleton and interactive model are created animation can begin.

(c)   With the help of the BBC a library of live action wildlife reference material was built up, which were used to help form ideas about the kind of movements and behavioural characteristics the dinosaurs would have lead. The first stage is to get the dinosaur walking. This initial animation helps visualise the animal's weight, size, posture and character. Each 'bone' is then individually animated to create realistic, fluid movement.

(d)   In a process called 'enveloping', the final model is attached to the animation skeleton. A walk cycle for the complete dinosaur is then rendered on a 'turntable' so that the skin and movement can be fully tested.

(e)   Extra 'bones' are added (ribs, for example). These make sure that skin, muscles and wobbling fat behave correctly. Finally eye blinks and breathing are added, these small details really help bring the creatures to life.

5. Lighting and rendering

Once the animation is completed for a shot it is ready to light. Lighting involves illuminating the computer-generated scene with virtual lights, to match the direct and ambient light in the live action back plate(s). This is first accomplished by using survey data and reference information collected on location at the time of filming. Range data enables the setting up of a virtual camera and set its position. Reference frames of a 'lighting ball' are filmed at the same time. Using a 'lighting ball' it is possible to understand the proper direction and intensity of the dominant light sources in the scene. After carefully balancing the virtual lights to match the graded live action scene the shot is ready for rendering. As part of this project proprietary methods were devised to maximize render throughout, but also to offer complete flexibility over lighting balance and shadow density, right through to the final composite. This enabled the generation of over 28,000 frame elements in one 12-hour period.

6. Compositing

Computer-generated three-dimensional elements are rendered to tape, with up to five layers for each creature. These consist of a colour, form, shadow, highlight and secondary shadow passes (as shown below). Each layer is added one on top of the other, and at each stage careful adjustments are made to ensure that the dinosaurs' shading and shadow density match those of the live action background plate. At this stage bluescreen elements such as extra tree ferns, rocks and other foreground items are added.

When colour grading underwater creatures, the colour saturation decreases with depth. By using a three-dimensional depth matte a creature can be made to appear and disappear from the blue depths. For the larger land-based dinosaurs we were also able to control the depth of field along the length of their bodies. The team of five Henry and five Inferno compositing artists produced over 1000 shots.

7. Mastergrade

When all the compositing is finished the final shots are dropped into the edit. In telecine any final 'look' or matching of colour balance is carried out. It was decided to make *Walking with Dinosaurs* future protected. This means safe for 4:3 and 16:9 widescreen viewing. The plates or backgrounds were shot on 35-mm film 'open gate'. This gave us excellent steadiness and detail. Prior to *Walking with Dinosaurs* almost all documentaries were shot 16 or S16mm, which was felt not to be high enough quality for this project. The film master was finally transferred to digital tape as '16:9 anamorphic', this is then unsqueezed at the point of broadcast.

APPENDIX 2.3: EXCERPT FROM BRAND GUIDE

Brand positioning:

—   the real life experience with the most extraordinary creatures that ever lived

Brand substantiators:

—   travel back in time and watch living, breathing dinosaurs in their natural habitat

—   it feels completely real; a primeval environment is created by leading-edge computer technology, animatronics and footage from locations around the globe where ancient plants still survive

—   story-led programmes which show us the anatomy, life-cycle and behaviour of dinosaurs – familiar favourites like Tyrannosaurus Rex, as well as less familiar creatures like Liopleurodon, the world's largest carnivore at 25 metres long

—   the latest palaeontological theories on the magnificent prehistoric animals which roamed the earth for
     160 million years

Target audience

—   broad family appeal – adults and children alike
—   everybody who loved *Jurassic Park*
—   everybody with an interest in natural history or palaeontology

How does it make me feel?

—   Wow, that was amazing
—   I feel I could reach out and touch them . . . the detail is fantastic
—   When you see the dinosaurs in the forest crashing through the trees, splashing in the water, chasing insects
     – it's like being on a dinosaur safari

Brand values

—   real, captivating, cutting edge

Associated products

—   home videos
—   adult trade books
—   children's books (photo book, sticker book, Q&A book, 3D poster book)
—   DVD
—   Music CD
—   Merchandise
—   Online site

APPENDIX 2.4: AWARDS AS OF 30 OCTOBER 2001

Walking with Dinosaurs – the Pilot

•   Prix Pixel-INA Monte Carlo 1998 'Content Graphics'
•   London Effects and Animation Festival (LEAF) 1997 'Education and Training Award'
•   Australian Effects and Animation Festival 1998 'Education and Training Award'
•   CGIX Amsterdam 1998 (category not recorded on the award, and I can't remember!)

Walking with Dinosaurs – the Series

•   3 Emmys (US)
     ○   Outstanding animated programme

- ○ Outstanding music composition for a miniseries, movie or special
- ○ Outstanding achievement for nonfiction programming – sound editing
- Royal Television Society – team award for Walking with Dinosaurs
- BAFTA – innovation award; also nominated for the Lew Grade Award (voted by readers of Radio Times)
- Voice of The Listener and Viewer Awards – best new television programme
- London Effects and Animation Festival (LEAF) Gold Award 1999
- Royal Television Society Craft and Design Awards 1999/2000 'Design and Craft Innovation Award'
- Royal Television Society Programme Awards 1999 'Team Award'
- Creative Freedom Awards 2000 'Factual Television Programme Award'

Framestore

- 2001 Outstanding Animated Programme: The Ballad of Big Al
- 2000 Outstanding Visual FX: Walking with Dinosaurs
- 2000 Outstanding Animated Programme: Walking with Dinosaurs
- 2000 Outstanding Main Title Design: The 10th Kingdom
- 1999 Outstanding Special FX: Alice in Wonderland
- 1998 Outstanding Special Visual FX: Merlin
- 1997 Outstanding Special Visual FX: The Odyssey
- 1996 Outstanding Special Visual FX: Gulliver's Travels

3 Structured processes for developing new products

For most companies wanting to become more innovative, which they will almost certainly associate with the development of new products, the starting point is the introduction – or revision – of a new product development process. While structured processes for the development and management of new products are no guarantee for improving innovativeness they are nevertheless an important part in an organisation's armoury to improve new product introduction rate and maximise the benefits from a company's product portfolio. One of the key dilemmas is described by one interviewee, "The problem with process is, if you provide too much detail you create information overload; if you have too little detail – people make mistakes and lose perspective." The processes should be about providing guidance, not dictating what needs to be done.

The last few years have brought a couple of new insights into processes in the context of innovation. First, a structured process alone is often not sufficient; the behaviours of the people will have to change alongside. Second, many companies have realised that one process is not enough, particularly if innovation is to go beyond the incremental. Incremental and radical innovation require different conditions under which they flourish. Leading innovators have started to address this by either having different pathways or by establishing a pre-process phase. We will come back to that in more detail in Chapter 21.

This chapter briefly reviews the evolution of the new product development process, expands on the stage-gate process and product portfolio management as well as the role of the project leader, concluding with some insights into best and worst practice.

THE EVOLUTION OF THE NEW PRODUCT DEVELOPMENT PROCESS

One of the biggest influences on how companies approach product development in the west has been a concept developed by NASA in the 1960s, introduced to make the management of large-scale, complex defence projects easier. The first version 'Phased Project Planning', as it was called, described a basically sequential approach consisting of four phases:

- preliminary analysis (phase A)
- definition (phase B)
- design (phase C)
- operation (phase D)

In addition checkpoint reviews were introduced to ensure that mistakes would not be carried forward into the next phase. While this approach was originally applied to complex, large-scale projects only, its principles were soon scaled down and translated for new product development in a more general way. The fundamental principles – phases and checks between them – are still valid today, and reflected in the now most commonly used kind of process, the stage-gate process, which we will look at in the following section. Figure 3.1 shows the NASA process as seen in Peter W.G. Morris's book *The Management of Projects*.

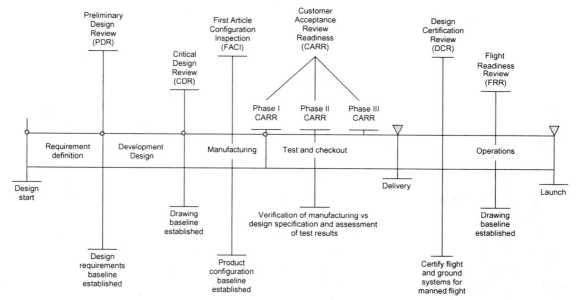

Figure 3.1   The NASA management process.
Source: Morris, P.W.G. (1994). *The Management of Projects*. London: Thomas Telford. Reproduced by permission of NASA.

A further influential study, with regards not only to the development process but also to new product in general, was undertaken by Booz Allen Hamilton (1982). When they researched how companies define product development stages they found the following steps:

1.   development of new product development strategy[1]
2.   idea generation[2]
3.   screening and evaluation[3]
4.   business analysis
5.   development
6.   testing
7.   commercialisation

---

[1] Aspects related to strategy are covered in Chapter 6.
[2] Aspects related to idea generation are covered in Chapter 21.
[3] More on the evaluation and measurement in Chapters 21 and 25, respectively.

These categories are used with variations throughout the literature and there is a body of literature discussing each of the steps individually. If more steps are proposed, they are generally a breakdown of one of the steps above. Cooper (1986), for example, describes 13 steps whereby the additional steps result from separating activities such as market research and business analysis. Another, broader way of segmenting the development process, identifying three main stages, is provided again by Cooper (1988):

1. pre-development activities
2. product development and testing
3. commercialisation

In his 1992 article Rothwell provides a useful summary of how the new product development process has evolved over time (shown in Table 3.1).

In the shift from a linear, sequential development process towards a more integrated and dynamic process the need for increased speed has been one of the main drivers. Takeuchi and Nonaka (1986) have written one of the most influential articles on this subject, alerting companies to the need to move away from the linear approach. The sequential approach is described as a 'relay race' where the baton is passed from one department to the next, often requiring changes to accommodate requirements of a downstream department. This approach could probably also have been called 'Chinese whispers' as information passed on is often incomplete or insufficiently explained, leading to misunderstandings and confusion. One of my favourite sketches on this subject stems from Michael Smith – see Figure 3.2 (reproduced as seen in Lorenz, 1990).

Table 3.1 Five generations of new product development models

Generation	Type of model	Characteristics of model
First	Technology push model	Simple linear sequential process; emphasis on R&D, the market is a receptacle for the fruits of R&D
Second	Need pull model	Simple linear sequential process; emphasis on marketing; the market is the source of ideas for directing R&D; R&D has a reactive role
Third	Coupling model	Sequential but with feedback loops; push or pull or push/pull combinations; R&D and marketing more in balance; emphasis on integration at the R&D/marketing interface
Fourth	Integrated model	Parallel development with integrated development teams; strong upstream supplier linkages; close coupling with leading edge customers; emphasis on integration between R&D and manufacturing/design for makeability; horizontal collaboration (joint ventures)
Fifth	Systems integrating and networking model	Fully integrated parallel development; use of expert systems and simulation modelling in R&D; strong linkages with leading customers (customer focus at the forefront of strategy); strategic integration with primary suppliers including co-development of new products and linked CAD systems; horizontal linkages; joint ventures; collaborative research groupings; collaborative marketing arrangements etc.; emphasis on corporate flexibility and speed of development (time-based strategy); increased focus on quality and other non-price factors

Source: Based on Rothwell, R. (1992). Successful industrial innovation: critical factors for the 1990s. *R&D Management*, **22**, 221–39.

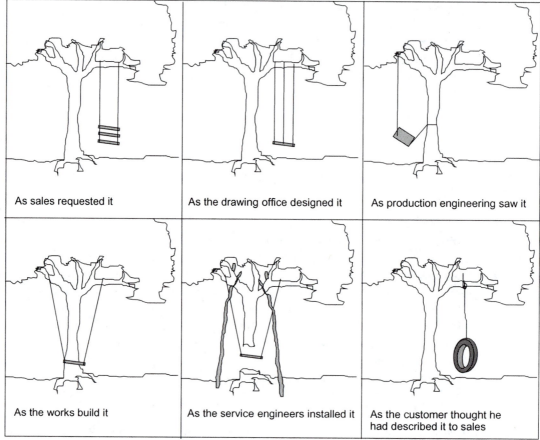

As sales requested it

As the drawing office designed it

As production engineering saw it

As the works build it

As the service engineers installed it

As the customer thought he had described it to sales

Figure 3.2 Barking up the wrong tree?
Source: Smith in Lorenz, C. (1990). *The Design Dimension*. Oxford: Basil Blackwell. Reproduced by permission of Basil Blackwell.

Takeuchi and Nonaka (1986) contrast the relay race with a then new approach they compare to a 'rugby game' in which the product is passed back and forth between the different departments, like the ball in rugby. They explain that the advantages of the new approach include not only increased speed but also lead to greater consistency and integrity of the product because of the early consideration of concerns and requirements from all departments involved in a product's development process.

Building on the insights and positive results that companies experienced through early and continuous interaction between all departments, a large number of articles in the early 1990s heralded the use of cross-functional teams as the solution to many a development problem (e.g. Ancona & Caldwell, 1990; Belbin, 1991; Faust, 1993; Nadler, 1991; Oakley 1990a). However, companies implementing teams as a consequence were often disappointed. This may have been attributable to a considerable extent to the fact that teams were told to work in teams – without being given any training or other kinds of support that would aid the shift in working practices and behaviours. I would also like to point out here that which is the most suitable structure to drive a project forward will depend on the level of innovativeness. Small changes can successfully be executed by moving the project through the different functions whereas highly innovative projects have more chances of success if they are executed by a dedicated team. We will come back to the subject of teams and structures in Chapter 10.

A final aspect that has received a great deal of attention in the literature is what is often described as the 'fuzzy front end' of the development process. Particularly for highly innovative concepts it tends to be difficult to predict how long the development will take, what kind of resources will be required and what exactly the outcome will be. On the other hand, the early stages of product development are quite fundamental as over 80% of a product's production costs are locked in during these early stages (e.g. Dixon & Duffey, 1990; Smith & Reinertsen, 1995). A lack of attention here can lead to costly and time-consuming changes later in the development process. Smith and Reinertsen point out, "The calculated cost of delay is often 500 to 5000 times higher than the visible cost of assigned personnel. Managers unaware of these costs will tend to ignore the fuzzy front end. Those who understand these costs will instead focus a great deal of attention on this phase." Khurana and Rosenthal (1997) who have undertaken research into this fuzzy front end of new product development found that success factors related to this stage can be grouped under two headings:

1.   Foundation – including aspects such as the existence of a product strategy, the management of the product portfolio (rather than individual projects), the existence of a specific product development organisation structure including a project leader, a core team, an executive review group, and a good communication structure.

2.   Project-specific – referring to the existence of the following: a concept statement, thorough evaluation, a product definition, value chain considerations, front-end project planning and definitions, and recognising interrelationships.

However, there are also those who emphasise that different stages of the development process require different cultures, particularly if innovation rather than incremental improvements are concerned. Zien and Buckler (1997) describe what they call three micro-cultures of innovation:

1.   The Fuzzy Front End (FFE): experimental and chaotic; requires high tolerance for ambiguity and uncertainty; for people with high structure needs it often seems 'unreasonable'; but people who like it enjoy it for the quest itself; it *is* unpredictable, and it depends on much individual activity.[4]

2.   The Product Development Process (PDP): which needs to be disciplined and focused on numerous quantitative goals and measurements; it requires commitment to the goal; is schedule oriented and urgent; can be trained, and is generally not receptive to new ideas; teamwork is of paramount importance.

3.   Market Operations (MO): here we seek predictability and order; it has a strong financial orientation; it relies on commitment to established values and businesses; is oriented to rules and routine and slow to change; has to be highly organised and does not welcome revolutionary ideas; tends to be of large size compared to FFE or PDP.

It is often at the intersections of the stages that problems arise. People from one stage have often little sympathy or even respect for those best suited to conduct the next stage. Essential aspects of a project can get 'lost in translation'

---

[4] This is very much the point made in the introduction about the difference of creativity which relies on individuals, and implementation which depends on teams.

when a project is passed on. I sometimes suggest establishing the role of 'the keeper of the essence', a person who ensures that the key aspects of the concept are maintained and protected through the different development stages. Some companies have started to address this issue by developing dedicated project leaders; however, disconnecting the ideator from the project can also lead to a watering down of the original idea.

THE STAGE-GATE PROCESS

I have mentioned earlier that the principles of the stage-gate process go back to the work undertaken by NASA on project management. As the original NASA process, the stage-gate process suggests that a project has to be reviewed at certain points in its development, and a go/no-go decision should be made. This way an organisation can avoid throwing good money after bad – it is never advisable to keep spending money on a project just because quite a lot has been spent on it already (sunk cost).

> **Sunk cost:**
>
> past expenditure, which is often thought to be irrelevant to future decisions as the best decisions tend to maximise future cash flow.
> *The Oxford Concise Dictionary of Business, 1990*

The stage-gate process as now known and used in product development has been devised by Robert G. Cooper. Both Figure 3.3 and the overview in Box 3.1 are based on Cooper and Kleinschmidt's 2001 article 'Stage-gate process for new product success'.

In their article Cooper and Kleinschmidt also share some insights into how to maximise changes for new product success. This includes the already-mentioned necessity to pay careful attention to the early stages, which includes doing background research as well as a 'sharp and early' definition of the product, and other points such as the

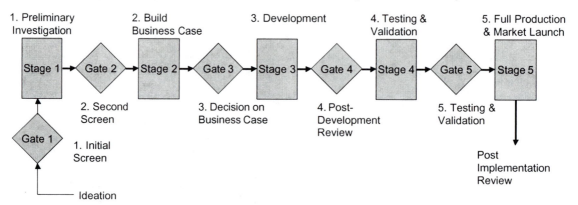

The Stage-Gate New Product Process by Robert G Cooper

Figure 3.3 Stage-gate process
Source: Reproduced from Cooper & Kleinschmidt, 2001.

Box 3.1   Process overview

Gate 1	Gate 2	Gate 3	Gate 4	Gate 5
First decision to commit resources, signalling tentative commitment; criteria tend to be qualitative and few in number: strategic alignment, technical feasibility, competitive advantage, opportunity attractiveness; looking at 'musts'	More rigorous screen; commitment of resources more substantial; often a scoring model is used to measure synergies, market attractiveness, competitive situation, product advantage, profit potential; looking at 'musts' and 'shoulds'	Last point to kill project before heavy spending; sign off of product specification; pass criteria should be tough and rigorous; looking at 'musts' and 'shoulds' again as well as financial and risk review	Recheck continued attractiveness of project; check against product specification and performance expectations	Criteria here are largely on quality of efforts to date, appropriateness of the production and launch plans, financial viability

Stage 1	Stage 2	Stage 3	Stage 4	Stage 5
Quick review of project, looking at technical and marketplace merits	Development of business case to verify attractiveness; 'critical homework stage' that is often neglected; studies may include: user needs/wants; competitive analysis; concept testing; technical and manufacturing appraisal; legal, patent and regulatory assessment; detailed financial analysis	Deliverable at end of this stage is a lab-tested prototype; emphasis is on technical work, marketing and manufacturing activities run parallel	Testing and validating: the product itself, production process, customer acceptance, economies; activities may include: in-house product test checks (quality and performance); user field trials; pilot production; pre-test market; revised financial analysis	Putting marketing launch plan and production or operations plan in motion

Post-implementation review

Often companies review the project and the products performance about 6–18 months after launch to draw out lessons learnt

Source: Cooper & Kleinschmidt, 2001. Reproduced by permission of Cooper & Kleinschmidt.

need for market orientation, teams and strong cross-functional cooperation and, most importantly, the need for a superior product. This last point is still the major differentiator between a successful and a less successful or even completely unsuccessful product. And finally, as we mentioned speed earlier, it is interesting that the authors warn to be careful with speed. Or rather, agreeing with the idiom 'speed not haste', they say that companies should be careful not to let speed become a goal in itself. The goal should always remain the intro-duction of a successful new product. Cutting corners, particularly in the early stages, generally has to be paid for, manifold, later.[5]

A further note of caution, in applying a stage-gate process companies should be careful not to let the process become an end in itself. If applied too strictly and rigidly it can hinder rather than help the development of new products; to quote one of my interviewees, "There can be a tyranny of the process!"

Leading-edge companies have come to realise this and now talk about using the process as guideline, rather than a 'bible' or 'rule book'. Gates become more fluid and more than one stage can be worked on simultaneously. This prevents individual gates from becoming bottle necks that delay progress of a project unnecessarily. In fact, Robert Cooper himself has pointed this out as early as 1994, announcing it to be time for the third-generation new product development process, one that is characterised by four 'Fs':

- Fluid: it is fluid and adaptable, with overlapping and fluid stages for greater speed.

- Fuzzy gates: it features conditional go decisions (rather than absolute ones) which are dependent on the situation.

- Focused: it builds in prioritisation methods that look at the entire portfolio of projects (rather than one project at the time) and focuses resources on the 'best bets'.

- Flexible: it is not a rigid stage-and-gate system; each project is unique and has its own routing through the process.

The four 'Fs' are not only important for the application of the process, they also apply to the treatment of the process itself. It is important to continuously assess and adjust a company's new product development process to make sure it reflects latest insights, the context of the organisation, and particularly its ambition. What I mean by the latter is that a process for the development of incremental improvements or routine projects should be different from one that aims to produce radical ones – as alluded to earlier. Changes in a company's structure can also have implications for the new product development process, for example, product development in a functionally oriented organisation is likely to be executed differently from an organisation with a project or matrix structure (for characteristics of functional, project and matrix-based organisations see Table 3.2). Whichever process is chosen, it is essential that reward systems support the behaviours required to fill the process with life – in fact, all systems and aspects of an organisation need to enhance and support each other, a theme to which we will come back to again and again throughout the book.

---

[5] Further articles on the stage-gate process are available on www.stage-gate.com.

Table 3.2 Types of organisational structure

Type	How it works	Appropriate for	Problems
Functional structure (basic structure)	The project is planned and executed within a functional structure with moves from department to department in a pre-arranged sequence (relay race) Responsibilities must be clearly defined Need for integration of sequential activities	Improvements of existing products New products of low innovation Sequential processing possible Fosters deep specialisation and expertise	Often strong pressure on the departments to give top priority to short-term projects Conflicting demands on staff (prioritisation of projects) Balance between short-term projects (order and discipline) and innovative projects (freedom and flexibility) Integration of functions
Independent project organisation	Self-contained group, full-time members from various different functions The project manager has full responsibility for the project and is given the necessary resources for planning and implementation Team should be co-located	Large projects which justify employing experts from different functions on a full-time basis For new solutions or new products Firms in dynamic markets	Issue of re-integration of staff Isolation from the rest of the organisation Dispensing people to the project full-time might cause problems in the basic organisation How to maintain specialisation and carry forward learning from previous projects
Matrix organisation	Decision-making responsibility rests with the project team Project manager negotiates with heads of functional departments on necessary resources (staff and equipment) Staff is assigned on a part-time or full-time basis Task often broken down into independent activities and allows simultaneous processing High demands on social and political skills of project manager Clear goals and well-understood technology will result in an effective balance of power	Complex projects which require simultaneous efforts of experts from several disciplines Large projects, here the project manager is often supported by team leaders within the individual functions	Authority can be split between the project manager and the functional manager Projects are cutting across the authority lines of the functional departments (leading to authority ambiguity) Conflict of loyalty of part-time staff who work on more than one project simultaneously Problems of re-integration into functional structure If project is broken down into sub-tasks the need for coordination goes up Competition for resources also leads to an increased need for coordination Time consuming decision-making process

Source: Based on Baker & Wilemon, 1977; Brown & Agnew, 1982; Davis & Lawrence, 1977; Earle, 1973; Greiner & Schein, 1981; Holt, 1987; Kingdon, 1973; Kolodny, 1979, 1980; Rowen *et al.*, 1980; Sayles, 1976; Ulrich & Fluri, 1988; Vasconcellos, 1979.

THE DEVELOPMENT FUNNEL AND PRODUCT PORTFOLIO MANAGEMENT

Next to the stage-gate process the best-known and a popular tool in the armoury to improve new product development is the 'development funnel', a tool developed by Harvard Business School professors Kim Clark and Stephen Wheelwright in the early 1990s (see Figure 3.4). It encourages managers to take an integrated approach to new product development. Rather than making decisions on individual projects, their approach suggests the management and coordination of product development activities from a company-wide perspective, starting with a link to company strategy. It is interesting to note though that much of the literature seems to treat the development funnel as a variation on the theme of stage-gate processes albeit with a strong emphasis on the need to generate many ideas, and to narrow them down quickly as the project is progressing through the process. I believe that the main advantage of the development funnel is the requirement to take a company-wide perspective.

In the following we will look at the factors behind each of the individual components of the development funnel.

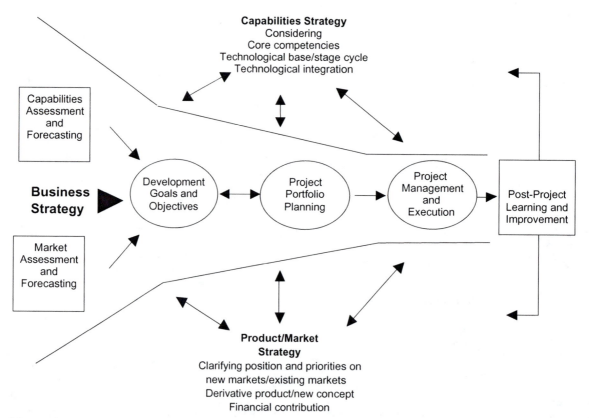

Figure 3.4 The development funnel.
Source: Reproduced from Clark, K.B. & Wheelwright, S.C. (1993). *Managing New Product and Process Development: Text and Cases*. New York: Free Press.

For *capabilities assessment and forecasting* a company would undertake an analysis of the current and future product/service capacity, look at current and planned new product/service developments, investigate the efficiency of current processes and review technologies to determine the company's current position.

Market assessment and forecasting would involve an analysis of existing clients to identify current needs and areas of improvements as well as an analysis of competitors to identify new areas of expansion, and finally, a trends analysis to capture the direction of the industry.

Development goals and objectives comprises the development of a set of specific measures and targets for key portfolio criteria including:

- strategic fit
- revenues and profits
- client fit
- dates of new product/service introductions and technology achievements
- new product/service performance objectives and criteria

This component also involves the establishment of targets for entering new segments, developing new technology and technical skills, or creating new markets as well as acting as a guideline for investment decisions.

Project portfolio planning involves the definition of a set of criteria against which projects are selected and resources are allocated to them. Box 3.2 gives an example of the criteria one particular company uses. There should generally be a strong link between the portfolio criteria and an organisation's overall strategy. When selecting projects the first question should always be, will it help us to achieve our ambition, followed by a second, does this project help us balance our portfolio or are we doing too much of one particular kind.

Box 3.2 An FMCG company's portfolio criteria

We balance out product portfolio at four levels:

1. Between brands/product portfolios – to make sure there is enough innovation in each area.

2. Between developed/non-developed markets; recognising that non-developed markets take longer for pay-back.

3. Between three levels of horizon which equate to different types of innovation: (a) product extension; (b) existing product into new market or changed product into existing market; (c) more of the blue-sky stuff, not necessarily fitting in at present.

4. Against strategy.

Careful resource planning and management are critical, as successful product development is prevented in many organisations due to 'project constipation': too many projects with too little resource. Clark and Wheelwright found that a person operates at their best when being able to focus on no more than two projects (Figure 3.5).

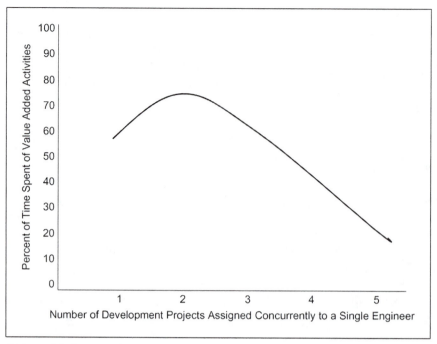

Figure 3.5   Value added per project.
Source: Reproduced from Clark, K.B. & Wheelwright, S.C. (1993). *Managing New Product and Process Development: Text and Cases*. New York: Free Press.

Companies should also consider:

- specifying the types and mix of projects along the key portfolio criteria
- explicitly linking projects to firm and service line strategies
- identifying existing capacity for development
- identifying capability requirements for development of current and future generation products/services
- providing a resource capacity plan for development efforts
- acting as the framework for communicating the portfolio

In the context of innovation it is particularly important to review the product portfolio in terms of the mix between radical and incremental innovation. Most organisations focus on incremental innovation, thereby putting the future of their organisation into jeopardy. Many organisations that have started out with a major innovation or with being very innovative become stale and complacent over time, neglecting three out of the four quadrants that a company's product portfolio should address (see Figure 3.6). Unless an organisation keeps putting new products into the far three quadrants, over time all its products or services will end up in the bottom left corner. What the appropriate split between the four different quadrants will depend on each company's specific context and innovation ambition – but without some activity in each, decline is certainly preprogrammed. And, by the way, most organisations concentrate their efforts with about 80% on incremental innovation, and about 10% each on incremental innovations for new markets and radical innovation for existing markets – and none on radical innovation for new markets.

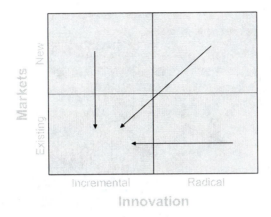

Figure 3.6   Innovation categories.

Project management and execution implies the definition of appropriate stages and gates a project must pass through. This process has to facilitate ideation, guide projects efficiently from idea to launch, ensure untenable product/service projects are terminated, identify tasks for each stage, specify clearly identified decision points, and provide information on required documentation and decision criteria. While some seem to view the development funnel as a substitute for a stage-gate process, I rather see the stage-gate process as a tool during the *project management and execution* stage. And what Cooper (e.g. 2001) calls 'post-implementation review', though not officially part of the stage-gate process as such, covers Clark and Wheelwright's last box, 'post-project learning and improvement'. However, the execution of a development funnel as described above seems to be an ideal scenario, and is not matched by what Clark and Wheelwright (1993) found (see Figure 3.7).

While their three scenarios certainly do not give the impression of a happy ending, companies should also be wary not to 'overdo things', particularly when it comes to perfecting a product before launch. Interviewees in large companies emphasised that working on the '100% right theory' can delay product introduction indefinitely! 'Failing early and often' is one of the mantras innovation consultancy IDEO promotes. Rather than trying to get something perfect they suggest getting exposure and feedback as early as possible, so the concept can be improved before being finalised.

One of the reasons for a lack of successful introduction of stage-gate processes and development funnels is that there is often insufficient support through training and holding people accountable to adhering to the new process. As one interviewee commented, "When the new product development process was introduced, my question was: where is the plan for the behavioural aspects? The consultants did not have any advice on attitude or any supporting training." Leading by example and rewarding people for the successful adaptation of new processes can also help.

Another is that top management's attention to any one particular project seems to come at the most inconvenient time: towards the end, when most parameters have been fixed and changes are costly and time consuming – as shown in another graph from the 1993 book by Clark and Wheelwright (Figure 3.8).

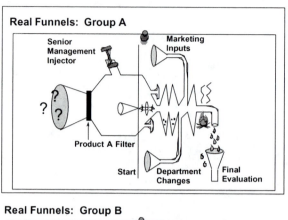

Real Funnels: Group A

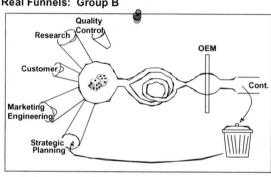

Real Funnels: Group B

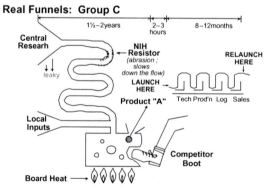

Real Funnels: Group C

Figure 3.7 Development funnel realities.
Source: Reproduced from Clark, K.B. & Wheelwright, S.C. (1993). *Managing New Product and Process Development: Text and Cases*. New York: Free Press.

If management comes in towards the end, wanting to change certain aspects of the project will have consequences for project costs as well as project timing. Early involvement and gaining buy-in can help prevent this from happening.

The responsibility for involving relevant parties and securing their buy-in falls generally to the project manager, who sits at the centre of the hour glass of management and the project team. This makes the project manager's role particularly important.

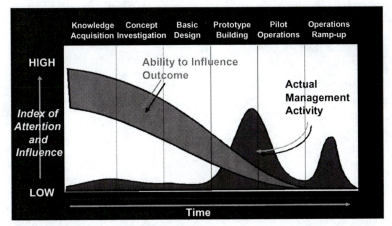

Figure 3.8   Senior management attention.
Source: Reproduced from Clark, K.B. & Wheelwright, S.C. (1993). *Managing New Product and Process Development: Text and Cases*. New York: Free Press.

THE ROLE OF THE PROJECT LEADER

"I believe that it is often the person driving the project who makes the difference between success and failure, particularly for innovative projects."

Quote from the Innovation Best Practice interviews, 2003

The issue of 'the project manager' or 'project leader' has first been brought onto management's radar through a 1959 *Harvard Business Review* article by Paul Gaddis. He was the first to alert management to the fact that a new breed of corporate animal was required, the project manager.

In his book on project management Harvey Maylor (1996) suggests that project managers should receive the following from their organisation/management:

- responsibility
- authority
- accountability
- credibility

Explaining that the exact role a project manager takes on will depend on aspects such as the nature of the project (complexity, scale, position in hierarchy of projects), the nature of the organisation that it is being carried out in (sector, activities, organisational structure), the personality of the project manager, and the specific constraints under which the project team is working. He also provides a list of characteristics desirable in a project manager (see Box 3.3).

That the project-specific context not only influences the role of the project leader but also that the project leader needs different characteristics depending on the context has been pointed out by a colleague of Clark and Wheelwright, Takahiro Fujimoto. In his 1991 article Fujimoto categorises products by looking at two aspects: the difficulty (a) of achieving internal product integrity and (b) of achieving external product integrity, and suggests that

Box 3.3   Characteristics of successful project leaders

- A desire not just to satisfy but to delight customers and stakeholders alike.

- Accepting of both challenges and responsibility.

- Being focused on action, rather than procrastination – getting the job done rather than avoiding critical or difficult decisions.

- A desire to make the best use of all resources – minimise waste in all activities.

- Does not lose sight of the light at the end of the tunnel – is goal focused.

- Has personal integrity – people find it very difficult to respect and take the authority of a person who has low integrity.

- Is flexible about the route that must be taken to achieve the stated end-goals.

- Has personal goals that are consistent with those of the project organisation – the project team perceives that the project manager and the organisation are going the same way.

- Ability to determine the real needs/desires of the customer; this is done through 'getting close' to the customer via visits and both formal and informal discussions, and asking the relevant questions.

- Analytical skills to turn data into information and break down the project into comprehensible component parts.

- Technical skills – the project manager need not be a technical specialist, but must at least be capable of comprehending the work that is being carried out and 'speaking the language' of the people involved.

- Team skills – many battles have been won against poor odds by the ability of an individual to motivate and enthuse a team.

- Ability to delegate effectively – not try to do everything personally.

- Ability to manage own time – you cannot expect to manage other people unless you can show that you can manage yourself.

- The balancing of stakeholders' perceptions of project progress (otherwise known as being able to 'sell ideas').

- Negotiation skills – resolve potential conflict situations to create a win–win.

- Problem solving/facilitating problem solving.

- Question all assumptions made by stakeholders at all stages of activities.

Source: Maylor, H. (1996). *Project Management*. London: Pitman

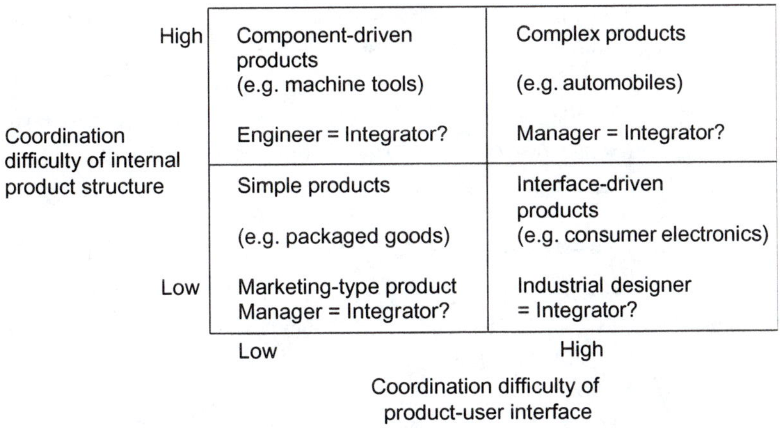

Figure 3.9 Types of products and project integrators.
Source: Fujimoto, T. (1991). Product integrity and the role of designer-as-integrator. *Design Management Journal*, 29–34. Reproduced by permission of *Design Management Journal*.

each of the four possible project types requires a different type of project manager, or 'integrator' as he calls them.[6] The four product categories he defines are 'Component-Driven Products', 'Complex Products', 'Simple Products', and 'Interface-Driven Products' (see Figure 3.9). To manage each product type a different set of skills is required; for example, for highly complex projects a manager might be the best integrator, that is someone with general, political and negotiation skills – rather than someone with for example a particular specialist technical expertise. The more complex a project – or the more innovative – the greater also the need for effective communication and internal selling.

But the skill set required of a project leader may not only vary from project to project, it may also change during the course of the project, particularly for large and complex projects. The following example from the Eurostar, the high-speed train that connects the capitals of Belgium, France and the UK, illustrates this (von Stamm, 1999a).

While the members of the central project team and most other key people remained unchanged throughout the project, the person for the manufacturing consortium changed twice during the development process. The first change took place in 1991 after time and cost overruns had come out in the open, the second in 1993 when the project went from the development stage into production. Each of the three project managers had a different skill set which was seen to be most appropriate at the time.

The first project manager had been responsible for the development of the TGV Atlantique, the latest version of the French high-speed train, which was seen to be the blueprint for the Eurostar. However, he had not managed international projects before and failed to acknowledge the issues and complications arising from this. He also seems to have underestimated the technical complexity arising from the need to operate the train on four different railway systems (Belgium, France, the UK, and the Eurotunnel). His withdrawal from the project was also meant as a signal

---

[6]With 'internal product integrity' he refers to problems in achieving consistency among the functions and structures of the product itself, and with 'external product integrity' he refers to the difficulty in coordinating the interface (functions and features) between product and user.

to the customers – the three national railways – that the imminent problems regarding time and cost overruns had been acknowledged, and that action for change and improvement had been taken.

His successor was chosen for his technical competence – he had high credibility with the engineers working on the project – and his extensive experience in managing international projects. His main aim was to bring the technical problems under control and the project back on track.

When the third project manager took over, the major technical problems had been solved and someone was needed who could make sure that production would progress at satisfactory speed. In fact, someone was needed who had sufficient authority with the French factories to ensure manufacturing would actually happen because here the Eurostar had to compete for capacity with the various TGV models.

An interesting insight from a workshop on project leaders in the context of innovation was that understanding and knowledge of an organisation's culture – how things get done and how to move through the system – was considered to be the most important factor by workshop participants; it was felt that this could not substituted by anything, neither expertise nor otherwise relevant experience.[7]

So whether it is the structure and design of the new product development process, or the choice of project leader, the company or project-specific context and requirements need to be taken into account. Off-the-shelf solutions can only be a starting point, not the final solution.

Perhaps one final comment on project leaders. The choice of the 'right' project manager is important for another reason: one of the key differentiators between projects that are successfully introduced to market and those that fail, or disappear into the black holes of an organisation is often quite simply the enthusiasm and passion of the project leader. This is particularly important for innovative projects where there is inherently a lot of uncertainty as well as potentially a lack of understanding of the concept, and therefore a greater need for selling and communication. And who is most likely to feel passionate about any particular project, extremely keen to tell anyone who may or may not want to hear about it? Who else but the originator of the idea. This has led some organisations, which have previously given innovative ideas to professional project managers for development, to reconsider their approach. They now provide the idea originators with the training necessary to bring them up to speed with project management best practice, or have a professional project manager work alongside them to complement their skills.

READING SUGGESTIONS

On new product development

Clark, K. & Wheelwright, S. (1992). *Revolutionizing Product Development: Quantum Leaps in Speed, Efficiency, and Quality*. New York: Free Press.

Comment: A classic on tools and frameworks for new product development, introducing the development funnel, among other things.

---

[7] Innovation Exchange workshop held 16 October 2003 at the London Business School.

Baxter, M. (1995). *Product Design, Practical Methods for the Systematic Development of New Products*. London: Chapman & Hall.

Comment: While it is written primarily with designers in mind, it provides useful insights into aspects on and around product development, including creativity and innovation. At the end of each chapter Baxter provides a useful summary of key concepts, as well as lists of 'Design Toolkits' for various aspects of the development process.

Smith, P.G. & Reinertsen, D.G. (1997). *Developing Products in Half the Time*, 2nd edition. New York: Van Nostrand Reinhold.

Comment: While focusing on the acceleration of new product development, what problems are and how they can be overcome, this book has lots of useful insights for new product development in general.

Bobrow, E.E. (1997). *The Complete Idiot's Guide to New Product Development*. New York: Alpha Books.

Comment: A bit basic but a good introduction to lots of subjects relevant to new product development.

On project management

Maylor, H. (1996). *Project Management*. London: Pitman.

Comment: I found this a very useful introduction to project management with all sorts of evaluation and assessment techniques.

SOME USEFUL WEBSITES

www.pdma.org

Comment: This website by the Product Development and Management Association provides a useful glossary on new product development terms, as well as book recommendations on and around the subject.

www.stage-gate.com

Comment: This is the website of the consultancy founded by Robert G. Cooper and Scott G. Edgett who are seen to be the originators of the stage-gate process: it provides useful articles, book references and latest insights on and around the stage-gate process.

4 A note on globalisation

While global aspects play only a secondary role in the BBC case study, I would nevertheless like to take the opportunity to expand on that subject as many organisations are grappling with the issue. Not least because in the 2005 survey of the Boston Consulting Group, globalisation was cited as one of the biggest challenges facing many companies in 2005.[1] There are some words that need explaining before one can start a discussion on it; like 'innovation', 'globalisation' is one of them. People have different expectations and concepts in their mind when talking about it. The varying perceptions cause confusion and misunderstandings about the scope and implications of globalisation. And as academic Wood (2000) points out, "Globalisation is fiercely controversial and triggers strong emotions."

Is globalisation a myth or reality? What does globalisation actually mean? What drives and hinders globalisation? What are the advantages and downsides? What does globalisation mean in the context of new product development – does a global product exist? Is globalisation for everyone and what are structures that might facilitate global innovation? This chapter explores these questions and attempts some answers.

MYTH OR REALITY?

Within five years there will be two kinds of managers – those who think in terms of a world economy and those who are unemployed.

Peter Drucker

Recent research suggests that globalisation is a myth.

Rugman & Hodgetts (2001)

Williamson stated in 1994 that, "Thinking and acting globally has become the order of the day in many corporations, both in the US and overseas. The proliferation of telephone service, fax, and electronic mail make it possible for even small companies to have a global reach." A more recent literature review by Ulijn *et al.* (2000) noted that, "Commentaries on organisational vision, effectiveness, direction, and mission usually noted the necessity to innovate and expand beyond normal limits and borders."

---

[1] Innovation 2005; Senior Management Survey by Boston Consulting Group.

Rugman and Hodgetts (2001) on the other hand, who define globalisation as "The activities of multinational enterprises engaged in foreign direct investment and the development of business networks to create value across national borders", declare that, "Recent research suggests that globalisation is a myth. Only in a few sectors, such as consumer electronics, is a global strategy of economic integration viable. For most other manufacturing, such as automobiles, and for all services, strategies of national responsiveness are required, often coupled with integration strategies. Successful multinationals now design strategies on a regional basis; unsuccessful ones pursue global strategies."

In his book *The End of Globalisation*, Rugman (2000) argues that the bulk of world trading activity is regional rather that global and that multinationals must improve their ability to analyse what drives success on a regional, rather than global, basis. In fact, he states that trade is taking place at primarily what he calls 'triad-based', meaning trade between the United States, the countries of the European Union and Japan – rather than globally. As a consequence, so Rugman suggests, companies need to develop a distinctive competence or sustainable competitive advantage within their home region.

During an Innovation Workshop held in spring 1999 this was certainly the view of a participant from an FMCG company who declared, "Global innovation does not work. We have experienced repeated problems in developing a global brand and found it much more useful to develop a product aimed – and fulfilling the needs – of one particular market." This seems to be supported by a survey of six multinational consumer product firms (Colgate-Palmolive, Kraft GF, Nestlé, Procter & Gamble, Quaker Oats and Unilever) in 67 countries on five continents undertaken by Boze and Patton (1995). Their findings indicate that fewer than 1% of brands were global brands, whereby global was defined as being found in 90% or more of the countries surveyed.[2] On the other hand, Nestlé does only 2% of its business in its home country, Switzerland, and the remaining 98% abroad (Espey, 1991).

There is evidence for and against the scope, or even existence, of globalisation. Two comments that might put this into perspective follow. First, what all these statements have in common is that they are backward looking which limits their predictive power for the future. While Rugman might be right that trade currently takes place primarily between three marketplaces, the European Union, the United States and Japan, it does not imply that it will be the same in the future. Could it not rather be argued that globalisation is happening, but that it takes time, just as all change? No one can expect immediate and complete globalisation just because academics have become aware of a trend. Change takes time. As Paul Judge wrote in *Management Today* in August 2001, "Most talk about globalisation is primarily economic. Human beings are even more complex than economies, and are much slower in going global."

Consider cross-functional cooperation and teamwork: these concepts were first promoted about 30 years ago, and as has been pointed out in the previous chapter, they are key to successful product development. But does this mean that today all organisations operate with cross-functional teams? Or rather, does the fact that not all organisations are operating this way mean a trend does not exist? One simple answer as to why not all organisations are following the trend may be that it is just not appropriate for all types of organisations or industries. It is certainly a fact that it has never been easier for a company to enter a marketplace beyond its national boundaries and promote its services or products abroad than today. There is little doubt that the interconnectedness between different parts of the world has increased. To quote Wood (2000) again, "The marriage of telecommunications and computers

---

[2] Procter & Gamble has the most global brands, with 8% of the brands studied distributed in 50% or more of the countries. The majority of brands (50% to 72%) are available in three or fewer countries.

greatly accelerates the process of global economic integration." The degree to which cross-border activities involve one or many countries will depend on product, industry and size of the company in question. And actually, I am not alone with my view, Bryan *et al.* state in their book *Race for the World (1999)*, "The process of economic integration is not new. It has been under way, at a slow pace, for thousands of years. What is new is the pace and the scale."

Secondly, some say globalisation exists, some that it has never happened. Maybe by looking at globalisation at different levels a high degree of agreement can be reached. What do people mean when they talk about globalisation and what are the implications for understanding global innovation?

DEFINITIONS

The term globalisation entered our language in the 1980s and the magazine *The Economist* defines globalisation, short and sweet as "international economic integration". In his book *The Lexus and the Olive Tree* the journalist Tom Friedman goes beyond the purely economic context stating that, "It is the inexorable integration of markets, nation states, and technologies to a degree never witnessed before in a way that is enabling individuals, corporations and nation states to reach around the world farther, faster, deeper, and cheaper than ever before."

Global or international?

But is this global integration a reality for companies today? And are we talking truly global or rather international? Where is the borderline? Williamson (1994) defines the difference as follows, "International organizations house only portions of functions at foreign sites or operate independent business units. In contrast, the global company locates functions based on economic advantage or regulatory considerations."

The discussion might become less confused when trying to understand globalisation at three different levels:

- the economic level
- the organisational level
- the product level

Between the developed world and emerging markets the dollar trade volume has gone up from $802 billion in 1986 to $2 trillion in 1996.

For globalisation at the organisational level we have to consider which industry we are talking about. According to a McKinsey report (quoted in Bryan *et al.*, 1999), the degree of globalisation in petroleum, timber, aluminium or chemicals is somehow higher than in shoes, luxury goods or legal services and definitely higher than in funeral homes or large-scale production materials. The question here is, in how many countries is an organisation operating and trading?

Finally at the product level the discussion is about whether or not it is feasible to: (a) develop products in a global team and (b) sell it to a global customer – we will come back to that later.

Assuming that a trend towards globalisation exists in at least the first two levels introduced above (economic and organisational), we now turn to what enables globalisation, what drives organisations to become (more) global and what are the advantages. This will be followed by an investigation of the obstacles to globalisation as well as some potential downsides.

ENABLERS AND DRIVERS OF GLOBALISATION

There are three main enablers of globalisation:

- deregulation
- new communications
- increasing mobility of capital

Governments are reacting to market pressure to deregulate and open markets to foreign trade. Trade alliances (EU, NAFTA, ASEAN (Southeast Asia), MERCOSUR (South America)) and changes in political climate (Cold War, China) help to open up new markets. Digital technology enables cheaper and faster communication than ever before, and also helps to overcome problems of geographical dispersion. And finally, more and more money crosses borders – foreign exchange transactions per day are $1.5 trillion.

If deregulation, technology and mobility of capital are enablers at the economic/national level, what are the drivers at the organisational level to pursue globalisation? Besides the usual drive to cut cost there are several other drivers underlying the quest for globalisation.

- **Competitive pressures** and a concern for remaining at the forefront of business development are one reason organisations are induced to start thinking globally.

- Access to new markets is not only used to increase trade. More and more companies locate departments based on the **best/most effective conditions** not just considering manufacturing. For example, Branscomb *et al.* (1999) found that the United States relies increasingly on foreign resources for its innovation efforts.

- Another driver is the need to respond to increased **consumer awareness**. Through travel consumers encounter new products or find out about product offerings from other countries through the media – the latter trend has been accelerated by the internet revolution (Gray, 2001). But there is also a dichotomy: people want variety and experience 'exoticness' when abroad but at the same time they want things they are familiar with and want to know exactly what to expect. This is particularly applicable to food.

ADVANTAGES OF GLOBAL INNOVATION

While cutting cost is often one of the reasons companies pursue globalisation strategies, increased efficiencies and reduced complexity and duplication in a company's product portfolio are some of the other benefits gained by the same token.

Along with globalisation strategies companies often increase centralisation as this is seen to be necessary to coordinate brand consolidation and reduction of product variety. Pooling of resources, better integrated portfolio management as well as closer alignment to the company's overall strategy can be further positive side effects of global product management. Operational benefits are the need for fewer manufacturing plants, longer production runs, reduced changeover time and fewer products to stock.

THE FLIPSIDE OF THE COIN

As with everything, global innovation has some disadvantages and problems. One of the most important questions is: does a truly global customer really exist? Judge (2001) points out that human beings are slow to change and that it will therefore take some time for them to become 'global'. The question then is: is it really possible to develop a product that satisfies the needs of a Danish consumer as well as those of a consumer in Nigeria, Chile and Korea? And even if we manage to develop such a global product, a product that must be blander if it wants to satisfy different tastes and needs, do we not leave too much room for a perhaps smaller competitor who focuses on the needs of one country only and can therefore match requirements much better? How many tastes can we satisfyingly integrate before the end result becomes something unexciting and meaningless?

On the other hand, an increase in the travelling population can cause a conflict if a company's strategy is to consolidate brands while maintaining a degree of local adaptation. A consumer used to a certain consistency of a cosmetic product or taste of a particular drink or food who encounters variations when consuming the seemingly same product in a different country will be confused and upset by the inconsistency. The variations between countries in the degree of sweetness in toothpaste is one example, the degree of spiciness in McDonald's food is another.

And while the consolidation of brands has great advantages, companies aiming to reduce their product portfolio by 300% create high pressure for those brands remaining to perform. It also brings up the question as to what criteria should be used for the development of future brands. Is it possible to identify brands with global potential early enough to ensure they are not weeded out by accident? The introduction of a new brand on a global basis is highly risky and costly. Will this result in boring products that are perceived to be safe? What will happen to the innovation aspect of globalisation? And again, will the global company leave its doors wide open for competition from the small and nimble?

Another of the advantages, the pooling of resources, has its disadvantages too. The coordination of development efforts on a global basis leads to increased complexities, where errors of judgement will have far-reaching and costly consequences. Under regional control local managers will have made decisions based on their local insights and their experience. Will this expertise be called upon or will decisions be made by people at the centre who just assume that they know what is best for the regional markets?

OBSTACLES TO GLOBAL INNOVATION

And beyond the potential downsides of global innovation there are also cultural issues within organisations that need to be addressed. Many of the organisations following the goal of globalisation have previously had strongly regionally oriented structures, with considerable power and autonomy given to the local managers. What actions are taken to ensure that 'we' within an organisation is perceived to encompass the entire organisation? Because when headquarters makes decisions on what projects to take forward it will do what is best for the entire organisation – which may not be what is best for any particular region. Will people be able to associate with the distant headquarters?

How much will the feeling of 'us and them' hinder successful development – and more importantly, implementation? Gray (2001) highlights the need to "Remove local subjective prejudices – often founded on old research data and myth – and focus on objective issues." In the Innovation Exchange workshop on global innovation the problems arising from local protectionism were emphasised too. Members of participating companies had experienced that local managers became protective of their organisation and previous power, using perceived regional differences in taste as a pretext to boycott the introduction of new products that had been developed without their involvement, as well as to justify local product development. In such a situation, are centres able to establish *true* rather than perceived or assumed consumer preferences? And more importantly, are these organisations capable of building a culture that overcomes such protectionism?

To achieve global innovation, existing structures will have to change. As Monge and Fulk (1999) point out, "A hierarchical, bureaucratic structure is less responsive in such an environment, and a flatter, more responsive organizational pattern is required." Have those companies seeking to become a global innovator flattened their hierarchies and implemented faster and easier ways of communicating?

Consistency of raw materials and quality of production are further criteria that can hamper globalisation. For example, 3M pointed out that minor variations in the raw material for its sandpaper production led to significant inconsistencies in the product's performance, requiring continuity of suppliers and in product formulation, making transfer of production and formula between locations difficult if not impossible (von Stamm, 1999a).

Finally, the perhaps greatest obstacles to global product development are the differences between nations in a variety of aspects. These include:

- **Differences in consumer preference and habits**. Take for example washing machines. Whereas front-loading machines seem to be the preferred option in most European countries this is not so in France. Here top-loading ones are the norm. Take food where there are also considerable differences in habits. Gray (2001) observes that clues to divergent responses can be found by looking at national attitudes to the environment. For example, Germans tend to be ecologically vigilant, while the French believe food and wine are more important than environmental campaigning. He also reports that when Unilever was developing a new chicken dish it had to bear in mind that in the US chicken is traditionally cooked in the oven, rather than on top of the stove which had implications for the consistency and ingredients of the sauce itself as well as for the instructions on the packaging.

- **Differences in environmental requirements** such as environmental regulations or attitude, for example emission levels in the US are different from those in Europe.

- **Differences in general legislation and company law**. For example, in Germany one cannot just decide to produce and sell leather belts, an accreditation by the responsible crafts guild is required otherwise the person will be liable to fines.

- **Differences in health and safety regulations** can mean that materials acceptable in one country cannot be used in another or that medication freely available in one country is a prescription drug in another.

- **Differences in patenting laws** also exist, for example, if an employee in the UK develops a product for which a patent can be registered within his normal remit of work, the patent will be held by the company, which will also receive the royalty payments. In Germany on the other hand the patent will be in the name of the inventor who will also be the beneficiary of royalty payments.

- Finally, even **differences in the physical environment** such as climate variations and variations in distribution patterns can have an effect.

Fundamental differences between countries remain which when ignored can cause significant problems at best, complete failure at worst. Barkema *et al.* (1996) point out, "Unexpected culture differences might lead to serious failures as demonstrated by a statistical study of foreign entry." Zuckerman (2001) emphasises the need to consider cultural issues when promoting change, "Nothing can sink a global logistics operation faster than ignoring the cultures and mores of any given region." Cultural differences are quite fundamental and will be explored in more depth in Chapter 15.

In the next two sections I will look at the considerations for the organisation of R&D in particular and new product development more generally.

HOW TO STRUCTURE FOR R&D IN A GLOBAL CONTEXT

I would like to start with an overview summary of aspects to consider when deciding upon an R&D structure and their implications – see Table 4.1.

Whatever the structure chosen, in the end the mechanisms that are put in place to facilitate exchange and communication between different parts of the R&D organisation are most critical. Some ways through which communication/exchange could be facilitated:

- Establish some groups that span all parts of the R&D organisations that meet for regular exchanges.

- Arrange regular rotation and secondment between R&D centres.

- Organise conferences/events for people from all R&D centres where they can showcase and discuss what they are currently working on.

In the context of innovation a drive towards bringing other functions, particularly marketing, closer to R&D are noticeable (co-location). However, due to the aforementioned possible misunderstandings particular care needs to be taken when establishing direct collaboration between these two functions.

Some key articles around organising for R&D, particularly in a global context, are summarised below.

Table 4.1 Global or local R&D – criteria for consideration

Aspect	Comment
Degree of innovation	Many organisations pursue radical from the centre, not least as money for these projects often comes from and is ring-fenced by the centre
Importance of speed to market	If speed to market is truly essential then having R&D located in the relevant key markets is important, as is close collaboration with marketing
Specificity of market knowledge	If success depends critically on in-depth and close market understanding then R&D is better delegated to the respective markets
Degree of uniformity of products across markets	Are the same products sold in all markets? If that is the case then it does not make sense to have R&D in all locations; it is more important to find mechanisms to allow those not directly involved to buy into what is being developed for them
Need for economies of scale	If economies of scale are critical then R&D might better be consolidated in one location (does not have to be close to headquarters)
Benefits of close collaboration between marketing and R&D	If close collaboration between marketing and R&D is important to the success, co-location between the two functions is important (it is probably difficult to argue that collaboration is *not* important)
Culture – possible threat of the 'not-invented here' (NIH)? syndrome	Is something rejected just because it was developed by a different country/continent? This should influence the mechanisms that facilitate exchange and communication rather than the overall structure. However, it is an important consideration as acceptance and buy-in from the different parts of the organisation will determine success or failure
Benefits from cross-fertilisation of different parts of the R&D organisation	Are there benefits of having the different bodies of knowledge that make up the R&D department in close proximity, e.g. to encourage boundary-spanning ideas? For example to come up with a Mars bar ice-cream? Then of course having the different parts together is beneficial (however, the benefit might be achieved by rotating people across the different parts of the R&D organisation)

The archetypal R&D function was located in a separate building, or even a separate site, and operated with a different culture and reward system from the mainstream organisation. It tended to be a culture where extensive interaction, peer group exchange and cooperation were emphasised (Fairtlough, 1994). Such groups could be viewed as 'islands of cooperation' operating in a sea of more transactional relationships. However, globalisation pushes organisation to facilitate better collaboration and sharing of knowledge, not only between different departments of an organisation but also between different divisions of an organisation (e.g. Nahapiet et al., 2005).

In his article on R&D strategies Khurana (2006) provides an overview of possible structures based on two dimensions: the first looks at where the primary focus of R&D is or should be, for example on the technology or the regional market, the second is whether R&D is decentralised or centralised. Figure 4.1 provides an overview of the R&D structures he has observed, including company examples.

However, Khurana's graphic does not really consider the degree of innovation that is pursued: some companies separate out research that is more 'blue sky' and keep that close to the centre whereas regional R&D centres deal with the short- to medium-term requirements of the organisation.

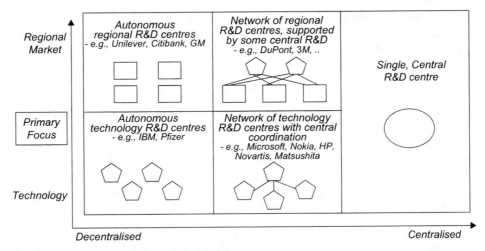

Figure 4.1 Approach to managing global R&D.
Source: Kharuna, A. (2006) Strategies for global R&D; Research Technology Management. Washington: **49**, Mar/Apr: 48–57.

An argument for the decentralisation of R&D, that is the need to undertake R&D outside an organisation's headquarters is made by De Meyer and Mizushima (1989). They argue that what they call the 'globalisation of R&D' has become a necessity for multinational firms as a result of aspects such as:

- the localisation of competition
- product life becoming shorter than development time, and
- the need to place laboratories near sources of new technological expertise

They continue by suggesting that when establishing a new foreign-based laboratory the following should be considered:

- Whether the activities are to be market- or process-oriented, (similar to Khurana's argument of technology vs. region).

- Where on the R&D scale the activities will be placed.

- How far the direction of the laboratory's programmes and work will be decentralised.

They also emphasise that global management requires special attention to the building of open communication networks among the laboratories. Unless good lines of communication are established R&D activities can become disconnected, which means that duplication can occur and potential benefits of the wider network are lost.

Next I would like to introduce three different approaches to R&D in a global context described by Chiesa (1996), which he describes as 'purely global', 'multi-domestic' and 'coordinated network'.

Companies that adopt the **purely global** model generally concentrate their operations in one or more countries. R&D is undertaken primarily at the headquarters of the parent organisation. This approach is based on the assumption that the concentration in one or few locations enables the acceleration of the organisation's learning processes by allowing for fast and effective communication on the one hand and reducing and improving economies of scale on the other.

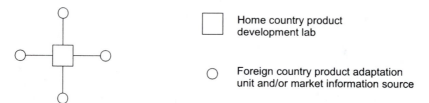

□ Home country product
    development lab

○ Foreign country product adaptation
    unit and/or market information source

1. *Global Central Lab* model: The product development is concentrated in the home country; product adaptation units and/or market information sources are decentralised

○ Global specialised lab

◇ Headquarters

○ Foreign country product
    adaptation unit and/or
    market information source

□ Home country product
    adaptation unit and/or
    market information source

2. *Global Specialised Lab* model: Product development is assigned to a foreign lab with a global mandate; product adaptation units and/or market information sources are dispersed in other countries.

□ Home country product
    development lab

○ Foreign country product
    development lab

3. *Global Integrated Lab* model: Each lab performs local innovations; labs work together on projects of common interest.

There are three different structures in the new form of multinational company called the coordinated netwrok company.

Figure 4.2   Chiesa's three models for global R&D.

Source: Chiesa, V. (1996). Strategies for global R&D. *Research Technology Management*, **39**(5), 19.

The second approach they describe as a **multi-domestic international strategy**. Following this approach companies maintain R&D facilities at their manufacturing plants and commercial affiliates in order to be able to offer local technical support as well as the capability of adapting products to the local needs. In some cases the reason for decentralisation is the desire to develop (rather than adapt) products locally. As the author points out, "these R&D operations are managed by individual subsidiaries on the local level".

The newest of the three approaches to the globalisation of R&D is the **coordinated network company**. As Chiesa describes it, "this model is based on the fact that companies must capitalize on the resources of the different subsidiaries, integrate the resources and capabilities of the different facilities, and exploit the uniqueness of each facility's resources so as to develop and exploit innovations worldwide". Here global R&D is distributed amongst different countries in order to benefit from the specific technical resources each facility or country has to offer. The aim is to further the organisation's overall technological capabilities and increase overall profits. Here individual R&D organisations follow their own, specific research agenda but as part of an overall, globally coordinated plan.

Chiesa proposes that the coordinated network company is the only effective approach, arguing that neither a multi-domestic nor a purely global strategy can facilitate successful management of R&D in a global context. His three approaches are shown in Figure 4.2.

Whereas the previous articles are mainly descriptive, Birkinshaw (2001) provides some insights on what should influence the choice of R&D structure. He suggests that the nature of knowledge pertinent to R&D should drive the organisational structure chosen for R&D and proposes the flow shown in Figure 4.3.

The nature of what he calls the 'knowledge asset' should drive the attributes of the R&D centre, which in turn is interdependent with the mandate of the centre, that is what kind of research is to be undertaken by the centre (time horizon, degree of innovation, etc.). This then has implications for the organisational structure chosen for R&D. In my view the relationship is more iterative and interrelated as the chosen R&D structure will in turn have implications for the knowledge generated.

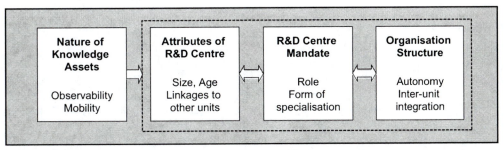

Figure 4.3 Deciding on an R&D structure.

Source: Reprinted from *Long Range Planning*, **35**(3), Birkinshaw, Julian, Managing internal R&D networks in global firms – What sort of knowledge is involved?, pp. 245–267, Copyright 2001, with permission from Elsevier.

In his research he focuses on two dimensions of knowledge: observability and mobility. **Observability** is the extent to which the knowledge base of the R&D centre can be understood through observation, for example by taking a tour of the facilities, by watching the employees at work, or by talking to some employees. It refers to "how easy it is to understand the activity by looking at and examining different aspects of the process or final product". **Mobility** is the extent to which the knowledge base of the R&D centre can be separated from its physical setting. The less the knowledge is associated with specialised capital equipment, the less the linkages with related activities such as manufacturing, and the less the linkages with the local community, the more mobile the knowledge is.

Looking at these two dimensions Birkinshaw observes three different types of R&D operations, the characteristics of which are described in Table 4.2.

Table 4.2 Typical characteristics of three types of R&D centre

	Self-contained R&D centre	Modular R&D centre	Home base R&D centre
Nature of knowledge assets			
Observability	High	Low	Low
Mobility	Low	High	Low
Attributes of R&D centre			
Size	Small–medium	Small–medium	Medium–large
Age	Relatively old	Relatively young	Relatively old
Knowledge assets are substitutable	Low	High	Mixed
Linkages to other units	Co-located with manufacturing	Not co-located with any other activity	Co-located with both manufacturing and business management
R&D centre mandate			
Role of R&D centre	Unique role – there are no other centres with this capability profile	Non-unique role – there may be other centres with similar capability profiles	Unique role
Form of specialisation	Vertical specialisation, i.e. working with a project through to commercialisation	Horizontal specialisation, i.e. focusing on one step in the R&D value chain	Vertical specialisation, working with several projects through to commercialisation
Organisation structure			
Level of autonomy	Relatively high	Relatively low	Relatively high
Level of integration with rest of network	Relatively low	Relatively high	Relatively high

Source: Reprinted from *Long Range Planning*, **35**(3), Birkinshaw, Julian, Managing internal R&D networks in global firms – What sort of knowledge is involved?, pp. 245–267, Copyright 2001, with permission from Elsevier.

Moving up a level to look at **networks of R&D organisations** Birkinshaw identifies two approaches as most common. The first he describes as an **integrated network of R&D units**. This type has physical representation in different countries which behave as if they were an integrated whole. The advantage of this approach is that it enables a coherent and structured R&D strategy to emerge. The downside of this approach is that it leaves relatively little freedom to the individual R&D units because they are basically acting as executing bodies of the headquarters. The second approach is a more loosely coupled network model whereby individual units act as **centres of excellence**, specialising on a particular technology or competency area and having much more freedom in terms of what they develop. This is what Chiesa describes as the coordinated network company. Characteristics and identification criteria and implications for managing two different kinds of R&D networks, loosely coupled and integrated, are shown in Table 4.3.

Table 4.3 Two models of R&D networks

	Loosely coupled network	Integrated network
Nature of knowledge assets in R&D	Low mobility; various levels of observability	Low observability; various levels of mobility
Nature of technology and products made by firm	Relatively stand-alone products	Relatively interdependent, greater reliance on technical standards etc.
Typical industries	Electrical, mechanical engineering, automotive, industrial products	IT, telecommunications, pharmaceuticals
Approach to R&D strategy	Strategy broadly defined; R&D centre roles shaped at corporate level, but defined through bottom-up process	Strategy defined in a top-down manner; R&D centre roles are defined at corporate level, with less bottom-up input
Management of R&D network	Broad areas of responsibility defined, interfaces managed to avoid unnecessary overlap. Resourced either through central funding process, or through long-term contracts with business units	Modularised system. R&D work assigned to specific centres. Resource allocation usually top-down, but can also be contracted
Management of individual R&D centres		
Degrees of freedom for R&D centre managers	Relatively high	Relatively low
Centralisation of decision making	Low	Moderate–high
Formalisation of processes and standards	Low	High
Informal patterns of interaction	Low–moderate	High

Source: Reprinted from *Long Range Planning*, **35**(3), Birkinshaw, Julian, Managing internal R&D networks in global firms – What sort of knowledge is involved?, pp. 245–267, Copyright 2001, with permission from Elsevier.

What is increasingly clear is that, as with everything related to innovation, there is no one right way, but different ones, depending on the desired outcome and the context. And more often than not it will not be a question of 'either/or' but of finding a way to facilitate both.

WHAT DOES GLOBAL MEAN IN THE CONTEXT OF NEW PRODUCT DEVELOPMENT?

Focusing on the product level, globalisation can take two meanings: (a) it can refer to a product that is developed for a global consumer – either by a central or by a global team; or (b) it can mean that a product is sold on a worldwide basis – be it exactly the same product or variations of a product under the same name (see Figure 4.4).

The difference is important as it has implications for the development of new products.

While the 'development team' aspect will have implications primarily during the design and development process, the number of nationalities that make up a product's 'market' is likely to have implications for the outcome itself. It is important to understand differences in two situations:

1.   When developing products for a specific country (one nationality).
2.   When developing products across countries (many nationalities).

The first is necessary to understand what the 'order winner' in that particular country is. The second is necessary to understand whether one and the same product can be a success in a number of countries or whether adjustment would improve the odds for success – or may even be necessary. This does not mean that one can expect people of a certain national background to behave exactly as predicted by the stereotypes! For example, I am German but I cannot stand beer. I believe I have some sense of humour (but I know what people mean when they refer to the Germans as not having one…). I am a freak for punctuality – but then I know Germans who aren't. What I tend to say is, if you meet a German, you will more likely or more frequently be able to observe certain behaviours and characteristics. Or put differently, when you have a group of 1000 French people and 1000 Danish people, you will find certain behaviours and values more frequently in one group than the other.

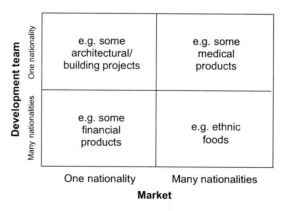

Figure 4.4   Degrees of globalisation.

Assuming that there is a global consumer means that marketers will aim to develop a product that appeals to people around the world. Such a product must therefore consider and address a great variety of preferences.

The most difficult scenario is probably the development of a product for a 'global' market developed by a global team. In such a scenario the result is very likely the result of a series of consensus decision, which most likely reflect the lowest common denominator. Such a watering down of concepts in the attempt to satisfy a global audience has been observed by Martin Smith, former Chief Executive of the advertising agency Grey Worldwide London. In his FT article (2001) 'Sorry, that's too interesting for us', he laments "A loss of subtlety and nuance in ads caused by risk-averse marketers dulling them down to accommodate a global audience."

Another consequence of aiming to find a consensus between varying design tastes can be a lack of ownership. Each party assumes that the result reflects the other parties' preference – while in actual fact it does not please anyone. A story from the development of the high-speed train connecting the capitals of Belgium, France and the UK, the Eurostar, in which all three countries were involved, may serve to illustrate the point. Those who have travelled on the Eurostar may recall the pink-frosted lampshades in the first class carriages. The French press referred to them as 'typical English pink', whereas the UK press associated them with 'typical bohemian French'. Each side thought it was the other country's taste that had influenced the decision while no one seemed to be happy with it. If that happens when coordinating tastes between three countries, and all of them European, what would happen to a global product?

There are products that might not necessarily have been developed with the 'global' consumer in mind but have ended up being sold globally – Coca-Cola or McDonald's foods are examples. Such products often have a strong national association – which is part of their attraction. Coca-Cola, widely cited as a 'truly global product', started off as a product that was developed in response to a specific local need in a specific local market. Marketing and the drink's taste that appealed to a wide audience mean it is today one of the most widely available products around the globe. Coca-Cola has become global but it was not developed with that intention in mind. And, as Rugman (2000, p.170) points out the Coca-Cola formula is not quite the same everywhere, the amount of syrup used is varied to cater for regional preferences in sweetness.

Another product often assumed to be global is the car. An example of a successful 'global product': Chrysler's PT Cruiser. As Tom Lockwood (2000) (Global Brand and Design Strategy Manager, StorageTek) writes, "A decade ago, the differences between cultural design preferences and the communication inefficiencies caused by geographical distance could have made this kind of international appeal difficult, if not unthinkable. But the internet now allows designers, engineers, and marketers to disseminate ideas globally in a matter of seconds and keep close track of cultural preferences, trends and design processes." The car is selling 175,000 a year instead of the expected 70,000 on both sides of the Atlantic. However, even here it may only hold true for the base model. Having been involved in an international exhibition by the motor company Ford I realised that different aspects of the car were highlighted as standards, depending on the nationality of the audience. Each country addresses national preferences by the varying offerings of fittings, colours and standards. Such adjustments can put a question mark behind concepts of global production and distribution.

While emphasising the need to understand the differences I would by no means like to suggest that the attempt to develop global products is always futile. In fact, Kleinschmidt and Cooper (1988) reported nearly 15 years ago that "industrial products that are developed for world applications and are targeted at export markets will have more success". It will depend on the industry and product in question, and to what degree consumer tastes are truly compatible. And again the issue might be one of definition. Does global mean *exactly* the same – or 'variations on a theme'? Products that vary at the following levels may still be considered 'global':

- different product formulations (e.g. cream, toothpaste, scents, etc.)

- product features (e.g. cars, washing machines, mobile phones)

- packaging varying to address different design preferences (e.g. toys, pharmaceuticals)

- different distribution channels, depending on the host country's existing infrastructure

- different approaches to marketing depending on consumer preference (e.g. different types of sales promotion, 2 for 1, vouchers, bundling, etc.)

- different approaches to advertising (different types of humour, play on words etc.)

None of the above is detrimental to the concept of a global product, the questions should be, how easy – effort (possibility) and cost – could we adapt an existing product? When faced with a decision of whether a product has global potential an organisation might want to consider the following aspects of new product development:

- Product ideas – Is there a consumer group to which the product is relevant that exists in more than one country? Are there differences at the systems level? E.g. regulation, power supply.

- Manufacture – Is manufacture possible in more than one country, if not, is transportation easy and cost efficient? Are raw materials sufficiently consistent across markets?

- Marketing/advertising – What are consumer preferences in approaches to marketing? Are tastes, preferences for advertising compatible?

- Approach towards sales and distribution – To what sales promotions do consumers react favourably? What distribution channels do they use?

- After-sales service – What are expectations towards after-sales services? What services are to be included in the purchase of the product, what is an 'extra'?

Depending on the degree of overlap, product managers might want to decide to launch a 'global' product or develop separate brands.

WHAT TO CONSIDER WHEN GOING GLOBAL

Larry Roelling (Executive Vice President at Enterprise IG consultants in San Francisco) has the following recommendation for developing a global brand:

- Create a captivating name, wordmark or symbol that is understood and has positive connotations around the world in all applicable markets.

- Determine whether it is best to accentuate or play down country associations.

- Be willing to modify strategy to accommodate cultural diversity.

- Devise packaging that strengthens brand impression.

- In the development and execution of product or service, be sensitive to environmental, social and ethical considerations.

- Research the laws of each country as they affect sales and marketing.

- Balance economies of scale with a local presence.

Gray (2001) has some similar advice, "What most global brands have in common is a powerful identity. Successful global brands often feature abstract brand names, as well as identities that are single-minded and memorable, but not literal." He continues to give the following recommendations:

- Develop a holistic brand brief that encompasses all communication of the brand at every consumer interface. This brief should be the bible against which everything is objectively measured – all research must be designed and implemented tightly against the objectives set out in the brief. Ensure that the bible is bought into at all relevant levels through all markets – failure to do this will invariably result in confrontation down the line.

- Create a strong, simple visual brand icon capable of instantly identifying the brand through all communication and flexible enough to incorporate local detail.

- Communicate the brand consistently, cohesively and repeatedly and do not allow creativity to get in the way of simple communication.

In addition, much of the best practice identified for new product development and innovation is equally applicable to global innovation. As for all initiatives that are to be taken seriously, it is important for **the top to lead the way**. Research by Heiss and Fraser (2000) found that top corporate executives who consider their companies very successful globally spend 40% of their time on global issues, compared with 25% for executives overall. A way to give weight to the importance and seriousness of global would be, for example, to give profit relief to global innovation projects which may take longer to become profitable – and to develop alternative metrics for innovation, for example the number of intellectual property rights gained.

If a **clear and focused strategy** is important in any scenario, it becomes paramount for the successful implementation of a globalisation strategy – more on the role of strategy and vision in Chapter 6. Communication plays a critical role, as emphasised by Heiss and Fraser (2000) in the following statement, "Best-practices companies are balancing the global–local challenge of overall communication – advertising, branding and media relations. These companies are synchronizing international operations and coordinating these activities in communicating information from local subsidiaries to headquarters. Globalization has increased the need for clear, consistent and central corporate messages with adaptation at the local level."

The desire to maximise benefits from globalisation companies tends to lean towards a **centralisation of new product development** activities. This was seen to be necessary to avoid duplication and allow maximisation of existing resources. A further advantage of a centralised approach was seen to be the opportunity for cross-funding over a longer time horizon. Projects that might otherwise have fallen prey to the consequences of quarterly or bi-annual reporting could be pursued for the long-term benefit of the organisation – and taking a global perspective on new product development might also help to smooth the waves of economic turbulences across countries.

The **sharing of knowledge** should be supported by establishing global networks and the facilitation of effortless communication between different parts of the organisation. As Heiss and Fraser (2000) found, "Best-practices companies are using research to develop a better understanding of their global constituencies – and communicators must immerse themselves in the research process."

Global innovation is built on **collaboration and relationships**. Without people working together, sharing insights and information global innovation cannot happen. Selectron's Vice President of Global Logistics, Jim Molzon, states that he can't get 'buy in' to company goals in overseas operations unless it's a collaborative process (in Zuckerman, 2001).[3]

Dedicated resources are needed. An Innovation Exchange member commented as follows (von Stamm, 2001) "We have a very limited number of global projects – or rather projects with global potential. At no time is the project managed from the centre, the leadership is always with one of our innovation centres. But as the local centre does not always have the right skills and resources to execute the project, we will second people or give part of the project to the central research facility, establishing virtual teams – but the leadership always stays local."

While it makes sense to centralise some activities, others should remain with the regions. Examples are accounting and payroll systems. In addition, to accommodate local differences in custom and law, some companies are sorting their application portfolios according to their applicability on a local, regional or global basis and obtaining economies of scale by rewriting those that can be used globally (Williamson, 1994). Best-practice companies are balancing the global–local challenge even though seeing the benefits of such an approach may take some time, as one Innovation Exchange company reports, "The matrix we are using to **balance global and local requirements** was time consuming to start with. And it was frustrating to get consensus and to get consistency across the process but we have managed it now. How have we overcome the initial problems? Because of the commitment of the people and the clarity everyone shares about business direction."

However, sometimes the findings will indicate that differences are so fundamental that the development of a product appropriate for a variety of markets will be impossible. For an organisation it is important to remain open and accepting of such situations – particularly if the product is widely believed to have global potential. Gray (2001) provides the example of research undertaken by a design consultancy that when charged with the development of a new stationery range for a global office products company came across significant differences in expectations of children's pencil cases: in the US, pencil cases had to be bigger to be best, while in Germany it needed lots

---

[3]Selectron is a contract manufacturer of computer boards and equipment for companies such as Dell and Compaq and has 60 manufacturing operations in 28 countries and five continents.

of compartments and in France there was a more haphazard approach. As the designer commented, "It became apparent there was no way we could design a global pencil case."

SUMMARY

This chapter has addressed the following questions:

- What does globalisation actually mean?
- What are the drivers and obstacles to globalisation?
- What insights do we have for structuring R&D?
- What does this mean for global new product development?
- What to consider when developing global products?

Globalisation means different things to different people but for the purpose of this chapter it refers to the fact that companies are increasingly broadening their geographical reach and adjusting their structures and processes, new product development in particular, accordingly. Planning and coordination takes place at a global/international level rather than the national/regional one – which does not preclude new product development at the regional level, it only means that decisions about which projects are taken forward are being made at the centre.

While globalisation may not have reached its full potential, strategic planning in companies considers actions and planning for the global (or at least international) level rather than the national/regional one. Truly global products, in the sense that the exactly same product satisfies consumer needs in countries around the globe, hardly exist. But sometimes quite simple and small variations will address varying consumer needs and in such situations the planning and developing of a 'global' product may make sense.

READING SUGGESTIONS

On globalisation in general

Rugman, A. (2000). *The End of Globalisation*. London: Random House.

Comment: In his book Rugman pursues the line that there is no globalisation and never has been, as the connectivity and exchange is primarily happening between three regions, North America, the European Union and Japan; the author discusses the implication of this different view of globalisation for managers and strategy planning.

Lowell, B., Frazer, J., Oppenheim, J. & Rall, W. (1999). *Race for the World*. Boston, MA: Harvard Business School Press.

Comment: Written by four McKinsey consultants, the book paints the picture of a world that is increasingly connected with any one company operating in more and more markets. The authors suggest how managers can prepare their organisation to be in the pack that 'leads the race for the world'.

Hill, C.W.L. (2004). *International Business: Competing in the Global Marketplace*, 5th edition New York: McGraw-Hill.

Comment: In his book Hill addresses the question, 'How does a business go global/international?' and offers insights on the process of internationalisation, why businesses chose to go global and the managerial implications of such decisions. He provides a lot of background of particular economic and other implications, probably slightly weaker on implications from an innovator's perspective.

SOME USEFUL WEBSITES

http://www.globalisationguide.org/

Comment: Starting more from an economic perspective, this site provides some insights on questions such as, 'What is globalisation and where did it start?', 'Who are the players?' and 'What are the costs and benefits of free trade?'

5 Innovation and branding for the web

CASE STUDY 2: IHAVEMOVED.COM[1] (A)

What next?

In July 2000 the four founders of ihavemoved.com sat at their boardroom table in the grip of a mild panic. Having launched their website in November 1999, secured £2.5 million finance in March 2000 – signed just before the NASDAQ crash – they were faced with significantly dropping registration rates. The advertising campaign they had run in May and June 2000 to raise awareness had had a positive impact on overall brand awareness and had attracted lots of visitors to their website but actual sign-ups to their services were dropping significantly. What were they to do next in order to secure the future of the company in which they had invested all their personal wealth?

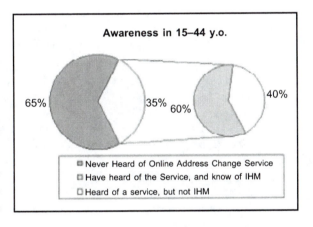

Awareness in 15–44 y.o.

65%   35% 60%   40%

- Never Heard of Online Address Change Service
- Have heard of the Service, and know of IHM
- Heard of a service, but not IHM

The starting point

The ignition point for ihavemoved.com (IHM) occurred during an MBA course at London Business School (LBS) in 1997. For their second-year project, David Anstee and Niko Komninos teamed up to develop a business plan. Internet ideas were still hip and cool back then so the original idea was to devise a website on which people could view properties for free and the company would make money from selling mortgages. Their idea got nominated to represent LBS at the European Business Plan competition at INSEAD, France in June 1999. As soon as they arrived they found out that people from Imperial College had a very similar idea which led, not surprisingly, to a lot of frantic activity on both sides to fine-tune presentations and impress the jury. Custom-made folders were produced for each judge and glasses of vodka with mango juice were handed out – a potent subliminal reminder of the company's name: 'MangoHomes'. But not only that, as David remembers, "We also did a fake *Business Week* cover

---

[1] The case has been prepared by Dr Bettina von Stamm as a basis for class discussion rather than to illustrate either effective or ineffective handling of a management situation.

with 'MangoHomes wins' which was put under the judges' hotel room doors overnight." But to no avail, whereas Imperial achieved third, they did not even get placed.

Also realising that the time lapse between identifying a property and dealing with the mortgage might cause problems, they started a major rethink of the original idea, deciding that they should find a value proposition that better integrated into the service.

MONEY Go Round

ONE of the biggest hassles for home-movers is making sure you've given everyone your new address including utilities, the DSS, Passport Office, DVLA and taxman.

Now a website will contact up to 600 organisations for you free. Just log on to **www.ihave moved.com** If you haven't got a computer, phone 0207 799 3300 for a form.

The revised idea was sparked by a breakfast conversation between flatmates David and Francesco Benincasa, one of the subsequent co-directors. Occasionally at weekends they used to sit down and go through all the mail that would pile up during the week. They used to get stacks of mail, addressed to other people, obviously previous tenants who for one reason or another hadn't bothered to tell their friends, debt collection agencies and utility suppliers that they had moved. Francesco and David wondered where the people had moved to and what they were missing out on through not receiving their post. They also thought about how much money companies were wasting by posting out information to people who would never receive it. They expressed their vision as: "ihavemoved.com will enable individuals and companies to change address for every piece of mail that crosses their threshold: quickly, easily and conveniently." The idea for a change of address service was born in summer 1999.

They presented their revised business idea at the London Business School in Kathy Hammond's class 'New Media Markets' but the feedback they got from students, who were concerned about privacy issues, was quite negative! However, this time they were not dissuaded by the negative feedback and decided to push on.

By this time, the team had grown to four, Onic Palandjian, a childhood friend of Niko's had joined, bringing his sales experience to the party, an ideal complement to David's background in finance, Niko's marketing expertise and Francesco's knowledge of internet business gleaned from running an internet consultancy (more details of their professional background can be found in Appendix 5.1). Not only were the professional skills complementary, they also got on well at a personal level, which was considered very important as Francesco emphasised, "I'd lived alongside David for a year before we worked together and Niko and Onic grew up together, so we all knew how each other would react in a fast-growing business."

To avoid complications and disappointment, the autumn was spent not only refining the idea, seeking lawyers' advice and developing a website, but also for lots of meetings to talk about where people felt they should be in five years' time and what they wanted out of life.

Market opportunity and competition

The population of the UK is just under 60 million, of which around 10% move each year. Nearly 80% of all movers are aged between 15 and 44. This corresponds closely to the demographics associated with internet usage, with

78% of users falling into the same age group. From this information, they deduced that there are at least 2.3 million online movers each year in the UK.

When ihavemoved.com launched its website there were about 100 property sites around but they were the only company offering an online change of address service in the UK. In contrast to mail forwarding with the Post Office, their service was free to movers. It was not until July 2000 that a competitor emerged, being a close copy of how IHM's site looked at the time. 'Company X' had started as an offline service but launched an online version just after ihavemoved.com's advertising campaign. As David remembers, "We responded to their threat by also

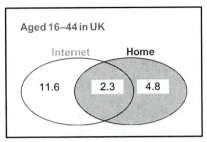

offering an offline form, figuring that if they were entering 'our' market, we would enter theirs and increase the pressure." In autumn 2000 Company X, employing six staff (of which five were directors drawing no salary) and averaging about three address changes a day, was seeking £750,000 in funding. With the very tough market, raising money was almost impossible, especially with a clear market leader in IHM distancing itself from them apace.

From idea to reality

ihavemoved.com Ltd was registered in July 1999. Then, to prove the concept and have a prototype to show potential partners and investors, Francesco built a functioning demo site. The founders skimmed the fax or e-mail addresses for customer service departments off bills and websites of key companies, and used this to pass on the trickle of change requests that came through the site. Whilst a bit cheeky and only marginally legal, this 'rapid prototyping' approach proved the concept, boosted the learning cycle and gave the impression of progress and credibility.

Jun 99	Leave LBS
Jul 99	Set up company
Aug 99	Demo site
	– put up companies
	– process first
	change of address
Sep 99	HSBC loan
Nov 99	Bluewave site launch
Dec 99	British Gas
Dec 99	PowerGen
Mar 00	Rothschild funding

Through the UK Government Guarantee Scheme, the company was able to raise £30,000 in an unsecured loan from HSBC, due to a relationship Francesco had from his previous company. This enabled IHM to retain Bluewave, a web design agency selected from a shortlist of three firms for its understanding of the opportunity and its enthusiasm for the project.

Equipped with initial screenshots from Bluewave and a healthy dose of enthusiasm, it was time to start selling. Two factors made the utility sector the most amenable to IHM's offering. Deregulation in the electricity and gas markets had resulted in intense competition for customers. Secondly, moving home requires disconnection and reconnection, and this is the perfect point to capture a new customer . . . or lose an existing one. Utilities were the companies to hit, and Centrica (British Gas) was the biggest game in town.

Value proposition

Basically, companies would pay for clean information delivered at the time of moving, in a format easily incorporated
into their customer database. This would save costs and
make it easier to stay in touch with customers. For movers,
this free service would save time and hassle, as well as
acting as an effective reminder for all the tasks easily for-
gotten during the stressful moving process. IHM made a
high gross margin revenue stream from notifications and
commissions. It also collected rich and timely information
about its users. This was seen as the likely real long-term
value of the company.

> ### Using the website
> - Log on
> - Enter old and new address
> - Select the companies which need to be informed
> - Enter specific data where required
> - That's it

The revenue model

The team came up with a number of revenue avenues, including charging users of the site; however, after investigating
the options, it seemed the following were the best options:

- **New customer commission**

    The service provider partners offer significant commissions on new customers, cross-sales and up-sales. In
    the case of a telecommunication company, this ranges from £5 to £90, depending on the product sold. From
    one energy company, a new dual fuel customer can generate up to £40.

- **Digital update service**

    IHM partners pay £1 per notification of a customer address change in a digital format compatible with their
    existing database. This pales in comparison to the expenses associated with call centres, data entry and
    administration.

- **Banner advertisements**

    The type of traffic IHM attracts, and the ability to target specific advertisements at very narrowly defined
    demographics, have enabled the company to sell banner and sponsorship space at above-average rates.

Looking for funding

Having the idea seemed easy, but how and where to get the money for the investments necessary to get the
business going? The four partners had used their own money – around £100,000 in total – to get the business off
the ground, but they now needed serious money to put the company on a proper footing: offices and more staff
were required to enable growth. In addition, they realised that they would have to upgrade the website which did
not work quite as they wanted. The usability both from the user as well as their perspective was not satisfactory, it
was inflexible and unintuitive.

With a website up and running, first customers and companies signed up and with first revenues coming in they had not anticipated how difficult it would be to find investors, especially as money seemed to be handed out to almost any business idea during this time, the dotcom boom. Initially they were quite protective about their idea – but got more relaxed as time went on. Without introductions it was impossible to get through doors – and even with an introduction it was hard work to get even the chance to present the idea. David remembers, "Rising above the noise was difficult. Venture capitalists were seeing so many business proposals and dotcom ideas that they were difficult to contact, were frequently rude and usually devoted very little time to each new idea. It did not help that many operate on a black-ball system where one vote against it is sufficient to reject the proposal. While we could usually convince the people we met of the merit of the idea, it was very difficult to get in front of people in the first place. In a way venture capitalists are quite risk averse, they want proof that something has worked before – but what if what you do is so new it does not have a point of referral?" It was an interesting experience to find that venture capitalists should prefer to invest in 'me toos'.

After contacting over 40 venture capitalists, and presenting at dozens of meetings, the breakthrough finally came on 18 January. First Tuesday was holding its regular networking evening at the Mermaid Theatre in London. CNN were filming the funding frenzy, and they followed the ihavemoved team as they worked the room. At the dinner that followed, Francesco sat next to Zoe Appleyard of Continuation Investments NV ('CINV' – the principal private equity vehicle for the Rothschild investment banking group). Zoe was the executive responsible for bringing in new business at the firm. Not only did she like the business concept immediately, it also fitted very well with CINV's investment strategy, which focused on investing in TMIT (telecommunications, media, internet, technology) businesses. While most investors had been sceptical about the business idea, CINV immediately saw some unique selling points such as a first-mover advantage, a good concept that was simple and obvious, and further possibilities once the data had been collected. In addition, there were synergies with another CINV investment, upmystreet.com (incidentally ihavemoved.com and upmystreet.com entered a business relationship in July 2001). The investment proposal went to committee mid-February and the contract was signed on 8 March 2000.

After a first investor was secured, others followed suit: Hyundai, who saw them on the 19 January CNN broadcast; Nicholas Negroponte whom they met through a Greek connection of Onic's; and Internet Indirect (later acquired by New Media Spark). By the time they signed the investment agreement for £2.5 million in March 2000, things were desperate: they had sold houses and stretched their credit cards to the limits, BT had already cut off the phone, and they were seriously short of cash. The timing was tight from another perspective too: just two days after they signed the agreement the dotcom crash happened and the NASDAQ index went into freefall.

Putting the money to work

With fresh money available, the founding team was now able to put structures and systems into place that would set the company for future growth. Immediate steps were to get offices and hire five more people (an operations manager, an operations assistant, a sales manager, a marketing assistant and a website manager). The total number of staff grew from seven in March 2000 to 12 in May and 17 in July.

Next on the agenda was an upgrade of the website by Bluewave to sort out problems with the functionality of the site and improve the user experience. Then they commissioned Conquest to design an advertising campaign to boost awareness and position the company as a first mover. This ran in June 2000, to coincide with the relaunch. Costing £600,000 this was quite a moderate amount for an internet start-up. So far they had only deployed a successful PR campaign with most major national newspapers covering the story.

To mark the relaunch of their website they decided to celebrate with a high-profile event at the Royal Opera House. Their breakfast seminar on 2 June 2000 – at which they had secured high-calibre speakers such as Nicholas Negroponte, founder of the MIT Media Lab and *Wired Magazine*, and Alex Allan, the UK e-envoy – was attended by their other investors, 200 delegates from the UK's largest companies, as well as CNN.

The results of the medium-sized launch produced good results, about a third of the target population of 18–44 year olds knew that they could change their address online, 60% of whom also knew that the place to do it was ihavemoved.com. The team were also pleased to find that all service providers they contacted seemed to have heard of ihavemoved.com. While the campaign had been great in promoting awareness of ihavemoved.com's services, it had also alerted competition to a great opportunity: in July 2000 a competitive site went online. Company X had previously offered their service offline and now decided to offer their services online too.

While the relaunch had been a great success, they had struggled greatly to get Bluewave to complete the redesign of the website for the relaunch, despite quite close operation and making extra funds available to boost resource input at Bluewave. Even with only two weeks to go to the start of the advertising campaign and the relaunch party, the website had been far from ready. Frustrated at the progress, they decided to get technical and design expertise in-house and hire a chief technical officer. However, this was quite a risky move as none of the directors had the knowledge necessary to assess the technical capabilities of the new recruit. Using their network they found Andrew

Andrew Day

Information technology has been a part of Andrew's life since he was 13 years old, when he wrote the first published machine code version of the game *Space Invaders* in 1977. After four years in the banking sector, in 1995 he founded a company to offer online information services – he could be viewed as one of the original dotcommers. Before joining ihavemoved.com in June, Andrew provided consultancy services to Virgin Mobile Phones.

Day, who turned out to be just what they needed. Not only was he able to immediately identify major flaws with the newly redesigned website, he was also able to fix them. Having the design resource in-house not only gave them more control, it was also much cheaper.

The need to accelerate growth

So far so good. The company had successfully secured funding, relaunched its website, and the advertising campaign had given the company a profile in the crowded dotcom scene. High levels of interest from the media had helped

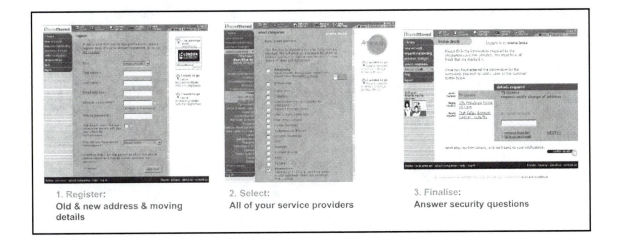

1. Register:
Old & new address & moving details

2. Select:
All of your service providers

3. Finalise:
Answer security questions

too: between 1 November 1999 and 31 August 2000, the company achieved 161 mentions in the press, averaging four a week. This reached a cumulative 46.7 million people in the UK. In addition, the company and website had won several awards. However, the high levels of awareness did not seem to be translating into actual customers, sign-ups to the services were lower than expected and they needed to grow faster in order to meet revenue projections and financial commitments.

When the directors were pondering what steps to take to accelerate growth, they revisited the arrangements they had with one company, PowerGen. In December 1999 PowerGen and ihavemoved.com had come to an arrangement under which PowerGen had incorporated ihavemoved.com's service into its own website. PowerGen had understood immediately the benefits that 'clean' and formatted data would provide and had wanted to ensure that more of its customers would be using the system. It also meant that it would be able to offer a better service to its customers who, when visiting PowerGen's website, would find an address changing service as part of the site's offerings. The website would of course be branded with PowerGen's look and feel. ihavemoved.com would lose its branding and the only reference to IHM would be 'powered by ihavemoved.com'. The question was, whether it would be feasible and sensible to offer such a structure to other customers. Many organisations had to re-acquire their customers when they move and these organisations are very keen to find newer, more efficient ways of doing this.

This was an interesting proposal but quite threatening too. If a strong brand was considered increasingly important for a 'bricks & mortar' company, it was said to be essential for a web-based one. Over the months they had managed to build up very good awareness for their brand, would they lose all that by having their concept integrated into another organisation's website?

And how would PowerGen's competitors react if ihavemoved.com put their services on PowerGen's site? Would they stay with ihavemoved.com or would they withdraw?

Finally, the production of custom-made pages for different providers took development time and resource, which cost money. Could ihavemoved.com get companies like PowerGen to pay for this production when essentially this initiative helped promote the ihavemoved.com service and create revenue for the company from the backend notifications? Would the partners instead seek to charge ihavemoved.com or request revenue share for promoting them on their websites and should ihavemoved.com pay?

Questions

1.   Why was it important to position ihavemoved.com as a first mover?
2.   What would you do to take the company forwards?

APPENDIX 5.1: BACKGROUND TO THE FOUR FOUNDERS

E. David Anstee

BCom (Melbourne), MBA (London Business School)

David has four years of experience in equity raising and corporate finance with Merrill Lynch Australia. He spent his summer break working with Arts Alliance, a London-based venture capitalist, vetting business plans, meeting portfolio companies and working on a business plan under a scholarship scheme. With a focus on entrepreneurial studies both at London Business School and while on

1997–99 London Business School
1995–97 Travel, National Geographic
1991–95 Merrill Lynch Australia
1994–99 3D World Newspaper, Sydney

exchange to the Haas School of Business at UC Berkeley, David is responsible for the financial performance of the company, German operations and investor relations.

Francesco Benincasa

BSc (Cardiff), IOD

As managing director and founder of the Chameleon Group, Francesco has worked in web communications and strategic planning since 1995. He has delivered pioneering web strategies to McKinsey Consulting, the BBC, NCR, Evolution Consulting, McGregor Boyall and TrustWorks. Francesco's responsibilities include online marketing, relationships with key partners and white-label integration.

1995–99 Managing director of Chameleon Strategic reviews for BBC, BT, Dixons. Online branding for Freeserve
1992 RAF Officer Cadet Pilot
1989–92 BSc Hons University of Wales

Nicholas Komninos

BA, BAS(Penn), MBA (London Business School)

Prior to his MBA, Nicholas was a Flight Sergeant for the Hellenic Air Force, dealing extensively with HR-related issues, and account executive for OgilvyOne advertising where he planned, conducted and evaluated international marketing campaigns. He has an academic background in psychology and practical experience in designing HRM systems during his summer internship at Qualco Management Consultants. Nicholas was one of the co-founders of a private tutoring service for the students of the American College of Greece. He is responsible for maintaining the fast growth of ihavemoved.com as marketing director and human resources manager.

1997–99 London Business School
1999 Qualco Consultants
1995–97 OgilvyOne Worldwide, Athens
1989–93 University of Pennsylvania USA
BA Computer Science & Psychology

Onic Palandjian

BSc (Bentley), Bus. Admin. (Harvard)

With experience as a venture capital executive in the US, Onic has evaluated and refined the business models of a variety of internet and e-commerce enterprises. He has conducted business in the former Soviet Union under uncertain and difficult circumstances and worked on the financial and operational areas of a global shipping company. Onic works on securing partners and alliances for ihavemoved.com, as well as the commercial offering.

1998–99 Eagle Venture Capital USA
1996–98 Dorian Ships, Piraeus & USA
1992–95 John Hancock Financial USA
1994–95 Harvard Extension School
1989–92 BSc, Bentley College USA

APPENDIX 5.2: FINANCIAL PERFORMANCE FORECAST YEARS 1–3

	Year 1	Year 2	Year 3
Top Line			
Revenue	£364,189	£1,699,929	£6,670,431
Expenses	£2,086,853	£2,136,678	£2,136,822
Profit	− £1,722,664	− £436,749	£4,533,608
Revenue	£350,194	£1,699,929	£6,670,431
COA Revenue	£139,821	£801,631	£3,288,730
Commission Revenue	£156,608	£837,669	£3,260,303
WL Sales Revenue	£20,000	£0	£10,000
Advertising Revenue	£33,765	£60,628	£111,397
Expenses	£2,086,853	£2,136,678	£2,136,822
Web Site	£71,812	£60,000	£60,000
Staffing	£1,105,250	£1,153,850	£1,153,994
Marketing	£455,210	£444,804	£444,804
Professional Services	£124,603	£102,000	£102,000
Equipment	£103,580	£166,000	£166,000
Operating Expenses	£226,276	£210,024	£210,024
Financial Expenses	£122	£0	£0
Ratios			
Revenue/User	£10.83	£7.45	£8.43
Expense/User	£154.00	£10.76	£3.10
Profit/User	− £143.17	− £3.31	£5.33
Marketing/User	£38.81	£2.24	£0.64
Revenue in €	0.6	2.8	11.1
EBITDA in €	−2.9	−0.7	7.6

6 Strategy – emergent or planned, and other issues

In the ihavemoved.com case study the attitude of the four founders towards the development of their company's strategy, and the flexibility they showed in responding to emerging opportunities were quite important to the success of the company. The decision to allow other companies to brand the website, acknowledging ihavemoved.com only through a reference to 'powered by' was not an easy one but essential for the company's financial well-being and growth. Flexibility and open-mindedness were required though and, in fact, the new offering did not distract from the founders' vision but rounded it.

In the first chapter of his book *Contemporary Strategy Analysis* Robert M. Grant introduces three stories of outstanding corporate success proposing that in each case success was due neither to access to superior resources nor accounted for by sheer luck. Though he continues, "In all three stories lucky breaks provided opportunities at critical junctures. But none of the three organisations was subject to a consistent run of good fortune. More important was the ability of all three [organisations] to recognise the opportunities when they presented themselves and to have the clarity of direction and the flexibility necessary to exploit these opportunities." (1991, p. 3) It is the openness towards opportunities, the mental and organisational flexibility that allows taking advantage of them, that are part of what differentiates innovative organisations from their less innovative counterparts.

In this chapter we first expand on the differences between emergent and planned approaches to strategy and what this means for innovation. We then take a closer look at what an innovation strategy is, what innovation best practice in the context of strategy looks like and follow up by discussing a few strategy frameworks that:

1. help companies to define their starting point and context (Porter's five forces)

2. provide insights for how companies can align their organisation to an innovation ambition (Higgins' application of Peters and Waterman's 7S framework to innovation)

3. suggest an approach that helps strategy implementation

The chapter concludes with taking a closer look at design from a strategic perspective.

STRATEGY – EMERGENT OR PLANNED?

The strategic aim of a business is to earn a return on capital, and if in any particular case the return in the long run is not satisfactory, then the deficiency should be corrected or the activity abandoned for a more favourable one.

Alfred P. Sloan Jr (1963)

There are probably two distinctive approaches to strategy development, the first is planned – top management devises the strategy, middle management translates it, and supervisors and employees implement it. This approach is also referred to as the rational model of the strategy process. The problem with this approach is that it represents a linear process, not allowing for feedback to be integrated in a flexible and timely fashion.[1] The second approach on the other hand combines top-down planning with structures that allow for reactions to insights and activities from all levels of the organisation. This approach is also referred to as an emergent strategy. Table 6.1 summarises the description of the sections on 'strategy as rational decision making' (planned strategy) and 'emergent strategy'.

One could argue that in today's fast-moving environment there is little choice but to follow an emergent strategy development process. It is important to point out that emergent strategy should not be confused with not having a direction or strategy at all. When embracing the white-label strategy ihavemoved.com did not change what their company was all about. They knew what they wanted to provide: a web-based offering that would provide a one-stop-shop address changing service to home movers. Had they insisted on providing the website itself that was offering the services they would not have entered into collaborative agreements with other companies. In a way,

Table 6.1 Planned versus emergent strategy

	Planned strategy	Emergent strategy
Starting point	External and internal context of the organisation (traditional SWOT analysis)	Action within the organisation, trial and error learning though still aimed at implementing an overriding strategy
Leading to	Identification of key success factors (external) and distinctive competencies (internal)	Insights from experiments that in turn influence future action
Resulting in	The creation, evaluation and implementation of a strategy	Review and revision of the overriding strategy
Flow	Top down	Bottom up as well as top down
Level of uncertainty (driven by complexity and rate of change)	Low	High

Source: Based on Hatch, M.J. (1993). The dynamics of organizational culture. *Academy of Management Review*, **18**, 657 and Mintzberg, H. (1990). The design school: reconsidering the basic premises of strategic management. *Strategic Management Journal*, **11**, 171–95.

---

[1] An approach to strategy development that addresses issues of nonlinearity, taking a more holistic and dynamic approach is called 'strategy dynamics'.

what they have changed is the way they deliver their service, not what the company stands for. So it is not only the ability and willingness to respond to unforeseen opportunities that lie at the core of innovative organisations but also a strategy that is formulated broadly enough to allow flexibility when necessary. It is probably the lack of a broad enough vision that prevented Xerox from exploiting the inventions coming out of its research lab in Palo Alto (see Chapter 1).

By the way, it is often the shift from a product to a service based strategy that can make the difference and create a competitive advantage. Think about train operators in the US. Had they thought of themselves as being in the business of transporting people from one place to another rather than being in the train business their chances for survival would have been much higher. Another example is Castle Cement, a UK-based provider of cement. In the past customers had called Castle Cement if and when their silos were empty or nearly empty. This required an immediate response and delivery from Castle Cement, often leading to half empty trucks racing around the countryside to ensure fast delivery. Rethinking the way it sold its product Castle Cement turned the process on its head: instead of delivering on demand they started to offer a guarantee that 'your silo will always be full'. This meant that they were monitoring their customers' silos, planning deliveries well ahead which meant that load rates of their delivery vehicles went up, and routes could be planned to maximise efficiencies.

However, being flexible and responsive can also be quite threatening. What if the new opportunity threatens the core of the existing business? In an interview by the magazine *Quisic* Peter Skarzynski, co-founder and CEO of the strategic consultancy Strategos, was asked, "You've been quoted as saying that for companies to innovate, they may have to stop doing some things that made them successful in the first place." His response was, "They have to critically look at the things that have made them successful and understand which of those keep them from radical growth, keep them from transforming the industry. So yes, sometimes it means stopping or changing the very thing that drove the success."[2] The larger the organisation, the larger the part of the organisation that is under threat, the less likely it is that the opportunity will be taken up.

It seems to me that the description of characteristics of a success generating a new product development process given by Robert G. Cooper (1994) is equally appropriate for a company's strategy. The four characteristics identified by Cooper are:

- Fluid: it is fluid and adaptable, constantly reviewing the company's environment to enable early identification and fast response to changes or opportunities.

- Fuzzy gates: it features conditional Go decisions (rather than absolute ones) which are dependent on the situation.

- Focused: it builds on the company's skills and capabilities (rather than on existing products and markets) and focuses resources on the 'best bets'.

- Flexible: it does not stick religiously to its formulated strategy if changes in the wider environment render it obsolete.

---

[2] For full interview see http://www.quisic.com/cgi-bin/ic/ic_article_display.pl?nav=2&channel_id=1&content_id=104.

I would also like to emphasise that one approach does not exclude the other and argue that both are needed. A company needs to have its overriding goal or ambition, but needs to be flexible in how it achieves it. No good in insisting in the production of typewriters when the world has moved on to personal computers – unless one wants to become a specialist and niche player. As has been pointed out, sometimes organisations need to give up what has made them successful in the past to be able to succeed into the future.

Companies aiming to become more innovative have to embrace the thought of allowing their strategy to emerge. To be innovative is to pursue opportunities that were neither known nor available before, and which cannot possibly be planned or scheduled. As research by Slevin and Covin (1997) found, "Planned strategies are positively related to sales growth among firms with mechanistic structures and operating in hostile environments. Emergent strategies, on the other hand, are more positively related to sales growth among firms with organic structure and operating in benign environments."[3]

These are fundamentally issues of whether or not companies are ready to embrace discontinuous or disruptive change and we will take a closer look at this topic in Chapter 31.

STRATEGY AND INNOVATION

Before looking at strategy best practice in the context of innovation in particular, some more general insights into strategy best practice in general. In his aforementioned book on strategy analysis Grant (1991) identifies the following four characteristics of successful strategies:

- They are directed towards unambiguous long-term goals.

- They are based on insightful understanding of the external environment.

- They are based on intimate self-knowledge of the organisation's capabilities.

- They are implemented with resolution, coordination and effective harnessing of the capabilities and commitment of all members of the organisation.

To become a successful innovator the first and last points are the most important. We have just discussed the importance of flexibility while maintaining an overall strategic direction. The first point also implies clarity and sharedness, and we will come back to that in a moment. The last requires determination and commitment – something that research by Repenning (2002) has found to be fundamental to innovation success. His research into understanding the dynamics of innovation implementation led him to the following conclusion, "Managers should not adopt an innovation unless they are prepared to be both fully committed to the effort and patient in the month between adopting the innovation and crossing the motivation threshold. A half-hearted approach or early termination can severely limit the value of an otherwise useful innovation" (See Box 6.1). What is true at the project

---

[3]See also Table 3.2 in Chapter 3 for a comparison between different types of organisational structure whereby 'mechanistic structure' corresponds with 'functional structure' and 'organic structure' with 'matrix structure'.

level is equally true for the company level. Managers should not embark on the journey of creating a more innovative organisation unless they understand the implications, and are prepared to continue on the path and commit the necessary resources.

Box 6.1   Repenning's experiment

Repenning conducted two experiments concerning the implementation of an innovation that were identical up to a certain point in time, and the only aspect varying after that was the level of senior management commitment. In one scenario visible senior management commitment was discontinued after 24 months, under the other scenario it was continued. Perhaps not surprisingly, in the first scenario the commitment among employees dropped to zero in a short period of time, leading to a failure, whereas in the second scenario employees remained committed, leading to a successful implementation of the innovation.

To clarify, in a vision a company states its goal. Its strategy is, as defined by James Brian Quinn in *Strategies for Change: Logical Incrementalism* (1980), "The pattern that integrates an organisation's major goals, policies, and action sequences into a cohesive whole. A well-formulated strategy helps to marshal and allocate an organisation's resources into a unique and viable posture based upon its relative internal competences and shortcomings, anticipated changes in the environment, and constant moves by intelligent opponents." Or in much simpler terms, a strategy is a plan for action. So if to become more innovative is part of an organisation's goal, managers will have to develop a plan of action to achieve this. Putting it into the annual report and adding it to the company's values is not sufficient. Most importantly, it ignores that becoming (more) innovative is about changing behaviour, and an innovation strategy provides 'a plan for action' on how to achieve this. Such a plan for translation of innovation intent into action is often made explicit in an organisation's innovation strategy.

In order to be effective an innovation strategy should provide the following:

- An explanation of how it fits in and feeds into the overall business strategy.

- A definition of what is meant by innovation in general and further definitions and information on different types and levels of innovation (see Box 1.2 in Chapter 1); it should further provide information in which of these different types and levels of innovation the organisation wants to engage in.

- A company-wide portfolio that outlines what types and levels of innovation the organisation wants to pursue, and what kind of resources, time frames, responsibilities, success criteria etc. are associated with each of the different portfolio segments.

- A structure through which innovation is managed and executed.

In order to develop such a strategy and reap its benefits it is essential that it is well communicated, and that buy-in is ensured early on in the process. Once such a strategy has been developed it will serve as a decision framework for the selection of project and the allocation of resources (people, time, money etc.). Box 6.2 outlines the three stages of innovation strategy development.

Box 6.2   Innovation strategy development

Definitions and framing (why and what)

- **Situational analysis** – to understand the context for innovation within the organisation as well as the external environment.

- A clear link to company **vision and strategy** – how does innovation help us to achieve our ambition? Innovation is ultimately a means to help an organisation achieve its goals and ambitions.

- **Goals and objectives** – what we want to achieve through innovation.

- **Definition of innovation** (with types and levels); definitions are often organisation specific, they also help to create a shared language.

- Define **'focus areas for innovation'** (or **platforms/themes**) around which innovation should be focused (often tie in with trends or insights/deductions from trends).

Portfolio and structures (how)

- Approaches to **idea management** – where do we get our ideas from (internal/external), how do we collect, assess and manage them, who is reviewing and responding to them?

- Different dimensions and clusters of the **portfolio**, outlining in which innovation types/levels (innovation fields) the organisation plans to engage; how much of overall **resources** will be allocated to each innovation field; the result is highly organisation specific.

- What kind of **people and capabilities** do we need for each of the different innovation fields and how do we build this up over time? How do we recruit (for diversity), assess (for creativity, different team roles and skills, e.g. Belbin, MBTI, KAI, IDEO 10 faces of innovation etc. – see appendices), train, reward, remunerate, incentivise people (careful with financial rewards).

- **Metrics and measures of success**, varying and specific to the different innovation fields (see appendices for more).

- The **processes** through which innovation is managed, e.g. idea management, stage gate, prototyping, capturing and sharing **learnings** from success *and* failure.

- The **structures** through which innovation will be managed, e.g. innovation roles, reporting relationships and responsibilities, where and how decision making takes place.

- Information on how innovations (of different kinds) are **transferred into mainstream business.**

Creating a receptive and fertile ground

- A strategy for how **buy-in and involvement** will be assured, particularly among middle and senior managers

- Identifying aspects of **corporate culture** that help or hinder innovation, and how they might be migrated/changed over time.

- How the **physical work environment** be used to encourage and foster innovation.

Such a strategy can also be used to develop a time-bound plan for culture change (with the aim of creating an innovative organisation), defining steps towards the ultimate goal.

While this book focuses on innovation, I do not want to ignore the fact that there are other positioning strategies companies can pursue. Jones (1997) identifies four different types of new product strategies (see Table 6.2), each of which will require a different approach, structures and strategies to realise its respective ambition.

Looking back at the characteristics of planned and emergent strategy (Table 6.1) and comparing them to the characteristics of the four different new product strategies shown in Table 6.2 we find that an emergent strategy is much better suited for achieving innovation.

However, somethings even the most innovative organisations need to balance are the diverging need of innovation on the one hand and operations on the other. It is the conflict between creativity and implementation introduced in the first chapter. Table 6.3 compares aspects of an operating organisation with those of an innovating organisation. However, how many organisations that claim to be innovative truly have all characteristics of the innovating

Table 6.2 Product strategies

Type	Characteristic	Examples
Offensive	Innovators Research intensive High risk/uncertainty Current information	Pilkington – float glass Du Pont – Teflon Polaroid – instant film Hoover – vacuum cleaner
Defensive	Followers Incremental innovation Production quality Market focus	Matsushita – VHS video IBM – personal computers WordPerfect – computer software Nissan – cars
Imitative	Low-cost manufacture Licensed technology No R&D Localised markets	Compaq – computers Molson – dry beer Daewoo – cars Samsung – microwave ovens
Traditional	Established markets Constant demand Niche market Low technology	Barbor – clothing Aga – cookers Zippo – cigarette lighters Mont Blanc – pens

Source: Jones, T. (1997). *New Product Development, an Introduction to a Multifunctional Process.* Oxford: Butterworth Heinemann. Reproduced by permission of Butterworth Heinemann; T. Jones.

Table 6.3 Comparing operating and innovation organisations

	Operating organisation	Innovating organisation
Structure	Bureaucratic, specialisation and division of labour; hierarchical control	Flat organisation without hierarchical control; task oriented project teams
Processes	Operating units controlled and coordinated by top management which undertakes strategic planning, capital allocation and operational planning	Processes directed towards generation, selection, funding and development of ideas; strategic planning flexible, financial and operating controls loose
Reward systems	Financial compensation, promotion up the hierarchy, power and status symbols	Autonomy, recognition, equity participation in new ventures
People	Recruitment and selection based upon the needs of the organisation structure for specific skills, functional and staff specialists, general managers, and operators	Key need is for idea generators who combine required technical knowledge with creative personality traits; managers must act as sponsors and orchestrators

Source: Based on Jay R. Galbraith and Robert K. Kazanjian (1986) as adapted by Grant, R.M. (1991). *Contemporary Strategy Analysis: Concepts, Techniques, Applications.* Cambridge, MA: Basil Blackwell, p 240. Reproduced by permission of Professor R. Grant.

organisation? And another question is, is there an innovative organisation that could survive long term without also providing the conditions of an operating organisation?

What does this mean for managers? For one it means that large, operating-orientated organisations that also want to be innovative have to find a way to balance the demands of both the operation and the innovating company which I have emphasised before. It might also mean that large operating organisations are just incapable of dealing with radical innovation – in the existing structures – and that in order to allow truly radical innovation to flourish they have to create alternative structures that meet the requirements of an innovating organisation. Again this is an issue we will return to in Chapter 31.

Finally, some insights into strategy best practice for innovation. Research into innovative organisation tends to highlight three aspects about strategy and vision that differentiate the innovative from the less innovative organisation:

- clarity
- sharedness
- attainability

If having a clear and shared vision and strategy is important for any organisation that wants to achieve an ambition, it is essential for an organisation aspiring to change – and what does the ambition to become more innovative imply but the need for change. While the implications of 'clarity' and 'sharedness' are quite straightforward – everyone in the organisation needs to know and understand, and share the same interpretation of the strategy – attainability is a bit more ambivalent and without explanation might be interpreted wrongly.

One could understand this third aspect either to read: it has to be easily achievable or, it has to be just about achievable. Theresa Amabile, whose framework was introduced in Chapter 1 refers to this with 'pressure' (represented by workload pressure and challenging work). The goal set needs to be attainable, but at the same time it needs to provide a stretch, a challenge. Something too easily attained does often not seem worth pursuing, whereas something too unrealistic puts people off. Having said this, if the external pressure is sufficient it is surprising what people can achieve. Think about the public pressure to perform created by Kennedy's public announcement that he wanted to put men on the moon, or the challenge to engineers at NASA during the *Apollo 13* flight, when the lives of their colleagues and the entire mission depended on their ability to create a pump that could convert carbon dioxide into oxygen out of the most bizarre array of objects imaginable. It is often that need, the urge, the crisis, however you would like to call it, that is missing in organisations wanting to become more innovative, companies where people tend to think, 'everything is going just fine, thank you, why change?'

People need a reason to change – and not just one that appeals to their minds. Kotter and Cohen (2002) emphasise, "People change what they do less because they are given analysis that shifts their thinking than because they are shown a truth that influences their feelings." It is 'getting people's hearts as well as their minds' that matters and management writer Charles Prather has translated this into a formula for change:[4]

$$\text{Change} = \text{Vision} \times \mathbf{X} \times \text{Felt need to change}$$

Change only happens when there is a vision of where to go, when there is a *felt* need for change, and when there are some specific steps to be taken ('$\mathbf{X}$'). If any part of the equation is zero, there is no change. This also enforces the point made earlier, that a clear strategy and vision is so important in realising an innovative organisation.

By the way, Rosabeth Moss Kanter's book *The Change Masters* (1985) explores the dilemma of change, and provides a host of useful insights as to why change may not be happening, and how to overcome the hurdles. Though the list of 'rules for stifling innovation' she provides in her book (see Box 6.3) might make you smile, I am sure there are some – if not many – that are true for organisations that you know.

Box 6.3   Rosabeth Moss Kanter's 'Rules for Stifling Innovation'

1. Regard any new idea from below with suspicion because it's new, and because it's come from below.

2. Insist that people who need your approval to act first go through several other levels of management to get their signatures.

3. Ask departments or individuals to challenge and criticise each other's proposals (that saves you the job of deciding; you just pick the survivor).

4. Express your criticism freely, and withhold your praise (that keeps people on their toes). Let them know they can be fired at any time.

5. Treat identification of problems as signs of failure, to discourage people from letting you know when something in their area isn't working.

---

[4] 'Leading Innovation: enabling your organisation', presentation given at the 2002 Innovation Network conference in Minneapolis, 22–25 September 2002.

6.   Control everything carefully, make sure people count anything that can be counted, frequently.

7.   Make decisions to reorganise or change policies in secret, and spring them on people unexpectedly (that also keeps people on their toes).

8.   Make sure that requests for information are fully justified and make sure that it is not given out to managers freely (you don't want data to fall into the wrong hands).

9.   Assign to lower level managers, in the name of delegation and participation, responsibility for figuring out how to cut back, lay off, move people around, or otherwise implement threatening decisions you have made. And get them to do it quickly.

10.   And above all, never forget that you, the higher-ups, already know everything important about this business.

So attainability means finding a balance between realistic but boring and unrealistic but exciting, and providing people with a motivation and ambition to achieve it.

One final point on innovation and strategy; there is often a debate as to whether it is better to be a first mover or fast follower – and the verdict is still out. In order for it to make sense to be first mover the reward needs to justify the risk. In some industries being a first mover has distinct advantages, for example, if this helps to set an industry standard or creates other significant barriers to entry. Exclusive access to a key resource can be such a barrier. In other situations, where the first mover can be easily and quickly copied, it might pay to be a fast follower and let the first mover establish and educate the market. We talk of a fast follower advantage when an organisation entering a market as second or third develops a leading position despite a later entry.

Hence there are advantages and disadvantages associated with each strategy and which are summarised below.

First mover advantages

- Technological leadership; e.g. through patent registration; this can be observed in the pharmaceutical industry.

- Pre-emption of scarce assets; e.g. geographical or shelf space; an example of the former might be if there is only room for a few competitors as for example for particular ferry routes.

- Scale effects; e.g. reducing unit cost through large production runs.

- Network externalities; e.g. the product is part of a wider offering, e.g. phones for free as part of buying network services.

- Buyer switching cost, e.g. the learning is specific to the first mover's product/the user has to make an up-front investment that would have to be repeated when switching, e.g. switching from one software to another.

- Brand loyalty; e.g. the first mover shapes and influences tastes and expectations of the users.

- Experience effects; e.g. the first mover moves up the learning curve and followers have difficulties catching up.

Table 6.4 To follow or to lead?

Product	Innovator	Follower	Winner
Jet airliner	De Haviland (Comet)	Boeing (707)	Follow
Plate glass	Pilkington	Corning	Lead
VCRs	AMpex/Sony	Matsushita/Panasonic	Follow
Diet cola	R.C. Cola	Coca-Cola	Follow
Instant camera	Polaroid	Kodak	Lead
Disposable nappy	Procter & Gamble	Kimberley-Clark	Lead
Paper copier	Xerox	Canon	?
Web browser	Netscape	Microsoft	Follow

Two obvious disadvantages to being the first mover are cost, e.g. investment in R&D and market education, and risk, e.g. there are no knowledge and mistakes of others to learn from.

Fast follower advantage[5]

• Free-rider effect; taking advantage of the learning and education of the market that has already taken place; the fast follower can focus on improving the product.

• Technological or market uncertainty have been resolved; it is often the fast follower who takes a product from niche to mass market.

• Government interference; e.g. change in subsidies to avoid monopoloes or introduction of deregulation.

• Resource homogeneity; if resources are the homogeneous and available to all then a first mover cannot establish a resource-based advantage

Table 6.4 gives examples of successful first movers as well as successful fast followers.

USEFUL CONCEPTS AND FRAMEWORKS FOR STRATEGY DEVELOPMENT

With all the above, managers are still facing three important questions:

1. Outward looking – no organisation operates in a vacuum. How do we understand our context and define our starting point?

---

[5] The advantage of the fast follower is explored in detail in the book *Fast Second* by Constantinos Markides and Paul Geroski – see book recommendations at the end of this chapter.

2.   Inward looking – what are the aspects that our innovation strategy should address?

3.   Once we have established our innovation strategy, how do we ensure implementation?

The three frameworks I am suggesting are:

1.   Porter's five forces to help companies to define their starting point and understand their industry context.

2.   Higgins' application of Peters and Waterman's 7S framework to innovation to provide some insights for how companies can align their organisation to an innovation ambition.

3.   Hay and Williamson's strategic staircase to provide valuable insights into strategy development and implementation.

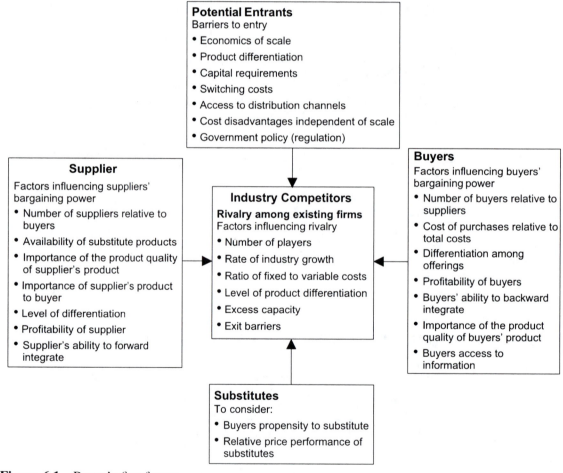

Figure 6.1 Porter's five forces.
Source: Porter, M.E. (1980). *Competitive Strategy: Techniques for Analyzing Industries and Competitors*. New York: Free Press. Reproduced by permission of The Free Press.

Before developing an innovation strategy for their organisation managers should make sure that they understand the context in which they operate and what their position in the playing field is relative to other players. Porter's (1980) five forces framework allows organisations to do just that by requiring managers to take a closer look at customers, suppliers, possible new entrants, possible substitutes for existing products and its industry's overall competitive position. Figure 6.1 summarises the aspects to be considered for each of the five forces. The insights gained from the analysis can inform both the company's overall as well as its specific innovation strategy.

Once context and positioning have been established the company's overall strategy can be developed. Closely linked to the overall strategy should be the company's innovation strategy. The 7S framework developed by McKinsey consultants Peters and Waterman in 1982 provides a useful reference point to make sure that all aspects of the organisation are aligned to the innovation ambition.

Higgins (1996) used the 7S framework to suggest how to implement an innovation strategy. He states that "Everything in business must start with strategy. Your organisation's innovation strategy reflects the demands of its future environment, and how the organisation plans on reacting to or changing that environment to meet its needs. Strategy leads to everything else. The other S's must be pointed in the same direction as strategy." He too suggests that the strategy determines and must be supported by values, which need to be set by top management and shared throughout the organisation. Based on the strategy and values, managers then need to set to work to develop and select the right structure, the right systems, the right style, and the right staff with the right skills. Table 6.5 lists what managers need to consider for each of the seven 'S'.

Once the context is understood, and plans have been made for how to change the organisation's 7S to reflect the innovation ambition, there is still the most difficult step – there are still two problems. First, how to develop the strategy from which the other six 'S' follow, and second, how to implement it and fill the strategy with life.

Table 6.5   The 7S framework

7S	To consider
Strategy	Should reflect the demands of future environment, and how the organisation plans to react to or change that environment to meet its needs; everything else must follow
Structure	Teams, innovation centres, lines for communication, alliances, idea evaluation
Systems	Align rewards and remuneration, management information systems, celebration of innovation and creativity, idea assessment beyond – financial evaluation, systems for implementing process, marketing, and management innovations
Style	Accepting of failure, suspending judgement, transformational leaders
Staff	Recruit creative people, develop innovation champions, train people, provide time for reflection, provide physical facilities
Shared values	Strategy determines the shared values; changing existing values will take time
Skills	Create opportunities, improve and innovate continuously, start knowledge management and organisational learning initiatives, invest in R&D

Source: Based on Higgins, J.M. (1996). A plan for innovation. *R&D Innovator*, **5**. Reproduced by permission of Innovative Leader.

I would like to refer to two articles written by Michael Hay and Peter Williamson in 1991 and 1997, respectively. Both articles investigate why strategy often fails at the implementation stage, and suggest an approach that might help to overcome the problems.

In their first article the authors identified lack of clarity, a preference to continue in accustomed ways and the fact that most organisations seem to use the past as predictor for the future as the main reasons underlying implementation failure. They found that many organisations describe a large number of priorities, each with several key performance measures, which means that it is difficult for managers to prioritise their efforts. If everything is first priority, where to focus resources? If innovation is not top priority innovative projects tend to get axed at the first signs of difficulties, partly because they are seen to be high risk, partly because benefits cannot be reaped in the short term.

In addition Hay and Williamson found that the different priorities can stay in direct conflict with each other, which they felt made implementation efforts even more difficult. In her book *When Giants Learn to Dance* Rosabeth Moss Kanter (1989) picks up on some of the contradictions managers face:

- Think strategically and invest in the future – but keep the numbers up today.

- Be entrepreneurial and take risks – but do not cost the business anything by failing.

- Know every detail of your business – but delegate more responsibility to others.

- Speak up, be a leader, set the direction – but be participative, listen well, cooperate.

- Continue to do everything you are currently doing even better – and spend more time communicating with employees, serving on teams, and launching new products.

While I agree that the contradictions are difficult to manage, I also believe that increasingly innovative companies and individuals have learned to do just that. Innovative organisations manage their existing business through structured and efficient processes while at the same time providing some flexibility and slack for creativity and innovation to flourish.

But back to strategy development. In their second article Hay and Williamson probe deeper into possible causes of implementation failure. Interviewing managers about strategy and delving into statements made about strategy they found that managers' perception of what strategy means and involves is the true show-stopper to implementation (see Table 6.6).

Realising that what seems to get distilled from the strategy are targets and forecasts they comment, "but what often gets lost in this distillation process is the broader strategic perspective". And it is just this broader perspective that is essential to innovation. From the above they distil three reasons for implementation failure:

1. Confusion about what exactly a 'strategy' is and, specifically, the difference between the various levels at which it operates. How, for example, should a mission, individual objectives and the budget be linked?

2. An abiding sense that episodic bouts of strategy and the reality of managerial life rarely connect. How therefore is one to link strategy to action?

Table 6.6 A deep-seated scepticism characterises the view from below

On the surface	Revealed below
Strategy is about the long term	Far enough in the future so that you don't need to do anything about it now
Strategy depends on forecasts	Strategy is about crystal ball gazing
Strategy influences profitability	Budgets are about profitability, strategy is about mountains of paper and thick folders
Strategy is about a common mission, pulling together	Everyone agrees we should have a strategy as long as it doesn't constrain any of our individual departments
Strategy needs periodic review	Strategic planning is a comfortable part of the corporate ritual; a once-a-year 'binge' and it's back to the in-tray

3. Frustration that the constituent parts of the organisation more often pull apart than together with department X thwarting the best efforts of department Y and vice versa. In other words, can strategy be coordinated and made consistent across the organisation?

The approach they suggest involves the following sequential approach:

- Step 1: Provide clear definition of goals, explain what they actually mean for day-to-day management, be specific about actions and targets.

- Step 2: Establish what the specific goals mean in terms of requirements on the firm's resources.

- Step 3: Think about what your company would look like when the strategy has been achieved. Then identify what specific actions you need to take to achieve your goal, working back from the future and considering all resources, skills, capacity, structure etc. required (now also known as 'backcasting').

With that process in mind they then suggest that companies develop the following in a strictly ordered fashion:

- **A vision** – that has two dimensions: external and internal; defining a vision provides the firm with an essential set of bearings: a map of the changing terrain on which it is competing; underpinning the vision there has to be a set of guiding beliefs and values.

- **A mission** – that should encapsulate an organisation's raison d'être or guiding purpose; the destination to which that purpose leads; and the rationale behind the purpose.

- **A plan** – that focuses on how it is to be done, identifying specific steps.

- **Key initiatives** – each step of the plan needs to be broken down into specific initiatives.

- **Individual objectives** – employees' objectives need to be derived from the set of initiatives being pursued; where individual objectives and strategic requirements are at odds with each other, then strategy will surely fail.

- **Budgets** – the revenues and costs identified in a budget have to be linked to individual initiatives.

In order to qualify what Hay and Williamson call a 'first-class strategy' it should provide the following:

- *Inspiration* in the form of a worthwhile, relevant goal.

- A *linkage* that helps individuals to connect their own task with the initiatives being undertaken elsewhere in the company.

- *Guidance* to individuals about the trade-offs and prioritisation decisions they have to make on a daily basis.

- *Discretion* for the individual to manoeuvre by loosening some existing constraints and generating some new options.

- The facilitation of *communication* by establishing a common language which everyone in the company can use.

If a strategy fulfils the criteria above it should provide a sound foundation from which managers can build an innovative organisation.

DESIGN AND STRATEGY

A design strategy is the effective allocation and coordination of design resources and activities to accomplish a firm's objectives of creating its appropriate public and internal identities, its product offerings, and its environments.

Olson *et al.* (1998)

In the final section of this chapter I would like to talk about design's role in and connection with business strategy. For the last 20 years management gurus have promoted the strategic value of design, starting with Kotler and Rath declaring in 1984 that design is "a powerful but neglected tool" quoting companies such as IBM or furniture maker Herman Miller as examples for companies that have used design to achieve a superior market position. Tom Peters (1995) soon joined the ranks of the illustrious promoters of design – and slowly it seems that their arguments are being taken on board.

Sony – one of the first companies to put design at the core of its strategy

For years Sony has been able to charge a premium of around 25% over competitors' products with similar technology. Design is widely acknowledged to have been the enabler of this. Norio Ohga, successor of Sony's legendary co-founder Akio Morita, had set up a centre as early as 1964 to bring together the product planning group and the design centre, the first Japanese company to do so.

There still remains some confusion about what design actually means, what its use involves, and how it can actually contribute to a company's competitiveness. However, as examples of Sony for some time and Procter & Gamble more recently show, more and more companies are starting to understand its potential and contribution in the context of innovation. Fewer organisations confuse design with styling – the latter being something that is applied to an existing product towards the end of its development process whereas the former is an integral part of a product's development process right from the outset.

Having said that, differences in education, resulting in different mindsets and different approaches to problem solving, are still to blame for a slow take-up of design's offerings. Managers are taught to think rationally, to analyse and measure. They are taught to avoid risk and focus on answering questions. Designers on the other hand are taught to express themselves (be emotional), to explore and experiment. They have a great tolerance for ambiguity and focus on understanding the question. Managers are concerned with facts and figures whereas designers are driven by intuition and inspiration. The lack of acknowledgement and understanding of the differences leads many managers to view design and creativity as something close to a black art, something that cannot be managed and is therefore better left alone. Creating an awareness for the differences and bringing designers on board as early as possible can help to maximise the benefits that can be gained by harnessing the differences.[6]

It also helps to communicate clearly the benefits that design and designers can bring to a business. Kotler and Rath explain that design and the conscious management of design can add value by:

- Creating corporate distinctiveness in an otherwise product and image surfeited marketplace.
- Creating a personality for a newly launched product so that it stands out from its more prosaic competitors.
- Reinvigorating product interest for products in the mature stage of its life cycle.
- Communicating value to the consumer.
- Making selection easier (standing out) and increasing consumer satisfaction.
- Helping to inform consumers in a more efficient way.

Kotler and Rath continue to identify what constitutes effective design, namely performance, quality, durability, appearance, cost benefits but state that to achieve this it is necessary that senior management recognises and understands the contribution design can make, and that designers are an integral part of the new product development team, right from the outset.

Considering the above and referring back to the Porter framework design can hence help:

- To create barriers to entry by providing product differentiation and creating emotional switching costs.

- To reduce suppliers' bargaining power by high levels of differentiation, enhancing product quality, increasing hurdles for possible substitutes.

- To reduce buyers' bargaining power by higher levels of differentiation, increased desirability and product quality, and decreasing price sensitivity by preventing direct comparability (due to differentiation and quality).

- To reduce customers' receptivity to substitutes and decrease price sensitivity.

- To reduce the impact of the number of players and excess capacity, e.g. Apple computers are less likely to be affected by excess capacity than bog standard computers.

But even if management realises the value of design, the next questions then are, how can it be harnessed, where does it apply and what part can design play in realising a company's strategy? Cooper and Press (1995)

---

[6]For a comparison of designers' and managers' preference please refer to Table 1.3, Chapter 1.

have identified three distinctive areas of design activity in an organisation and associate specific design strategy issues with each:

- The development of corporate identity – this is about communications and of course identity; it requires the understanding of the corporate values, the relationship between corporate image and corporate goals, whether the focus lies on the corporation, the division or the product line, what the necessary design competencies are, and what the intangible messages of the corporation are. To implement these strategic issues designers need to work with members of the PR, advertising, HR, finance, R&D, marketing and IS departments.

- The design of saleable products and services – this is about the relationship between the factors involved in product or service design (price, quality, standardisation) and corporate goals and requires the understanding of price point constraints and production costs and capacities, about having insights into the features that are valued by customers, about having the competencies necessary to design and deliver the planned products, and understanding the intangible messages that designed products and services carry. To implement these strategic issues, designers need to work with members of the marketing, R&D, operations, and, to a lesser extent, finance and accounting departments.

- The design of operating environments – this is about the relationship between corporate values, image, environment and goals. It requires the understanding of the competitive strategy adopted by the firm or division, knowing how work is conducted within the firm and the critical interrelationships between functions, understanding consumer shopping preferences, having the competencies necessary to design corporate environments, and understanding the intangible messages that corporate environments

Corporate identity is the reality of what the company says and does, be this visual, verbal, environmental or behavioural.

Corporate image is how the organisation is perceived. These perceptions may not necessarily reflect the reality.

Corporate identity is translated into corporate image via direct (advertising, corporate literature, etc.) and indirect (employee behaviour, service quality, etc.) corporate communications.

Tangible elements of corporate identity are the physical manifestations of visual identity and communications, e.g. corporate logo/name, publications, web site, exhibitions, buildings. Intangible elements are management style, procedures, general attitude and service quality. Intangible and tangible messages have to be consistent whereby the intangible ones are the most important as people will trust their experience more than what they are told.

Summary of design management process (based on Olson et al., 2000):

1. Clearly articulate the firm's competitive strategy to designers and design managers.

2. Develop a detailed understanding of the design requirements inherent in the adopted competitive strategy.

3. Ensure open lines of communication among the design group and other functional units.

4. Create, review and approve design briefs.

5. Compare performance outcomes against the objectives established in design briefs.

carry. To implement these strategic issues, designers need to work with members of the marketing, operations, and HR departments, as well as architectural firms and public zoning agents.

However, having said all that, and emphasised the contributions design can make, I would like to give voice to a designer (!) who, while many seem to suggest that design should take over the world, suggests that "In a successful relationship, you will often find a dominant partner and a quiet one – a leader and a supportive follower. In the business–design relationship, business must be the leader, and design must be the supportive follower." For that to happen, Turner (2000) realises, design has to redefine "its relationship with business – not in terms of design strategy versus business strategy, but at a much more fundamental level". He suggests that design takes the role of coordinator, facilitator and interpreter, rather than that of the leader it often aspires to. He also suggests that, as design touches so many parts of a business, "It can bridge the gap between a company's ambitions and the things that go on every day in the factory, the showroom, or the office in a way a mission statement never can." This certainly is a strong argument for design, and for the potential to become reality companies need to integrate design into their DNA – or treat design as, what Gorb and Dumas (1987) refer to as 'design as infusion' (see Table 1.3 Chapter 1), which means everyone in the organisation understands and values the contribution design can make.

I would like to conclude this section with some questions senior management might want to ask about design that I have extracted and adapted from the British Standard 7000, 'Guide to Managing Product Design':

- Have the corporate objectives for design and new product development been properly defined and, thereafter, periodically reviewed?

- Are these corporate objectives understood by all involved and have they inspired enthusiasm?

- Is the company's product strategy compatible with its corporate objectives?

- Have significant resources been provided to match the product strategy?

- Are procedures in place to ensure that up-to-date information about market requirements are available to the design and development team?

- Are the collaborative, information and evaluation links between the design and development team and other parts of the organisation operating properly?

- Are the organisational policies and procedures for managing the design and development process adequate?

- Is there a sincere and visible commitment to high standards of product design?

- Are achievements and expenditure being monitored against time?

- Are results being properly evaluated and is this evaluation being communicated to all concerned?

READING SUGGESTIONS

On strategy

Grant, R.M. (1991). *Contemporary Strategy Analysis: Concepts, Techniques, Applications.* Cambridge, MA: Basil Blackwell.

Comment: Introduction to strategy analysis and development, it makes several references to innovation
                and the innovating organisation.

                Markides, C. & Geroski, P. (2004). *Fast Second: How Smart Companies Bypass Radical Innovation
                to Enter and Dominate New Markets*. San Francisco: Jossey Bass.

Comment: Arguing for and elaborating on the fast follower advantage.

                Warren, K. (2007). *Strategic Management Dynamics*. Chichester, UK: John Wiley & Sons, Ltd.

Comment: A book on the theory and practice of applying system dynamics to strategy development in a
                business context.

On change

                Moss Kanter, R. (1985). *The Change Masters*. New York: Touchstone Books.

Comment: One of the classics on change, with particular insights for and emphasis on innovation.

                Moss Kanter, R. (1989). *When Giants Learn to Dance*. New York: Simon & Schuster.

Comment: On how large organisations manage to become innovative, and thrive on change.

SOME USEFUL WEBSITES

                www.strategos.com

Comment: Strategos is the consultancy set up by management guru Gary Hamel, site provides a listing of
                its publications as well as insights into its research findings

                www.smsweb.org

Comment: This is the website of the Strategic Management Society which provides a list of useful
                links (www.smsweb.org/reference/web_sites.html), as well as influential books on strategy
                (www.smsweb.org/reference/inf_books.html)

                http://www.systemdynamics.org.uk/ (UK)
                http://www.systemdynamics.org/ (US)

Comment: Websites of the organisations promoting a dynamic approach to strategy development. As
                they state, "System dynamics is a methodology for studying and managing complex feedback
                systems, such as one finds in business and other social systems."

7 Branding and innovation

Our brand is our most important asset. It's more valuable than all the other assets on our balance sheet. It is more valuable than our factories, our buildings, our warehouses and our inventory.[1]

Joe Middleton, European president of Levi Strauss

Strategy and branding issues were closely related in the ihavemoved.com case study, and brands can provide a shared framework within which innovation can take place. This chapter looks at what 'brands' and 'brand equity' actually mean, what their role in innovation can be, and what role brands play for web-based companies.

WHAT IS A BRAND?

Some may ask, why actually talk about brands in the context of innovation? On its website the British Brands Group (www.britishbrandsgroup.com) declares, "In a world that is ever more complex and sophisticated, brands stand out as beacons of familiarity and reliability. As reference points with known characteristics with which consumers can identify and trust. As symbols of hope and new prosperity in the fast emerging markets of the world. As vehicles for delivering continuously improving value." People might want to argue that if familiarity is a major characteristic of a brand, than surely brands must be a rather unsuitable

"A brand starts its life as a statement or guarantee about a single product. As the reputation of that product grows, the brand may be used as a promise of assurance in relation to products launched under the same umbrella. The brand has also developed a third and more subtle role, in which it says something both about the product and about its users and their lifestyles."

The British Brands Group

subject to discuss for innovation? Well, I think that is just why it is important to discuss brands. There are two reasons. First, as Haigh (1996) points out, "It [the brand] must be separable from the underlying product or service, permitting transfer of loyalty between products and categories over time", which means that a brand can be used as a platform from which to launch innovation. The advantage of using an existing brand as a springboard for innovation is that consumers, customarily slow to embrace something entirely new, might transfer the trust and liking they have for the existing products or services associated with the brand to new ones, hence accelerating its acceptance.

---

[1] Quoted in the article 'Consumer Products – Branding' which can be found on http://www.sgs.co.uk.

The second reason is, in understanding the power of a brand, managers launching an innovative product or service should focus on building a strong brand quickly, thus accelerating the development of trust and acceptance rates among its potential customers. The Orange campaign comes to mind. By the time the services were launched consumers already seemed to have a good familiarity with the brand, leading to a faster take up of the product than might otherwise have been the case. Don't forget, what influences people's decision making is first and foremost experience, then feelings, and rationality only comes in when absolutely necessary (often as post-purchase rationalisation). Focusing on developing a strong brand can help acceptance and market penetration.

What else do brands do for consumers and companies? As the British Brands Group's booklet *A Guide to Brand X* points out that when brands were 'invented' around the middle of the nineteenth century, their main purpose was "to differentiate a product from its competitors by stressing particular features such as quality, consistency and reliability". Also, "Brands help us to decide what to wear, eat and use, how we shop, travel and manage our money."

Now that we have established why we should talk about brands, what does 'brand' actually mean? Allen (2000) suggests a rather short and straightforward definition of a brand: reputation = brand = behaviour, which I understand to mean that a brand rises and falls with its reputation, which in turn depends on the behaviour people associate with it. However, his definition seems to confuse 'brand' and 'brand equity', which need to be differentiated. *A Marketing Glossary for UK Public Companies' Annual Reports*[2] offers the following definition for 'brand':

A brand is a name, term, symbol or design (or a combination of them) which identifies one or more products (mostly used in the US).

Or

> "A brand is a specifically defensible piece of legal, intellectual property manifested in logos, identities and advertising to which an incremental stream of revenue is attached. It therefore represents a secure flow of future earnings."
>
> Haigh (1996)

The identification plus the product itself and its packaging, i.e. the gestalt (mostly in the UK), e.g. "A product is something that is made, in a factory; a brand is something that is bought, by a customer. A product can be copied by a competitor; a brand is unique. A product can be quickly outdated; a successful brand is timeless." Stephen King

To put a bit more flesh on this definition it might help to take a look at the characteristics of brands as identified by a non-executive director of one of the world's largest advertising companies, WPP, Jeremy Bullmore (2002):

- Products are made and owned by companies – brands [images] on the other hand are made and owned by people ... by the public ... by consumers.

- A brand image belongs not to a brand – but to those who have knowledge of that brand.

- The image of a brand is a subjective thing – no two people, however similar, hold precisely the same view of the same brand.

---

[2] The glossary has been edited by Tim Ambler, London Business School, and can be downloaded from www.london.edu/marketing/glossary.

- People come to conclusions about the brand as a result of an uncountable number of different stimuli – many of which are way outside the control or even the influence of the product's owner.

- Much of what influences the value of a brand lies in the hands of its competitors.

- It is universally accepted that brands [brand equity] are a company's most valuable asset, yet there is no universally accepted method of measuring that value.

With his list Bullmore also makes clear the difference between a product and a brand but even though most of the above seems to imply that the management of a brand and its reputation are beyond a company's control, this is certainly not the case. This rather means that companies have to consciously manage their brand (whether this refers to the product or the company level) and take actions to reinforce the desired image of the brand, counteracting any negative reflection competitors' action might cause if necessary.[3]

> **Brand image**
>
> Perceived impression of a brand by its audience. A multidimensional concept that is hard to measure precisely but can be defined by its associations, e.g. Martell cognac is associated with expensive sporting activities.

In his last point he refers to brand equity which the *Marketing glossary* defines as:

An important tangible asset for the company, it can be seen as the reservoir of results gained by good marketing but not yet delivered to the profit and loss account.

Awareness, attitudes, associations, memories and habits, which cause people to choose/recommend the brand more often and/or in larger quantities and/or at higher prices than would otherwise be the case.

'Customer brand equity' is part of the total brand equity in the minds of customers as distinct from other stakeholders, e.g. employee brand equity which is the reputation of their employer in the minds of employees.

Similar to reputation which is often used for corporate brand equity but excludes product availability. Can also be described as 'goodwill'. The financial value of brand equity cannot (in the UK) be included on a balance sheet although the cost of acquired brands may be so long as the cost is not more than their financial value.

What then are characteristics of brands, particularly successful ones? The following traits have been combined from Ambler (1997) and the website of the British Brands Group (BBG):

- They provide a strong bond of trust between the brand owner and the consumer – successful brands meet or even exceed consumer expectations and aspirations.

- They come with an implicit guarantee of quality.

---

[3] In his book *Company Image and Reality* David Bernstein (1986) makes a persuasive argument as to why companies should communicate: people will talk anyway so you might as well influence what they have to say.

- They are consistent – the assurance is not only about quality but also about consistency, wherever and whenever the product or service is bought the experience is the same.

- Leading on from the previous point, successful brands are also widely available.

- They have a distinctive difference – successful brands stand out from the crowd. As the BBG points out, "Consumers will not purchase a product that is simply a mild variation on a theme, a brand should provide a distinctive difference."

- And finally, they have a clear personality – consumers are clear what the brand stands for and what its rational and emotional values are.

You will find out about the true strength of a brand really when disaster strikes. The question is, is the mistake considered to be 'typical' or is it an 'honest' mistake? If the brand in question is a strong one customers will often give the benefit of the doubt. If the brand is less well known retributions from customers are much more likely. Think about the Elk test disaster of the Mercedes A-Class. Though there was a lot of negative press, the Mercedes brand, and of course how the crisis was managed by the company's management, meant that the success of the product was merely delayed, not prevented. I believe that the saving grace was not the brand in itself, but the consistency of the management's behaviour with the brand values: admitting the problem and acceptance of responsibility, open communication and rectification of the problem in the shortest possible time.

> The four dimensions of 'brand manners' as identified by Pringle and Thompson (1999) are:
>
> - **Spiritual**: the brand must make the consumer feel a better person.
>
> - **Political**: consumers must feel comfortable with how the brand was made etc. (was it right for me?).
>
> - **Emotional**: the brand must give us the feeling 'I would like to do that again'.
>
> - **Rational**: the brand must function, perform and overdeliver.

Given that consumers seem to be obsessed with labels – spending £20 billion on branded fashion goods in the UK alone – and that brands are increasingly seen to be a company's most valuable asset, there are increasing attempts to put a value on brands and to measure the brand equity.

So what then is brand equity, and where does it come from? In his aforementioned presentation on innovation and brands Ambler says, "Brand equity is a marketing asset, it is the consequence of good marketing. It is primarily formed by the brand experience, but also by advertising and marketing, and can be described as 'What everyone has between the ears about the brand'." Or as David Aaker (1991) defines it, brand equity "is a set of assets (and liabilities) linked to a brand's name and symbol that adds to (or subtracts from) the value provided by a product or service". He identifies aspects that feed into brand equity: brand loyalty, brand awareness, perceived quality, brand associations, other proprietary brand assets.

But how to put a value on a brand? David Haigh, author of the report 'A Review of Current Practice – Brand Valuation' (commissioned by the Institute of Practitioners in Advertising, IPA, in 1996) has observed four different financial valuation methods:

- Cost based – based on what it would actually or theoretically cost to create the brand; Haigh suggests that this approach is backward looking and no guide for current value.

- Market based – this approach assumes the existence of comparable transactions of brands or companies against which a brand can be valued; however, he identified two problems with this approach, the difficulty of making direct comparisons between brands, and the availability of sufficiently detailed data to make a judgement.

- Income based (royalty relief) – assumes that brands are licensed to operating companies which in turn pay royalties which in turn could be used to determine the value, using net present value (NPV) or discounted cash flow (DCF) calculations; problems with this approach are that (a) brands are more often than not 'used' by the companies that own them and (b) if brands are licensed it is often difficult to get the data necessary to make a judgement.

- Income based (economic use) – based on estimating the difference in gross profit from selling a branded as opposed to an unbranded product; an approach generally using the discounted cash flow approach (a method pioneered by the brand consultancy Interbrand); this approach evaluates the brand against a number of different aspects such as geographic spread and protection, using the identified 'brand risk' to discount future cash flow.

BRANDS AND INNOVATION – A CLOSER LOOK

For owners of brands . . . , the successful management of brands depends on a never-ending quest to bring the brand closer to the consumer's ideal. In a dynamic economy, brands are not only a guarantee of quality and replicability, they are also the means for delivering innovation. Innovation which depends on the long-term commitment of brand owners to make substantial investment in the future of their brands.

http://www.britishbrandsgroup.com

Earlier in this chapter we established why it is worth taking a closer look at brands and branding in the context of innovation, that is the provision of focus for innovation around an existing brand, and the need to establish a strong and consistent presence quickly if a new brand is concerned. In this section we take a closer look at what this actually means.

In the chapter about strategy and vision the need to provide some focus for innovation was emphasised. A strong brand is one way of providing such focus. As SGS, a company specialising in the verification, testing and certification of new products declares, "Innovation and brands are interdependent. A brand can focus innovation on the requirements and aspirations of the consumer which can help build brand equity." If everyone is familiar with the brand and what is often referred to as the brand's DNA (the core values reflected by the brand) this will make it easier for them to come up with new ideas that strengthen the brand and move it forward. Although companies must ensure that the new product and services are aligned with the brand promise – unless the innovations are to be used to help reposition the brand. Allen (2000) describes the brand promise as the intersection of three aspects: corporate communication, corporate behaviour, and corporate strategy (see Figure 7.1).

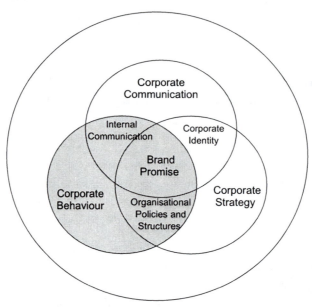

Figure 7.1   Brand promise.
Source: Allen, D. (2000). Living the brand. *Design Management Journal*, 35–40. Reproduced by permission of *Design Management Journal*.

But the question is not only, 'What can the brand do for innovation', it is also, 'What can innovation do for the brand'. To quote from the British Brands Group's website again, "In order to meet the changing needs of consumers and to stay ahead of the competition, the manufactured brand must strive for continuous innovation and improvement." Ergo, innovation and brands are interdependent. Innovation is not only a means for staying ahead, it also helps to achieve another criterion for brand success: differentiation.

However, the associated of brands and innovation is not all positive. A strong and clearly defined existing brand can limit innovation, restricting the avenues that can be explored. It becomes a question of how far a brand can be stretched – the issue of 'brand extension'. Recent research into this topic by Hem et al. (2001) led to the following insights:

• Perceived similarity of brand extension and parent brand is crucial for the acceptance of brand extension of services.

• The reputation of the parent brand is a crucial factor: a favourable reputation of the parent brand has a positive impact of the success of the brand extension (this is true for FMCG, durable goods and services alike).

• The perceived risk[4] associated with the brand extension is an important influence for brand extensions of durable goods and services.

---

[4]The authors identify two components of perceived risk: (a) uncertainty about the consequences of making a mistake and (b) uncertainty about the outcome. Consumers rely on brands to minimise perceived risk.

- Consumers who have generally a positive attitude towards innovation tend also be more open towards brand extensions.

So it is important to decide what kind of strategy a company wants to pursue, innovation within or outside existing brands, and in deciding a company's strategy towards branding, a categorisation by Vishwanath and Mark (1997) might be useful, particularly as they comment on each quadrant's position on innovation (see Figure 7.2). They suggest that a company can have one of four approaches towards brand positioning:

- **Hitchhikers**: gain share by lowering prices dangerously, it is usually in their best interest to follow the leader's pricing moves. Innovation might help.

- The **high-road brands**: key to success here is innovation, consumers tend to be loyal and willing to pay a premium.

- The **low-road brands**: feature inflated cost structures and lack of differentiation, to improve situation review cost structure.

- The **dead-end brands**: according to the authors you don't want to be here and should try anything to get into a different quadrant!

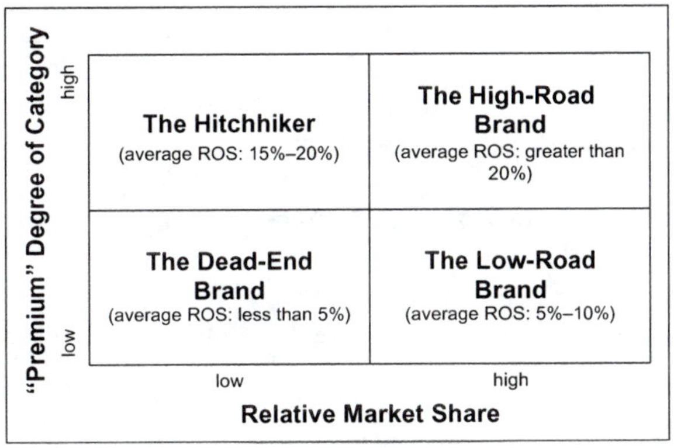

Figure 7.2 Branding categories.
Source: Based on Vishwanath, V. & Mark, J. (1997). Your brand's best strategy. *Harvard Business Review*, 123–9.

Each of the four types of brands is associated with a different level of innovation, and in the end the success of a company will depend on the level of alignment that is achieved across all aspects of the organisation.

Finally, not all brands live up to expectations and Lane Keller *et al.* (2002) have identified five possible reasons as to why that might be:

- Walk before you can run – companies sometimes attempt to build brand awareness before defining a clear brand position. The authors suggest that many dotcoms have succumbed to this kind of pitfall.

- Identify what matters – sometimes companies focus on promoting something consumers don't care about. The authors give the example of analgesics where companies focused on the length of the relief – rather than what mattered really to the customer: the speed with which it took effect.

- Focus on differentiators – a brand will get into trouble when the main selling point can easily be copied, e.g. price advantage.

- Watch what you are copying – copying a product feature because a competitor has been successful does not mean that you will benefit too. The authors quote the example of General Mills introducing Honey Nut Cheerios, based on the perception that honey is healthier. When Post decided to re-brand its Sugar Crisp into Golden Crisp it actually lost market share.

- Think carefully before rebranding – trying to reposition an existing brand can be very difficult if not impossible. The authors give the example of Pepsi-Cola's attempt to move the brand away from its youthful image, only to revert back to it when it became clear that the repositioning only led to a loss in market share.

BRANDS AND THE WEB

This final section briefly looks at brands in the specific context of the web, finishing with some considerations about website development in general.

What do companies planning to set up a website need to consider? In their article 'E-Branding: Leadership Strategies'[5] Plant and Willcocks (2000) have identified four components:

- Technology – how are you attempting to leverage the technology, and with what consequences for your brand?

- Service – what level of service at what cost will we deliver through this channel, and how will this affect the brand?

- Market – what is our segmentation strategy, and how can we define brands across our segments?

- Brand – what is the website to do for your brand, create a new one, reinforce or change an existing one, or are you just following what everyone else does?

The authors found that market leaders will not focus on one or a few of these aspects but address all of them. While branding cannot compensate for shortcomings in the competitive positioning, the pricing strategy or levels of service provided, it can play a powerful role in creating a successful web presence.

As indicated above, the authors have identified a number of different strategies a company can pursue in setting up its website:

---

[5] The full article can be found on http://www.brandchannel.com; see also Plant (2000).

- The creation of a new brand – e.g. the setting up of a new company such as amazon.com or eBay.com. The strength here comes from being the first mover, developing a high visibility fast and, most importantly, adding value for the consumer.

- The reinforcement of an existing brand – giving the BMW website as example (www.bmw.com) the authors describe this as an "intermediate strategy for organisations that have established distribution channels and cannot risk alienating existing customers and distributors", or that can inform but not sell to certain segments such as drug manufacturers (www.genentech.com).

- To support the repositioning of a brand – e.g. United Parcel Services (www.ups.com) move from a parcel delivery company with a rather static site in 1996 to being a logistics solutions company whose website reflected the 'information delivery component' of the brand.

- To be a brand follower – the 'me-too' approach, driven by the fact that everyone else in the market has done it, often mimicking the first mover without adding any particular value that would be specific to their site.

Needless to say that the authors believe that the last option is least likely to create value for the company.

But, independent from which strategy a company pursues, what should managers consider when setting up an internet site? Upshaw (2001) points out that managers of dotcoms seem to fail to realise that "in a selling environment in which the product is not touchable and services are promised by companies that came into being only months before, businesses must entice prospects into active involvement with their brands, not just their sites". His advice for companies seeking to develop a web-based brand includes:

- Adopt a name that will provide maximum flexibility for the brand.com business model, e.g. if the 'click' business is to move into 'mortar' too.

- Establishing marketing strategies that are self-sustaining, e.g. make sure that all marketing and advertising activities reinforce each other.

- Construct a masterbrand that creates superiority online, not just differentiation, e.g. not only the choice but also the legendary service of amazon.com.

- Design a user interface that is specifically suited to create maximum brand involvement, not just simple interaction, e.g. personalised pages when the site is revisited.

- Forge a proactive customer service operation that is an integral part of a greater relationship-building engine, e.g. live online support.

And whether the company is entirely web-based or whether it is a 'mortar' company that decides to set up a website, what are the aspects to consider when maximising chances of a success? Lorraine Justice (2001) has some suggestions. First she recommends reviewing who should be involved during the web development. Quite obviously the website development team, which should include representatives from a number of different disciplines such as design, computer programming, marketing, social science, information architecture and those related to production. The second group are the visitors (one-off) and users (repeat) of the site, ideally the website should be designed in a way that people who have visited once would come back. The third group, and not to be underestimated, are the decision makers, who may or may not be the client. She further suggests that it might sometimes be advisable to bring in an independent expert team, which has the expertise to comment on technology and usability, and which is not prone to *betriebsblindheit*, a nice German word for describing the problems that arise from being too close to a situation to be able to see its problems and limitations. Even though this might incur some extra costs, getting the site wrong is much more expensive.

Justice has also identified a number of issues that often go wrong in website development – though looking at the list it seems to me that it is not only website development that suffers from these ailments, these are characteristics of projects that are not planned properly, and that do not have a high profile in the organisation:

- Poor team development caused by personal conflict, control issues, politics and power struggles.

- Poor definition of the website's purpose, varying views on what it is to achieve, a lack of hierarchy/importance to guide the structure, and poor research methods.

- Poor development process, namely being overly descriptive, or too unstructured, e.g. missing clear stages and sign-off points (see also Chapter 3).

- Lack of technical or artistic support, which are both essential for the successful development of a website.

- Unrealistic time or cost constraints.

Beyond the more procedural contributors to website success Robin Cleland (2000) has identified the following 10 elements of web-branding success:

- A compelling value proposition.

- A high-quality online experience (convenience, content, customisation, community, connectivity, customer care and communication).

- A reputation for excellence (delivering their e-promise).

- Strong communications programme and efficient customer acquisition strategy.

Web development process (Justice, 2001)

Define the site purpose

- Corporate communication tool?
- Provide which content to which audience for what experience

Research/information gathering

- Set the information hierarchy, navigation system, and ideas for visual/emotional appeal to use for the prototype

Ideation/problem solution

- Informal prototype and site solutions generated

Production of the site

- Pulling components together, visualising the site

Final evaluation

- Successful, not successful, partly successful
- Plans for future updates and redesigns

- Unique positioning concept and distinct brand image.

- Strong partnership and strategic alliances.

- Intense customer focus.

- First mover and early mover advantage.

- Relentless innovation.

- Ability to leverage offline brands and assets.

READING SUGGESTIONS

On branding

Upshaw, L.B. & Taylor, E. (2000). *The Masterbrand Mandate*. Chichester, UK: John Wiley & Sons, Ltd.

Comment: The book identifies what differentiates successful from less successful branding strategies. Emphasising the need to foster a sense of community both within and outside the organisation the authors analyse successful megabrands, such as Sun Microsystems, Charles Schwab & Co and America Online.

Kapferer, J.-N. (2001). *Reinventing the Brand: Can Top Brands Survive the New Market Realities?* London: Kogan Page.

Comment: A review in the Market Research Society's publications described the book as, "Useful insights into brand strategy and management. Kapferer provides a holistic overview of the marketing industry and market research's place within it."

Klein, N. (2001). *No Logo*. London: Flamingo.

Comment: High profile and controversial book suggesting that 'ever powerful brands' reflect a potential danger; provides a historic account of the development of brands.

Plant, R.T. (2000). *E-Commerce: Formulation of Strategy*. London: Financial Times/Prentice Hall.

Comment: Drawing on his interviews and research with leading e-commerce organisations it explores four key drivers of e-commerce success: brand, technology, service and market. Aimed at the board level to develop an understanding of all aspects associated with internet strategy development and execution.

Bedbury, S. (2002). *A New Brand World: Eight Principles for Achieving Brand Leadership in the 21st Century*. London: Viking Books.

Comment: Written by the former Head of Advertising at Nike and more recently Senior Vice President of Marketing at Starbucks the book provides a counterpoint to Naomi Klein's book, this book tells the behind-the-scenes success of Nike and Starbucks and how it can be applied to any growth business.

Dowling, G. (2000). *Creating Corporate Reputations: Brands, Identity, and Performance*. Oxford: Oxford University Press.

Comment: Corporate reputations are a valuable strategic asset for every company. Good reputations have been shown to help firms attain and sustain superior financial performance in their industry. This book outlines how high-status companies become corporate superbrands, and it presents managers with a framework to enhance their corporation's desired reputation.

SOME USEFUL WEBSITES

www.interbrand.com

Comment: The Interbrand website has lots of useful and interesting articles on the subject of brands most of which you can either view or download. Interbrand are the pioneers in brand valuation.

www.britishbrandsgroup.com

Comment: The British Brands Group website has a host of useful information on and around brands.

8 The value of market research

CASE STUDY 3: BLACK & DECKER'S QUATTRO[1] (A)

If I only had time . . .

We need a decision soon, the trade fair in Cologne is in March next year and we need to commission tooling if we want to be ready on time. We do not have time to market test the new design. The original design had great results so we know people would like it. I know this new design is a bit different, but . . .

Nigel Robson, an industrial designer at Black & Decker's design centre in Spennymoor, UK, had been working furiously to produce an alternative design for a new cordless multifunctional tool that was to be introduced to the world at the trade fair in Cologne in March 1998. It was already April 1997 and a decision on the design needed to be made soon.

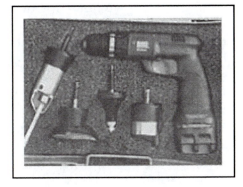

Due to internal resource constraints the initial design had been developed by an external consultancy with which Black & Decker had worked successfully before. The result was all right but Lawrie Cunningham, Director of Innovation and Industrial Design, thought it quite traditional and felt that this new product category could be made more exciting. Even though marketing were very happy with the original design – which had researched very well – he decided to ask Nigel Robson from his industrial design team to refine it. Nigel, who was relatively new to the company, felt very strongly about not just "rounding the corners", as he put it.

In his view this new multipurpose tool ought to look different from what already existed, and it was certainly not to look like a drill. He pointed out, "The question for the designer is always how to differentiate your product on the shelf." The main reason the existing design looked like all other cordless drills was the location of the batteries. Nigel started looking for alternative locations. At the same time he reviewed the ergonomics of the product. It was not very well balanced making it uncomfortable to use. By reconsidering ergonomics and battery location he not only achieved better handling of the product but also increased functionality.

---

[1] The case has been prepared by Dr Bettina von Stamm as a basis for class discussion rather than to illustrate either effective or ineffective handling of a management situation.

However, there were not only upsides. The new design was more expensive, it needed some extra parts, and was less able to rely on existing – hence proved and tested – parts. On top of that there would not be time to market test the new design. At least with the first design they knew that customers would like it.

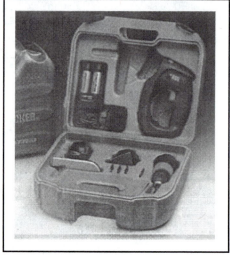

A new consumer trend

Lawrie Cunningham explains, "Black & Decker are always keen to stay in touch with changes in customer preferences, to react to or even anticipate consumer trends." He continues, "We are continuously trying to get a portrait of our buyers and take time to look carefully at what exactly it is the consumer wants." As a consequence most new product ideas are researched intensively by marketing who define what is needed but generally leave it up to the designer how to execute it. Concepts are developed around user profiles that are defined by motivation, knowledge and ability.

In addition to the desire to respond to market demands there were also other reasons for Black & Decker to pursue the concept. They were operating in a market with a lot of competition where prices had dropped considerably. A significant manufacturing base had grown in China and, for example, in 1996 sanders were priced at £19.95, a product that had previously been two to three times that price. So the opportunity to introduce a product that was different and would offer new benefits to consumers was very welcome.

Marketing had become aware that in the DIY tools market the emphasis was increasingly on multifunctionality. Earlier in 1996 Black & Decker had already introduced a multifunctional sander, which had been very successful. Their aim was now to develop another even more successful tool around the concept of multifunctionality. The multipurpose tool was a response to an ever-increasing need for simple tools that users of limited experience could feel confident working with. The challenge was to create a product that would be truly innovative and exciting in a highly competitive market – particularly as in the past add-ons had been perceived to be inferior. This meant that they would have to ensure that performance for all functions was equally high – which would be a challenge, given that the battery available would only have 7.2 volts.

> Millions of people rely on powered hand tools to make their lives easier. All of these people have different needs. Tool manufacturers have responded with a seemingly bottomless toolbox of powered drills, grinders, sanders, saws and so on. To keep their customers satisfied, and attract new ones, manufacturers have been offering lower-cost tools with improved ergonomics and a wider range of features. One of the most popular features is battery power. Battery-powered or cordless tools are one of the fastest-growing categories in power tools, with advances in rechargeable batteries spurring development.
>
> *Machine Design*, 17 April 1997

Black & Decker – the company

Black & Decker had been founded in 1910 by S. Duncan Black and Alonzo G. Decker in Baltimore, Maryland. In the 1920s the company started its global expansion by setting up wholly owned subsidiaries in Canada (1922), the

UK (1925) and Australasia (1929). Interrupted by the Second World War, expansion continued so that today Black & Decker sells its products in 130 countries around the world (see also Appendix 8.1). In 1996 the consumer products division of Black & Decker was operating in three distinct areas: Consumer Power Tools (CPT), Outdoor and Household of which CPT was the largest.

In 1965 the British subsidiary purchased a 100,000 sq ft plant at Spennymoor near Durham, which is recognised as one of Black & Decker's flagship sites. One of the company's three design centres is located here. Of the other two design centres one is in Black & Decker's homeland, Maryland, the other in Hong Kong. Each centre designs products not only for its region but also for the global market. One hundred people work in the European Design Centre, as Spennymoor's design department is known. However, only about 40 of these are designers/industrial designers, the rest are technicians, 3D specialists and so on. But, as Danny Bone, innovation manager, emphasises, "We all share a passion for power tools."

> Power tool maker Black & Decker has been drilling away at plant optimisation using kaizen. The continuous improvement programme at the Spennymoor plant under the guidance of US consultant TBM has proved so successful that last month the company hosted a week-long event to demonstrate the kaizen approach to 43 senior managers from Rolls-Royce, TRW, Alstom, JCB, Polaroid and others.
> *Professional Engineering*, 10 May 2000

At Spennymoor about 14 million tools are produced every year – the equivalent of 360,000 tools per week – 79% of which are exported. The throughput as well as the number of different products – about 2000 product variations leave Spennymoor every month – creates much opportunity for process improvement. This is why Black & Decker embraced first Kaizen and then Six Sigma.

Besides quality, branding is very important to Black & Decker. To allow a clearer brand proposition Black & Decker had separated its consumer and professional lines in 1994, relaunching its professional products under the brand name 'DeWalt'. In the US this move pushed it from number three to number one in professional power tools.

From its inception Black & Decker was an innovative, market-led organisation with focus on new product development. Today about 65% of its products are less than three years old, and as Danny points out, "We often have products that are ahead of the market." To facilitate innovation they have established flat structures and work through peer-led groups, use product- and process-based teams, and have mechanisms to maintain close contact with their customers.

To facilitate sharing of knowledge and the dissemination of ideas Black & Decker has established a database to which every engineer has access. Into the database, which has been upgraded recently, all test data is entered. When asked about how people would find out about projects or find people with a particular expertise, Shaun Loveless, a senior electrical engineer, answered, "You find out about existing projects by contacting other people, by emailing around. How to find some special expertise? Project files are created at the end of each project. The files used to be microfilmed, but today it is all put onto CD-ROM. If you look there you can find out who was on the project." He adds, "And, everyone here at B&D is happy to go and ask for help and advice."

To help minimise common conflicts between marketing and engineering and ensure that the two functions would work together, both departments, as well as the director of industrial design Europe, report to the same person, the European Marketing Director. Though Stephen Bird, European Marketing Director and Vice President of Consumer

Power Tools at the time, remembers, "There used to be a lack of cooperation between marketing and engineering as well as between the UK and the rest of Europe. Particularly the latter has improved since we have started bringing people from all over Europe to work with us at Spennymoor."

Developing concept and prototype

The idea for the new product was conceived on the 1 November 1996 during a video conference involving Stephen Bird, European marketing director, Lawrie Cunningham, Director of Innovation and Industrial Design and Danny Bone, Innovation Manager. They were discussing the success of the recently introduced multisander and felt that there should be further scope in developing multifunctional or perhaps even multipurpose tools, although in the past the argument had been that having different function heads would not be technically feasible.

Still, intrigued by the idea, Stephen asked Lawrie and Danny to think about it – and, as Stephen remembers, "Danny had this gleam in his eye and I knew he already had something in mind. Danny came back a fortnight later with this rough but fully working prototype. The idea was great and he could prove that interchangeable heads were technically not a problem. Danny's trick was to develop a separate gearbox in front for each of the tools. Although each feature already existed in many guises from a number of manufacturers, we wanted to combine forward-thinking views of changing marketplace requirements with highly innovative patent pending design solutions."

The idea for a multipurpose tool was based on:

- A strong DIY market in Europe with an increasing number of men and women doing DIY.

- Main trend: less experienced females on the increase; more people living on their own; growing number looking for small products (space constraints).

- People do a small number of small DIY tasks; in contrast, many existing B&D products had the tendency to be over-engineered.

- Market for drills is mature – need to do something different.

- Recent success with the multisander (combining three functions), sold at a premium price.

Danny, who had been working in the area of new product development since 1989, had been promoted to product innovation manager in 1995. While nominating an individual to be the 'Innovation Champion' can cause problems, not least because of the 'not-invented here' syndrome, this did not seem to be the case in Black & Decker. Danny attributes this to a culture where design and innovation are valued and appreciated. It also helps that Danny has a track record in successful new product development, which gives him credibility with colleagues across all functions. He describes his role, "One aspect is that I act as catalyst between engineering and marketing." He also points out that he has many colleagues with whom he can discuss ideas and who are able to ask each other the right questions.

He strongly believes that in new product development it is important to move to prototypes and models quite quickly as it helps marketing and other departments to understand how an idea could work. He says, "I see being a translator as another important part of my job. If you have a model to show people they are much more likely to buy into the idea and get a feel for the benefits we are trying to achieve through the new product. The great benefit of my position is that I am given time to explore and experiment. My scope goes across all product groups within the consumer business." Though there can also be a problem with prototypes as Danny points out, "Sometimes there is a necessity to translate between the different functions, for example, marketing don't always understand the difference between a prototype and a product; if they see a working prototype they think it can be in the shops the next day which of course is not true."

Once the concept had been developed the next step was to present it at one of the worldwide product meetings. When Stephen went to the global new product development meeting in the US later in November 1996, it was clear that he was very excited about the idea. However, the meeting did not go well. In fact, they did not like the idea at all, and not only that, he was told to stop working on it. Thinking about it afterwards Stephen reflected, "The market in the US is very different from the market in Europe, much more macho, powerful, and about tools for a specific use – rather than easy to use and multifunctional." But he said, "It is a rare occasion for me to call something 'my baby' – but if ever there was one, this was it. I really wanted to do this." So he disobeyed the ruling and decided to develop the tool one step further.

He commissioned an external industrial design consultancy to develop the concept into a model and did some preliminary market testing. When he re-presented his idea at the next meeting six months later in March 1997 with some positive market response to back him up the response was, "We thought we had told you not to do it!" But he dug in his heels and focused on communicating the

> "We wanted our industrial design execution to make the tool desirable to own and use by both male and female consumers. For example, comprehensive flexibility and neat storage was seen as a clear user benefit."

importance and potential of the new idea. In the end he got the go-ahead for at least some further development. Looking back he comments, "The good thing about Black & Decker is that people are not afraid to throw up ideas and fight for them, that's nothing unusual. I even had a few disasters, but this was OK. As long as it does not become a habit, B&D accepts a bit of failure."

The plan was to introduce the new product complete with a 'kitbox' at the big trade fair in Cologne in spring 1998. Meeting that deadline was important if they wanted to make it into the shops for Christmas 1998. This meant that they had to work towards a tight time schedule, having less than a year for development and tooling. It could take about 16 weeks alone just for the tools to be made, and as this had to be outsourced, it was out of the hands of the Black & Decker team. Taking it to a trade fair would also mean that it had to be very robust, as visitors at a trade fair – particularly from competing organisations – would test the product thoroughly.

However, when Lawrie saw the prototype based on the design consultancy's design he was not quite happy. He felt that they should be able to do better with the design. Given the time frame, Stephen was not too pleased with going for a second design, in fact as he recalls, he was quite negative about it – but he was also open minded and in the end Lawrie persuaded Stephen that there would be some value in giving it another go.

So when industrial designer Nigel Robson came back from a two-week holiday, Lawrie asked him "To come and see me once you have sorted yourself out." Nigel knew something was up and went to see him straight away. Lawrie explained the project to Nigel and outlined his thoughts on the need for a rethink of the industrial design. A project of such scale was a first for both Nigel and senior design engineer Brian Wadge: both were very excited by the idea. Nigel recalls, "The first thing I did was to familiarise myself with competitor products. Power tools as a category tended to be quite traditional – but consumers were not. I felt that we could do with being more innovative and daring."

However, he also pointed out that, "If it had been just a sander we would have had a lot of time to develop the product – but the product would have three different heads which all needed careful design and engineering input."

Chris Burke from purchasing commented on the time schedule as follows, "Was time pressure a good thing? In a way, yes. There was no room for things to go wrong and we knew we had one shot at things, true. But then, if you have six months you fill the six months, if you have six years you fill them too. It really focused our minds."

A first team meeting was held early in April 1997 with representatives from engineering, purchasing, manufacturing, finance, marketing, industrial design and quality, other people would join the group if and when needed. While Brian was dedicated full-time to the project, for other people it was one project among others. However, it was soon made clear that this project should get first priority. Brian went to great lengths to ensure that everything was documented and made available for future access.

For many people on the team such as Andrew, Brian and Nigel it was their first big assignment and Davie Skaife remembers, "The key players were all keen and ambitious – and being relatively new to the game they did not have any preconceived ideas." The group was quite closely knit and many people knew each other from previous projects.

After the initial meeting the group would meet on a weekly basis, chaired by the programme manager, Andrew Eyre. Outside contractors would be brought in for tasks such as model making – they used a lot of 3D, as opposed to 2D, as there was seen to be much less margin for (wrong) interpretation. Using selective laser sintering (SLS), they were able to get a prototype within three days – rather than the 16 weeks it used to take. The models were not only for demonstration purposes but also for communicating with other departments. Brian comments, "As the models are made straight from the drawings you can see mistakes straight away."

The Project Team:	
Department	Representative
Programme manager	Andrew Eyre
Innovation manager	Danny Bone
Senior design engineer	Brian Wadge
Senior design engineer	Richard Jones
Industrial designer	Nigel Robson
Senior electrical engineer	Shaun Loveless
Finance	Alan Baldwin
Quality engineer	Davie Skaife
Purchasing	Chris Burke
Manufacturing engineer	Norman Spence
Marketing Europe	Etienne Bourgeois
Marketing North America	Kirsten Smith

While Nigel was working on the design the rest of the team were putting the information together for the CAR – the Capital Appropriation Request. The document combines information from all disciplines, outlining resource requirements for the development and manufacture of a new product, which can be quite time consuming. Alan Baldwin from finance comments, "Marketing being based in Slough

> Up to $400,000 a project can be signed off in Slough, generally within a couple of weeks, above that it has to go to the US where sign off can take up to a couple of months – if no changes are required.

can be a bit of an issue. They can take an awful lot of time at the outset and we here do not get into the project soon enough, they don't always involve us early enough. At times we also have to wait for artwork and packaging which are marketing's responsibility. However, we are trying to remedy this by bringing some marketers here to Spennymoor."

Getting costing right for new products has a high priority at Black & Decker which means that purchasing gets involved very early on. Once a design is available Chris Burke from purchasing starts working back from the launch date to determine what needs to be available when. For the Quattro he worked closely with Brian to ensure everything would be available as and when needed.

A lot of the costs are driven by the purchasing agreements Black & Decker has with its preferred suppliers. But project teams tend to cooperate closely with the suppliers to ensure best possible solutions, both in terms of functionality and cost effectiveness. David Skaife explains, "We visited the suppliers and involved them early on. We went as a group, design engineering and quality engineering, which meant that there was always a good level of knowledge around the table. We went through all functions of new parts before doing anything else."

With the new design Nigel had clearly moved away from the traditional pistol handle generally found for drills. The new handle also added extra functionality, Nigel had put quite some effort into making it stand up, which was particularly tricky for the top-heavy jigsaw module. While the two designs were not too different in terms of the mechanics, the second required some new tooling – which had cost and time implications. The newness also implied that it was more difficult to get accurate cost estimates, they could not use previous projects as a benchmark. First estimates ended up well above the original target cost – whereas the original design, with a greater number of existing parts and no additional costs for tooling, came out much cheaper.

When Nigel first showed the 2D drawings of his new design to marketers they did not like it – but his reaction was, stuff it! He was convinced that his design had benefits to offer and continued to refine it. Once he had modelled both designs the development team went back to present it to marketing and management. Many people had a vested interest in sticking with the traditional design not least because it seemed less hassle, would be cheaper, quicker to develop, and was based on tried and tested components. But Nigel kept arguing vehemently for the radical and at every opportunity.

Management was faced with a difficult decision, the traditional design had researched very well – and no one outside the company had seen the new one, and there was no time to conduct lengthy market research. Then there were also the additional new parts that would require tooling and extensive testing (all components need to be tested for consistency, gauge reliability and reproducibility, whereby the variation between two measurements has to be less than 9%) and marketing had already started 'selling' the initial design and was reluctant to go back on it. On the other hand, as Brian pointed out, "In order to get innovative products you have to take risks. You have to move away from what you have always done." But then again, individuals were rewarded on successful market introduction and were answerable to any costs occurring from repairing damaged products, so there was not much incentive to take too much of a risk. Nigel sums it up saying, "There was no confidence to make a clear decision."

Questions

1.   Given the situation, what would you do, which design would you take forward and why?

2.   What is your definition of market research and what is/should be the role of market research in new product development?

APPENDIX 8.1: COMPANY HISTORY

1910	B&D founded by S. Duncan Black & Alonzo G. Decker in Baltimore, Maryland
1911	First advertisement placed in *Manufacturers Record and Horseless Age*
1912	Adopted B&D hex as company trademark
1913	First cash dividend paid
1914	Filed application with US Patent Office for pistol grip and trigger switch drill (patent awarded in 1917)
1917	Built new plant at outskirts of Towson, Maryland
1918	Opened first company-owned product service centres in Boston and New York
1919	Passed the $1 million sales level
1922	Incorporated B&D Mfg. Co in Canada
	Expansion of factory
1924	Erected two-storey admin building in Towson, still B&D International HQ
1925	B&D as wholly owned subsidiary in London, UK
1927	Listed B&D on the Baltimore Exchange
1928	Production starts in leased plant in Slough, UK
1929	Established B&D Australasia
1933	Reorganised sales operations to promote regional management control
1939	Built a 65,000 sq ft plant in Harmondsworth, UK
1942	Formed B&D post-war planning committee; decision to develop the do-it-yourself market for power tools
	First use of plastic by company (replacing metal drill housing)
1946	Introduced world's first line of popularly priced drills and accessories
	Opened sales, service and warehousing facilities in São Paulo, Brazil
1948	Subsidiary in Mexico
1951	S. Duncan Black dies
1955	Subsidiary in South Africa
1956	Alonzo G. Decker dies
1957	Subsidiary in Belgium
1958	Subsidiary in New Zealand
	Subsidiary in Germany
	Subsidiary in The Netherlands
1960	Acquired DeWalt
1961	French subsidiary (bought out company)
	British company opens sales and service branches in Denmark and Sweden
	Acquired Italian company
1962	Subsidiary in Norway
1964	Passed $100 million sales level
	Began multi-programme schedule of US network television to advertise the broad range of B&D products
1965	British company purchased 100,000 sq ft plant at Spennymoor, Durham, UK
	Subsidiary in Venezuela
1966	Subsidiary in Austria

1967	Subsidiary in Spain
1968	Introduced new management concept which established geographical areas of operations, each under a vice president who serves as general manager with responsibilities for all markets in the group
	Subsidiary in Finland
1969	Passed $200 million sales level
	Subsidiary in Japan
	British company opens sales and service branch in Israel
1970	British company opens sales and service branch in Portugal, Cyprus, Greece, Iran
	180,000 sq ft added to Spennymoor
1971	Subsidiaries in Nigeria, Argentina, Singapore
1974	Introduced management concept which establishes four operating focuses, US Power Tool, European International, Pacific International and McCulloch Corporation (acquired in October 1973), each under a corporate officer
	Joint venture in Yugoslavia
	Subsidiary in Zambia, Panama, Philippines

Products

1916	The world's first portable 1/2" electric drill with pistol grip and trigger switch utilising a universal motor
1922	First electrical screw driver
1936	First electric hammer developed with a special B&D patented design proved more effective and easier to handle
1940	First electric Quick-Saw with table and radial arm attachments
1946	First portable electric 1/4" drill for consumers
1953	First finishing sanders and jigsaws for consumers were marketed, thus expanding the consumers' ability to do-it-yourself
1957	Move towards outdoors with first lawn edgers and hedge trimmers
1961	First cordless electric drill powered by nickel-cadmium cells
1962	First cordless outdoor product (hedge trimmer)
1963	First all-insulated drills and sander grinders
1968	First power head for the Apollo Lunar Surface Drill used to remove core samples from the moon
1973	Workmate (combination of workbench, vice, and sawhorse)
1979	Introduction of the Dustbuster, a hand-held cordless vacuum cleaner for household markets
1981	Heatgun – introduced into consumer markets
1984	Powerfile
1992	Snakelight
1996	Multisander
1998	Quattro
1999	Mouse
2000	Quattro selected as Millennium Product by Design Council

APPENDIX 8.2: CAPITAL APPROPRIATION REQUEST

Summary extracts

- Marketing overview:

  - Driven by the desire to dramatically improve the penetration of the VersaPak business by providing a hero product for 1998 and beyond

  - Multifunctionality has been extremely successful in the sanding category (575,000 sold in Europe in 1996 at 179 DM)

  - The concept has been extensively researched, with outstanding results, being 'better than multisander' and in the top 5% of projects researched by the research company

  - The multisander was received as new, interesting and highly giftable

  - Price point of 249 DM with gross margins of 45% within Europe

  - High promotion spend (15.3% NSV year 1) will support the launch and volumes of 1,290,000 are anticipated over three years

  - TV media spend will commence in November 1998 for European launch countries

  - Cannibalisation of volumes has been shown within the CAR as the Quattro will replace the majority of multi-tool kitboxes sold.

Competitive position

- No competition at point in time
- Designs will be heavily patented for future protection

Global requirements

- Major market is seen to be Europe (up to 400,000/annum) with a level of interest in the US and Eastern hemisphere (up to 80,000/annum)

- Spennymoor will provide the global requirements

Engineering plan

- Project is fast track, therefore the intention is to use as many existing components as possible
- Use of modern draughting and rapid prototyping techniques

Manufacturing plan

- Incubated in Spennymoor for approximately 12 months and then relocated to an attack plant
- A new production line will be laid down, using low levels of assembly automation to facilitate transfer

Purchasing plan

- Complete analysis of capacities of current components has been undertaken and there will be no requirement to extend these as part of this project

- For new components, tools will be laid down with minimum capacities of 864,000/year versus 475,000/year anticipated annual sales volumes

Quality plan

- Aligned to Milestone process

- All of the 'critical to quality' performance dimensions are detailed in the plan

- Test programmes will be discussed and utilised to simulate high levels of customer abuse modes of operation, so that failure potential is minimised

- Ongoing quality post-bulk will be controlled through clearly defined standards, test bench data and market feedback through the early warning system

Financial summary includes:

- Exchange rates
- Capital investment
- Sales potential
- Product cost/profitability
- Return measures
- Sensitivity analysis
- Alternative production plant

Signed-off in June 1997

9 Approaches to market research

Market research tends to be an important part in a company's armoury to develop and verify new products, services and business ideas. Not least because best practice literature has shouted for years about how important it is to meet consumer needs in order to be successful. In the past most companies have translated this into the need to conduct market research; the more inspired organisations have sought to involve consumers throughout the development process. However, what managers need to be careful about is what kind of approach to market research they take, and how much they let results influence their decisions. In the case of Black & Decker, should the market research data dictate which design to take forward? Rather the devil you know?

Particularly in the context of innovation there is a considerable problem with market research: if you ask people what they want, they will refer to something they are familiar with. Kaplan (1999) comments, "Customers seldom articulate needs they don't know they have. Ten years ago, how many people would have asked for a subscription to anything like America Online? Thirty years ago, how many people would have asked for a calculator that fits into a shirt pocket, or a microwave, or a VCR, or a Walkman?" So it is important to understand the limitations of more traditional forms of market research and focus. As Henry Ford used to say, "Had I asked people what they wanted they would have told me: faster horses!" When choosing a market research approach it is essential to understand the need to match that approach to the development ambition on hand. If it is a small adjustment then a focus group or other forms of more traditional market research will be just fine. If it is something entirely new we are thinking about we need to be much more careful how we elicit consumer intent.

There are two main approaches: quantitative and qualitative. The former involves surveys and questionnaires; the latter interviews, focus groups and observations. After some general insights on market research, this chapter looks first at traditional market research methods and then at some more recent developments and approaches better suited to innovation.

WHAT IS IT ABOUT MARKET RESEARCH?

Research with members of the Best Practice Research revealed that most companies are dissatisfied with the results of current market research practices. Taking a closer look at how many companies conduct their research gives an indication why more often than not the activity is outsourced to an external agency. This means the information that the company gets back has been filtered through the market research agency's lenses, or as a member of the Innovation Exchange put it, "You generally only get a summary of the research but researchers do not necessarily have the knowledge and understanding of the market to interpret the results 'correctly.' " As Bobrow recommends in his book *Complete Idiot's Guide to New Product Development* (1997), "Use it [market research]. Don't believe it." You may have heard the following story that illustrates this point before:

> A car manufacturer, just having finished a prototype of its new small car, commissioned a market research agency to find out what consumers would think about it. When the research report came back the engineers were surprised to read that consumers were not quite happy with the engine performance. It was only a small car and the engine was already quite powerful. But still, give the consumer what the consumer wants. So the engineers reworked the engine, and the revised model was market tested again. But still, the results said that consumers wanted more power. This circle was repeated a few times until the engineers threw their hands up and said, 'This cannot be true! Let us speak to the researchers or even better, be present when they conduct their research.' And indeed, a good idea it was. When the engineers were present and could actually observe the consumer and talk to them directly they realised that it was not that the **real** power of the engine was an issue but it was the **perceived** power. What consumers were missing was the feeling of gently being pushed back into the seat when accelerating – something that could be fixed easily – and quickly as well as cheaply – by changing the upholstery.

This story illustrates very clearly that it is not about getting information, it is about being able to interpret the feedback correctly, and applying insights and expertise to come to the right conclusions. When selecting a particular method for a piece of market research the two critical questions are: Will this type of research be able to collect the data we need? And secondly, will the way the data is treated maximise its value?

Another issue with market research is that it is often undertaken to confirm results or beliefs, rather than to gain new insights. Market research is sometimes commissioned with the aim to generate some 'ammunition' to help sell a particular idea – and when the answers are not as desired, they often get ignored.

But, even if market research is taken seriously and conducted appropriately, the results are not necessarily a good indicator for what is going to happen upon the introduction of the product. Let me just give you a few examples:

- 190,000 consumers testing the *New Coke* against the existing formula overwhelmingly declared that they preferred the new taste, but its launch was a failure (Martin, 1995).

- In consumer research McDonald's found that consumers wanted healthier burgers – but when they launched their diet burger, McLean, it was a flop. People continued to buy the nice fatty, greasy burgers (Martin, 1995).

Even when it is the consumers themselves who make a particular request, it does not necessarily mean that they do as they say they would if faced with a decision, as the following example illustrates. Consumer electronics company Philips had heard customers complain over and over again about how boring the black and silver boxes of the hi-fi equipment was, and how much nicer it would be to have something bright and colourful. Philips invited some of these consumers to a workshop and as a thank you offered them a small radio to take home. Participants could choose between lovely bright-coloured ones as well as the more traditional black or silver versions. The ones left on the shelf were the brightly coloured ones.

If market research does not seem to be a good predictor for market success, its predictive power of market failure is similarly (un)impressive: Kaplan (1999) reports, "When tested through market research, the HP35 calculator, the first videocassette recorder, the fax machine, and Federal Express all received negative ratings!" or as another story from Martin's (1995) article shows:

> When Compaq first thought about introducing Systempro, PC-based servers, everyone in the industry declared that this, surely, was beyond the possibilities of a personal computer and had to be done on a mainframe. Gary Stimac, then Compaq's senior vice president who led the team recalls, "By the end of 1990, Systempro's first year in the market, it generated only $200m in revenue. But we did not give up and continued to educate the market. It typically takes 12–18 months to get good read on whether what you are hearing is surmountable scepticism or a downright lack of market acceptance." In 1994 Compaq sold $1.8 billion worth of Systempro, equalling 17% of the company's revenue.

These insights – failure of current market research practices to deliver accurate results and the problems of misinterpretation through external research agencies – lead companies to reconsider their approach. Involving people from within the organisation in market research exercises is a possible solution, as a quote from a US government website on best practice in service acquisition illustrates,[1] "In the past, it was not unusual for technical staff to conduct market research about marketplace offerings, while contracting staff conducted market research more focused on industry practices and pricing. A better

> "The starting point for innovation is to connect with the consumer. This has been a weakness over the past 4–5 years, we were too removed from the consumers. We are now asking our people to go and talk to consumers where they spend their lives – in bars, sports fields, shopping centres – to find out how they actually live. We can already see that where we understand the consumer more we have great success."

approach is for the entire integrated solutions team to be a part of the market research effort. This enables the members of the team to share an understanding and knowledge of the marketplace – an important factor in the development of the acquisition strategy – and a common understanding of what features, schedules, terms and conditions are key." Another is to send out your staff to observe your product or service in action.

Compaq's story also brings out a very important point: innovation can take some time to get a foothold in the market. Offerings not flying off the shelves initially does not necessarily mean that they are a failure. Particularly, if something is very different from what people are used to it might take some time to get accepted. Finding ways to educate and excite the market are what is called for in such a situation. Viral marketing is one such approach.

Viral Marketing – how to infect consumers

Managers are becoming dissatisfied with the impact of traditional marketing and advertising campaigns. Particularly for highly innovative products which can require extensive educating of the consumer traditional methods take a long time and can be very costly. Think about the following:

In today's world we have tremendous information overload: we get bombarded with advertisements every moment of our waking lives from radio, television, newspapers, bill boards, magazines, mail shots, etc.;

---

[1] From http://www.acquisition.gov/comp/seven_steps/step3_take.html, a government website on a project on developing best practice for service acquisition.

More and more people expect to be treated as individuals rather than as part of the big crowd;

As a consequence people get immune to mass marketing approaches;

Insight: About 67% of consumer purchases are influenced by peers (McKinsey & Co, 2000).

A different approach: use *viral marketing* to create a *Social Epidemic*. A *Social Epidemic* refers to the rapid spread by social contagion of an idea, emotion, or behaviour through a population. A distinct advantage of this approach: it tends to require much smaller budgets than traditional marketing approaches. Creating a consumer epidemic is about stealth marketing; there are three principles to consider in the creation of a consumer epidemic:

- **Who** – law of the few; i.e. who are the influential few who will be imitated and followed by the many?

- **What** – stickiness; what is it about our offering that is highly attractive and easy communicable?

- **Where** – context; i.e. adapt your idea to piggy-back on a trend so its fits the context of existing ideas

Another good source for customer insights that many organisations ignore are the frontline sales people. They have direct contact and can often observe the customer using the product. However, mechanisms need to be put in place to ensure that the feedback from the frontline is honest and straight. Most sales people are not motivated to feed back if there are any 'problems' or they are not rewarded for ideas, but are rewarded for sales. This may also influence their listening ability: they listen to sell, not to learn. Companies can improve the process by putting systems in place that encourage sales staff to feed back any useful information, for example introduce customer visit feedback forms and ensure that rewards are not counterproductive – but don't forget to train the sales people so they know what they are expected to do and look out for. An approach to filter back insights from the frontline taken by a large fast-moving consumer goods company is shown in Box 9.1.

Box 9.1   Capturing insights from the frontline

The Global Business Intelligence team

- At the core of the Global Business Intelligence (GBI) are three people who are focused on market and competitor intelligence. It is championed by the executive vice president of marketing.

- The team produces reports for senior management (corporate and country) every 6–8 weeks updating them on the latest developments world wide.

- The work of the team is reactive as well as proactive. Under the 'reactive' umbrella falls the monitoring and tracking of large as well as small and local competitors. In the selection of their focus they also ensure that the categories they are investigating are relevant to the company. In their work they collaborate closely with a technology scouting group.

- They have also set up a network of 'internal correspondents' who feed into the central team what is happening in their market.

- About 20% of information goes into the regular bulletin. In writing their report they are looking at the wider context not just at specific and individual products.

The process looks like outlined below:

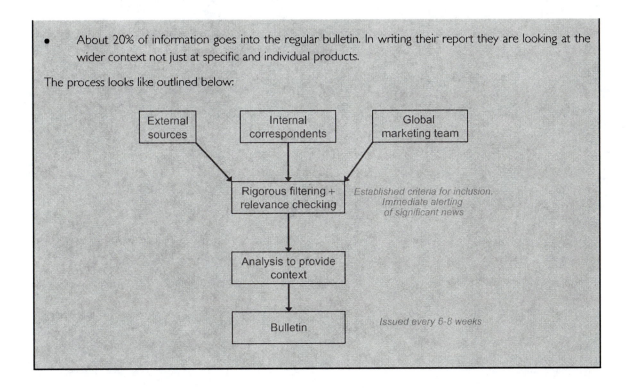

TRADITIONAL APPROACHES TOWARDS MARKET RESEARCH

Keeping the above in mind, what are the traditional approaches to market research? They all have one thing in common, they are based on asking the consumer what he or she wants, either through the collection of quantitative or qualitative data. Under the category of quantitative research we find different distribution methods of surveys and questionnaires: per mail, over the telephone, in person, either in home or office, or 'on the street' and more recently, via email or on the internet.

The three main qualitative market research methods are interviews, focus groups and observation – or in fact a combination. Qualitative approaches have the advantage that they generate a deeper level of understanding of consumer needs and viewpoints. Artefacts such as drawings, prototypes or the finished product can be used for either. As mentioned before, it is horses for courses. Table 9.1 by Steven Cohen (1996) compares methods of quantitative market research whereby the latter two columns also shed some light on the benefits of qualitative interviewing.

However, there are not only different approaches to consider, managers should also think during which stages of the development process they seek to involve consumers. Bruce and Cooper (1997, p. 86) suggest that market research has a part to play in all stages of product development. Conveniently, Mahajan and Wind (1992) provide a matrix with different approaches to market research on one axis and different new product development stages on the other, suggesting which approach is appropriate for what stage (see Table 9.2).

Table 9.1 Comparing approaches to market research

	Survey method			
	Mail	Telephone	In person (home or office)	In person (intercept)
Use of incentives	Recommended	Not necessary except in rare cases	Recommended	Recommended
Cost per interview	Low	Depends on population to be reached	High	Moderate
Ability to use visuals and physical prototypes or do taste tests	Visuals only	Not possible	Yes	Yes
Possible interview complexity	Few skip patterns, many complex question types possible	Complex skip patterns, many question types not possible	Both complex skip patterns and question types are possible	Both complex skip patterns and question types are possible
Awareness, open-ended questions, and probes	Not possible	Possible	Possible	Possible
Speed of response	Slow	Fast	Moderate	Moderate
Security	Low	High	Moderate	High
Survey length	Long surveys possible	Moderate length	Long surveys possible	Long surveys possible
Control over who responds	Low	High	High	High
Control over conduct of interviews	Low	High	Moderate	High

Source: Cohen, S.H. (1996). Tools for quantitative market research. In M.D.J. Rosenau, A. Griffin, G. Castellion & N. Anschuetz (eds), *The PDMA Handbook of New Product Development*, volume 1 (pp. 253–67). New York: John Wiley & Sons, Inc. Reproduced by permission of John Wiley & Sons Ltd.

Another question is, how many people need to be asked to get some meaningful insights? Cohen (1996) has collected data that provides some guidelines on typical sample sizes for different types of quantitative marketing research studies (Table 9.3):

The reliability of the data will vary from industry to industry, and with varying user groups. For example, research that involves professional users and buyers tends to be much more reliable than research undertaken with consumers stopped in the street, and insights from research for fast-moving consumer goods (FMCDs) tend to be more reliable than those from research regarding capital expenditures goods.

Table 9.2 Use of models and methods of market research across new product development activities

	Focus group	Limited rollout	Concept tests	Show test/ clinic	Attitude, usage studies	Conjoint analysis	Delphi panel	QFD	Home usage test	Product life-cycle models	Synectics
New product idea generation	x	x	x				x	x		x	x
New product screening	x	x	x	x	x	x	x				
Market study for concept development	x	x	x	x	x						x
Market identification positioning, marketing strategy specification	x	x	x		x	x		x		x	
Business/finance analysis			x		x	x				x	
Product development	x	x	x	x		x		x	x		
Consumer test of products	x	x	x	x		x			x		
Pre-market volume forecasting				x		x					
Market test/trial sell		x		x							
Market launch planning	x	x	x	x	x					x	

Focus group – in an interactive setting people comment on a particular product, service, concept, advertisement, idea, packaging, etc.
Limited rollout – rather than launching the product across all markets the organisation operates in a few but significant markets selected to gauge consumer reaction.
Concept tests – elicits consumer responses to a particular concept; can be used as part of field surveys, personal interviews and focus groups.
Show test/clinic – where consumers are asked to evaluate different concepts/ products.
Attitude, usage studies – also known as **decile analysis** or **Pareto analysis**; segments users by level of use (heavy vs. light) or by time and place.
Conjoint analysis – Bobrow (1997) describes conjoint analysis as "A technique for separating and measuring respondents' judgements about complex alternatives, usually product characteristics or attributes, into distinct components."
Delphi panel – elicits ideas from participants by means of a series of highly structured and progressively more focused questionnaires; initial questionnaire is sent out, questions are summarised and rephrased into a new set of questions which is resent to initial participants; process is repeated.
QFD (Quality Function Deployment) – a matrix with product characteristics and attributes on the one axis and customer needs on the other is used to determine where to focus development efforts.
Home usage test – based on realistic exposures to the product, generally in the home of the user.
Product life-cycle models – looking at the product in question from a cradle to grave approach.
Synectics – I would not necessarily classify Synectics as a tool for market research, I would rather describe it as a structured team approach to problem solving and idea generation, promoted originally by a company of the same name.

Source: Mahajan, V. & Wind, J. (1992). New product models: practice, shortcomings and desired improvements. *Journal of Product Innovation Management*, **9**, 128–39. Reproduced by permission of Blackwell Publishing.

Table 9.3 Sample size for market research studies

Study	Minimum size	Typical size (range)
Market studies	500	1000–1500
Strategic studies	200	400–500
Test market penetration studies	200	300–500
Concept/product tests	200	200–300/cell
Name tests	100/name variant	200–300/cell
Package tests	100/package variant	200–300/cell
TV, radio commercial tests	150/commercial	200–300/commercial
Print advertisement tests	150/advertisement	200–300/advertisement

Source: Cohen, S.H. (1996). Tools for quantitative market research. In M.D.J. Rosenau, A. Griffin, G. Castellion & N. Anschuetz (eds), *The PDMA Handbook of New Product Development*, volume 1 (pp. 253–67). New York: John Wiley & Sons, Inc. Reproduced by permission of John Wiley & Sons Ltd.

THE FUTURE

Given that traditional approaches to market research do not seem to work too well in the context of innovation, what then are approaches that might help? Sanchez and Sudharshan (1993) recommend what they call 'real-time market research'. In their words, real-time market research involves, "To offer batches of actual new product models to consumers to learn their exact and varied preferences as to alternative product configurations, features and performance levels." This approach, so they claim, overcomes some of the limitations and time requirements of traditional market research methods – for a list of what Mahajan and Wind (1992) consider to be the major shortcomings please see Table 9.4.

Table 9.4 Traditional models of market research and their shortcomings

Models	Major shortcomings
Focus group	Market complexity not captured
Limited rollout	Too much time to implement
Concept tests	Forecast inaccuracy
Show test/clinic	Too much time to implement
Attitude, usage studies	Forecast inaccuracy
Conjoint analysis	Expensive, complexity not captured
Delphi panel	Market complexity not captured
Quality Function Deployment	Forecast inaccuracy, too much time
Home usage test	Expensive, too much time
Product life-cycle models	Forecast inaccuracy
Synectics	Expensive, forecast inaccuracy

Source: Mahajan, V. & Wind, J. (1992). New product models: practice, shortcomings and desired improvements. *Journal of Product Innovation Management*, **9**, 128–39. Reproduced by permission of Blackwell Publishing.

However, real-time market research does not really overcome the problem of people knowing what they like and liking what they know. There are two possible ways of addressing this issue. The first is, if innovative products or ideas are concerned, work with a group of people who are known to like change and new things, don't work with traditionalists who always prefer the 'good old days'. Find the 'Vorreiter', the pioneers of new products and technologies who like nothing better than a new toy. They are more likely to be open and positive towards new things. The most leading-edge market research and launch strategists go even further, rather than launching a product or service and leave it to advertising and other sales-enhancing techniques to establish the product in the marketplace, they aim to identify trend leaders and let them promote the product instead. If the right people can be identified, marketers can achieve a market pull – instead of the company push – for their innovation, an approach called 'viral marketing'. The art lies in identifying who are the right people to create a market. However, it is also very expensive.

We talker earlier about involving users and this has in fact become increasingly an area of interest. However, the question is always, how to find the right users? To ensure they work with the right kind of user some organisations have developed particular strategies seeking out and working with those users who actively want to change and improve existing offerings. One of the first questions is often, what does 'active' mean? Eric von Hippel (2005) at MIT, who has been working on this topic for a long time, put the main emphasis on what he refers to as users who are at the 'extreme' end; it is often those users who invent and improve things. One example is an enthusiastic long-distance cyclist who designed a rucksack that could be filled with water and had a pipe directly to his mouth so he could cycle for hours without having to stop for a drink.

> A German supplier to the car industry **Webasto** went through a systematic approach to understand what lead users are and how to identify them. Building on existing literature they identified four aspects that really drive people's propensity to innovate (cognitive complexity, team expertise, general knowledge, willingness to help). Based on those aspects they developed a questionnaire that they sent out to 100 people from their database. About 20% returned the questionnaires, there were several selection steps (e.g. age bracket, innovation potential) before they arrived at a lead user group of 11. The lead users committed to come for an entire weekend, and without pay.

Some things to consider when engaging with active users are:

- Choosing people who really care about the product and are emotionally engaged – but passion alone is not enough; people need to have a certain level of understanding/expertise/insight to be able contribute.

- Proactive approach to addressing intellectual property issues.

- Finding ways to 'reward' active users. Recognition tends to be infinitely more effective than purely financial rewards (Lego names the 'inventors' on the product packaging; BMW has invited those who came up with the top 20 ideas to their design studio).

The second way is not to ask people what they want, but observe what they actually do. This approach is particularly useful at the idea generation stage as it helps to identify latent consumer needs – those needs of which even the consumers might not be aware – but if you are able to identify such a need, and develop a solution for it, you are on to a winner. One company well known for this approach is IDEO (www.ideo.com). Harvard academics Leonard and Rayport (1997) called this approach 'emphatic design'. They explain, "Emphatic design calls for company representatives to watch customers using products and services in the context of their own environments. By doing so, managers can often identify unexpected uses for their products. They can also uncover problems that customers do not mention in surveys. Companies can engage in emphatic design, or similar techniques such as contextual inquiry, in a variety of ways. However, most employ the following five-step process: 1. observation, 2. capturing data, 3. reflection and analysis, 4. brainstorming for solutions, 5. developing prototype of possible solutions." In Table 9.5 Leonard and Rayport contrast the traditional approach of asking people what they want with the observation approach.

It is approaches such as 'emphatic design' and 'viral marketing' that are more likely to identify seed for innovations than market research methods that count 'ticks in a box' and rely on statistical analysis.

One final approach which is more about understanding the future than actual market research is scenario planning. This is about looking at a world which does not necessarily follow the current trajectory. These can be trend extrapolation or 'standard' forecasting techniques but can also be more advanced scenario-based approaches.

Table 9.5   Comparing the traditional approach with emphatic design

Inquiry	Observation
People can't ask for what they don't know is technically possible	Well-chosen observers have deep knowledge of corporate capabilities, including the extent of the company's technical expertise
People are generally highly unreliable reporters of their own behaviour	Observers rely on real actions rather than reported behaviour
People tend to give answers they think are expected or desired	People are not asked to respond to verbal stimuli, they give nonverbal cues of their feelings and responses through body language, in addition to spontaneous, unsolicited comments
People are less likely to recall their feelings about intangible characteristics of products and services when they aren't in the process of using them	Using the actual products or a prototype, or engaging in the actual activity for which an innovation is being designed, stimulates comments about such intangibles as smells or emotions associated with the product's use
People's imagination – and hence their desires – are bounded by their experience, they accept inadequacies and deficiencies in their environment as normal	Trained, technically sophisticated observers can see solutions to unarticulated needs
Questions are often biased and reflect inquirers' unrecognised assumptions	Observation is open ended and varied; trained observers tend to cancel out one another's observational biases
Questioning interrupts the usual flow of people's natural activity	Observation, while almost never totally unobtrusive, interrupts normal activities less than questioning does
Questioning stifles opportunities for users to suggest innovations	Observers in the field often identify user innovations that can be duplicated and improved for the rest of the market

The concept of 'scenario planning' is often associated with Shell, which has taken a pioneering role in this approach. It is the process of building plausible views of a small number of different possible futures, generally for an organisation operating in conditions of high uncertainty. Companies have come to realise that it is not only about predicting the future but to a certain degree also shaping and influencing the future. One example where a certain future is created is the fashion industry where certain styles and colours are promoted to the exclusion of any others.

Different industries use different kinds of scenarios; the car industry for example uses concept cars to test and influence a 'future'.

BASF went through a multi-stage process, using the megatrend 'ageing population' as starting point. The process started with a discussion of experts from a wide variety of professions (e.g. airline industry, newspapers, medical profession etc.) about what life for the aged would be and feel like in 2020. Next internal experts looked at the results of the discussion and related these results to BASF's industries. Further steps were verification of conclusions internally as well as externally. **GSK Consumer Health** used a process quite similar to strengthen their medium- to long-term pipeline.

More recently companies have started to see value in developing such scenarios jointly with other organisations and discover exciting opportunities for cross-industry collaboration (which often means the creation of an entirely new market.

READING SUGGESTIONS

Kelley, T. (2001). *The Art of Innovation*. London: HarperCollins Business.

Comment: Written by one of the founders of one of the leading innovation consultancies, IDEO, this book provides some great insights into the company's practices and processes. An anonymous reviewer on amazon.com wrote, "The key strength of this book is Kelley's hands-on experience that crackles through every page. This book is not permeated by academic detachment but a bubbling and infectious enthusiasm."

Hague, P. (2002). *Market Research*. London: Kogan Press.

Comment: Aimed at practitioners and students alike, this book does not require previous knowledge of the subject. It provides advice as well as real-life case studies that provide insights about how to set up market research. It covers all steps from planning, desk research, qualitative and quantitative research, oversampling and questionnaire design to data collection and analysis. Also useful is the listing of research agencies, codes of practice, quality schemes and a contact list.

De Geus, A. (1997). *The Living Company*. London: Nicholas Brealey.

Comment: A classic on the topic written by the former head of Shell's Strategic Planning Group, which has developed and pushed the boundaries on this topic.

SOME USEFUL WEBSITES

www.rbg.org.uk

Comment: The Research Buyer's Guide is a directory of organisations offering market research and related services.

http://www.marketresearch.org.uk

Comment: With over 8000 members in more than 50 countries, the Market Research Society is the world's largest international membership organisation for professional researchers and others engaged or interested in market, social and opinion research.

10 A note on teams

Since the early 1990s teamwork, which played an important role in the Black & Decker case study, has found widespread attention in the management literature in general and the innovation and new product development literature in particular. Teams are often described as the backbone of innovation. For example, Tidd *et al.* (2001) certainly agree, stating that, "Innovation is primarily about combining different perspectives in solving problems, and there is thus much potential value in team working." But what actually is a team?

We believe that organisations only truly innovate and grow when three fundamental elements are all firmly in place (http://www.innovaro.com):

- The ability to conceive and exploit new ideas
- A clear strategic vision focused on value generation
- Aligned and empowered teams to drive progress

In their work Katzenbach and Smith (1993) define a team as "A small number of people with complementary skills who are committed to a common purpose, performance goals and approach for which they hold themselves mutually accountable." They differentiate between five different types of teams whereby the distinguishing factor is the degree to which performance can be delivered (see Box 10.1).

For teams to succeed in innovation they have to be at least Real Teams. But while there is general agreement that teams are essential for innovation, companies often complain that they do not seem to work. Henke *et al.* (1993) suggest that most firms are not using teams as effectively and efficiently as they could and should. Majchrzak and Wang (1996) provide one explanation, "Managers often underestimate the difficulty of breaking the functional mindset. Many managers do away with functions but fail to change their own positions. Our research indicates that if companies are not ready to take the steps required to change their culture they may be better off leaving their functional departments intact." A further problem is that more often human resource levers are not adjusted to reflect the shift from individual to team. Reward and recognition systems continue to support individual performance whereas the working reality is based around teams. In the end individuals will demonstrate the behaviour that they are rewarded/remunerated for rather than the behaviours they are told to display.

However, Henke *et al.* (1993) also found that organisations participating in their research experienced the following to be benefits of using teams:

- The shortcomings of hierarchical structures are overcome by the team's ability to cut across traditional vertical lines of authority.

Box 10.1   Different types of teams

Working Group   "There is *no significant, incremental performance need* or opportunity
                        that would require it to become a team." The purpose is exchange
                        of information, best practice, perspectives etc.

Pseudo Team   "There is no significant, incremental performance need or opportunity,
                        but *it has not focused on collective performance and is not trying to
                        achieve it.*" There is no real interest in shaping a common purpose,
                        and the sum of the whole tends to be less than the parts. Of all
                        types of teams this performs worst.

Potential Team   "There is a significant, incremental performance need, and *that really is
                        trying to improve its performance impact.*" Often lacks clarity of
                        purpose and collective accountability.

Real Team   "A small number of people with complementary skills who *are equally
                        committed to a common purpose, goals, and working approach for
                        which they hold themselves mutually accountable.*"

**High-Performance   "All conditions of the real team, and has *members who are also deeply
Team**   committed to one another's personal growth and success.*" This type of
                        team outperforms all others.

Source: based on Katzenbach, J.R. & Smith, D.K. (1993). *The Wisdom of Teams.* Boston, MA: Harvard Business School Press.

- Decision making is decentralised and therefore faster.

- Hierarchical information overload is reduced at higher levels.

- Higher quality decisions can have a significantly greater potential of occurring than with individual decisions.

To what extent the benefits can be reaped depends to a large degree on team composition, structure and level of responsibility, and that all of the aforementioned is appropriate for the task at hand.

When Wheelwright and Clark (1995) took a closer look at teams in the context of product development they found four different types of teams:

- Functional Team
- Lightweight Team
- Heavyweight Team
- Autonomous Team

Each team has its advantages and disadvantages, and each is better suited to different kinds of problems. Table 10.1 summarises their characteristics, strengths and weaknesses and Figure 10.1 provides a visual representation of the different team structures.

Table 10.1 Types of New Product Development Teams

Team structure and associated characteristics	Strengths	Weaknesses
Functional Team Members are answerable to their respective functional heads; team is abandoned upon completion; projects evolve in a serial fashion as tasks pass from one function to the next; assessment not as team but by functional managers	Brings functional expertise to problem solving Function managers control resources for the tasks they own Clear career path Clear control, functional accountability	Judged based on adherence to functional processes rather than overall project results Cookie-cutter approach to solving varied problems Team does not own business results Narrow levels of expertise Disjointed development Turf battles possible
Lightweight Team Most common; heightened degree of coordination due to 'administrative' oversight; individuals continue to be focused primarily on their function, not on overall project results; improved communications	Same as functional Oversight of collective functional responsibilities helps to ensure timely project completion	Same as functional The lightweight manager has little organisational clout and little power to affect critical decisions
Heavyweight Team Core team members are representatives of their functions on an integrated development team; heavyweight manager is the heavyweight in the organisation	Heavyweight manager has broad control over the decision-making processes, resources used and targets established	Team members still report to functional head; rewards and responsibilities are disconnected from project deliverables Political tightrope – project manager has about the same stature as functional heads
Autonomous Team Team members are co-located and answer only to the heavyweight project manager; the team has extreme latitude to devise solutions to the problems it has responsibility for; sets own objectives; truly integrated cross-functional structure	Focus on results No conflicting forces pulling at team members Speed and ability in solving challenging, novel problems Complete functional integration, the broadly skilled team is independent	Less control; team tends to expand on original project description Little use of existing process solutions Independent/lack of integration with others Unique product and process solutions may be difficult to integrate into existing business

Source: Based on Wheelwright, S.C. & Clark, K.B. (1995). *Leading Product Development: The Senior Manager's Guide to Creating and Shaping the Enterprise*. New York: Free Press.

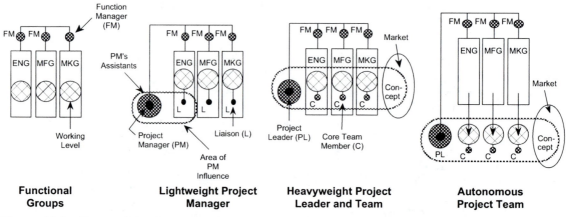

Figure 10.1 Types of development teams.
Source: Reproduced from Wheelwright, S.C. & Clark, K.B. (1995). *Leading Product Development: The Senior Manager's Guide to Creating and Shaping the Enterprise*. New York: Free Press.

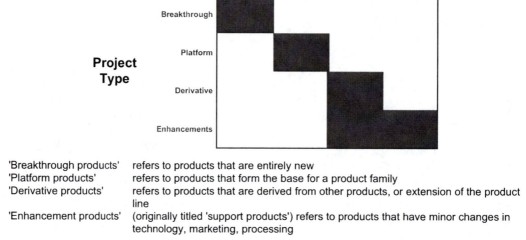

'Breakthrough products'	refers to products that are entirely new
'Platform products'	refers to products that form the base for a product family
'Derivative products'	refers to products that are derived from other products, or extension of the product line
'Enhancement products'	(originally titled 'support products') refers to products that have minor changes in technology, marketing, processing

Figure 10.2 Levels of innovation.
Source: Reproduced from Wheelwright, S.C. & Clark, K.B. (1995). *Leading Product Development: The Senior Manager's Guide to Creating and Shaping the Enterprise*. New York: Free Press.

Wheelwright and Clark have also identified four different levels of innovation – breakthrough, platform, derivative and enhancement – and by combining the two sets of insights they provide a matrix that suggests which type of project team is particularly relevant and appropriate for which type of innovation (see Figure 10.2).

These categories relate to the portfolio categories introduced in Chapter 3 on new product development and Figure 10.3 shows how both categorisations relate to one another.

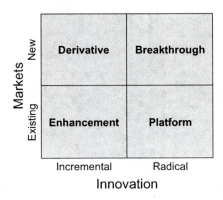

Figure 10.3 Levels of innovation and product portfolios.

Beyond structuring and composing a team that is appropriate for the development challenge, there are some more general rules for team success. Tidd *et al.* (2001) found that successful teamwork tends to depend on the following:

- clearly defined tasks and objectives
- effective team leadership
- good balance of team roles and match to individual behavioural style
- effective conflict resolution mechanisms within the group
- continuing liaison with external organisation

While Smith and Reinertsen (1995) looked at how to accelerate the execution of new product development products in particular, their insights are valid for successful teamwork in general. In their experience the more of the following criteria the team satisfies, the faster it will develop products:

- A team should have fewer than 10 members.
- Members should volunteer to serve on the team.
- Members should serve on the team for the time of product concept until the product is in production.
- Members should be assigned to the team full time.
- Members should report solely to the team leader.
- The key functions, including at least marketing, engineering and manufacturing, should be on the team.
- Members should be located within conversational distance of each other.

I would like to point out that it is generally the case that the more innovative a project the more difficult it is to give accurate time predictions. It is in the nature of innovation to carry a degree of uncertainty and unpredictability – if everything was known and predictable it would hardly be innovative!

There is one characteristic that is particular to innovation teams that did not show up on either of the above lists: diversity. During a speech at the 2002 Innovation Network (www.thinksmart.com) conference held in Minneapolis, Doug Hall, author of *Jump Start Your Business Brain* (2001) provocatively – but quite to the point – said, "If you have complete consensus within a innovation team of ten, nine of these people are a cost savings opportunity!" Innovation happens when you connect different bodies of knowledge. If there is no intellectual tension and questioning of each other's assumptions, there will be no innovation. Hence, team composition is very important and it pays to consider carefully whom to second to the team. And that is why in the last section of this chapter we take a closer look at different personality and preference tests that might help you to compose a diverse team.

TEAM COMPOSITION

In this last section of this chapter we will investigate tools for determining and understanding team diversity. By the way, one point that is also essential when putting together a team is to select its members based on their merit, that is on the skills they have to offer, rather than just choosing someone who happens to be available at the time (which seems to happen rather a lot). This is something the innovation consultancy IDEO sees as a cornerstone of its continued innovation success, even if it requires bringing together people from across their eight offices around the world for the duration of a project. It is also important to acknowledge that the best possible team composition will change over the different stages of the innovation cycle.

The six instruments introduced here are:

1.   *Belbin* suggests eight different roles that should be represented in a team to ensure all necessary skills are available.

2.   *Myers–Briggs* investigates four opposing pairs of behaviour and attitudes.

3.   *CARE*, developed by Allen Fahden and Srinivasan Namakkal, identifies individual behavioural and thinking approaches.

4.   *Kirton's KAI* inventory looks at people's preferred problem-solving style.

5.   *Innovation Potential Indicator* (IPI), a tool for the assessment of individuals' potential to innovate, developed by Dr Fiona Patterson.

6.   *The Adversity Index* (AQ), developed by Paul G. Stoltz, is based on the theory that how a person responds to adversity is a valid and broad predictor of, among other things, individual and team performance and capability for change.

(1) Belbin's team roles

Dr Meredith Belbin and his colleagues developed his tool specifically to help organisations to compose better teams. They found that in a 'perfect team' eight different roles are represented, whereby one person can hold more than one role, that is a team does not necessarily have to have eight members. The test they developed is based on four principal factors:

- intelligence
- dominance

Table 10.2 Summary of Belbin's Team Roles

Title	Characteristics	Upsides	Downsides
Chairman	Calm, self-confident, controlled, tolerant, warm, enthusiastic	Capacity for welcoming all contributions and treating them on their merits without prejudice. Strong sense of objectives	No more than ordinary in terms of intellect or creative ability
Company worker	Conservative, dutiful, predictable	Organising ability, practical common sense, hard working, self-disciplined	Lack of flexibility, unresponsiveness to unproven ideas
Shaper	Full of nervous energy, highly strung, very high achievement motivation, wants to win, aggressive, extrovert	Drive and a readiness to challenge inertia, ineffectiveness, complacency or self-deception	Prone to provocation, irritation and impatience
Plant	Innovative, introverted, independent, individualistic, serious minded, unorthodox	Genius, imagination, intellect, knowledge	Up in the clouds, inclined to disregard practical details or protocol
Resource investigator	Extroverted, warm, enthusiastic, curious, communicative	Capacity for contacting people and exploring anything new. An ability to respond to challenge	Liable to lose interest once the initial fascination has passed
Monitor evaluator	Sober, unemotional, prudent, detached, intelligent	Judgement, discretion, hard-headedness	Lacks inspiration and the ability to motivate others
Team worker	Socially oriented, rather mild, sensitive, trusting, perceptive, diplomatic	An ability to respond to people and situations. Promotes team spirit	Indecisive at moments of conflict
Completer finisher	Painstaking, orderly, conscientious, anxious, consistent	Capacity for follow-through, perfectionism	Tendency to worry about small details. A reluctance to 'let go'

- extroversion/introversion
- stability/anxiety

Table 10.2 lists the eight roles, their specific traits, as well as their benefits and downsides.

(2) Myers–Briggs Type Indicator (MBTI)

The second instrument is the MBTI, developed by Isabel Myers and Katharine Briggs in the 1950s. It has been designed to facilitate the understanding of psychological types as described by psychologist Carl Jung. The MBTI identifies four individual preferences:

- extroverts versus introverts (E vs. I)
- sensers versus intuitives (S vs. N)

Table 10.3   Characteristics of the Eight MBTI Types

Extroverts (E)	Introverts (I)
Are action-oriented and impulsive Like to think out loud and tend to present rough drafts Outgoing and social	Enjoy privacy and quiet time Tend to prefer fully developed ideas
Sensers (S)	**Intuitives (N)**
Look at what is known and real Rely on actual experience and proven results Approach change slowly, carefully, incrementally, and critically	Perceive abstract things, meanings, relationships and possibilities through insight Like complexity, theoretical relationships and connections between things Able to see future possibilities, often unusual and abstract ones, using imagination and theory
Thinkers (T)	**Feelers (F)**
Use the process of logical and impersonal decision making Apply logical analysis to weigh facts and examine consequences objectively	Arrive at conclusions through process of appreciation with a system of subjective personal values and standards Typically exhibit a warm understanding of people, compassion, empathy and the need for harmony
Judgers (J)	**Perceivers (P)**
Convergent, driving towards closure and results Organisation, schedules, plans, and priorities are important	Divergent, open, flexible and unconstrained Tries to keep things open for new possibilities as long as possible and does not want to miss anything

Source: Adapted from Hipple, J., Harde, D., Wilson, S.A. & Michalski, J. (2001). Can corporate innovation champions survive? *Chemical Innovation*, 14–22.

- thinkers versus feelers (T vs. F)
- judgers versus perceivers (J vs. P)

The first three choices describe a person's orientation towards life, the last choice a person's orientation to the outer world, resulting in 16 possible types. The MBTI is considered one of the oldest, most reliable and valid of the personality instruments. It has been tested on millions of people, and has proved to be a useful tool in understanding human dynamics both at work and on a social level. The authors suggest that it is an effective tool in team building, communication and career exploration. Table 10.3 provides a summary of each of the eight preferences.

In Kenneth Allinson's book *The Wild Card of Design* (1995) I found the reproduction of some typical professional profiles for some of the 16 MBTI types which I thought interesting in the context of this book (see Box 10.2).[1]

---

[1] Originally from G. Macdaid, M. McCaulley & R. Kainz (1986). *Atlas of Table Types*. Gainsville, FL: Centre for Application of Psychological Type Inc.

> **Box 10.2   How professions score on the MBTI**
>
> - Architects   INTJ   - Computing professionals   INTJ
> - Designers   ENFJ   - Managers, administrators   ESTJ
> - Fine artists   INFJ   - Engineers   ISTJ
> - Craft workers   ISTJ   - Accountants   ISTJ
>
> *Source:* Based on Allinson, K. (1995). *The Wild Card of Design – A Perspective on Architecture in a Project Management Environment.* Oxford: Butterworth-Heinemann.

(3) CARE Profile

The third instrument, the CARE, was developed by Allen Fahden and Srinivasan Namakkal. It identifies individual behavioural and thinking approaches using four categories:

- Creator – likes to come up with new ideas, reframe problems and explore alternatives; good at visualising the bigger picture, prefers to focus on the future.

- Advancer – recognises ideas and new directions early on and advances them; when thinking about implementation prefers to rely on past experience; works within existing norms and expectations.

- Refiner – likes to challenge concepts and wants to understand consequences before acting; prefers order and being methodical.

- Executor – focuses on high quality and ensuring the implementation process runs smoothly; prefer proven to the new and pays attention to detail.

The instrument is based on the theory that those working together towards a common goal combine their behavioural preferences and thinking into a specific approach. Identifying individual approaches to teamwork, clarifying roles, understanding and encouraging innovation and problem solving are all components of CARE. The authors suggest that over the course of a project the idea is passed back and forth between the four different roles, each bringing a particular skill to the party.

(4) Kirton's Adaption-Innovation inventory (KAI)

Developed by Dr Michael Kirton, the fourth assessment tool is primarily focused on thinking styles with particular interest in how people show their creativity, solve problems and make decisions. It measures style, not level or ability. Scoring takes place on a continuum that includes *Highly Adaptive* (low score) and *Highly Innovative* (high score) at opposite ends of the scale. The three components measured are: originality, attention to detail and conformity to rules, with each receiving a numeric designation placed on the continuum. Each of the components is added to arrive at the total KAI score. The KAI takes an in-depth look at problem-solving styles, and is useful

Table 10.4 Summary of KAI inventory

Adaptor (Conserver)	Innovator (Originator)
Efficient, thorough, adaptable, methodical, organised, precise, reliable, dependable	Ingenious, original, independent, unconventional
Accepts problem definition	Challenges problem definition
Does things better	Does things differently
Concerned with resolving problems rather than finding them	Discovers problems and avenues for their solutions
Seeks solutions to problems in tried and tested ways	Manipulates problems by questioning existing assumptions
Reduces problems by improvement and greater efficiency; aiming at continuity and stability	Is catalyst to unsettled groups, irreverent of their consensual views
Seems impervious to boredom, able to maintain accuracy in long-term spells of detailed work	Capable of routine work (system maintenance) for only short bursts; quick to delegate routine tasks
Is an authority within established structures	Tends to take control in unstructured situations
Tends to view innovators as:	Tends to view adaptors as:
unsound, impractical, abrasive, undisciplined, insensitive, one who loves to create confusion	dogmatic, compliant, stuck in a rut, timid, conforming, inflexible

Source: Based on Hipple, J., Harde, D., Wilson, S.A. & Michalski, J. (2001). Can corporate innovation champions survive? *Chemical Innovation*, 14–22. Reproduced by permission of American Chemical Society.

in team work when coping behaviour is needed between team members with diverse styles. It also provides knowledge and awareness of both individual style and team style, and can thus be a useful tool in providing the right balance of adaptors and innovators in a group. Table 10.4 shows their characteristics, and what they think of each other.

Looking at their propensity to embrace change – and what is innovation but change – each type is very different as Figure 10.4 shows.[2] This difference can lead to quite some conflict, depending on the level of respect between individuals involved, as Prather (2002) indicates in Figure 10.5.

(5) Innovation Potential Indicator (IPI)

This test for identifying the innovation potential in existing and potential employees was developed by Dr Fiona Patterson. It looks at four main areas of behaviour which can be used to establish whether a person is an innovative thinker:

- Motivation to change (MTC) – describes whether an individual is open to frequent change and new ways of tackling issues at work.

---

[2] Adapted from a presentation by Charles Prather at the 2002 Innovation Network conference in Minneapolis, 21–25 September.

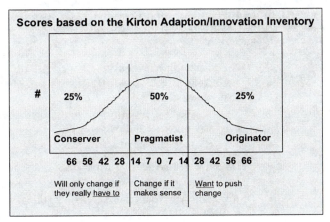

Figure 10.4 Adaptor versus innovator

Source: Based on Kirton, M.J. (1980). The way people approach problems. *Planned Innovation*, **3**, 514.

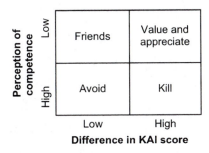

Figure 10.5 Acceptance of person.

Source: Reproduced from Prather, 2002.

- Challenging behaviour (CB) – describes an individual's degree of active engagement in championing change or maintaining the status quo.

- Consistency of work styles (CWS) – describes an individual's preferred approach to work.

- Adaptation (AD) – describes an individual's preference to adopt tried and tested work methods as opposed to doing things differently.

The behaviours identified by the scales are shown in Table 10.5.

(6) The Adversity Index (AQ)

Finally, the Adversity Response Profile, developed by Paul G. Stoltz, PhD, is based on the theory that how a person responds to adversity is a valid and broad predictor of individual and team performance, capability for change, ability to learn, persistence, motivation, productivity, and mental and physical health. The profile looks at four factors:

Table 10.5 Innovation Potential Indicator

Scale of behaviour	Characteristics
Individuals with a high MTC	• Are tolerant of ambiguity and issues that are less 'clear-cut' • Are likely to be interested in new ways of thinking and to strive for achievement • Show intellectual curiosity and enjoy solving problems for the challenges they may offer • Actively seek change and are open to new experiences
Individuals with low MTC	• Do not welcome shifting work goals and too frequent change • Prefer stable environments and are keen to resolve ambiguity • Approach new ideas and ways of working with caution and prefer the familiar
Individuals with a high CB	• Believe it better to seek forgiveness than to ask for permission • Are unlikely to bow to authority if they hold strong beliefs about a particular issue • Will challenge others' points of view
Individuals with low CB	• Strive for group consensus • Are less likely to take risks • Will accept the group consensus and harmony even if they hold strong beliefs about a particular issue
Individuals with high CWS	• Prefer to engage in a disciplined and structured work style • Are highly conscientious • Actively seek organisation and a structured environment
Individuals with low CWS	• Prefer an unstructured environment and variety • Prefer to juggle lots of conflicting demands • Do not enjoy situations that require a methodical and planned approach
Individuals with high AD	• Do not believe they need to be radical to achieve significant progress • Prefer analytical step-by-step approaches and 'precision'
Individuals with low AD	• Are more likely to work outside current systems and parameters to find new ways of tackling problems • Look for novel ways to achieve solutions and aim for originality

Source: Based on Patterson, F. & Silvester, J. (1998). Counter measures. *People Management*, **4**, 46–8.

• Control dominance – how much control a person believes they have over a given event or outcome.

• Origin and ownership dominance – how much a person feels ownership for the outcome even when the origin of the event was someone or something else.

• Reach dominance – the extent to which a person lets bad events impact on other areas of his or her life.

• Endurance – how long a person allows adversity to last.

The tool provides a measure of a person's adversity capacity call AQ^{TM} (Adversity Quotient). A person's AQ also measures their subconscious patterns of response to adversity. It is plotted on a scale of low to high, the higher the AQ the greater the tendency to outperform others, learn from mistakes, take risks and stay emotionally healthy. The lower the AQ the tendency is to repeat mistakes, feel helpless, avoid risk, become depressed and be debilitated by stress.

Except the last tool, which seems to imply a 'right versus wrong', all the tools are just describing different approaches and preferences. When reading through the description you will find that some roles and preferences are better suited to radical innovation, step changes, challenging etc. and others are ideal for situations where incremental innovation, continuous improvement and increased efficiency are required. In the end, to bring a project to a successful conclusion all skills are needed at some point or other. The question each manager needs to ask is where is the emphasis and what are the characteristics of the project for which a team is being assembled? To ask someone with an ESTJ Myers–Briggs profile to come up with a radical innovation is as inappropriate as it would be to ask an INFP type to bring a project to a successful conclusion! What all these tools do is provide some help in: (a) putting the right person on the right job or project and (b) giving people a means through which they can explain and understand their differences. Differences in preferences and language, if not understood and acknowledged, can cause major misunderstanding between individuals as well as disruptions in the execution of projects.

One last observation on this subject, Prather and Gundry (1995) comment on the tension that can exist within commonly used job classifications. We often put accounting and finance or sales and marketing under one person's responsibility. If we look at how they actually score on the KAI we find that individuals focusing on one of these positions actually score quite differently. So people in positions that combine responsibility for both spend a lot of energy doing work they'd rather not be doing. Prather and Gundry call energy expended on such tasks 'coping energy' (see Figures 10.6 and 10.7). They explain, "Essentially, coping energy is zero-return energy – that is, it brings you up to zero so you can begin doing the work." I really liked this concept as it helps to explain why it takes one person for ever to complete a task while another can do it in the shortest period of time – it is about liking what you do, doing what you like, and therefore being good at it.

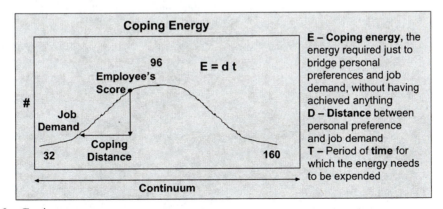

Figure 10.6 Coping energy.
Source: Prather, C.W. & Gundry, L.K. (1995). *Blueprints for Innovation*. New York: American Management Association.

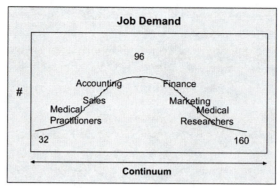

Figure 10.7   Professions across the spectrum.
Source: Prather, 2002, based on Kirton.

For characteristics of team leaders you may want to refer back to the Team Leader section in Chapter 3.

READING SUGGESTIONS

Skopec, E. & Smith, D.M. (1998). *How to Use Team Building to Foster Innovation Throughout Your Organization*. New York: McGraw-Hill.

Comment: In their book the authors discuss how to develop and organise a well-balanced, productive team; how to lead, motivate and reward teams; and deal constructively with mistakes and obstacles to successful team building

Katzenbach, J.R. & Smith, D.K. (1993). *The Wisdom of Teams*. Boston, MA: Harvard Business School Press.

Comment: The authors provide a very valuable insight into a great variety of aspects surrounding teams. In part one they address questions such as why teams are useful, why they might be resisted, how to define a team and what its characteristics are. Part two is concerned with different types of teams, how teams work, what kinds of leader do they need, what might prevent them from performing and how to address this. The third part looks at the role of teams in major change, the role of teams at the top and why they are different, and last not least the role of management.

Kelley, T. & Littman, J. (2005). *The Ten Faces of Innovation: IDEO's Strategies for Defeating the Devil's Advocate and Driving Creativity Throughout Your Organization*. New York: Currency.

Comment: As Kelley explains, this book is "about innovation with a human face. It's about the individuals and teams that fuel innovation inside great organisations." As well as case studies the authors define 10 different personas that are involved in making innovation happen (see also http://www.tenfacesofinnovation.com).

SOME USEFUL WEBSITES

http://www.ccmd-ccg.gc.ca/research/publications/html/innovation/focus_e.html

Comment: The Canadian Centre for Management Development argue for and explain the use of teams
             in innovation
             http://www.american-book.com/Articles/arwilsonp3.htm

Comment: Phil Wilson introduces his book, *Inspired Innovations: A Guidebook to Highly Efficient New
             Product Development*, in which he discusses how development teams can be used to routinely
             produce award-winning, commercially successful innovations. The book is available from
             http://www.pdbookstore.com.
             http://www.kdla.net/statelib/SLS_GSCResources_DHPT.htm

Comment: On this webpage of the Kentucky State Library there is an extensive list of books relevant to
             creating high-performance teams.

11

Collaboration – innovation in manufacturing

CASE STUDY 4: THE LOTUS ELISE[1]

The philosophy behind Lotus and the Elise

A proper sports car should weigh little, handle and ride superbly, and deliver high levels of driver satisfaction.

Lotus founder Colin Chapman

The Lotus Seven, launched in 1957, was Chapman's first car to be built on a commercial scale – previous models had been built exclusively for racing purposes. By taking his cars to market he wanted to transfer some of the excitement of racing cars to the road.[2] The Lotus Seven offered racing-car qualities at kit-car prices, with performance achieved through light-weight construction rather than a powerful engine. Chapman was quoted to have said, "It is a bit like a four-wheeled motorbike."

In 1966 Lotus, which had started off on a site in Tottenham, London, moved to its current site in Hethel, Norwich. The site, which had been the home of a USAAF Liberator squadron in the Second World War was chosen not only because it offered ample room for expansion, but also because it allowed the building of a great test track on what was the former runway and the airfield perimeter road. While keeping the driving fun, Lotus moved decidedly upmarket with the development of the £60,000 Esprit in the 1970s, a direction that was substantiated through the introduction of the Elan, a two-seater sports car, in the 1980s. Neither of the cars has ever been built in large quantities.

Group Lotus plc consists of two parts: Lotus Cars Ltd building the Lotus vehicles, which at the time of the Elise development had about 500 staff; and Lotus Engineering, acting as a consultancy to the automotive industry, with about 800 employees. Both parts of the business, each generating about half of the company's revenue, are located on the same site. While they normally operate quite independently, they operated closely on the development of the Lotus Elise.

Although the company had taken on engineering work for outside companies on a consultancy basis before, a separate Design and Engineering side of Lotus was set up in 1986. In 1998 35 designers and modellers were

---

[1] The case has been prepared by Dr Bettina von Stamm as a basis for class discussion rather than to illustrate either effective or ineffective handling of a management situation.
[2] Interesting to note that 25% of all Lotus Seven built have, at some point or other, been driven in races.

employed by Lotus. Russel Carr, Chief of Design, explains, "50% of all the work that Lotus Design does is for third parties. The volume of work has increased several-fold over the last five years." At Lotus's new design centre in

> The only other car manufacturer that entertains an automotive engineering consultancy is Porsche.

Hethel with its two independent units, officially opened by the Prime Minister of Malaysia in October 2000, they can now run two vehicle programmes independently of each other.

In its drive to deliver light-weight, fast cars innovation has always played an important part. Says Kenneth Sears, Head of Vehicle Engineering, Lotus Engineering, "One of the things that people identify with the company is gaining some performance advantage through the development of new technology." Explaining what Lotus means by innovation a company representative explained, "Innovation must combine elements of knowledge, information and creativity. This means that engineers now and in the future need to combine individual and team working skills." It also means that the company is strongly committed to research and development, and the development of new products.

Previously owned by the Italian company Bugatti International, which had bought Lotus Group in 1994, the Malaysian car manufacturer Proton took a 64% stake in the company for £51 million in October 1996 with its Chairman, Tan Sri Yahaya, buying an additional 16%. When Yahaya died unexpectedly in a helicopter crash his share was bought by Proton in June 1997, bringing the company's share in Lotus to a total of 80%. The remaining 20% is still held by Romano Artioli (previously of Bugatti).[3]

Conception and concept

Don't follow the crowd and copy what they are doing.

Alastair Florance, Lotus Cars

There were several threads that together led to the conception of the idea for the Lotus Elise, or project M1-11 as it was originally called. The company was looking for a follow-up product to the Lotus Elan, which had proved far too expensive to produce and was rather complex to manufacture. The last straw had been when the Japanese company that had supplied the engines for the Elan closed down. With the discontinuation of the Elan in June 1992 200 jobs were lost.

The Elise started with a clean sheet, the only guideline was that it had to be true to the spirit of the founder. To fund the experimentation and development necessary for an entirely new car it was agreed that money would be diverted from the research budget of Lotus Engineering under the condition that the new car should be a demonstration of Lotus's engineering and technology skills. In fact, it was the research budget of two years that was 'liberated' for the development of the Lotus Elise.

It was agreed that the money available should be invested in the development of those parts that would really make a difference, parts that would contribute to the car's character and advancements in technology. In addition a member of the development team was tasked with maximising the number of components that were readily available and would not compromise the car's design and character. For example, the cost involved in developing a

---

[3] In the late 1990s Artioli sold Bugatti to the German car manufacturer BMW.

door mirror in-house would have been in no proportion to the value created through its uniqueness, so a readily available model, from the Rover Metro, was used instead.

The design brief started from a corridor conversation of a few people – including Kenneth Sears, Head of Technology Strategy, and Roger Becker, Head of Vehicle Engineering – about what a new Lotus car should look and feel like in November 1993. Soon after the design team began its discussion about the philosophy for the new car concept. Unusually, rather than starting with an engineering specification, this project started in the design centre. A few parameters were clear from the beginning: it had to be an open two-seater sports car that would be fun to drive, and it should not cost the earth. Three years were anticipated from conception to production, as was a production run of a couple of thousand cars.

The designers started by putting together theme boards through which they explored customer characteristics and defined the mood and feeling that the car should have. Such boards were covered with pictures of cars, aircraft, fashion items, celebrities, advertisements and motorcycles such as Ducati, a passion for which was shared by Richard Rackham, Head of Engineering, and Head of Lotus Design, Julian Thomson. Richard went into raptures about it, "The bike has some awesome performance. You will never use all of it, but you know it is there. It is a bit of a toy that you just love owning. And if you take the clothes off a Ducati you see lots of nice things, that's what we wanted to achieve with the Elise." Richard and Julian kept discussing the concept in all its aspects during work as well as when they met socially.

Once a philosophy had been agreed the designers spent about six weeks developing sketches. Through the sketches key aspects were discussed and agreed: it was to be a step-in two-seater with the engine located at the back, set quite low. The question always asked was, is this in the spirit of Lotus, would driving such a car be fun? The team also used a buck made out of fibreboard, mounted on a wooden frame called the 'seating buck', through which the relationship of driver to driving controls, such as the steering wheel, pedals and gear stick, could be explored. In addition to mood boards, sketches and the cardboard model the team brought in a whole host of previous Lotus models.

With some key aspects and overall lines agreed, a first scale model was developed. This initial 1:3 scale clay model would demonstrate how the car was anticipated to

A very clever aspect of the models is that only half a car is built – and then set against a mirror.

look and what the basic elements would be. Rather than using the clay model for presentations a plaster case was taken from it from which fibreglass models were made. This had the advantage that the original clay model could be used for further development while the presentation model would be much more attractive and representative of a real car than a clay model could be. Once completed the fibreglass model showed some flaws. For example, the proportions of the car did not seem right, it was too short and the overall height had to be reviewed.

Even though the Lotus Board had approved the development of a new car in-house in January 1994, the team faced its first big challenge only a month later. Unbeknown to the Lotus team, Artioli had commissioned other design consultancies to come forward with designs for a new Lotus car. Julian recalls, "Mr Benedini, Bugatti's representative, got the Lotus Board down to decide which design they liked best." It was fortunate for the in-house team that their idea was considered to be the most progressive, innovative and different – and more aligned with the

key brand values of the company than the other designs. While following a similar philosophy to the Lotus Seven, the design team had made a conscious effort to differentiate the new product from the existing ones.

During a body review meeting held in spring 1994, for which a refined second 1:3 scale model was used, questions were posed as to the feasibility of a step-in design. Finding a satisfying engineering solution, mainly to achieve the necessary stiffness, would require time and was likely to add weight to the car. On the other hand, developing doors and windows would be quite costly too and particularly the designers were very keen to stick to their original idea. As a compromise it was decided to give the team four weeks to come up with a solution. But before the four weeks were up vehicle legislation engineer Ken Evans dropped a

bombshell: legislation decreed a maximum step-in height of 750 mm off the ground, a running board, i.e. a step, would be required. Ken pointed out that the line would only have to come down by 30 mm but the designers felt it would compromise the lines of their design. A major rethink was required resulting in additional costs of about £1/2 million.

While the second-generation design changed several times, it showed many aspects found in the final car such as the side air scoops, the top-exit radiator duct, the character of the headlights and the round indicators.

The surface of the 1:3 scale model was scanned to develop a set of drawings from which a full-scale model could be developed. Developing a full-size model is quite an involved process and often scaling problems mean that proportions have to be revisited. Richard compared this to scale toy models where certain aspects of the car look right only because they have been overemphasised. In developing the first full-size model wood and foam were

applied to a steel frame which was then sent away
to a specialist. At the specialist the foam was milled
to 40 mm below the surface and spiked with pegs
sticking out 60 mm, making the model look like a giant
hedgehog. Upon return to Lotus, the model makers
applied clay to the height of the pegs before sending
it once again to the specialist who then copy-milled
it into the final but still only initial clay buck. At the
time Lotus employed 10 model makers, bringing in
additional modellers on a contract basis if and when
required. A team of four to six worked on a full-size
clay model at any point in time, each on a specified

area. The role of the model makers was to help designers and engineers to refine the design. Based on the clay
model that returned to the factory in May 1994 the design was signed off, both Romano Artioli and Gianpaulo
Benedini of Bugatti were part of the decision-making body.

A lot of the actual design was done 'on the object', for example height and positioning of the headlights. Clay had
the great advantage of being easy to manipulate and change, bits could be taken away and added back on. By doing
so any curve or shape could be achieved. Refinement can take quite some time and might leave some people
wondering whether anything has actually changed but spending time and effort here could make the difference
between the end result being 'great' or 'exceptional'.

While the full-size clay model was developed, the
latest 1:3 scale model was tested in the wind tunnel
by aerodynamicist Richard Hill. For lightweight cars to
achieve high speeds efficient aerodynamics are particularly important. Hill found what he had anticipated
when first seeing the low, stubby design: the car had
quite a high drag factor. Another aspect contributing
to the high drag factor was the radiator duct. By reducing the lift at the front, the radiator duct caused an
imbalance at the back, meaning that the car would lift
under aerodynamic load. Not something one would

want to experience in a rear-drive car. To address the problem Richard Hill used clay, Styrofoam and tape to build
up the surfaces until the optimum aerodynamic performance was achieved.

Julian, when presented with the result, was quite taken aback. Not only did he feel that the design had been
spoilt, there was also the question of whether this meant that the design had to go back to the board
for renewed approval. Richard Hill explained that he had taken the changes to the ultimate limit and that a
compromise would have to be found. Project manager Tony Shute commented, "The car was as aerodynamic
as a brick! However, the car had style and whatever happened, we did not want to lose that." Richard
Rackham too was a strong supporter of Julian's design and keen to help find solutions that would maintain the
visual identity. Under the mediation of other team members a compromise was finally reached, and a spoiler
added.

Julian commented on the design process, "The important thing is to remember that all those decisions governing the size and layout of the package that are given by the body engineering department are relevant to us. We talk about the styling but my group is very much involved with the concept of the car; you find that all companies offering truly innovative products have to have a level of

> Occasionally they would come up against what founder Colin Chapman had described as, 'the old school engineers' of whom he had said, "The trouble with experts is they know what can't be done."

understanding between both groups. You can't just have engineers produce something and then decorate it with different styles, they have to complement each other." Richard agreed saying, "Chassis design is more than just a structure, it's part of the style of the car as well, because it's so visible in the design." The team worked to progress engineering and design issues in parallel, as well as considering interior and exterior as each would impact on the other. The efforts were supported by the geographical closeness between the design and the engineering department, and a presence of key concept engineering personnel in the design studio.

A lot of attention was paid to detail. Having a single windscreen wiper was part of the desired look. But not only would it look racy, it was also cheap, and most efficient aerodynamically. The choice of a single wiper had implications for the size of the windscreen and with it the

> Later in 1997 the French company approached Lotus, being interested in buying the wiper mechanisms Lotus had developed.

proportion of the whole vehicle. There were many legal requirements and from the outset there had been some doubts internally as to whether a single wiper would work. Julian remembers, "Our engineers were more interested in developing wiper systems that would fit any car." Lotus had also approached a French company specialising in complex wiper systems. But the tight schedule for the project meant that Lotus was looking for a solution within four months – rather than the 12 the French company declared necessary – which meant that they decided not to get involved. Determined not to give up, Richard Rackham experimented until he found a solution that worked. He commented, "The fact that I was familiar with the Citroen AX system probably helped to see what would be possible. I just tilted the wiper motor spindle and it worked." For the manufacture they eventually found a UK-based company but the design was, in the end, done entirely in-house by Richard.

Probably the biggest challenge for the team was to achieve all other ambitions within a limited budget – if you have lots of money you can achieve almost anything! To make the car widely affordable the price tag had been set at the £20,000 mark. To meet all challenges the team decided to

> We wanted to make the frame out of as small a number of components as possible. We wanted to join each piece. directly to the next piece.

strip out anything that was not absolutely essential, and have as many parts as possible with more than one function, so for example the front structure of the car, which was crash structure, support for the radiator, aerodynamic wing and attachment for a tow hook.

Chassis development

While Julian and his team were working on the overall design, Richard Rackham, who had been involved in the development of the M1-11 even at seating buck stage, started to think about the chassis design. The target weight for the new car had been set at 650 kg – to put this into perspective, a Renault Spider Sport weighs about 930 kg and the MGF brings about 1.1 tonnes to the scale.

> **Some key players in the development team set up in January 1994 and their roles:**
>
> - Tony Shute – project manager, product engineering background, philosophy behind the car, its gestation period, has done a lot of the development driving.
>
> - Julian Thomson – head of Lotus Design, designing the shape, styling process.
>
> - Richard Rackham – head of engineering design, responsible for the design of the chassis and suspension, engineering issues, issues during production process.
>
> - Luke Bennett – manufacturing engineering manager.
>
> - Morris Dowton – manufacturing manager, Lotus production.
>
> - Ben Wright – purchasing & procurement manager.
>
> - Dave Minter – executive engineer, responsible for honing the ride and handling.
>
> - John Miles – details of damping set-up.
>
> - Alastair McQueen – chief test driver.

To determine the dimensions of the chassis Richard and his team, together with Julian, started with a full-size plastic sheet onto which the outline of the car was pasted. The tapes that were used for the lines could be moved and reapplied whereby different colours were used for different parts, i.e. chassis, engine and passenger. "Using this", said Richard, "helps us understand the interaction between car and 'agent orange', so called because for the occupant we use orange lines." From the full-size drawing computer drawings were produced which then allowed working with the chassis and the positioning of individual components.

Before the start on the MI-11 project Lotus had been working with a British car manufacturer on exploring the use of lightweight extrusions for car structures, a liaison that had been set up by Hugh Kemp, Technical Director at Lotus at the time. When Lotus's collaboration partner was taken over by a German manufacturer the relationship

> The aluminium is shipped to England for bending, then goes back to Denmark for heat treatment, machining and the assembly of the chassis before being shipped to Lotus.

ended rather prematurely. However, Richard had got hooked on the idea and decided to explore possibilities for the MI-11 and Tony commented, "It is nice to have a big brother when exploring new territory but we are quite used to doing such things on our own. Our Board saw the visionary product and felt that our people had not only the necessary expertise and knowledge but also a good dose of enthusiasm to see the project through." Richard contacted a company they had worked with previously, the Danish company Hydro Aluminium, whose core expertise was in the building industry but who had recently set up a new division, Hydro Automotive Components.

Welded aluminium had been used for car structures before, but not to the extent Richard planned to use it. Using extruded aluminium would not only mean that the frame would be lightweight but also durable and corrosion resistant. A constraint inherent in the choice was that extrusions tend to be straight. Any bend would not only cost time and money, it would also create a weak point in case of a collision. Finding a solution that would use only straight parts and be aesthetically pleasing turned out to be impossible and in the end two bends had to be integrated into the back part of the chassis. Hydro's experience and expertise came into its own and a special and complex piece of equipment was developed for the bending. However, the bending had to take place in a part of Hydro located in England, this meant that the chassis parts had to be shipped back and forth a few times. It was agreed that once Hydro's new plant in Worcester was completed, production would be moved to the UK. While open cars are often compromised structurally, requiring extensive stiffening to make them sufficiently rigid, the Lotus Elise with its aluminium chassis needed no additional measures. Despite its structure weighing as little as 70 kg, it met all safety standards and proved to have great torsional rigidity.

> **Aluminium versus steel**
>
> The most critical aspect of strength in automotive structures is for safety. Modern vehicle structures must retain the integrity of the occupant cell without significant distortion in crash conditions and provide controlled energy absorption. Aluminium alloys have a range of strength to weight ratios which is broadly similar to typical automotive steels whereas the dynamic behaviour may be different. Aluminium, for example, tends to exhibit no effect or a softening. Aluminium generally cannot support such high values of elongation before failure.
>
> Tooling for a particular aluminium extrusion can cost as little as £2000 whereas tools for a pressed steel part can require as much as fractions of millions.

However, welding aluminium tended to reduce its strength, which would have to be counterbalanced by thickening the material. And there were more downsides: (a) welding would only hold the parts together at the seam; (b) as welding changed the properties of the material there was also the concern that corrosion might occur here; and (c) heat-induced distortions could occur. The team did a lot of investigating and much research took place into possible solutions. In the end, to avoid an increase in material, and inspired by the use of glue in the aircraft industry, Richard decided to explore bonding. He found a partner in crime in Peter Bullivant-Clark at Hydro

Aluminium Automotive Tønder, Denmark, who had been involved in Hydro's previous explorations of the use of aluminium extrusions for vehicle spaceframes. He spent two years with the Lotus engineers encouraging them to 'think extrusion' and 'think bonding'.

Hydro had used chemicals for bonding aluminium before but there were no industry standards, which meant that there would be no ready-made solutions. Several companies were visited and interviewed before they signed up Ciba, based near Cambridge, UK, to help address the problem. Bonding had several advantages: rather than just holding different parts together at the seam it would bind

> The material used for the bonding does not cure entirely until the chassis has been into an oven for 4–5 hours. This means that parts could be adjusted and even dissembled during experimentation stage.

them together through a patch. Bonding would also not be given to distortion. However, a downside was that once a bonded joint started to peel it would have the tendency to separate suddenly – and the idea of the

Lotus Elise disintegrating suddenly in the case of an accident was not particularly appealing. In order to overcome the problem special aluminium screws were used right at the edge of the joints. In fact, the screws, which were made of soft aluminium, when driven into the parts were actually slightly melting, so they acted more like rivets and were hence called 'screw rivets'. These screw rivets did not have to be very strong as their main function was to prevent the onset of peeling. Testing took place to ensure that corrosion would not be likely to happen.

But not only was the chassis made of aluminium. Richard recalls, "Once I got hooked I started looking at every part thinking, could this be an extrusion? For example, I looked at the ugly Metro pedal box we had initially intended to use. Next to it I had sketched an idea pedal – and suddenly thought 'extrusion'! The resulting pedal did not only look elegant, simple and functional but also turned out to cost a fraction of their steel equivalents." Other parts that were made of extruded aluminium included the door hinges, suspension uprights and the steering column mounting bracket.

The Elise derived part of its structural stability from two high-sided members on either side of the car, which were connected in front and rear by torsion boxes. Attached to the chassis were front and rear clamshell body sections made from lightweight composite materials.

> The pedals and brake discs are aluminium, the aerodynamic body is made from lightweight composite material and the oil dips are made of plastic. And, because of its weight, the car does not need power brakes or power assisted steering.

The body panels were made of very light composite materials. Lotus had been involved in fibre glass reinforced composites since the 1950s. About 20 different types of matting were used in the production of the panels. There are two different ways of producing panels. One was to use a closed mould, the other to use a number of moulds

> The switch-over point where the high investment in machinery for steel panels becomes preferential to the high labour cost for glass fibre panels is around 20k–30k units per year.

that are joined together. The latter required layering of the glass fibre by hand which was time consuming but had the advantage that several sections could be joined together and would come out as one piece. For example, for the front panel eight sections are joined together, 11 for the back. Matting was laid up in a mould that had been prepared with a gel that formed a smooth, paintable surface. Sufficient curing times for the panels were important, the panels had to remain in the oven for 5–6 hours at 60°C, then stand for 24 hours before being put into the oven for another hour at 80°C. If cured too fast the panels would develop a tendency to buckle and distort.

Once the body parts had cured they were prepared for painting. The first step was cleaning up and smoothing the edges, which was done with a water jet cutter. Next the panels received two coats of primer, after which imperfections were sanded off and another coat of primer applied. After that panels were checked once more for flaws before a colour and clear coat were applied. That done the panels were placed into an oven to dry for 80 minutes at 80°C. Another quality check was made before panels were moved on for assembly. In total there were 16 build stages for the Lotus Elise, each lasting between 7 and 36 minutes.

Another type of composite material was used for the brakes, aluminium and silicon. It was much lighter than the conventionally used cast iron, and, given that it conducts rather than absorbs heat, it had the additional benefit that such brakes would not overheat.

> The brakes were produced by Lanxide. When the company went under in mid-1998 Lotus quickly changed to race car specification cast iron discs.

Getting approval

Getting approval for a new model can be a lengthy and frustrating process. There were about 25 major tests a car had to pass to obtain European type approval. More often than not a new type would fail in several of them, which would mean that the programme could be put back by as much as six months. The Elise team had worked hard and systematically to anticipate and avoid any major reasons for a reject. They tested everything they possibly could under a range of circumstances and conditions. The testing facilities at Hethel, such as the track and rigs, were used extensively to ensure any problems would be detected before the car went for approval. One example was noise emission. Instead of measuring noise emission on the finished product, a silencer was incorporated right from the outset, meaning that it was an integral part of the product as well as the production process – rather than having to be put in as an afterthought.

Several internal measures supported quality control efforts. People from engineering and process control met at the end of every day to discuss any issues that had come up during the day. Everyone could find out performance criteria such as production cost, delivery against targets, materials issue and so on from noticeboards that had been distributed around the shop floor. To ensure everyone could see how their work fitted into the whole an instruction booklet was available, providing information on the parts used, sequence of assembly, move-up times, duration of each build stage and so on.

Some of the initiatives had been prompted by the preparations for QS 9000 certification which Lotus obtained in 1997. QS 9000, the car industry's equivalent of ISO 9000, had been a requirement from some of their major clients such as Ford and General Motors.

The team decided to go for approval in the Netherlands – not that the tests there were much different from those in the UK but the team there had been particularly cooperative and helpful. There was only one aspect that had to be redressed for the Elise, the angle of the front windscreen which was considered to be too shallow. This had escaped the attention of the team as it became only obvious in the prototype – today, where everything would have been done on CAD, it could have been identified earlier.

But even that did not prevent the Elise from becoming the first car in the world to obtain the full European vehicle type approval the first time around.

> Lotus has copyright, design registration, trademark and patents for the Elise, and several items on the car are subjects of new patents.

The market and results

Strong design requires strong leadership.

Richard Rackham

When the car was first shown at the international motor show in Frankfurt in 1995 it caused a bit of a stir. Not only because of its exciting design but also because of the extensive use of aluminium in a way thought impossible before. Richard recalls standing next to the car and being approached by someone who turned out to be the project

> 1997: *Car* magazine named the **Lotus Elise** as the 'Most Innovative New Car In Production' in its 2nd Annual Design and Technology Awards. The chassis and brakes on the Elise also picked up the 'Best Innovation in Production' award.

manager for the Renault Spider. The French project manager was completely taken aback by the fact that Lotus had managed to come up with a bonded aluminium chassis – just as he had aimed to do, but he had been told by his engineers that it was entirely impossible. Upon which Richard commented, "The car would probably not have been as daring both in terms of its design and components had decisions been made by consensus."

While it had originally been planned to produce around 700 cars per year, since the start of production in August 1996 it had become obvious that demand would by far exceed this mark. In May 1997, with a daily production of eight cars expected to go up to 12 by the end of that year, Lotus had an order book of 2000, which translated into a waiting list of 18 months. In handling that kind of demand Lotus's dedicated, well trained dealership was seen to be essential. Increased demand also meant that Lotus had to invest significantly in increasing production capacity but even in January 2002 they had waiting times of approximately three months. And all that despite, as Tipler writes, "While other cars seem to have a clearer customer profile, it is not quite clear what attracts someone to Elise ownership." But Lotus were not too worried about customer profiles at that point in time, to quote Julian, "We don't want to get overly involved in marketing, market research and clinics, that sort of stuff; that's a lot of hassle. But I think what is important is how you pitch our car in terms of its image, how you separate it, how you use a brand. The luxury for us is that we don't have to find hundreds of thousands of customers, we only need to find a few thousand. And the product we do can be even stronger for those people. That's what we've done with the Elise: we've found a product that isn't for everyone but definitely is for some people. And those people would never be seen dead in an average sports car. That's our luxury. We've got a fantastic name. We've only got to find a maximum of 5000 customers a year, and we know there are nuts who'll put up with all sorts of things. And we can build our brand and make it stronger. We can do a total enthusiasts' car, we don't need to do electric windows or NHV, or worry about a walnut facia. We can get away with blue murder compared with the others, and we can make a fantastic car that enthusiasts are going to love."

The future

In *Autocar* magazine of 12 February 1997 Proton, the company's Malaysian owner, outlined the following agenda for the company:

- Treble Elise production at Hethel.
- Establish Elise assembly in Malaysia.
- Launch third model, possibly slightly larger Elise-based V6 coupe, by 2000.
- Replace Esprit with V8 supercar by 2000.
- Establish post-graduate college for automotive engineers at Hethel by autumn 1997.
- Consider Lotus re-entry to F1 for Malaysian GP of 1999.
- Double earnings from engineering.

Questions

1. What can be learned from the use of prototypes at Lotus?
2. Discuss the role of collaboration with external companies.
3. Given the demand for the new product, what steps should the company consider?

12 The role of prototypes

On a list of, say, five things would-be-innovators should do, working at creating a full-blown culture of rapid prototyping surely merits inclusion.

Tom Peters (in Machlis, 1996)

During the development of the Lotus Elise the team made extensive use of different types of prototypes, from very simple ones made of cardboard, to highly sophisticated computer-generated ones. Extensive experimentation and the use of prototypes are firmly at the heart of innovative organisations, and it is not only restricted to tangible products. While it can be a bit more difficult to apply the concepts of experimentation and prototypes to processes and services, once understood and internalised they can prove invaluable in keeping an organisation agile.

In this chapter we investigate what makes experimentation and prototypes so invaluable to innovation, provide a brief overview of different categories of prototypes, and conclude with Michael Schrage's (2000) insight that innovative teams do not create innovative prototypes but in fact, innovative prototypes create innovative teams.

WHY USE PROTOTYPES?

By now prototypes in their various forms and guises are acknowledged to be one of the key tools for successful innovation. And Michael Schrage (1993), research associate at the MIT Media Lab and a Merrill Lynch Forum Innovation Fellow, declares, "Companies that want to build better products must learn how to build better prototypes." Companies renowned for their innovativeness, such as IDEO (www.ideo.com), Hewlett Packard (www.hp.com) and Sony (www.sony.com) to name but a few, are firm subscribers.

> Almost immediately after thinking of a promising concept, a development team at a place like IDEO or Design Continuum builds a prototype, shows it to users, tests it, and improves it. The team then repeats the sequence over and over.
>
> Hargadon & Sutton (2000)

So what are reasons that more and more companies subscribe to prototyping, particularly innovative ones? In the following we will look at each of the arguments listed below in turn:

- It helps to bridge language barriers between departments and create a shared vision.
- It provides focus.

- It facilitates involvement and creates buy-in.
- It allows failure at the early stages.
- It contributes to the learning process.
- It saves time.
- It helps to communicate the unknown.
- It works for services too.

It helps to bridge language barriers between departments and create a shared vision

Leonard Barton (1991) likens today's development teams to the seven blind men of the fable describing their encounter with an elephant. As each of them has touched the animal they all believe to have shared a common experience and to talk about the same thing. However, as they have each touched a different part of the elephant – having had a different starting point – each has come to a different conclusion as to what the object in question is. The one who has touched the trunk thinks he felt a snake, the one who has touched its flank asserts he has touched a wall and the one who has touched a leg believes to have encountered a tree trunk.

The diverse people involved in new product development today are like a group of blind men touching an elephant, each assuming they are discussing the same thing while each perceives a different aspect of the whole (you may want to refer back to Figure 3.2). Working with prototypes makes sure that all members of a project team share the

> Language barriers between disciplines can inhibit a team's productivity in the early stages of a development process, when that productivity is important.
> Sisodia (1992)

same vision for the outcome when discussing and developing a new product. This can be particularly important in the early stages, when there is a need to develop an understanding of what the project is all about and what its aims are.

Prototyping specialists IDEO go a step further. Whereas most organisations would start with a specification as the foundation for product development, founder Kelley comments (in Perry, 1995), "We believe in a prototype-driven culture, not a specification-driven culture." This means that they 'get physical' as early as possible, putting together rough mock-ups of initial ideas rather than waiting for the concept to be developed through discussions first.

It provides focus

But beyond establishing a shared vision there is another benefit to using prototypes as early as possible. Sisodia (1992) points out, "In addition, the involvement of engineering and production people in the team at early stages can lead to emphasis on product capability instead of usability and can build unnecessary manufacturing costs into the final version of the product. Some of these difficulties can be mitigated by using early-stage models and prototypes (getting physical fast) as a way of spanning language barriers and increasing the likelihood of developing consensus among team members." Prototypes are tangible and easy to understand, which means that they are also useful for resolving crucial questions quickly and unambiguously.

It facilitates involvement and creates buy-in

But it is not only within the development team that prototypes prove useful, they also help communicate with other constituencies within and outside the organisation. Many people have difficulties visualising what is described to them and, as the saying goes, a picture says more than a thousand words. True, but if you can offer something three-dimensional, even better. How many times has someone described something to you and in the end said, let me draw it for you. And if you can touch the object, it becomes even more convincing and real. So being able to show a prototype can help in the explanation and selling process, and to get buy-in.

For example, BMW was initially not too keen on the idea of developing estates. It felt that it was not quite consistent with the car's brand image. To convince senior management a small group of staff welded together an estate car made up of a BMW front and the back of a competitor's existing estate car. Creating a 'reality' which proved to be more convincing than any other argument could have been. Needless to say that the model has gone on to be a great success and opened up new market space.

Prototypes also allow a constituency larger than the project team to contribute to the development, Leonard and Rayport (1997) comment that prototypes "enable the team to place its concept in front of other individuals who work in functions not formally represented on the team". This means that prototypes make it easy for 'outsiders' to contribute and provide feedback to a project under development. Of course this applies not only to 'outsiders' within the organisation but also those outside, that is potential customers.

It allows failure at the early stages

The possibility of getting early feedback from a wide range of audiences (internal and external) has a further benefit, it allows mistakes to be weeded out early. Mistakes or even failure as a result of feedback in the early stages can play an important role in putting the team on the right track. Steve Deak of Hasbro says (in Perry, 1995), "[By using prototypes] we do design iterations a heck of a lot quicker. We can weed out wrong ideas much earlier. Once you get a prototype, a lot of things become obvious, because you can hold it and feel it."

Avoiding 'barking up the wrong tree' and early elimination of mistakes are quite important, as about 80% of manufacturing costs are decided during the early design stages of a product (e.g. Sisodia, 1992).

It contributes to the learning process

Insights into mistakes and wrong approaches early on also feed into an organisation's learning process. However, this requires that the process is carefully recorded with iterations and reasons for rejection or improvement being noted and stored in a form that is easily accessible to later project teams. This is also pointed out by Barkan and Iansiti (1993) who say, "When effectively exploited, prototypes are an essential part of the learning process – providing benefits in speed, quality, and productivity."

It saves time

Being able to put product ideas to internal and external audiences early also means that time can be saved. According to Perry (1995) organisations that used rapid prototyping – generating prototypes directly from 3-D CAD data – cut between 10 and 15% off development time. A great benefit in many industries where time to market is a significant contributor to the successful introduction of new products.

It helps to communicate the unknown

What I find particularly important in the context of innovation is that it helps to sell the unknown. Let me tell you
a story to illustrate what I mean. Imagine you, a person of
the 21st century, are meeting a person of the middle ages,
and have to explain to them the benefits of products such

> "What use could the company make of an electric toy?" Western Union upon turning down rights to the telephone in 1878

as a car or a microwave. You may want to role play this and experience first hand how difficult this can be! This is how people with an innovative idea feel, like someone from the future trying to sell people the benefits of a product they just cannot imagine or understand. Personal computers, telephones and small photocopiers are famous examples where people just could not see the value – and hence the potential the product had. So the more radical an innovation, the harder it is to understand, the more important and valuable are prototypes.

It works for services too

And though it might seem strange, prototypes do not only work for tangible products, they can be a great help for intangible products too.[1] Rettig (1994) for example suggests the use of paper-based prototypes for the development of software and websites. Pointing out that the development of 'real', that is computer-based versions is expensive and time consuming, he suggests the use of paper-based versions which allow potential users to play with possible elements (see Box 12.1).

Box 12.1   Problems with hi-fi prototyping in software development

- Take too long to build and change
- Reviewers and testers tend to comment on 'fit and finish' issues (wrong focus, they should focus on usability etc.)
- Developers resist change – once they got so far they are probably not willing to change anymore
- A prototype in software can set expectations that are hard to change
- A single bug in the hi-fi can bring a test to a complete halt

Source: Based on Rettig, M. (1994). Prototyping for tiny fingers. *Communications of the ACM,* **37**, 21–7

Hargadon and Sutton (2000) illustrate the benefits of using prototyping for website development through the following story. Inspired by Dell Computers Bill Gross of Idealab! thought of selling cars online, using the internet

---

[1] More insights on insights specific to innovation in the service industry can be found in Chapter 24.

not only to send customers to a dealer but also selling cars directly. While other companies often spend as much as $10,000 to $250,000 on temporary websites to find out how many people might be attracted to the website and its offerings, Gross quickly assembled a group to try out the idea. Rather than building a complex website that would be able to link dealers or handle large numbers of visitors, the team built something simple just to test the idea. Gross hired a CEO for three months and explained that his only job was to sell one car. The idea was that in the case of an order Idealab! would buy the required car from a dealer and resell it to the customer, accepting that this might incur a loss of about $5000. To his surprise Gross found that over 1000 people visited the website on its first day, resulting in the sales of four cars.[2] So there are different ways of using prototypes in the service environment.

PROBLEMS WITH PROTOTYPES

However, as ever it is not all roses – or rather, no roses without thorns. Two problems associated with the use of prototypes are (a) the need to manage expectations and (b) the need to manage intellectual property rights.

If you are showing a prototype to external audiences – external to the project team – you have to manage expectations quite carefully. Think about the prototype of the Lotus Elise exhibited at the motor show. Many people would probably think that having a working prototype means that the car will go into production shortly. Far from it. It took another 12–18 months before the first customer received the finished product. The same is true for the use of prototypes internally, if a company is not familiar with the use of prototypes, and the different types of prototypes. In the Black & Decker case study it was mentioned that sales assumed the product was ready to go into the shops whereas it was only a working prototype, which meant that all tooling, resourcing and manufacturing had still to happen. So in showing a prototype it needs to be made quite clear what the purpose and scope of it is. Another consequence of a mismanagement of expectations is that people might comment on functionality – 'But this button does not work . . . ' – where the prototype is about form and usability, or vice versa.

Machlis (1996) on introducing rapid prototyping:

Benefits:

- weeding out wrong ideas much earlier
- being able to see, touch, feel helps evaluate concepts better and with more confidence

How to implement rapid prototyping:

- move to 3-D CAD
- determine if you are interested in concept models, functional prototypes and/or a process for speedy toolmaking
- test various processes by prototyping at one or more service bureaus
- don't underestimate the resources needed to run an in-house RP system, including infrastructure and technicians

---

[2] The experiment led to the founding of CarsDirect.com.

How to begin using solid modelling:

- investigate benchmarks and ease-of-use claims made by software vendors
- invite vendors to demonstrate their software's ability to solve one of your common design problems
- analyse packages for ease of model creation, editing, assembly modelling, and available complementary software packages

---

The second issue is around the protection of intellectual property. In his article 'Is your prototype yours?' Berner (1997) points out potential problems that can arise when a prototype is shown at trade shows before all important patents are registered. There is not much then that prevents competitors from picking up unique aspects and using them in their products. The timing of patent application and registration generally stirs some debate, and will be explored in more detail in Chapter 19.

WHAT PROTOTYPE?

Prototypes can be anything from crude gadgets to elaborate mock-ups.

Hargadon and Sutton (2000)

From the previous section it has already become clear that there are many different kinds of prototypes, and which one is most appropriate will depend on the aim and the stage of the project's development process at which it is to be used. In the development of the Lotus Elise a number of different kinds of prototypes were used, for the development of the body shell as well as the development of the chassis. Box 12.2 lists the different kinds of prototypes used during the development of the body shell.

Box 12.2   Prototypes used during the Lotus body shell development

- The team started with mood boards to capture the essence of what the new car was to be about

- This was translated into a 'cardboard buck' which gave a first impression of the overall lines of the car

- Once this was refined a 1:3 scale clay model was built – but for presentation purposes a plaster case was made which in turn was used to build a fibreglass model which would be much more realistic than the duffer clay model.

- There were several iterations of the 1:3 model, which was also used for testing in the wind tunnel

- The development of a full-size clay model using digital technology (the model is cut directly from the digitised drawings), which was then refined by hand

---

Today computers and computer-driven machinery tend to play a important role in facilitating fast and cost-effective prototyping. Machlis (1996) comments that "A decade ago 'rapid prototyping' was little more than a laboratory curiosity."[3] Today leading companies make extensive use of the possibilities opened up by computer-aided prototyping. For example, IDEO has computerised milling machines that allow rough sketches as well as detailed drawings to be turned into either rough first concept models, or sophisticated and refined prototypes. They are also known to have built a full-size foam model of an Amtrak train to play with seating arrangements, layout and signage.

In her 1991 article 'Inanimate integrators: a block of wood speaks' Leonard-Barton lists the basic categories of prototypes, suggesting that the further down the list the more senses are addressed. Table 12.1 summarises the different categories, their manifestations and what their main purpose is.

It has already been emphasised that the use of prototypes can be particularly useful at the outset of a product's development process. An approach which I find particularly powerful is 'totem building', a process developed by Angela Dumas that combines words and visual images to create a 'totem' that summarises and illustrates the vision for a product, product group, service, building – or any kind of project for that matter. Dumas described totems as "Object-based metaphors for product development, using words and pictures; helping to build up a vocabulary which strengthens the sense of belonging to the family to which the product belongs." Box 12.3 summarises the totem-building process as described in her 1994 article 'Building totems: metaphor-making in product development'.[4]

Box 12.3 Angela Dumas' totem-building process

The situation: A shoe maker who wants to be innovative/fashionable but despite trying seems to come up with the same kind of shoe again and again

Phase 1

Step 1: Building the context:

Company teams were teamed up with fashion design students to go around a circuit of selected shoe shops whereby students were asked to talk about their likes and dislikes, resulting in the purchase of the pair of shoes the student liked most (regardless of price). To enable the company people to get to know the students a little bit better, this was followed by lunch.

The idea was not to copy the desirable shoes but to understand what made them attractive, and translate that into a shoe that would fit into the same product category; the results would be appraised by the fashion students.

Step 2: Defining the context

Each company team discussed the shoes chosen by the students, agreeing on subset and 10 words associated with the shoes; each person then drew the shoes and put underneath his or

---

[3] 'Rapid prototyping' generally refers to prototypes generated straight from digitised drawings whereby the model is cut out of blocks of foam or other material that is cut by laser or shaving drill, eliminating the need for hand-crafted mock-ups or expensive tooling.
[4] For a reprint of her article please contact the Design Management Institute (www.dmi.org) in Boston.

her own selection of associated words; the drawings reflected the personal preferences, e.g. some drew the entire shoe, others just a detail – a balance between individual and team work is seen to be critical.

Step 3: Building a vocabulary

Each team receives five sets of slides each with different objects (furniture, interiors, textiles, consumer products, and industrial products) with the task to select one slide from each set that matches the set of 10 words established in Step 2.

Once the slides are chosen each team member drew separate pictures to represent the objects shown on the slides, again each individual choose a selection of words from the original 10 to apply to each picture.

Participants then drew a picture of what a shoe would look like if the object on the slide became a shoe.

Again the balance between team and individual input is important: the choice of slide was a team decision, the drawing of the shoe based on the slides and the selection of words is an individual act.

Step 4: Refining perceptions

Each team reviewed the 10 words originally agreed upon; any words added by individuals were also discussed until a revised list of 6–8 words was agreed.

This is followed by a discussion on the physical qualities of the slides to establish which qualities are shared by five slides; this leads to a description of the 'family' to which the object (shoe) belongs.

Step 5: Distilling the totem

Each team reviews caricatures drawn in step 3 (what if this object became a shoe) comparing them to the five slides to decide which 5–6 caricatures best fit into the 'family'.

Finally, slides, words and caricatures are reviewed and those items that are least relevant, powerful or helpful are taken out; the remaining words, slides, caricatures and shoes become the totem.

Phase II

Design and prototyping of new products developed from the totem.

The Results: A range of new shoes very different from the company's traditional range eliciting a very positive (surprised) response from fashion design students.

Table 12.1 Categorisation of prototypes

2-D (flat) models	Non-functional 3-D models	Functional prototypes	User test models	Organisation/System models
• Concept sketches	• Simulations	• Engineering prototypes	• Working prototypes	• First production units
• Drawings	• CAD models	• Feasibility models		• Pilots
• Blueprints	• Finite element analysis – graphical representation	• Simulations		• Production models
• Specifications • Engineering layout	• Site models • 'Soft' models	• CAD models • Finite element analysis – graphical representations		• 'First article' • 'First article'
Generally require some understanding of 'expert speak'	Emphasis on form and aesthetics, how it feels and looks	Emphasis on functionality/how it operates	Combining form and function; foretelling interaction between user and product	Primarily focusing on the interaction between product and company (e.g. manufacturing)

● ——— Address an increasing number of senses ———→

Source: Leonard-Barton, D. (1991). Inanimate integrators: a block of wood speaks. *Design Management Journal*, 61–7. Reproduced by permission of *Design Management Journal*.

It was mentioned earlier that the kind of prototype will vary from stage to stage, and audience to audience. In a way Michael Schrage (1993) turns the process on its head when he suggests that by looking at a company's use of prototypes one can tell much about the company's culture, and whether or not it is innovative. The questions he asks are, how and where are prototypes used: internally or externally, to identify opportunities or manage risk, and are they formal or informal? In his experience, "Within some innovation cultures, prototypes effectively become the *media franca* of the organisation – *the* essential medium for information, interaction, integration, and collaboration. In other cultural contexts, prototypes are little more than sales tools and technical stalking horses for the politically adept." For understanding prototypes he looks at three different axes:

- Formal versus informal – refers to the degree to which the prototype is polished and comprehensive, in the case of the Lotus Elise it would be the cardboard buck versus a clay version.

- Risk management versus opportunity – do we use the prototype to explore and understand potential risks and problems or to identify opportunities?

- External versus internal – is it to be used within the company or shown to the outside world?

His framework, shown in Figure 12.1, illustrates this.

In his book Schrage (2000) goes even further, commenting that "Several companies discovered that, instead of innovative teams creating innovative prototypes, innovative prototypes create innovative teams." This implies that appropriate and extensive use of prototypes can help an organisation to improve its innovativeness. Schrage continues, "It means that innovation requires improvisation. It means innovation is not about rigorous following 'the rules of the game', but about rigorously challenging and

> "Prototypes are a way of life."
>
> IDEO founder David Kelley in Schrage (1993)

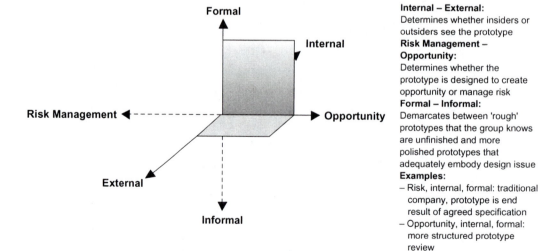

Figure 12.1 A framework for understanding prototypes.
Source: Schrage, M. (1993). The culture(s) of prototyping. *Design Management Journal*, 55–65. Reproduced by permission of *Design Management Journal*.

revising them. It means innovation is less the product of how innovators think than a by-product of how they behave." He concludes that the value of prototypes lies not so much in the models themselves as in the interactions they encourage and provoke. So perhaps the choice of prototype should be influenced by the kind of interaction and collaboration that it should facilitate.

And on the comment on collaboration, this is another differentiating factor for innovative organisations: they engage extensively in collaboration, internally as well as externally, which we will explore in more detail in the following chapter.

READING SUGGESTIONS

Kelley, T. (2001). *The Art of Innovation*. HarperCollins Business.

Comment: Also listed under the reading suggestions of the Market Research Section, this book is helpful when wanting to find out more about how an innovative organisation uses prototypes.

Schrage, M. (2000). *Serious Play – How the World's Best Companies Simulate to Innovate*. Boston, MA: Harvard Business School Press.

Comment: The entire book is dedicated to the promotion and explanation of the value of prototypes, and their role in the innovation process.

SOME USEFUL WEBSITES

http://www.radical-departures.net/2001/serious_play_full.asp

Comment: Here you can find a good summary of Schrage's book *Serious Play*.

http://home.utah.edu/~ asn8200/rapid.html~ ACA
http://www.paperprototyping.com

Comment: Under these links you find some information about rapid prototyping, and paper prototyping respectively

13 Collaborating for innovation

$$1 + 1 + 1 = 5$$

This is how a company participating in the 2001 survey of the Confederation of British Industry (CBI) summed up the benefits of collaboration.

One aspect that made the development of the Lotus Elise such an innovation success was the company's willingness to collaborate, internally as well as externally. Collaboration is yet another arrow in the quiver of innovation. When considering that innovation happens through the connection of previously unconnected bodies of knowledge, and when assumptions are challenged, it is easy to understand why innovative companies are keen collaborators. It is often the assumptions we carry about what we can and cannot do that prevent us from innovation – and if someone comes along and just questions as to why we do things the way we do, it can help us to realise the mental models we have, and hence enable us to change them.

This chapter will shed some light on issues around collaboration, looking at reasons as to why companies collaborate, what benefits they gain, what can be in the way of collaboration, how collaboration can be encouraged, and what different forms of collaboration there are. This edition also has an additional section that looks at particular forms of collaboration in the context of innovation: user-led innovation and open innovation.

> "The best innovators aren't lone geniuses. They are people who can take an idea that's obvious in one context and apply it in not-so-obvious ways to a different context. The best companies have learned to systematize that process."
>
> Hargadon & Sutton (2000)

SOME BACKGROUND

For decades companies used to pursue development activities – be they a new product or a new strategic direction – within their own boundaries. Collaboration seemed too risky, and if a company decided to collaborate, this would generally be manifested in the form of mergers or acquisitions, on a permanent basis – though the reason underlying most of the M&A activities was the desire to grow rather than collaborate. In the more recent past collaboration has gained increasing attention in the management literature and 'open innovation' has become one of the latest management buzz words. Managers have come to realise the benefits of teaming up with other companies for selected projects or developments rather than 'for life'.

One of the reasons that collaboration has become so much more popular is that many organisations feel that they have come to the end of the path of growth through mergers and acquisitions, and that future growth will have to come from new avenues, including innovation and collaboration. France *et al.* (2001) quote a Booz Allen Hamilton survey that reports that four out of five executives said they saw alliances as one important strategy for future growth and refer to another study that states that by 2002 participating companies expected 35% of their revenues to stem from alliances.

M&A – do they create or destroy value?

Mega mergers destroy value. A survey by the Boston Consulting Group found that deals above $1bn destroy twice as much value than deals below that value – there were 450 such deals in 2006. It seems that for 58% of acquiring companies their M&A activity results in a loss.

Source: Financial Times Deutschland, 16 August 2007; see also www.ftd.de/fusionen

---

That collaboration is not only a plan for the future, but is actually happening is shown by the figures of the 2001 annual survey of the Confederation of British Industry, which found that about 75% of companies surveyed had been involved in external cooperation, with 44% describing themselves as regular collaborators (five or more collaborative ventures per year). Most collaborations lasted between 2 and 5 years, whereby larger organisations tended to have longer cooperation periods than small organisations. Most likely collaboration partners were other companies (see Box 13.1) though I thought it quite interesting that while partnerships with consultants were almost always described as problematic, the least problems were reported in business–academia relationships – despite the commonly held view that academia may be too slow and not to reliable in meeting deadlines.

Box 13.1   Collaboration partners

Who to collaborate with?

Other companies	73%
Academia	48%
Consultants	35%
Government or private research institutes	25%

CBI survey (2001)

An interesting trend is that towards collaboration with competitors, as a survey undertaken by the Innovation Exchange in spring 2002 found out (von Stamm, 2002). Thirty-seven percent of firms indicated that they were currently collaborating on a small percentage of their projects with direct competitors, and in future as much as 49% envisage this form of collaboration (see Box 13.2).[1]

---

[1] However, there were also 4% of firms which had undertaken a small percentage of their development work with direct competitors in the past but indicated that they would not do so in the future.

Box 13.2   Collaboration today and in future

Within the supply chain		With the competition	
• With distributors & retailers:	Past→Future	• Non-direct:	Past→Future
– A small percentage	53%→60%	– A small percentage	47%→53%
– Majority	11%→18%	– Majority	4%→9%
– Not at all	31%→20%	– Not at all	49%→36%
• With suppliers:	Past→Future	• Direct:	Past→Future
– A small percentage	64%→60%	– A small percentage	38%→49%
– Majority	11%→22%	– Majority	9%→9%
– Not at all	18%→13%	– Not at all	56%→42%
With customers		**Other**	
• Lead Users:	Past→Future	• Universities:	Past→Future
– A small percentage	44%→33%	– A small percentage	51%→53%
– Majority	23%→47%	– Majority	7%→11%
– Not at all	24%→13%	– Not at all	42%→29%
• Customers generally:	Past→Future	• Consultancies:	Past→Future
– A small percentage	51%→33%	– A small percentage	58%→62%
– Majority	33%→44%	– Majority	16%→20%
– Not at all	13%→13%	– Not at all	22%→13%

Source: von Stamm, B. (2002). *Innovation in Turbulent Times*. London: Innovation Exchange, London Business School

But of course, for innovation not only external innovation is important, at least if not more critical is internal collaboration. The use of cross-functional teams has long been heralded as a cure for many ailments of new product development, and the issue of teams and their role in innovation has been discussed in Chapter 10. While most of this chapter focuses on issues relevant to external

> Realising the potential of collaboration between different business units, particularly in the context of innovation, BASF has someone who is dedicated to spotting and facilitating projects that span business unit boundaries.

collaboration, the discussions of obstacles to collaboration and some of the insights on how to make collaboration work are as relevant for internal collaboration as they are for external collaboration. In the case of large companies the question of 'internal or external' can be a little blurred: does 'internal' mean within one business unit or within the overall business? Collaboration across different business units is often as difficult and rare as collaboration with external partners. However, it is here that the most impactful and exciting innovations happen, and it is through collaboration across industries that entirely new markets are created (rather than existing ones being extended). Think about the collaboration between Swatch and Mercedes, creating the SMART which opened up an entirely new market for micro cars.

The value of innovating across industry boundaries has been realised by some leading organisations who have set up an initiative called the 'Emerging Leaders for Innovation across Sectors' (www.elias-global.com). As it says on their website, "Co-founded by BASF, BP, Oxfam, Nissan, the Society for Organisational Learning (SoL), Unilever, the UN Global Compact, UNICEF, the World Bank Institute, and the World Wildlife Fund (WWF), the ELIAS project was launched at MIT in March 2006. ELIAS is a network and prototyping platform that links twenty leading global institutions across the three sectors of business, government, and civil society in order to co-create and test profound system innovations for a more sustainable world."

REASONS FOR AND BENEFITS OF COLLABORATION

There are many reasons why companies collaborate externally, and the following will be discussed below:

- To share risk and cost.
- To access and create new or different markets.
- To obtain additional resources.
- To gain access to knowledge and expertise.
- To reduce development time.

The desire to share risk and cost

When asked, 'what motivates companies to collaborate', the most frequent answer is that it allows the sharing of costs and risks involved in new ventures – and more often than not risk and cost are invariably linked. It seems the higher the risk, the greater the openness towards collaboration. This is supported by recent research findings which indicate that those companies that engage in R&D activities that aim to introduce new to the market (rather than new to the firm) innovations are more likely to engage in cooperative arrangements for innovation than those that engage in more incremental innovation (Tether, 2002). But costs can also be an important factor, particularly in industries such as pharmaceuticals where development costs are prohibitively high.

There is always a brand risk attached to collaboration. If the collaboration fails, or the results are too far removed from the image and positioning of the parent companies, it might cause some confusion among customers or even worse, damage the parent brand.

Accessing and creating new or different markets

There are also many organisations that seek collaboration to expand into new and different markets. As we have read in Chapter 4, globalisation is an issue many managers have to contend with. Not many companies have the resources available to expand into new countries at the rate they would like to. Collaboration with companies in the target market, or companies that operate in the target markets, can help to accelerate the process of expansion as well as provide valuable local insights and expertise.

But some organisations are much more ambitious in their collaborations: they collaborate to create new markets. One example is the collaboration between Consumer electronic giant Philips and sports-ware manufacturer Nike, announced in March 2002.[2] In the announcement it reads, "Royal Philips Electronics and Nike, Inc. today announced

---

[2] Press Information 25 March 2002, from Philip's website http://www.philips.com.

Table 13.1 Benefits and pitfalls of cross-industry collaboration

Possible pitfalls	Possible benefits
• Not making the right match of partners (how to find them in the first place?) • Not hitting the decision makers when seeking and promoting collaboration • Not defining clear 'success' objectives: hit & run or visionary inspiration? • Not visualising as soon as possible (to create a shared understanding and vision) • Not understanding instability of '3-some'; making such a relationship work is not easy; it generally benefits from a facilitator or arbitrator • Not recognising durability of relation: what are we interested in, a one-night stand or long-term relationship	• Corporate strategy – external partners can be a positive inspiration • Breakthrough innovations – potential for something that has not been before • Perfect partners • Energy of networking – inspiration comes through exposure to different bodies of knowledge • Future perspective – creating a new stream of business/opportunity • Brand image – positive association of innovation • Market success – across-industry products and services tend to open up new markets rather than extend existing ones

Source: Based on workshop contribution of Jens Jacobsen Marketing4U, 2005.

an alliance to merge their athletic and digital technology expertise to develop innovative technology product solutions which create a richer, more motivating environment for physical activity." The article continues, "Nike and Philips bring unique strengths to the venture. Nike has exceptional expertise in sports and material technology, marketing and innovation. The company transformed athletic footwear with the invention of air technology. Philips is a leading innovator of 'wearable electronics' technologies and has a long heritage of technology innovation, especially in the digital arena, as well as intimate knowledge of consumers. Philips originated the idea of wearable electronics in 1995 and has a reputation for introducing high quality, cutting edge electronic products." Again, it is the bringing together of disparate bodies of knowledge to create something that has not existed before.

Jens Jacobsen, a colleague of mine, has developed an approach to facilitate 'threesome' collaboration between companies from different industry sectors. If collaboration is normally quite tricky it becomes even more difficult if three partners are involved – and three egos need to be satisfied. However, as in the example of Philips and Nike above, the outcome has the potential to be truly new, and to create an entirely new market. Table 13.1 describes some of the benefits and potential pitfalls.

To obtain additional resources

Most organisations will have been through one – or even several – rounds of downsizing, generally with the preamble to have to refocus.[3] This has often led to the contracting out of activities previously undertaken in-house. Whereas there are some activities that almost any organisation would have sought collaboration anyway, such as advertising, some companies have extended this to R&D and product development activities. Even if the functions

---

[3] A consequence of downsizing with negative implications for a company's ability to innovation, the destruction of trust, is addressed in the section on what gets in the way of collaboration.

may have not been disbanded entirely, these departments have often been reduced to a size that makes effective in-house development difficult. During interviews conducted by von Stamm (2001) one participant commented on his company's staffing policy, "It seems to be a good idea to get a company 'lean and mean' but I think we might have gone too far and have become anorexic." If such organisations want to engage in the development activities, collaboration often becomes a necessity.[4]

Access to and transfer of knowledge

Closely related to the previous point is the lack of the skills or technologies necessary to execute a particular project. In the case of the Lotus Elise the company did not have the skills necessary to manufacture the aluminium frames, or to glue the aluminium parts together. Instead of trying to develop the skills in-house they looked for other companies who they could partner with.

While collaboration can be used to access additional resources – staff or expertise – it does also provide the opportunity to transfer skills between organisations. For example, new product development agencies often use collaboration on particular points to gain insights into and better understanding of aspects relevant to a particular project as the following story illustrates (Hargadon & Sutton, 2000). New product development agency Design Continuum was commissioned to improve the tools and techniques used in knee surgery. Rather than read up or being told about how it works the engineers decided that observation would provide the most relevant insights. Joining surgeons at a convention they asked doctors to simulate the surgical procedure so they could observe and ask questions during the process. Hargadon and Sutton report how one of the engineers described the scene: "We wanted to observe the procedures, so we had a cadaver lab, which was actually in a swank hotel. One room was the lecture room and the other held 12 cadavers. They had the room chilled to 50 degrees, with the cadavers in there and a guard 24 hours a day making sure nobody accidentally walked in. We just wanted to see how doctors used the tools, the little blocks and stuff they use for doing the procedures." From their observation the designers concluded that surgeons often needed a 'third arm' which inspired them to develop a new surgical tool that would function as such. So collaboration can provide some learning by doing – or, in the case above, observing.

To reduce development time

When Lotus decided to experiment with aluminium frames they had one of two choices: first, develop the necessary skills in-house – after all, they were also a manufacturing company. Second, they could seek out a company that had an expertise in this area and engage in collaboration. Following the first route Lotus would have had to spend significant resources, time and money, to develop the skill to a standard necessary to apply it to their new car. By taking the latter approach Lotus avoided wasting valuable time and energy on the development of a skill that, while useful, would not be core to their activities. So collaboration is a quick way of gaining access to skills that would take a long time – or at least too long a time – to develop in-house.

---

[4]Much of the discussion on the collaboration with external designers in Chapter 28 is relevant to collaboration with external partners more generally.

And finally, an interesting reason to increase collaboration internally was brought forward in an Innovation Exchange interview (von Stamm, 2001), "The company is split into separate business units and the (cultural) glue is beginning to unravel. To prevent this from happening we are trying to become more interactive and collaborative." So internal collaboration can help create shared culture and help bind different parts of the organisation together.

If you would like to find out how supportive your organisation is towards collaboration you may want to take a look at a set of questions published in Lynne Snead and Joyce Wycoff's book *To Do, Doing, Done!* (1996) (see Box 13.3).

Box 13.3   What's your organisation's collaborative quotient?

The following evaluation will help you determine how well your organisation supports collaboration. Rate your organisation from 1 to 5 on the following questions:

1 = terrible/never   2 = poor/seldom   3 = average/generally   4 = good/often   5 = excellent/always

1. We stimulate communication by providing conference rooms, whiteboards, bulletin boards, open work areas.

2. We share information widely through group meetings, newsletters, e-mail, closed circuit TV, financial and performance reports.

3. We have a high level of trust and respect for each other.

4. We encourage people to collaborate on projects and allow them to identify potential projects even when it takes time away from 'normal' duties.

5. We have a compensation policy that rewards collaborative efforts as well as individual efforts.

6. Our organisation's values, vision and objectives are clearly understood by all and we encourage groups and individuals to clarify their own values and vision.

7. Rewards and risks are shared equitably by everyone in the organisation.

8. We have computer-enhanced collaboration tools and groupware in place and everyone in the organisation has access to these tools.

9. We encourage informal interaction across departments and functions and have an 'open access' policy for everyone in the organisation.

10. Most of the time, most of our people feel pride in their work and frequently talk about work being 'fun'

Total scores:

50 Congratulations! Check your perceptions with the first 5 people you meet. If they rate these questions the same way you do, call us . . . we would like to hear your story!

45–49 Yours is a rare organisation. Somehow you've managed to do what everyone else is talking about doing. Keep up the good work!

40–44 You're on the right track but you need to open your lines of communications. Ask people (all people) what would make their work life better? What tools do they need? What information do they need? Do they understand the work processes and how they fit into the whole?

39 or less Organise a collaboration group to discuss ways to stimulate collaboration . . . before it's too late.

G. Lynne Snead, vice-president with FranklinCovey can be reached at lynne.snead@franklincovey.com

Source: Snead, G.L. & Wycoff, J. (1996). To Do, Doing, Done! A Creative Approach to Managing Projects and Effectively Finishing What Matters Most. Simon & Schuster

WHAT GETS IN THE WAY OF COLLABORATION?

While there are compelling reasons to collaborate, not everyone is into collaboration, not least because there are often great obstacles to be overcome – a study conducted in 1999 by Kalmbach & Roussel, Accenture, found that about half of all alliances fail. But not only external collaboration is prone to failure, often less obvious internal collaboration has its problems too, ranging from project delays due to a lack of timely responses or lack of provision of information, to suboptimal results, to things just not happening. In the following we will look at some obstacles to collaboration:

- Lack of trust and respect.
- Restrictions to knowledge sharing.
- Non-supportive reward systems.
- One-sided benefits.

Lack of trust and respect

If there is one key ingredient for successful collaboration that cannot be overemphasised it is trust. Without trust between the collaborating parties – be they within one organisation or across company boundaries – there will be no way that the collaboration will yield the best possible results and that other benefits of collaboration can be reaped.

The CBI survey found that reasons for not collaborating were:

- Had not really thought about it (48%)
- Do not want to share ideas (36%)
- No need, have all resources in-house (32%)

In some organisations where collaboration is second nature you might find that trusting one's colleagues is second nature, and that this may even be extended to external collaboration partners. But for people in a great many organisations trust is not something that exists naturally – particularly if these organisations have gone through periods of change induced by mergers or acquisitions, or restructuring. Climate surveys undertaken after such a period of change will almost invariably show a reduction in levels of trust – trust between colleagues as well as trust between management and staff. This means that trust is something that needs to be built and nurtured carefully.

I would like to elaborate a bit more on the negative impact of downsizing – or 'rightsizing' as it was subsequently called when the inevitable redundancies had caused too negative an association with downsizing. Consider the atmosphere in a company that goes through 'a round of downsizing'. First people are insecure about their jobs, then they get upset by close colleagues leaving, in the end they are left with an increased workload because the reason for downsizing tends to be the need to cut cost, rather than underutilised resources. So what are the consequences?

⇒   the destruction of trust
⇒   the destruction of internal networks
⇒   the elimination of slack

In times where everyone fears about losing their job they are not likely to be at their most trusting. Sharing ideas and knowledge might lead a colleague to look better or more useful, so people tend to withhold their insights and ideas – not exactly conducive to good collaboration.

Losing people through downsizing is detrimental to innovation and collaboration for two reasons. First, innovation often relies on the ability to locate people with the right skills within the organisation if and when they are needed – more often than not this relies on internal and informal networks. Such networks develop over long periods of time, and when people from the network are removed, particularly if they have been key players or holders of specialist expertise, it will take a long time to close the gaps. The second reason is that those who leave are often the more experienced and knowledgeable people, either because they are close to retirement and are encouraged to take up financially incentivised offers for early retirement or are happily taking up redundancy packages because they know that they can easily find another job somewhere else. In their research Dougherty and Bowman (1995) identified the destruction of informal networks, impacting on a company's capacity to successfully develop new products, as a major negative effect of downsizing.

Finally, while it is generally argued that downsizing decreases slack and duplication more often than not the people left in the organisation will feel stretched and overburdened with work. I believe that many organisations who downsize take it too far, cutting out what I call the 'creative fat'. As a consequence people tend to be so busy that they do not have the time to contemplate, to have a chat in the corridor, to network outside their own organisation, be it to attend external events, see customers or meet up with colleagues from inside or outside the organisation. They have to 'do' all the time. Why do I think that is a problem? Because to come up with new ideas, to make new connections and to be innovative people need time to doodle and think. But not only that, under time pressure people tend to focus on the most urgent things at hand – this quarter's budget, this month's sales figures – and not things that are long term – as innovation initiatives tend to be.

The issue of respect is critical as this determines to which degree participants believe that their colleagues' actions and words are their best efforts. If I tell you that something can or cannot be done, and you do not respect my professional qualifications and capabilities, you may believe either that I am entirely unrealistic or that I am just too lazy or ignorant to carry out the task. More likely than not you will try to find a way of making it happen, finding someone else to do it, get a second opinion and so on. If, on the other hand, you trust my professional judgement, you will either trust me to get on with it, or there will be no time (and money) wasted in exploring the possibility further.[5]

---

[5] I would also like to emphasise that highly innovative teams will make possible what others have believed impossible before. Accepting and respecting someone's expert opinion should not be confused with giving up at the first hurdle.

Restrictions to knowledge sharing

If people are asked to collaborate but at the same time are told, 'but don't give away any of our company's (department's, team's) secrets' this can create problems – not least as it undermines the development of trust which, as has just been emphasised, is essential in making collaboration work. In collaboration the willingness to share and contribute – on both or all sides – is important. If one party holds back, the other(s) are likely to do the same.

Reward systems

How to incentivise and reward for collaboration is another important issue. If the contribution to a successful collaboration is not part of the assessed performance, chances are slim that people will give themselves entirely to the collaboration. In the end, people deliver and focus on what they are assessed. Reward and assessment systems have to be set up to encourage and support collaborative behaviour.

There is also an interesting discussion as to the percentage split between collaborators. Some say that it is important for someone to have a majority. Others, such as The Technology Partnership, which is our case company in Chapter 29, swear on 50/50 joint ventures. Their argument is that only equal shareholdings will result in equal interest to make the venture work. They also have the policy of joint ownership of intellectual capital – and in their extensive collaboration experience have achieved great results by following these principles.

One-sided benefits

Following on from the previous point, collaboration will not work when the benefits are one sided. The attitude 'the winner takes it all' is not one that is appropriate for collaboration. Unless both parties gain from working together, the collaboration will not be sustainable. Some companies wanting to engage more in collaboration experience that their past is coming back to haunt them. An Innovation Exchange company interviewed about their attitude towards collaboration answered: "Our cooperation with customers is limited, and with suppliers it is quite difficult as we have generally screwed them for cost in the past." Similarly difficult is the situation of another company interviewed who admitted, "Our company negotiates too hard with its suppliers which often causes problems during the contract period, sometimes even going bust. This means in the end we have to pay more than we would have had we been less aggressive in the first place" (von Stamm, 2001).

HOW TO MAKE COLLABORATION WORK

There are a number of things managers can do to help overcome the obstacles discussed in the section above. These include:

- Rationale for collaboration.
- Open and frequent communication.
- Facilitation of face-to-face meetings.
- Dedicated collaboration rooms.

Rationale for collaboration

Any collaboration should be undertaken for the right reason – just because everyone else engages in collaboration does not qualify – and the type of collaboration should be matched to the objective in mind. France *et al.* (2001) from Ernst & Young recommend asking the following questions:

- Does each of our alliances align strongly with our corporate culture and business goals?

- How well is our portfolio performing, in the aggregate? Are we leveraging our alliances to capture maximum value?

- Do we need additional alliances? Are we missing key areas of opportunity? Should some be eliminated?

- Are we reaching the best universe of prospective partners?

- Does our alliance portfolio create any new risks?

If it is an external collaboration addressing a strategic need a joint venture might be the most appropriate form. Tidd *et al.* (2001) have assembled a table that provides an overview of different types of collaboration and their advantages and disadvantages (see Table 13.2).

And as everything within an organisation that is to be taken seriously, collaboration requires if not the active involvement then at least the support of top management.

Everyone needs to be clear that the reason for engaging in collaborative efforts is its relevance and importance to the company's future – and not because it is the latest management fad that everyone else seems to be doing at the time. Objectives need to be stated clearly, and measures need to be put in place to monitor progress against

Table 13.2 Types of collaboration

Type of collaboration	Typical duration	Advantages (rationale)	Disadvantages (transaction costs)
Subcontract	Short term	Cost and risk reduction, reduced lead time	Search costs, product performance and quality
Cross-licensing	Fixed term	Technology acquisition	Contract cost and constraints
Consortia	Medium term	Expertise, standards, share funding	Knowledge leakage; subsequent differentiation
Strategic alliance	Flexible	Low commitment, market access	Potential lock-in; knowledge leakage
Joint venture	Long term	Complementary know-how Dedicated management	Strategic drift; Cultural mismatch
Network	Long term	Dynamic learning	Static inefficiencies

Source: Tidd, J., Bessant, J. & Pavitt, K. (2001). *Managing Innovation; Integrating Technological, Market and Organisational Change*. Chichester, UK: John Wiley & Sons, Ltd. Reproduced by permission of J. Tidd.

them. The reward and assessment structure should also be designed to recognise and encourage collaborative behaviours.

As important as a good and thought-through rationale for entering a collaborative agreement, it is wise to think about time frames and possible exit scenarios. Is the collaboration for the duration of a project, or for a certain period of time? What happens to equipment and machinery at the end of the collaboration? How are people integrated back into the parent organisation? There are many important questions to be considered not least to reassure the people delegated to the collaborative venture.

Open and frequent communication

Open and frequent communication between the collaborating team and the parent organisations is very important. The parent organisation needs to be assured that progress is made against set objectives, and team members need to be reassured that they are still part of the main organisation.

In order that the collaborating team is flexible and can respond quickly to changing requirements, it is beneficial to limit the number of people who have to be involved in the decision-making process.

Working in a collaborative venture also means that you bring together different cultures, which is bound to lead to some conflict. It is therefore important that structures are in place that allow for these conflicts to be resolved, this includes mechanisms for constructive feedback.

Facilitation of face-to-face meetings

Trust requires a degree of familiarity, and familiarity that cannot be built via e-mail or through video conferencing. So to build trust and allow mutual respect to grow there is only one way, facilitate face-to-face meetings so that those who are expected to work together have the chance to get to know each other.

If you cannot allocate people to the collaboration whose reputation precedes them, you might want to try to find ways that allows collaborations to respect each other's expertise. One way might be to organise exhibitions or presentations of their work, another to develop a game or simulation that allows participants to display their expertise (without 'showing-off').

You may also want to consider the use of facilitators to start the collaboration off. One Innovation Exchange member commented on their use of teams, "We have a strong commitment to teams and this year we are using extra facilitators to help our teams work together – teams don't just happen."

Space dedicated to collaboration

In addition to supporting the process of collaboration through facilitators, organisations should provide some space where collaboration partners can meet and work together. If such space cannot be allocated to the team for the entire course of the collaboration, it should at least be made available at frequent intervals. The aforementioned company IDEO places great value on its project spaces. All project teams have a space dedicated to their exclusive use. One of the benefits of dedicated space is that everything to do with the project can be left on display. IDEO finds that it helps people to start off where they have left off, and it also has the added benefit of allowing others to come in and contribute their ideas – particularly as there are always some prototypes around (see also previous chapter).

It is also important to understand that collaboration spaces are different from other office spaces such as meeting rooms or workstations. The layout of the room should facilitate and encourage collaboration, offering whiteboards, easel pads, pens and sticky notes, and a selection of tables and chairs chosen for comfort rather than adherence to office furniture norms (see Box 13.4).

Box 13.4   What collaboration rooms should convey

Beauty – Goethe recommended that every day you should read some poetry, see a beautiful picture, get into nature so that we don't lose the sense of the beautiful that's in all of us.

Fun – Play is an important part of creativity and collaboration. Fun breaks down barriers and frees us from the inhibitions that keep us 'in the box'. Bean bag chairs, toys, bright graphics, crayons and silly hats all help create an atmosphere of fun.

Abundance – of snacks and drinks as well as all kinds of stationery.

Tools – for example, internet connection, a computer with mindmapping and project management software, a printer, an overhead projector and VCR.

Source: Snead, G.L. & Wycoff, J. (1996). *To Do, Doing, Done! A Creative Approach to Managing Projects and Effectively Finishing What Matters Most.* Simon & Schuster

---

In his book *Orbiting the Giant Hairball* (1996), Hallmark's jester and 'creative paradox'[6] Gordon MacKenzie describes how he created the space of the creative design group he led. Instead of selecting from the company's office furniture catalogue he went round antique shops collecting rolltop desks, using stained glass windows and doors as space dividers and milk cans as wastebaskets – even if getting the milk cans – which were not on the list of approved furniture – past the accountants required declaring them as part of the company's art collection! The environment was not only much more imaginative than any standard office environment it also cost 20% less.

Exactly how much structure needs to provided will vary from company to company, and according to the individuals involved. Companies who are used to collaboration and people with tolerance for high levels of ambiguity will need less instructions and structure than those who do it the first time (see Box 13.5). However, too much structure and bureaucracy can prevent people from focusing on the task at hand, being too busy managing the bureaucracy and reporting requirements.

---

[6] This was a title Gordon created for his job at Hallmark's headquarters – read the book to find out what it entailed!

Box 13.5   Collaboration between TTPcom and Hitachi SIC

The set-up:

- Mutual compatibility: one had what the other needed

- Royalty based building on a common objective

- Joint intellectual ownership to ensure each party would be equally interested and protectionism in engineering teams would be dispelled

- Broad areas of responsibility (not bogged down in detailed definitions as to who does what)

Getting started:

- Teams were established with complementary as well as overlapping skill sets and direct links from engineer to engineer

- Started by bringing the two teams together for four weeks

- Six face-to-face meetings per year

- Audio and video conference calls

- Both parties being aware of other culture's specifics

- Use of simple English

- Ask face-saving questions etc.

- Working with secondment to transfer skills

OPEN INNOVATION AND USER-LED INNOVATION

Open innovation is the use of purposive inflows and outflows of knowledge to accelerate internal innovation, and expand the markets for external use of innovation, respectively. [This paradigm] assumes that firms can and should use external ideas as well as internal ideas, and internal and external paths to market, as they look to advance their technology.

Henry Chesbrough (2003)

User-led innovation is the process by which a person develops a personal or in-house innovation because existing products do not meet their needs.

Eric von Hippel (2005)

For me the notions of open innovation and user-led innovation are quite closely related. Open innovation is about an awareness that great ideas can come from anywhere, not only from top management or people inside the organisation. The lead-user approach then goes a step further arguing that there is a particular group of people out there that is particularly likely to come up with great ideas for our products or services: the so-called lead users. According to Franke and von Hippel (2003) lead users have two key characteristics that set them apart from your 'standard' user, namely:

1.   a high expected benefit from a solution to their leading edge needs which may induce them to innovate; and
2.   needs that are ahead of the marketplace demand.

The two approaches are by no means exclusive, rather they are complementary. One could almost describe the 'open innovation' approach as a primarily passive approach – where we are looking for users to come to us with suggestions – whereas the lead-user approach is more proactive – we make a conscious effort to identify those users who may have an interest in working with us.

The case of the development of the Linux software was an open innovation approach. In fact, it was very much a trigger that helped to create the awareness of the knowledge that is out there. In 1991 Linus Torvalds, at the time a student at the University of Helsinki in Finland, started to develop a computer operating system – Linux. Instead of working behind closed walls, carefully guarding his development secrets he published his code on the internet and invited others to contribute and improve his programme. He realised that he might have some good ideas – but that by exposing his ideas to others the ideas could be improved upon and the usability of the product would improve at a much faster rate than otherwise possible. It also has the advantage that any user can adopt the existing software for his or her specific needs – though part of the agreement is that the improved version is made equally open available for others to use. This kind of collaboration helps both the user and developer, and leads to fast, efficient improvements of functionality as well as quality of the software.

In a way one could say that the Linux example illustrates a case of 'passive lead user identification' whereby the users find the product they want to improve. In the case of the company Webasto, mentioned in Chapter 9, the identification of lead users was a very deliberate and conscious one.

Inspired by the Linux experience companies started to develop tools for tapping into that external knowledge, generally using the web as medium for interaction. Some examples are:

•   In June 2001 **Ely Lilly** launched the internet site **Innocentive** as a space Ely Lilly and other companies could access a large pool of scientists and invite them to work on problems/challenges posted on the website. Innocentive CEO Darrel Carroll says, "Lilly hires a large number of extremely talented scientists from around the world, but like every company in its position, it can never hire all the scientists it needs. No company can."

•   **Microsoft** makes extensive use of user communities, particularly for the development of new products, not only for support and but also for further development of existing products.

•   Lego has set up the **Lego Factory** website where visitors can build their own model online and then have the ready-to-assemble set sent out to their homes (http://factory.lego.com/). This facilitates direct communication with enthusiasts that can be difficult to identify otherwise. The benefits, Lego gets feedback from the most advanced users and lets this information influence and educate its mainstream products.

- **Procter & Gamble** has set itself the target of sourcing 50% of its innovations from outside the company as it pursues its 'Connect and develop' open innovation approach. In order to achieve that they make use of multiple websites such as http://www.homemadesimple.com (for consumer ideas) and http://pg.t2h.yet2.com/t2h/page/homepage (for technology ideas).

- This kind of approach is being explored by the **British Broadcasting Corporation (BBC)** – a major producer of broadcast media now trying to deal with the discontinuous challenges of the new digital media environment. Attempting to second guess a massively complex world 'out there' from within the confines of a small R&D group is rather difficult. One alternative is to try to engage a rich variety of players in those emerging spaces via a series of 'open innovation' experiments. BBC Backstage is an example, trying to do with new media development what the open source community did with software development. The model is deceptively simple – developers are invited to make free use of various elements of the BBC's site (such as live news feeds, weather, TV listings, etc.) to integrate and shape innovative applications. The strap line is "use our stuff to build your stuff" – and since the site was launched in May 2005 it has already attracted the interest of hundreds of software developers. Ben Metcalf, one of the program's founders, summed up the approach. "Top line, we are looking to be seen promoting innovation and creativity on the Internet . . . if someone is doing something really innovative, we would like to . . . see if some of that value can be incorporated into the BBC's core propositions" (see www.bbcbackstage.com).

READING SUGGESTIONS

Chesbrough, H. (2003). *Open Innovation: The New Imperative for Creating and Profiting from Technology.* Boston, MA: Harvard Business School Press.

Comment: The book describes an approach to innovation that is based on allowing idea flow into as well as out of organisations.

Von Hippel, E., (2005). *Democratizing Innovation.* Boston, MA: MIT Press.

Comment: In his book von Hippel argues that companies should redesign their innovation processes in a way that will allow them to tap into and engage with innovations that have been developed by users. He explains why and when users find it profitable to develop new products and services for themselves, and why it often pays users to reveal their innovations freely for the use of all. True to the spirit of his message you can download his book free on http://web.mit.edu/evhippel/www/democ.htm.

A Question of Culture? Collaborative Innovation in UK Business. CBI in cooperation with 3M and the Design Council, February 2001.

Comment: This report provides insights into what differentiates innovative from less innovative organisations, focusing on culture and collaboration in particular. To obtain a copy please contact the Confederation of British Industry, Centre Point, 103 New Oxford Street, London WC1A 1DU.

Doz, Y. & Hamel, G. (1998). *Alliance Advantage: The Art of Creating Value Through Partnering.* Boston, MA: Harvard Business School Press.

Comment: The book introduces three possible approaches to creating value through alliances and shows how they evolve over time. Illustrated through case studies on companies such as Xerox, JVC, Corning, Siemens, Airbus, GE, Thomson, Boeing and many others.

14 Innovation and industry context

CASE STUDY 5: ROCHE–SAQUINAVIR[1] (A)

1995 – a new class of HIV antiviral

On 6 December 1995 the US Food and Drug Administration (FDA) cleared Roche's new HIV drug, Invirase® (saquinavir) for use in combination with approved nucleoside analogues for selected individuals with advanced HIV disease. This decision to approve Invirase as quickly as possible was addressed in the US media as, "Some of the most hopeful news in years for people living with AIDS. This approval introduces a new class of drugs for treating AIDS." Until 1995, HIV therapy had been limited to the use of combination regimens comprising two drugs that were designed to prevent the virus from infecting the cell. The introduction of Invirase enabled the use of new combination regimens that would target the virus at two steps in the replication cycle – providing a "one-two punch" approach. Like many other infectious agents, immunodeficiency viruses had an unfortunate tendency to mutate in such a way that they would become resistant to individual substances used to attack them. As many as 40% of HIV/AIDS patients had failed multiple treatment regimens or had developed resistance to existing options.

While AIDS-related deaths had declined since the introduction of Invirase and subsequent HIV protease inhibitors, the number of people living with HIV continued to grow. The use of triple combination therapy, pioneered in Roche's Phase III clinical trials became known as HAART (Highly Active Antiretroviral Therapy). The use of HAART therapy has been shown to significantly prolong the survival of people living with HIV and reduce the incidence of opportunistic infections.

Criteria for selecting an ideal anti-retroviral combination:

- Synergistic or additive anti-HIV activity
- No cross-resistance between drugs
- No overlapping toxicities
- Antiviral activity in multiple cellular and tissue reservoirs of HIV
- Lack of adverse interaction between component drugs and other commonly used agents
- Ease of administration

While Invirase provided significant clinical benefits, full potential (antiviral effect) could not be realised due to limited bioavailability of this formulation. When Merck launched Crixivan in late spring 1996, a third protease inhibitor, they focused their marketing activities against Invirase upon the greater viral load reductions achieved with their drug.

---

[1] The case has been prepared by Dr Bettina von Stamm as a basis for class discussion rather than to illustrate either effective or ineffective handling of a management situation.

In addition a company called Agouron had picked up Roche's patent and had managed to develop a similar compound in just five years with the advantage of achieving higher drug concentrations and showing a unique drug resistance profile that allowed other protease inhibitors to be used following failure of a Viracept-containing treatment regimen.

Moving into HIV drug research – the situation in 1986

In 1982 an unusual collection of clinical symptoms observed in a small number of homosexual men in urban areas of San Francisco was recognised and classified as acquired immunodeficiency syndrome (AIDS). There-after, the number of individuals diagnosed with AIDS increased rapidly and it became apparent that AIDS was widespread in many western countries and sub-Saharan Africa, and had evolved into a worldwide epidemic. AIDS manifests itself as a severe impairment of the human immune system, leaving those affected vulner-able to a wide range of opportunistic infections, resulting in a dramatic loss of weight and ultimately death. At this early stage in the history of AIDS the life expectancy of an infected individual was around two years.

The search for the infectious agent responsible for AIDS attracted the attention of scientists around the world. In 1983 two research groups, one in the USA the other in France, independently isolated the same retrovirus which later became known as human immunodeficiency virus (HIV), the causative agent of AIDS.

Molecular cloning and gene sequencing elucidated the composition of the HIV genome, from this data it was proposed that much of the genetic information required for replication of the virus was contained in just three distinct genes: *gag, pol* and *env*. From the nucleotide sequence of these three genes a number of enzymes were proposed to be encoded by the HIV, giving scientists the first indication that it may be possible to design specific chemotherapeutic agents capable of inhibiting the replication of this deadly virus.

The sheer scale of the problem and the potentially devastating threat to world health mobilised worldwide cooperation. In 1986, six United Nations organisations took the unprecedented step of joining forces to form the 'Joint United Nations Programme on HIV and AIDS

Scientific background

HIV is a retrovirus. Like all retroviruses, the genetic material of HIV is RNA rather than DNA. When HIV infects a cell, the viral RNA is transcribed by a spe-cific enzyme, called reverse transcriptase (RT) into DNA which is then integrated into the host cell genome. After that viral DNA is copied to produce components of new viral particles which are assembled at the cell membrane where budding and maturation result in the formation of a new HIV particle.

Scientists continued to isolate and study HIV from in-fected individuals in those areas where the disease was of epidemic proportions. It became apparent that two sig-nificantly different strains of the virus existed and were classified as HIV-1 and HIV-2. The latter, most pre-dominant in Africa, is less virulent.

Scientists were comparing the genetic composition of HIV with other closely related viruses in an attempt not only to trace its origin but to better understand its replication and also to identify possible model systems to facilitate the evaluation of potential inhibitory agents. The transmission of viruses from animals to humans is known but is not common and is an inefficient process. Most notable is the transmission of influenza from avian species to man, which until the 1997–8 Hong Kong outbreak was thought to require the intermediacy of hogs. Since HIV infects the chimpanzee attention turned to other primates and viruses that infected primates. There is a high degree of homology between HIV and simian immunodeficiency virus (SIV) which infects the African green monkey, this led to the suggestion that HIV may

(UNIAIDS). Its role is to monitor, facilitate exchange and spread knowledge related to HIV and AIDS. The organisation also publishes annual estimates on the spread and scope of HIV infection as well as mortality rates, with the objective to help direct efforts to control the spread of the virus and those infected by it. From a few known cases in the early 1980s the number of people living with HIV and AIDS was estimated by UNIAIDS and the World Health Organisation (WHO) to have grown to 36.1 million worldwide by the end of 2000, with 1.4 million of them being children. This equates to approximately 15,000 new infections every day. The geographic region most affected by HIV is sub-Saharan Africa with about 70% of all known cases. A further 16% or 5.8 million live in South and Southeast Asia.

The first two drugs on the market, Retrovir® (or ATZ) introduced in 1987 by Burroughs Wellcome and Hivid® introduced in 1992 by Roche, were both designed to hinder the viral RNA from being transcribed and integrated into the cell. However, they could not prevent the virus from reproducing once the cell had been infected. Other concerns were that these drugs could only be taken in relatively small quantities as they tended to interfere with the metabolism of human cells causing side effects such as diarrhoea, vomiting, nausea, fatigue and headaches. In addition problems started to occur with strains of the HIV that had mutated in such a way that they had become resistant to the drug.

be derived from SIV that may have crossed the species barrier as early as the 17th century and emerged as HIV in the 1930s.

Roche takes up the gauntlet

Even in the mid-1980s the speed with which the virus was spreading focused pharmaceutical companies' attention on the problem. All major pharmaceutical companies seemed to be racing against time and each other to find an angle that would allow them to be first in bringing an HIV drug to market. In late 1985, around the same time Glaxo and SmithKline started to engage in research into HIV, Roche's antiviral chemotherapy group in Welwyn, UK, initiated a programme to develop a drug that would prevent the virus from entering the cell. There were also rumours that Burroughs Wellcome was about to introduce an HIV drug.

Rick Kramer, a Roche scientist working in collaboration with the American Health Authorities performed experiments in which parts of the HIV virus could be produced in yeast cells. In these experiments he deleted parts of the virus to see what effect that had on the other components. He showed that deletions in one gene, suspected of being a protease by analogy with the SIV gene, prevented proteolytic processing of the *gag* and *pol* gene products. This confirmed that the virus encoded a protease which had an essential function in virus maturation and he proposed that this protease could therefore represent a target for an anti-HIV drug.

In May 1986 the current status of the AIDS pandemic was discussed in Roche Nutley with a call for a corporate commitment to AIDS research and the formation of an AIDS Task Force. Various aspects of research into AIDS therapy and diagnosis were assigned to different Roche research centres. It was decided that Roche Discovery in Welwyn would take on the HIV protease and reverse transcriptase as therapeutic targets. The prior experience of many Welwyn chemists and biologists in the inhibition of proteases from sources other than HIV underpinned this decision.

Chemist Joe Martin who had set up Roche's virology department in the early 1980s remembers, "Management told us to drop everything else, I guess about 80% of the virology team were working on or were even dedicated to this project." It was clear that the input of both chemists and biologists, both located in the same building, would be essential. The first task of the chemistry group, headed by Joe, was to review all molecules to identify possible targets that would allow preventing the virus either from entering the cell or from reproducing. One problem when developing a drug is to find an area for attack that is as specific as possible. If a sequence of events is targeted that can be found in aspects of human biology, then healthy cells will be attacked along with the targeted ones, leading to high levels of toxicity.

Information about the structure and function of HIV protease was far from complete when the inhibitor programme began in 1986. The virology team in Welwyn had little prior experience with protease biochemistry, although there was considerable experience in Welwyn in related areas. Some clues could be obtained from a study of similar viruses in birds and Ian Duncan, a senior virologist at Welwyn, was able to suggest potential cleavage sites, including one that was particularly unusual.

It was the unusual one that caught the imagination of the scientists. From Ian's perspective the enzyme responsible for splitting the viral proteins into building blocks for a new virus, seemed a good starting point but he felt that he needed input from a colleague to assess biological aspects. Scientists from all backgrounds

Protease acts like a pair of scissors cutting into pieces the long protein chains produced by the cell under the influence of the virus. These pieces are needed for the production of a new virus that bursts out of the host cell and then infects new cells. If the protease fails to do its job the resulting immature virus particles are non-infectious.

The protease had been provisionally classified as an aspartic protease on the basis of an Asp–Thr–Gly amino acid motif in its sequence but this was not confirmed and there was a problem in that all previous aspartic proteases contained two such motifs and this contained only one. The possibility of the enzyme being formed from two identical sub-units was proposed and later confirmed by X-ray crystallography.

The cleavage site specificity of the enzyme was also unknown, i.e. between which amino acids did the enzyme cleave the gag and pol proteins? One of the cleavage sites suggested by Ian Duncan was the unusual cleavage between the amino acid pairs Phe–Pro and Tyr–Pro. (The cleavage sites that Ian Duncan

had been discussing their work on HIV all the time and from their internal networking they knew that biologist Noel Roberts had worked for the past 12 years on the biochemistry and inhibition of proteases other than HIV. Noel was invited to join the team to advise and participate on that aspect of the work.

Noel recalls, "I started by investigating the literature and did some thinking and then gave my thoughts to management. In my view it was essential to get the enzyme into the test tube so we could start working on it." He observed that the unusual cleavage sites, between Phe and Try–Pro, were unique for HIV and similar virus proteases and that no human proteases, including the mechanistically similar human aspartic proteases, could make such cleavages. Thus, an inhibitor of HIV designed using chemistry based on the amino acids Phe–Pro should be able to produce an inhibitor of HIV protease which would not inhibit the human proteases. This was important as unwanted inhibition of human proteases could result in drug toxicities.

Thus the strategy was set. However, it was largely based on hypothesis and on the belief that they would be able to achieve a number of significant scientific challenges. When the teams presented to the Hoffman La Roche Senior Research Management Team in October 1986, the project was fully approved. The timing of the programme was very tight and required simultaneous working on several aspects at once, each group working on the assumption that all the other groups would be successful. The programme that was agreed to in November 1986 read as follows:

1. Clone and express enzyme (protease) and demonstrate cleavage of Phe–Pro in a peptide (short piece of protein) substrate (mid-1987).
2. Purify enzyme; develop a rapid assay; achieve a potent and selective inhibitor (mid-1988).
3. Demonstrate antiviral activity (end 1988).
4. Select a drug candidate (end 1990).

After that a method for the large-scale production of the compound would need to be found and clinical trials would be the final test-bed for the quality of the drug.

speculatively proposed were later confirmed by researchers in Roche Basle directed by Jan Mous.)

They had no HIV protease in a test tube to inhibit (no one had achieved that at the time), there was no assay to test for the inhibition of the enzyme once they got it, and no test for the inhibition of whole HIV replication (a special high containment laboratory would have been required to work with whole HIV and Welwyn did not have such a facility at that time).

Attempts to clone and express the HIV protease in a bacterium (*E. coli*) using molecular biology techniques were pursued simultaneously by Jan Mous in Basle and by Mary Graves and her group in Nutley; Noel Roberts with help from peptide chemist Raj Handa, set about devising an assay first to detect the activity of the protease and then to assay its inhibition; Ian Duncan established a collaboration with St Mary's Hospital, Paddington, which had the facilities to set up an antiviral assay using HIV and Joe Martin and his chemistry team started to make at first relatively simple compounds which could provide the basis for an inhibitor.

Employing some very old chemistry from the 1930s, Noel showed that proline (the Pro part of Phe–Pro) at the end of a peptide would react with a compound called isatin to give a blue colour, but while in the middle of the peptide it would not. Thus, if a peptide were made with a Phe–Pro bond in the middle and this were then cleaved by HIV protease a blue colour could be formed with isatin and the resultant smaller peptide. Soon, bacterial cultures potentially containing genetically engineered HIV protease were coming from the Basle and Nutley labs. In September 1987 a bacterial lysate (broken-up bacteria) added to a Phe–Pro containing peptide, incubated and then reacted with isatin turned blue. They had active HIV protease in the test tube! This assay then needed further refinement to make it both sensitive and quantitative so that they could use it to assay for HIV protease inhibition with the compounds Joe's team were already making. That took about another two months.

Tackling the challenges

In 83 the virus had been completely unknown and by 89 it was probably the best understood virus in the world. To be part of this activity was exciting, to make headway even more so.

In order to take their investigations further they needed the enzyme. But as it was not possible at the time to grow HIV to get the enzyme – not least because no one wanted to get anywhere near large quantities of live HIV viruses – they would have to synthesise it by getting bacteria to produce it which was a complicated process in which both Basle and Nutley were involved. After the cloning of the HIV protease had been achieved successfully, an assay was needed firstly to prove the activity of the enzyme and then the effectiveness of inhibition.

Noel decided to try to devise a colorimetric assay for the protease, that is one in which a colour change in the test tube would indicate the presence of the active enzyme. That would enable rapid assessment of results at least semi-quantitatively, by eye. Noel remembered about his first breakthrough, "Between Christmas and New Year 1986 I spent three days in the lab, when it was nice and quiet and no phone would ring. It was then that I first managed to observe the formation of a blue colour in the test tube which could be used to detect the presence of the enzyme." By November 1987 they had a working assay (test) that allowed visual assessment which meant that they could tell within a few hours whether a compound was inhibiting or not. But even nine months before Noel got the assay working Joe had developed compounds based on the link identified and the first proteinase inhibitors had been synthesised as early as spring 1987.

When working on compounds, past experience came in handy again. Roche had applied a process, called transition state mimetics (TSM), before. What this means is making a chemical compound which looks to the target protease to be like molecules that it usually binds and cleaves but which cannot be cleaved.

The concept of transition-state analogues is that short peptides containing a stable dipeptide mimetic should bind competitively to the active site of the protease, thus preventing the natural substrates (gag and gag–pol polyproteins) access to the active site of the enzyme and therefore from being processed. The use of crystal structures of enzymes, with and without inhibitors bound in the active site had been used successfully to aid the design of enzyme inhibitors in other therapeutic areas. Unfortunately, at this early stage there were no crystal structures of HIV protease. Therefore, to assist in their search for novel structures that may bind in the active site of the HIV enzyme, the team began studies to produce crystals of the protein and determining its three-dimensional structure. Meanwhile, homology modelling of the HIV protease active site was initiated using computer graphics which had been developed in the Physics Methods Department at Roche Welwyn. The use of homology modelling enabled the team to look at a three-dimensional structure of the enzyme, from all angles, but also to dock structures of potential inhibitors into the putative structure of HIV protease. This is an extension of the early concept of the 'lock and key' approach to the design of enzyme inhibitors.

In the lead generation process a series of transition-state mimetics was prepared and incorporated into small peptide-like molecules and evaluated as inhibitors of HIV protease. Very rapidly, a range of molecules from different structural classes were identified that had modest inhibitory activity. One of these which was of particular interest because of its novelty and small size (a tripeptide analogue) was considered a lead structure.

Thus the mimetic (inhibitor) binds to the enzyme and gets stuck there – 'the wrong key in the right lock'. The challenge was to find a key that would fit the HIV protease without fitting other locks, leading to toxic side effects. In the search for such a key the computer-based modelling tool developed by the Physics Methods Department at Roche Welwyn was of great help.

A systematic approach to lead generation and lead optimisation was adopted. Some of the structures were inhibitive but not all of them were selective, meaning that they would interfere with other processes too, leading to undesired side effects.

A systematic process of chemical modification to the lead Phe–Pro mimetic structure was guided by assaying the potency of the compounds to inhibit HIV protease and their activity against whole HIV virus. Potent inhibitors were rapidly achieved and to a large degree potency against the enzyme was accompanied by potency against the virus. Potency as an antiviral in the test tube is only part way to identifying a drug candidate. The compound must also have an acceptable pharmacokinetic profile (i.e. if you take it by mouth does it get to the parts of the body where it needs to act in sufficient concentrations to be effective) and it needs to have low (ideally no) toxicity. Two or three potential development compounds had been identified by the autumn of 1989.

To get to this point the team had synthesised about 250 compounds, normally they would have expected the need to have made thousands. From the decision to commence the project to this point it had taken the team only about three years though Joe points out, "At that time it was incredibly fast and we were even three months ahead of schedule but today things can be done even quicker, mainly due to advances in technology."

Patenting of course was a critical activity but it also presented some difficult decisions. A patent can be filed immediately after the discovery has been made but this sets the clock ticking. Alternatively, one can delay filing which will give a longer protection period after marketing. Also, the longer patent filing can be

The next step was to begin the lead optimisation phase. First, six key structural features were identified in the lead structure; each of these were considered essential for activity. Next, each of the six key elements was modified separately keeping the other five constant. Thus, in this first round of optimisation a number of preferred structural fragments at each of the six critical sites in the lead structure was identified. The next phase of lead optimisation was to assemble individual molecules each containing permutations of all of the best fragments into individual molecules. It was very satisfying to find that the contribution of each of the optimised fragments was additive when incorporated into a final molecule. We then had a number of compounds that were very potent inhibitors of the HIV protease. This was the first step towards finding a medicine to inhibit HIV infection.

The next stage involved evaluation for antiviral activity in a cell-based assay that had been set up in collaboration with scientists at St Mary's Hospital, Paddington, London. Again, it was very gratifying to find that the very potent inhibitors of the HIV protease display excellent activity in the antiviral assay. Furthermore, there was a good structure–activity relationship (SAR), that is, the level of activity in the antiviral assay followed in parallel the potencies in the enzyme assay. This was another major advance in the project. Next, it was important to assess the compounds for selectivity and hence potential toxicity. Since there were no animal models available to assess the toxicity of these inhibitors the team took a different approach to assess the toxicity potential. Collaboration was established with Professor John Kay, an expert on mammalian aspartic proteases, at the University of Cardiff. Professor Kay measured the potency of the optimised compounds against a panel of important human aspartic proteases, which gave the Welwyn group a measure of the toxicity potential of their inhibitors. Yet again, they were delighted to find that their potential development candidates were totally selective for the viral enzyme. Thus, none of the compounds inhibited any of the key enzymes in Professor Kay's panel of important human enzymes.

delayed the stronger the patent can be made by inclusion of additional examples. The downside of delaying is that the competition might file a patent first, which means they would have sole rights to the invented compounds. As competition was fierce in this field, a patent was filed in 1988 covering the genetic aspects of the Roche inhibitors but the team's preferred compound was specifically claimed in a new patent filed in December 1989.

During the entire research phase less than 10 g of material had been available, with most of the *in vitro* studies having been completed with no more than 25 mg.

The next step was to select one of the compounds to be the development candidate. A key step was to determine whether any of these compounds had sufficient oral bioavailability to enable the molecule to be taken in tablet form and achieve adequate levels of substance in the blood to be an effective anti-HIV agent. A number of studies were carried out in rats, dogs and monkeys from which it was concluded that these compounds did achieve adequate blood levels to be an effective drug. At this point the compound whose code number was Ro 31–8959 was considered to be the likely development candidate.

Development – from test tube to mass production

Noel recalls, "In autumn 1989 we had two or three components but one seemed to work best, it was more potent than the others. The problem with that compound, Ro 31–8959, was that it was the chemically most difficult to produce. We had a meeting, myself, Joe, Ian Duncan, David Clough (Director of Research who had given the project unlimited support throughout) and Peter Machin, Director of Chemistry. Intuitively we all wanted to go for the most difficult one but it was really for Peter to decide whether it could be produced on a large scale. Most of the building blocks were able to be purchased or readily prepared but the decahydroisoquinoline moiety that replaced the proline residue found in the substrate was extremely difficult to make."

Even though the synthetic tractability was not proven at that time and, on the contrary, it was expected to be rather difficult if not impossible. Nevertheless, and despite the fact that only one out of 10 drugs that enter development makes it to market, Peter felt quite confident that they would be able to produce the compound in the quantities required and the decision was made to follow gut feelings. The compound, later to become known as saquinavir, was handed over from the research team to an International Project Team (IPT). The IPT was responsible for the development of the compound into a product and also for taking that product to market. The stages involved were: pre-clinical development and formulation, toxicity studies in animals, evaluation in healthy volunteers (Phase I), clinical studies (Phase II and Phase III), registration and marketing (see also Appendix 8.2).

In 1990 experts in chemical process research and production chemistry found themselves confronted with the difficult task of producing the complex molecule on an industrial scale. The elements of the molecule had to be assembled in a specific order to afford the correct molecular structure. Only one out of 64 possible scenarios was wanted, which meant that ways of detecting the one desired outcome were needed. Dieter Krimmer, a development chemist based in Basle, had the task to develop a viable synthetic process that could produce saquinavir on a much larger scale than had previously been undertaken. At the time many competitors knew the compound and its structure but all of them had declared that it would be impossible to manufacture the compound on production scale and at an acceptable cost to be profitable. If choosing the Phe–Pro mimetic as the core of inhibitors had already been considered very risky developing a production process was now seen as an outstandingly difficult challenge.

At the same time, other companies such as Merck and Abbott had much larger teams working on similar products. Abbott had chosen to focus on symmetrical inhibitors, whereas, Merck and SB were working on renin-like molecules. In fact, Roche had looked at these options as well but had, in the end, decided to focus on protease inhibition based on the more difficult but potentially more selective Phe–Pro moiety. Separately, a group of scientists in Roche at the Nutley site in New Jersey were studying TAT antagonists as an approach to HIV therapy. Both project teams identified development candidates at approximately the same time but because the protease inhibitor had a higher chance of success the decision was made to concentrate on that approach.

The challenge facing the development chemist is not simply a matter of producing material on a larger scale but also to improve the synthesis to be more efficient by reducing the number of steps in the process. The initial synthetic route deployed in the research phase involved 26 steps but by the time early clinical studies were being initiated batches of 30 kg of bulk material were being prepared using a process that had been improved to involve just 17 steps. Another advantage arising from the shortened synthesis was that the time required to produce a batch of saquinavir was reduced by a third from 15 months to 10 months.

In the early phases of research and development the physical characteristics of the active substance does not affect the outcome of experimental studies but by the time large-scale manufacture is reached the final product has to be made available in a physical form that is suitable for the preparation of capsules and/or tablets. The physical characteristics of early batches of saquinavir were such that it was very difficult to fill capsules needed to conduct the early clinical studies. Fortunately, the problem was easily overcome and in 1991 when the production process had been optimised the final compound was obtained as a free-flowing crystalline powder.

Clinical trials and introduction

Another challenge was to determine the right dose. The question was how much needs to be given to ensure that the patient receives enough of the drug for it to be active but not so much of the drug for the patient to experience un-acceptable levels of side effects. Phase I clinical trials were undertaken with healthy volunteers, and took place in 1990.

Following the completion of Phases II and III a daily dose of three times 600 mg was recommended, and Invirase was brought to market in 1995, creating the first of a new class of HIV drugs.

In the Phase II clinical trials the drug was given to HIV-infected individuals, providing the first indications for the product's efficacy. Phase II involved double-blind studies with a total of 200 patients in the UK, France and Italy. The results were good: the number of CD4 cells (the cells of the immune system, which HIV destroys) increased. It seemed to work even better in combination with AZT (the first anti-HIV drug available for clinical use which inhibited another enzyme in the virus, reverse transcriptase). A further study took place in the US with 300 trial participants, exploring three different drug combinations. Finally, in Phase III, which began in the US in 1994, the aim was to detect clinical improvements as well as changes in surrogate HIV markers. In this study 978 patients were involved who were given either saquinavir or Hivid (another AIDS drug from the first class of compounds – the reverse transcriptase inhibitors) or both. A second part of Phase III began in August 1994 in 200 centres in 24 countries around the world with 3500 patients (the largest combination drug study ever to be carried out in the HIV area). In this study triple drug therapy for HIV was used for the first time. This is now the treatment norm. Side effects were detected in less than 4%, indicating very low levels of toxicity. The Phase III studies showed that Invirase significantly improved the patients' clinical status by delaying the progression of AIDS and improving survival.

The fact that Roche was in the process of creating a new class of HIV drugs had also put the company into the limelight early in what was a whole new ball game in the pharmaceutical industry. One of the first groups hit by the HIV epidemic was the gay community. The gay community had established advocacy networks and lobbying experience and soon began to focus on HIV. HIV treatment advocacy groups began to gain strength, their intention being to reduce the negative stigma associated with HIV, to initiate public awareness, to halt the spread of the virus through education about safe-sex practices and to pressure pharmaceutical companies and regulatory authorities for early access to life-saving medications. Initially there was a lot of anger. The advocates were literally fighting for their lives and there was no established basis for communications between the advocates and the industry. As a result, there were often public displays of anger. All of the drug companies involved in HIV in the early days experienced such action, as did the regulatory authorities and leading HIV physicians.

There was considerable public pressure on Roche to make its new drug available before all clinical trials had been completed. After first hints on the development of a new class of drug had been published in 1993, demands were made to make saquinavir freely available to HIV sufferers by allowing them to participate in Compassionate Use Programmes. Compassionate Use Programmes pushed companies outside of their comfort zone as these programmes required that companies make their drugs available before clinical studies had been completed and evaluated while at the same time maintaining full responsibility for the consequences. In addition, the usage of the drug in such programmes tends to be less well controlled and monitored than in clinical trials. Compassionate Use Programmes often include patients with more advanced HIV disease who may suffer more acutely from adverse drug reactions. Roche was initially cautious in agreeing to such a programme. In 1993 AIDS activists had demanded

> Recognition:
>
> 1995
>
> - Roche International Research Prize
> - Prix Galien (UK)
>
> 1997
>
> - Prix Galien (Spain)
> - Prix Galien (Portugal)
> - SMR Drug Discovery Award
> - Innovation Award (Pharmazeutische Zeitung)
>
> 1999
>
> - International Prix Galien
> - PhRMA Discovers Award (USA)

that a different HIV drug Roche had been working on, based on TAT inhibition, should be released. However, Roche had refused – and later clinical trials revealed unacceptable levels of toxicity in the drug, which eventually led to the discontinuation of development of the TAT inhibitor. However, in the case of saquinavir Roche agreed to set up a Compassionate Use Programme ahead of approval and the programme got under way in July 1995. By the end of August 1996 some 12,000 patients had been included.

Thanks to the close cooperation of the teams at Roche with various authorities in relevant countries from an early stage, approval of the drug was more rapid than could normally have been expected. The NDA (New Drug Application) Dossier delivered to the FDA on 31 August 1995, consisting of 600 volumes and 160,000 pages, was approved in record time. Approved in the US in December 1995, by the end of 1996 the drug had been approved in North and South America, Australia, several countries in Europe and Asia.

Questions

1. Drug development normally takes up to 15 years; Invirase was developed much faster. What has enabled the speedy and successful execution of the project?

2. Given the situation in 1996, how would you have taken this part of the company forward?

Additional information on AIDS can be found at:

> http://www.medicalfutures.co.uk/

Comment: This is the website of *Medical Futures*, a venture aimed at promoting innovation among healthcare professionals and facilitating the successful commercialisation of these innovations. Medical Futures operates through three main channels: innovative events, a high quality magazine and database-driven websites.

> http://www.aidsmeds.com/

Comment: This website, run by people infected with the HIV virus, offers up-to-date information on treatment, developments, readings, conferences etc.

APPENDIX 14.1: TEAM MEMBERS

Chemistry

J.A. Martin	A.C. Freeman	W.C. Spurden	M.P. Gunn
B.K. Handa	R.A. Hopkins	S. Redshaw	J.H. Merrett
C. Kay	K.E.B. Parkes	J.C. Gilbert	I.R. Johns
R.W. Lambert			

Biology

N.A. Roberts	I.B. Duncan
A.V. Broadhurst	J.C. Craig
A.J. Ritchie	L. Whittaker

Virology (Roche, Basle)

J. Mous

Molecular biology (Roche, Nutley)

M. Graves

Virology (MRC Collaborative Centre)

A.S. Tyms

D.L. Taylor

X-ray crystallography (Roche, Nutley)

B. Graves

Biochemistry (University of Cardiff)

J. Kay

A.D. Richards

Pharmacokinetics

S.L. Malcolm

A.F. Clarke

A. James

Molecular modelling

W.A. Thomas

A. Kroehn

APPENDIX 14.2: DRUG DISCOVERY VALUE CHAIN

10–15 years from Exploratory to Launch

Decisions

Expl.	Target Selection	Lead Selection	Early Development Compound	Phase I/IIa	Phase IIb	Phase III	Subm.	Launch

Phases

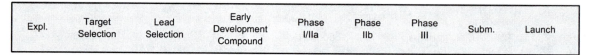

Target Ident.	Lead Ident.	Candidate Ident.	Preclinical	Phase I	Phase IIa	Phase IIb	Phase IIIa	Phase IIIb	Phase IV

Principles

Proof of Concept	Proof of Efficacy

APPENDIX 14.3: GLOSSARY

AIDS Acquired immunodeficiency syndrome

Amino acid Although more than 100 amino acids occur naturally, only 20 are commonly used in protein synthesis; these are the same in all living organisms, from protozoa to plants and animals. Amino acids are joined covalently in long chains by peptide bonds to yield proteins (including enzymes and hormones; structural, transport and contractile elements; and molecules of special biological activity) or in shorter chains to give 'peptides'

Analogue A compound with a molecular structure closely similar to that of another

Aspartic protease Proteases (proteinases) are enzymes which cleave (digest) proteins. Aspartic proteases are a sub-class of proteases in which the amino acid aspartic acid is part of the structure of the enzyme and critical to the function of the enzyme

Assay Set-up to test for the existence of a certain substance or that a certain process has happened

Bioavailability The 'availability' to the body of various dosage forms of drugs

Cleavage Separation of a chain of molecules (peptide bonds/amino acids)

Colorimetric assay Test where results can be assessed based on a change in colour

Compound Any substance composed of identical molecules consisting of atoms of two or more elements

Dipeptide Peptides are amides derived from two or more amino acids. The amino acids may be the same or different. The number of amino-acid molecules present in a peptide is indicated by a prefix: a dipeptide contains two amino acids; an octapeptide, eight; an oligopeptide, a few; a polypeptide, many

DNA Deoxyribonucleic acid is present in all independently-living organisms in the chromosomes. It is the carrier of genetic information. It is a very long chain composed of four different nucleotides. The genetic code is read from these four nucleotides in groups of three at a time

Enzyme Practically all of the numerous and complex biochemical reactions that take place in animals, plants and micro-organisms are regulated by enzymes. These catalytic proteins are efficient and specific – that is, they accelerate the rate of one kind of chemical reaction of one type of compound, and they do so in a far more efficient manner than synthetic catalysts. They are controlled by activators and inhibitors that initiate or block reactions. All cells contain enzymes, which usually vary in number and composition, depending on the cell type; an average mammalian cell, for example, is approximately one one-billionth (10^{-9}) the size of a drop of water and generally contains about 3000 enzymes

Genome Every cell of an organism has a set of chromosomes containing the heritable genetic material that directs its development, i.e., its genome

HIV Human immunodeficiency virus

HIV virus   Like other viruses, HIV enters a cell in order to multiply. Viruses cannot replicate on their own and instead rely on mechanisms of the host cell to produce new viral particles. HIV is a retrovirus, a unique family of viruses that consist of genetic material in the form of RNA (instead of DNA) surrounded by a protein envelope. HIV infects helper T cells by means of a protein, called gp120, in its envelope. The gp120 protein binds to a molecule called CD4 on the surface of the helper T cell, an event that tricks the cell into letting the virus in. Once inside the T cell, HIV uses the cell's machinery to copy its RNA into DNA by means of the enzyme reverse transcriptase. The newly produced viral DNA is then inserted into the chromosomal DNA of the host cell. It was thought for some time that when HIV integrated into the host DNA it became dormant, a theory that accounted for the long lag time between infection and the development of AIDS. Although this is true of other viruses, it is not the case with HIV. Rather, during the latent period HIV multiplies, usually at breakneck speed. As the virus replicates, many mutations in the RNA arise, a situation that complicates the task of the immune system in combating the virus. Eventually, the large numbers of new virus particles produced are able to debilitate or destroy helper T cells more rapidly than those cells can be produced by the immune system

Homology   In biology many organisms are closely similar and/or their components are similar. The degree to which they are similar is their homology. Thus, for example. The genome of HIV has about 50% homology with the equivalent monkey virus, SIV, but within those genomes there are parts (usually the critical functional parts) where the homology is much higher (80%+)

Isatin   A pale yellow crystalline compound used in the manufacture of dyes

Mimetic   Something that pretends to be something else

Moiety   Individual compound or individual part of a larger molecule (compound)

Nucleotide   Any member of a class of organic compounds in which the molecular structure comprises a nitrogen-containing unit (base) linked to a sugar and a phosphate group. The nucleotides are of great importance to living organisms, as they are the building blocks of nucleic acids, the substances that control all hereditary characteristics

Pandemic   Prevalent over a whole country or the world

Peptide   Any organic substance of which the molecules are structurally like those of proteins, but smaller. The class of peptides includes many hormones, antibiotics and other compounds that participate in the metabolic functions of living organisms. Peptide molecules are composed of two or more amino acids joined through amide formation involving the carboxyl group of each amino acid and the amino group of the next. The chemical bond between the carbon and nitrogen atoms of each amide group is called a peptide bond. Some or all of the peptide bonds, which connect the consecutive triplets of atoms in the chain regarded as the backbone of the molecule, can be broken by partial or complete hydrolysis of the compound. This reaction, producing smaller peptides and finally the individual amino acids, is commonly used in studies of the composition and structure of peptides and proteins

Pharmaco-   Study of the factors that influence the movement of drugs throughout the body is called
kinetic   pharmacokinetics, which includes the absorption, distribution, localisation in tissues, biotransformation and excretion of drugs

Phase I clinical trials	Trials with healthy volunteers (safety and pharmacokinetics)
Phase II clinical trials	Double blind studies with infected individuals (short-term safety and efficacy proof of concept)
Phase III clinical trials	Optimising drug doses and frequency (long-term safety and efficacy)
(Poly)protein	Highly complex substance that is present in all living organisms. Proteins are of great nutritional value, constitute a large part of the composition of all living organisms and are directly involved in the chemical processes essential for life
Potency	Here: how effective the drug is in achieving its objective
Proline	An amino acid which is a constituent of most proteins, especially collagen
Protease	An enzyme which breaks down proteins and peptides
Protease inhibitor	Prevents the final processing of a number of important HIV proteins carried out by the enzyme HIV protease
Proteolytic enzyme	Also called proteinase or protease, any of a group of enzymes that break the long chainlike molecules of proteins into shorter fragments (peptides) and eventually into their components, amino acids
Renin	An asparic protease secreted by and stored in the kidneys which promotes the production of the protein angiotensin. This in turn controls blood pressure
Retrovirus	Retroviruses are so named because, by means of a special enzyme called reverse transcriptase, they use RNA to synthesise deoxyribonucleic acid (DNA). This constitutes a reversal of the usual cellular processes of transcription of DNA into RNA. The action of reverse transcriptase makes it possible for genetic material from a retrovirus to become permanently incorporated into the DNA genome of an infected cell
Reverse transcriptase	An enzyme which catalyses the formation of DNA from an RNA template transcription
RNA	Ribonucleic acid, a nucleic acid present in all living cells. Its principal role is to act as a messenger carrying instructions from DNA for controlling the synthesis of proteins, although in some viruses RNA rather than DNA carries the genetic information
RNA virus	A virus in which the genetic information is stored in the form of RNA (as opposed to DNA)
Selectivity	The drug does not inhibit or interfere any other processes
TAT antagonists	An approach to HIV therapy based on blocking the actions of TAT, a viral protein component which controls the expression of viral genes
Toxicity	Caused by a drug attacking/reacting with cells/processes other than the ones intended

Transition state mimetics   The transition state, or activated complex, is the fleeting molecular configuration that exists at the top of the energy barrier that the reactants must surmount to become the products. Strictly it is not a component of the reaction system and it cannot be examined directly in the way that an intermediate (however unstable) can because it lasts no longer than the duration of a molecular collision. The transition state may have properties of its own, not reflected in those of the starting materials or of the products and of the reaction, and so it is of vital importance in determining the course of reaction. Inference concerning the nature of the transition state is the essence of mechanistic study

A method to prevent the successful completion of a viral reproduction cycle by introducing, via a drug, a chemical structure that replaces one of the natural building blocks, thus preventing the reproduction process to be completed

APPENDIX 14.4: INTRODUCTION OF HIV DRUGS

1987	Welcome – nucleoside analogue reverse transcriptase
1992	Roche – nucleoside analogue reverse transcriptase inhibitor – Hivid (zalcitabine; ddC)
1995	Roche – proteinase inhibitor – Invirase (saquinavir)
1996	Merck protease inhibitor – Crixivan (indinavir)
1996	Abbott protease inhibitor – Norvir (ritonavir)
1997/8	Agouron/Roche – protease inhibitor – Viracept (nelfinavir)
1997	Roche protease inhibitor – Fortovase (saquinavir soft gelatin capsule formulation)

15 The effects of industry and cultural context

The concerns and issues in the Roche case study seem somewhat different from the ones of the earlier case studies. In the BBC case study the issues were about internal selling of an idea, about collaboration and to a certain degree about considering a multinational audience. The ihavemoved.com story was about branding and strategic flexibility. The Lotus Elise and the Quattro were about more traditional new product development related issues such as prototyping, internal and external collaboration, processes and market research. Most of the above are under the control or at least strong influence of the people within the organisation. Many of the influences in the development of saquinavir – industry regulations, pressure groups – were externally and mostly outside the influence of the people within the organisation. Understanding the context at four levels – national, industry, company and project – is an important part of innovation success. As we have already looked at company context in Chapter 6, this chapter will focus on the project, industry and national level.

WHY THINK ABOUT CONTEXT?

In recent years people have become increasingly aware of the importance of the context in which individual products are developed as an element that should be considered in shaping the design and development process. There are a wide range of factors that can – not necessarily will – have an influence on a product's design and development process.

The terms 'design process' and 'new product development process' often assume generic applicability to a very wide range of products – tangible and intangible, large and small – involving all sorts of different skills and types of design. While I agree that the basic components of the design management and development process will be applicable for most situations there are also aspects that require different approaches and tools, depending on the product in question. In his book Baxter (1995, p. 143) compares four products along different dimensions, just have a look at Table 15.1.

And, from a design perspective, these are all the same types of projects, that is most of them will require primarily product design. Having said that, the first two will also involve packaging design, the latter interior and engineering design – I am sure we could find other design types too. But that is not the main point. The main point is that these projects vary considerably in terms of their requirements, in terms of what is needed for them to be completed successfully. And success here means primarily on budget and on time (see also Chapter 25 for a discussion on success and failure). It is important to understand the differences as it is advisable to adjust approaches, tools

Table 15.1 Different types of products

Company	Stanley	Hewlett-Packard	Chrysler	Boeing
Product	Jobmaster Power Screwdriver	DeskJet 5 000 Printer	Concorde Automobile	777 Aeroplane
No. of unique parts	3	35	10,000	130,000
Development time	1 year	1.5 years	3.5 years	4.5 years
Development team	3 people	100 people	850 people	6 800 people
Development costs	$150,000	$50,000	$1 billion	$3 billion
Sales price	$30	$365	$19,000	$130 million
Annual production	100,000	1.5 million	250,000	50
Sales lifetime	4 years	3 years	6 years	30 years
Development costs/lifetime sales	1.2 %	3 %	3.5 %	1.5 %

Source: Ulrich, K.T. & Eppinger, S.D. (1995). *Product Design and Development*. Singapore: McGraw-Hill. Reprinted by permission of McGraw-Hill Companies, Copyright © 1995 McGraw-Hill Companies. From Baxter, M. (1995). *Product Design – Practical Methods for the Systematic Development of New Products*. London: Chapman & Hall.

and techniques to the particular situation in question. For example, consensus decisions are considered to play an important role in the successful completion of a project. This is great – but while in the case of the screwdriver consensus can be achieved between all members of the team it would be more difficult for the printer and certainly impossible for the Chrysler. This might seem fairly obvious but illustrates the issue that it is not possible to take a tool or 'golden rule' and just apply it slavishly, regardless of the specific context.

It should also be pointed out that in the context of innovation a consensus decision can lead to a dilution of the essence of the concept. So in innovation buy-in is essential, consensus should be thought about carefully. Later we will have an example where the aim for too much consensus led to a mediocre outcome that turned out to be dissatisfying for all involved.

UNDERSTANDING CONSTRAINTS

One reason why understanding the specific context is important is that out of the context arise constraints. So in order to define its response to a particular innovation task, an organisation needs to understand (a) the context and (b) the resulting constraints. The relationship between these three is shown in Figure 15.1.

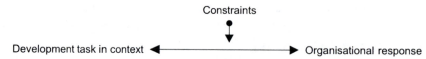

Figure 15.1 Development task in context and organisational response.
Source: von Stamm, B. (1999a). The effects of context and complexity in new product development. Doctoral thesis, London Business School.

Every project will face some constraints, some very obvious – e.g. a given budget – some less so and they may become apparent only later in the process. Constraints arising from the use of a certain material or its characteristics often fall into the latter category. It seems obvious that the development team should want to be aware of as many constraints at the outset as possible but it does not seem that many organisations take the time upfront to investigate the specific context and related constraints. However, unless conscious decisions are made to address constraints, they can become an impediment to the best possible execution of a project. Constraints can be related not only to the organisational response but also to the task itself. An example of a constraint related to the task could be the existence of a dominant design – limiting the choice of technology and we will come back to that in the section on industry context. An example of a constraint related to the organisational response might be the skills or technologies readily available in-house.[1]

While a brief generally defines the objective of a project, reference to constraints is more often than not limited to financial and time aspects. But there are generally many more constraints, implicit in the brief and arising from the company's skills and knowledge, structure and processes, competitive and market position. The organisation has to take these constraints into consideration when deciding on how to approach a development task. Interestingly, it is the innovators who find ways around constraints and sometimes redefine industry norms in the process.

Hence constraints need careful consideration as to whether or how their impact might be minimised or even neutralised, for example by changing the dominant design or employing additional skills. Generally a trade-off will be required. For example, if in order to get a better product you want to change the machinery involved in production you have to invest additional money. If you put more people on a project you might be able to complete it in a shorter time span – but it will be more expensive. Changing the dominant design for a product might grant tremendous income – if it is successful in replacing the existing dominant design, but will cause tremendous losses if it does not.

A reference to constraints in the context of product development can be found in Goel and Pirolli (1992). Their research into the structure of design problem spaces has identified a number of features that are overt in design task environments. They state that, "The constraints on design task environments are generally of two types: (a) nomological and (b) social, political, legal, economic, and so on. The latter consist of rules and conventions and are always negotiable. The former consist of natural laws and are never negotiable. However, the laws of natural law vastly undermine design solutions."

It might be true that legal and economic constraints are negotiable in principle but it is doubtful if the range of actual negotiability is wide. For example, safety regulations for a high-speed train will not be relaxed because they pose a significant constraint on the development of a new train. Each product development takes place in a specific context and there are constraints related to that context.

Gause and Weinberg (1989) refer to a constraint as 'a mandatory condition'. They continue, "in order for the final design solution to be accepted, every constraint must be satisfied". They perceive a constraint to be part of the specification that has to be adhered to, but I consider constraints to provide the initial boundaries for a project. While some constraints are truly unmoveable (e.g. government regulations), it generally depends on the parties involved in the development whether they seek to address them, or operate within their boundaries. In other words, an organisation needs first to identify the constraints, and secondly, it needs to establish whether or not a constraint can be changed and, if it can be changed, what the costs and benefits are.

---

[1] This assumes that the organisation is unable or unwilling to buy in additional expertise.

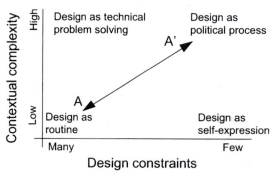

Figure 15.2   Contextual complexity and design activity.
Source: Based on Boisot, M., von Stamm, B. & Griffiths, D. (1995). Integrating design and organisation: a research proposal. Submitted to the Design Council.

A closer look at the interaction between the project beginning, design constraints and the complexity inherent in the design task (contextual complexity) – Figure 15.2 – associates high levels of complexity with 'design as technical problem solving' whereas low contextual complexity and few design constraints tend to be associated with 'design as self-expression'.

However, projects may have elements of both types of design, and a key issue in the management of design is to balance the claims of both. For example, a combination of high contextual complexity and few design constraints will require intense negotiation between the stakeholders involved, that is the further up the curve A–A' a project is located, the more political the negotiation process becomes and designers will find themselves confronting and negotiating with 'silent designers' (see the section on Design in Chapter 1).

The distinction between design as self-expression and design as technical problem solving is made in a similar way by Crawford (1994) – albeit in a different context.[2] His concept, shown in Figure 15.3, bears some resemblance to Figure 15.2 and relating the two one could say that the 'engineer/chemist' represents 'design as technical problem solving' and 'painter/composer' represents 'design as self-expression'.

When a product is fairly new, there are likely to be only a few constraints in terms of standards and regulations. However, over time dominant designs emerge that constrain an organisation's choice of technology and design while at the same time reducing complexity. As the number of constraints on choice of technology increases, a shift takes place from a focus on solving technical problems to a focus on product features and aesthetics.

The point is: an organisation should aim to match the complexity of the task and the complexity of its response. The complexity of organisational response is seen to be reflected by the degree to which cooperation and coordination are facilitated. Looking at existing research for a suggestion on how best to achieve this, one insight is that highly innovative or complex projects are more likely to be successful when conducted within a matrix structure, whereas incremental

---

[2]Crawford developed these categories when discussing idea and concept generation and identifying different types of creativity. He argues that research has identified two types of creativity (artistic creativity and scientific creativity), and that both are required to develop new products.

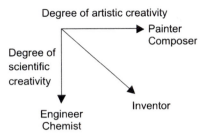

Figure 15.3 Types of creativity.
Source: Crawford, C.M. (1994). *New Product Management.* Reading, MA: Addison-Wesley. Reprinted by permission of McGraw-Hill Companies from Crawford C.M. (1994). *New Product Development.* Copyright © 1994 McGraw-Hill Companies.

innovations can be addressed within a functionally oriented structure (see also Table 3.2, Chapter 3). Two extremes of the spectrum are represented by a functional structure on the one hand and a matrix structure on the other.

One indication useful for determining the most appropriate choice of organisational response can be found in the 'Law of Requisite Variety' (Ross Ashby, 1964). This law states that if a problem is to be solved, the variety of the response must be equal to or greater than the variety of the problem, that is the complexity of a response must at least match the complexity of the problem. The line where contextual complexity equals complexity of organisational response, the 'Line of Requisite Variety', represents an optimal match between the complexity of a given problem and that of the response.

If a company is below the Line of Requisite Variety, it does not – or cannot – use its competencies to its full potential; if a company is above the line, the problem addressed is likely to be addressed in an inadequate way. Positioned either above or below the line the company has two choices:

Above the line:

1.   Enhance organisational response capacity to match design task complexity (either by developing competencies internally or by bringing in outside expertise).
2.   Reduce the complexity of the design task (by breaking the system down into subsystems, i.e. by devising components that can be looked at separately).

Below the line:

1.   Work on products with higher complexity (i.e. of an untapped potential for adding value).
2.   Reduce internal skill base (i.e. outsource less complex tasks).

Examples of products that are above the line are those that have failed to meet their performance requirements – technical or otherwise – such as the early version of the British tilting train, the Advanced Passenger Train (APT). Examples of overemphasising the technical or design aspect of the task could be a Japanese electronic consumer product that has more features than anyone would want to use (overengineered product), and of overemphasising

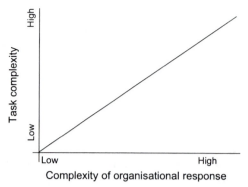

Figure 15.4 Task complexity and organisational response.
Source: von Stamm, B. (1999a). The effects of context and complexity in new product development. Doctoral thesis, London Business School.

the aesthetic aspects of the task could be a building by the Spanish architect Ricardo Bofill such as the airport in Barcelona which looks very good but is highly nonfunctional (overdesigned product).

In other words, being on this line would mean that a company applies just the right structure, competencies and resources necessary to deal with a given task. So the relationship between the task complexity and the organisational response could be illustrated as shown in Figure 15.4.

One issue with an innovative project is that levels of complexity and uncertainty are often not well understood at the outset when the project structure and the key players are chosen. Some actually say that this is a good thing, as project might never get off the ground were problems known at the start.

CONTEXTUAL FACTORS AT THE INDUSTRY LEVEL

While the discussion above referred primarily to the project level, there are also contextual factors at the industry level that are worth considering. We will take a brief look at the following:

- dominance of a particular profession
- speed of change
- related to the above, product life cycles
- norms and industry standards
- the degree of globalisation

In addition we will look at the role of different types of design in different industries.

Professional dominance

Different industries are dominated by different professional backgrounds. For example, fast-moving consumer goods and foods tend to be dominated by marketers, electronic consumer goods by engineers, and pharmaceuticals by researchers and scientists. Why is it important to be aware of that? Let's say that you are an organisation that has its roots in science, with scientists' values dominating the company culture. According to some interviews I conducted scientists can view collaboration as a sign of incompetence. If this is the case, how likely are we to get high-quality internal and external collaboration? And, given that collaboration is a cornerstone of innovation, it is important to be aware of potential internal resistance, and the underlying reasons for it.

Speed of change

A critical influence is the frequency at which new products are brought to market. Think about the computer industry with products introduced today being out of date tomorrow – and Moore's law about computing power doubling every 18 months – whereas the car industry experiences much longer product life cycles. Short product life cycles require different structures, processes and approach than long cycles. To me it seems that aesthetic aspects fall by the wayside of short-lived, technology-driven products such as computers. Is the success of the new Apple due to its technological superiority or its different, appealing design?

But increased speed is not only observed with regards to individual product introduction rates. It seems that more generally the pace of change in business is increasing, requiring organisations to respond to it and adapt. Changes can be induced from within an industry but they are more likely than not triggered by an event outside. Again, participants in the innovation best practice interviews named 'unexpected competition from outside own industry' as one of the major challenges of the future. The internet has been enabled by computer technology – but think about the industries on which it has had an impact: retailing, banking and so forth. So it is not only about bringing products to market faster, it is also about addressing, responding to and countering changes in the wider industry environment quickly.

One word of caution though. Managers often seem to be so caught up in the desire to bring products to market as quickly as possible that shortcuts are taken. But taking shortcuts, particularly during the early stages of a project can have time-consuming and costly consequences later on. Aristotle has said, "Understanding the problem is half the solution." So managers urging project teams to go straight into developing solutions would better be advised to ask the team to verify first that the problem thought to be the issue is indeed the problem for which a solution should be sought. Speed not haste is the motto.

Life cycles and industry norms

Product and industry life cycles have already been referred to above but I'd like to look at them in a bit more detail. They are important for two reasons. First, they determine on what aspect of a product an organisation focuses its effort in order to compete successfully, for example technology or features, product or process. Second, they influence the number of players within an industry. At the birth of a new product category or market there will only be a few players. If the new category is profitable, more players are likely to enter the scene. With increased competition prices decline, often leading to a phase of mergers and acquisitions, that is a reduction in the number of players (see Figure 15.5).

Demands on product development will change over the five stages of a product's life cycle (development, introduction, growth, maturity, decline). With the maturation of the product, a better understanding of customers'

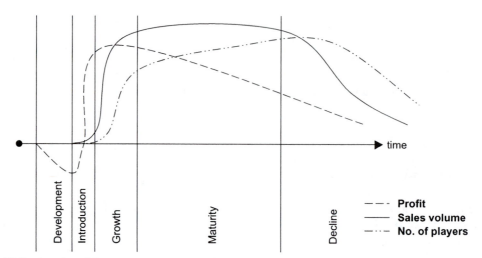

Figure 15.5   Product life cycle.
Source: Adapted from Wright, I. (1998). *Design Methods in Engineering and Product Design*. London: McGraw-Hill.

requirements and an associated shift from product to process innovation demands on product development change and different skill sets are required. This is as true for the overall skill mix in general as for the design skills in particular. But not only that, as Henke *et al.* (1993) state, "As the product moves through its life cycle, fewer functional areas tend to be involved on a continuous basis."

The Sony Walkman may serve as an illustration of design skill requirements changing over time. In the early phases the miniaturisation of the technology was the major concern, that is developing components small but powerful enough to satisfy both the space constraint and quality of sound. Hence, the main focus was on engineering design and technical aspects of the product. At a later stage, when Sony modified the product to capture different market segments – a Walkman for different activities such as jogging, e.g. a waterproof one, customer segments, i.e., for children, and so on – industrial design or even graphic design (packing) became most important.

A further phenomenon of a product's life cycle is the emergence of a dominant design. A dominant design is a single architecture that establishes dominance in a product class. It reduces uncertainty, permits firms to design standardised and interchangeable parts and to optimise organisational processes for volume and efficiency. However, at the same time it also limits the number of choices a company can make in pursuing the development of a particular product. As a consequence of the reduction in uncertainty and a better understanding of the technology, which are characteristic of the emergence of a dominant design, organisational standards, systems and managerial practices evolve.

The very fact that makes the development of existing products easier and allows for continuous incremental improvements can be an obstacle to creativity, radical innovations and openness to change. Because organisational structures, processes and procedures are established and people have become used to certain working methods and being able to rely on their existing knowledge, there can be a tendency to continue working in old ways within new contexts.

We have talked about the fact that the emergence of a dominant design causes a shift from a focus on solving technical problems to a focus on product features and aesthetics. Similarly, Tushman and Anderson (1986) describe a shift from radical to incremental innovations over the course of a product's life cycle. This shift is generally driven by a change in market dynamics, whereby the basis for competition shifts from product innovation to product improvement and differentiation, implying a stronger focus on product features and styling.

A further shift associated with a product's life cycle briefly mentioned above is that from a focus on product innovation to a focus on process innovation. Tidd et al. (2001) comment on the fact that different stages of a product's life cycle are associated with different foci for innovation. While early phases are seen to be characterised by rapid and frequent product innovation and an emphasis on variety, later stages are more likely to be characterised by a fairly stable product concept and a stronger emphasis on process innovation.

Similar to products, industries go through life cycles too and the number of players competing in any industry generally depends on the stage of its life cycle. Think about cars. In the beginning, there were few who believed in the future for the car, it was a product for the rich and famous. With time, more and more competitors entered the market, unit cost came down, and with advancements in other areas (production lines, etc.), the number of cars on the road began to increase. And now, about a century later, we have just been through a phase of consolidation, the latest being the merger of Daimler and Chrysler. A more recent example of a new industry opening up is the worldwide web. We talked about speed earlier. The time to move from 'product of the few' to 'product of the many' has certainly accelerated a lot (think mobile phones, think MP3 players).

Industry norms and standards I would also consider here. While not all of them are binding, adhering to them is often seen as minimum requirement from the customer's point of view. You may be familiar with the concepts of 'qualifier' and 'order winner'. The former refers to a criterion that the minimum requirements have to be fulfilled in order for consumers to consider the product at all; the latter refers to characteristics that sway the consumer's decision in favour of a particular product. Adhering to industry standards and norms is generally considered to be a 'qualifier'. For example, a survey undertaken by the London Business School in 1996 (Temple & von Stamm, 1996) showed that the two most important reasons for introducing ISO 9000 were (a) company reputation and (b) customer requirement.

Globalisation

We have already talked about globalisation and its implication for innovation in Chapter 4. With increasingly instantaneous exchange of information and falling trade barriers, organisations need to look beyond their own national boundaries to understand what is going on in their industry. Even products that were formerly perceived to be tied to national boundaries, such as perhaps cement, have to compete on an increasingly international basis. So while there are still products that are designed

> **No more local goods?**
>
> On the contrary, products will be sold across countries because of their local association: potatoes from Jersey, maple syrup from the east coast of the US, white consumer goods from Germany. Why else do most products have a label declaring where the product has been made?

for and bought in a local market, internet and travelling make it increasingly likely that the number of products to which such conditions apply will shrink. Competition does not only come from within the own national boundaries, it can come from any other country around the globe. Even for perishable products such as fruit, butter and milk. Which makes me wonder what kind of processes these products go through to arrive in our shops looking fresh. In terms of product development it means primarily that for gathering market intelligence companies need to cast their net wider.

One final point in this section of contextual factors at the industry level: innovative companies do not let existing industry constraints hold them back. An example here is BT which has developed a new strategy that can only work if they can influence and change existing industry conditions. In order to being able to realise their strategy they had to collaborate not only with suppliers and customers but also with the government, regulators and even competitors. With their new strategy, announced in June 2004 and called 21CN (21st century network), they have responded to the convergence of IT-based and IT-supported products and services. Traditionally different services such as voice have required their own discrete networks with discrete infrastructure, systems, management and services to support them. This, resulting in numerous different devices, phone numbers, services providers, has been highly inconvenient for consumers. 21CN has been designed to provide an end-to-end Internet Protocol (IP)-based network, consolidating BT's 16 separate network platforms into one. Crossing the boundaries of a number of industries would not have been achieved by BT working behind closed doors. Only opening up and involving all parties affected by their strategy in its implementation allowed BT to translate their plans.[3]

Types of design and types of industries

The four aspects above – professional dominance, speed of change, life cycle and industry norms, and degree of globalisation – will vary from industry to industry. Another aspect that varies from industry to industry are the kinds of design services that are typically used. We will briefly look at different types of design likely to be most used or most appropriate in the following:

- fast-moving consumer goods
- white consumer goods
- investment goods
- luxury goods
- pharmaceutical products
- services
- non-profit and government organisations

Fast-moving consumer goods

Fast moving consumer goods, packaged consumer goods and foods will most likely have significant input from packaging and brand design. More recently structural packaging has gained popularity and this often means that the packaging is becoming part of the product offering, for example pump sprays being used instead of the chemical, environmentally harmful versions. Products are sold based on the strength of their individual brand – often consumers don't even know which company is behind the product. Would you necessarily know who is behind

---

[3]For more information please visit BT's website on http://www.btplc.com/21CN/.

Bounty, Ariel or Pear's Soap? The success of such products is generally quite sensitive to the advertising spend. Such products are purchased frequently and repeat purchase generally depends on the quality of the previous experience.

White consumer goods

In terms of design, white consumer goods will require input primarily from engineering and industrial design. Bought less frequently, they rely more on the reputation of the manufacturing company. Quality and reliability are traits for which many a consumer is willing to pay a premium. However, it also seems that these products are often particularly technology driven which can mean that design aspects – usability, aesthetics, sometimes even functionality – may suffer. Think about washing machines with endless programmes no one ever uses or the confusing number of buttons of a remote control. However, companies that can combine great technology and great ergonomic and aesthetical design, such as Apple or BMW are on to a winner.[4]

Investment goods

Even more so than with white consumer goods, investment goods rely on the quality of the engineering design, and company reputation is even more important. Solutions are often bespoke and one-off (plant and machinery). Here 'how it looks' is even more frequently compromised for technical capability and functionality. Managers in such companies often underestimate the contribution design can make to functionality, and user friendliness.

Luxury goods

I have listed this category separately, even though you can find top of the range products as a sub-segment in most of the other categories too. This is probably the category where the aesthetics, quality and brand name are the most important. The brand name is often that of the designer behind the luxury brand/company – think about fashion houses. Succession and institutionalisation of the brand name can be difficult challenges facing such organisations. Products are bought not only for what they are but perhaps even more importantly, what they stand for. It is often the lifestyle represented by the product that customers acquire. People are willing to pay a premium to be seen to be part of the club. I sometimes wonder whether it is perceived rather than actual quality that persuades people to buy ... it is interesting to note that the association you buy with a product seems to become more and more important.

Pharmaceuticals

Again, I feel this merits a separate category as specific conditions apply here: long development lead times, high R&D expenditure, the reality of patent implications. Many products are dependent on being prescribed by doctors which means that the end user and 'purchasing unit', for example the doctor, are different. This has implications for marketing and advertising. Unlike prescription drugs, over-the-counter (OTC) products rely increasingly on graphic

---

[4] Though of course it is debatable whether BMW belongs in this category or rather in the category of luxury goods.

and packaging designers to help sell their products. The quality and success of the product depends primarily on the quality of the R&D staff. At least in prescription drugs design (by designers) plays a very limited role. Having said that, if the drug is administered through a device as is the case with asthma inhalers, involving industrial designers can be of huge advantage.

Service providers

Here people often think that design is not so important – but have you tried to fill in any forms of insurance companies or banks? How many times have you despaired at nonsensical questions or bad layout? It is here that graphic design plays an important role and can make a huge difference to the perceived quality of the service.

Non-profit organisations (including charities and government)

Design here probably takes mainly the shape of graphic design (publications, posters, etc.) and architecture. One difference I can think of is that such organisations need to ensure more than others that any design reflects 'political correctness' or is aligned with and representative of what the organisation stands for. If Greenpeace were to use highly glossy brochures it would make their arguments less credible. I would like to emphasise the 'even more so' as all good design should support the image and value of the organisation it represents.

CONTEXTUAL FACTORS AT THE NATIONAL LEVEL

There are certain aspects of the wider national environment that can influence an organisation's approach to design and development such as:

- Economic and legislative conditions:

    ◦ the overall economic conditions, i.e. boom or bust, tax and investment policy (e.g. government policy towards subsidies)

    ◦ legislation, including patenting laws, environmental as well as health and safety regulations

    ◦ business-specific conditions such as company law and structure of company ownership.

- Cultural differences

    ◦ national characteristics, preferences and values (culture), e.g. focus on design and aesthetics in countries such as Italy, focus on engineering and quality in Germany, focus on natural materials in Scandinavian countries, and so on

    ◦ attitude towards environmental issues, i.e. recycling of packaging is the responsibility of the manufacturer (in Germany), penalties on not separating rubbish (Denmark), speed restrictions in many countries, etc.

    ◦ cultural differences at the company and departmental levels.

These aspects will be explored in a bit more detail below.

Table 15.2 Differences in the wider economic environment

UK	France
Conservative government	Socialist government
Hands-off approach to industry	National hi-tech projects
Let the market decide	Mixed industries
Privatisation	Joint state–industry projects
Competition for capital projects	National champions

Source: Based on Kemp, R. (1993). *The European High Speed Rail Network*. Manchester: GEC Alsthom Transport

Economic and legislative conditions

To illustrate the point, Table 15.2 compares the wider political and economic environment in the UK and France.

These differences impact, for example, on investment decisions and the availability of public funding for projects 'of national interest'. This means that if a project is considered to be of national importance, such as the high-speed trains, significant amounts of money are made available to pursue the idea. The risk and uncertainty associated with innovative projects are accepted – and financed – for the greater good.

But the influence of governments can come in various shapes and sizes. Not only the attitude towards investment and subsidies has an influence, there are also regulations and legislation that can have a profound impact. Take for example health and safety regulations. They impact on various aspects of the design and development of new products: they can impact the choice of material, on thickness of glass for windows, fire-resistant quality of upholstery material, what materials are usable in conjunction with food, and so on. Such restrictions can act as a damper for innovation as many organisations might be reluctant to follow the lengthy and expensive testing procedures that are necessary to get a new material or technology approved. For example, to have a new and different disc joint for shaft couplings in cars approved the company would have to go through crash tests and procedures before it would be acceptable to a car manufacturer (see GKN case study in Chapter 20).

Some of these contextual issues might be known at the outset, others will arise during the course of the development. Needless to say that to avoid costly changes later on, it is important to be aware of what might be applicable to the product in question at the outset of a development process. This is especially important for innovative products where parts may have to go through a separate approval process.

But, particularly for large-scale projects, governmental influence can go beyond this. Let me give you another example from the Eurostar, the high-speed train connecting the capitals of the UK, France and Belgium. One critical determinant during the set-up phase of the project was the involvement of the governments. As the tunnel project was seen to be highly prestigious, not least because it was a milestone in engineering history, the governments of both France and the UK were determined that 'their' companies should have an involvement not only in the development of the tunnel but also in the train that would run through it. They therefore applied pressure on the initially competing consortia from the UK and France to get together and submit a joint proposal. When a bit later the Belgian government decided that Brussels too should be linked into the high-speed train network, it was more or less self-explanatory that Belgian companies would join the consortium. In the end the manufacturing consortia, calling itself the Trans Manche Super Train Group (TMSTG) consisted of 10 companies, four each from the UK and France and two from Belgium. It seems hardly accidental that the split more or less reflects the split of the financial backing for the project: UK and France 44% each, Belgium 12%. This split did not only apply to the engineering task, it was also applied to the design task, resulting in the British design consultancy, Jones Garrard, being asked to design the nose of the train and the driver's cab, the French designer, Roger Tallon, ADSA, being responsible for the interior and the livery (i.e. exterior) and the Belgian designer for the toilets, overhead luggage racks and the seats. It is not difficult to imagine that the multi-company, multinational set up had far-reaching consequences for the management and execution of the project as well as the results.

Well, does it? Thinking about it, for the successful completion of any project cooperation between all parties involved is essential. Successful cooperation generally does not come easy but in this particular situation it is made more difficult because the partners did not come together on their own accord. The individual companies forming TSMTG had not been selected primarily based on what they would have to contribute to the team but because they had been part of the original competing consortia. It was not 'what skills do we need and who has them' but 'that is who we have, who can do what'. Admittedly, the original consortia had each been assembled to represent all skills required – but of course that meant that individual tasks could be performed by either a French or a British company. So a way was needed to be found to split the workload that was acceptable to all. Again, the financial backing was used to decide what percentage share should be carried out by each country. As a consequence tasks were allocated not only on expertise but also to fulfil the quota. For the manufacture this meant that some parts were dual sourced, that is produced on two different sites. For example, half of the main transformers were manufactured in Stafford, UK and half in St Ouen near Paris.

Even though the split of the workload according to the financial involvement was very fair, it also caused additional costs due to transporting components back and forth across the three countries. One example of components being shipped around several manufacturing sites was the inverter module which is part of the motor bloc. Its odyssey is shown in the Figure 15.6.

On top of that they had to overcome language barriers and cope with geographical dispersion, which brings us to the last point, the cultural context.

Cultural context

Culture is an important factor to consider. But what is culture? Kroeber and Kluckhohn (1952) give the following definition: "Culture consists of patterns, explicit and implicit of and for behaviour acquired and transmitted by symbols, constituting the distinctive achievement of human groups, including their embodiment in artefacts. The essential core of culture consists of traditional (i.e. historically derived and selected) ideas and especially their attached values. Culture systems may, on the one hand, be considered as products of action, on the other, as conditioning elements of future action."

In understanding the concept of culture three aspects of this definition are of particular importance: (a) that some of the cultural patterns are implicit; (b) that those patterns have evolved over time (historically derived); and (c) that these patterns influence future behaviour. What it actually means is that people have developed patterns of behaviour that are based on their experience and influenced by their environment. This means two things: firstly,

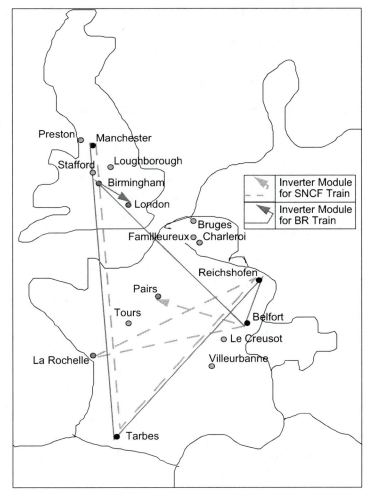

Figure 15.6   Odyssey of the inverter module.
Source: von Stamm, B. (1999a). The effects of context and complexity in new product development. Doctoral thesis, London Business School

to someone within a country, within its culture, particular traits might no longer be obvious. He or she is so used to them that certain values are built into products without questioning – that's the way they've always done it. At the national level one might want to think of engineering-driven solutions in Germany, with an emphasis on quality and durability, design-driven solutions in Italy, and so on. This means that when people go out to buy a product these often implicit values are the 'qualifiers' according to which products are selected for closer consideration. And, as such aspects are implicitly expected, they may not be raised as an issue in traditional market research – it is so obvious that no one will mention it. Similar values exist at the company level. If not acknowledged and understood, they can prove to be major obstacles to innovation.

And secondly, more often than not, people will approach a task in the way that they are accustomed to without investigating alternative approaches. Generally, alternatives are only then considered when the normally followed approaches fail. If that is true for cultural behaviour at the national level, it is likely to be equally true at the company level. This is also pointed out by Adler (1986), "Our ways of thinking, feeling, and behaving as human beings are neither random nor haphazard but are profoundly influenced by our cultural heritage. [...] For years people have thought that organisations were beyond the influence of culture and that they were only determined by technology and task. Today we know that work is not simply a mechanistic outgrowth of either technology or task. At every level, culture profoundly influences organisational behaviour."

It seems that organisations still have to address three issues: (a) they have to acknowledge that there actually are some cultural differences between people of different nationalities; (b) they further need to be aware that cultural differences can exist between companies of the same national background; and (c) they have to move away from assuming that one way is superior to the other. Instead they should focus on finding ways that combine the strengths of each culture, taking advantage of the diversity. Hence, it is important to understand that there is no 'right' and no 'wrong', just different approaches and each approach will have its merits and problems.

Within cultural differences, differences in language deserve particular mention. 'Language differences' here refers to the fact that different groups of people tend to use different vocabularies. Such groups of people can be defined by national or geographical boundaries, by social boundaries, by company boundaries or even departmental boundaries. Or even worse, people with different backgrounds may have different meanings and associations with certain words – which are not necessarily shared by others who nevertheless use the same words. This can make people believe that they have established a shared understanding while they are actually talking about different things. You may want to have another look at Figure 3.2 in Chapter 3. The acknowledgement of the existence of such differences is important as ignoring them can lead to costly mistakes. Language is also important in another context, corporate headquarters must ensure that a consistent and clear message is presented throughout its global operation. To quote Patrick Sim, Vice President of Nortel's Supply Chain Materials Management, as saying, "Everyone, no matter who they are globally, must get the same information and get it in a consistent fashion" (in Zuckerman, 2001).

But it is not only cultural differences at the national level that have an impact. Cultural differences at the company and departmental level are of equal importance.

Departmental and professional level

Research has been undertaken into cultural differences between a variety of departments: between designers on the one hand and engineers and scientists on the other (Cross, 1993; Dormer, 1993), between designers and managers (Walker, 1990), between marketing and R&D personnel (Griffin & Hauser, 1996), as well as between marketing and engineering (Workman, 1995). Any inherent differences have been reinforced over time through training and exposure to other like-minded people.

For example, Biemans (1993, in Ulijn et al., 2000) lists common mutual misperceptions of engineers and marketers: "The latter believe that scientists/engineers have no sense of time, costs, service, or competitive advantage. They hide in the lab and continue developing a product without strategic planning, holding standardization and technology sacrosanct, and expecting the client to adapt. The marketers are, in the eyes of the scientists/engineers, aggressive, demanding, and unrealistic. They want everything NOW, want to deliver a product before it is ready, are always in a hurry and impatient, or cannot decide what they want. As a result, they promise more than they can guarantee, often change the specifications because they have no sense of technology, have no trust in scientists/engineers, and are not interested in their problems. Finally, scientists/engineers think that marketers focus on unrealistic targets." You may want to have another look at Figure 3.2.

An interviewee from the innovation best practice research pointed out that in their experience, "Scientists may understand the rationale for collaboration but in their hearts would not buy into it. To scientists collaboration is a sign of weakness." For global innovation, for which collaboration is paramount, such an attitude can provide a significant obstacle.

Company and national levels

There is little doubt that each organisation has its own unique style. Procter & Gamble and Unilever may both be in the FMCG business but each has a quite different set of values and behaviours. Compatibility of company culture is an important aspect for successful intercompany collaboration, be it on a project basis, through joint ventures, mergers or acquisitions.

An additional layer of complexity is added when a company operates in more than one country in which case managers have to understand and manage the interface between their own and the host country's culture. As Uljin et al. (2000) point out, "When a multinational firm, such as Philips, operates in the United States, it is accepted almost as a U.S. firm since it is loosely related to the individualistic U.S. society where interaction is explicit, low context, and monochronic. On the other hand, to be successful in Japan, Philips should behave as a Japanese firm, where national culture and corporate culture overlap in a tight, collectivistic society where interaction is implicit, high context, and polychronic. High context cultures use informal implicit ways of communication, while low context cultures need to state messages explicitly in written text."

And perhaps most significant are differences at the national level. Hofstede (1980, 1991) has written extensively on the issue of national differences. The five dimensions of culture he has introduced (power distance, collectivism versus individualism, femininity versus masculinity, uncertainty avoidance, and long-term versus short-term orientation) are used widely to understand and explain differences between cultures. For example, most Western countries are individualistic cultures whereas consensus and group-oriented behaviour can be found in East Asian countries.

These cultural differences are reflected in how meetings are run, what form of communication is acceptable, and, especially important in the context of new product development, how relationships and collaboration are approached. Uljin et al. (2000) cite Weggeman (1989) and Nonaka and Takeuchi (1995) who suggest that Japan pursues an innovation strategy quite different to the West. The Japanese learn implicitly through oral communication, rather than explicitly by written instructions. He also points out that other dimensions such as uncertainty avoidance and power distance, loose/tight individualistic/collectivistic and implicit and explicit might affect the innovative capacity of a firm, and poses the question, "How important are uncertainty avoidance and power distance to the innovative capacity of a firm?"

When asked whether he would carry out a multinational project again, Daniel Brun, the representative of SNCF (the French railway company) on the International Project Group said, "I would say, probably not, it's very time consuming. Trying to reconcile what I'd call Latin culture and British culture is still very difficult" (Evamy, 1994). It also seems that this was the most underestimated challenge. While the differences in project management styles and design preferences were most obvious, there were also differences regarding the judgement of who the customer would be, and the wider economic environment.

Table 15.3 Differences between SNCF and BR

SNCF	BR
Is the design authority	Is customer, supplier is responsible for design
Approval of drawings	Design scrutiny
Loose contracts	Strict legal contracts
Established contacts are important	Lowest bid wins
Informal contacts to resolve problems	Disputes resolved by the contract
International technological leadership	—

Source: Based on Kemp, R. (1993). *The European High Speed Rail Network*. Manchester: GEC Alsthom Transport

Let me give you some examples from the Eurostar of the consequences resulting from differences in national culture, and a lack of understanding them.

Project Management

An aspect not fully anticipated by participants – at least not initially – was the fact that each country had a different approach to project management. Differences of approach showed in the tendering process and even more so in expectations of how the relationship between railway and manufacturer would be managed. While SNCF was used to taking a very active role in the design process, BR was used to giving a design specification to the manufacturer and seeing him, again, more or less, once the product is delivered.[5] Some of the differences between BR and SNCF are shown in Table 15.3.

Meetings

The French and British had also quite differing views on the meaning and conduct of meetings. The French would have a series of informal meetings, sounding out options and then go into a meeting where a decision would be reached without too much further discussion. The British, however, would expect to share information and facts during the meeting, have a discussion to elaborate on different options and views, and then make a decision based on the preceding discussion. The two expectations could not be more opposing. As a result participants were confused and actual decision making took a long time.

Different Design Taste

Even though there might have been an element of national pride, there were certainly real cultural differences in taste. Bob Illingworth, BR's representative on the IPG, commented that, "the talk about regional differences wasn't all bullshit. There were big differences in taste" (in Evamy, 1994). An illustration of the 'cultural differences' in design taste might be the market testing of the seat for the Eurostar. Both the French and Belgian designer suggested a seat for the Eurostar. The two models were then market tested. Without knowing which designer had designed which

---

[5] In this context it is quite interesting that the English word 'scrutiny' was until 1993 translated with the French word 'approbation' (approval).

seat the French preferred the seat designed by the French designer, the Belgians preferred the one designed by the Belgian designer. Despite all the talk about internationalisation or even globalisation of consumer taste and despite the fact that the European market is becoming more and more integrated, there seem to be differences in national taste that cannot be denied.

Industry journalist Michael Evamy (1994) commented, "An excess of widely diverging advice on the design, colours and finishes in the train has left its mark. Cultural divides between the three railways were wider than anyone anticipated. The resulting entity is a frenzy of old, new, cool, warm, kitsch and hi-tech; it's all there, and the disappointment is all the greater after the excitement of the highly individual external styling." Hence the attempt to combine design input from three countries into a unified, well-balanced whole led to an amalgamation of design tastes, resulting in a compromise at the lowest common denominator rather than a combination of best designs.

The Customer

Finally, there also seem to have been differing views as to which customer (end user) the Eurostar would be serving and whose marketing information was more trustworthy. Tony Howard, who was BR's deputy head of design at the time said, "The French were very good on engineering. I think we brought a commercial realism to the project. We were ahead in our knowledge of the commercial market of the future. BR had split up into sectors, so we were already tailoring the interiors of Intercity trains to be very different from, say, regional trains in North Wales" (in Evamy, 1994). However, Roger Tallon, who had a different view, said, "SNCF have been carrying out qualitative studies of their client's expectations since 1973. BR, on the other hand, have been practising a marketing of 'conviction', which varies according to changes in personnel or situation."

In the end the layout of the interior was very closely modelled on the TGV. However, the Eurostar serves a different customer profile, that is the Eurostar has far more leisure travellers than the TGV, and problems arose from a lack of luggage space. During the summer season problems became so severe that the railways had to employ extra staff to administer luggage storage and eventually had to take out some seats to provide additional luggage space.

Of course there are many more areas where cultural differences exist – for example, another is how companies measure corporate success. But I think these examples from the Eurostar case study make clear how important it is to understand and acknowledge national differences.

I'd like to finish with an anecdote from the Eurostar case study that illustrates what happens when cultural differences are not acknowledged and discussed and decisions are based on assumptions rather than a deep understanding. Those who have travelled on the Eurostar may recall the pink-frosted lampshades in the first class carriages. The French press referred to them as 'typical English pink', whereas the UK press associated them with 'typical bohemian French'. Each side thought it was the other country's taste that had influenced the decision while no one seemed to be happy with it. If that happens when coordinating tastes between three countries, and all of them European, what would happen to a global product?

16 Informal networks and the management of knowledge

Another part in the jigsaw that makes an innovative organisation are informal networks. It is about knowing who to go to when you need a particular bit of information or a particular skill, who can do a particular job for you – or who is the right person to influence decision makers. Such informal networks played an important role in the Roche case study – but also in others. In the BBC case study it was Mike Milne's web-based discussion groups that helped to find people with the right skills and attitude. In the Black & Decker case it was Lawrie Cunningham knowing that Nigel Robson would take the design task and turn it into something really exciting.

In this chapter we will look at the role of informal networks for innovation and the way managers attempt to formalise such information networks, namely what is generally known as knowledge management.

INFORMAL NETWORKS

The reason why informal networks are so important for innovative projects is that it is often not possible to identify what kind of skills will be needed in the course of the project at the outset. Therefore being able to find the right skills if and when required can be essential.

There is one issue with informal networks: they are 'owned' by individuals, and when these individuals move on so does their knowledge. In Chapter 13 we have already mentioned the negative implications downsizing and restructuring have for innovation, exactly for that reason. In the past informal networks have been severely disrupted when round after round of downsizing and restructuring have taken out layers of middle management – those people who often know who knows what in the organisation – and has allowed experts to leave – those who know what. People close to retirement with a fast body of tacit knowledge acquired over the working life, and those who can easily find new jobs elsewhere, specialists and experts are the ones most likely to take up redundancy and early retirement offers, leaving gaping holes in informal knowledge networks.

Only slowly are managers beginning to realise the value of informal networks, and the consequences of destroying them. One consequence of a nonfunctional informal network can be the hiring of external expertise even though the skills required might readily be available in-house (Hodgson, 1999). Those managers who are aware of the value of such informal networks are seeking ways to understand informal networks better, and find ways to draw on their value.

A tool widely used for understanding networks is the so-called Social Network Analysis. It basically maps the interactions between different members of a team, within the team as well as outside. Figure 16.1 illustrates the outcome of such an analysis whereby the large circles signify team members and the small circles represent external ties.

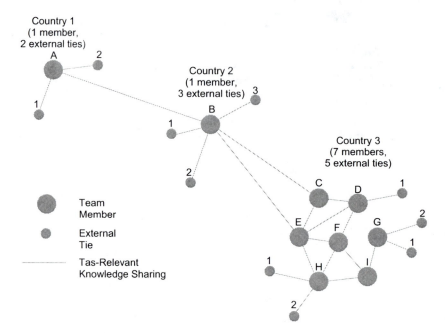

Figure 16.1   Example of Social Network Analysis output.

Through the analysis critical network nodes can be identified. Nodes tend to be the people who know everyone, and everything. Knowing who is at the centre of informal networks can help in several ways. For one, managers can try to ensure that an effort is made to keep these people, for example in the case of voluntary redundancies.[1] Knowing who the network nodes are is also helpful when seeking a person with a particular competence; the nodes are likely to know where to find them.

Understanding informal networks and identifying key people only seems to have moved up the agenda more recently. While the awareness of the value of informal knowledge has been around a long time, ways to access or capture it have changed. In the past the focus was more on putting infrastructures in place, which aids the capture of such knowledge.

Expert databases are one way of capturing people's areas of expertise. Hodgson (1999) has identified the following advantages of such databases:

- Elimination of rework and duplication of effort by linking together individuals working in similar areas.
- A reduction in cycle time and costs through quicker resolution of problems.
- Increased transfer of best practices.

However, she also points out that managers establishing such a database must be clear about its purpose. Is it an experts database or a skills database that is needed? A list of other questions to be asked before starting to set up an experts database is shown in Box 16.1. Hodgson describes an experts database as selective, assuming that some

---

[1] Though it is of course also these people who often volunteer to go first as they are the ones having a great network through which they can find a new job.

Box 16.1   What managers should ask when setting up an experts database

- What is the purpose of the database?
- How will experts be identified and selected?
- Will inclusion be voluntary?
- What are the responsibilities of the experts who are listed?
- What information will be included in the expert's profile?
- What keyword list/thesaurus will be used to standardise expertise descriptions?
- Will profile information undergo a review process?
- What security and access controls will be needed?
- How will data be maintained, by whom, and how often?

Source: Reproduced from Hodgson (1999)

---

people have more knowledge than others, due to their education and/or experience. Such a database is used to create networks and linkages between different parts of the organisation. She also suggests that expert databases can facilitate the elicitation and sharing of tacit knowledge.[2]

A skills database on the other hand is more inclusive and can provide information on just about anyone in the organisation. Hodgson suggests that such a database would generally be used by the human resource department to identify personnel for project teams of particular job placements.

In my view the problem with the experts database is who actually identifies the experts. While Hodgson suggest five possible avenues (see Box 16.2), I would argue that it is sometimes the most unlikely people that have some relevant experience, and this may only be known by a few. Another reason for being more inclusive, especially in the context of innovation, is that you may not be aware what kinds of skills you may need for an innovative project. Giving people the opportunity to provide insights into skills and expertise, areas of interest and involvement in past projects (possibly even outside work) will ensure that all that employees have to offer can be harnessed. However, this means that the database can be quite large which makes good and easy-to-use search facilities absolutely necessary. The last section of this chapter, 'The management of knowledge' gives the example of BP, which have successfully introduced a knowledge management database. Before we go into deeper into why the management of knowledge is important, and what companies can do about it, let us have a brief look at what 'knowledge' actually means.

Box 16.2   How to select experts (based on Hodgson, 1999)

Peer Recommendation
Experts are identified by their peers.

---

[2] Tacit knowledge is knowledge that exists in people's heads and that is difficult to codify, i.e. make accessible for other people. It is most likely to be shared and passed on through 'learning on the job' and observation. See also section below on 'What is knowledge?'

Management Recommendation
Based on the assumption that management has insights into their staff's areas of expertise through annual reviews etc.
Awards Recognition
Identifying individuals that have received awards, e.g. for innovation or quality improvements.
Publications
Internal and external publications such as articles, patents, internal reports.
Self-Nomination
Can help to ensure that an important person is not missed but assumes that everyone would be confident enough to put themselves forward.

WHAT IS KNOWLEDGE?

We can know more than we can tell.

Michael Polanyi (1966)

There is often confusion about what the following three terms mean – data, information and knowledge, and knowledge management – and how they are different from one another. Data is basically the raw material, the facts and figures, without any categorisation or analysis. For the latter three Quintas *et al.* (1997) provide the following definitions:

- Information is organised facts and data.

- Knowledge consists of truths and beliefs, perspectives and concepts, judgement and expectations, methodologies and know how (Gurteen suggests a much simpler definition of knowledge. It reads: "A [more useful] definition of knowledge is that it is about know-how and know-why"[3]).

- Knowledge management is the process of continually managing knowledge of all kinds to meet existing and emerging needs, to identify and exploit existing and acquired knowledge assets and to develop new opportunities.

So knowledge is distinguished from information and data in that an interpretation is applied to it. This also means that knowledge is something that is developed by individuals, and that the quality of the knowledge depends on that individual's insights and expertise. Nonaka (1991) comments, "Creating new knowledge is not simply a matter of processing objective information. Rather, it depends on tapping the tacit and often highly subjective insights, intuitions, and hunches of employees. The means of making use of such knowledge are often soft – taking the form of slogans, metaphors, and symbols – but they are indispensable for continuous innovation."

He distinguishes two different types of knowledge: tacit and explicit. He describes explicit knowledge as follows, "Explicit knowledge is formal and systematic. For this reason it can be easily communicated and shared, in product

---

[3] Brackets inserted by author.

specifications or a scientific formula or a computer program. Tacit knowledge on the other hand is not separable from the individual who holds it, it is very personal." Nonaka comments, "It is hard to formalize and, therefore, difficult to communicate to others. Tacit knowledge has an important cognitive dimension. It consists of mental models, beliefs, and perspectives so ingrained that we take them for granted, and therefore cannot easily articulate them." He suggests that the ability to tap into tacit knowledge is one that characterises what he calls 'knowledge-creating' companies. The four patterns of knowledge creation Nonaka identifies are described in Box 16.3.

Box 16.3   Nonaka's four basic patterns for creating knowledge

- Tacit to tacit – socialisation (person to person – because their knowledge never becomes explicit, it cannot easily be leveraged by the organisation as a whole).

- Explicit to explicit – combination (combining existing pieces of knowledge which does not really extend the company's existing knowledge base).

- Tacit to explicit – articulation (learning and sharing it with a group).

- Explicit to tacit – internalisation (new knowledge becomes part of thinking pattern).

He considers figurative language and symbolism (e.g. metaphors) to be the most powerful tool for converting tacit knowledge into explicit knowledge as it provides a clear sense of direction.

The ability to access tacit knowledge is very important – but there are also problems associated with it, as Quintas et al. (1997) point out, "Lots of what employees know (their tacit knowledge) reflects the past that we are trying to escape." This means that existing knowledge can often hold innovation back. If people are too aware of constraints, of what is possible and what is not – or rather, what they consider to be possible or not, based on their previous experience – they might miss great opportunities to innovate. It is those who believe that the impossible is possible, despite of what everyone is telling them, who are the great innovators.

THE IMPORTANCE OF KNOWLEDGE MANAGEMENT

Lots of innovations depend on knowledge which has long been known but not applied to the current problem.

Quintas *et al.* (1997)

Minimising the impact of the destruction of informal networks through redundancies and retirement is one reason why managers engage in knowledge management. But there are other reasons that organisations striving to become more innovative should consider a formal knowledge management process. Innovation happens when making new connections, connections that have not existed before – applying laser technology to fix eye problems or using microwaves to heat food.

In his 'Report on the Second Comparative Study of Knowledge Creation Conference', held June 1998 in St Gallen, Switzerland Rumizen (1998) uses the Unliever case study as an illustration of the fact that "Many organisations are beginning to recognise the need to manage knowledge asset to meet business needs." A summary of the Unilever case study is shown in Box 16.4.

Box 16.4   The Unilever case study

Unilever has realised that making its knowledge access fully productive is one of the preconditions for fulfilling its corporate purpose, as well as helping to avoid the repeating of mistakes. They have identified four stages of organisational development in the management of knowledge:

1.   Sharing – improve sharing of knowledge and best practices which often involves the changing of cultural norms and creating social networks to create an open mindset.

2.   Leveraging – emphasise ways in which knowledge can be made more productive, including releasing experts from the routine work of re-answering frequently asked questions, and identifying ways of gaining new revenue streams from knowledge-related services and products.

3.   Creating knowledge – gain new knowledge from genuine insight, creativity and the ability to recombine existing sets of knowledge in new ways. This requires a tolerance for failure, time for reflection, high levels of trust and organisational mechanisms for the cross-fertilisation of different knowledge cores and ideas.

4.   Competing with knowledge – examining the knowledge potential of an organisation or business unit to uncover an opportunity to reposition the business in terms of competitive capability or customer/consumer value proposition.

Solving the problems and meeting the opportunities in each of these stages involves three convergent elements:

1.   Knowledge processes – including identification, acquisition, mapping, storing, accessing, distributing, leveraging and using knowledge.

2.   Technology enablers – including information systems, document retrieval, groupware, corporate intranet, knowledge-based systems, etc.

3.   Organisational alignment – leadership is a critical part of alignment, together with rewards, roles, mind set, structure and openness.

Source: Based on Rumizen, M.C. (1998). Report on the Second Comparative Study of Knowledge Creation Conference. *Journal of Knowledge Management,* **2**, 77–81.

THE MANAGEMENT OF KNOWLEDGE

The capture of 'who knows what' has become one important aspect of knowledge management. Another aspect is to store and make available any information on past and current projects, and in a way idea management[4] can be

---

[4]Idea management and suggestion schemes will be discussed in more detail in Chapter 21.

classed as another aspect of knowledge management. In fact, I would suggest that all major stages of new product development should be covered in a company's approach towards knowledge management:

- idea management (from idea generation to idea selection)
- development and review
- commercialisation and monitoring

I will explain briefly what I mean and why I believe it is important.

Idea management

Idea management involves the storage of ideas generated in focused sessions as well as through those coming from suggestion schemes. To keep track of ideas, what happens to them, why a certain idea is selected, and why others are rejected can provide a powerful trail that helps understand an organisation's innovation projectory. Keeping information on ideas that have been rejected as well as those that have been selected is important for two reasons. First, when the same or similar idea comes up again it can be checked why it has been rejected previously, and whether the reasons for rejection are still valid. The other is that ideas that do not fit within an organisation's innovation strategy might still be great ideas, which means it should be investigated whether they can be sold off. The earlier example of the Xerox lab comes to mind, which generated so many significant inventions but did not realise their potential.

Development and review

Once ideas have been chosen for development again there is great value in tracking their progress. What went right and what went wrong during the development, and why? What lessons can be learned and how can they be fed back into future projects? It is at this stage that the experts or skills database comes in handy. Who has been working on similar projects, who has the right skills? Quick access to such information at any time during the project can save a lot of time and money (particularly if it helps to avoid buying in outside experts). Finally, while most organisations are getting better at generating data and information on projects due to the use of the stage-gate process (though often this is not stored in a systematic and easily accessible way), it seems true that most organisations could increase their learning by undertaking 'post mortems' of those ideas that have not made it to market.

Commercialisation and monitoring

But even once the product has been introduced to market the learning is not over. What is the reception in the market, how does the product or service perform? Is there anything to be learned from competitors' reactions? Are sales or market shares targets met? And so on.

Despite powerful arguments for the use of knowledge management many organisations struggle with it. Systems are put in place but are not used. The most frequently used arguments as to why companies are not engaging more in the active management of their knowledge asset is the lack of time. However, my question would be, is it not more

Table 16.1 Knowledge Management – Challenges and Possible Solutions

Challenge	Possible solutions
• How to ensure consistency of the quality of information inputted into the system	• Provide guidelines to what kind of data is to be entered, provide glossaries or thesaurus • Train people to use the database; one company asks people to sign a 'code of conduct'
• How to keep information up to date and relevant	• Ensure that time is scheduled for maintenance and upkeeping tasks • Appoint a dedicated database manager
• How to make sure that learnings and insights are fed back into future projects	• Schedule consultation of database during the early stages of a project's development • Close projects properly, i.e. a review of activities and issues should be undertaken

time consuming *not* to manage knowledge, repeat mistakes, and spend time and money on finding the right skills if and when needed?

However, there are also some challenges for the database-based management of knowledge. Table 16.1 lists the three major ones, and suggests some.

Box 16.5 summarises an interview and an article with John Browne, CEO of British Petroleum, both published a few years ago in the *Harvard Business Review* (Anonymous, 1997a; Prokesch, 1997).

Box 16.5 BP's approach to knowledge management

John Browne, CEO of BP explains, "The aim of this computer network is to allow people to work cooperatively and share knowledge quickly and easily regardless of time, distance, and organizational boundaries."

The network consists of a large number of high-specification personal computers (including videoconferencing capability, electronic blackboards, scanners, faxes, and groupware) that allow their users to work virtually, and access the company's rich database of information.

In addition BP has established an intranet on which everyone within BP can create his or her own home page which serves a number of purposes.

• Functional experts describe the experience they have to offer.
• The sharing of technical data on a wide range of subjects

- The sharing of contacts.
- Information about programs and processes available for technical areas relevant to oil extraction and refinement.
- Dedicated sites for each technology discipline.
- Sites for the general managers of all the business units in BP Exploration and Production (BPX), listing their current projects and performance agendas.

The realisation that working virtually would require new behaviours meant that about one-third of the $12 million spent on the pilot programme in 1995 went to behavioural scientists.

Interesting also that signing up to the network was voluntary. Browne commented, "After about six months, we suddenly found out that a lot of people in other groups were asking, 'How do we get one?' Some people were bootlegging and buying the stuff on their own."

In the year following the pilot Browne made virtual networking available to everyone in BP; however, they had to pay for it out of their own budgets. No one seemed to mind which means that today people from the most disparate parts of the world can work together.

But the network is not restricted to people inside BP, collaborative partners such as for example Shell in the Gulf of Mexico can join the virtual team too.

Browne states that some of the benefits of the virtual team network are quite easy to measure:

- A big drop in the person-hours needed to solve problems as a result of improved interactions between land-based drilling engineers and offshore rig crews.

- A decrease in the number of helicopter trips to offshore oil platforms.

- The avoidance of a refinery shutdown because technical experts at another location could examine a corrosion problem remotely.

- A reduction in rework during construction projects because designers, fabricators, construction workers, and operations people could collaborate more effectively.

BP estimates that the virtual team network produced at least $30 million in value in its first year alone.

Source: Extracted from Prokesch, S.E. (1997). Unleashing the power of learning: an interview with British Petroleum's John Browne. Harvard Business Review, **75**, 146–68.

READING SUGGESTIONS

Nonaka, I. & Takeuchi, H. (1995). *The Knowledge-Creating Company*. Oxford: Oxford University Press.

Comment: A classic on this subject.

Polanyi, M. (1983) *The Tacit Dimension*. Gloucester, MA: Peter Smith.

Comment: Might want to go back to the origins of the concept of tacit knowledge. By the way, his notion of tacit knowledge is that it is impossible to illicit, that is its very nature.

SOME USEFUL WEBSITES

www.knowledgeboard.com

Comment: Knowledge Associates provide some useful articles and other information on their website, and are also organisers of a conference on knowledge creation.

17 Innovation for the environment

CASE STUDY 6: PLASWOOD BY DUMFRIES RECYCLING[1]

Plastics recycling and recyclate is good for the environment and good for business. Recycled material is a largely untapped resource. It is an additional resource stream waiting to be exploited by Industry and an opportunity which many businesses are currently missing out on.

Rt Hon Michael Meacher MP, Minister for the Environment during a conference on recycled plastics, London, 6 March 2000

Invest or sell?

British Polythene Industries (bpi) PLC, of which Dumfries Plastic Recycling (DPR) is a 100%-owned subsidiary, have always placed strong emphasis on recycling. In fact, in 1999 about 25% of the company's £452 million turnover came

> Approximately 60% of total plastic waste is packaging which typically has a 'life' of less than 23 months.

from recycled products, £5 million of which are contributed by the products manufactured and sold through DPR. Cameron McLatchie, Chairman and Chief Executive, declares on the company website, "As the leading manufacturer of Polythene Film Products in the UK we accept that we have a responsibility to manufacture products which meet recognised environmental criteria, and to produce them in a way that fully meets our social commitments." With its business being in the manufacturing and selling of polythene products – primarily thin materials such as films, plastic bags and wrapping materials – McLatchie had recognised the need to recycle plastic early on.

In the early 90s bpi produced about 400,000 tonnes of polyethylene (PE) a year and it was felt that it should be possible to make some use of the wastage generated in the process. In addition there had been enquiries from their customers about recyclability of PE products, most of which have a very short lifespan. It was also anticipated that legislation would be introduced to enforce recycling on a wider scale – and being able to make use of recycled material would put bpi in a competitive position.

Over the past 5–10 years the company had invested significantly in its recycling facilities – about £15–20 million in the past five years alone – but so far returns on investment had not been quite as expected. The reasons were manifold. Government regulation had not panned out the way it had been anticipated and the government's

---

[1] The case has been prepared by Dr Bettina von Stamm as a basis for class discussion rather than to illustrate either effective or ineffective handling of a management situation.

expectations of the market regulating prices had not happened – and were not likely to either with existing legislation. Instead of encouraging recycling related industries to be established in the UK, British interpretation of EU legislation (EU Directive on Packaging and Packaging Waste) which states that in 2001 50% of packaging waste has to be recovered, resulted in much of the 'raw material' being exported to the Far East.

From BPI's 1999 Annual Report & Accounts

Despite years of experience in the recycling of post consumer waste films, we have yet to see an acceptable return for this activity. The current system of Producer Responsibility may indeed be delivering compliance with Packaging Regulations at the lowest cost for retailers and packer-fillers, but it has done nothing to improve the infrastructure for recycling of genuine post-use waste polyethylene film in the UK. This has a direct bearing on our post-use retail waste film plant at Heanor which is currently operating at a loss. Our agricultural film recycling plant at Dumfries survives on waste film sourced from Eire, the Channel Islands and Mainland Europe, all of which subsidise local collection of material for recycling. In the UK, farmers cry out for help with their waste polyethylene films, but so far all we have is some marginal help for a pilot collection scheme in Wales. There is clearly a discontinuity in the Government's thinking in this area.

The idea of recycling plastic was not new but previously manufacturing processes had been restricted to the use of reasonably clean recycled plastic. A high percentage of recycled plastic was highly contaminated, requiring extensive and costly washing procedures. Backed by strong senior management support, a team of bpi engineers, led by David Butler, Operations Director of bpi.recycled products, started to work on developing processes that would allow processing of stronger contaminated materials, and to identify new applications for such a material. The company's efforts, combining two previously separate technologies of washing dirty, low-grade plastic waste and recycling it, resulted in a material called 'Plaswood' which could be manufactured into multipurpose plastic blocks. The material was used to develop a range of replacement products for items made previously from timber, metal or concrete such as fence posts, benches and bollards. In 1995 Dumfries Recycling Ltd was set up to manufacture and sell Plaswood products.

There were some conflicting indicators. On the one hand the overall cost structure as defined by legislation and 'raw material' prices meant that parts of the recycling division operated at a loss. On the other hand there were the

> Contamination refers to labels on plastic bottles, soil and other waste on agricultural films.

company's firm commitment to recycling, consumers' increasing environmental consciousness and their interest in products made from recycled materials, and requests by users of PE products for environmentally friendly solutions for the disposal of plastics.

Plastic recycling in the UK

Recycling: to reclaim a product after its primary use, for the manufacture of either the same or another product.

UK's Producer Responsibility Obligations (Packaging Waste) Regulations passed by the House of Commons, March 1997

Worldwide production of plastic materials has gone up annually from about 5 million tonnes in the 1950s to about 80 million tonnes in 1997 of which 3.5 million are consumed in the UK. As most plastic products have a fairly short lifespan they contribute hugely to waste disposal problems. Out of the approximately 2.8 million tonnes of plastic waste generated in the UK in 2000, about 60% or 1.7 million tonnes are packaging waste. With landfill being the primary means of disposing of plastic waste, this is a major problem.

In an attempt to address increasing environmental concerns and the increasing shortage of landfill sites, the European Union had introduced a directive in 1994 that requested each member to put systems in place to recover 50–60% of all packaging waste by 2001 (94/62 EC). The minimum quota for each type of packaging material was set at 15%. How countries would achieve the target was left entirely up to them.

> The legislation defines packaging as "All products made of any materials of any nature to be used for the containment, protection, handling, delivery and presentation of goods from raw materials to processed goods from the producer to the user or the consumer."

It is important to distinguish between 'recovery' and 'recycling'. Recycling is one method of recovery, others being incineration and what is called feedstock recovery, that is returning packaging to its original raw material or components as long as it would involve diverting the waste from landfill. These targets were incorporated into UK legislation on packaging in 1997. With waste from plastic packaging amounting to around 1.7 million tonnes in 2000 it meant that 255,000 tonnes of the total amount to be recovered (850,000) would have to be mechanically recycled into new products. For 2001 the anticipated volume of plastic actually recycled lies between 150,000 to 180,000 tonnes, well short of the target.

Plastic recycling and recovery methods

• Mechanical recycling by producing new finished plastic products (melting and moulding, manufacturing regranulate).

• Feedstock recycling by breaking polymers down into their constituent monomers which in turn can be used again in refineries or petrochemical and chemical production.

• Incineration with energy recovery, where plastics can be burnt to release electricity or heat.

The UK is concentrating on mechanical recycling.

Who recycles and how much

Raw material manufacturer	
e.g. a manufacturer of sheet steel to be made into packaging	6%
Converter	
e.g. a manufacturer of steel cans for the food industry	9%
Packer/Filler	
e.g. a company filling cans with food	37%
Seller	
e.g. a retailer selling canned goods to their customers who throw away the cans	48%

(Companies generating less that 50 tonnes of packaging waste per year are exempt.)

Products made from recycled plastic

Polyethylene bin liners and carrier bags; refuse sacks; bottles; water and sewer pipes; flooring; fibre-fill duvets; audio, video and compact disc cassette cases; fencing and garden furniture; office accessories; seed trays and building insulation board. It is possible to buy scissors and knives with handles of recycled plastic. Recycled plastics are also used in multi-layer containers for fabric softeners, engine oil and paint. Even fleece clothes, e.g. jackets, hats and gloves are made up of recycled PET bottles.

The UK legislation introduced a system of Packaging Recovery Notes (PRNs) which shares costs of recovery between producers of the raw material, converters, users and sellers, each part of the chain has an obligation to recover. Andrew Green, MD of bpi.recycled products explains that the PRN system is, "Based on the legislation a compliance scheme has developed. It is like a non-profit making club, in the end it is the club's responsibility to ensure recycling. Members pay the club, thereby buying off their organisation's obligation. The club outsources recycling to companies such as bpi." This means that a company does not necessarily undertake any of the recycling itself, it just needs to show proof – by purchasing PRNs – that a certain amount of packaging waste has been recycled. PRNs are sold by companies (reprocessors) who turn recycled materials back into raw materials or new products. However, Green also points out that at present the scheme is not working very well, the main reason being that the value of PRNs is very low. This means that a company taking on other organisations' obligations to recycle by selling PRNs can only realise small incomes while on the other hand the process of recycling is expensive and finding markets for products made of recycled plastic is not easy. Green indicated that a company would have to charge about £150 per tonne to make recycling financially viable – the price realised per PRN per tonne of material was £45–55 and £45–60 in October and November, 2001 respectively.

In establishing their recovery responsibility companies can **discount** the following:

- Packaging that is thrown away.
- Packaging that is exported.
- Packaging that has been used before.
- Packaging a company does not legally own.
- Production residues (from production process).

There are several aspects of the plastic industry that make the recycling less straightforward than one might expect:

- There are about 50 different family groups of plastics, with hundreds of different varieties; the number of different plastics makes sorting complicated and requirements for successful recycling vary.

- Methods have yet to be developed to process different types of plastic together.

- Most post-use plastic is contaminated, e.g. by labels, soil etc., and cleaning can be difficult and costly.

UK estimates of post-use recycling plastic in 1997	
Polyethylene (PE) film	66,000 t
Polyethylene (PE) other	10,000 t
Polypropylene (PP)	20,000 t
Polystyrene (PS)	5,000 t
Expanded Polystyrene (EPS)	2,500 t
Acrylonitrile Butadiene Styrene (ABS)	2,000 t
Acrylics	1,200 t
Polyvinyl Chloride (PVC)	10,000 t
Polyester (PET)	3,000 t
TOTAL	119,700 t

- Plastics are light in weight which means that transport costs for waste plastic to a recycling centre are relatively high.

- Quality of recycled plastic is never as good as virgin material and also more variable.

- Virgin material is about £400–600 per tonne for polyethylene, recycled polyethylene costs about £300–500 per tonne.

In addition, less packaging than anticipated has been used resulting in a lower UK obligation to recycle as shown in Box 17.1.

Box 17.1   UK obligation to recycle plastic at 15% of packaging volume predicted versus actual

Year	1997	1998	1999	2000	2001
Predicted	45	119	170	231	272
Actual		90	125	178	240

But there were also other factors causing problems. During a conference in London in March 2000 Keith Stenning, Group Resources Director of bpi, criticised current legislation stating that, "PRN funding has now reduced to a level which will only support the simplest of recycling processes. Regulations have merely sustained activity through the last plastic price cycle without significantly increasing the infrastructure of capacity in the UK." He further referred to a study that concluded that there would be no ecological benefit in plastic packaging recycling rates above 15% and urged greater focus on energy and feedstock recovery options adding: "If we are to sustain plastic recycling programmes in a free market environment we need markets and applications which can realise beneficial use at an affordable cost. If the packaging chain cannot or will not support the costs of current recycling routes within the UK, and significant waste holders opt to export waste, then this not only puts the UK recycler at commercial risk but also cuts off his waste resources. Does the answer lie in low cost third world economies becoming the recycling partners of developed economies? I cannot believe that this was the intention of the global drive towards sustainability."

While bpi has a number of competitors within the UK, the biggest threat comes from the Far East – both for the picking up of the 'raw material', e.g. plastic waste, and supplying products which would in the UK be made out of recycled material such as plastic bags (albeit plastic bags

> Today almost all carrier bags come from the Far East, and at a very good price, but most of them are made from virgin material.

from China tend to be made from virgin material). Andrew explains, "The Far East seems to have an almost unlimited demand for waste plastic which keeps the price of waste artificially high. It pays to ship plastic waste over there because of the vast number of empty containers that travel back – so transportation costs are not an issue. Once over there they have lots of cheap labour they can throw at segregating the waste." bpi used to get plastic from Sainsbury who charged them £150 per tonne to collect it but now it ships all its plastic recycling to the Far East. The plastic sent to China tends to be recycled into plastic pellets that are used for rigid products such as the casing of electronic consumer goods. As a consequence of the competition from the Far East a number of plastic washing plants all over Europe have closed down in recent years.

Another distinction is important, scrap and post-use plastic. The former is 'process scrap' from industry, which is easy to recycle as the ingredients are known, and it is clean as it has not entered the waste stream. Many companies working with recycled plastic concentrate on this – and have done so before legislation was introduced. It is generally recycled

> A lot of other companies make pellets from rigid products, under the government scheme they were getting PRNs for what they had been doing all along anyway.

in-house or with a local processor. Post-use plastic on the other hand is defined as 'plastic material arising from products which have undergone a first full service life prior to being reclaimed'. This plastic waste requires collecting, sorting and in most cases cleaning which means it is more difficult and costly to recycle. In 1997 bpi recycled about 14,000 tonnes of post-use packaging and about 34,000 tonnes of process scrap.

One of the flaws of the existing system is that it does not differentiate between different sources for recycling plastics. While processing scrap plastic is comparatively straightforward and easy, the tricky bit is working with post-use plastic. It can cost about £200 per tonne to have the recyclable material delivered to the factory alone – in comparison, the cost for other recyclable materials such as

> A neighbouring plant was filling containers with plastic material and having to pay for its removal. bpi offered to take it off their hands and save them the container charges – but they were not interested unless bpi would pay them for it.

paper, glass or steel is around £20 per tonne. The problem here is that people see post-use plastic as raw material and price it accordingly. In addition one does not get 100% return out of the material that arrives at the plant. For example, at Dumfries Plastic Recycling they get about 40% PE out of 100% delivered material. This is due partly to the fact that not all of the material delivered is usable, partly because the contamination (a) is 'dead' weight and (b) incurs costs as the material needs to be cleaned before it can be processed.

Other companies focus more on bottles from the domestic waste stream, which are relatively easy to separate, but machinery is expensive. Bottles tend also to be contaminated by paper and different plastics are used in the production of plastic bottles, which means that it is generally necessary to sort bottles by type of plastic. To avoid problems arising from the mixing of different types of plastic Germany has introduced legislation that attempts to prevent mixing at the source.

	2005/06	2006/07
Municipal waste:		
Collected	28.7 mt	29.1 mt
Recycled	27.1%	30.7%
Recovered	37.2%	41.8%
Incinerated	10%	11%
Landfilled	62%	58%
Household waste:		
Collected	25.5 mt	25.9 mt
Recycled	26.7%	30.9%

Source: http://www.letsrecycle.com (13.11.07).

One final distinction is that between rigid and flexible plastic. Rigid plastic has the advantage that it tends to be easier to segregate and clean and many domestic or consumer rigid plastic packaging contains an identification marking. David Butler, Operations Director, Refuse & Recycling, bpi Recycled Products explains, "As long as products are rigid they can be sorted. For example, US grain sorters are good for sorting different coloured pellets. There are also machines that can identify different plastics. But at present there are no machines for sorting films, it tends to go all over the place." Plastic film, even if it were marked, remains a problem as it tends to be mixed with other waste. At present the only working plant in the UK for processing recycled plastic film is bpi's plant in Dumfries.

Background to British Polythene Industries

Between 1983 and 1997 British Polythene Industries had grown significantly. As David Butler, Operations Director of bpi.recycled products recalls, "In 1987 we consisted of five to six small companies. By the late 90s, after we had completed a number of mergers and acquisitions, we had grown to 50. The expansion of the company had started with the acquisition of Anaplast Limited by Scott & Robertson in 1987 after which its current Chairman Cameron McLatchie joined the board, which was also when the company became its current name, bpi. This was followed by further important steps:

- Purchase of PCL Recycling in 1986.
- Acquisition of Visqueen from ICI in 1988 – more than doubling group size.
- Merger with Alida Holdings in 1989 – moving into the retail sector.
- Acquisition of Brithene Bridgewater from Courtaulds in 1991 – expanding the stretch film sector.
- In 1992 acquisition of Novathene Films from BP – expanding the collation shrink sector.
- Acquisition of Parkside Flexible Packaging in 1995 – moving into the high quality flexible packaging sector.
- Acquisition of polythene film business of Wavin and Low and Bonar – establishing significant presence on the continent and market leadership in silage stretchwrap.

In 1999 bpi was the largest producer of polythene products in Europe, generating a turnover of £452 million and £27.5 million operating profit (before employee share scheme) with just under 4000 employees. The group is now split into seven strategic businesses:

- Recycled Products   Manufacture and sale of recycled products including refuse sacks, construction films; recycling of post-consumer waste (~19% of group turnover).

- Industrial Products   Manufacture and sale of heavy duty sacks and pallet covers for the fertiliser, chemical, animal feed, construction and horticulture markets (~18% of group turnover).

- Stretchfilms   Manufacture and sale of film on the reel products including hand and machine pallet stretchwrap, silage stretchwrap and agricultural and horticultural sheeting (~16% of group turnover).

- Films   Manufacture and sale of collation shrinkfilm, converter, lamination and overwrap films (14% of group turnover).

- Packaging Services   Provision of services for a range of polythene related products through manufacturing, converting and merchanting operations; products include polythene film and bags, pallet stretchwrap, paper sacks and tape (~13% of group turnover).

- Consumer Packaging   Manufacture and sale of polythene and paper bags for the food, petcare and consumer markets (~12% of group turnover).

- Belgium   Manufacture and sale in Europe of printed films, industrial stretch films and silage stretchwrap and agricultural sheeting (8% of group turnover).

McLatchie had always felt strongly about the company's obligation to recycle. Since 1995 the company had invested £16 million in state of the art recycling and film extrusion technology and, as stated on the company website, "We remain at the forefront of innovative and environmentally responsible high-performance products." However, David points out, "It seems that we have made a lot of long-term investments and are taking a long-term view", but of course the city does not like that and they were seen to be weak and a take-over target. The website further contains a statement on bpi's environmental policy: "I consider it important that we let you know in a clear and concise manner the environmental policy of British Polythene Industries Plc" (see also Box 17.2).

Box 17.2   bpi's environmental policy

We will ensure that:

- **all** our products will be manufactured to conform in every respect to prevailing Government environmental standards.

- **we will** seek to minimise the use of non-renewable raw materials.

- **our products** will be manufactured from materials which are capable of being recycled.

- **recycled products** will be offered where they can be demonstrated to be fit for purpose.

- **we will** provide, wherever practicable, the facilities for the collection and recycling of polythene film products.

- **we will** be a responsible employer and a good neighbour.

- **we will** manage our operations and processes in a way which respects and protects the environment.

- **our operations will** conform to current legislation.

- **we will** be in the forefront of developing new environmentally responsible initiatives, where it is economical and practical to do so.

In 1999 the company discharged its recovery obligations on paper through the national compliance scheme, but plastic recycling obligations were met through its own resources. Seven sites were accredited by the Environment Agency which meant that they could sell PRNs to generate additional income. However, while the legislation on packaging waste recovery had originally been thought to give this aspect of the business a significant boost, the company had to learn to the contrary at its cost. Deteriorating prices of PRNs and cheaper processing in the Far East meant two things. Firstly, volume throughput was likely to go down, and secondly, access to suitable waste would become increasingly difficult.

While the Annual Report 1999 still mentioned seven sites dedicated to the recycling business, 2001 saw the closure of two, partly due to difficult circumstances in the recycling industry – competition from the Far East – and partly to consolidate bpi's recycling efforts. In addition one of the five sites has been reassigned to the production of high-quality refuse sacks made from virgin material (see Appendix 17.2 for the use of the remaining four sites).

The competition from the Far East is particularly felt in the market for carrier bags – and this is true for the retail as well as the recycling side. Whereas bpi used to have a business recycling bags from stores, that part of the company was closed down in June 2000 as supermarkets preferred to ship their waste plastic east; Sainsbury, formerly being a customer of bpi, being one of them. As David explains, "To ship a 24-tonne container from the UK to Hong Kong costs about $500; to ship 1 tonne back costs $150. Once the container gets to China the contents get dumped into the streets of small villages where the villagers sort the plastic by hand. Polyethylene goes to one village, polypropylene to another. The people sort it by colour and degrees of contamination (paper etc.). Labels and other paper-based contaminations are then cut out by hand and used as fuel. The plastic is then hand-stuffed into the extruders – something that would be forbidden for safety reasons here. The pellets resulting from this process can then be blown into good film." He continued, "Our Chairman Cameron McLatchie has tried to explain it to the government and other interested parties how short-sighted it all is – but no one wants to listen. So the UK allows massive exports of recyclable plastic. Ireland on the other hand is much stricter. Its exports to Dumfries are the exception and allowed only because Ireland does not have its own film recycling plant."

In order to be allowed to issue PRNs bpi had to be accredited, by the Environment Agency for England and the Scottish Environmental Protection Agency in Scotland. Through accrediting companies the government maintains a certain degree of control and can collect the data necessary to prove to the EU that they are fulfilling the UK's post-use packaging recycling commitment.

bpi product range from recycled plastic

Rigid products

- Geoblock ('porous' pavement system)
- Plaswood (fencing, street furniture, sign posts, garden furniture, marine use, playground furniture)
- Reblocks (traffic bollards)
- Pallets
- Cable ducting

Flexible products

- Envirolope (genuinely recycled envelopes)
- Carrier bags
- Waste sacks
- Collation and transit packaging (shrinkfilm and pallet stretch film
- Tissue overwrap (for toilet paper)
- Mailing film
- Multibags (crisps and snack food)
- Refuse sacks and bin liners
- Kerbside collection sacks
- Polly Teen (educational scheme for primary school children developed by bpi)

Dumfries Plastic Recycling

The Dumfries plant is now solely dependent on imported agricultural plastic waste from subsidised collection schemes in Southern Ireland and Continental Europe. As yet there is no sign of any Government support for a Farm Plastic Recycling Programme in the UK.

bpi 1999 Annual Report

In 1995 bpi spent £5 million to set up Dumfries Plastic Recycling as a subsidiary to manufacture and sell rigid products made of Plaswood. Between 1992 and 1995 bpi had produced Plaswood on the company's site in Stroud, Gloucestershire. Dumfries had been chosen for its closeness to Ireland, a major source of its 'raw material', post-use agricultural film. But there were other favourable conditions, the process of recycling plastic needs an abundance of water – and the site was right next to the River Nith, the previous owner of the plant had been trying to

> Plaswood, a substitute for wood, concrete and metal, is made from 100% recycled polyethylene. It is produced in a wide variety of shapes, lengths and colours, and can be customised to match clients' requirements. It is extremely durable, rot proof, maintenance and splinter free. Applications include children's play areas, harbour decking, park fencing and floating pontoons.

sell it off for quite some time and was therefore willing to negotiate the price, and finally, some grants were available.

When bpi first entertained the idea of producing rigid products from post-use plastic waste, they had hoped to be able to sink large amounts of recycled material in the process. However, they soon found out that it would not work like that. To arrive at a 'raw material' that is suitable for the production of rigid products the recyclate going into the process had to be homogeneous with its characteristics known, otherwise the outcome would be too variable both in terms of quality and performance. They found that only certain plastics were suitable – and segregation is a costly and labour-intensive process.

Interest in the new material was extremely slow to pick up. When they reassessed the market after about one year, they decided that they would need something that people could see which would help them to understand the benefits of the material – and they needed something that would bring in money quickly. In 1993/94 they decided to build a set of street furniture: a park bench, a picnic table (adult and junior) and a backless bench. These were

> A competitor of DPR had recently gone bankrupt mainly because they did not understand the importance of segregation and that one could only achieve good results from recycling if materials are separated; otherwise the resulting material is too inconsistent and not suitable for producing film.

some very basic products but people reacted positively saying, 'Now I see what you were talking about.' Kim also remembers, "The street nameplates introduced in 1995 were our first big hit, not least because people did not need much imagination to see how that would work."

While bpi have invested a lot in recycling technology, they tend not to spend on R&D. Andrew explains, "We are doing very little R&D in this area. Some of the machinery manufacturers and raw material suppliers are doing a lot but this will not continue if the commercial viability of recycling continues to be very poor." However, DPR have developed processes that allow for the recycling of lower grade plastic waste than other companies are using. When asked whether they did some research before going into the production of rigid products Andrew answers, "Very little research was done before developing the process. We embarked on it primarily because we were looking for a product that would accommodate lower grade waste than was necessary for making film. The technical and market strategy was developed in conjunction with a Dutch manufacturer of similar products with whom we began a licensing agreement some 10 years ago. The agreement ended about five years ago although we continue to work together and continue to buy product from them. The Dutch effectively sold us their process technology in return for a royalty on the products we make and sell."

The end of the collaboration agreement with the Dutch company and the decision to specialise in the recycling of agricultural film were the trigger for setting up DPR. After David, who had been charged with preparing the plant for the production, had remodelled the plant it was capable of producing 5000 tonnes per year of pellets from post-use agricultural stretchfilm. However, as bpi.recycled products Managing Director Andrew Green remembers, while they had been part of the plant in Stroud, "There was no real allocation of costs." Once they had moved production to Dumfries this became all too obvious, the washing plant lost money from day one. Only recently had it started to make a small contribution. In fact, DPR came under serious review about four years ago, and the question was asked, do we really need to be in Plaswood? Strongly influenced by the company's commitment to the environment it was decided to continue production – but that product prices would have to start reflecting true production costs. Kim remembers, "When Andrew took over and realised how much money they were losing, one of the first things he did was to put up the price for our products by 30%. It was quite remarkable, we explained to our customers that the reason for the price increase was the need to cover cost – rather than to increase our profits – and we lost hardly any of them." Another reason customers stayed with them was that their products were of a quality superior to competitors' products.

Concerning the competition, there was agreement that there was in fact quite little – at least in terms of similar products made from recycled plastic. David comments, "There is not much competition, certainly not for street furniture. One company is making flat panels for pigsties but that's a niche market. There are a few companies on the continent, one in the Netherlands and two in Italy, the latter also making furniture from recycled plastic but only on a small scale. As transport costs are quite high, there is not much cross-border trade. On the other hand, for flexible recycled plastic products, such as refuse sacks, there is horrendous competition."

> In agricultural stretchfilm about 58–60% are sand, soil and water.

With 45 employees DPR processes about 60,000 tonnes of polythene a year, about half of which is post-use plastic. After the recyclate has been washed it is 'reduced in size' – which means it is shredded – and then melted in an extruder. In the extrusion process the liquid plastic is pressurised into moulds. Once the material has cooled down in water, it is pushed out by compressed air. David points out, "Make sure that you don't stand in the way when it is pushed out, it is like a torpedo!" It is important to give sufficient time to the cooling process. Again David explains, "The outer skin has to be 'frozen' before the product can be taken out of its form; it must be kept in its mould until the outside is sufficiently hard, otherwise the product will disintegrate."

Over the years the Plaswood product range had expanded continual. Asked about where product ideas come from David comments, "They come from within the organisation as well as from our customers. We also scan the market for existing products and ask whether making them from Plaswood would bring any advantages to the consumer." Kim Williamson, Sales Manager, adds, "We are working very closely with our customers, for example Safeway and Waitrose. We supply Waitrose with all their car park requirements and also take their old plastic bags back – it is a win–win situation." Kim continues, "It is important to be reactive to customer needs – and listen. It is also important to keep the sales team informed and provide them with the latest insights, knowledge and developments. We at Dumfries aim to give very good service and delivery. My philosophy is, get in front of customers as much as you can. Honesty is very important too. Say if you believe something does or does not work. You have to know the product inside out so you don't make promises that cannot be delivered. For example, if the customer requires something for which Plaswood is not the ideal solution, we do not hesitate to recommend a combination with other materials." About 75% of products sold are off-the-shelf solutions, 25% are bespoke to customer requirements.

bpi's products from recycled materials are sold predominantly into the following markets: the building industry, local authority and private waste contractors, as well as catering and janitorial. However, most of these markets are interested in flexible rather than rigid products. DPR's main customers tend to be local authorities. In fact, the four top accounts are with local authorities and about 40% of DPR's business is conducted with its four major customers. "Keeping in constant contact with the local authorities is very important," says Kim. "Our sales staff

> Waitrose is a very enlightened company, they have 'bags for life' which customers buy, use until they are worn out and can then exchange for a new 'bag for life'; the worn out bags get collected and come back to Dumfries who then produce Plaswood products with them which in turn go back to Waitrose who use them either for their shops or donate them.

contact all local authorities with the latest product info etc. about twice a year. In fact we conduct much of our sales activity over the phone. Persistency, and the fact that our organisation has been around for some time, delivering high quality products and good service, had led several local authorities to start specifying products made from recycled materials in their tender documents. Of course they cannot request our products but it is a step in the right direction."

The material characteristics – maintenance free, non-rotting, resisting vandalism, immune to infestation by insects and salt water resistance – make it ideal for the outdoor/marine environment. Hence the product focus is on outdoor furniture – benches, bollards, street signs – and other outdoor products such as children's play environments, fencing and decking products for wet environments (band revetments, floating pontoons, fendering, etc.). DPR also supply people/companies with 'raw material' for them to do their own furniture.

The team at Dumfries are keen to identify new applications and product ideas for Plaswood material. One recent move was to add different colours. Kim comments, "Originally all of our products were black. Since we have developed brown Plaswood in addition to the black the market for fencing has taken off." They have just started the production of some Plaswood products in brighter colours such as yellow, green, red and blue which gives the customer more choice and makes them particularly attractive for playgrounds and nurseries. Early in 2001 DPR introduced a new product called Post Saver. Post Saver is a boot of recycled plastic lined with bitumen which can be heat-shrunk onto a wooden post which means that the part of the post that is under ground is protected and

Fancy a sturdy Kung Fu partner?

Dummies, traditionally made from wood, are an important part in Kung Fu training. When Simon Brooker, dedicated Kung Fu disciple, wanted to acquire his own he ran into unexpected difficulties: price, quality and size were not encouraging. Having heard about Plaswood he approached DPR who were, while initially sceptical, happy to help. Assuming that more people were struggling with traditional wooden training dummies, he set up his own company, Immortal Creations, now selling four variations.

hence less likely to rot. Environmental concerns had motivated the product as previously posts had to be treated with a highly toxic wood preservative containing copper chrome and arsenic.

While this was all very exciting, and DPR had just finished a record quarter, there were some concerns. Plaswood was not a cheap material, neither was production nor were, consequently, any products made of it. In fact, while they were much easier to maintain and of longer durability (expected life time is a minimum of 50 years), they would sell at about the same retail price as hardwood. In addition, despite the advantages many customers would still prefer wood to plastic, and Kim points out, "One of our biggest challenges is how to change the consumer's perception of our product." Andrew points out that "Manufacturing cost for the products would have to come down by 50–70% to make them commercially viable. In order to achieve that we would need to increase throughput considerably." DPR had plans to recycle 10,000 tonnes of plastic by 2006. "But", Andrew asks, "would there be sufficient customers for our products?" On top of that recent checks had revealed that the washing plant in Dumfries had lost between £500,000 and £1 million between 1994 and 2000.

Questions

1.   Putting yourself in Andrew's shoes, what decisions would you take regarding Dumfries Plastic Recycling?
2.   What are factors underpinning success for 'green' products?
3.   Discuss the difference between 'green' and 'sustainable'?

APPENDIX 17.1: ALTERNATIVES TO RECYCLING

Source: bpi website

1. Biodegradable plastic

Biodegradability is an exciting and potentially very useful technology used in the correct applications. However, until EC standards are set any manufacturer of biodegradable products can make untrue and misleading claims about their products. This means that some degradable products may be marketed for use in inappropriate applications. Currently, biodegradability is suitable for products which will be composted, not for products going to landfill or being recycled where the effects of biodegradability on the recyclate are unknown. Biodegradability is expensive. Environmentally it is acceptable in some specific applications but at present it is generally undesirable

2. Call for incineration

Incineration might be an alternative to land fill but there is some public resistance against it, it is a question of education. Arguments for and aspects of incineration include:

*   Is safe and clean; modern plants control emissions by the installation of devices such as acid gas scrubbers, bag filters and electrostatic precipitators

*   A minimum temperature of 850°C is needed

- Incineration converts nearly all carbon to CO_2 while in landfill under normal conditions methane is predominantly formed; methane gas contributes to the greenhouse effect 30 times more than CO_2

- Incineration of municipal solid waste (MSW), i.e. domestic refuse, drastically reduces the volume of waste by up to 90%

- Plastics have a calorific value greater than coal, make up 7% by weight of MSW, and produce 50% of all energy produced during incineration, making plastic a vital component of MSW (Switzerland, Denmark and Sweden rely heavily on energy recovery from waste)

- Plastic waste can also be used to manufacture high calorific fuel pellets, termed Refuse Derived Fuel; RDF can be transported and stored and are used to generate heat for industrial processes.

APPENDIX 17.2: RECYCLING AT BPI

The six recycling related sites and their activities are:

- Dumfries   Washing plant; production of rigid products from recycled plastic.100% is post-use

- Stockton   Refuse sack plant; processing about 12,000 tonnes per year of refuse sacks; selling mainly to the NHS; the plant process bpi scrap; bpi own the site

- Heanor   Used to be part of bpi retail; recycling has taken over half of the site since January 2001; this plant too is scrap based, scrap here comes from inside bpi as well as outside; the washing plant at Heanor has been moth-balled

- Stroud   Production of flat sacks for local authorities; part of company since 1987; also scrap based, some stems from Dumfries and more is bought from other companies within the UK

- Rhymney   Production of building films from 100% recycled plastic about 60% of which is post-use

- Witney   Production of building damp proof course from 100% recycled plastic about 80% of which is post-use

18 Green design – clean environment or clean conscious?

Companies can minimise environmental impact by reviewing and adapting their corporate and marketing operations policies and strategies, and their management styles and training to integrate environmental expertise.

Dermody and Hammer-Lloyd (1995)

Pressures on companies to become more environmentally conscious come from two sides. First there are increasingly tougher environmental regulations introduced by government; secondly, and perhaps more importantly, consumers are becoming increasingly environmentally aware. Concerns about global warming, food-related scandals and oil prices that have gone far beyond what seemed possible only four to five years ago, have motivated the consumer to questions around environmental impact and sustainability. In response to this external pressure organisations have increasingly started to emphasise the 'triple bottom line'. Rather than being just concerned about the profit (economic results), organisations are starting to consider their impact on people (human capital/social implications) and planet (environmental impact/issues of sustainability).

In a way it is an extension of the concept of corporate social responsibility (CSR). CSR is defined by the World Business Council for Sustainable Development as "... being the continuing commitment by business to behave ethically and contribute to economic development while improving the quality of life of the workforce and their families as well as of the local community and society at large".

Organic – great idea, but . . .

You may recall that Iceland, the producer of frozen foods, announced a few years ago that all their products would be based on organic ingredients, at prices that would match non-organic foods. Their decision was driven by consumer demand and, I am sure, extensive consumer research that indicated that such a policy should significantly increase the demand for their products. However, after they had introduced their 'all organic' policy, consumers behaved differently from what they had expected, production cost did not decrease at the rate anticipated, and as a result Iceland had to reconsider its position.

It seems that they were ahead of the time; today they might be more successful.

While only a small group of consumers seems willing to pay a higher price, all else being equal they'd rather buy an environmentally responsible product. But it is not only external pressures that motivate managers to look into 'greener' development, it is also about positioning the company as responsible and proactive – and the insight that environmentally conscious development makes business sense.

In this chapter we make the argument for increased environmental consciousness, take a closer look at what environmentally friendly actually means, introduce the concept of natural capitalism, and conclude with some suggestions on the designer's role in making environmentally responsible products a reality.

THE ARGUMENT FOR ENVIRONMENTALLY RESPONSIBLE DESIGN

Unprecedented consumption of natural resources, an increasing pollution, desertification, ozone depletion, acid precipitation, global warming, and loss of habitats and species diversity.

Dermody & Hammer-Lloyd (1995)

With an ever-growing world population and decreasing natural resources, also caused by more and more obvious signs of environmental problems – piles of rubbish and toxic waste (see Box 18.1), dying trees, extinction of already rare breeds of animals and plants, global warming – there is an increasing concern with the impact of our consumer society on our environment.

In order to achieve global ecological sustainability the environmental impact of products and services has to be reduced by factor X. Biologists Ehrlich and Ehrlich (1990) have proposed the following formula:

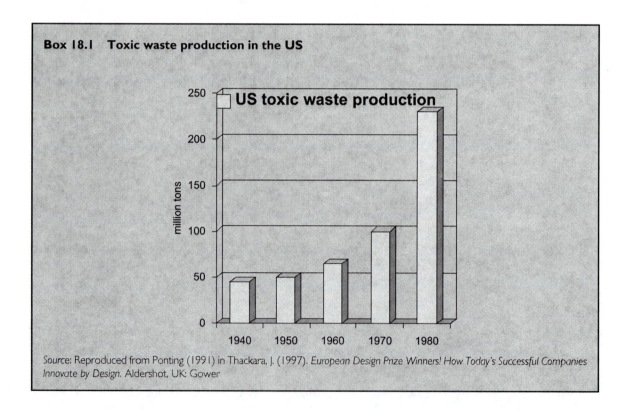

Box 18.1   Toxic waste production in the US

Source: Reproduced from Ponting (1991) in Thackara, J. (1997). *European Design Prize Winners! How Today's Successful Companies Innovate by Design.* Aldershot, UK: Gower

$$\text{Total environmental impact } (I) = \text{Population } (P) \times \text{Capital stock per person or affluence } (A)$$
$$\times \text{ Environmental damage done by particular technologies } (T)$$

Building on the premise that the earth has a limited capacity to carry environmental impacts sustainability can only be achieved if the negative environmental impacts worldwide are less or equal to, the earth's capacity. Needless to say that today our consumption and demands exceed capacity, the world's population keeps growing, and affluence continues to increase, particularly in developing countries. As it seems difficult to control population growth, and particularly the developing countries need to be allowed to increase their affluence, one important lever to balance demand and capacity is to minimise the environmental damage caused by particular technologies. The specific factor which describes these reductions is also known as factor X. Depending on the assumptions made about the earth's capacity and future population and consumption factor X is estimated to lie between 4 and 50. A simple principle and hierarchy on where we should focus our efforts is:

- reduce
- reuse
- recycle

Just think about the amount of waste produced from each shopping trip. Unpacking after one trip to the supermarket generally fills the rubbish bin easily with plastic bags, containers and cardboard items. As usual there is a debate as to who should address the problem, the consumer or the supplier. In Germany for example regulation has been introduced that placed the responsibility for disposal of packaging firmly with the providers of goods. This means that consumers can leave all superfluous packaging material at the shop or supermarket. And as the managers of shops and supermarkets do not like to end up with piles of cardboard boxes and other packaging materials, and carry the cost for their disposal, they in turn put pressure on the suppliers to cut down on the packaging. In Denmark waste segregation laws are very strict and

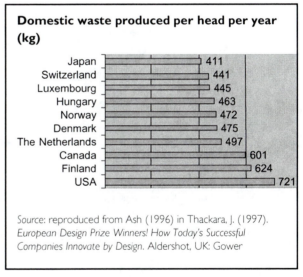

Domestic waste produced per head per year (kg)

Japan	411
Switzerland	441
Luxembourg	445
Hungary	463
Norway	472
Denmark	475
The Netherlands	497
Canada	601
Finland	624
USA	721

Source: reproduced from Ash (1996) in Thackara, J. (1997). *European Design Prize Winners! How Today's Successful Companies Innovate by Design.* Aldershot, UK: Gower

people have to pay penalties if they are found to put rubbish in the wrong containers. In both cases the consequence seems to have been some reduction in waste.

More and more regulations and legislation are passed to encourage – or force – organisations to consider the environmental impact of their activities both at production and usage level. However, there is always a fierce battle between industry and government as to how strict regulations should be, and how quickly they are to be implemented. Industry generally argues that improving environmental performance would add costs, endangering jobs and putting them at a disadvantage in international competition. However, much of this is based on assumptions, and companies that have embraced sustainability have actually experienced great benefits, in terms of cost, profit, market share and reputation. Some examples will follow later in this chapter. So most of the time compromises need to be reached, generally leading to a dilution of the original intentions and the stretching of time frames. However, it seems that leading firms take the initiative in talking to government and defining the rules. This, of course, has not only the advantage of being seen to be proactive but with it comes the benefit of being able to influence what kind of regulations and legislation are being put into place.

Still, much of activity in this area has been driven by government and even more so the European Union where particularly the Dutch government with its eco-design initiatives has been pushing the frontiers. However, nations' view on the importance and urgency of responding to the environmental challenges varies. Lewis et al. (2001) state that "In Australia, environmental protection is still viewed by some (vocal) parts of industry as just another potential burden that will increase costs and reduce profits. In the European context (and to a great extent in the USA and Japan), regulations and policies to increase environmental protection appear to have become a new stimulus for innovation and to have led companies to identify new business opportunities." They name companies such as Xerox, Electrolux, Bosch, BMW, Philips, Volvo, AEG and Wilkhahn as leaders in this area. These companies have invested heavily in new processes, systems, production technologies and design methods in the search for dramatic reductions in the environmental impacts of their products. Lewis et al. have found that companies invest in reducing their environmental impact because they:

- Want to position themselves as market leaders and innovators.

- Do not want future surprises (they want to anticipate the changing regulatory and market context rather than to react to changes as they are upon them).

- Recognise the emergence of a new business paradigm and a new competitive terrain.

- Desire to act responsibly (to have a clear conscience on the part of directors).

- Desire to influence the direction of regulations and legislation (in partnership with government and to secure their investment).

- Desire to strengthen technical competence and develop new areas of technical competency.

- Want to change or improve the market image of the whole company.

WHAT ARE ENVIRONMENTALLY RESPONSIBLE PRODUCTS?

Because our problems are caused by industry and the solutions must be found by industry, environmentalists have got to roll their sleeves up and get stuck into working with industry.

Elkington and Burke (1989)

So there are a number of good reasons why leading companies engage in environmental issues. But what exactly is an environmentally responsible product?

One of the results of an increased environmental consciousness is that more and more companies are starting to use terms that indicate 'environmental friendliness' in their marketing and product literature. Therein lies a problem: anyone can describe their products in whichever way they see fit. OK, within limits, but many of the claims made on promotional literature and packaging are difficult for the consumer to check, leading to confusion. In response to this problem, and to provide consumers with some guidance, labels such as the 'green point' (Europe-wide), the Blue Angel (in Germany), the Soil Association (UK) or the Forest Stewardship Council have emerged. But even labels require a certain degree of education, and not all of them are backed by legislation or clear definitions. For a less knowledgeable consumer it remains difficult to differentiate between empty logos and labels that are backed by official schemes. For example, while the Soil Association and the Forest Stewardship Council stand for specific products, with the Blue Angel on the other hand, being associated with all kinds of products, the consumer does not quite get as much information and help.

Take for example organic food. There are so many products on the market that claim to be produced organically – which makes the consumer feel good, but if asked, how many consumers would actually be able to respond to what 'organically produced' means?[1] Having just recently looked it up on the government's website www.food.gov.uk I now know that organic food should be produced under the following conditions:

- No fertilisers (unless approved for organic production).
- No pesticides (unless approved for organic production).
- The land has been farmed organically for a minimum of two years.

An inspector has to verify the above, and the labels of organic produce need to state the certifying body that has issued the certification. The code number and name or trademark of the certification body may also be shown. As there may be some problems obtaining all ingredients required for a product from organic origins, manufacturers of organic food are allowed to use up to 5% non-organic ingredients. While this is certainly a start there still seem to be some loopholes that can be exploited by those who jump onto the bandwagon purely for financial, rather than for ethical reasons. How many people would know which institution or organisation is qualified to certify organic food and which one is not?

Casting the net wider than food, what does it generally mean: 'an environmentally responsible product'? A whole host of terms are used and I would suggest that people are not quite sure what they actually mean, and what the differences are – see Box 18.2 for a list of the most common buzzwords. Is 'environmental design' better than green design? What is the difference between a socially responsible design and ecologically oriented design? I would suggest leaving the terminology to one side and looking at what actually characterises an environmentally responsible product instead. Many organisations claim to follow an environmentally responsible philosophy. But is it really environmentally friendly to buy softener in plastic pouches – instead of bottles? Is the question rather, do we need this additional product at all (which, by the way, was developed out of byproducts from the washing powder production)? Is it environmentally responsible to buy pencils that are made from plastic cups? Would it be better not to produce these plastic cups in the first place? There are a whole host of products out there that are appealing at our 'green' conscious – but that are really doing just that, making us feel better – not helping the environment. When Honda's president Nobuhiko Kawamoto stated in 1992 that making cars more environmentally friendly was the most important challenge facing manufacturers he followed the statement with specific action: in

---

[1] If you want to read more on 'What organic really means' visit www.food.gov.uk.

Box 18.2   Palette of buzzwords

- Eco design
- Sustainable design
- Design for sustainability (DfS)
- Design for the environment (DfE)
- Green design
- Dematerialisation
- Life cycle design

August the same year Honda withdrew from motor racing to focus more on environmental aspects of development (in Lamming, 1993).

Companies that are serious about protecting the environment go beyond glossy annual report statements. For example, Dermody and Hammer-Lloyd (1995) highlight the following as noteworthy from Procter & Gamble's environmental quality policy:

- They assess the environmental impact of their products following the cradle to grave concept (see below).
- They have set themselves the goal of exceeding environmental laws and regulations.
- They subscribe to a continual assessment to meet environmental goals.

However, the fact is there are hardly any products that are truly good for the environment. All products take up resources, use energy and produce waste that has to be processed, leaving a 'footprint'. Lewis et al. (2001) state, "Every product we make and use contributes to environmental degradation in many different ways. It has an 'ecological footprint' that extends well beyond national boundaries and long after a product has been used and discarded." So the best companies can do is to ensure minimum impact of their products. One way of achieving it is to consider all inputs and outputs, stage by stage of a product's life cycle.

The 'cradle to grave' approach mentioned above is one tool that facilitates this (Box 18.3). It encourages companies to consider the environmental impact of a product from its conception to its disposal, looking at a number of different possible areas of impact. Only when a product is looked at over the period of its useful life can the true environmental impact be assessed.

A different representation of the same idea is shown in Figure 18.1. With the environmental impact in mind it suggests considering the input demands as well as the outputs at each stage of a product's life cycle.

The following list of questions by Burall (1996) helps to minimise the environmental impact over a product's life cycle:

- Consider from the outset what the ideal life might be for the proposed product: calculate data cradle to grave (minimum packaging, energy efficient, using renewable resources).

- Ensure that the product will be easy to use and repair, and that product manuals encourage repair.

Box 18.3   Cradle to grave matrix (used in the Assessment for Eco-labelling Schemes)

Product Life Cycle / Environmental Fields	Pre-production	Production	Distribution (incl. packaging)	Use	Disposal
Waste relevance					
Soil pollution & degradation					
Water contamination					
Air contamination					
Noise					
Consumption of energy					
Consumption of natural resources					
Effects on ecosystems					

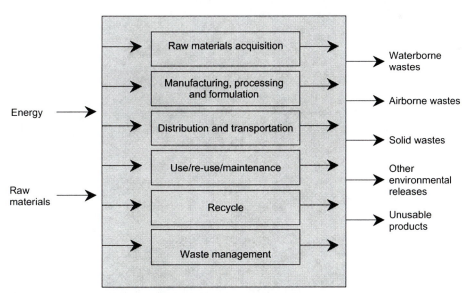

Figure 18.1   Product system from a life cycle perspective.
Source: SETAC, 1992, in Lewis *et al.* (2001). *Design + Environment – A Global Guide to Designing Greener Goods.* Sheffield, UK: Greenleaf. Reproduced by permission of Greenleaf Publishing.

- Increase the 'service intensity' of the product.

- Avoid trendy designs that encourage early product replacement (designed to last, fulfilling real needs).

- Design to facilitate upgrading (e.g. modular components).

- Consider from the outset how the product is to be disassembled (minimum non-reusable waste).

- Check that any fixing methods and finishes do not inhibit recycling.

- Ensure that plastic components carry permanent identification of materials.

- Avoid toxic materials.

- Optimise high-turnover goods (e.g. food) for low transport intensity (using local resources).

- Investigate setting up a destination for recycled elements in advance.

- Ensure that materials do not create hazard on disposal.

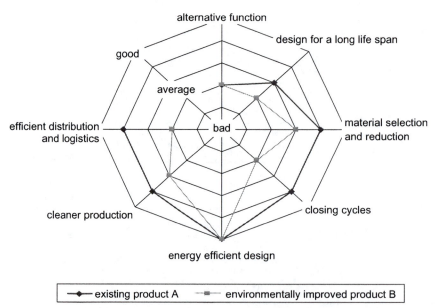

Eco-wheel diagram
(C.G. van Hemel, Delft University, The Netherlands, 1995)

Figure 18.2 Eco-wheel diagram.
Source: Reproduced from van Hemel (1995) in Thackara, J. (1997). *European Design Prize Winners!*
How Today's Successful Companies Innovate by Design. Aldershot, UK: Gower.

However, when there are different options neither of the above is too helpful for assessing different types of environmental impact relative to one another. Is it more damaging to use more energy during consumption or use more non-renewable resources? A tool that might provide some help with the comparison of different options is the Eco-wheel developed by Brezet and van Hemel (1997) (Figure 18.2). By mapping different options on the spider diagram it helps managers identify the option with the least environmental impact. Although the challenges remain to define the scales in a way that allows a sensible comparison of the different axes of the spider diagram.

NATURAL CAPITALISM VERSUS 'GREEN DESIGN'

When we talked about factor X earlier in this chapter, what was really referred to was sustainable development. Sustainable development goes beyond environmental responsibility. It is not about developing products that use a bit less energy or are easier to recycle. It is about developing products in ways that will not deprive future generations. A similar notion is expressed in the definition

Taking responsibility for future generations:

An Indian tribe measures its decisions against their impact for the people seven generations hence.

by the Bruntland Commission (the World Commission on Environment and Development) in 1997: "Sustainability is about meeting the needs of the present without compromising the ability of future generations to meet their own needs." The implication is that for development to be sustainable, it must take account of not only economic factors, but also environmental and social factors, and must access long-term consequences of actions as well as short-term results (in MacKenzie, 1997).

To achieve the step from environmentally responsible to sustainable a previously omitted factor has to be integrated: costing the impact on the environment. Lovins *et al.* (2001) state, "The reason that companies (and governments) are so prodigal with ecosystem services is that the value of those services doesn't appear on the business balance sheet. But that is a staggering omission. The economy, after all, is embedded in the environment. Recent calculations published by the journal *Nature* conservatively estimated the value of all the earth's ecosystem services to be at least £33 trillion a year. That is close to the gross world product, and it implies a capitalised book value on the order of half a quadrillion dollars. What is more, for most of these services there is no known substitute at any price, and we cannot live without them."

'Costing the earth', and taking this cost into consideration when pricing projects would make many a project that is undertaken today unrealistic, even irresponsible. Think about nuclear energy. The costing of nuclear power stations has never included the cost for the storage and impact of nuclear waste, or of the decommissioning of nuclear power plants. Had this been the case nuclear power would never have been able to compete with solar or wind energy, and if the money that has gone into the research and development of nuclear energy had gone into alternative energies, effectiveness and efficiency of wind and solar energy could have been improved sufficiently to make them a viable alternative. However, the field of nuclear power was pursued not only to provide new sources of energy, political and military considerations also played their part in these decisions.

Lovins *et al.* (2001) suggest a new approach called natural capitalism. This approach would help to protect the biosphere but also improve profits and competitiveness. It is no good trying to try to persuade managers to adopt a different approach for ecological reasons only. However, Lovins *et al.* emphasise – and have ample convincing examples – that natural capitalism is good for both the environment *and* business. They have identified four steps in the journey towards natural capitalism:

1.   Dramatically increase the productivity of natural resources
     This is achieved primarily by reducing waste through changes in the product design and production processes. In their experience companies that pursue such options have increased yield 10 or even 100 times. With such efficiency improvements the initial investment required pays for itself in short periods of time. Looking at the wider system (systems approach), and all aspects of a product's life cycle can provide the insights necessary to achieve such reductions.

Example: Interface Corporation

When designing a new carpet factory in Shanghai interface engineer Jan Schilham realised that two simple design changes could reduce power requirements from 95 horsepower to just seven, while costing less and without requiring any new technology. His approach was to use fatter pipes, causing less friction and hence less pumping energy. Traditional costing would have looked at the cost at the fatter pipes and decided against them as they are more expensive than thinner ones. Schilham took a systemic approach, looking at the system and costs over the product's life cycle. The second insight was to make the pipes short and straight. This was achieved by positioning the pipes first and then positioning the other equipment. This did not affect the workflow – all it did was improve the energy efficiency of the entire system. One of the reasons that no one had looked at it this way before is that the pipes seem to be the least important part of the system, so they were considered last. However, the systems approach requires all aspects of the system to be considered at the outset hence allowing optimisation of the whole *system* rather than any one aspect.

Source: Based on Lovins, A.B., Lovins, L.T. & Hawken, P. (2001). A road map for natural capitalism. In J.V. Henry, 2nd ed., *Creative Management*. London: Sage

---

2.   Shift to biologically inspired production models
     Aim to eliminate waste by trying to achieve closed-loop systems as seen in nature, e.g. compost; if the closed-loop system does not work for a single product, perhaps the waste from one product can be used as input for another. This approach can reduce a company's materials' requirements by up to 90%.

Example: Interface Corporation

Interface have developed a new material called Solenium that not only lasts four times longer and requires 40% less material than ordinary carpets, it can also be remanufactured into identical new products. It is also free of chlorine and other toxic materials, can be cleaned with water and does not grow mildew. The chairman of the company has an interesting definition of waste: any measurable input that does not produce customer value and all inputs until they prove otherwise. The zero-waste approach led to an increase in revenue of

> $200 million while resource requirements remained constant. $67 million of the revenue increase were a direct result of reduced landfill changes (down 60%).
>
> *Source*: Based on Lovins, A.B., Lovins, L.T. & Hawken, P. (2001). A road map for natural capitalism. In J.V. Henry, 2nd ed., *Creative Management*. London: Sage

3. Move to a solutions-based business model

    Shift from an emphasis on sales of goods to sales of services; example: agricultural chemical producer who sells weed-free fields instead of bags of chemicals, hence ensuring that a minimum rather than a maximum of chemicals are used – it is in the interest of the manufacturer to use as little as possible, rather than to sell as much as possible.

> **Example: Interface Corporation**
>
> Realising that people want to use and see carpets but not necessarily own them has led Interface to sell the service of providing carpeted floors, rather than carpets. Monthly inspections identify and replace tiles that are worn out. This leads to a 35-fold reduction in the flow of materials needed to maintain a carpet covered floor.
>
> *Source*: Based on Lovins, A.B., Lovins, L.T. & Hawken, P. (2001). A road map for natural capitalism. In J.V. Henry, 2nd ed., *Creative Management*. London: Sage

4. Reinvest in natural capital

    As the costs arising from deteriorating ecosystems rise, businesses need to invest in renewable resources. Companies face direct costs from the consequences of deteriorating eco systems, resulting in climate changes, e.g. high winds and floods. Lovins *et al.* mention the example of the deforestation in China's Yangtze basin in 1998 which triggered floods that killed 3700 people, dislocated 223 million, and destroyed 60 million acres of cropland. The total costs of the disaster amounted to £30 billion, forced a logging moratorium and required a $12 billion crash programme of reforestation.

> **Example: California Rice Industry Association**
>
> Companies are increasing efforts to live with nature rather than against it. Rather than focusing on a single product the Association has discovered the value of diversity. Instead of burning the rice fields they allow 150,000–200,000 acres of the Sacramento valley rice fields to flood after harvest. This not only creates seasonable wetland which is ecologically valuable, but creates other benefits such as the replenishment of the groundwater, improved fertility. Through the flooding the straw that was previously burned (polluting the air) has increased silica content which means that its resistance to insects has improved which means it can be profitably sold as construction material.
>
> *Source*: Based on Lovins, A.B., Lovins, L.T. & Hawken, P. (2001). A road map for natural capitalism. In J.V. Henry, 2nd ed., *Creative Management*. London: Sage

THE ROLE OF THE DESIGNER

Lovins *et al.* (2001) give impressive evidence that considering the environment makes commercial sense. In the section before that we looked at several tools and questions that help assess a product's environmental impact. The question is, who should take responsibility of ensuring

> Interestingly but not surprisingly much of the writing on environmentally responsible products can be found in the design literature.

minimum environmental impact of products? Of course senior management buy-in and leadership are essential. Life-cycle consideration and a systems approach will be new to many organisations, and a significant departure from how things have been done in the past cannot happen without top management support. However, at the project level environmental considerations need a champion too. Designers – industrial designers, design engineers, packaging designers and so on – are well positioned to take up such a role. MacKenzie (1997) comments, "For many years, designers have been asserting their influence and demonstrating the power of design. The new demands on designing for minimum ecological impact will provide an ideal platform from which designers can justify their claims and acknowledge their responsibility. Why should so much responsibility fall to the designer? Design is one part of a holistic process, which involves a wide range of other skills. However, design is a pivotal part of the process." And Lewis *et al.* (2001) point out, "The designer, as the principal determinant or creator of the product itself, has a direct influence on the amount of damage which will occur at each state in the process." Designers often determine which materials and processes are used, and these determine to a large degree how environmental friendly – or not – a product is. Take for example a recent example of Nike who have emphasised the 'eco-design' aspects of one of their recent products: snap-in soles that recycle easily, 100% recycled laces and rubber that has 96% fewer toxins than previously used kinds.[2] It is also designers who manipulate consumption indirectly as influencers of trends and fashions.

Toys are a great (negative!) example. How many toys are created as a fashion, to last only a season, to be thrown away as soon as the batteries run out or the next toy comes along. How many clothes are designed to last – one season instead of a lifetime? Who would like to buy one high-quality suit rather than two or three cheap ones even though they will last only a fraction of the time? Of course it is not just the designers that need to reconsider, looking at their output with sustainability in mind. Consumers, all of us, will have to rethink our values and priorities if we are serious about handing the planet to the next generation in a healthy and liveable state. Sounds dramatic? People joke about selling fresh air – people joked about selling fresh water less than a century ago. Just something to keep in mind.

Designers should have knowledge about characteristics of materials, they can influence the number of different materials used, they influence the number of components, they are involved in the design of systems and so on. Lewis *et al.* have in fact identified nine major environmental problems that designers should keep in mind when making their choices:

- global warming
- ozone depletion
- reduced biodiversity
- resource depletion
- water pollution
- air pollution

---

[2] As reported, for example, in *Fast Company*, March 2007.

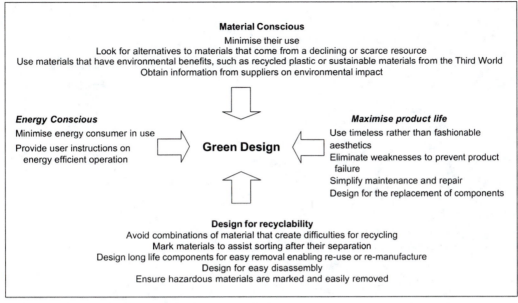

Material Conscious
Minimise their use
Look for alternatives to materials that come from a declining or scarce resource
Use materials that have environmental benefits, such as recycled plastic or sustainable materials from the Third World
Obtain information from suppliers on environmental impact

Energy Conscious
Minimise energy consumer in use
Provide user instructions on energy efficient operation

Green Design

Maximise product life
Use timeless rather than fashionable aesthetics
Eliminate weaknesses to prevent product failure
Simplify maintenance and repair
Design for the replacement of components

Design for recyclability
Avoid combinations of material that create difficulties for recycling
Mark materials to assist sorting after their separation
Design long life components for easy removal enabling re-use or re-manufacture
Design for easy disassembly
Ensure hazardous materials are marked and easily removed

Figure 18.3 A framework for achieving green design.
Source: Burall, 1992. Reproduced by permission of Design Council, copyright Paul Burrall.

- land degradation
- solid waste
- acidification

Burall (1992) suggests a framework for achieving what he then called 'green design' which mirrors his questions introduced earlier in this chapter summarising aspects that designers should consider in the design and development of environmentally conscious products into four categories (see Figure 18.3).

All the above are influenced through product design. Lewis *et al.* suggest that one way of sharing responsibility for assuring that products are based on sustainability principles is to write environmental/sustainability criteria into the design brief (see Box 18.4).

Box 18.4   The design brief

Introduction

- Define the aim of the (design) project
- List specific objectives

General requirements

- Define primary function of the product
- State the durability requirements

- List aesthetic considerations
- Define ergonomic requirements
- List the safety requirements and issues
- Outline the required performance and quality

Environmental objectives

- List specific strategies relating to materials, efficiency, recovery at end of life and so on
- Include quantitative targets where relevant (e.g. 'use 50% recycled materials')

Production requirements

- Specific manufacturing requirements or limitations
- Include any objectives or targets (e.g. minimise components to streamline assembly process)

Regulation and standards

- List any mandatory regulations, standards or codes of practice relevant to the product

Cost

- Specify limits on cost of production to ensure that the product is competitive

Source: Lewis et al. (2001). Design + Environment — A Global Guide to Designing Greener Goods. Sheffield, UK: Greenleaf

It is also important to point out that it is not only the product design that needs to be considered. Process design, and in fact business design as we have seen in the case of the Interface Corporation, need to be considered.

And one final comment, many organisations are wondering where to concentrate their innovation efforts and what selection criteria to establish for choosing concepts to be taken forward. Focusing on ideas that combine a minimisation of environmental impact and maximisation of cost efficiency might provide a viable framework. Such products not only provide extra value for the consumer, but also positioning yourself at the forefront of environmental consciousness and thinking can become a differentiating factor for your organisation.

READING SUGGESTIONS

Hawken, P.A. & Lovins, L.H. (1999). *Natural Capitalism: The Next Industrial Revolution.* London: Earthscan.

Comment: If you want to read one book on the subject, this is the one.

Papanek, V. (1991). *Design for the Real World,* 2nd edition. London: Thames & Hudson.

Comment: When the first edition came out in 1971 it was well ahead of its time in terms of highlighting the social and ethical responsibility of design and designers. Should be required reading for all designers, and gives ammunition to those who want to want to argue for better and more responsible design. You may also want to look at his 'sequel', *The Green Imperative: Ecology and Ethics in Design and Architecture* (1995). London: Thames & Hudson.

Charter, M. & Tischener, U. (eds) (2001). *Sustainable Solutions*. Sheffield, UK: Greenleaf.

Comment: Addressing the need for suitable management structures and practical tools to address increasing environmental concerns, the book addresses the following: (a) issues of business sustainability; (b) methodologies and approaches towards organising and developing more sustainable products and services; (c) a collection of global case studies; (d) a list of literature, resources and addresses of useful organisations.

Lewis, H., Gertsakis, J., Grant, T., Morelli, N. & Sweatman, A. (2001). *Design + Environment – A Global Guide to Designing Greener Products*. Sheffield, UK: Greenleaf Publishing.

Comment: This book is very 'hands-on', reviewing many tools, comparing the use of recycled and non-recycled raw materials, lists hazardous materials etc. also reviews specific design areas such as packaging, clothing and textiles, furniture and electronic and electrical products.

Mackenzie, D. (1997) *Green Design: Design for the Environment*, 2nd edition. London: Laurence King.

Comment: MacKenzie starts her book by explaining the designer's contribution to creating products that are more environmentally responsible, provides some background for creating the urgency, and then looks at how 'green design' should be reflected in different design disciplines (architecture and interior design, product design, packaging design, print and graphic design, and textile design).

SOME USEFUL WEBSITES

http://www.wbcsd.ch

Comment: Website of the World Business Council for Sustainable Development (WBCSD) which was founded in 1992. It is a not-for-profit organisation whose mission it is to "... provide business leadership as a catalyst for change toward sustainable development, and to support the business license to operate, innovate and grow in a world increasingly shaped by sustainable development issues".

www.eea.eu

Comment: The website of the European Environment Agency where you can download useful information such as a guide on Life Cycle Assessment (see http://reports.eea.europa.eu/GH-07-97-595-EN-C/en).

http://gm.com

Comment: On this website by the Global Recycling Network you can find company directories, processes, publications and news about recycling.

                http://www.ends.co.uk

Comment: Environmental Data Services Ltd (ENDS) is an independent publisher which has served environmental professionals since 1978.

                www.gemi.org

Comment: The Global Environmental Management Initiative (GEMI) provides some guides and tools for starting organisations in a sustainable direction, including the Sustainable Development Planner™ as a starting point for planning how to integrate sustainability into your business.

19 Note on intellectual property rights (IPR)

The basic Bell patents for the telephone were defended in court and the survival of Bell Telephone was ensured by a few crude notes made by Bell on the back of an envelope which (luckily) had been properly signed, witnessed and dated.

http://www.quantumbooks.com/Creativity.html

As innovation is often risky and costly, most companies are quite keen to protect their innovations for as long as possible through patents and other forms of intellectual rights protection. How important, and how effective, the protection of intellectual property is will vary from industry to industry. In the pharmaceutical industry where research and development costs are immense, patents play an important role in paying for future R&D activities. The exclusivity for the duration of the protection also allows companies to charge a premium which tends to get eroded once 'generics' come onto the market. This makes timing quite critical: registering a patent too early means that the company is losing out on profits, if the team wait too long there is a danger that a competitor might get a registration first. This conflict was alluded to in the Roche case study.

On the other hand, there are people who believe that making intellectual property freely available can be greatly beneficial. During a recent workshop at the leading edge innovation consultancy IDEO one of their staff commented, "We believe that ideas are free. It is what you do with them that creates the value." This is certainly a trend that is gaining increasing momentum – and we have talked in Chapter 13 about the movement towards 'open innovation'. IBM made the papers in 2005 when it announced that it would release 500 of its software patents into the open development community.[1]

I also found it quite interesting to hear CD sales went up during the period when music titles could be copied freely – at the same rate as the downloads – just to drop again when downloading became prohibited.

This chapter provides an overview of different types of IPR protection, summarises the general requirements and process for patenting, comments on filing patents internationally, takes a brief look at issues around patenting in the pharmaceutical industry, and comments on some recent changes to design rights.[2]

---

[1] BBC News, Tuesday, 11 January 2005.
[2] The content of this chapter was originally based on the following sources:
http://www.medicalfutures.co.uk
http://www.cipa.org.uk

TYPES OF INTELLECTUAL PROPERTY RIGHTS

There are a number of different ways of protecting intellectual property, applicable in different contexts and for different types of products. Below we will review the following:

- patents
- copyright
- designs
- trademarks
- databases
- 'know-how'

PATENTS

While a patent gives its owner the legal right for the exclusive use of an invention for up to 20 years, its main purpose tends to be to prevent others from using it – or at least using it without consent.

To qualify for patent application the following criteria need to be fulfilled (from the UK Patents Act of 1977 and the related European Patent Convention):

- The invention must be new, i.e. it must not have been disclosed by the inventor(s) prior to filing the application – we explore this issue in a bit more detail later.

- It involves an inventive step, which means it is not blatantly obvious.

- It can be described in an enabling fashion (so that others can reproduce the invention).

- It is capable of industrial application.

- Is not specifically excluded from patent protection (see sections below).

Patent law specifically provides that the following subject matters as such are not patentable inventions:

- A discovery, scientific theory or mathematical method.

- A literary, dramatic, musical or artistic work or any other aesthetic creation.

http://www.derwent.com/patentfaq/process.html - no longer active
http://crct.oyster.co.uk/pat_matt/pat_req1.html - no longer active
http://www.designcouncil.org/design/content/fact.jsp?contentID=09009e0d8003e9d8 – no longer active; you may want to look at http://www.designcouncil.org/en/About-Design/Business-Essentials/Invention/Invention6/
'Legal matters, software and the patent trap', *Innovation Business,* issue 2, publication by the NatWest & The Royal Bank of Scotland, p. 5.
E. Bobrow (1997). *Complete Idiot's Guide to New Product Development.* Alpha books, pp. 211–33.

- A scheme, rule or method for performing a mental act, playing a game or doing business, or a program for a computer.

- The presentation of information.

Patent law further provides that a patent shall not be granted:

- For an invention, the publication or exploitation of which would be generally expected to encourage offensive, immoral or anti-social behaviour.

- For any variety of animal or plant or any essentially biological process for the production of animals or plants, not being a microbiological process or the product of such a process.

The patenting process

The patenting process is time consuming and somewhat costly: it can take in excess of two years from filing the initial application to granting the patent and cost around £25,000. Figure 19.1 illustrates the process, cost and time lines.

Filing patents internationally

The filing and recognition of patents is truly international – in January 2000 the Paris Convention for the Protection of Intellectual Property of 1883 (revised and updated many times) had 157 signatory nations. While there are some national differences, most processes and procedures share a large degree of communality. As a rule of thumb, you have to ensure for patent protection in those countries in which you would like to see your patent protected, and in most countries patent laws would expect you to commercially exploit your patent within three years.

Where the US patent law differs

There are actually some differences in patenting law between Europe and the US. While an invention is considered non-patentable if it has been disclosed in public before the patent is filed in Europe and most other parts of the world, the US patent law allows for one year to lapse between the first public disclosure and the filing of the patent application.

Related to this is the other main difference: the importance of the filing date for priority. Unlike in other countries where the critical moment for deciding who owns a patent is decided the moment a patent is filed – 'first-to-file' system, the US operate a 'first-to-invent' system. If someone can prove that they have made the invention before the person that has filed the patent application, they may be entitled to that patent after all. This means that keeping dated, signed and countersigned records of any documentation or drawing that could prove that you have been the first to come up with a particular invention is critical. For example, research scientists should be encouraged to keep laboratory notebooks documenting their work whereby they have to ensure the signing, dating, peer scrutiny and countersigning.

The Patenting Procedure

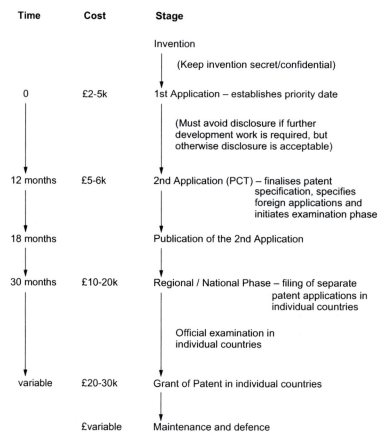

Time	Cost	Stage
		Invention
		(Keep invention secret/confidential)
0	£2-5k	1st Application – establishes priority date
		(Must avoid disclosure if further development work is required, but otherwise disclosure is acceptable)
12 months	£5-6k	2nd Application (PCT) – finalises patent specification, specifies foreign applications and initiates examination phase
18 months		Publication of the 2nd Application
30 months	£10-20k	Regional / National Phase – filing of separate patent applications in individual countries
		Official examination in individual countries
variable	£20-30k	Grant of Patent in individual countries
	£variable	Maintenance and defence

Figure 19.1   The patenting procedure

However, there are further details to be aware of, concerning the conception – "the complete performance of the mental part of the inventive act", and the reduction to practice – "when a working model is made and a practical utility demonstrated". The filing of a patent application is considered to be the point when an invention is reduced to practice. If there is a conflict about who has come up with the invention first ('interference' in legal terms), the rules shown in Box 19.1 apply.

Box 19.1

The person who can prove the earlier date of conception and reduction to practice wins.

    Party A conception first   reduction first
    Party B   conception second   reduction second
    A wins

> However, if A can prove conception before B but reduction to practice occurs after B, then A will have to prove 'reasonable diligence' in reducing the invention to practice. Reasonable diligence generally requires 'reasonably continuous activity'.
>
> | | | |
> |---|---|---|
> | Party A conception first diligence | | reduction second |
> | Party B conception second | diligence | reduction first |
> | A wins | | |
>
> | | | |
> |---|---|---|
> | Party A conception first insufficient diligence | | reduction second |
> | Party B conception second | diligence | reduction first |
> | B wins | | |

Patenting and the pharmaceutical industry

If patent protection is important in most industries, it is quite critical to the pharmaceutical industry. Nowadays it can easily take £100–200 million in R&D investment to bring a new drug containing a new chemical entity (NCE) to the marketplace – and not every NCE is a blockbuster. To get one blockbuster pharmaceutical companies have to develop thousands of compounds and materials, most of which will get discarded before they reach the market. Even drugs that make it successfully into the market often fail to generate return on investment. Escalating development costs and stricter regulatory and safety demands have led to the shortening of the period from bringing a product to market to the expiry of the patent. For example, recent estimates of the Centre for Medicines Research suggest that the effective patent life in the UK (from market introduction to patent expiry) is on average only about eight years. It is very much due to decreasing returns even from successfully introduced drugs that has led to a drop in annually introduced NCEs from 90 in 1969 to fewer than 40 in 1989. Legislation in the US and Japan (1994 and 1988, respectively) has been changed to address this issue, it is now possible to extend the period of protection. Similar legislation has also been introduced in Europe where pharmaceutical companies can apply for a Supplementary Protection Certificate (SPC) which provides a maximum of 15 years legal protection, counting from the first marketing authorisation in the European Union.

COPYRIGHT

Whereas a patent protects an idea, copyright protects the way in which the idea is expressed. So you cannot copyright an idea, only its expression. Typical candidates for copyright are books, musical compositions, artwork, illustrations, films, records, broadcasts and typographical arrangements, including computer software. Copyright laws prevent other people from copying or exploiting the originator's work without permission. It is a weaker but wider form of protection than a patent. Infringement has to involve proven copying of a substantial part of the work. Unlike patenting copyright applies automatically which means it is quicker and cheaper. Once the material is created, it is protected. However, it is still worth registering to ensure protection in some circumstances, especially in the US. The owner of the copyright tends to be the originator though when the work has been undertaken as part of an employment, the employer will be the owner. For literary works the copyright will generally continue for 70 years after the author's death. For other works the time span of protection is different and the rules of ownership are more complex.

DESIGN RIGHTS

(a) Registered

Registered design rights become relevant when the novelty lies in the appearance rather than the new idea or principle itself. A registered design gives the owner excusive rights to a certain appearance of a certain article. This means he or she can stop anyone else from making, using and selling a product of the same design without permission. This kind of protection generally applies to commercial objects with a unique or aesthetic appearance. To achieve the status of 'registered design' the originator has to submit drawings or photographs showing the item to the Designs Registry. The main costs associated with obtaining a registered design are the initial filing costs. Upon registration the design is initially protected for five years, with the possibility of extending, five years at a time, up to 25 years.

(b) Unregistered

Besides the registered design rights there are also unregistered design rights. These are not directly associated with appearance but protect internal and external features. However, they only give protection against the copying of the features, e.g. the brand name, the company logo, the physical design of computer chip or architectural drawings. Design right exists automatically – you do not need to apply for it. However, to prove that you are the originator it is advisable to sign and date the original drawings and/or prototypes and keep them in a safe place. While design right can be relied upon in the UK, overseas protection is not necessarily guaranteed unless further protection is sought.

(c) Recent changes

Towards the end of 2001 a new European Directive was implemented bringing a number of important changes to Design Registration law. The six key changes to the law are:

1.   Instead of the article bearing the design it will be the design that is protected. In the past the protection of a pattern would be linked to the particular object for which it was registered, if the pattern was to be applied to a different object or material a separate registration would be required, e.g. if the original registration was for a cup, a new registration would have been required for bed linen or a table to which the same patterns would be applied. Since the change it is the pattern that is protected, independent of the product to which it is applied. This means that graphic symbols, such as desktop icons can now be registered.

2.   Whereas there was previously a minimum number of units (50) that had to be produced before a design could be registered, the change allows the registration of unique products, e.g. a sculpture or any handicraft item. This enables the artist to keep control of licensing arrangements.

3.   Whereas previously the entire object had to be registered – it had to have an 'independent life of its own' – now any visible part of a product can be registered. For example, you can now register the lid of a pot, be it applied to a teapot, a sugar bowl or a biscuit tin.

4.   Previously the application for a registered design would be checked against existing UK registrations. Now a disclosure in any other country in the world would similarly cause an application to fail on grounds of lack of novelty. So if the designer of a particular piece of period jewellery sought registration, he or she might be refused because such a piece exists in a museum somewhere in the world.

5.   The rules for what is classified as 'novel' have been tightened. Registration is refused if the object in question evokes a 'déjà vu' in the eyes of an 'informed user'. The informed user will not be a design expert but someone familiar with the object in question, e.g. a waitress would comment on the degree of familiarity with a new cup design.

6.   Whereas before only designs that had not previously been disclosed could be registered, now designers have a 12-month 'grace period'. In the past many a designer only realised the value of his or her design when it became a success in the market – by which time it was too late to register it. However, designers should be aware that if someone discloses the same or similar design, which this someone has created independently, first, then the designer will have lost his or her opportunity to register the design.

TRADEMARKS

Trademarks can be registered or unregistered. Registered marks afford better legal protection. Registered trademarks are the only intellectual property right which can exist indefinitely – provided the mark is used and periodic renewal fees are paid whereas copyright and patents expire after a given time. A trademark is a sign, name or symbol that distinguishes one product or services from similar competitive products or services. Good trademarks seem to share in common that they are easily pronounceable (if they are words), memorable and pleasing to the eye. An example for a trademark is the Coca-Cola bottle. A trademark could be anything from the design of a label to the shape of a product's packaging or even the sound or smell of a particular product. Having a registered trademark means that no one but the registered owner or someone with his or her consent can use the image or shape for their product – which can be extremely valuable in maintaining a market leader position. Trademarks like patents are territorial, i.e. you have to apply for them in the country or group of countries in which you want to use them. You usually have a grace period after the first country filing to register in other countries as well.

KNOW HOW

'Know how', sometimes also referred to as 'confidential information' or 'trade secret', is a fairly new type of intellectual property protection. Unlike other international property rights, it is not based on a statutory scheme but is rooted in case or judge-made law. Any process, technique, formula, information, device, design or even client list can be a trade secret as long as it is not generally known (i.e. a secret) and represents a competitive business advantage. You do not need to do much to secure a trade secret, generally you would only need to prove that you have done everything to ensure confidentiality (e.g. have employees or other people who come in contact with the trade secret sign confidentiality agreements). The problem with trade secrets is that they are only protective while the information is secret. If the secret information is made public by legitimate means, e.g. reverse engineering, disassembly or chemical analysis, there is no way to protect it. It is only when the secret has been obtained illegitimately, e.g. though industrial espionage, that protection might be enforceable.

READING SUGGESTIONS

Bouchoux, D.E. (2001). *Protecting Your Company's Intellectual Property: A Practical Guide to Trademarks, Copyrights, Patents and Trade Secrets.* Amacom.

Comment: This is a detailed look at how to protect the four key areas of intellectual property: trademarks; copyrights; patents; and trade secrets (including customer lists, marketing plans, and other in-house documents). Written for a general business reader, the book shows that intellectual property is often a company's most valuable asset.

Jacob, R., Alexander, D. & Lane, L. (2004). *A Guidebook to Intellectual Property.* Sweet & Maxwell.

Comment: Aimed at students and business people alike; main emphasis on patenting; brought to life with case studies; includes reference to European and international applications.

SOME USEFUL WEBSITES

http://www.cipa.org.uk

Comment: For information and questions around patents in the UK, the website of the Chartered Institute of Patent Agents (CIPA), the professional and examining body for patent agents (also known as patent attorneys) is the right one for you. The web address for the UK patent office is http://www.patent.gov.uk and for the US patent and trademark office it is http://www.uspto.gov.

20 Innovation in large organisations

CASE STUDY 7: GKN – LIGHT COMPOSITE DISC JOINT[1]

Decisions, decisions

To spin or not to spin, that was the question that senior management of GKN's Automotive Driveline Division (GKN ADD) was facing in October 2001. Over the past decade an innovative product – the Light Composite Disc Joint (LCD) – had been developed internally, offering a number of customer benefits. But there were two main reasons why GKN was hesitant to embark on full commercialisation within the Group, the first was that there was not widespread confidence that sales would be of a scale acceptable to GKN; and secondly, it was felt that the product was not close enough to its core.

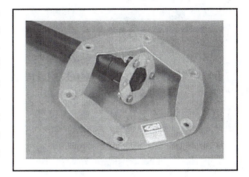

Dr Andrew Pollard, GKN ADD's project champion who had been involved in its development since the early 1990s, had spent about one year developing a business plan which had recently managed to attract the interest of two investor consortia: one based in London, one in the Midlands. Particularly the London-based one was very keen to proceed. In the business plan the concept of Spinning-Composites Ltd, as the business was to be called, read as follows:

> Spinning-Composites Ltd is a spinout operation from GKN plc with the aim of exploiting composite shaft and coupling technologies developed in GKN's Automotive Driveshaft Research and Development centre. Confidence in the potential of the new business is underlined by GKN's commitment to invest and retain an equity stake. In particular, Spinning will produce and market the GKN Light Composite Disc Joint (LCD), an innovative new kind of shaft coupling that has been awarded Millennium Product status by the Design Council in the UK. Spinning is being established to exploit the identified business potential for industrial and non-automotive driveshafts, which is non-core business for GKN Automotive Driveline Division

Since the original decision that the only way forward for the LCD would be to spin it out, GKN had started to review its policy towards 'non-core' business concepts. But had the success in attracting investors put some doubts into

[1] The case has been prepared by Dr Bettina von Stamm as a basis for class discussion rather than to illustrate either effective or ineffective handling of a management situation.

the minds of GKN ADD senior management as to whether a spin-off would be the best solution? Might there be a solution internally to take the business forward after all? Andrew Pollard was wondering what would be decided.

- In the automotive business it is essential to be a global player and to provide consistent products wherever they are produced – which means engineering standardisation of material/components/processes/suppliers is a big issue

- GKN has 38% of world driveshaft production worth about £1.7 billion; a further 31% is done in-house by car manufacturers but many of them licence GKN products. GKN have worked on convincing car manufacturers that they have more in-depth knowledge and expertise in driveshaft development than anyone else in the world; recently acquired in-house production of driveshafts from Fiat, Opel, Nissan

- Due to size of operation and complexity of customer relationships (global etc.) the management structure is complex and heavily focused on standard constant velocity joint products

- R&D is aligned closely to products

How the project had started

In the late 1980s GKN had started an initiative to investigate the use of composite materials as a replacement for the metal used for its core products, shafts and joints that transmit power from a car's gearbox to its wheels. Composite materials offered some potential advantages in the area of noise, vibration and harshness (NVH), particularly for longitudinal propeller shafts that are used in rear-wheel drive vehicles. In addition, lighter components would also aid car manufacturers in their quest to improve the fuel efficiency of their cars.

Though the main focus of the efforts was to develop shafts made of composite materials, applications for the joints were considered too. In the late 1980s Wolfgang Löbel of GKN Löhr & Bromkamp (LBO) in Germany, a producer of constant velocity joints (CVJs) developed a constant velocity joint made from composite materials, later to be known as the light composite disc joint. The new product concept was aimed at enabling a much lighter form of CVJ for automotive propeller shafts. Although metal CVJs are very effective at transmitting power through big misalignment angles (e.g. when a car's wheels are turned), they are rather complex and heavy. A small-scale development had been progressed in Germany before the project was transferred for further development and the identification of applications of the product within the automotive sector to GKN Technology (GKNT), GKN ADD's R&D facility in the UK, in 1991.

Even in the early 1990s ADD had a very globally integrated structure so everyone could find out what other people in his or her area of interest were working on. Andrew, who had joined the company in 1986 with a degree in mechanical engineering and who had since developed an expertise in composite products, had already heard about the concept through the company grapevine and was keen to take it forward. Between 1991 and 1996 the project

The LCD is an innovative lightweight and flexible coupling suitable for use in power-transmitting driveshafts, and delivers a range of technically exciting competitive advantages. It comprises a composite of glass fibre in an epoxy matrix, with controlled orientations of glass fibres throughout the laminated structure of the disc.

was part of the regular development programme for automotive couplings in GKN's R&D facility in Wolverhampton in the UK.

As technical questions (product design, materials, process, performance) were answered, the focus of the development programme moved to the commercial potential of the LCD for automotive applications. Although the total potential automotive market for this type of product was estimated around four million units per annum, the manufacturing investment required to achieve low enough costs and win a significant share of this market were prohibitive in relation to the expected commercial return. In 1996, it was decided to stop the development programme for automotive applications.

Those involved in the development of the LCD remained fascinated by its extraordinary performance within a particular sector of technical coupling requirements. Additional avenues were found more or less by accident. LBO was at that time also selling their CVJ products for non-automotive applications. Wolfgang Löbel believed that the LCD might help to solve application problems that they were suffering from due to overheating and maintenance needs of CVJs used in wind turbine driveshafts. However, there was one problem, company rules said that GKN Technology could not talk to customers directly – not even to GKN Business Units outside of Automotive Engineering for that matter. Determined not to let company rules get in the way Andrew worked with the GKN design engineers in the German driveshaft business, the engineer from the German company in turn talked to the GKN people in Denmark who then spoke to the potential customer, the producer of wind turbines.

The Danish GKN engineer succeeded in persuading the Danish wind turbine producer to test the disc, which was a great step towards moving the project forward. But trying the new product required a leap of faith: imagine offering to replace a hefty, somewhat complicated assembly of steel parts weighing 20 kg with an extremely thin 390 gram 'plastic' disc! The response from the wind turbine manufacturer though was positive and, although accessing this additional market still meant the LCD business was trivial in GKN terms, Andrew got a green light for further development. This was due not least to the fact that LBO had considerable political power within the GKN organisation, were interested in finding an improved replacement for the CVJ joint used in wind turbines at the time, and were ready to invest £60,000–70,000 in the tooling and testing of the LCD.

History of GKN

Under its current name GKN had started trading at the beginning of the twentieth century when three companies got together: John Guest whose ancestor had started iron smelting in Wales in 1767; Arthur Keen who had started a bolt company in the 1860s; and John Sutton Nettlefolds, specialising in woodscrews, wire and metal rods. Soon after that the company added forging, rolling and stamping to its portfolio. The company rode on the increased demands for automobiles in the first half of the last century, complementing its existing expertise in the 1960s through acquisitions. In the late 1960s GKN expanded its operations into Germany by acquiring a stake in Uni-Cardan AG, maker of constant velocity joints (CVJs). International expansion continued during the 1970s with business acquisitions in Australia, the US and France.

In the 1980s GKN diversified its service operations and strengthened its automotive business through further acquisitions while disposing of most of its interests in steel. It was also in the late 1980s that GKN acquired a stake in Westland, a UK helicopter maker (bought outright in 1994). When Hong Kong-born Sir C.K. Chow took over as Chief Executive in 1996 he found a GKN that looked, as the *Economist* described, "More like an Asian mini-conglomerate than a textbook firm focused on a core business." In the 1997 Annual Report Chow wrote, "We redefined our corporate values earlier this year. GKN's traditional values, to which we have a firm and continuing commitment, relate to our dedication to our customers, respect for and development of our people, and a sense of responsibility towards the communities in which we operate and the environment in which we all live. To these we have added a commitment to fostering entrepreneurship and innovation. We encourage our people to create wealth by being innovative and resourceful in meeting the needs of our customers. We want them to be commercially agile and to manage risk carefully. We also want to create an environment which allows them to perform at a high speed."

> In 1999 GKN had three main business lines:
>
> 1. Automotive including: automotive driveline, powder metallurgy, auto components, off-highway vehicle systems; 51% of business or £2394 million in 1999.
>
> 2. Aerospace including aerospace structures and helicopters; 31% of business or £1439 million in 1999.
>
> 3. Industrial Services including Chep (pallets etc.), Cleanaway (waste disposal), Meineke (exhaust replacement chain in US); 17% of business or £810 million in 1999.

The drive towards entrepreneurship and innovation was reflected in a three-horizon approach. The aim of Sir C.K. Chow to transform the old-established UK engineering company into an innovative, fast-growing leader in its chosen markets resulted in the divestment of the Industrial Services business in August 2001. With consolidation achieved GKN also revised its approach to innovation. GKN's top management decided that Horizon 3 projects should no longer be pursued, but that increased emphasis should be placed on Horizon 1 and Horizon 2 developments (perhaps including the LCD coupling) that related to the core automotive and aerospace businesses.

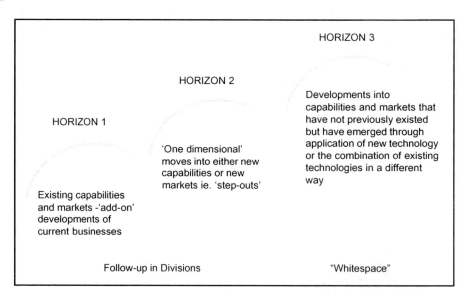

Full steam ahead

In September 1997, after LBO committed funds for further development of the LCD, Ian Leadbetter, Engineering Director GKN Automotive Driveline (ADD), agreed that to enable the project to move forwards Andrew should be allowed to communicate directly with the Dansk Uni-Cardan, the Danish GKN company that supplied to the wind turbine producer. Until this point, the communication and product engineering chain ran from GKN Technology through ADD Engineering to the Engineering Department in LBO (one of the ADD Business Units), and back down through the Aftermarket Operations (AMO) organisation to Dansk Uni-Cardan.

Andrew spent 1998/99 communicating with other AMO companies within GKN, to explore other potential application areas for the LCD coupling, as it was thought that GKN AMO would be the customer-facing unit – and they were quite enthusiastic about it. Andrew was pulling strings wherever he could, which meant working to get the helicopter division interested, and (successfully) applying for a 'Millennium Product' award. Receiving the award was particularly helpful in protecting the project internally. In the meantime, Dansk Uni-Cardan were successfully win-

> In 1998 Ian was succeeded by Graeme Walford who in turn left GKN in August 2001. (He was replaced in November 2001 by Al Deane, previously responsible for Engineering in the USA.) While not convinced personally, Graeme was fairly supportive of the project and gave advice and inputs to the ADD Financial Director between April and August 2001.

ning new business for the application of the LCD in wind turbines, while AMO UK were making inroads into motorsport applications. All these activities led Andrew to feel that he was successfully sowing the seeds to a viable business.

There was a small structural change to GKN Automotive in January 1999, which was helpful to Andrew's project. The AMO companies had previously operated as quite independent national units, mainly after-sales services and the distribution of spares, and reporting at the Divisional (GKN Automotive) level. In 1999, they were formed as a Business Unit within ADD. This made it more legitimate to cultivate direct links between GKN Technology and the AMO companies.

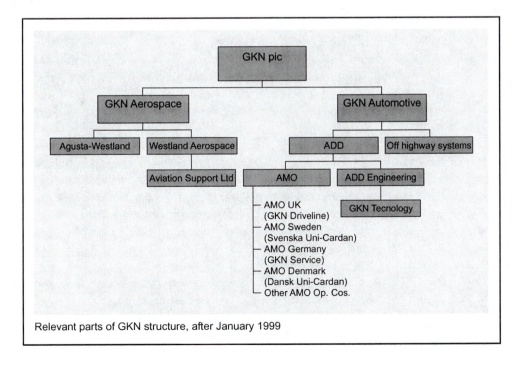

Relevant parts of GKN structure, after January 1999

A significant problem arose in late 1999 when Graeme Walford made organisational changes within ADD Engineering, which resulted in Andrew reporting to a different director. The new R&D Director was adamant that only projects directly relevant to automotives were to be continued; all others had to be wound up.

End or beginning?

Early 2000 there was a whole host of arguments as to why the project should be discontinued, not only the lack of relevance to automotive:

- The manufacturing process had nothing in common with existing ADD operations.

> Andrew recalls, "All in all, I was generally able to persuade people that it was a worthwhile project. But those I could not persuade made things quite difficult for me."

- A product aspiring to sales of £5 million was seen to be too much of a niche product in an organisation with total sales approaching £2000 million.

- It was seen to represent a distraction to ADD management time.

- Drawing on resources that could be used better to support existing business.

- The organisation was not set up to cater for start-up businesses.

In short, the LCD was not able to meet company criteria and did not fit into any of the existing GKN boxes. It seemed that in an organisation set up for maximising returns from existing products and delivering against set customer expectations the culture was such that, as someone put it, "It would crush anything that is in its wake."

Andrew realised that if he could not come up with an alternative solution, the project would soon be officially stopped. Explaining his determination he said, "In R&D about 95% of the work you do disappears without trace so, if you hit on something, you really want to pursue it; it is about making something real out of an idea." Another personnel change did not help much either: in December 2000, AMO got a new CEO who was supportive of the project in principle but felt that AMO's business was about sales, not the manufacture of a technical product.

One aspect of the strategy for GKN set out by Sir C.K. Chow though was very much to Andrew's advantage: the drive to increase innovation. In 1999 GKN had set up an Innovation & Learning Group (ILG) that was responsible for coordinating and stimulating innovation and learning activities from a central level and one aim was to identify potential new lines of business. After finding out about it and developing his case Andrew emailed Jenny Smith (Manager, Innovation & Learning) of the ILG. She recalls, "Andrew felt that what he was doing was not quite strategic enough and that if he was released from his 'normal' activities he could do more. I could tell he felt quite strongly about it." She raised the issue with Marcus Beresford, the Chairman of the ILG and an Executive Director of GKN plc, and it was decided that this project might serve as a good example for what GKN wanted to achieve with its drive for entrepreneurship in the organisation. They felt that it would be a good project to trial processes and concepts they planned to develop for the incubation of new businesses.

In October 2000 the GKN PLC Board decided that Andrew should be given the mandate to develop a business plan to spin off the LCD business as an independent company. He was taken out of line reporting and given six months to find, finance and launch as an independent business. The assignment was signed off by two of the company's board directors, Marcus Beresford – his responsibilities included the ILG – and Ian Griffiths, the board member responsible for GKN Automotive. Andrew made sure the announcement would be made publicly as he knew that top management's officially declared support would be instrumental in securing the help and input from other people within the organisation. In addition KPMG were hired in January 2001 to act as independent advisers to Andrew – rather than GKN – to help develop a viable business plan and add credibility with external investors.

The business plan

To validate the idea Jenny also asked Andrew to present to the St John's Innovation Centre near Cambridge. The St John's Centre is linked to Cambridge University Science Park and its aim is to encourage and help incubate new businesses, the Centre works with about 400 businesses per year. Financially the Centre is backed by the University and draws additional funds from leasing space in its buildings outside Cambridge. The presentation in July 2000 went very well and Walter Herriot, its director, recalls, "The business plan Andrew brought was pretty good. It was clear that Andrew was well motivated, intelligent and had a business background. He was mature in age as well – as opposed to most other people who come here to present their business plan. This meant that his business plan was much higher up in the chain of probability. His proposal required much less input than most others."

St John's College is an educational charity and has set up the St John's Innovation Centre Ltd in order to:

- Enable the College to maximise the return on its investment by the efficient professional management of the Park

- Provide a supportive environment for tenant businesses by providing quality, cost-effective services

- Provide an environment in which technology transfer and innovation are promoted to assist small and medium sized business at a local, national and international level

According to Walter Herriot the majority of spin-outs did not come from universities as widely believed but from within companies. Discussions with Walter emphasised the importance of clarifying IPR issues. In the case of the LCD this was complicated by the fact that some patents were registered in the name of the German inventor – and that in fact German patenting laws were different.

The development of the business plan took Andrew up to April 2001, somewhat beyond the target completion date of March 2001. As he recalls: "They realised that it was not a straightforward process, but that I was getting somewhere so they continued to support me." The plan also set out a need for commercial expertise and input; whilst Andrew had all the technical expertise necessary to make a success of the business, it was obvious that additional management and business skills would be needed. Investment was needed to procure tooling to produce a full product range of the LCD coupling, to carry out tests on the prototype couplings to obtain data needed to publish specifications, to improve some of the production processes and to undertake commercialisation.

It was reckoned that the LCD had potential to be applied to a wide range of industries. Industrial driveshafts are used in a huge range of applications, typically to transfer power between motors, gearboxes and loads. Some applications, for example, are the driveshafts between gearbox and generator in a wind turbine, fan driveshafts in cooling towers, pump driveshafts, rail traction driveshafts, marine driveshafts, cranes, escalators etc. The overall potential world market for flexible couplings needed for such driveshafts was estimated to be $1.1 billion to $1.4 billion. Unlike automotive applications (dominated by couplings capable of working at big angles), the industrial market is dominated by couplings optimised for small angles. The real uncertainty was how big a share of this market might be taken by the LCD, particularly considering that in many industries lengthy testing is required before a component's safety and reliability is accepted. There were also two other companies, both based in the USA, that could be considered competitors in using composites to produce flexible driveshaft couplings, but none in Europe.

Finding investors

After finishing his business plan Andrew started campaigning to investors in May 2001; all in all he gave over 20 presentations. KPMG had contacts with investors but Andrew was also fairly proactive in identifying possible parties. He went to a few DTI events and made contact with Investor Champions, a network of Business Angels. Through Investor Champions he did a presentation in July 2001 on site at GKN Technology to about 12 participants who had enquired about the business plan. Rather than being venture capital funds or companies this group was made up predominantly by individuals of means. A few followed up further and Andrew continued discussions with one particular individual around whom a consortium based in the Midlands developed.

He also went to the British Venture Capital Association website and did a search to find venture capitalists who might have an interest in similar products/businesses. The names of the individuals identified he passed on to KPMG who then wrote a letter introducing the idea. About one-third of the 20 parties approached requested the business plan and one contact led indirectly to a London-based consortium.

By September 2001 Andrew and some senior members from GKN had had several conversations with the two interested consortia. However, while the initial interest had been very positive, both consortia now wanted to renegotiate the venture's structure, and requested that the new company should be given the freedom to pursue automotive applications of not only the disc, but also other products based on the composite, to exploit the technical know-how that would be transferred to the new company.

Questions

1.   What would your decision regarding the LCD have been and why?

2.   What are alternative approaches to dealing with highly innovative or marginal products within large, established organisations?

APPENDIX 20.1: MANUFACTURING FLOW
FOR THE COMPOSITE DISC JOINT

Manufacture of pre-preg: resin + glass fibre base material

A unique epoxy resin formulation has been developed to suit the LCD product and processes.
Pre-Preg is widely used as the material for high performance composites. Pre-preg is a
lifed material (−18°C storage) and available from commercial suppliers.
Spinning benefits from just-in-time manufacture of material to exclusive specification.

Kiss cutter – limbs and core daisies

Rolls of pre-preg are fed into a rotary die kiss cutter. Cylindrical steel dies rotate as
the material is fed through and punch out the limb and core daisy shapes. This
in-line cutting process, developed by GKN Technology and not available elsewhere,
is a highly effective method of producing thousands of identical cut shapes.

Core production

Several core daisies are laid up and cut to produce core segments with the required fibre
orientation sequences. These segments provide reinforcement and increased thickness around the
both position. This process is protected by patent GB9804771, also US and Denmark.

Disc assembly: cores + limbs = composite disc pre-form

The discs are laid up by hand. The cores and limbs are laid up in controlled sequences
to produce a disc pre-form. The sequencing of the fibre orientation is protected by patent
DE3725957, also France and Japan.

Moulding

The disc pre-form is enclosed in nylon film and transferred to steel compression moulding tool. Each disc is moulded at high temperature (165°C) and high pressure for a floor-to-floor cycle time of 15 minutes. Compression moulding of high performance composites is not widely used, but is suitable for producing thousands of parts per annum. The use of nylon film is protected patent GB9901394

Post curing

The discs are placed in an oven and post-cured for several hours as a batch process in order to fully develop the material properties.

Finishing

Finishing operations comprise machine routing and hard finishing

Inspection and Packaging

Each disc is measured, inspected visually and weighed. The discs are then marked, packed and logged for despatch to the customer

APPENDIX 20.2: SUMMARY OF TECHNICAL AND COMMERCIAL ADVANTAGES AND TECHNICAL LIMITATIONS

LCD Joints - Technical Competitive Advantages	
High operating efficiency, joints run cool	Key for wind turbines, motorsport - any application where high power is sustained for long periods or absolutely minimum energy losses desired
Low axial stiffness	Minimises force transmission between connected systems; can be important for gearboxes, noise and vibration transmission
Low weight, low inertia, no backlash	Low weight is often desirable. Can be extremely important for high acceleration systems, eg positioning servo drives
Good tolerance of angular misalignment	Better than most alternatives, eg steel disc couplings typically restricted to 0.75° continuous angle
Good tolerance of harsh environments	eg humidity, temperature, salt water, ozone, oils - all of which can cause problems for other coupling types
Non-conductive, non-magnetic, radar transparent	Electrical isolation is often important
No wear, maintenance free	Major advantage over gear couplings
LCD Joints - Commercial Competitive Advantages	
Comprehensive patent cover	Appendix C
Exclusive, vertically integrated m/f process	Section 7
Resin system exclusive to GKN	With m/f process, prevents product copying
GKN brand and driveshaft knowhow	
LCD Joints - Technical Limitations	
Restricted axial load capacity	Consequence of low axial stiffness
Torsionally stiff, no torsional damping	In common with gear couplings and laminated steel couplings, but torsional compliance and damping can be important for a significant share of the market
Can't accept radial misalignment as a single coupling	Some (low speed) coupling types can, but in mitigation the thinness of the disc enables very short spacer couplings which is important for a significant range of applications, eg rail

Organising for innovation

In a way, much of the GKN case study is about how large organisations approach innovation. What are the structures and processes they could use to infuse organisation, and are different kinds of processes needed for incremental versus radical innovation? Should venture capital be sought? The following two chapters address these issues.

There are a number of different ways organisations can approach innovation which seem to crystallise around two fundamental starting points: the people route or the process route. If the people route is chosen then there are three further options:

- the innovation champion (standalone)
- the dedicated innovation team (bolt-on)
- the central innovation department with 'ambassadors'

Only very few organisations manage a holistic approach that combines and goes beyond either the process or the people approach and achieve innovation as infusion.

Each approach has its merits and issues – and which choice a company makes will generally depend on its specific circumstances. Rather than being exclusive the four steps (innovation champion, innovation team, innovation ambassador, innovation as infusion) can also be seen as stages of an overall innovation journey.

In this chapter we will take a look first at the process-based route, whereby the main focus will be on idea management. This is followed by some considerations about the differences between incremental and radical innovation, and their implications. We will then take a look at different possible people-based structures for infusing innovation, which includes looking at different roles that creating an innovative organisation might require.

THE PROCESS ROUTE

Companies following the process route generally start the innovation journey with the introduction of a formalised innovation process – and this is often assumed that it is the same as the stage-gate process. A second avenue of the process route is the introduction of a process for generating and managing ideas. As we have already talked about the new development processes in Chapter 3 I will focus here on issues around idea management.

Idea management

The issue of idea management, already mentioned in Chapter 16, will be investigated here in more depth by looking at five aspects:

- suggestion schemes
- other forms of idea generation
- idea selection
- managing 'unsuitable' ideas
- rewards and recognition around ideas

Suggestion schemes

Based on the insights that great ideas can come from anywhere within the organisation, most companies operate, or have at some point operated, idea suggestion schemes. Getting these right, however, is quite critical for making them a success. Many companies are reporting a paradox around suggestion schemes: they say that they get more ideas than they can cope with while at the same time lamenting that the ideas they have are not good enough. It is all less paradoxical when understanding that the ideas companies get through suggestion schemes are plenty, but that often none of these ideas are really exciting or would really make a difference.

For many organisations a 'call for ideas' is the first step on their innovation journey. More often than not, such calls result in a flood of ideas; many people in the organisation will have been waiting for an opportunity to bring forward the great idea they have had for a long time. The organisation is then faced with at least two challenges: first, how to assess the submitted ideas and second, how to communicate with those who have submitted the ideas.

About the first challenge, not many organisations launch into ideas suggestion schemes with firmly established assessment criteria set out. This has two negative consequences: first, the people submitting ideas do not really know what kind of idea is wanted; and secondly, they often do not understand why their ideas are being selected or rejected.

The second challenge results from the fact that not many organisations provide sufficient manpower to review and assess the flood of ideas in a timely manner. Those who have submitted ideas then get frustrated and the original enthusiasm often changes to an attitude of 'I have told you it would not make a difference', or 'It was just another of these initiatives that do not really mean anything'.

Hence it is important to set out clear guidelines and assessment criteria at the outset, and ensure that those who submit ideas are receiving a timely response and are kept informed about what happens to their idea.

I observed a very powerful approach of dealing with the dilemmas of calling for ideas in a retail organisation in the UK. They too wanted to start an innovation initiative but instead of asking the open-ended question 'have you got any good ideas?' they decided that ideas that would help the company deliver its strategy and mission were wanted. A first step was to ask employees whether they could not only recite the mission statement but were actually able to say what it meant in their daily business life. Once it became clear that this was not the case they set out to dissect what the company ought to be known for. Once this had been established they used these values to call for ideas that would help communicate and deliver these values to the organisation's customers. A great many ideas were submitted and rather than considering each idea to be the potential starting point for a project these ideas were organised into themes.

The beauty of this approach was that the organisers could go back to everyone who had submitted an idea and could say, 'thank you for helping us to shape the landscape in which we ought to innovate'. Secondly, it gave the organisers an opportunity to combine ideas and develop them into much more powerful concepts. And finally, it gave them platforms or 'innovation hot spots' from which to start serious idea generation and development for meaningful and impactful innovation.

There is a further issue related to the volume of ideas coming through the system. There is the danger of allowing too many projects to start, as the initial resource requirement tends to be quite low. This can give a false sense of security and lead to problems when the project needs to be scaled up. It is therefore important to have mechanisms in place that allow consideration of the entire product portfolio, the identification of projects that best complement existing activities, and killing off projects that fail to meet set criteria.

Finally, there are issues that are related to the debate around incremental versus radical innovation. Suggestion schemes tend to be great for the former but bad for the latter. While ideas coming through suggestion schemes can often save a lot of money, they rarely generate ideas that create top-line growth. This is partly due to the way such suggestion schemes operate. Ideas tend to be reviewed either by a small team of people, or by peers who have an expertise relevant to the suggestion made. This is fine for incremental innovations but less likely to work for radical innovations for the following reasons:

- If the idea is really radical it may be difficult to fit a description into the standard submission form.

- If something is really new existing expertise is more likely to cause a rejection – 'We have tried this before', 'I know that it does not work because . . . '

- Radical ideas tend to need room to grow and develop, they tend to change shape and scope.

- Selling radical ideas requires persuasion and explanation, neither is easily done on a single sheet of paper.

Generating incremental innovations need not be a bad thing. Even small improvements or changes can result in significant cost savings although, as mentioned before, NOT new income streams. As cost cutting seems to be an issue with most companies most of the time, suggestion schemes are a valuable source for identifying cost-savings opportunities. In their book *Corporate Creativity* Robinson and Stern (1997) give many great examples of how small changes have resulted in big cost savings. The following one is from American Airlines. A cabin crew had noticed that most people (72%) do not eat the olive in their salad. Big deal, one might say. But when knowing that the salad is costed based on the number of items included, it starts to make a bit more sense: four different items cost 60 cents whereas five different items were priced at 80 cents. Serving the salad without the olive saved the airlines around $500,000 per year. So the fact that idea suggestion schemes generate incremental rather than radical ideas does not mean that they cannot generate great financial savings.

Many companies run very successful suggestion schemes and Box 21.1 shows the example of the idea suggestion scheme run by the University of Arizona. All people need to know fits onto one page: a focus and clear evaluation criteria, what information is required when submitting an idea, how, when and by whom suggestions will be reviewed and taken forward, and assurance that senior managers support the scheme.

Box 21.1   The University of Arizona Employee Suggestion Program

PURPOSE

Bright Ideas! is a University-wide program designed to encourage all employees of the University of Arizona community to contribute innovative suggestions that can enhance campus life and working conditions.

Suggestions should be creative and should benefit the University by:

- improving the quality of working conditions and campus life;
- eliminating inefficiencies, waste or duplication;
- saving money, resources or time;
- streamlining administrative procedures and operating methods; and
- increasing safety, promoting health, or improving morale.

Suggestions must be realistic, cite a specific area for improvement, include a brief analysis of the intended results, and recommendations for potential implementation strategies.

Bright Ideas! will be reviewed by a committee made up of various University employees from all over the UA campus.

HOW DO I SUBMIT MY *BRIGHT IDEA?*

Any UA faculty, staff, or student employee – or group of employees – may submit a suggestion at any time. Suggestions made be submitted on-line, via e-mail, campus mail, or fax by using a suggestion form and including all pertinent information outlined below.

Suggestions should include:

- a description of the problem to be addressed or the area to be improved;
- a detailed description of the solution; and
- an analysis of the benefits to the University.

The Suggestion Coordinator will immediately acknowledge, in writing, the receipt of each suggestion. The suggestion is encoded to ensure anonymity and then forwarded to the Bright Ideas! Suggestion Team. Each Bright Ideas! suggestion will be reviewed at the Team's bimonthly meetings.

The Suggestion Team will submit results and recommendations of appropriate ideas to the Program Sponsors. Ideas that are more appropriately dealt with at the college or unit level will be referred to a suitable individual for further evaluation and action.

Bright Ideas! will be awarded and recognized upon implementation. The Suggestion Team will present employees with cash awards, plaques, or other great gifts for meritorious *Bright Ideas!*

THE *BRIGHT IDEAS!* TEAM

The following individuals are the current team members. They represent a wide cross-section of the University community; faculty, staff, students and appointed personnel.

[This is followed by a host of names and telephone numbers and the names of the program sponsors, in this case the Senior Vice President for Business Affairs and the Associate Vice President for Administrative Services]

Source: http://w3.arizona.edu/%7Ebright/index.html

If a suggestion scheme does not work one of the following might be the reason:

- Political games – decisions for which ideas to take forward are based on personal preference, nepotism or budgetary considerations rather than clear selection criteria and merit of the ideas.

- Overload – the flood of ideas has been underestimated and resources to manage and assess incoming ideas are insufficient, leading to people not being kept up to date with progress which in turn destroys positive energy and trust.

- Lack of sincerity – if the scheme has been in place 'because everyone does it' instead of the true belief that it creates value and if managers are not really interested at all in the ideas brought forward.

- 'Illiteracy' – the inability to express (from the person submitting the idea) or understand (by the person reading the suggestion), particularly if the idea is more radical or 'off the wall'.

Having said earlier that suggestion schemes tend to produce incremental rather than radical ideas, there are also ways to set up schemes as to be more conducive to the submission of more radical ideas. An example of such a scheme that seems to work quite well is given in Box 21.2.

Box 21.2   Innovation fund

The underlying principle is, 'no risk, no money'. This is a significant change in our culture and in the first year about 30% of applications emphasised the low or no risk factor of the idea – we rejected them for that particular reason to make sure people understood that we were truly looking for different, more risky projects. The fund is non-bureaucratic. Initially all that is needed is to fill in a 2-page form, available either as hard copy or on the intranet, which will be turned around in 2 days. We have some set criteria – known by everyone – against which the suggestions are evaluated:

- Business and strategic fit
- Substantial potential benefit to business – BIG
- Not business as usual, think high risk

- Needs to have a senior business sponsor
- Potential substantial technology capability acquisition

Other things we are looking for are:

- Commitment, enthusiasm, vision (use virtual groups, wide range of backgrounds etc.)
- Client/customer involvement (think early about realisation and implementation)
- Supplier support/participation

The funding process involves 4 stages:

1.   Enrolment (that's when senior business person's support is required)
2.   Concept – concept development (what support would be needed to get to market)
3.   Demonstration
4.   Pilot

From stage 4 onwards 50% of cost are to be carried by a business unit, i.e. there is tapered funding – but these rules are not written in stone, people can jump to any stage. All suggestions are stored electronically – the database is not available internally yet but will be. We also have plans to publish projects that have won awards on our website.

Source: von Stamm, B. (2001). Innovation Best Practice and Future Challenges: A Study into Innovation Best Practice in Innovation Exchange Member Companies and the Literature. London: Innovation Exchange, London Business School.

Other forms of idea generation

Suggestion schemes are only one way to generate ideas. Best practice companies combine continuous idea generation through suggestion schemes with 'bursts of idea generation', for example through focused brainstorming sessions.[1] Such 'bursts of idea generation' are generally time bound, i.e. run for a specified period of time, and generally have a predefined question or challenge. Research by the company Imaginatik from 1998 showed that such focused, time-bound events not only produce a higher volume of ideas but that the ideas produced are also of higher quality. Running events should be preceded by strategic debate about what the idea generation should be.

A large fast-moving consumer goods company wanted to find out how its big break-through innovation had come about. They were quite astonished to find that each of the products that had made a huge difference to the company over time could be traced back to a particular individual. What was a bit worrying though was that over the course of downsizing, eliminating slack and tightening controls all of these individuals had left the company, or had been pushed out.

Unless only small numbers are involved such events are generally hosted on the organisation's intranet. One of the reasons why such event-driven idea generation sessions create better results is that participants can see, comment and build on other participants' ideas. The richness and depth of the ideas is much greater than in linear events. Research also indicates that such sessions are more likely to generate some radical ideas. It is worth remembering

---

[1] See also Chapter 1, Table 1.2 on different idea generation techniques.

Table 21.1   Idea generation – continuous versus bursts

	Employee suggestion system	Creative problem-solving workshop
Use when...	To involve all employees On a particular problem from a wide range of perspectives	Known problem, particularly difficult
Potential number of participants	Limited only by the number of people who have access to the system	Small group of people, diversity and lateral thinking are important
Type of ideas generated	Tactical rather than strategic Usually easy to implement Tend to be of incremental rather than radical nature Cost saving rather than new business	More strategic than tactical Implementation often more difficult and time consuming Of radical rather than incremental nature New business rather than cost saving
For success, this is required...	Visible and continued top management support Clear and easily understood structures and procedures for input as well as selection Sufficient resources to manage suggestions	Strong team leader Problem is real, important, no easy solution, specific, requires action Needs dedicated time for the team (the authors suggest two days) Benefits from experienced facilitator

Source: Building on Prather, C.W. & Turrell, M.C. (2002). Involve everyone in the innovation process. *Research Technology Management*, 13–16.

though that every radical idea originates with one person. A team is necessary to develop and implement the idea, but the seed stems from one particular person.

One of the participants in the innovation best practice research commented, "How do we come up with genuine innovation? We use cross-country teams, a good mix of genders, people who are experienced and have strong subject knowledge. We also emphasise consumer contact. This is the kind of blend we are trying to create."

Whether it is in small teams or large-scale internet-based idea generation sessions, the common denominator for the successful creation of great ideas is diversity of insight and input.

Building on an article by Prather and Turrell (2002), Table 21.1 provides a comparison of 'continuous' and 'bursts'.

Finally, I would like to point out that the question or challenge in such a situation is critical. The answers you are likely to get are only as meaningful as the question you ask.

Another vehicle for stimulating innovation is to set up a dedicated fund for innovation. Such a fund does generally have some clear rules and procedures – but is generally quite open to the kind and topic of idea submitted. In a way it is like a small-scale venture capital fund. The purpose of such a fund tends to encourage and support more radical ideas, ideas that would not find funding and support inside existing business units – see example in Box 21.2.

> **Root cause analysis** is a particular approach to solving problems or identifying issues. When challenged with a problem or issue we have the tendency to deal with the symptoms rather than making the effort to understand the underlying causes.
>
> **5 Whys**, originally developed by Toyota, is one method for getting to the root of a problem. To quote Taiichi Ohno (1988), architect of the Toyota Production System "... the basis of Toyota's scientific approach ... by repeating why five times, the nature of the problem as well as its solution becomes clear." To illustrate the point, imaging the situation that your car is not starting. Upon investigating the issue you find that the battery is dead. You could now replace the battery – but was this the real problem? Asking why the battery is dead might lead you to find that the alternator is not functioning. Asking 'why' again you may find that it has broken beyond repair. Asking 'why' again you may find that it has come to the end of its useful life. And a final 'why' might lead you to the insight that you have failed to maintain the car regularly so the alternator was not replaced at the appropriate time.

Idea selection

I have already alluded to the problem of selection above. This is often seen as a greater challenge than that of generating ideas. The *Innovation Trend Survey* conducted by the Confederation of British Industry (CBI), published in February 2001, came to the same conclusion, "Idea generation may not be a problem for most, but how effective are companies in picking up these ideas, recognising their worth and turning them into innovations?"

This is why having a clear vision of where the business wants to be in three, five or ten years time is important. Everyone in the organisation should have a clear understanding of that. Unless they do it is rather difficult for them to come up with meaningful ideas – and disappointment of idea generators is pre-programmed. From the vision assessment criteria should be developed and widely publicised. In this context it is also important to emphasise that the assessment criteria should vary for different aspects of the overall portfolio. We have talked in Chapter 3 about the need for an organisation to balance its portfolio (e.g. across time horizons, innovation levels, product categories etc.). If assessment criteria for radical innovations are the same as those for incremental innovations no one should be surprised if no radical innovations are being pursued.

Looking at the company's overall product portfolio is one way, the 'Buyer Utility Map' (see Box 21.3) developed by Kim and Mauborgne (2000) is a variation on the theme of portfolio management. They suggest looking at the different stages of the buyer experience cycle and a number of product aspects that create value to customers. Existing products can be mapped onto the matrix, giving an indication for the fields that are already addressed through existing products. The managers can then decide which of the 'open windows' they might want to address with their new developments. In this way the matrix can be used as starting point for idea development. However, it can also be used to map existing ideas, identify where hotspots are, and check that against existing offerings. A great way of ensuring that development efforts are focused on satisfying a new or different need, rather than being 'yet another one of these'.

Kim and Mauborgne give Starbucks as an example of a company that has used a different lever at the same stage (offering fun and image instead of competing on prices), where Dell is an example of a company that has used the

Box 21.3   The buyer utility map

The six stages of the buyer experience cycle

	Purchase	Delivery	Use	Supplements	Maintenance	Disposal
Customer productivity						
Simplicity						
Convenience						
Risk						
Fun and image						
Environmental friendliness						

The six utility levers

Source: Kim, C.W. & Mauborgne, R. (2000). Knowing a winning business idea when you see one. *Harvard Business Review*, Sept–Oct, 129–37. Reprinted by permission of *Harvard Business Review*. Copyright 2000 by the Harvard Business School Publishing Corporation; all rights reserved

same utility lever in a new stage (competing via distribution rather than faster computers). Finally there is of course the option of using a new lever in a new stage. Here the authors give the Alto light-bulb developed by electronics giant Philips as an example (offering environmental friendliness and convenience at the disposal stage).[2]

Managing 'unsuitable' ideas

Not all ideas collected are of immediate value. In the previous section we looked at ways of identifying the right ideas. However, there might be great value in those that were not selected. In Chapter 16 we have already suggested that there is value in storing unused ideas in a meaningful way in a database. Making most of those is an art that not many organisations have discovered yet. There are a number of options:

- Ideas can be revisited periodically to see whether their applicability or the reasons for rejection have changed.

- Ideas can be sold off to parts of the company or other organisations that are closer aligned to the concept.

[2] In their article 'Knowing a winning business idea when you see one' the authors offer two further tools: the 'price corridor of the mass', which helps managers to identify the pricing level with the maximum number of customers and 'the business model guide', which offers guidance in assessing the company's ability to deliver the new idea at the optimum price.

- New ideas can be checked against the database to see whether something similar has been tried before, what the result was, and why.

- Even if individual ideas might be difficult to realise, they might be indicative of an emerging theme that is worth pursuing.

In addition there might be cases where a product has been developed, be it through skunkworks or regular project work, that no longer seems to fit with corporate objectives – as in the GKN case study. The question is, what to do with ideas that have great potential but do not really fit with what we are doing? One way is to set up a separate business unit and/or spin it out. Table 21.2 by Lord *et al.* (2002) provides managers with a checklist of questions for each stage of the development process that will help to make and execute the critical decision of whether or not to spin.

Some best practice for idea management includes:

- **Scan high and low** – involving customers as well as suppliers; using suggestion schemes as well as bursts of idea generation.

- **Provide focus for idea generation** – which can be cutting cost; the identification of high risk/high reward projects; a particular topic or for a particular part of the business.

- **Be clear about the innovation ambition** – e.g. how radical should the suggestions be, how closely do they need to fit with existing business; are you really interested in taking forward something that is outside your organisation's core?

- **Offer a clear structure** – a simple process, information requirements, time lines etc.

- **Start with lots of ideas and encourage experimentation but narrow down quickly** – select an idea and create lots of variations around that particular idea rather than develop loads and loads of ideas.

- **Summarise and combine** – to reduce the total number of ideas you may want to group them together under emerging themes; these themes can also be used to start focused idea generation sessions.

> "A lot of trial and error goes into making things look effortless."
>
> Bill Moggridge. IDEO, *Financial Times*, 30 July 2002

- **Make submission of ideas easy and provide good support** – don't ask for complete business plans.

- **Ensure that rejections are not taken personal** – people need to know why ideas are selected or rejected which means that the selection criteria are known by everyone in the organisation.

- **Manage and store <u>all</u> ideas** – provide mechanisms that allow getting most value out of your pool of ideas, whether it is by using them yourself or selling them off (at whatever stage of their development) and be prepared to sell off those ideas that do not fit with your corporate strategy.

Table 21.2 Challenges and considerations for spinouts

Stage	Key challenge	Critical consideration	Recommendation
Conception	The decision: why and when to spin out (or not)	Is spinout really the right strategic choice? Or should we develop internally, form partnerships, licence, sell, or simply cut the programme? What is the best way to maximise value creation?	Make sure the spinout has a sound strategic logic behind it. Ensure that it is not driven by short-term financial gimmicks and that it is indeed a non-core asset with a solid case as a standalone business
Gestation	The team: leadership and championing	Who will lead and champion the nascent venture? Should the leader come from outside or inside the corporate parent? Which key managerial and technical people should go with the spinout and which should stay with the parent?	Initially, a leader from the ranks of the parent company may best be able to navigate the process; later, increased external leadership likely will be required or negotiated, especially as the spinout's independence grows
	The strategy: focus and purpose	What will be the specific strategic scope and direction of the spinout? What are its vision, mission, goals, and objectives, especially vis-à-vis the parent?	The spinout should have a clear understanding of what it is and what it will do, reduce future tension and conflicts with the parent by defining its focus and boundaries up front.
	The organisation: creating internal autonomy	Is it necessary to create internal legal, financial, and organisational autonomy for the spinout as a prelude to its eventual separation from the parent, and if so, how?	Create a legally separate subsidiary or affiliate with its own management, organisation, and books. Minimise complex parent–offspring ties
Separation	Alliances: attracting and negotiating with outside partners	Who should we pursue as partners? How can we convince them to join? How can the parent and spinout best tackle the three-way negotiations?	Gather outside partners to validate and accelerate the separation process. Remember that spinout partners don't want to be entangled in complex or subordinate relationships with the parent
	Funding: attracting and negotiating with outside investors	Who should we pursue as investors? How much should we sell and at what prices? Again, how can the parent and spinout best tackle the three-way negotiations?	As with partners, outside investors should be brought in to validate the merits of the venture and to accelerate the separation process. But investors need to know that they are on a clear and level playing field when investing in the spinout, not one skewed by entanglements with the parent
	Freedom: achieving true independence	What should be the nature of the relationship between parent and offspring? How can the spinout be free to chart its own course while still allowing the parent to recoup its investment?	The parent should drop to a minority stake and should not dominate the spinout's management or board. Any remaining umbilical ties should probably be severed so that dealings between the parent and the spinout stay at arm's length

Source: Lord, M.D., Mandel, S.W. & Wager, J.D. (2002). Spinning out a star. *Harvard Business Review*, 5–11. Reprinted by permission of *Harvard Business Review*. Copyright by the Harvard Business School Publishing Corporation.

Rewarding and recognition for innovation

Some managers feel that employees will only come forwards with great ideas when suitable financial rewards are given although there is still some controversy about the effectiveness of financial rewards in eliciting innovative ideas. The consensus seems to shift towards the view that financial rewards do not make a difference and that in fact they might even have a negative effect. Recognition of some kind, on the other hand, is essential; otherwise people feel ignored and undervalued. We will come back to the issue of reward and remuneration towards the end of the section on idea management.

This is very much aligned with the findings of Harvard Professor Theresa Amabile's finding. In an article by the magazine *Fast Company* in December 2004 she said, "Bonuses and pay-for-performance plans can . . . be problematic when people believe that every move they make is going to affect their compensation. In those situations, people tend to get risk averse. Of course, people need to feel that they're being compensated fairly. But our research shows that people put far more value on a work environment where creativity is supported, valued, and recognized."[3] Hence, creativity and innovation are driven primarily by intrinsic motivation and the feeling of being able to make a contribution, to make a difference.

What should be noted is that what works in terms of reward and recognition for innovation will vary from organisation to organisation. How innovation is encouraged and rewarded should also change over the development cycle, i.e. an idea or a concept should be acknowledged in a different way from a new business unit, up and running. In short, the reward should match the risk the individual takes and the contribution he or she makes. Suggesting an idea does not involve a huge amount of risk whereas giving up one's job to set up a new business unit involves greater risk. The insert gives examples for intrinsic and extrinsic motivation.

> **Intrinsic**:   Challenge,   independence,   self-actualisation, wanting – and being able to contribute, etc.
>
> **Extrinsic/recognition**: Awards, chairman's dinner, mentioning in newsletters, employee of the month, choice of next role/job/project, promotion, etc.
>
> **Extrinsic/reward**: Bonus, shares, pay rise, etc.

One final point on the idea management section: ideas alone are not innovation. Only once they have been implemented and have had an impact do creativity and ideas become innovation. In my experience it is at the hand-over between the different stages of the development cycle that ideas wither and die: when being passed from research to development, from development to scale-up from scale-up to launch, from launch to support and maintenance in

> Sales and marketing of new products or services requires more effort than flogging well established products. Unless sales staff are motivated and rewarded for supporting and selling the new, chances of success are seriously undermined. This seems to be forgotten all too easily.

the marketplace. It is also at each of these handovers that there is a danger of the concept being diluted. What can companies do about it? Involve all those affected by the development as early as possible to gain understanding and buy-in; have a strong project leaders – or someone else on the team – who takes the role of the 'keeper of

---

[3] 'The six myths of creativity', by Bill Breen, *Fast Company*, 89, December 2004.

the essence' – a person who ensures that the essence of the idea does not get diluted and watered down over the course of development and implementation; ensure that the 'keeper of the essence' remains involved until the project is well established in the market; and ensure that everyone who is part of the journey is encouraged and rewarded for playing his or her role in the success.

Incremental versus radical – what's the difference?

Most organisations would probably argue that they are quite good at incremental innovation – idea generation as well as implementation. Where companies seem to struggle more is radical innovation and again this applies to idea generation as well as implementation. However, there are probably not too many organisations that use different processes, depending on which type of innovation they pursue. We have pointed out above that some approaches to infusing innovation are more likely to generate radical innovation than others. So why is it important to make the distinction, and what are differences in requirements for each kind? In their valuable book *Radical Innovation*, Leifer et al. (2000) provide some great insights as to why so many organisations struggle with radical innovation. They provide a comparison of conditions and facts for each type of innovation (see Table 21.3) from which becomes crystal clear that these two different types cannot be approached the same way.

The important point is, incremental and radical innovation require very different business conditions, skills, structures and processes. So if most organisations aim to achieve the two different types through the same systems and processes it is not surprising that it does not lead to the desired results. Managers that are serious about radical innovation should set up separate structures, with different process, time frames and evaluation criteria. There are a number of options and the innovation team introduced above can be one of them. Other distinct approaches are:

- Internal venturing – tends to be opportunistic; new companies are created internally and are wholly owned initially; possibility of spin-out or spin-in.

- Venture incubators – as opposed to internal venturing a separate unit is set up with the aim to create new business; new companies are seeded internally with a spin-off or spin-in as options; examples are BT Brightstar or the P&G Ventures Group.[4]

> Two-thirds of the US Top 100 companies are thought to be either using or thinking of using corporate venturing as a means of finding new customers, new markets and new technologies.
>
> CBI (2002)

- External venturing – equity is purchased in external companies; can also be explored through joint ventures; often leading to acquisition; Intel Capital or Novartis' Bioventures are examples hereof, you may also want to refer to the TTP case study in Chapter 29.

However, even when setting up a separate venture unit it is still important that there is some unique link and contribution from parent to venture unit, be it synergies in R&D, distribution or existing industry relationships. If a project is completely outside the competencies of the parent organisation the question is why it should be linked

---

[4] The latter has been written up by Dean Whitney as a Harvard Business School case study (1997, No 9-897-088).

Table 21.3 Incremental versus radical innovation

	Incremental	Radical
Time frame	Short term – six to 24 months	Long term – usually 10 years plus
Development trajectory	Step after step from conception to commercialisation, high levels of certainty	Discontinuous, iterative, set-backs, lacking information, high levels of uncertainty
Idea generation and opportunity recognition	Continuous stream of incremental improvements readily available and tend to come up through systematic idea development or suggestion schemes; idea fully formed at outset; critical events large anticipated	Ideas often pop up unexpectedly, and from unexpected sources; it is important to have structure in place to allow the ideas to surface; slack tends to be required; focus and purpose might change over the course of the development
Process	Formal, established, generally with stages and gates	A formal, structured process might hinder rather than help, companies complain about large ideas becoming small
Business case	A complete business case can be produced at the outset, customer reaction can be anticipated	The business case evolves throughout the development, and might change; predicting customer reaction is difficult
Players	Can be assigned to a cross functional team with clearly assigned and understood roles; skill emphasis is on making things happen (Kirton's adaptor)[1]	Skill areas required will evolve during the development, key players may come and go; finding the right skills often relies on informal networks; flexibility, persistence and willingness to experiment are required (Kirton's innovator)
Development structure[2]	Typically, a cross-functional team operates within an existing business unit	Tends to originate in R&D but could start anywhere in the organisation; tends to be driven by the determination of one individual who pursues it wherever he or she is
Resource and skill requirements	All skills and competencies necessary tend to be within the project team; resource allocation follows a standardised process	It is difficult to predict skill and competence requirements; additional expertise from outside might be required; informal networks are important and flexibility is required
Operating unit involvement	Operating units are involved from the beginning	Involving operating units too early can again lead to great ideas becoming small

Notes: [1]See reference to Kirton's work in Chapter 10; [2]Please see also Table 3.2 in Chapter 3. *Source*: Building on Leifer *et al.* (2000). *Radical Innovation – How Mature Companies Can Outsmart Upstarts*. Boston, MA: Harvard Business School Press

at all (see also Table 21.2 about 'Challenges and considerations for spinouts'). There are powerful examples that external venturing can be extremely profitable. For example, in 1999 Intel's external venture unit contributed 15% of company profits – though managers should be aware that many more radical innovations will take at least five years before starting to pay back.

THE PEOPLE ROUTE

While some organisations start by introducing innovation-specific processes, others start by introducing innovation-specific roles into their organisations. Here we will discuss first what kind of people-based approaches companies use to infuse innovation, and second is, what kind of innovation they are hoping to achieve through the chosen structure. Companies do not always proceed to ask the second question which can lead to problems. A third topic discussed here are different roles that might be useful in the context of innovative.

Let us start with looking at some of the different structures that companies use to infuse innovation. Some key options and their implications are summarised in Table 21.4.

Innovation champion

Establishing the role of an Innovation Champion or Innovation Manager is often the first step on an organisation's innovation journey. The Innovation Champion tends to be a bit of a lone fighter, often tasked with infusing innovation into an organisation single-handedly. Such a position tends to come with a wide remit and lots of freedom – but generally little authority. As one champion explained, "At present I feel I am just adding to people's work load. I can only ask people to do things, not tell them – but then, people are generally very cooperative. We have very good people but they don't (yet) understand the value and role of innovation so it's often hard work."

The individuals, generally very enthusiastic and highly committed to their course, tend to report to a senior manager – which seems to indicate that it is a top management priority. In enlightened organisations the Innovation Champion is used to develop a plan for action for further steps on the innovation journey. In less inspired organisations the position of an Innovation Champion is somewhat of a token gesture. One is seen to be doing something – but the belief that things will really change is quite limited.

The interesting question is, what happens to the Innovation Champion once the initial scoping work is done? It seems that one of two things can happen, either the position disappears or a team is put in its place. If the former is the case, the organisation goes 'back to normal' – the attempt of infusing innovation has failed. In the latter, management has realised both the value of innovation and that a lone fighter – depending on the size of the organisation of course – cannot by him- or herself turn attitudes and behaviours in an entire organisation around. What does not seem to happen is that there is a series of individual innovation champions.

Table 21.4 Structures observed in other organisations

Summary	Responsibilities	Location	Reporting to	Who/Team members	Success factors	Comments
Fragmented Generally found in organisations before innovation moves up the agenda; one department or function is seen to be responsible for improving the existing and developing new ideas	'Normal' NPD; within FMCG companies generally with marketing as driver; in technology oriented companies generally driven by R&D; decisions made by functional managers	Activities take place primarily within departmental/ functional boundaries	Head of function/ department who also makes decisions; little senior management attention	Generally from within one function only	Works really only for incremental innovation – but even there cross-functional work is often beneficial (though majority of functions only needs to be involved at key stages)	Little integration, projects often passed on across functional boundaries – also known as 'relay race'; tends towards multifunctional teams but with aim to improve speed and reduce rework, not innovativeness
Innovation champion Often the first step when senior management decides that something needs to be done about innovation	Investigate possible structures for innovation; identify best practice inside and outside the organisation; generally advisory function, no real decision making	Generally from HQ/business unit	Senior management/ board	Generally just one person; often not particularly senior	Choose enthusiastic, open and communicative person; ideally with some respect and clout in the organisation; make senior backing very clear	Often seen to cause additional burden; no authority, advisory function only
Innovation team A small group of people (around 10), representing different functions and backgrounds	To come up with 'the next big thing'	Often outside the existing structure to ensure independence of bureaucracy and other constraints	Senior management/ board; sometimes functional director	People from different parts of the organisation; additional members are often recruited from the outside; fresh perspective and attitude more important than in-depth expertise	Develop mechanisms that ensure exchange between team and rest of organisation to avoid NIH; diversity is important (e.g. KAI, MBTI, Synectics Kingdom)	Principal ability to focus on innovation and new things, but can sometimes fall back into more routine type developments which can then cause resentment in rest of organisation

Skunk works Often set up for a particular project, e.g. after identification of idea; small team of experts	Radical innovation, often outside existing boundaries; time pressure can also lead to the setting up of a skunk works team	Outside existing structures; generally off-site	Senior management/board	Highly autonomous, highly competent, best people, experts; strong team leader	Leads often to the setting up of a new business unit/independent business	Only appropriate for certain kinds of project; lack of integration with existing business; often problems with 're-entry'
Innovation department Variation on the innovation team, larger in scale, more integrated into the organisation	Development of big impact concepts and new business ideas	Within existing business	Innovation director	People are drawn from different departments,	High level of freedom to develop own structures, processes and culture yet still part of the organisation	Once successfully established, the aim is to transfer learning into other parts of the organisation
Innovation ambassadors Innovation specialists who support projects in all parts of the organisation on a temporary basis	Providing support and inspiration to teams; versed in innovating and best practice; brings company-wide perspective;	Generally located and financed at HQ	Innovation director/innovation steering committee	Well respected, often senior people, experts; good communicators; skilled facilitators; creative	Have to be seen as positive contributors, not spies from HQ; need to have the respect and trust of the team	Seen as additional resource; can lack authority
Innovation as a mind-set Everyone feels responsibility for innovation; it has become part of the company mindset; often using a combination of approaches listed above	Innovation is everyone's responsibility	Everywhere	CEO takes overall responsibility and is approachable by anyone who has an idea	Everyone	Has to be driven and 'lived' by the top; commitment in deeds not only words; innovation budgets available at various levels; vision of company very clear	Is a long-term process; requires willingness to experiment and learn

One last comment on champions, the literature generally highlights the importance of a champion or strong project leader in order for projects – innovation or otherwise – to be successful. This literature tends to refer to new product development and the individual project level, not necessarily to a company-wide initiative. However, looking at the list of desirable attributes for project leaders, taken from *Project Management* by Harvey Maylor (1996) (see Box 3.2, Chapter 3), this is true for larger projects too – as long as the two balances are kept:

- ○ no responsibility without authority
- ○ no authority without accountability

Dedicated innovation team

A different approach is the setting up of a separate innovation team. This tends to be driven by the insight that innovation requires a different culture from day-to-day business but that establishing an innovation culture may take too long – or a change in the overall company culture does not seem desirable.

In this situation responsibility for innovation is delegated to the Innovation Team – whereby it has to be said that the kind of innovation an organisation is looking for when setting up a separate, dedicated Innovation Team tends to be radical rather than incremental. Incremental and 'day-

> The culture in our innovation group is very different from the rest of the company, less driven by procedures and processes – and deliberately so.

to-day' stuff happens within the existing business – though people can interpret the fact that a dedicated Innovation Team exists as releasing them from any responsibility to think 'innovation'. We will come back to the differing requirements of radical and incremental innovation in the last section of this chapter.

The reaction of the rest of the organisation to the establishment of an Innovation Team is often mixed – at all levels. Such teams often encounter great scepticism from people in the parent organisation who do not believe that they could actually have an impact. And even though top management tends to subscribe nominally to such teams, real belief is often lacking.

A very important consideration when setting up an independent Innovation Team is what mechanisms to develop to bind the group back into the main organisation, how to ensure that there remains sufficient common ground to avoid any not-invented-here syndrome when transferring concepts back from the Innovation Team into the main organisation. Communication, establishment of mutual understanding about what each part of the organisation can contribute to the whole, and constant exchange between the two parts of the organisation are key in preventing the Innovation Team from becoming 'too independent'.

The way a company participating in the innovation best practice research has structured the Innovation Team seems be a very good approach for addressing such issues. The small team is made up of a number of dedicated full-time staff from different functions of the business – not necessarily innovation experts but excited by the idea, open-minded and creative. These are joined by: (a) a number of part-time people who spend the other half of the time in their 'normal' jobs in the main organisation and (b) secondees from the main organisation who spend 1–2 years with the team. In this way a continuous flow of communication is ensured, which brings with it insights into what is happening in the group and it might even spark an interest in people within the company to want to join the group.

A challenge for Innovation Teams is to remember that they have been set up to be different, and must therefore resist the development of stifling processes and procedures.

Central innovation department and innovation ambassadors

The third approach combines a very senior team or individual (seems to depend on company size) at central level with a team of 'Innovation Ambassadors'.[5] The role of the central team/individual is to coordinate innovation activities across the entire organisation, evaluate and select projects, resource projects and monitor their progress, often beyond launch.

The Innovation Ambassador(s), while being part of the centre, will work alongside local teams and provide them with expertise, a company-wide perspective and company best practice. This role means that these people tend to be quite senior, more often than not with a track record for innovation. This seems to be the approach preferred by multinational innovative companies as it allows them to achieve a balance between 'central' and 'local'.

Interesting too is the difference in the selection criteria for people on the Innovation Team versus Innovation Ambassadors. Where characteristics for the first included 'very young', 'fresh perspective', 'not caught up in company traditions'; characteristics for the latter are focused more around 'experience and expertise', 'track record' and 'good company knowledge'. But looking at the purpose behind each approach might help explain the differences, a separate Innovation Team tends to be set up to *generate and explore ideas* and be radically different whereas the Innovation Ambassador is brought in to help with the *implementation of ideas* and concepts.

> The (central) innovator is part of the team and works jointly with them. The innovator brings experience, knowledge, a company-wide perspective and awareness of best practice to the party. The local team provides closeness to the consumer and, of course, local insights. That way we get the best of both worlds.

This approach to infusing innovation is also quite different from the Innovation Champion where innovation is seen to be an additional burden, the Innovation Ambassadors are an additional resource. And as the Innovation Ambassador tends to work alongside the local team rather than spreading his or her wisdom from the lofty heights of headquarters, he or she tends to become accepted as a part of the team and a welcome extra pair of hands.

While each company needs to identify its particular needs around innovation and develop an approach to innovation that is specific and suitable to its context, there are some insights that might be useful for any of the three options, as well as different contexts:

- **Establishing credibility** – while support from the top is generally important, it is equally important that the people driving innovation have credibility within the organisation.

- **Create urgent need for innovation** – innovation has to be seen as a necessity, not a nicety; this might involve creating a 'crisis' or making the need explicit in any other way (e.g. future growth predictions, collapse of the product pipeline, competitor action, profit warnings).

---

[5] This kind of approach was pioneered by Nestlé.

- **Top-level sponsorship** – is critical but note that the most appropriate and effective sponsor might not necessarily be the most senior one; look for a sponsor who can influence others, make funds available, has credibility etc.

- **Generate small successes** – it might be necessary to 'prove' the success of an innovation team/initiative before being able to secure funds; 'liberating' funds to create these initial successes might be required; it is also important to pick the time for talking about the innovation initiative and successes, people need to want to listen – better to be asked about it than trying to do a 'hard sell'.

- **Work with volunteers** – when starting a drive for innovation working with people who want to be involved and who are enthusiastic is more likely to lead to success; if people are 'press-ganged' into innovation services they will do the minimum, not go the extra mile as often required; it might also help to make being involved in innovation something special: make involvement difficult but not impossible, people like a challenge.

- **The right skills mix** – while volunteers are great, it is also important that they have the right skills and the right mix of skills; you need innovators as well as adaptors (see Chapter 10).

- **Mix new and old blood** – involve people who are new to the organisation as they are not infected by 'the way we do things around here' and hence can challenge assumptions and habits, at the same time you want people around who know the organisation inside out and can explain why things are done a certain way and more importantly, how things work.

- **Understand different needs** – understand different needs and what people might want to get out of innovation, be they caused by differences in either national or departmental cultures.

- **Clarify risk** – make sure people on the team are aware that it is a 'fire escape job' – though management should also make sure that there is a safety net for people to return into other jobs in the organisation.

- **Find ways of ringfencing innovation budgets** – if times get tough and resources are scarce, don't necessarily stop the innovative project, ask people whether they can liberate resources somewhere else.

- **Adjust HR** – make sure innovation is integrated into people's performance measures; make sure it is not seen as an overhead, separated from day-to-day business.

- **Fun** – make it fun, it not only attracts people and makes them want to be part of it, it makes risk more acceptable.

- **Space as symbol** – you may want to dedicate some space to the innovation activities, it is a visible commitment and focal point for those who want to contribute (see also Chapter 27).

A HOLISTIC APPROACH TO INNOVATION

Not many organisations take a holistic approach to infusing innovation. Examples of organisations that take an approach that touches all relevant aspects of the organisation, i.e. strategy and vision, leadership, processes, culture and the physical work environment, are far and few between. Taking a fragmented approach might achieve the odd innovation, but only a coherent and consistent approach leads to the creation of an innovative organisation. What is the difference? If I walk into an innovative organisation and ask, 'who is responsible for innovation?' I will get the answer: 'every one of us'. If I walk into an organisation that has the occasional innovation success with the same question I will be pointed towards the R&D department, or the marketing department – or senior management.

Creating an innovative organisation requires a people-centred approach; after all, it is people who come up with ideas and transform them into innovations, not processes. It is impossible to command innovation, you have to inspire people to want to contribute. The author Antoine de Saint-Exupery puts it so well, "If you want to build a ship, don't drum up the men to gather wood, divide the work and give orders. Instead, teach them to yearn for the vast and endless sea."

I would like to share a brief summary of one company who has taken a holistic approach to creating an innovative organisation, Whirlpool – see Box 21.4. The case study illustrates that it is not just about process, not just about people, not just about money. It is a combination of numerous things, and all aspects of the organisation have to support and enforce each other.

Box 21.4   The Whirlpool story

The innovation journey started for the 61,000-employee white consumer goods company Whirlpool in September 1999 when CEO David Whitwam announced: "I want innovation from everyone and every-where; we need to make innovation a core competence." The vision Whitwam had for innovation was comprehensive:

- It must be possible from anyone.
- It goes beyond product.
- It must permeate to the fabric of our culture and business.
- It must create new business opportunities.
- It is not be focused on individual- or functional-level creativity.
- It must be sustainable.

He really meant business: he introduced the role of Global Vice President Innovation and pulled 25 people from the organisation's three regions to receive nine months of innovation and creativity related training; after that one-third went back to their old jobs, one-third became leaders of innovation projects, and one-third set out to teach others (I-Consultants). Impressively his comment was, "I don't really care if any innovations come out of the first 75 as long as they learn the skills of innovation."

Then they set out to ensure everyone knew about it, and identified things that needed to change. Finding ways to express the needs and journey visually was felt to be important. They also put some structural elements into place which included:

- Create an innovation board of which innovation mentors are a part.
- Create an innovation e-space with tools etc. Around innovation.
- Work innovation into the balanced scorecard.
- Make training mandatory for everyone in the organisation.
- Support proactive, cross-functional and hierarchy idea generation.

To embed innovation into the core of the organisation they also took the following steps:

- Exposing everyone to innovation through reading, joining an innovation project, or some other means of engagement.
- Establishing new career paths in innovation.
- Ensuring that innovation is written into people's job descriptions.
- Including diverse people on innovation teams.
- Measuring the number of people involved in innovation projects.
- Counting the number of innovation mentors (I-Mentors, part-time innovation consultants) available to help on innovation projects.

In order to monitor whether they were achieving their ambition they introduced the following measures:

- New revenue generated from innovation.
- Number of projects in the innovation pipeline.
- Number of IP rights generated.
- Number of people in the process.
- Number of new customers.
- Number of new methods of distribution and doing business.

They further looked at:

- Amount in seed funds set aside and used to fund innovation projects, administered with a minimum of bureaucracy and administration.
- Number of or diversity of people certified in levels of innovation expertise.
- Number of change management projects defined to drive innovation.
- Number of key barriers removed to allow innovation to thrive.
- Number of job changes due to innovation.

Rewards and recognition were also aligned to support the creation of an innovation culture – whereby they noted that the informal measures were more successful than the formal ones:

- Individual level: the individual innovator or leader who participates or promotes innovation.
- Team level: the effort of innovation teams or work units that worked on an innovation.
- Organisational levels: for rewarding people who address the systems and processes that focused the organisation on risk taking, culture change, the customer, new business opportunities, and embedment itself.

In addition there were benefits such as:

- Getting invited to 'the party'.
- Becoming a strategic thinker.
- Increased marketability and job potential.
- Extending networks.
- Being free to think outside the box.
- External recognition.

Insights from the journey were:

- Has to be led by example from the top.
- Top has to listen.
- Make resources available.
- Introduce fast experimentation (low budget, 10-day experiments).
- Recruit people who make you comfortable.
- Understand that both innovation and routine are needed.
- Recognition, not financial reward.
- Has to be 'three-line whip'.
- It takes time.

Results:

- Record results in 2005: profit of $422 million on sales of $14.3 billion.
- Share price to an all-time high.
- Innovation pipeline valued at $3.3 billion today (up from $2 billion a year earlier and $1.3 billion two years ago).
- 60% of the products sold in 2006 are new to some extent, accounting for $1 billion in sales.
- Profits are expected to increase by at least 13% to $475 million.

Sources for the summary:

- Anonymous (2004). Why Whirlpool is cleaning up. *Business Week*, 8 February.
- Driscoll, M. (2003). Whirlpool: innovation and organizational learning, March 2003; http://www.clomedia.com/content/templates/clo_inpractice.asp?articleid=135&zoneid=88.
- Foley, J. (2004). Center of creativity. *Information Week*, March 15.
- Meltmuka, K. (2004). Innovation democracy. *Computer World*, 16 February.
- Pomeroy, A. (2004) Cooking up innovation: when it comes to helping employees create new products and services: HR's efforts are a key ingredient. *HR Magazine*, November.
- Snyder, N.T. & Duarte, D.L. (2004). *Strategic Innovation*. Chichester: John Wiley & Sons, Ltd.
- Warner, F. (2001). Recipe for growth. *Fast Company*, 51, October.

Table 21.5 Innovation-specific roles

Possible title	Responsibility	Key requirements	Reporting to	Seniority level
Innovation Director	Setting the overall innovation agenda, i.e. developing an innovation strategy in alignment with the company's overall strategy 'Selling' innovation and innovative projects throughout the organisation Keeping innovation on the agenda and the forefront of senior and middle management Leading by example	Good understanding of the company strategy and ambition Good communicator High level of respect and acceptance throughout organisation	Company board	Senior
Innovation Leader	Basically the role of a project leader but with an additional, special skill set Leading projects beginning to end, primarily of the 'discontinuous' category: 'progressive' if felt appropriate	High level of respectability and trust from different functions Experienced and knowledgeable and good project management skills Open-minded, good negotiator and communicator Understanding of the overall company strategy in general and the innovation strategy in particular	Innovation Director	Quite senior
Innovation Coach	For projects that do not have a dedicated innovation leader, working alongside teams and helping them with innovation tools and processes Identifies behavioural and process-related gaps/obstacles to innovation, works closely with HR on the development of an innovation-related training agenda Provides and facilitates innovation-related training, e.g. different ways to generate ideas, how to use the process, asking questions, etc. Acts as change agent	Good communication skills Good trainer/facilitator A deep understanding of innovation and creativity, and related tools and techniques Understanding of HR processes and tools (that could be used to help create an innovation culture, e.g. training, assessments, reviews, rewards and recognition etc.)	Innovation Director Close collaboration with HR	Relatively senior

Internal Innovation Scout	Identifies innovation opportunities that span internal business unit/ business or departmental boundaries. Presents and 'sells' ideas to business unit/departmental heads. Works closely with the Innovation Director	Good internal connections ; knows 'who does what'. Ability to make connections. Good matchmaker. Persuasive and good communicator	Innovation Director. Regular meetings with business/ departmental heads	Not that critical but does need some clout within the organisation
Innovation Catalyst	Helps to create a shared view and understanding of what innovation is throughout the organisation. Organises innovation events, e.g. lunchtime lectures. Helps create an innovation culture	Good networker and organiser. Imaginative. Good listener and communicator	Innovation Director	Not that critical but does need some clout within the organisation
Future Scout	Keeps abreast of new developments that might affect the organisation in the future. Links happenings outside and in the future to the here and now of the company	Curious, good communicator. Not a specialist in any particular area but very broad and interested in a wide range of topics and issues. Ability to see the broader picture and to make connections. Good networker internally but even more so externally. Good understanding of the company's overall strategy and ambitions	Innovation Director. Regular meetings with business/ departmental heads	Not that critical, drive and skills are more important

INNOVATION ROLES

I would like to present a few innovation-related roles that I have observed in organisations, or that I believe would be useful. The list does not aim to be exhaustive, and some of the different roles might be combined in the same person. Key points are also summarised in Table 21.5.

First of all I believe that innovation needs to be represented at the highest level in the organisation. The role of what I would call **Innovation Director** is to set the overall innovation agenda, i.e. he or she has to be fundamental in developing the top-level innovation strategy, ensuring that it is aligned with the company's overall strategy. This means it is important that the Innovation Director has a thorough understanding of the future ambitions of the organisation. The top-level innovation strategy should define the different categories and levels of innovation the organisation wants to cover, which will result in an overall portfolio. The innovation strategy should further define assessment/selection criteria associated with the different aspects of the portfolio, and give an indication of the percentage of resources to be allocated to each aspect.

For this role a holistic understanding of innovation is essential: this includes an awareness of latest development around innovation and a good understanding of innovation and innovation-related tools and processes. Further prerequisites are the ability to sell innovation and innovative projects throughout the organisation and ensure that innovation is on the agenda of senior and middle management. This requires good communication and influencing skills as well as being able to lead by example. High levels of respect and acceptance throughout organisation are important for the Innovation Director to operate successfully. The Innovation Director should report directly to the CEO or the company board.

A second role is that of an **Innovation Leader**. This is basically the role of a project leader but with an additional, special skill set around innovation and creativity. Ideally the Innovation Leader should take projects from concept to implementation. The higher the level of innovation the more important the end-to-end involvement of the Innovation Leaders becomes. The Innovation Leaders should play a critical role in assembling the innovation team. In order to win the best people for the innovation teams Innovation Leaders need to have the respect and trust of their peers and department leaders – which tends to come with a track record, experience and a good understanding of how the company operates. In addition Innovation Leaders need good project management as well as communication and negotiation skills. These are a rare breed and organisations should make sure to hold on to them if they find them! Given the requirements these people tend to be relatively senior; they ought to report to the Innovation Director.

A third role is the **Innovation Coach**. While the Innovation Leader would lead projects with high innovation levels, less innovative project might still benefit from the input of someone who is trained in innovation tools and techniques. He/She would work alongside teams and help them with innovation tools and processes. It would be the role of the Innovation Coach to identify behavioural and process-related gaps/obstacles to innovation and to work closely with the HR department on the development of an innovation-related training agenda. By exposing team members with innovation tools he or she also acts as a change agent. The benefit of this role is that it is an additional help to the project team. Again, good communication skills are required, as are good facilitation skills. The Innovation Coach should report to the Innovation Director, and keep a close relationship with HR.

An **Internal Innovation Scout** is relevant primarily to large, multi-divisional or multi-business organisations. His or her role is to spot opportunities for cross-boundary collaboration. The most exciting innovation happens when connections are made between previously unconnected bodies of knowledge. Connecting two different industries/business lines is more likely to create an entirely new market than a 'within-business' innovation. However, the level of complexity created by matrix structures combining product lines and geography is generally the limit of what organisations tackle. An example of an organisation that is quite successful at innovating across different aspects of the business is 3M, which achieves this by encouraging a very good internal, cross-business network of the research community and an intranet that makes finding a particular competence relatively easy. For this role to be effective the person has to have extensive contacts throughout the organisation, and some clout to be listened to, if and when an opportunity is identified. Reporting should be to the Innovation Director but regular communication with business heads is also important.

A role that should really be taken on by all senior managers in the organisation, but might need a 'specialist' initially is the **Innovation Catalyst**. The main role of the Innovation Catalyst is to help create a shared view and understanding of what innovation is throughout the organisation. Part of the role is organising innovation events such as lunchtime lectures to inspire people about innovation and help them to understand what is meant by innovation in the context of their organisation. It can also be used to expose people to new concepts, ideas and innovation projects that in turn might help to spark further new ideas. This role would also involve activities that help to create a culture of innovation; such activities might be organising cross-functional events, e.g. 'trade fairs' to showcase projects, ideas, questions, developments, or collect and spread stories that illustrate the kind of culture the company aspires to. Being good at networking, listening and communication are important, as are organisational skills and imagination. Again, such a person should report to the Innovation Director. Seniority is again not so essential but the person needs to be professionally respected in the organisation.

More externally oriented is the role of the **Future Scout** who is the outside ears and eyes of the organisation. While people in research and development as well as sales people might stay abreast of developments that are relevant to the organisation's industry, the role of the Future Scout is to look at and outside the industry borders for new developments, e.g. akin technology, social trends, economic trends, customer trends, that might become relevant to the organisation in the future. While subscribing to newsletters, reading blogs and searching the internet are one approach; it is also to be 'out there', at leading edge conferences and 'hanging out with the cool guys'. Such a person would not be a specialist in any particular area but have very broad and a diverse range of interests. A good dose of curiosity and good social and networking skills are key. A further key skill is the ability to make connections between things that are currently not connected, i.e. to see the relevance of digital photography for the mobile telephone industry. In order to understand which bits of the soup of developments are relevant there also needs to be a good understanding of the company's overall strategy and ambitions. The person should report to the Innovation Director but should keep regular contact with department heads/category leaders.

READING SUGGESTIONS

Leifer, R. et al. (2000) *Radical Innovation – How Mature Companies Can Outsmart Upstarts.* Boston, MA: Harvard Business School Press.

Comment: Focusing on issues around how to implement and nurture radical innovation – extremely useful book for those interested in radical innovation in particular.

Robinson, A.G. & Stern, S. (1997) *Corporate Creativity – How Innovation and Improvement Actually Happen*. San Francisco: Berrett-Koehler.

Comment: In their book the authors advocate the view that financial rewards are actually counterproductive. Full of examples and case studies.

SOME USEFUL WEBSITES

http://www.imaginatik.com

Comment: Imaginatik are one of the leading companies providing software based solutions for idea generation and management. Their website provides a number of useful links, articles, and other information.

22 Venturing – beyond company boundaries

In the previous chapter we looked at different approaches for infusing innovation into an organisation. All options explored rely entirely on internal funding. However, as in the GKN case study, external funding can play an important part in making innovation happen. After providing a brief overview of the spectrum through which innovation can happen and some background to the subject of venture capital, we will address the following questions:

- What are venture capitalists looking for and what to remember when negotiating with venture capitalists?
- What are other sources of external funding?

AVENUES FOR REALISING INNOVATION

For existing organisations there are a number of different avenues for pursuing innovation. Most traditional, and undertaken by all but the most stagnant organisation, is what is widely referred to as new product development. Most companies will have processes and structures in place to accomplish this.

In the introduction we have already established that most organisations have innovation firmly on their agenda; incremental improvements are no longer enough to ensure survival into the future. This comes with two realisations. First, it tends to be small start-up companies that are good at radical innovation, leading to realisation number two: it does not seem easy to pursue more radical departures from the existing through established organisational structures and processes. This is why many managers seek avenues other than traditional product development.

One approach is to encourage employees inside organisations to behave like entrepreneurs. This is also referred to as 'intrapreneurship'. Dollinger (1999) describes intrapreneurship as follows:

- Entrepreneurship within an existing business.

- The development within a corporation of internal markets or autonomous or semi-autonomous business units which produce products, services, or technologies in a unique way.

- An opportunity for corporate managers to take initiative and try new ideas.

- An internal corporate venture.

He argues that intrapreneurship gives corporations the ability and opportunity to experiment in the market. However, while the theory sounds easy, the practice is much more difficult to achieve within existing structures for the following reasons:

- Corporate bureaucracy.
- Internal product competition.
- Competing demand for resources.
- Resistance to change.
- Absence of internal venture capitalists for guidance.
- Employees' lack of ownership reduces commitment.
- Corporate environment not as free for creative ventures as entrepreneurial environment.

This is why many organisations are trying to develop different vehicles that allow people to 'think outside the box' and find 'new themes'. Rather than just encouraging employees to behave like entrepreneurs, organisations set up special funds to finance the fruits of entrepreneurial activities: internal venturing funds. Employees with ideas that do not suit the traditional development channels can seek finance from such a fund, just like entrepreneurs would from venture capitalists. Under this scenario development still takes place inside the organisation's boundaries.

External ventures unit or business incubators are one step removed from the organisation. Here ideas are developed outside the core business, in a dedicated business unit. Under this scenario an organisation will often also consider ideas that originate from outside the organisation.

A step further removed still is external venturing whereby an organisation invests in small start-up companies. Sometimes with the intention to 'spin-in' the organisation at a later state, sometimes to keep an eye on emerging technologies.

In my research I have come across one company that has established three different venture vehicles to achieve different ambitions. The first vehicle is a fund for buying start-ups from entrepreneurs in order to scale them up quickly and accelerate their market presence. The fund is owned 40% by the company and 60% by banks and investment funds. The company keeps an open mind as to what will happen with the investment; options are to keep it as a standalone company, to allow a management buy-out or integrate in the parent organisation. The company seconds senior management into these start-ups, which has resulted in a greater awareness of the concept of private equity onto senior managers' agenda.

The second vehicle is a technical venture unit based in Silicon Valley. This is wholly owned by the company and its purpose is to invest in early stage technology start-ups and take a minority stake. The main purpose is to be exposed to latest technological developments; it is about seeing 'stuff'. Investment decisions do not involve the company; there does not even have to be a fit with what the company currently does. A secondary objective of this vehicle is to support cultural change in the company. On the advisory board to the technical venture unit are three R&D senior vice presidents of the company plus their second in line who spend about 10 days per year in Silicon Valley. In addition 4–5 researchers are seconded to the venture unit every year.

The third vehicle is the company's venture unit. Its purpose is twofold: invest in technical spin-outs; and invest in businesses that are close to the core.

Each of the three vehicles has a different time frame, level of innovativeness, and degree of closeness to the core business. It illustrates clearly that organisations need to be clear about the intent and purpose of their venturing vehicle.

In addition to the three options listed above there is the traditional new product development we have already mentioned as well as mergers and acquisitions. All five approaches are compared across a number of criteria in Table 22.1.

Table 22.1 Different avenues to innovation

Category	Outcome/ Aim	Financed through	Initial location	Type of innovation anticipated	Learning	Main concern
Traditional, continuous new product development	Improved or new products	Regular budgets within functions	On site, within departments	Incremental, in line with existing business	Low	Unsuitable for generating radical innovation
Internal venture unit	New products or new businesses, can lead to spin-out	Ringfenced budget within existing business	On or off site	Incremental or radical, within or outside existing business	Potentially high	Can a distinctly different culture be maintained? Is it relevant to existing business?
External venture unit or business incubator	New businesses, intention often to sell off	Investment fund set up by parent company, often with contribu- tions from external investors/ investor groups	Off site	Radical, within or outside existing business	Potentially high	If too far removed, can investment be justified?
External venturing	New businesses, intention to spin-in	Investment by parent company in external businesses	Off site	Any, most likely radical	Potentially high	Can the new venture successfully be integrated into existing business?
Mergers and acquisitions	Integrated into existing business	Investment by parent company	Off site	Any	Potentially high	Can the new venture successfully be integrated into existing business?

For companies who are aiming to simulate a competitive funding environment for new business ideas it is helpful to understand how the venture capital industry operates. This will be the subject of the remainder of this chapter.

THE VENTURE CAPITAL INDUSTRY

Venture capital is money provided by professionals who invest alongside management in young, rapidly growing companies that have the potential to develop into significant economic contributors. Venture capital is an important source of equity for start-up companies.

Original source: http://www.indiainfoline.com/bisc/veca/

The concept of venture capital is not a new one, in fact, it probably existed before banking: an entrepreneur seeking finance to realise his (as generally 'his' it was) venture, promising the lender a share of the gains in return. A famous example from the fifteenth century is Christopher Columbus who first asked the King of Portugal to fund the voyage to discover a new route to India in return for the usage of this new route for the lucrative spice trade. When the Portuguese king refused he tried the Queen of Spain, who was more agreeable. In the old days getting access to funding depended on who you knew and whose ear you had. Today, while personal connections are still important, there is an established industry for bringing entrepreneurs and investors together.

This industry stared to take shape after the Second World War with the American Research and Development Corporation and J.H. Whitney & Co, both founded in 1946, leading the way. From what was probably considered to be an eccentric's fancy in the 1940s and 1950s, an asset class developed that today is considered mainstream. In 1998 the capital committed by venture firms in the US amounted to $25 billion and venture capital has become an important source of funding for start-up companies. Companies such as Digital Equipment Corporation, Apple, Federal Express, Compaq, Sun Microsystems, Intel, Microsoft and Genentech are all examples of companies that received venture capital in the early stages of their development. Many of the venture capital firms are privately owned but the money can come from a number of different sources:

- Private and public pension funds, currently about 50% with the remained split between the following:
  ○ endowment funds
  ○ foundations
  ○ corporations
  ○ wealthy individuals
  ○ venture capitalists

While the money can come from a variety of different sources, venture capitalists tend to have the following in common, they:

- finance new and rapidly growing companies
- purchase equity securities
- assist in the development of new products or services
- add value to the company through active participation
- take higher risks with the expectation of higher rewards
- have a long-term orientation (return is expected in 5–7 years)

FINDING VENTURE CAPITAL

Whether someone is trying to sell a new business idea within an organisation, or externally, to venture capitalists, the considerations and concerns will be more or less the same. The first step is to develop a convincing story and a business plan. The resulting document should include information about the product or concept and the management team, a marketing plan, market potential predictions and of course finance requirements. As venture capitalists tend to go through a large number of proposals – venture capitalist Arthur Rock (1992) reports that he looks at about 300 business plans a year – they have to be clear, concise and to the point. It is also interesting to note that Rock invests in about one or two per year with about half of his investment meeting performance expectations.

One problem when seeking venture capital is to find the venture capitalist who is actually in a position to make a fair judgement of the proposal. In Chapter 1 we talked about the problems of selling something that does not exist. If you are trying to sell a new pharmaceutical device to someone who is an expert in farming equipment he or she will have difficulties assessing the potential of your idea. This is the reason why over the recent past more and more venture capital funds have started to focus their investment activities on areas where the evaluators of business plans have a certain expertise. The investment fund set up by two people from the case study company *The Technology Partnership* is one example (see Chapter 29).

Purcell suggests that there are 10 vital questions potential investors need to ask:

1.   Is there a need – or is this a technology looking for a problem?

2.   Is the proposed solution compelling enough to overcome people's inertia?

3.   Is the potential market large enough?

4.   Has the company the potential to become the major player?

5.   Has the competition been assessed properly – and does the entrepreneur understand where future competition might come from?

6.   It is easier to expand from a niche than to enter a major market head on – though if it is a niche market, is it big enough to be of interest?

7.   What are the anticipated routes to market – have sufficient allowances been made for customer acquisition costs?

8.   Is there a strong management team – does the team have the right skill mix, balance, energy and drive?

9.   Does the revenue model stack up – what influences the break-even point, are key assumptions valid?

10.   What does the cash flow look like – how long can the company survive?

I would just like to point out that answering some of the questions can be rather tricky if the idea in question is a radical one. If an idea is radical indeed, how can one provide precise information on market size? For the very early stages of such ideas, when the perceived risk might be too high for professional investors, entrepreneurs often rely on so-called 'seed funding'. More often than not this will come from family and friends. Government grants and other organisations supporting start-ups, such as the Prince's Trust and Nesta in the UK, are other possible sources of funding.

For venture capitalists all 10 questions need to be answered positively, there is one that seems to be key in influencing a go/no-go decision: is there a strong management team? Rock (1992) elaborates on this point when commenting about what criteria he uses when assessing business proposals. He says, "Good ideas and good products are a dime a dozen. Good execution and good management – in a word, good *people* – are rare." Therefore when talking to entrepreneurs his questions very much revolve about people issues including:

- Whom do you know?
- Who do you admire?
- What is your track record?
- What mistakes have you made and what have you learned?
- Whom are they planning to recruit and how?
- What are your motivation, energy and commitment?

He also tries to assess whether the entrepreneur is driven by the desire to make their business a success or only in making 'a fast buck' and whether they are realistic in assessing potential problems, and have thought about possible solutions. And finally, he seeks to understand what the person's attitude towards him as an investor is.

So it will be a combination of the merit of the idea proposed and the quality of the entrepreneur and his or her team that will influence an investment decision. However, having said that, there are also external aspects that will influence an investment decision. First, an investor's decisions can be influenced by who else is showing an interest in the business proposition. It can end up in a vicious circle where the entrepreneur finds that several potential investors say, 'If you find someone else who is willing to invest, we might consider investing too.' It is also a reflection of the fact that a fair proportion of the venture capital industry is quite conservative in the investment decisions.

Second, the general economic conditions also influence an entrepreneur's likelihood of obtaining funding as well as the structure of the deal. Supply and demand will determine price. If there is plenty of investment money around it will be easier to get access to finance and to negotiate a deal that favours the entrepreneur. A shortage of venture capital money can mean that he or she has to give up a larger share of the business than in times when cash flows are ample. The structure of the deal will also depend on how desperately an entrepreneur needs money. If economic conditions are tight investors also tend to stick with safer investments – which generally means less innovation.

Finally, what is considered to be 'flavour of the month' will also have an influence on the investment decision. For a while everything that was a dotcom received funding. Many investors were getting careless in the attempt to get a stake in the booming market for e-commerce. After the crash in spring 2000 no one with a dotcom idea, however clever and promising, could find an investor.

Interestingly, for corporate investors some additional rules apply. A study by the American venture capital firm VentureOne observed interesting investment rules for large corporations. If the investment resulted in a strategic advantage such as access to technologies, products or markets large corporations were willing to double that which professional venture capitalists were willing to pay for a given ownership position in a company. It is worth noting that although many venture capitalists take a minority stake they often increase their powers by negotiating blocking rights on certain critical decisions.

For the investor the investment cycle tends to involve the following steps:

- Generating a deal flow – building up a portfolio of investment opportunities that are attractive to the investor.

- Due diligence – industry term that means assuring that everything possible is done to avoid mistakes, i.e. checking the qualitative as well as the quantitative aspects of a business plan, including the checking of references and background of the management team.

- Investment valuation – calculation of future revenue streams and anticipated profitability, prediction of the future value of the business, identification of preferred ownership structure to maximise return on investment.

- Pricing and structuring the deal – negotiating the financial instruments (see Table 22.2) and the pricing with the entrepreneur.

- Value addition and monitoring – this is where the venture capitalist – as opposed to a bank – can add value: he or she can advise, bring in some extra expertise and experience.

- Exit – the exit strategy will have been agreed in the initial investment agreement and can take a variety of forms, the entrepreneur might buy back the stake, find a different investor to take up the stake, or put the company through an initial public offering.

Table 22.2 Instruments of finance

Instrument	Issues
Loan	Clean vs secured
	Interest bearing vs non-interest bearing
	Convertible vs one with features (warrants)
	1st Charge, 2nd Charge,
	Loan vs loan stock
	Maturity
Preference shares	Redeemable (conditions under Company Act)
	Participating
	Par value
	Nominal shares
Warrants	Exercise price, expiry period
Common shares	New or vendor shares
	Par value
	Partially-paid shares
Options	Exercise price, expiry period, call, put

Source: http://www.indiainfoline.com

Venture capitalists are one source of funding for entrepreneurs, and probably the one that most seek in the first instance. However, there are other avenues which will briefly be explored below.

SOURCES OF EXTERNAL FUNDING

Rather than approaching individual venture capitalists for finance, entrepreneurs can investigate the following avenues:

- business angels
- venture capital trusts
- corporate venturing

Business angels

In addition to venture capitalists there are also private investors who invest directly in small companies or start-ups in return for a share of the equity. Quite frequently these investors, also referred to as 'business angels', also join the company's board to provide managerial expertise and other insights to the management team. They tend to bring industry experience as well as independent funds to the party. They are more likely than venture capitalists to invest at the very outset, sometimes even in the development of a product concept. They might be as excited about the idea as the entrepreneur, and are driven as much by the desire to realise the idea as to achieve a positive return on their investment. The presence of a business angel on an entrepreneur's management team can also have a positive influence on the assessment by venture capitalists at a later stage.

Venture capital trusts

More and more trusts tend to specialise in certain industries or technologies and also have set selection criteria. The process tends to be more formalised than with individuals, in fact, the type of investment they can make is regulated. The fact that such trusts underlie legislation means that they can offer tax incentives to private investors. After the initial fundraising the shares of such funds are quoted on the Stock Exchange and can be found in the listing of financial broadsheets such as the *Financial Times*.

Corporate venturing

In corporate venturing a non-financial corporation makes money available for investment in other companies, either directly or through a venture fund that is set up as subsidiary. Usually the investments are in line with the company's strategy, and the idea is to gain access to a particular technology or market, or to obtain other benefits that enhance the investing company's competitive position. The fact that the difference in objective between corporation (strategic benefit) and venture capitalist (make money) leads to different pricing strategies has already been mentioned above.

If a corporation engages in venture capital activities it is important to ensure that people with appropriate skills are in charge of such programmes. Running a venture capital fund and understanding issues in small and start-up companies requires a different skill set from running a mature company.

An example of a corporate venturing programme is that of Apple Computers. Established in 1986 the objective was twofold: to earn high financial return, and to support the development of Macintosh software. The structures – compensation mechanisms, decision criteria, operating procedures – were modelled on those of venture capital firms and funding decisions were made to maximise financial returns. Although the programme delivered an internal rate of return (IRR) of 90% it did little to improve the position of Macintosh.

Besides being a potent route to new revenues, diversification and flexibility, corporate venturing is also one way of experimenting with radical innovation without threatening the core business – unless, of course, too much money is lost in the process.

READING SUGGESTIONS

Hill, B.E. & Power, D. (2001). *Inside Secrets to Venture Capital*. New York: John Wiley & Sons, Inc.

Comment: To quote a reader's review from amazon.com: "A complete guide to venture capital covering all aspects from understanding what venture capital is, to writing the business plan to negotiations, written in an easy to understand, practical manner."

Lerner, J. (2001). *Venture Capital and Private Equity: A Casebook*. New York: John Wiley & Sons, Inc.

Comment: In its four modules the book looks at the following issues: (i) how private equity funds are raised and structured; (ii) the interactions between private equity investors and entrepreneurs; (iii) how private equity investors exit their investments; (iv) a review of the key ideas developed in the volume.

Camp, J.J. (2002). *Venture Capital Due Diligence: A Guide to Making Smart Investment Choices and Increasing Your Portfolio Returns*. New York: John Wiley & Sons, Inc.

Comment: Takes the reader through all aspects of due diligence in venture capital.

SOME USEFUL WEBSITES

www.bvca.co.uk

Comment: On the website of the British Venture Capitalist Association you will find information on private equity and venture capital in the UK, sources of funds and professional advice as well as a number of publications, information on research and other relevant material

http://www.nvca.org/def.html

Comment: On the website of the US-based National Venture Capital Association you will find information and articles on and around the venture capital industry as well as some useful links to related website. The association is also involved in research in this area.

                  www.firsttuesday.com

Comment: First Tuesday cities hold monthly events, such as: the **OOOClassic** event, which traditionally brings together the full range of a city's membership on the first Tuesday of the month; **OOOThought Leadership** events, which bring together leading experts to brainstorm on issues in the technology sector; or **OOOWireless Wednesday** events, which are focused on the wireless segment of the telecom sector.

23 Innovation in financial services

CASE STUDY 8: SHARED APPRECIATION MORTGAGE – BANK OF SCOTLAND[1]

The UK housing market is thought to have an aggregate value of about £1,200bn, greater than the combined value of the UK's stock and bond market.

Financial Times, 14 November 1996

The idea – rationale and getting buy-in

"There must be a way of giving investors access to one of the largest asset pools there is, the housing market", thought Craig Corn, working at Merrill Lynch at the time as a director in structured finance. The UK housing market was dominated by owner occupation with private rental playing only a small role. This meant that for many households, a large proportion – in some cases well over 100% – of their net wealth was tied up in a single il-liquid asset. The housing mortgage, which plays an essential role in financing housing purchase, does nothing to help householders reduce or diversify their risks. At the

	Owner Occupied	Private Rented	Housing Association Rented	Public Rented	Total
1960	7.0		5.2	4.4	16.6
1970	9.6		3.8	5.9	19.2
1975	10.6		3.1	6.2	19.9
1980	11.7	2.4	0.4	6.5	20.9
1985	13.2	2.3	0.5	5.8	21.8
1990	15.1	2.1	0.7	5.0	22.9
1995	15.9	2.4	1.0	4.5	23.8

Stock of dwelling by tenure in the UK (in millions)
Source: Department of the Environment

same time, commercial investment in residential property was very limited, discouraged by the cost of managing rented property and the difficulties of getting repossession of the asset. Pulling these thoughts together Craig was convinced there should be some value in designing a financial device that would somehow open up the enormous asset pool and give homeowners an opportunity to leverage their asset. What if one could find a way of linking an investment to a real mortgage? An alternative option would have been to have call options – but he felt that they would be more difficult to understand – and the mortgage market was not so tightly regulated. The seed for what was to become the Shared Appreciation Mortgage was sown.

---

[1] The case has been prepared by Dr Bettina von Stamm as a basis for class discussion rather than to illustrate either effective or ineffective handling of a management situation.

When Merrill Lynch's management felt that, while quite exciting, such a product would not fit into their existing product portfolio Craig decided to look for takers of his idea elsewhere. When the Swiss Banking Corporation (SBC), one of the companies he approached, were immediately interested, he decided to move there. Once at SBC he was looking for people to join his team, in particular for a person who would have knowledge of the UK mortgage and capital markets. David Garner, who had previously been with a building society and had joined SBC in late autumn 1995 fitted the bill perfectly. Over the next months David and Craig worked on putting the product together and seeking legal opinion. Quite soon the idea emerged that homeowners could perhaps give up a share in the appreciation of their property in return for a fixed-term, low-interest mortgage. The second part of the equation would be an investment vehicle that gave investors access to the shared appreciation in return for their investment, which would be paid by homeowners.

Competitive products at the time

Common Home Income Plan: allows people over 69 to remortgage up to £30,000 of capital from their homes and buy an annuity; part of the income from that is used to repay the loan, set at a fixed rate for the rest of the borrower's life, and part is paid as income to the person concerned. But the income is limited. A woman of 75 would receive only around £1240 a year or £1400 if a non-taxpayer.

Home Reversion Scheme: involves selling all or part of the property at a discount to its full value in return for a cash lump sum (or, in some cases, annuity) and rent-free occupancy for life. Upon death, the buyer becomes owner or part-owner. The price paid depends on how long the buyer waits for the property – and that will depend on how long the owner lives. A 70 year old selling his entire property would get 40% of its value now; an 85-year old would get 55%. The rest is kept by the provider because it might have to wait many years for the home to be sold.

While it was important to secure support from SBC, having an investment bank willing to take the idea forward would not be sufficient, a mortgage lender would be needed to market and manage the mortgages. As Craig and David were looking for a mainstream, respected lender with a solid reputation, they started talking to building societies. But they also talked to the retail oriented banks. Among these was the Bank of Scotland (BoS), which was not only highly reputable but also considered to be innovative. They had been the first to introduce pension backed lending stabilisers and special status lending. As John Lloyd, Director of Sales, Mortgages commented later, "We are amongst the top 10 lenders, but nevertheless think of ourselves as a niche player. We are not competing solely on price but on product differentiation and quality of service. We want to be known as an innovative and specialist lender."

Corporate Statement (from BoS Report & Accounts 99)

The Bank of Scotland Group aims

- To meet customers' needs by providing friendly, prompt, professional and imaginative service

- To deliver a range of distinctive financial products and services throughout the United Kingdom and internationally

- To train, develop, inform, encourage and respect staff so that they can perform an effective and fulfilling role

- To maintain its reputation for integrity and stability

- To make a particular contribution to the cultural and economic prosperity in the local communities in which it operates

- The achievement of these aims will result in long term growth in profits and dividends for the benefits of its proprietors

Craig's first contact at the Bank of Scotland in February 1996 was Willie Donald, who had recently joined the bank as Director of Sales. Willie immediately took to the idea and decided to go right to the top to George Mitchell, Divisional Chief Executive of Personal Banking via George While, Head of Mortgages, knowing that management was always willing to listen to new ideas. They too liked the idea, and George Mitchell felt that such a product could enhance their reputation as an innovator in the mortgage market. For the same reason he felt it would be a good idea to put the concept to the main board, who after some consideration gave their approval in principle in June 1996. Sanctioning from the top was important for another reason, they had been working on a new product for about the past year and it was clear that the bank would not be able to resource and support both projects. John Lloyd, who had been with the bank for a long time, was on the project team and succeeded Willie later in the role of Director of Sales. He commented, "Had Craig approached me at the time I would probably have said no. The current business was being very successful with high levels of growth and I would have feared that resourcing/servicing might become an issue."

Getting started

The SBC and the Bank of Scotland reached agreement to cooperate quite quickly with broad-based letters of intent being signed at the outset. After that the Bank of Scotland set up a team for the development and implementation of the product. When George Mitchell thought about who should work alongside Willie to take the concept further, Neil Forest came to mind. Neil had been with the bank for about 7–8 years and needed a new challenge. With his expertise in securitisation, mainly purchasing MBS notes for BoS, he would complement Willie well, who had just successfully completed the introduction of the Personal Choice Mortgage. Neil remembers, "I came from structured financing into retail, which meant that I could ask 'stupid' questions which challenged everyone and made them think." He continued, "Within our small group Craig and Willie were the visionaries, they would dream things up, many of which would not work – but that did not matter. We all got to know each other very well in the process. David Garner and myself were more on the technical side, translating their ideas into something realisable."

After Neil joined the team in March 1996 they spent about 4–5 months going down what Neil now describes as a blind alley. "But", he continues, "we learned many lessons from it that were very useful later on. And despite having spent quite some time going down the wrong track the top management still had the vision and belief in the product so we got another try." The first version of the product had not involved securitisation. One reason was that securitisation had a bad reputation – one only did it if one could not afford direct financing. Another that the interest rate swaps originally suggested would have meant that the bank would have retained a substantial taxation risk, which they did not like. By the time SBC suggested securitisation again the Bank's Executive was quite excited about the retail product, and so decided to give the go ahead.

Once the concept was finalised Neil and Willie presented to the senior management team, just in time for a board meeting in September 1996 where the product was approved. After that Neil and Willie sat down together to decide who should be on the implementation team but asked George White to actually nominate the people. Neil recalls, "Initially people had to be told to show up to the first meeting, but when they found out about the product they got quite excited about it and really wanted to be involved. Everyone was clear about what we were trying to achieve, we might have had plenty of arguments along the way, but in the end everyone did what was necessary to make the product happen." The implementation team, also referred to as steering group, was pretty senior, consisting of:

○   Willie Donald and Neil Forest, responsible for the product
○   Ian Dickson and John Lloyd, sales
○   John Trouten, customer care
○   Dave Smith, process area
○   Three people from systems

Meetings were held on a weekly basis with interim meetings taking place if and when required. Gary Gordon, Manager, Operations at the time, joined the team after their first meeting in early October 1996; meeting notes were copied to all heads of functions and regular progress reports were given to the board. In addition to the implementation team a second team was dedicated to developing the processes surrounding SAM (Shared Appreciation Mortgage), as the product was called.

Throughout the development confidentiality and timing were a concern. To ensure that as little as possible about the product would be known before the launch, the development area within the Bank of Scotland was declared restricted access. At the same time there was agreement that informing all relevant audiences – staff, intermediaries, branches, financial advisors, etc. – simultaneously would be very important. During the first steering group meeting, 25 September 1996, the launch date was set for 4 November 1996.

Product and markets

Once the concept had been signed off the team quickly decided to focus on two different types of interest rates only. John said, "Two interest rates were sufficient for the launch as we were trying to keep things as simple as possible given some of the product features were complicated enough to communicate as it was. In fact, initially we asked that applicants seek advice from a financial advisor or a solicitor to ensure they really understood what they were signing. Applications that came without the input of a financial advisor were sent back. On the insistence from the Executive we also included sentences to make sure the customer really knew in return for a low interest rate they would forgo some of the future appreciation in their property in both the approval in principal and the formal offer letters."

Bank of Scotland SAM product criteria

- Life-time fixed interest of either 5.75% or 0%

- Shared appreciation levels depending on choice of interest rate

- 5.75% interest rate – maximum loan to value is 75%, the shared appreciation level is equal in proportion to the percentage loan to value (1:1)

- 0% interest rate – maximum loan to value is 25%, the shared appreciation level is three times the loan to value (3:1)

- Purchase or re-mortgage – repayment method interest only

- Properties without existing mortgages accepted

- Minimum/maximum valuation £60,000/£500,000 (higher values may be considered on an individual basis)

- Minimum/maximum loan is £15,000/£375,000 (higher values may be considered on an individual basis)

- Arrangement fee of £500 which can be added to the loan

- No maximum term

- No maximum age

- Partial redemptions – minimum £10,000

- Early repayment fee if the mortgage is redeemed within the first three years: 5.75% SAM – 3 months gross interest, 0% SAM – 1.5% of loan

- Termination charge – administration fee of £300, plus the cost of the sale valuation to establish the level of appreciation

Strongly influenced by sales' point of view the two scenarios chosen were: (a) a 0% mortgage where the borrower could borrow up to 25% of the value of the property and would give up future appreciation worth three times the percentage borrowed (i.e. a maximum of 75%) and (b) a 5.75% mortgage – which was very competitive at the time – whereby the homeowner could borrow up to 75% of the property value, forgoing future appreciation at a rate of 1:1. Any improvements on the house would be discounted from the appreciation calculations, to calculate this homeowners would have to inform the bank in advance of any major improvements made to the home. As the product was designed with specific customers in mind, people who would want either to remortgage or raise capital, they were expecting to get a customer profile of asset rich, cash poor. They were also expecting to see lots of older people who needed to top up their pension interested in the product. For that reason consultations with Help The Aged and SAGA had taken place throughout development. Neil commented, "We did not market test but rather relied on input from our sales people and other experts."

For the investor side the product would work as follows: the 5.75% SAMs would be securitised into fixed-rate notes with a coupon of about 55% of the10-year gilt yield. The zero-interest SAMs would be securitised into floating-rate notes with a coupon of about 60% of three-month Libor. According to SBC's marketing literature, "Trading in the familiar form of Eurobonds, SAMs offer all the benefits of

	Equities	Government Bonds	Residential Property
Return	15.1%	7.5%	8.4%
Volatility	20.4%	11.3%	4.9%

Source: SBC Warburg Dillon Reed

involvement in residential property, with some protection from downside property exposure." Coupon payments to investors would be made on a quarterly basis and would consist of a fixed or floating element plus a supplemental interest element to reflect price gains for SAMs terminated that quarter; in addition, debt would be amortised each quarter as the number of underlying homes in any SAMs pool would become smaller. Willie Donald commented, "The step up coupons were designed to offer some attraction to investors who were buying something without a fixed maturity; but we were calculating on the basis that it would amortise after 25 years." The issuer had the option to sweep up the paper should the note size outstanding fall below 20% of the original total, or if a withholding tax were imposed.

With SAMs being like equity but less risky it was thought that they should be attractive to pension funds. A SAM would be long term and earnings-linked rather than being linked to the RPI. Craig felt that the product could enable pension funds to manage their long-term liability and improve earning power. In *Euromoney* December 1996 Craig commented on potential takers for the bonds, "Pension funds should be interested, because historically house prices have not only outperformed inflation, but matched increases in earnings. Most pension fund liabilities are earnings-linked. Property funds should certainly be interested. And there's enough equity in the bonds to encourage some equity investors as well, although the mortgages are being sold on the basis that stock markets have historically outperformed house prices."

Main features of SAMs:

- Asset diversification into a significant asset class
- Upside exposure to a superior performing asset on a risk-adjusted basis
- Asset/liability matching by means of an excellent wage inflation hedge
- A legally efficient and cost effective means to enter the owner-occupied residential property market
- Joint economic interest to preserve the value of the home
- Greater diversification than direct investment
- Extra value derived from a 'portfolio of options' effect
- Direct support of and investment in the local housing market

---

The Bank of Scotland would be taking no interest in the loans. 100% of debt and equity would go to bondholders with the Bank of Scotland receiving a fee. SBC released one issue per company. A separate Book ID on the BoS system would enable tracking of transactions between companies. The money from the mortgages coming into the Bank of Scotland would get cleared on a monthly/weekly basis to SBC. At the time SBC was one of the few financial institutions that had a triple A rating, the highest. It effectively stated that the likelihood of default was very slim. (At launch all SAM notes were AAA rated.) In the absence of a suitable model initial pricing for the bonds was based largely on SBC's research, which incidentally also indicated high levels of interest from investors in the SAM bonds.

In order to keep funds associated with the SAMs separate from its main books, the Bank of Scotland set up an independent company for each SAM with the Bank of Scotland acting as an agent for the BoS SAM (legal charges were in the name of the BoS SAM rather than the BoS). For the Scottish SAMs special arrangements were needed, a special service vehicle company was set up which originated both rated and zero SAM, the two books were sold to SAM3 and 4. The company was not involved in the securitisation but sold to one of the English companies who then securitised the assets.

Trials and tribulations

During development and implementation the team had to be aware of a number of acts and regulations. For example, they needed to ensure that the offering would not be in conflict with the betting act. Then there was the risk that while interest might be legally enforceable the appreciation aspect was not likely to be. Many of these issues had been identified during the first session where the team had a brainstorming session about what things could go potentially wrong. While many of the possible problem scenarios were familiar from previous projects and the team had the bank's new product development process and internal check lists as reference points, for example the Critical Sheet for Actual Lending, there were a number of issues no one had encountered before.

During their second meeting in early October the IT people alerted the implementation team to the fact that Unisys, one of the bank's IT systems on which all accounts would be domiciled and through which all transactions were managed and recorded, would only accept loans up to 50 years. With the SAM set up as an open-ended mortgage – until death (or sale) – this was potentially a problem. But this was not the only IT-related challenge. Unisys would not accept an interest rate of 0%. The suggestion to run SAM with 0.0001% interest, which would have meant that no statement would be issued, was not acceptable as it would still have had an impact on the account. With a separate company for each of the SAMs there was a concern that processing, which was done overnight, might overrun, particularly at the end of the month. The decision to upgrade processing capacity was made quickly. Setting up a standalone system for mortgages on Unisys had the advantage that they would not affect the mainframe and would avoid any loss of time and interference with priorities.

The team was aware that due to the fact that the SAM would be externally securitised they would have to design the infrastructure for SAM in such a way that would make it distinct from BoS with a clear and separate audit trail. Normally most documents would be microfilmed and only some key documents would be kept. But this was seen not to be sufficient for SAMs, they would have to satisfy external auditing requirements; this drove decisions on what kind of documentation would be required and for setting up separate companies. They even chose a special colour for the folders so they would be easily identifiable.

With appreciation being calculated on the difference between the initial valuation and exit valuation, valuations were an important issue. Countrywide was appointed to administer the panel of valuers who would provide all valuations.

During the team meeting on 9 October it was decided to launch on 11 November and announce the launch in the *Sunday Times* on 4 November 1996 – the team was quite positive that this would be front-page news.

Market introduction and reaction

The deal represents the first chance for many institutions to gain access to the £850bn pool of UK housing equity, rather than the housing debt market.

Euroweek, 6 February 1996)

It would make sense for individuals to own less housing, and for institutional investors, such as pension funds and insurers, to own more (they now own almost none).

Economist, 17 January 1997

As no similar product had existed before George White had informed many of BoS's large intermediaries directly about the product. As the magazine *Euromoney* pointed out in its article of December 1996, "It isn't like anything the capital markets have seen before." The article continues by quoting Craig Corn, "It's a convertible bond wrapped up in a securitisation vehicle; it's a property-linked bond; it's an equity securitisation; it's a mortgage-backed security; it's equity in retail housing; if I had to pick one bond which it was like, I'd say it was most like an index-linked gilt, linked to house prices instead of inflation."

The team also made sure that marketing material would be available to intermediaries ahead of the launch. Several other steps were taken in preparation of the launch: people were nominated to man the phones within the bank's mortgage area on the day of the press release which was a Sunday, more people had to be added when it turned out that telephone calls would last up to 45 minutes – rather than the 2–3 minutes normally spent on customer enquiry calls. A memo was sent out requiring all enquiries to be forwarded to the dedicated team within the mortgage area. The board too was kept fully informed and had asked that nothing be released that had not been approved by them.

By the time the product was launched – which was actually before contracts with SBC Warburg had been finalised or terms and conditions had also been copy-written – the bank was already receiving around 2000 phone calls per day, the majority of callers being interested in the 0% option. The interest had been stirred prematurely by a press leak in a Sunday paper on 20 October, which had put additional pressure on the team to launch – and which had meant that by the time the product was launched the bank had already a database of about 2500 individuals

> **From internal BoS memo to all sections**
>
> All enquiries should be diverted to the Business Development teams who have been briefed and have in-depth details of the product. As far as existing customers are concerned they should be transferred to the SAM Implementation team, who will respond as follows:
>
> "SAM is a new product and concept and at the present time there is a limited amount of funds available for this. Consequently it is not available for existing customers but it is our intention to review this after 6 months once we have had some experience of the likely demand and availability of funding which is provided through issuing Eurobonds. I would also mention that in the event this does become available to you, any transfer will involve a full re-mortgage with all the costs associated with this such as legal costs, valuation and arrangement fees given the mortgage is only available through a separate subsidiary of the Bank which has its own documentation"

who had requested information on the product. Demand far outstripped what the team had anticipated and by the second week of December they had run out of brochures. The first two tranches were launched in England with the first moneys drawn on 31 December 1996. The team at the Bank of Scotland was quite keen to keep the momentum going and launch the following tranches as quickly as possible.

But not only were the borrowers keen on the new product, most of the press wrote enthusiastically and Warburg's[2] first issue was, in fact, oversubscribed. For the 5.75% option, the BoS SAM1, bonds worth £27.2 million were issued; for the 0% option, the BoS SAM2, bonds worth £105.6 million. However, pension funds were not among the takers.

After the initial enthusiasm

Shared appreciation mortgages, a way of selling part of a property while continuing to live in it, are temporarily off the market after demand from borrowers outstripped the supply of money from the bonds market. Demand for the bonds has dried up after £750m worth from the Bank of Scotland plus a first launch of bonds from Barclays, which offered a SAM briefly this year.

Financial Times, 11 July 1998

While the bank's new product had caused great interest from borrowers, after just having lived through the problems of the pension funds, intermediaries were much more sceptical. As the bank received many calls from borrowers who felt quite strongly that they were quite capable of making decisions without legal advice, the bank decided to relax its requirement for applications to come through intermediaries. To their surprise applicants were also more often than not asset rich as well as cash rich, and they received several requests for what Willie Donald termed 'jumbos', huge properties. They also received calls from homebuilders building retirement homes who were enquiring on behalf of their customers, a group that had not been anticipated. In addition the age profile was different from what had been anticipated, applicants tended to be in their fifties and sixties rather than seventies, and they found that many Muslims were interested in the 0% option.

With interest from borrowers unabated, investor interest began to slacken after the first two issues. The bank had been keen to maintain the momentum but SAMs 3 and 4 could not be launched until securitisation of SAMs 1 and 2 had been completed because of limited warehouse funding lines. Also, due to the different legal system in

> But how interested will investors be in the securitisation of an asset with no track record because it has not existed before?
>
> *Euromoney*, December 1996

Scotland introduction of the product had to be delayed and it was not until mid-February 1997, with a financial crisis looming in Asia and Russia, that the SAM was introduced in the bank's home country. This coincided with the launch of tranches 3 and 4. While the emphasis had originally been on the innovativeness of the product and the great potential of the housing market at the time, the following tranches tried to present the SAM as an established product that was there to stay.

Tranches 3 and 4 took much longer to place and tranches 5 and 6 had to be taken up by SBC Warburg itself despite the fact that based on Halifax house price indices it could be expected that BoS SAM1 would have a

---

[2]Warburg merged with UBS in 1998.

return of 4.3% and BoS SAM2 a return of 4.4% against an overall increase of 3.4% in the UK as a whole. During the preparations for the issue of SAMs 5 and 6 SBC Warburg went through the merger with UBS and while the team at the Bank of Scotland was hoping SBC Warburg/UBS would find a way to interest investors in the product, in the end, they had to take the product off the market.

> "We have been educating investors about a whole new asset class. This deal is a hybrid, and the job has been to find the part of an institution which will buy it."
>
> Craig Corn, *Euroweek*, 18 July 1997

Within the bank Neil, as Director of Product Development, was given the remit by top management to pursue the idea for a further year and to expand the product development department.

Competitor's reaction

While applauding the ingenuity of the project, rival bankers said many hurdles needed to be overcome before the bonds could see the light of day. Some structuring issues were within the compass of SBC Warburg, such as coming up with a model that would convince investors they could accurately predict the rate at which mortgage holders paid off the loans – a crucial component of measuring return on asset-backed securities.

Euroweek, 15 November 1996

Corn predicted that some of the UK's top 10 lenders would launch rival products in the second half of the year with a view to securitisation in 1998.

Euroweek, 18 July 1997

In March 1998, after the Bank of Scotland had taken their product off the market, Barclays Capital launched their first securitisation of shared appreciation mortgages with a £98m triple-A rated zero coupon bond. The Millshaw SAMs No I Ltd issued a 55-year deal that was backed by 3253 first charge mortgages that Barclays had signed up between May and July 1998. These loans had a maximum loan to value ratio (LTV) of 25%. Like BoS SAMS 2, 4 and 6 no interest was charged but once borrowers sold their house, paid off the mortgage or died, they would have to surrender a share in the appreciation of the value of the property, calculated as three times the LTV. While progress was slow, Barclays found that institutions were buying the bonds for their high returns. If real property inflation ran at 2%, slightly below its long-term average of 2.2%, and retail inflation was 2.5%, Millshaw would yield 7.8%, around 330bp over Gilts. Barclays expected that any significant growth would only come with familiarity and that a retail bid for the assets could eventually play a part in making this theoretically persuasive market a reality.

Questions

1.   What would your advice have been to both the Bank of Scotland and UBS Warburg after the issue of SAMs 3 & 4?

2.   Do you consider the product to be a success or failure: (a) from the BoS perspective; (b) from UBS Warburg's perspective; and why?

APPENDIX 23.1: ADDITIONAL INFORMATION

- The time available to applicants to accept a mortgage offer set at 14 days, 3 months was normal; they decided to cut it in order to maintain a tight control of the money going out as there were only certain funds available for each phase.

- After acceptance borrowers had 6 weeks to draw the funds, normally they could do that any time – for the same reason as above.

- Allocation was on a first come first served.

- For normal mortgages they have a 60% conversion rate (from offer to being drawn), for SAM they had a 95% conversion rate; disagreement with valuations was the only reason that led people to withdraw.

- Borrowers were expected to meet all valuation costs (at outset, in between in case of home improvements, etc.).

- No proof of income was required for the 5.75% mortgage as applicants had to go through intermediaries who were expected to be able to judge whether the people were creditworthy or not; the requirement was not reinstated even when the intermediaries were no longer required.

- No life cover was required for the 0% option; for the 5.75% option it had initially been required but was later waived.

- The APR for the 0% was 8.6% and 8.9% for the 5.75%.

- It was not possible to add dependants onto the mortgage.

- Borrowers were required to undertake any major repairs before the initial evaluation.

- If people wanted to make improvements to their property they had to inform the BoS beforehand; valuers, paid for by the borrowers, would assess what percentage of future appreciation would be due to the improvement so it could be deduced on exit.

24 Innovation in the service industry

The case study of the shared appreciation mortgage is an example of innovation in the service industry. It also provides some interesting insights into innovative organisations' perspective on what constitutes 'success or failure'. This chapter takes a closer look at particularities of the service industry, the role of design in developing services, and compares factors that underlie successful service development. Issues around success and failure in new product development and innovation in general are addressed in Chapter 25.

PARTICULARITIES ABOUT THE SERVICE INDUSTRY

Let us start with a few observations before we start looking at the particularities of the service industry. First, increasingly the boundary between tangible and intangible products becomes blurred. For many products it becomes more and more difficult to say whether it is a service or a product. Think about any form of leasing (a service) versus buying the product, for example, cars. Is a programme providing internet access a product or a service? Is the selling of 'weed-free fields' referred to in Chapter 18 a product or service? The second observation is that services tend to be much more profitable than products. Blumberg (1989) reported that service obtain margins of 15–25% before tax whereas product can demand only 7–11%. Not least for this reason more and more companies are either trying to tie in products with services or switch to selling services altogether. Interestingly many of the examples for companies that have switched from products to services have been motivated by sustainability arguments (e.g. the company that offers the service of keeping your floor covered instead of selling carpets – see Chapter 18). Another reason is pointed out by Terrill and Middlebrook (1996) who state that, "When a product is offered in conjunction with a service it is often the service that adds value, not the product."

And, finally, in many developed countries the service industry has overtaken manufacturing by quite a margin. For example, in the UK the service sector today delivers some three-quarters of UK GDP and some 80% of employment, having grown by an average rate of 3.5% this decade.[1] Services industries also spend heavily on innovation (most is not formal R&D). In services, expenditure on innovation is highest in Iceland, Denmark and the United Kingdom (4% or more of total sales).[2]

---

[1] Speech by Rod Eddington to the Commonwealth Club in London, 1 December 2006 (http://www.dft.gov.uk/162259/187604/206711/speech).
[2] Source: Eurostat; OECD, STI/EAS Division, May 2001.

But how is 'service' defined? Johne and Storey (1998) provide a number of definitions that might be useful:

- Service product – the predominantly intangible core attributes which customers purchase.

- Product development/innovation – the development (or improvement) of tangible or service products.

- New product development (NPD) – the development of tangible products which are new to the supplier. Sometimes NPD is expanded to include new service development (see below).

- New service development (NSD) – the development of service products which are new to the supplier.

- Offer development – the development, by the supplier, of core product (or service) attributes plus the development of the processes by which the product is evaluated, purchased and consumed.

Many of the considerations for new product development and innovation are the same, whether the end result is tangible – i.e. a product – or intangible – i.e. a service. The usefulness of a formalised development process, the early involvement of all parties involved throughout the development, and the need for senior management to signal clear support for development and innovation activity, to name but a few. Given the aforementioned I found it quite interesting that an article published in 1997 (Sundbo, 1997) describes the innovation process in the service industry generally as an "unsystematic search-and-learning process", while it seems that most companies engaged in the development of tangible products have formalised product development processes by now. The description of the process for developing new processes by Terrill and Middlebrooks (in Kuczmarski & Associates, 1995) does not look very different from that for the development of tangible products (see Box 24.1).

Box 24.1   New service development process

1. Problem description
    2. Idea creation
        3. Concept definition
            4. Analysis & screening
                5. Concept design
                    6. Delivery and operations test
                        7. Broad market testing
                            8. Infrastructure scale-up
                              9. Introduction & launch
                                10. Post launch check-up

Source: Kuczmarski & Associates Inc (1995). *Winning New Products and Services for the 1990s.* Chicago: Kuczmarski & Associates Inc. Reproduced by permission of Kuczmarski & Associates Inc

---

However, there are also aspects of services and service development that are different and which need to be understood in order to innovate successfully. Most of the differences arise from the fact that services tend to be intangible by nature but the exploration below is broken down under the following headings:

- Consequences of the intangibility of services
- 'Manufacture' and delivery happen simultaneously
- Difficult to protect
- Easy to innovate

Consequences of the intangibility of services

The most obvious difference between a tangible product and a service is that the latter is intangible. This means that you cannot look at them or touch them and that they are difficult to assess before a purchasing decision is made. At a basic level service innovations might be easier to understand, for example internet banking means that you conduct all your banking activities on the computer instead of going into the bank or posting letters. However, the real test comes in the experience, when actually using the online service. No description of the product is likely to point out the problems of establishing a connection, problems with setting up transfers to accounts that are held at a different bank or the difficulties one can have in speaking to a real person to discuss a problem. A friend from Germany just reported that his bank would allow 'either or', that is he would either have to do *all* his transactions via the internet, or all the traditional way. As he spends time travelling for longer periods, which means that access to the internet cannot always be guaranteed, subscribing to the internet services is not really an option for him.

The fact that by the time that you are able to assess the quality of the service you have already paid for means that reputation and word of mouth are of critical importance. Reputational issues were a major consideration for the Bank of Scotland in the development of their innovative product. Senior management were quite adamant that everything possible should be done to ensure that purchasers of the shared appreciation mortgage would be absolutely clear about the conditions and implications of entering into such a mortgage agreement. This was the reason why a dedicated, well-trained team was set up to answer questions about the new product, and why applicants were initially asked to seek professional advice before submitting their mortgage applications.

'Manufacture' and delivery happen simultaneously

Because the product is consumed upon delivery there is no manufacturing as such and ergo neither the possibility to 'manufacture' in advance and put into an inventory. Unlike with tangible products, where quality controls can be built in at several stages during the manufacturing and delivery process, if there is a lapse in quality for intangible products the customer is probably the first to notice. As a consequence the medium through which the service is delivered – be it an IT system or people – are critical for the quality of a service as well as for its consistency.

On the note of IT systems, it seems that many organisations are introducing new and expensive IT systems under the umbrella of improving customer services. However, anyone who has tried to get through a system of options after options in automated telephone answering systems will be aware that most of these systems have little to do with customer service and are implemented for cost reasons only. My own recent experience with the provider of financial services for lease purchases of cars is an example of how 'improvements' of IT systems can backfire significantly if not designed and executed carefully (see Box 24.2).

Box 24.2   Experiencing service quality . . .

Contact from financial service provider	Response by customer
Letter of 16 May 02 informing customers about a new computer system, asserting that the customer does not need to take any action; electronically generated signature by 'A'	No action taken
Letter of 19 June 02 informing customer that 'due to lack of funds in your account your bank has been unable to make your last payment . . .' electronically generated signature by 'B'	Upon return from a holiday 2 July the customer telephoned the financial service provider, after checking that the account in question had been in credit throughout the period in question. A flash of inspiration led the customer to ask what account details were used which resulted in the insight that an account that had been used for the first months of the contract, back in late 1998, had been used; correct account details were given
Letter dated 1 July informing the customer that the bank had rejected the request for the second time; electronically generated signature by 'B'	No action as the customer assumed that phone call and computer generated letter had crossed
Letter dated 4 July asking the customer to provide correct bank details signed by 'C'	Customer received and sent letter 8 July AND spoke to 'C' 8 July confirming AGAIN the correct bank details
Letter dated 11 July signed by 'D' acknowledging customer letter of 8 July	No action taken – though customer quite annoyed as it is yet another computer generated letter referring to correspondence as 'complaint'.
Letter dated 11 July electronically signed by 'B' informing customer yet again that they were unable to draw from customer's account, setting an additional charge	Received and called 15 July, spoke to 'E' again giving current bank details. Customer requested a return call to confirm that problems had been resolved. No such call came Customer called again 18 July and requested to speak to the most senior person; explained the situation again and was yet again promised that problems had been sorted out
Letter dated 19 July identical computer generated letter electronically signed by 'A'	Received 25 July, 12.00; customer asked to be put through to 'A' and was told 'A' does not take customer calls, spoke to 'F' instead; Customer (!) suggested that if they had used the wrong bank details they might also have sent a letter notifying the bank of the changed arrangements to the wrong address; 'F' was very helpful and seemed, again, to be able to sort out the problem and promised that the customer would get no more computer generated letters

Letter dated 26 July, signed by 'A' informing the customer that a new account has been set up	No action taken
Two identical letters dated 31 July, electronically signed by 'B' requesting that the customer should call him	Upon receiving the letter 5 August the customer attempted to call 'B' (although of course the customer had previously been told that 'B' does not talk to customers); after several attempts and time spent in waiting loops the customer gave and wrote letter including a summary of all above correspondence
Letter dated 7 August, signed by 'G', apologising	Customer called 20 August upon returning from travels abroad, spoke to 'H' and confirmed that the company should continue with direct debit until all instalments were paid; 'H' agreed to call should there be a problem (there was only one left)
	Customer called 6 September when she found that her account had been drawn on twice; 'I' explained that they were the penultimate and last payment but that due to the problems in drawing from the account in June there was still one payment outstanding; customer decided to send cheque the same day to sever all relations with that company, the cheque was drawn from account 12 September
Two identical letters dated 23 September electronically signed by 'B' stating 'we refer to the arrangement for payment of the arrears on your account. The promised payment has not been made and we therefore require immediate payment. If full payment of the arrears or contact, is not received within 10 days, legal proceedings may be taken by this company without further notice'	Customer writes rather angry letter to the financial service (. . .) provider with copies to the British Consumer Association, the CEO of the car manufacturer associated with the financial service provider, and the MD of the UK branch of the financial service provider
Telephone call from the personal assistant of the car manufacturer's CEO, as well as from the PA of the MD of the UK company of the financial service provider	Customer demands letter to acknowledge that all claims had been deleted from her account; letter received 1 November 02, signed by the MD of the UK company

Particularly with financial services, frustration caused by IT systems seems common – and the big problem is that it seems the same everywhere. From personal experience I also know that being dissatisfied with bad service is one thing, actually doing something about it is something entirely different. How many people are dissatisfied with their banking arrangements but stay with their existing supplier – out of convenience, rather than conviction? The example of Egg shows that there is a tremendous opportunities for service quality improvements.

Difficult to protect

Unlike tangible products, which are often built around complex technologies or formula that can be patented, services are very difficult to protect. It is literally impossible to patent services or service components and not only that, it is generally very easy for a competitor to copy and improve existing offerings (Naslund, 1986). Having investigated innovation in the banking industry, Naslund explained that, "In my project several respondents suggested this fact [that service innovations are easy to imitate] as a reason for the low number of innovations in banks. A bank that innovates will not receive much of the profit from the process because competitors quickly imitate the new product." Many service providers are therefore attempting to develop new offerings in secrecy – as was the case for the shared appreciation mortgage. While the product was under development the bank tried to ensure that only a few people knew about the development, and were also quite selective about which customers and intermediaries to involve. Herein lays a conflict. On the one hand innovative services are difficult to understand unless they are explained in detail and preferably experienced, and a lack of customer involvement can lead to services being designed based on assumptions rather than real needs. On the other hand secrecy is important to prevent competitors from introducing the same or similar product first and hence steeling the thunder. The aim of the Bank of Scotland was to be first to market, to be seen as innovator and to create a level of bind-in of customers that would help them to establish a market leader position. Interestingly though, once the product was on the market the bank would have been quite keen for competitors to take up the product to help create a market, particularly for the bonds that were issues to securitise the mortgages. Unfortunately, while customers were very keen to take up the product, the interest among investors was insufficient to create an effective market for the bonds.

Having said services are easy to copy it should be pointed out that it is the 'what' that is easy to copy. The 'how' is often more difficult to replicate. If a service provider can establish an innovation in the marketplace through delivering a high-quality service, a competitor might be able to offer the same service, but if customers are satisfied with existing services levels they are not very likely to switch to a different provider. Providing superior service levels through training and building expertise can be as effective in fending off competitors as are patents.

Easy to innovate

The fact that new service development is often quite inexpensive – there is no R&D expenditure to speak of or any investment requirements for plant and machinery – means that anyone can come up with a new service proposition. While it is frequently pointed out that it is easy to innovate in a service context, the fact that much of the success of establishing a new service in the market depends on reputation and trust means that the 'coming up with ideas' is the easy part but implementation can be quite difficult, and often depends on an established and trusted brand underwriting the new offering. For Craig Corn, the ideator of the shared appreciation mortgage, the reputation of the Bank of Scotland as an innovator was an important selection criterion. He was looking for a bank that would have a high level of credibility in bringing an innovation to market, which customers would trust and believe would fulfil their promises.

As with the development of tangible products there are certain organisational characteristics that support innovation whereas others hinder the flow and realisation of innovations. In their research into innovation in the banking industry Johne and Harborne (1985) found that banks are traditionally characterised by tight, bureaucratic structures involving high levels of standardisation, formalisation, centralisation, and limited flexibility and specialisation. They saw this as one of the reasons as to why there is little real innovation in the banking industry. This argument is supported by further insights from their study which indicate that those banks that were innovating successfully were characterised by flexible operating structures.

Terrill and Middlebrooks (1996) propose five possible angles to service innovation:

1.   positioning innovation
2.   process innovation
3.   service offering innovation
4.   people innovation
5.   communications innovation

Using the first, positioning innovation, they suggest developing a unique positioning that differentiates the product or company from existing offerings. Restaurant chains offering a particular service are one example. Think about Starbucks coffee which has changed the fast and cheap caffeine intake into a lifestyle experience for which it charges a substantial premium.

With the second angle, process innovation, they refer to the removal or addition of a process step to improve the customer experience. Being able to use credit cards directly at the petrol station pumps is an example. However, this option is less likely to be sustainable than the first.

The third, service offering innovation, encompasses three options: first, the creation of a unique set of benefits of features by bundling or repackaging existing offerings; second, the adding of new benefits to an existing service; and third, the creation of a totally new service offering. As an example they quote garages that offer a service that includes life-time oil changes, thereby locking customers into future servicing and creating real switching costs.

The fourth, people innovation, is based on the concept of increasing or decreasing the discretion individuals have to improve a customer's service experience and provide individualised services. Walt Disney's message to their theme park employees is, "It is up to you to exceed customer expectations."

And finally, with communications innovation Terrill and Middlebrook refer to the branding of a service offering or the use of a unique communication approach to differentiate a service. The example the authors give is that of consulting firm CSC/Index, which branded their approach to cost reduction 'reengineering', and created awareness through articles, books and seminars.

Part of successful service innovation is the ability to identify the right customer segment. Kennedy (2001) points out that effective service innovation can generate top-line revenue growth as well as bottom-line profits. He argues that in order to realise this the following are essential:

•   understanding customer value creation
•   targeting high-value customer segments
•   choosing the correct customer interaction model
•   creative pricing
•   understanding cash flow

He emphasises that his research showed that "selling to the wrong customers, poor retention, failure to deliver value, and delivering service to customers who do not appreciate it destroyed value". I was impressed when a service provider suggested that the value of changes and innovations should be assessed as to whether it was introduced to serve and please the customer – or the company.

However, I found it interesting that de Brentani and Kleinschmidt (1999) concluded from their research that realising radical innovation can be quite difficult for service companies. They explain that, "For new industrial services, moving into fields that are unrelated to the firm's known capabilities and resource can be particularly problematic. Especially for highly intangible professional or expert services – where customers use the firm's reputation and past experience as a proxy when evaluating the new service itself – a low level of synergy with the company's known capabilities can have a detrimental effect. Conversely, new products involving adaptations, refinements and enhancements of existing products and/or service delivery systems often achieve a higher level of success because they leverage the unique resources and skills of the firm."

And finally, it is noteworthy that Johne and Storey (1998) found from their review of the literature that, "Leading edge new service development practice seeks to marry organisational aspiration with the aspirations of individuals." It confirms the importance of the project leader, and his or her enthusiasm to drive the project forward. We will find in the case study on the Technology Partnership, presented in Chapter 29, that the practice of following individuals' interest and passion has also proved a great contributor to the success of the company.

DESIGN AND SERVICE DEVELOPMENT

Hollins and Hollins (1991) start their book *Total Design* with the following:

Services are products

Products need to be designed

Design is a process

This process must be organised

This organisation is the job of management

While there is an increasing awareness among managers of the contribution design can make to the success and impact of tangible products, the realisation that design can play an equal part in the successful design and development of services is less common. However, the involvement of designers can improve the experience of many services significantly. For most services there is a tangible component. Be it forms to fill in when applying for mortgages or insurance policies, be it a computer interface or the physical environment at a hairdresser's or an advertising agency. Design can help to make the experience as smooth and easy as possible, and all things being equal – as they often are with services – people will be more likely to fill in a form they understand immediately, than one where they have to spend hours finding out what exactly is required, or go to a website that is easy to navigate than waste a lot of time searching around different pages.

Increasing competitiveness, as for example in the financial services industry, should also motivate managers to consider all the levers they can pull to differentiate their product.

SERVICE DEVELOPMENT – WHAT DRIVES SUCCESS?

Given the particularities of the service industry there are a number of considerations managers can should keep in mind in order to maximise their chances of success.

The first is to involve customers as early as possible and to attempt to get as close to prototyping as possible. A study conducted by Martin and Horne (1995) suggests that increasing direct customer participation in the development process in general and the use of information about the customer at specific stages increases the potential for success. But even though there seem to be great benefits to be gained from involving customers, Gadrey et al. (1994) point out that, at least in their research in the early 1990s, the service firms were not very efficient in establishing and using external networks, and involving customers in the innovation process.

Often it might even be feasible to engage customers as development partners. This is a way of ensuring that there is a real market for the new service. However, it is worth taking a closer look at what kind of customer is participating in the development. If the service is innovative it is advisable to involve early adopters and those who are known to be open to new ideas and risk taking, rather than a group of customers who are known to be laggards and highly risk averse.

Secondly, as it is the 'how', not the 'what', that makes it difficult to copy services, particular attention needs to be paid to the quality of the service delivery, be it through IT systems or people. This is why internal and external communication as well as advanced training and customer education are essential. In fact, in her research into innovation in the financial service industry de Brentani (1989) found that ineffective communication between the different parts of the service organisation caused major problems. Insufficient external communication, particularly for radical innovations, can lead to unrealistic or false expectations of the customer, which in turn will have negative implications for the acceptance of the new service. This is again something that the Bank of Scotland took very seriously during the development of its innovative product. And if it is indeed the 'how' that makes a difference it is also critical to keep service delivery in mind throughout the design and development process. This is also where design – interface design, the design of forms and brochures etc. – can make a significant difference, something that we address in the following section.

The third concerns the development process. De Brentani and Kleinschmidt found that successful service innovations have the following in common:

- They address a specific market need, e.g. close contact with and intimate knowledge of customers' needs and operations.

- They follow a formal up-front process as well as a formal and detailed launch process which includes test marketing, frontline training and internal marketing, developing a formal promotion and launch plan.

Table 24.1 Success factors – incremental and radical service innovation compared

	Incremental	Discontinuous
Market/need fit	XXXX	XX
NSD: planned launch	XXX	+
Frontline expertise	XX	X
Corporate synergy	XX	X
NSD: culture & management	X	XXXX
NSD: formal up front process	+	ns
Improved service experience	+	ns
Standardised service	+	ns
Service complexity/cost	ns	ns
Service quality evidence	ns	X
Competition	ns	ns
Market potential	ns	ns

XXXX < 0.0001; XXX < 0.001, XX < 0.01, X < 0.05, + < 0.10; ns – not significant

Source: de Brentani, U. & Kleinschmidt, E. (1999). Achieving new product success in highly innovative versus incremental new industrial services. Paper presented at the 28th European Marketing Association Conference, Humboldt University, Berlin.

- They explore corporate synergies and build on frontline expertise; corporate synergies refer to fit with managerial skills and preferences, expertise and human resource capabilities, delivery and behind-the-scene competences, marketing and financial resources and frontline expertise, the extent to which the new service uses high-level expert/professional resources in performing judgemental tasks during service delivery.

In addition they found that, particularly for radical service innovation, an internal innovation environment (e.g. effective new service development culture and management) is critical. Table 24.1 shows the aspects investigated and their potency in explaining success or failure in incremental and radical service innovation.

READING SUGGESTIONS

Zeithaml, V. & Bitner, M. (2000). *Services Marketing*. New York: McGraw-Hill.

Comment: Dedicated to enabling the reader to understand issues in service development including customer expectations and behaviours, the development process, service delivery and pricing

Hollins, G. & Hollins, B. (1991). *Total Design, Managing the Design Process in the Service Sector*. London: Pitman Publishing.

Comment: Even though the book is dedicated to the service industry, much of the reading covers ground that is equally relevant to the development of tangible products

SOME USEFUL WEBSITES

http://www.csfi.org.uk/

Comment: This is the website of the Centre for the Study of Financial Innovation which is an independent London-based think tank, funded by the world's top banks. It explores the future of the financial services industry. It has an active agenda of meetings, seminars and research projects which are of wide interest to all who work in, or use, the financial markets. Contact details are: 18 Curzon Street, London W1Y 7AD, United Kingdom; Tel: +44 171 493 0173, Fax: +44 171 493 0190

http://www.serviceinnovation.org/

Comment: The Consortium is a non-profit alliance of support organisations focused on innovation for the support industry.

25 Failure, risk and measurement in innovation

Many people might consider the Shared Appreciation Mortgage to be a failure because it did not stick in the marketplace. Interestingly though, both the Bank of Scotland and UBS Warburg rejected the idea that the development had been a failure. Both companies emphasised the valuable learning and insights that the experience had provided them with. While it is also true that neither organisation lost any money, which might have influenced their assessment on success or failure, such an attitude is characteristic of innovative organisations. Innovative organisations will not try to brush 'failures' under the carpet but will look at them carefully with the aim of extracting as much learning as possible. We will also explore other reasons why failure isn't always such a bad thing.

However, it is of course the aim of any organisation to minimise the failure rate and this is why I will start this chapter with taking a closer look at factors known to influence success or failure in new product (and service) introductions.

WHAT UNDERPINS SUCCESS AND CAUSES FAILURE?

Despite more than 30 years of research into the design and development process of products, the issues surrounding success and failure remain much the same. The importance of the early stages is constantly emphasised, because mistakes made at this point prove costly and time consuming later on. While there are some suggestions in the existing literature as to what can be done to improve this part of the development process (market research, careful screening) the issue is not dealt with sufficiently and the same loop is experienced time and again.

In their review of the literature on success and failure in new product development Balachandra and Friar (1997) comment that, "The review shows first that even with a conservative approach to listing significant factors, the list is very long. Second, comparing the factors across studies demonstrates that different authors have found that the magnitude of significance and the direction of influence vary. Third, given the differences in context, the meaning of similar factors may also vary."

While the individual factors identified underlying success and failure in new product development may vary considerably, overall the factors underlying success and failure seem to have remained the same over the past 30 years. Suggestions on best practice published by Karger in 1960 are not very different from those published by Cooper and Kleinschmidt in 1996. As early as 1957 Carter and Williams identified good people at all levels, willingness to take on new knowledge and sharing of knowledge, and cost consciousness as factors underlying successful product development. Consequent studies analysing product failure have generally identified the mismatch between product offering and market need as main culprit (see Box 25.1).

Box 25.1   When do products fail?

Basing their figures on findings of various researchers Hollins and Hollins (1991) have found that projects tend to fail at the following stages:

Ideas	Product design specification	Concept	Production preparation	Selling	Success
100%	20.6%	17.5%	17.0%	12.25	4.75

Source: Hollins, G. & Hollins, B. (1991). *Total Design: Managing the Design Process in the Service Sector*. London: Pitman

---

Urban and Hauser (1993) have contemplated the reasons of failure and suggest some safeguards against those most commonly observed (see Table 25.1).

Table 25.1   New product failures and safeguards

Failure reason	Elaboration	Suggested safeguard
Major shifts in technology	'Blind-sided' by radical change in technology; stayed with old technology too long	Monitor new technologies; look for new benefits they can produce; continuing education for R&D; have a contingency plan for shifts
Changes in customers' tastes	Substantial shift in customer preference before product achieves market penetration	Frequent monitoring and updating of customer preferences in the design, testing and launch phases
Changes in environment constraints	Drastic change in some key factor such as economic conditions or material costs	Analysis of environmental constraints in opportunity identification; monitoring in testing and launch; adaptability in design
Poor repeat purchase or no diffusion of sales	Customers buy the product in the beginning, but sales never reach potential	Trial and repeat, and diffusion measured in design phase and monitored in testing and launch; product designed to deliver real benefits; advertising matched to product's benefits delivery
Poor after sales service	Product complex or not reliable and service not delivered	Service considered as an explicit designed in benefit; monitored in testing and launch
Insufficient return on investment	Poor profit relative to investment	Careful selection of markets, forecasting of demand, design of product for low-cost production; value maps facilitate profit maximisation

Table 25.1

Failure reason	Elaboration	Suggested safeguard
Lack of coordination in functions	R&D develops a product that does not meet customer needs; marketing identifies benefits that cannot be delivered; design changes make production difficult	New product process is used to coordinate marketing, R&D, engineering and production; the input from the customer drives the design
Organisational problems	Conflicts between marketing, R&D and production; inadequate communication of key aspects of design and marketing	Careful attention to communication and explicit programmes to coordinate with quality design programmes; management involvement and review at various stages of the process; careful go/no go decisions with objective criteria
Market too small	Insufficient demand for this type of product	Market is defined and rough potential estimated in opportunity identification; demand forecasts in design and in testing
Poor match for the company	Company capabilities do not match the requirements for producing and marketing the product	In opportunity identification the company's capabilities are matched to the strategic plan; this is then tested in pre-launch, pre-test and test markets
Not new/not different	A poor idea that really offers nothing new to the customer; the technology may be new, but the benefit to the customer is not evident	Creative and systematic idea generation in opportunity identification; product designed with a focus on the customer; product and position tested before launch
No real benefits	Product does not offer better performance vis-à-vis customer needs; under-investment in core technologies	In design, a strategic benefit position is identified and the product engineered to deliver these benefits; R&D designs real product performance improvements; product test with customer assure adequate benefit delivery
Poor positioning vs competition	Perceived benefits from the product are dominated by a mix of competitive products; low value	The use of perceptual mapping, value mapping, and preference analysis identifies gaps in the market relative to competitive products
Inadequate support from the channel of distribution	Products fail to generate expected channel support; demonstrations not provided if needed; product not available to customers; after purchase service not available	The channel is considered in opportunity identification; service delivery is part of the product design; the channel reaction is monitored in testing and in launch

Table 25.1

Failure reason	Elaboration	Suggested safeguard
Forecasting error	Excess production due to overestimation of sales; opportunities are lost because of underestimation of sales and low production and marketing	Systematic methods in design, pre-test. And testing phases of the process improve earlier forecasts as the product and marketing strategy near completion
Poor timing	Enter too late in market; cycle time too long; miss window of technology or market opportunity	Design process to get to market fast; monitor changes; trade-off risks of go or delay
Competitive response	Competitors respond quickly before the product can achieve a success in the market; price and promotion; competitors copy design and improve it	Strategic positioning vis-à-vis competition; consideration of competitive response in design, pricing, and marketing plans; 'what-if' scenarios; monitoring of test and launch; move aggressively to establish first in market advantages

Source: Reproduced from Urban, G.L. & Hauser, J.R. (1993). *Design and Marketing of New Products*. Prentice-Hall

Looking on the other hand at factors that support success Barclay (1992) provides a still valid summary – perhaps not surprisingly all five aspects represent good current management practice.

1. An open mind and professional management.
2. A good market knowledge and strategy.
3. A unique and superior product that meets customers' needs and wants.
4. Good communication and coordination.
5. Proficiency in technological activities.

Much of the same is reflected in other reviews of the literature, for example Craig and Hart (1992) and Balachandra and Friar (1997). There is generally also a great emphasis on the importance of top management commitment, for example Booz Allen Hamilton (1982) and McGrath (1996). However, all these ingredients seem fairly obvious and for me the question is, this knowledge has been around for a while, and best practice is generally known, why does it still not happen?

> **Variations between incremental and radical innovation**
>
> Brentani and Kleinschmidt (1999) have identified a number of variations in success factors for incremental innovation on the one hand and radical or discontinuous innovation on the other. Demonstrated product superiority is likely to play a key role in the success of *discontinuous innovation* because these incorporate new technologies which often solve previously unsolved problems or handle customer concerns in completely different, more effective, ways. For *incremental* improvements or adaptations, an overwhelming product superiority is much less likely to be achieved and, in the case of services – due to their intangible, conceptual, nature – is even more difficult to effectively demonstrate.

It seems that insufficient analysis of the task and an underestimation of change, or a preconceived idea about what the task would be like, can be a major influence on blinding companies to potential problems and issues at the outset. Unexpected events are in the nature of innovative projects but to build in slack for accommodating such events, an awareness of potential problems areas and the overall level of innovation need to be understood at the outset. Research (von Stamm, 1999a) found that what tends to get in the way of a realistic assessment at the outset are two things: habits and assumptions. We will take a closer look at both.

Habits are accustomed ways of doing things and the problem with habits is, we tend to be unaware what our habits are, and how much they drive our behaviour. Most people in most situations will approach a new task building on what has worked in the past. Not many projects start with a reflection and questioning whether the task has been understood sufficiently, and the identification of aspects that are different from what had been done before.

The literature attributes such behaviour – approaching a new problem with established mindsets and procedures – to human nature. For example, looking at developments of new concepts in science Bohm and Peat (1991) observe that there is a general tendency of people to, "become accustomed to using their tacit skills and knowledge in subliminal and unconscious ways; there is a tendency of the mind to hold on to them and to try to go on working in old ways within new contexts". They continue, "Scientists attempt to press on by putting 'new wine in old bottles'. But why should this be? It involves a psychological factor, the mind's strong tendency to cling to what it finds familiar and to defend itself against what threatens seriously to disturb its overall balance and equilibrium. Unless the perceived rewards are very great, the mind will not willingly explore its infrastructure of ideas but will prefer to continue in more familiar ways. One way of defending the subliminal structure of ideas is to overemphasise the separation between a particular problem and other areas."

Basically, what they are suggesting is that existing knowledge and existing approaches can get in the way of the creation of new knowledge and new approaches. This observation has not only been made in the context of science. In the context of new product development, Leonard-Barton (1992) has made a similar observation. She argues that the source of strength of an organisation – its knowledge base or as she calls it, 'core capabilities' – can also act as a barrier to the development of future strength. Because core capabilities are part of what an organisation has known to work and what it takes for granted, they dictate how projects are approached. She concludes that, "because core capabilities are a collection of knowledge sets, they are distributed and are being constantly enhanced from multiple sources. (...) They are not easy to change because they include a pervasive dimension of values, and as Weick (1979) points out, 'managers unwittingly collude to avoid actions that challenge accepted models of behaviour'."

In his book, *Science of the Artificial*, Simon (1992) uses the concept of 'bounded rationality' to explain such behaviour. He argues that problems are often too complex to be solved within the time available. As a result, humans tend to rely on patterns of behaviour that were successful in the past. These patterns are only reviewed if problems are encountered – or someone questions them.

Moving on to the subject of assumptions we find that Schein (1992) argues that beliefs and assumptions form the core of an organisation's culture. Many projects run into problems because existing assumptions have not been challenged. These assumptions, which were either explicitly or implicitly understood, influenced choices, decisions and actions throughout the development process. Assumptions are needed at the beginning of any project because not all the necessary knowledge and information is available at the outset – which of course is particularly true for innovative projects. However, these assumptions need to be acknowledged and decisions taken on the basis of assumptions recognised as such.

The consequence of habits and assumptions is illustrated in Figure 25.1.

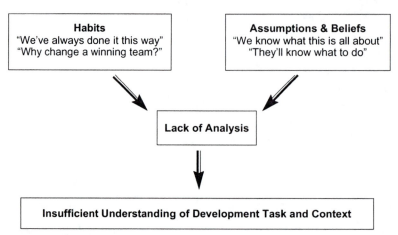

Figure 25.1   Consequences of habits and assumptions.
Source: von Stamm, B. (1999a). The effects of context and complexity in new product development. Doctoral thesis, London Business School.

You may want to refer back to Box 1.1 in Chapter 1 where insights from Guy Claxton's book *Hare Brain Tortoise Mind* are summarised. His insights help to understand different modes of responding to a situation and how people's unconscious exerts an influence in the classification of a new situation. The framework introduced in the following section suggests a way of eliciting habits and assumptions at the outset of a development process.

THE COMPLEXITY FRAMEWORK[1]

The framework is designed to aid members of an organisation in understanding any particular new development task in its specific context, and to elicit potential problem areas and constraints and help them to design the organisational response to a specific development task. It does so by requiring its user: (a) to evaluate the requirements of the new development task against the eight elements and (b) to assess the current status quo of the organisational context, again, against the eight elements, and with the particular requirements of the task in mind. It should bring out present knowledge levels as well as implicit habits and assumptions whereby former and latter are closely linked.

Eight common elements identified as having an impact on a development task are:

- time frame
- technology
- skills
- financial resources
- participants
- processes

---

[1] The complexity framework was developed by Bettina von Stamm as part of her doctoral thesis, 'The Impact of Context and Complexity in New Product Development', 1999.

- cultural aspects
- customers and markets

Besides understanding product-related aspects, it is further important to understand the organisational context in which the development takes place. We have discussed the implication of context and constraints in Chapter 15. Each of the eight elements contributes to the overall level of complexity of a development task. The specific context in which the development takes place will have considerable influence on the assessment. Therefore, the development team needs to look at: (a) the requirements of the new development task and (b) its own starting position, that is the current knowledge base, company processes and procedures, typical approaches and preferences, and so on.

Time frame

Ulrich and Eppinger (1995) comment on time pressure in new product development, "any one of the difficulties [in product development] would be easily manageable by itself given plenty of time, but product development decisions must usually be made quickly and without complete information". Time pressure not only requires decisions to be made based on assumptions rather than facts, but it can also force an organisation to develop components of a product in parallel (McGrath, 1996). This in turn will necessitate careful planning and close cooperation of all parties involved.

The time constraint under which a product is developed will also have a considerable influence on the approach an organisation takes. The tighter the time frame, the more likely it is that an organisation will try to fall back on existing components, solutions and concepts, thereby often neglecting the fact that the new problem task requires a different approach and a different solution (Bohm & Peat, 1991). Along similar lines Amabile (1998) points out that "organisations routinely kill creativity with fake deadlines or impossible tight ones".

Tight time frames have also become more of an issue in recent years, not least owing to the debate on 'time to market' and the need to shorten development cycles, which was strengthened by an influential article by Bower and Hout (1988). They state that high-tech products that come to market late, but on budget, earn 33% less profit over five years whereas products coming out on time being 50% over budget decrease company profit by only 4%. The views on the impact of reduced development times differ. Kuczmarski (1988) suggests that unrealistically short time frames, introduced as a consequence of the 'race to market', have become more of a problem in new product development. More recent publications also caution and point out that the trade-off between speed and quality needs careful consideration (e.g. Calantone et al., 1997; Cohen et al., 1996). Cutting corners to achieve shorter development times is found to be negatively related to product success. Contrary to a commonly held view, it is not always true that a speedy market entry secures financial success. Cooper (1994), for example, points out that it is more important to bring out the right product than to bring out a product at the right time.

The importance of timing is likely to vary from product to product. The race to bring products to market as quickly as possible is particularly obvious for rapidly changing markets such as computers and mobile telephones. Here new product features and improved performance can render existing products obsolete and promote the establishment of a new market leader.

Table 25.2 Constraints – time frame

Constraint	Implication
Externally or internally imposed time frame (e.g. competitor has announced timing for the introduction of a similar product; being part of a system; product introduction required for company's survival)	Restricts the ability to experiment and explore different options Increases the likelihood that an organisation will rely on existing and proven designs and technologies

Generally, a tight time frame, particularly when externally motivated, acts as a constraint. However, a lack of understanding of the complexities arising from the other elements of the framework can lead an organisation to agree to a particular time frame – because it is assumed to be realistic (see Table 25.2).

Technology

Technology-related issues were found to arise from two aspects: (a) the interdependencies, between components or between a product and the wider system of which it is part; and (b) the degree of innovation which, by nature, is associated with corresponding levels of uncertainty (Smith & Reinertsen, 1995). Both Adler (1992) and Fujimoto et al. (1991) have found a link between high levels of innovation and uncertainty and the need for interactive integration mechanisms.

For example, if a project is developed in the traditional, sequential fashion, interdependencies between components can result in the need for substantial reworking of components that have been developed during earlier stages. Thus, a high level of interdependency leads to an increased need for coordination and integration. Holt (1987) suggests that, in cases where the degree of innovation is high, there will also be an increased requirement for slack (in terms of time and human resource) to accommodate unforeseen events. The useful translation of this insight faces two problems: (a) an organisation would have to be aware of the degree of innovation inherent in the development task – which does not seem to have been the case in any of the three case studies; and (b) pressures on companies to bring products to market in ever shorter cycles make it less likely that companies will accommodate this need.

A constraint related to technology is the existence of a dominant design. Unless an organisation can be certain that its new concept would be capable of replacing the existing dominant design, it is not likely to take the significant risk. Having to adhere to an existing dominant design can pose a considerable constraint. At the same time the existence of a dominant design permits a firm to design standardised and interchangeable parts and to optimise organisational processes for volume and efficiency, hence reducing complexity. Though complexity is reduced, so are the number of choices an organisation can pursue in achieving a particular development task (Utterback, 1994).

Company internal standards – resulting from the company's plant and equipment, knowledge of technology, structures and procedures, or a combination of these – can also act as a constraint.[2] This type of constraint is

---

[2] Here is a link to the 'Culture' element. According to Schein (1992) culture is "the pattern of basic assumptions that a given group has invented, discovered, or developed in learning to cope with its problems of external adaptations and internal integration, and that have worked well enough to be considered valid, and therefore, to be taught to new members as the correct way to perceive, think, and feel in relations to these problems" – i.e. it defines the 'way we do things around here'.

Table 25.3 Constraints – technology

Constraint	Implication
Dominant design	Restrict the choice of design and technology High risk is attached in deviating from the dominant design
Industry standards	Restrict the choice of design and technology
Company internal standards	Restrict the choice of design and technology Can prevent experimentation with different approaches and technologies
Government regulations (environment, health and safety)	Restrict the choice of design and technology Changes in regulation may require re-design of existing components
Being part of a system	Restrict the choice of design and technology

most difficult to deal with because it is not explicit and, hence, often not perceived as a constraint. If an existing procedure or internal company standard hinders rather than aids the development effort, Leonard-Barton (1992) would describe this as a core rigidity.

Beyond industry and company standards and dominant designs, there are also government regulations, for example on environmental or health and safety issues, which can act as constraints.

Finally, Tidd et al. (2001) point out that whether or not a product is part of a system is an important factor. If the product to be developed is part of a larger system, this can act as a constraint. Consider the Eurostar, the high-speed train is part of not one but four different railway systems and many parts of that system are non-changeable, such as the signalling systems, track widths and platform heights. While these were changeable in principle, in reality it had to be accepted that they were not only non-changeable but also different from country to country. This inevitably had constraining consequences for the design and development of the train. Constraints related to 'Technology' are listed in Table 25.3.

Skills

The greater the range of skills required to complete the task, the greater the need for coordination and cooperation. However, it is also important to look at potential changes in the skill mix as compared with previous projects, that is it is important to understand where and how demands on skills have changed. In some cases it might be necessary to consider bringing in external resources.

Changes in the mix of design skills will also differ at different stages of a product's life cycle. We have referred earlier to the example of the Sony Walkman where skills required changed over the product's life cycle.

The skills available within the company and, even more specifically, skills available for each individual project, will also influence the approach.[3] It might be that, owing to the number of projects undertaken at any one time, the

---

[3] On this subject Tidd et al. (2001) have commented, "We have shown how firms are inevitably constrained by their choice of innovation strategies by their accumulated skills."

Table 25.4 Constraints – skills

Constraint	Implication
Skills available within the company	Company finances and politics will influence the freedom to bring in external expertise; company politics can also decide who is involved in the project (prestige projects tend to get the best people)
Skills available to the project	Due to other projects the most appropriate skills may not be available to the project
Existing knowledge base	May prevent a critical assessment of a new task

most appropriate people are not available to the project. Also, while it is important to have people with relevant experience on the project to avoid a replication of existing knowledge, such people are also more likely to refer back to concepts and approaches that were useful to them. This can lead to problems of a 'fixed mindset'.

A further issue is that the problem might be seen through one function's particular 'glasses', that is issues relating to that function's area of expertise might be highlighted while others remain unexplored. Constraints related to the 'Skill' element are listed in Table 25.4.

Financial resources

A very obvious constraint which needs little explanation is financial resource. While most project ideas can be realised technically, it is often a question of whether or not the cost can be justified. Most companies have guidelines regarding the payback period of their investments and apply these during the project selection process (see Table 25.5).

Participants

Today, alliances, joint ventures and supply-chain issues mean that it is common for more than one company to be involved in the process of designing and developing a new product (see also Chapter 13). The greater the number of participants, the greater the need for coordination and integration. The same is true for a single-company project where the varying interests and needs of the different departments involved need to be coordinated and integrated. As the number of participants increases more politics get involved. The more complex a project, the greater the

Table 25.5 Constraints – financial resources

Constraint	Implication
Budget	If financial resources are not available even the most congenial idea cannot be realised There is a technical solution to most problems but the result may not justify the investment

Table 25.6 Constraints – participants

Constraint	Implication
Distance between partners	The distance between partners can act as constraint on the communication flow
Split the work load	If more than one company is involved, each partner will expect a 'fair' share of the work whereby the 'fair' share might not be equivalent to the distribution of expertise but is often related to the financial backing by the companies involved
Partners (externally) imposed	Particularly in international projects the choice of partner might be externally influenced, e.g. by government; in national multi-company projects headquarters or other institutions of power might influence the choice
Politics	As the number of participants increases politics between differing interests are likely to impact on speed and efficiency

need for arbitration – you may want to refer back to the reference to work by Fujimoto in Chapter 3 (section on 'Project Leader'). The need for cooperation and coordination may decrease with increasing familiarity between the various parties involved. One might compare this with someone learning a foreign language: the more the language is practised and experienced in the national context, the greater the understanding of the meaning and use of words.

For multi-company projects and geographically dispersed organisations, the distance between sites is also an issue to be considered. Even additional expenses and time requirements for both travel and negotiations are a factor and are not entirely mitigated by today's technology (teleconferencing, e-mail, networked computers, etc.). If a joint venture or other form of partnership is chosen, it might be necessary to break down the workload so that each of the partners gets a 'fair share'. This can lead to the work being shared according to each partner's financial involvement rather than each partner's expertise and knowledge. For constraints related to 'Participants' see Table 25.6.

Processes

Unless the implications of a particular organisational or manufacturing process for the development process are understood, the project is likely to suffer. Barclay and Lunt (1987) argue that a holistic approach that considers issues of finances, technology, people and management, is important when investigating the introduction of new processes. The constraints related to organisational and manufacturing processes are closely interlinked with other elements of the framework such as financial resources, skills and culture (see Table 25.7).

Table 25.7 Constraints – processes

Constraint	Implication
Existing plant and machinery	Unless financial resources are available to alter existing plant and machinery, they can significantly constrain the choice of materials and technology
Existing organisational processes and procedures	The implications of a change need to be understood, i.e. how does the new process require the 'ways we do things around here' to change

Cultural aspects

Where different cultures are involved, cooperation and coordination need to be planned more carefully. Cultural differences exist between companies of different national backgrounds, between different companies and even between different departments within an organisation. The literature on design management and product development comments on cultural and language differences between several different functions such as between designers on the one hand and engineers and scientists on the other, between designers and managers, between marketing and R&D personnel, as well as between marketing and engineering. This has also been discussed in Chapter 15.

At company level, each party involved will have developed its own rules and procedures that are likely to differ from those of partner companies. Time and effort will be required to establish a shared understanding and find mutually agreeable solutions. Company culture will also have a profound influence on how people interact, what values they follow – and not least what habits and assumptions they share. While this thesis has identified the crucial influence of company culture it will remain the challenge of future research to investigate its influence on contextual complexity further.

At the national level, differences might be found in design taste and also in the wider economic environment, that is differences in the relationship between state and industry. Finally, in a cross-border project the need to converse in two or more languages can be a major constraint. Either interpreters are needed, which can prove difficult if technical vocabulary is required; or only people with a command of the languages in question are used on the project. This can result in a compromise on expertise (see also Table 25.8).

Customers and markets

Important factors here are the existing customer base and a company's reputation. While it is not suggested that a company is restricted to its existing customer base, the way the company is perceived by its customers, that is its reputation, needs to be taken into consideration. A whole body of literature is concerned with brand extension (see Table 25.9).

Table 25.8 Constraints – culture

Constraint	Implication
Language	The need to share a language might restrict the choice of people working on the project If different cultures (national as well as company or departmental) are involved, more time and effort has to be spent on ensuring shared understanding (objectives, procedures, etc.)
Different procedures and systems	Can slow a project down owing to the need to 'translate' between different systems; alternatively investment might be required to ensure compatibility
Habits and assumptions	Can influence, for example, the realistic assessment of a new task, how people interact and how decisions are made

Table 25.9 Constraints – customer and markets

Constraint	Implication
A company's reputation	How a company and its product are perceived by its markets and customers can be a constraint on the kind of product and the pricing strategy
Regulations	Regulations in different markets can also impact on the choices an organisation can make, this aspect has the most severe impact on technology

OVERCOMING CONSTRAINTS

While constraints can have a significant, impeding impact on a product's design and development process, few of them are insurmountable. However, in order to overcome a constraint an organisation needs to be aware of its existence. Meaning, for example, a team has to be aware of a lack of time to ask for more resources, or, a team needs to be aware that it is lacking a certain skill essential for completing the task to take steps to redress the problem. Once there is an awareness, the people responsible can then make a conscious choice and decide whether or not a trade-off should be made. Interviewees from the research underlying the development of the framework felt strongly that most of the above would not have been possible without the determination and foresight of an individual or small group of people who pursued their goals in spite of obstacles, and against the conviction of others.

THE FRAMEWORK

The assessment of a project for each of the eight elements has to be based on the company-specific context. In order to gain a better understanding of the development task the project team should first look at the requirements of the new project along the dimensions of the eight elements of the framework and then consider the company-specific context in which the task is to be executed.

The importance of the company's specific context in association with the management of innovation is emphasised by Tidd *et al.* (2001). They suggest that, "Innovation management is about learning to find the most appropriate solution to the problem (...), and doing so in the ways best suited for particular circumstances in which the organisation finds itself." This is an important point, as what seems simple to one organisation may be complicated to another. Table 25.10 summarises the eight elements and their subcategories, what they refer to and suggests a scale for their assessment. The aim of the framework is not to provide an instrument for exact measurement of objective complexity but to elicit the levels of complexity as they apply within an organisation's specific context.

In order to do this the project team will have to ask itself how the new development task compares with its existing position, previous projects and past knowledge. Asking about the conduct of previous projects and comparing this with the plans for the execution of the new development task will help people understand more about 'the way we do things around here'. Consideration of past knowledge is a critical point. As has been pointed out before, it can obstruct a clear assessment of the development task. It is essential to establish which part of existing knowledge is beneficial to the project and which aspect may be an obstacle.

Table 25.10 Components of contextual complexity

Element	What it refers to	Scale
Time frame	In comparison with projects of similar scope	Long/Short
Technology		
Interdependencies	Can arise from (a) interdependencies between different components and (b) being part of a wider system (e.g. trains, computers);	Few/Many
Degree of innovation	The percentage of new components; the level of technological uncertainty is generally related to the degree of innovation	Low/High
Skills		
Level	Number of different skills required	Low/High
Mix	In comparison with previous projects	Same/Different
Financial Resources	The degree to which financial resources are available to the project	Ample/Tight
Participants		
Number	Number of departments and/or companies involved in the design and development process	Few/Many
Proximity	Proximity of sites (departments and/or companies)	Close/Far
Familiarity	Familiarity of parties involved, i.e. have they worked together before, both at the individual and company level	Intimate/None
Processes		
Familiarity	The degree to which an organisation – and more specifically, the part of the organisation that is to develop the new product – is familiar with (a) organisational processes and (b) manufacturing processes	Familiar/Unfamiliar
Appropriateness	The degree to which the processes chosen are appropriate for (a) the task at hand and (b) the organisation's context	Appropriate/ Inappropriate
Cultures	Number of different cultures involved (cultural differences can arise between departments, companies and/or nations)	Few/Many
Customers and Markets		
Familiarity	Whether the product is aimed at an existing or a new audience	Same/Different
Reputation	The degree to which the product reflects the existing reputation of the organisation, e.g. the degree to which the new product has credibility with the customer	Established/ Has to be Built

To use the framework for a project, the template shown in Figure 25.2 is useful. The template has been filled in for the comparison of an imagined product to facilitate the discussion. Such a comparison not only highlights where differences have to be understood, but also where the gap between present and future is greatest.

In the example given, the time frame is tighter than for previous projects but at the same time more financial resources are available. This would mean that the organisation might be able to allocate more resources to

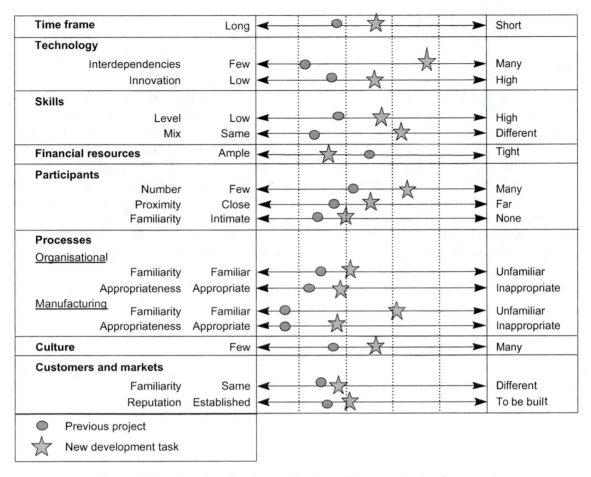

Figure 25.2 Template for the application of the complexity framework.

the project in order to compensate for the tighter schedule. The framework suggests how trade-offs can be made – which Ulrich and Eppinger (1995) consider to be an essential part of the new product development process.

The example also suggests unfamiliarity with the chosen manufacturing processes, which generate a cross-check into whether the degree of unfamiliarity is reflected in the assessment of the 'Skill' element. Using the proposed framework is not a one-step approach, but an iterative process that can be continued throughout the design and development process.

The framework aids in the correct assessment of any particular new development task – and it is the often the underestimation of the level of innovativeness that leads to problems later during development. It also provides an organisation with knowledge about itself and facilitates insight into its habits and assumptions. In eliciting these, an organisation can make an educated choice as to whether its present ways are still appropriate for the future or whether its 'core capabilities' are in danger of turning into 'core rigidities' (Leonard-Barton, 1992).

IS FAILURE REALLY FAILURE?

I like fiascos because they are the only moment when there is a flash of light that can help you see where the border between success and failure is. It is a precious experience in the development of new products. Our most beautiful fiasco was the Philippe Starck Hot Bertaa kettle. I did not realise that we had gone too far. Inside the kettle was some complicated but very intelligent engineering that prevented steam from escaping when the water was being poured. On the prototypes it worked well but when we produced thousands and thousands and thousands it did not work so well. The kettle was very much criticised. But it was never a stupid project. We just went too far. There were so many positives, not least the courage of the designer. He wasn't playing a joke on the customers. He just felt the need to experiment. Our customers seem happy to take risks with us, probably because they realise that we are always sincere. They like walking the borderline with us. Customers are much more progressive than marketing people, distributors or retailers believe. Society is much more exciting than just a target market. A target market is a cage where people try to put society. It bears no relation to what people feel and want.

Alessi, quoted in Wylie, 2001

Three of the big secrets of innovation are embedded in the above story, to innovate you need to take risks, to innovate you need to experiment, and to innovate you need to accept or even love failure. The story also shows that innovations can be valuable for different reasons. It is not only immediate and significant success in the market – though that is of course the main reason companies innovate. But even if the success in the marketplace is not as big as desired, there may still be benefits such as:

- Increased market share – in the fight against competition increased market share can actually be as valuable as large profits.

- Learning experience – the Bank of Scotland and UBS Warburg valued the experience of developing the Shared Appreciation Mortgage as it provided them with valuable insights and learnings.

- New expertise – through working on the recycling products BPI developed a number of new skills that position them to take good advantage of future emission and recycling regulations.

- Enhanced reputation – innovation specialist IDEO develops products to illustrate and demonstrate their innovation capability.

In their research into new service development Storey and Kelly (2001) found that companies were undertaking new service development for the following reasons:

•	To increase profit	88%	•	To develop distribution	14%
•	To increase sales	53%	•	To improve an existing product	12%
•	To increase revenue	40%	•	To improve the product range	12%
•	To satisfy customer needs	35%	•	To respond to regulation	9%

- To develop new markets   26%
- To address a new customer segment   23%
- To fill a gap in the market   23%
- To improve the strategic position   19%

- To improve customer satisfaction   7%
- To improve the image   7%
- To reduce costs   7%
- To increase market share   5%

Why failure can be a good thing

Before moving on to measuring innovation success I would like to share Petroski's (1997) view on failure as he puts a different spin on it saying, "We actually want certain things to fail and break, for otherwise we would be frustrated in their use and possibly even harmed by their existence." He illustrates his argument with examples of products that are actually designed to fail drawing on nature as well as manufacturing. Think what would happen if eggs did not break – there would be no reproduction. Other examples of products that are deliberately designed to fail – albeit under desired conditions – are sprinkler systems and fuses. And sometimes I would actually wish that the peanut bags served on aircrafts were more disposed towards failure as, more often than not, the contents of the crafty little bags end in my drink or on the floor rather than my stomach.

MINIMISING RISK OF FAILURE – RISK MANAGEMENT

The revolutionary idea that separates modern from ancient times is the mastery of risk: the notion that the future is more than the whim of the gods and that men and women are not passive before nature.

Peter Bernstein in *Against the Gods: The Remarkable Story of Risk* (1996)

Understanding the principles of sound risk management is the foundation for successful innovation in decision making.

Survey of the National School of Government (2006)

In the debate around innovation 'risk' and 'uncertainty' always come up as reasons why innovation does not happen; 'it is too risky', 'we do not know what return we will get', 'we don't want to take chances' are typical comments in this context.

Risk management as such is not a new discipline, and 'decision science' is part of most management degrees. So there is a lot of knowledge about the management of risk out there – but somehow that knowledge does not make people more comfortable with innovation. Perhaps it does have to do with the difference between 'risk' and 'uncertainty'. To quote economist Frank H. Knight on the difference between 'risk' and 'uncertainty' for the economic context. He describes risk as being "characterised by randomness that can be measured precisely" whereas "uncertainty creates friction that organisations may not be able to accommodate". Or also (in his book, *Risk, Uncertainty, and Profit* (1921):

- **Risk** is present when future events occur with measurable probability.
- **Uncertainty** is present when the likelihood of future events is indefinite or incalculable.

If risk is high on the agenda on the list of innovation deterrents this might be due to the perception that – particularly radical – innovation has high levels of uncertainty (rather than risk). Below I would like to draw together a few insights and thoughts around risk management in the context of innovation from academic and practitioner literature alike.

The overall picture to date

Let us start by having another look at definitions of risk and risk management. In a publication of the Government office (2006) of the UK, risk and risk management are defined as follows:[4]

- **Risk** is 'uncertainty of outcome, whether positive opportunity or negative threat, of actions or events: the combination of likelihood and impact, including perceived importance'.

- **Risk management** is 'all the processes involved in identifying, assessing, and judging risks, assigning ownership, taking actions to mitigate or anticipate them, and monitoring and reviewing progress'. Risk management involves taking a structured view about the most important risks to a business, assessing their likelihood and impact, and making sure that thought has been given to how these risks can be minimised, and to how they would be dealt with if they materialised.

And very kindly they also provide a link between risk management and innovation:

- Understanding the principles of sound risk management is the foundation for successful innovation in decision making.

In fact, between January and December 2005 the National School of Government led a consortium study "to research, identify and promote outstanding practice in achieving extraordinary performance through innovation and effective risk management". Here are a couple of insights from the study:[5,6]

- Whereas nearly all organisations had a definition of risk management, 43% of respondents did not have a clear definition for innovation.

- Typically, there are processes for managing risk but not for innovation – 87% of respondents reported that risk management was embedded in their core processes, and was commonly deployed, reviewed and improved, whereas innovation was considered less systematically.

- In looking at organisations that excel, we have identified ingredients that appear to be common to those that achieve success through innovation and well-judged risk taking. These ingredients are:

    ○ an imperative to innovate

    ○ a culture of accountability and responsibility for delivering results

---

[4] http://www.fco.gov.uk/servlet/Front?pagename=OpenMarket/Xcelerate/ShowPage&c=Page&cid=1007029395186.
[5] An electronic copy of the final report, which can also be downloaded from http://www.nationalschool.gov.uk/publications_resources/irers.asp.
[6] The results are based on a sample of 56 organisations from both the public and the private sector.

   o   an environment where organisational learning is systemic and systematic

   o   clear and simple risk management processes that are embedded in decision making and in the way the
        organisation works

   o   a decision-making culture where the expectations are to challenge and be challenged about assumptions
        and evidence

   o   an emphasis on developing the capability and capacity to innovate and take well-managed risks

   o   a systematic and reliable mechanism for delivering change.

The final extract from the report is most interesting – and at first glance might be seen to undermine the argument
that risk gets in the way of innovation:

● One of the issues explored was whether a strong emphasis on risk management suppressed innovation by
  encouraging risk aversion, but this proved to be the case in only 7% of the responses.

As so often, I think it might have to do more with the way the question was asked rather than the view that risk
does not get in the way of innovation. What the study's participants were asked was whether the *management* of
risk gets in the way of innovation – not whether (perceived or otherwise) risk gets in the way of innovation.

A further article links risk aversion to HR policies (Frances, 2003). The article argues that HR policies get in the way
of innovation; while innovation requires the taking of risk, failure is generally punished – and taking a risk always
implies a possibility of failure. This actually sits very nicely with a comment I found in the article 'A Question of
Risk' (Anonymous, 2003), "Since we cannot know what is safe unless we are willing to find out what is unsafe, the
only way to reduce risk in the long-term is to take risk in the short-term. Risk management is the process, both
analytical and subjective, of understanding, measuring and predicting risk. In this sense risk is a choice, rather than a
fate. Risk management transforms risk from something to be avoided or faced armed only with bravery, into a set
of opportunities open to choice (options) and direction (maneuverability)."

Before moving on to what to do with risk a brief detour on what kinds of risk exist. Fundamentally two different
types of risk are distinguished:

● technology risk
● market risk

Fortunately I have found an author (e.g. Understanding Firm Level Management of Innovation Risk, Tolga Yilmaz,
Economics of Science and Technology, Term Paper, Professor Jeff Parke) who spent some time thinking about this
and who provides the following insights:

Technology risk

This refers to the set of technical problems associated with a new or emerging technology, for instance, whether
those technical questions have already been solved to an extent at the time the firm receives the project, and if

not, whether the parts of the general solution exist somewhere (maybe the project at hand is composed, to some extent, of inventions that have already been made through a 'proof of principle' process, been patented, and can be achieved through licensing). Typically, innovative projects that are the results of a 'market pull' are subject to relatively higher technical risk, while those from a 'technology push' have, by definition, low technical risk.

Availability of competencies and complementary technologies: development of a new technology may require new technical skills, tools, processes or some complementary technologies. Sometimes these are not available to the firm and must be developed in the course of the project at hand. Clearly, this raises the technology risk greatly. But sometimes these exist somewhere outside the firm, and can be acquired, with lower risk, through a development contract or forming a partnership.

Specification achievability: as the product is developed, its performance in terms of the targeted product specification (user-friendliness, quality, reliability, environmental-friendliness, government's safety requirements) must be quantified. Here, the risk does not refer to whether the firm has chosen the proper (suitable for marketing) product specifications or not, but to the possibility that, through the course of the project, the goal of the project is understood to be actually incompatible with the specifications, once they has been chosen.

Marketing risk

Availability of value chain elements: the marketing of an innovation engages not only the R&D department, but also the activity of product engineering, manufacturing, marketing, distribution and sales organisations, which may not be ready for the innovation, especially as, in real life, these risks are entangled. For example, 'specifications' are certainly *not* fixed in the beginning of the innovation process and then remain so throughout. On the contrary, they are very much subject to change, depending on the market, in particular, the innovative activities of the rival firms. Or the innovator firm's understanding of the market requirements may simply improve through the course. Such previously unknown information will lead the firm to revise its perception of the 'technical risk' in the project, too, and may even cause cancellation of the project. More commonly, though, specifications will change when the performance of the technology turns out to be different from what was expected of it in the beginning. If the innovation involves opening into a new market where the innovation was not previously available. Then, the possibility that these elements of the value chain may not be incorporated in time to the marketing process of the innovation in question contributes to the marketing risk for the innovation.

Product vector of differentiation: this refers mainly to the competitive risk from the unknown innovative activity by the rival firms. For instance, it is possible for the innovating firm to underestimate the rate of innovative activity of the rival firms during the course of its own innovation process, which may raise the specifications of the market too quickly or make the project of the former obsolete through introduction of a superior technology to the market. Or else, the consumers may simply fail to see the wonder the innovating firm saw in its technology.

Market acceptance: the magnitude of this risk depends on how much prior experience the innovating firm has with the market it is introducing its innovation to, in particular, whether the firm has a business model that has previously been seen to work in similar markets and conditions.

Strength of intellectual property protection: there is usually a risk of imitation of the innovation by the rival firms, which decreases the lead time and the first-mover advantages the innovator firm has. From von Hippel's work (*The Sources of Innovation*, 1994), we know that patent protection is found to be 'relatively ineffective' in many industries except pharmaceuticals and chemicals. The top-left quadrant describes projects that aim at displacing some established existing technology in the market, which usually involve a significant amount of technology risk, and are said to cause a 'discontinuity' in the market. Those that target new markets (whether the new markets previously existed or not) to commercialise the already existing technology do not typically involve technical risk and are referred to, in the bottom-right quadrant, as innovations aimed at 'leveraging base'. Incremental improvements in the already existing products or processes marketed in the already existing markets

In addition there is the issue of '**reputational risk**' which, from an organisational perspective, is becoming increasingly important. One might argue that it is part of the 'market risk' – though I believe it is quite different from the 'credibility with customers' that is mentioned in the literature.

So how to deal with risk? Dorfman (2004) has identified four options. The first is to *tolerate* (retention), which means to accept the loss if and when it occurs. The second is to *treat* (mitigation), which means to reduce the severity of loss, e.g. to install water sprinklers to mitigate the damage caused by fire. The third and rather radical option Dorfman identifies is *termination* (elimination), which means not to go ahead with the risky event, and the final one is *transfer* (buying insurance), which means to hedge the event by getting someone else to take the risk.

While there are many quantitative tools to assess risk, Bernstein (1998) concedes that quantitative analysis is not always accurate or even appropriate. He suggests that risk management, in the end, is as much art as science, and must include, even integrate, subjective belief. This view is also proposed by Leigh Buchanan in *Inc.* magazine in which Buchanan states that people looking at risk believe that risk is ultimately a byproduct of uncertainty, and continues to suggest that the best weapon against uncertainty is knowledge. Buchanan suggests that to judge wisely decision makers should have four kinds of knowledge:

- Their own personal biases, and how those biases might influence their judgement. This way they can consider multiple assumptions about the present, their points of comparison, and the nature of their motivation.

- The statistical probability of success and the magnitude of potential failure.

- They should overcome groupthink by consulting a wide range of experts. Diversification as a risk-management tool works for stock portfolios, revenue streams, and also, it appears, expert opinion.

- Their own company's organisational Achilles' heels that might imperil a desirable outcome.

The article continues that, "Ultimately, the goal isn't to get 'the right answer' (because often there won't be one), but to gain a fundamental understanding of how risk works, and to use that understanding to make good decisions. When all else fails, intuition and improvisation must prevail."

Some more insights on how to deal with risk are laid out by Edward Barnholt (2002). He recommends the following:

- Be patient. If you really are making a high-risk bet, you have to give it enough time to play out.

- Look for markets or businesses that are going through discontinuous or disruptive change. This doesn't reduce your risk as much as it expands the potential reward.

- Look for 'white spaces', which are opportunities or markets you're not addressing now but could move into. These are usually growing or emerging markets with no entrenched leader. Such markets can offer enormous opportunity for companies who can innovate to both address and create customer needs. They also contain lots of risk.

- Keep ethical considerations at the centre of all our thinking and behaviour.

I find one of his lessons on risk particularly interesting: "This is one key to managing risk and change: understanding the difference between good managers and good leaders. Managers are good at supervising what exists or what has existed. They are effective stewards of the status quo – a valuable skill in many situations. But leaders take an organization on a new path." That is why innovation requires leadership more than it does management.

In the context of innovation and discovering what kind of products might excite the market, recent developments indicate that there is a new approach companies are taking: let the customers be the judge! Ogawa and Piller (2006) propose that bringing in customers very early in the development process allows the reduction of the risk of market failure – but perhaps not in the way traditionally assumed. Companies such as Threadless (www.threadless.com), an internet-based company that sells printed t-shirts, posts potential designs (generally suggested by customers) on its website. People can see it and place a pre-order. Only when a certain level of interest is achieved does the t-shirt actually go into production. The authors call the approach 'Collective Customer Commitment'. Companies such as Japanese *Muji* operate on a similar principle.

I would like to close with some thoughts from a workshop on risk management in the context of innovation held by the Innovation Leadership Forum, March 2007:

- A multifaceted approach to risk management is needed – there is no 'one-fits-all' approach to risk management.

- There are some no-go areas; i.e. there are areas where a company would not want to take any risk, e.g. severe health risk for a pharmaceutical product.

- Diversity is key – people who think alike tend to have the same blind-spot for potential risks.

- Some industries have a singular strong/dominant professional group which may colour the attitude towards risk (e.g. an approach of wanting to get 120% certainty before making any move).

- Technical risks are often easier to address than market risks.

- Risk assessment in the past was primarily about products; it has now shifted also to managing risks around brand, communication etc. connected to building experiences.

- Remuneration and other HR tools can get in the way of a willingness to take risk as does the general expectations on short-term performance.

- When talking about innovation (and risk) a common language is very important; what seems risky to one person might not seem risky to another.

- Different aspects of the innovation portfolio require different approaches to risk.

MEASURING SUCCESS

Innovation effectiveness is of perennial concern. At the same time most companies do not have a systematic way of capturing either investments in, or returns from, innovation.

Eric Mankin, Babson College, January 2007

As more and more companies see innovation at the heart of their growth strategy it is not surprising that more and more companies also seek to identify ways to measure the impact of their innovation activity. The critical questions are what to measure and how. Before summarising the insights by Thomas D. Kuczmarski, who has addressed just these questions in his article 'Five Fatal Flaws of Innovation Metrics' (2001), I would like to share a few observations. It is generally the view that 'what gets measured gets done'. This is mostly true, and clear and widely known measures can help employees to focus their efforts and make sure that resources are used most effectively. However, there are also the cynics who say, 'what gets measured gets fiddled'. If employees are rewarded based on the number of new products that are brought to market, they might invent all sorts of minor product changes, packaging changes, simple changes in colours etc. to fulfil their quota. This does not make sense, clutters up the product portfolio and can even confuse the customer. A similar effect can be observed with suggestion schemes where teams or departments are asked to provide a certain number of suggestions in a certain period of time.

In his article Kuczmarski (2001) has identified five problems with innovation measures and suggests if these are addressed measuring innovation should become both easier and more successful. The five 'flaws' he has identified are:

1.   Too many metrics – most likely this is caused by addition lots of new measures to already existing performance measures. This can lead to either everyone being confused as to what is really important and people giving up on measurement or the measuring in itself becomes an end in itself, rather than the means to an end. He suggests a three-step process: (i) identify what is essential and what the reason for measuring is; (ii) decide on how to measure; and (iii) ensure that they link together and actually provide you with useful insights into what affects your success. To avoid problems arising from too many metrics he advises establishing a thorough planning and review processes starting with "One metric per use and per screening criterion/operating function, and then expand this system by developing subsets as appropriate. Part of this process should include review against existing and emerging needs to identify measures that are no longer relevant."

2.   Too focused on outcome – expectations that innovation activities result in concrete outcomes each and every time can cause projects to be considered failures even though they may have proved to be springboards for other innovations, He suggests that viewing innovation as a continuous activity and process that does not go in a straight line can help to overcome the problem. He sees this as a problem of attitude and perspective. He quotes the example of Chrysler's K-Car which was considered to be less successful than its individual parts such as the basic frame, structure and design. Related to the outcome focus is the expectation of immediate financial results. While the aim of innovating is of course to improve the long-term financial performance of an organisation, it might be necessary to allow different time frames to realise the benefits. His antidote for problem number two is to "Develop innovation platforms to serve as the springboards for spawning groups of ideas that will generate new products and services."

3.   Too infrequent – he considers this to be indirectly related to the absence of a clearly defined innovation programme or an outlook that is based on finances only. The innovation programme should constantly seek

to identify customer needs and develop solutions for them. To overcome the problem he suggests setting up cross-functional teams as they help to ensure that the innovation agenda is for the best of the entire organisation, rather than following the interests of just one or two departments.

4. Too focused on cutting costs – for Kuczmarski customer-focused innovation is very likely to lead to cost cutting, whereas cost-cutting exercises hardly ever lead to exciting innovations. To overcome problems arising from a cost-cutting mentality he suggests focusing on customer needs and product quality.

5. Too focused on the past – while I am not sure that I agree with the headline chosen for this last point, I certainly agree with the message. Kuczmarski argues that many of the reporting systems associated with measuring are used to "identify the guilty and punish the innocent" and continues to say that only a change in attitude can overcome this problem. His suggested antidote is leadership that emphasises the value of experimentation and learning and rewards rather than punishes failure.

In their article on how to evaluate and measure firm performance Kaplan and Norton (1992) introduce the concept of a 'Balanced Scorecard'. The aim of using the Balanced Scorecard is to provide a set of measures that balances different needs and benefits. The four areas that are covered by the Balanced Scorecard are: (a) financial; (b) customer; (c) internal business process; and (d) learning and growth. Success measures found in the context of new product development and innovation have been identified by Hultink and Robben (1996) – see Table 25.11.

I believe that the work by US academic Thomas Kuczmarski provides some of the most useful insights in this area. In his 2000 article he groups the metrics in two categories:

Table 25.11 Performance indicators

Measurement level and performance indicator	Short term	Long term
Firm		
Percent of sales by new products	X	X
Market acceptance		
Customer acceptance	X	X
Customer satisfaction	X	X
Net revenue goals		X
Net market share goals		X
Net unit sales goals		X
Product level		
Launched on time	X	
Product performance level	X	X
Net quality guidelines	X	X
Financial		
Attain margin goals		X
Attain profitability goals		X
IRR/ROI		X

Source: Hultink & Robben, 1996. Reproduced by permission of John Wiley & Sons

Table 25.12 Kuczmarski's performance metrics (2000)

Metric	Components	Potential implications
Return on innovation investment	Cumulative net profits generated from new products launched Research costs + development costs + incremental production costs + initial commercialisation pre-launch costs	Single, standard measure for comparing performance between divisions over time and within industry
Cumulative profits	Cumulative (3–5 years) profits from new products	Impact on income statement
Cumulative revenues	Cumulative (3–5 years) revenues from new products	Impact on income statement
Growth impact	Revenues from new products over 3–5 years 3 year revenue growth	Contribution to firm growth
Success rate	Number of new products exceeding 3-year original forecast Total number of new products commercialised in last 3 years	Indicates quality of planning
New product survival rate	Number of new products remaining in the market (time period X) Total number of new products launched (time period X)	Provides insight about the demand of new product introductions relative to total new product efforts

Source: Reprinted with permission from *Marketing Management*, published by the American Marketing Association, Kuczmarski, T.D. (2000), Measuring your return on innovation, **9**(1): p24.

- **Performance metrics**: looking at long-term performance and impact of the NPD programme; including return on innovation investment, new product success rate, new product survival rate, cumulative new product revenue, cumulative new product profit, growth impact – see Table 25.12.

- **Programme metrics**: used to understand operational concerns reflected by the innovation performance metrics; including R&D innovation emphasis ratio, innovation portfolio mix, process-pipeline flow, innovation revenues per employee, and speed to market – see Table 25.13.

Interestingly, Kuczmarski suggests ROI as a valid measure for innovation though he mentions "too focused on outcome" and "too focused on cost cutting" as possible problems arising from innovation measures and measuring. In my view ROI can encourage both as the following story, shared through the American Innovation Network (www.thinksmart.com) illustrates. Innovation Network founder Joyce Wycoff quotes Robert D. Shelton, Vice President with the former Arthur D. Little consulting firm, who includes ROI in his list of symptoms of an anaemic internal market for creativity and innovation and illustrates the point through the following imaginary conversation:

Manager: I think we should invest in innovation.

VP: What's the ROI?

Manager: Uh . . . I don't know but I'll see if I can find out.

Actually, this isn't a conversation at all. It's a one-act play. The Manager is trying to be an innovation champion but doesn't have the confidence, and perhaps the understanding, necessary to sell the concept. The VP is using the ROI sledgehammer to avoid making a decision and possibly a mistake. Imagine another version:

Table 25.13   Kuczmarski's programme metrics (2000)

Metric	Category	Components	Potential implications
Speed-to-market	Speed	Σ (time from idea generation to market launch for new products) Total number of new products	R&D process efficient?
R&D innovation emphasis	Amount	Cumulative (3−5 year) R&D expenditure allocated solely in new products Cumulative (3−5 year) R&D expenditure	Focus on innovation? Innovation strategy executed?
New product portfolio mix	Type	Number of new products of type X Total number of new products Revenues from products of type X Total revenues from new products Expenditures for products of type X Total expenditure on new products	Balanced? Aligned to strategy?
Process pipeline flow	Amount	Number of new product concepts in each stage of development	How full is pipeline? Future revenues and expenses? Bottlenecks?
Innovation revenues/employee	Success	Total annual revenues from commercialised new products Total number of full-time equivalent employees devoted solely to innovation initiatives	Provides insight about the effectiveness of additional resource allocations

Source: Reprinted with permission from *Marketing Management*, published by the American Marketing Association, Kuczmarski, T.D. (2000), Measuring your return on innovation, **9**(1): p24.

Manager: I think we need to deepen our capability to innovate. We have very few new products in the pipeline and our revenue from new products and services has dropped dramatically in the past few years.

VP: What's the ROI on innovation?

Manager: I'm not sure that's the right question. Here's some different questions we might ask:

- At our present rate of new product and service development, where will we be in five years? Is that good enough and where do we think our competition might be?
- How much new business do we need to generate and how are we going to do that? What resources and capabilities do we need to develop to generate that new business?
- What new business or technology might actually put us out of business? Where might that come from?
- If we looked at ourselves from the eyes of our competitors, what would we do to put us out of business?

VP: So what should we do to address some of these questions?

To conclude this chapter I would like to draw on Brenner (1994) who reports how and why the company Air Products measures its innovation success. He argues that in order to get value from the measuring process and use it to gain valuable insights for future innovation programmes the question is not only what measures to use, but also which products to track. He reasons that "Attention must be paid to definitions, relevance to the businesses, consensus-building, analysis techniques, and communication mechanisms." He believes that data gathered in such a way over a period of time can provide insights for future innovation programmes. He reports that the "monitoring of new product sales at Air Products has resulted in significant actionable conclusions regarding the impact, life cycles, and returns from the innovation programs".

It actually starts with selecting products to be tracked. Air Products use the following criteria to define 'new products':

1. A threshold sales level of $100,000/year to start the tracking period – this avoids confusing the picture with products that are short-lived or superseded quickly by follow-up versions.

2. Products are 'new' for five years – once measurement starts products are considered to be new for five years. They found that it actually takes about five years to get an accurate picture of the success of a product. This is likely to vary from industry to industry.

3. New product sales can be the result of a number of different internal or external sources, for example, new products or processes coming out of their own R&D department, or product lines established through acquisition.

They emphasised that the definitions evolved over a period of time as the company strived to develop criteria that would be stable over time, be relevant to both current and envisioned business activities, and allow benchmarking against similar companies. They found that by collecting information on the source and type of the new product as well as the sales per year the company has identified the following benefits from their data collection:

*   It provides meaningful input for senior management decisions.
*   They are able to quantify the impact of new products on the corporation's growth.
*   They gain insights into trends, product life cycles, and returns from product investments.

In their annual reporting they consider the following:

*   Total new product sales in dollars as well as percentage of the corporation's overall sales.
*   Dollar and percentage change in new product sales (year to year as well as cumulative).
*   The number of new products introduced in past year (new as defined above).
*   Highlights – recent introductions, largest, superior performance, special features of new products.
*   Growth rate analyses and projections (mostly by trend).

Some lessons they have learned over the course of their experience since 1980 are:

*   Significant actionable conclusions from new product tracking are unlikely until five years after starting. If the commitment for this long-term effort cannot be made, it is probably not worth beginning.

*   Real data must be used – the new product sales must be the same data that financial and business managers recognise as sales.

*   The data should be collected with the participation of the business organisations that 'own' the products and the sales and performance that result from them. The analyses that are performed should be structured to be helpful to the operation of these businesses.

- The new products definition should be consistent across the corporation and relevant to the company's businesses, but some flexibility is always necessary for exceptional cases.

I would like to close this chapter with two final comments:

- When defining measures/metrics organisations need to ensure that the measures are addressing the underlying causes, not just the symptoms.

- What measures are set (and what the attitude towards risk is) should fundamentally be determined from the context of company culture.

READING SUGGESTIONS

Measurement

> Ambler, T. (2000). *Marketing and the Bottom Line*. London: Pearson Education.

Comment: The entire book is concerned with metrics albeit primarily from the marketing perspective. The book summarises a 30-month research project into marketing metrics, carried out by London Business School and sponsored by the Marketing Council, the Marketing Society, the Institute of Practitioners in Advertising, the Sales Promotions Consultants Association and London Business School.

Risk management

> Crouhy, M., Galai, D. & Mark, R. (2004). *The Essentials of Risk Management*. New York: McGraw-Hill.

Comment: The book offers an introduction into the field of risk management for readers without getting into too much detail of the mathematics.

> Lam, J. (2003). *Enterprise Risk Management: From Incentives to Controls*. Chichester, UK: John Wiley & Sons, Ltd.

Comment: The book is described as, "Text offers insights, practical advice, and real-world case studies exploring every aspect of enterprise risk management. Organised into four comprehensive sections: Risk Management in Context; The Enterprise Risk Management Framework; Risk Management Applications; and A Look to the Future."

> Office of Government Commerce (2002). *Management of Risk: Guidance for Practitioners*. London: The Stationery Office.

Comment: The report sets out "a framework for taking informed decisions about risk at a project, programme and strategic level to ensure that key risks are identified and assessed and that action is taken to address them".

26 Building for innovation

CASE STUDY 9: JOHN MCASLAN & PARTNERS [1]

Background

We always insist in having a look at a client's existing buildings and examining the client's company culture, we consider this standard good practice.

Andrew Hapgood, John McAslan & Partners

After having spent some time with the Richard Rogers Partnership in the early 1980s, John McAslan, born in Glasgow in 1954, set up his practice in 1984, originally with partner Jamie Troughton who left the company in 1996. He has always had a particular concern for history, which has led his studio into restoration and adaptive projects for classic modernist icons such as the Peter Jones store in London and Wright's extraordinary campus at Florida Southern College. He comments on his office, "Working with the past is second nature to the practice, but our central concern is a timeless one: insistence on the proper use of materials and the creative use of space and form. We seek to make an honest, accessible modern architecture for the twenty-first century, rooted in the past but looking to the future."

Today John McAslan & Partners has 50 staff based primarily in its Notting Hill office but also in its Manchester and Milan studios. The company operates in the UK and overseas, often in association with local executive architects, who

> John McAslan & Partners has undertaken a wide range of commercial and operational projects for international clients such as the Yapi Kredi Bank's operations centre near Istanbul, Turkey (completed in 1998) and Max Mara's headquarters and distribution facilities in Reggio Emilia, Italy (completed in 2002), to projects for the educational sector such as the new performance and teaching facilities for the Welsh College of Music and Drama in Cardiff; transportation schemes, for example the Jubilee Line Extension stations at Canning Town and Stratford; residential projects and redevelopment of existing buildings, including the adaptation, restoration and extension to 78 Derngate, designed by Charles Rennie Mackintosh in 1916–19, and the on-site remodelling of the Royal Academy of Music in London's Regents Park within the shell of a Grade I listed 1822 villa designed by John Nash.

assist in statutory procedures and documentation and management. The practice has a number of units specialising in landscape, interiors, industrial design, computer visualisations and model building.

---

[1] The case has been prepared by Dr Bettina von Stamm as a basis for class discussion rather than to illustrate either effective or ineffective handling of a management situation.

The role of the built environment

Whereas there was a time where most organisations would have been happy to move into speculatively built, readily available office space, today there is an increasing number of companies who are keen to ensure that there is a close fit between the way they operate and the physical work space environment. Part of the reason for McAslan's success is that in their work the company places strong emphasis on ensuring that its architecture is closely aligned to what a company stands for.

> "A strong-minded client can be both good and bad, depending on the level of insight and 'expertise'."
> Andrew Hapgood

Three examples from McAslan's work show how companies are trying to gain most benefits from their built environment and use it to communicate messages about their organisation and culture.

Helping to create a new culture – the operational centre for the Yapi Kredi Bank in Istanbul

The new operational centre with its open streets and courtyards communicates national culture – and that the company cares. When investing into office space managers should always remember that happy people are more productive.

John McAslan

When the Yapi Kredi Bank, one of the leading banks in Turkey, produced the brief for the invited competition in 1993 they requested that the design should address the following issues:

- Geography of site – 23 hectares on a sloping site with differences of 40 m, located on an earthquake fault.

- Expandability – to accommodate anticipated growth, initially 45,000 square metres.

- Environmentally friendly – consume as little energy as possible.

- Influence workplace culture – facilitate exchange and 'bumping into each other' of people from different departments.

Considerable time was spent understanding and clarifying the brief. Though delighted with winning the competition Andrew Hapgood, lead architect acknowledged, "It was quite a brave decision of the bank to go for a UK-based architect!" To address the challenges McAslan worked with a multi-disciplinary team based in London and Istanbul, liaising very closely with a proactive client representative, who participated fully in the project. In fact, in addition to frequent meetings and Andrew's presence in Istanbul for much of the time, for the detailed design stage the entire consultant team moved out to Turkey for six months, working closely with a local architectural practice. Throughout the project a number of independent consultants including specialist engineers, façade engineers, landscape architects, security consultants, construction specialists and artists were involved.[2] An engineering studio was asked to test the design and structure through computer modelling, physical models, drawings and calculations. As Andrew Hapgood recalls, "The main problem was to overcome technical challenges within an achievable and acceptable standard of construction. One thing the project has highlighted is the importance of fostering a positive atmosphere within the design team as well as the contractor and client."

The result was a modular molecular plan of usable office floor space linked by a three-dimensional circulation network of bridges, stairs, ramps and lifts. This had many benefits: it allowed for future growth and expansion that would not look like an 'add-on'; it meant that buildings could be moulded into the ascending hill and an integrated structural approach to earthquake resistance.

The fact that the centre was erected on a greenfield site with limited access to infrastructure, meant that to a large degree the centre had to be self-sufficient in the provision of water, power, as well as the management of waste. The result was an integrated service system designed to maximise the potential of the limited resources available on site. The structure they chose minimised exposed surface, with external and internal shading preventing exposure to direct sunlight, thereby reducing requirements for extensive air conditioning. The semi public street areas linking the modular buildings act as climate balancers for the air-conditioned office spaces, utilising waste heat and 'cooling' to optimise energy use. The irrigation system currently in place is intended to eventually become redundant as native plants take over and the self-sustaining ecosystem is re-established as it was in classical pre-goat times.

The bank was designed in response to the bank's company culture and its desire to change its workflows and patterns. With their new operations centre the bank wanted to bring together some previously independent

[2] See Appendix 26.1 for a list of participating companies.

administrative functions and, while they wanted to allow each function to retain its own identity, they wanted to facilitate a new culture of collaboration between all functions. McAslan's team engaged in detailed discussions with members of Yapi Bank's groups, not only to understand their current ways of working but also to develop an architecture that would facilitate the introduction and development of new ways of working.

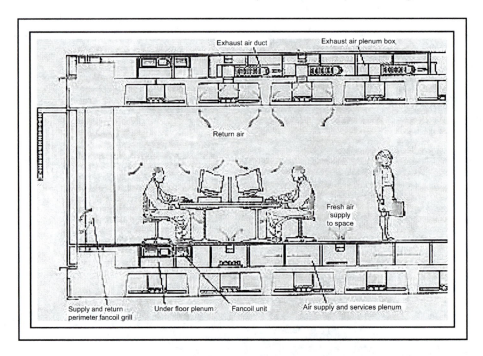

Addressing the needs for both connectedness and independence McAslan, picking up on the oriental theme of street bazaars, developed a system of modular units that are linked by internal streets and walkways. And, according to Andrew, "The streets are what really matters and facilitate the exchange and contact between departments. Here you find all the communal activities: moving and arriving, eating and drinking, chatting and meeting." Each street is designed and landscaped differently, offering variety and helping orientation within and around the building. That the streets became a synonym for the company's new culture is illustrated by John McAslan's comment, "At some occasions Burhan Karacam, President of Yapi Kredi Bank, could actually be found with his secretary, sitting in one of the streets, working away."

Perhaps the greatest compliment Yapi Kredi pays to its host country, however, is not to be condescending. The design does not pilfer local motifs or assume a fake vernacular or a needless grandiosity. Instead, it honours, with modesty, certain traditional responses to conditions in that part of the world that the modern architect would be wise to learn. The house of the family of Yapi Kredi is a harmonious one.

Architectural Record, March 1999

The bank was pleased with the result: "The Operations Centre Complex undertakes an enormous mission in transforming the efficiency of our Bank to an extraordinary level," said Karacam. And as the bank felt 'Operations Centre Complex' did not do the centre justice they renamed it 'Information Age Banking Base'.

The 10 courtyard office buildings are linked by covered courtyards and walkways that imitate the traditional Ottoman marketplaces.

Max Mara's HQ in Reggio Emilia – local groundedness and corporate vision

Within the fashion industry, there is a belief that because you are able to innovate, you must destroy what has come before and that innovation is entirely about change. Max Mara stands alone in their belief that, in fashion, 'good designer style' is closer to architecture, instilling a culture of working towards the permanent. As a company, Max Mara look for the 'well designed' incorporating a close and strong element of functionality. At the same time, our working method is aimed at creating tools for human beings to reinforce their identity and not to overcome their personality.

Luigi Maramotti in an interview with Andrew Hapgood, spring 2001

The roots of Max Mara's roots go back to the middle of the last century when in 1951 Achille Maramotti presented his first Italian-styled prêt-à-porter collection under the name Max Mara. Quite a daring step at a time when fashion was dictated by Paris and dressmakers' ateliers. By the late 1970s Maramotti had brought together a number of autonomous companies under the name Max Mara, producing a range of different collections and styles for the working woman. Today Max Mara consists of six design and production companies, has its own distribution company which supplies to over 1000 Max Mara stores worldwide, and employs some 2700 people. With the commissioning of a new headquarters for Max Mara, the current generation of Maramottis running the company, Luigi and Ignazio, wanted to achieve the following:

- Provide a physical and emotional anchor point for the organisation.

- Be a focal point and representation of the company's values and beliefs.

- Continue its commitment to the region (in the Po Valley in Pianura Padana, northern Italy).

- Demonstrate its belonging to the region through a design that would respect and integrate into the existing landscape.

John McAslan remembers, "One aspect that was very close to Maramotti's heart was that the building looked as if it belonged to the land." On their choice of McAslan & Partners, who had teamed up again with the American landscape architect Peter Walker, as a result of an invited design competition between three architects, Luigi Maramotti commented, "The McAslan/Walker team had the greatest sense of a belonging to the land. The team's response provided a more urbanistic than architectonic approach at the competition stages together with an integration with the site which set the scheme apart from the others. JMP Studio submitted a conceptual design that had

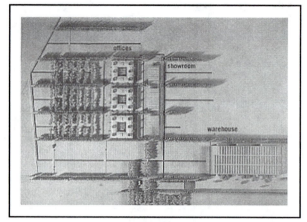

fully interpreted our brief with a great understanding of the importance of integration with the landscape. The project was chosen also for its coherence and clear vision of the relationship between buildings, functions and people."

The 42,000 m^2 headquarters facility was to be located on a 30-hectare agricultural site just south of Milan. The brief consisted of offices for each of Max Mara's five companies as well as showrooms and a 15,000 m^2 distribution warehouse located in an ecological park setting. Andrew Hapgood describes their approach, "Each of the principal buildings are individually expressed in a distinctive modernist architectural vocabulary of concrete, steel, brick and glass."

While the company did not have much experience in preparing an architectural brief they felt that cultural aspects would have to be an important element. As the chairman Luigi Maramotti felt strongly about the importance of company as well as regional culture, Andrew was invited to spend two weeks with the company observing. Andrew commented, "It is difficult to provide a brief that conveys that." This echoed McAslan's emphasis on culture and Andrew recalls, "We began working with each of the companies in the group to understand their differences as well as their parts of common identity." The challenge was not dissimilar to the one McAslan had been facing with the

Yapi Bank and again modularity offered opportunity for both diversity and communality. The 18-by-18 m pavilion buildings provided a sense of individuality while the overarching design, based on a grid that echoed the irrigation systems characteristic for the region, provided the connectivity and unity of a whole. While each company had its own office space, other components such as the showroom, the warehouse and the spacious staff restaurant with its panoramic views were shared.

Andrew comments of the main components of the complex, "The three principal elements in the development were each designed to a highly specific brief. The offices and studios can be seen as the heart of the operation.

The three linked blocks which house them are highly flexible in form, a mix of cellular and open-plan space which eschews dated ideas of rank and hierarchy. While offices look out to semi-public external spaces, with courtyards which echo the squares of nearby Reggio Emilia, the first-floor design studios form a sanctum where the ideas which drive the business emerge. Lofty and generously day-lit, these spaces, where new designs are drawn up and specimen garments assembled, have a gravitas and intensity. In contrast, the showroom block is Max Mara's window on the world, where its products face the scrutiny of the customer. Simple but refined, this building makes no attempt at superfluous display but offers a series of clear and flexible spaces in which the products speak for themselves to retail trade buyers. The great warehouse finally, with its sophisticated mechanised racking and storage system, is the first part of the scheme to be completed and is, on one level, frankly and unapologetically industrial in its aesthetic, a place of constant movement, served by an endless succession of vehicles. Nonetheless this building has not been identified as a place apart. The location there of the restaurant, which services the entire site, removes any sense of isolation with most staff visiting the building daily."

Company internal considerations were only one part of the equation, ensuring that the buildings would correspond with the surrounding landscape was essential to the Chairman. High quality, simplicity and connectedness were sought inside and out. Andrew explains, "The buildings on the site are elements within an overall landscape which extends into the 'groves' of parking and which gives the development its essential unity. Like the traditional city, this is a place of constant movement, interaction and human contact. From the autostrada to the individual workspace, it is connected by a landscape designed to encourage easy circulation and a sense of constant activity. The squares, avenues and streets of the complex are, like those of the city, the domain of communality, where the individual meets the community and where the community meets the outside world. In its balance of private and public space, Max Mara is nothing less than a city in miniature, a place with a collective life of its own but equally one where individuals can flourish. The desire was for connectivity, and the final landscape design achieves a penetration of the geometry of the fields through the buildings and out the other side. The penetration is achieved with insistent rows of poplar trees which, in fact, become a site element as powerful as the buildings themselves."

> "Two themes, both fundamental to Italian culture, are equally basic to the project. The first is that of the family, Max Mara is a family enterprise, a 'family' in itself, moreover of closely associated but distinct companies, working together under the same roof. The second theme is that of the city. The project builds on the civic and urbanistic ideals which have typified Italian architecture and flexible sense of purpose and hierarchy to a diverse range of activities. From these themes the scheme has evolved a new and radical approach to the design of the workplace."
>
> Andrew Hapgood

Redevelopment of Peter Jones – bringing the founder's vision up to date

I am very anxious that our shop shall make an impression of cheerfulness, gaiety, modesty and good-fellowship.

Spedan Lewis, 1934

The entire philosophy and culture of the John Lewis Partnership, of which Peter Jones is part, was formed by Spedan Lewis who took over the direction of his father's company in 1914. And even though Spedan died over 40 years ago in 1963, Beverley Bolton, Managing Director of Peter Jones comments, 'It is staggering how John Spedan Lewis influences what we are doing today."

The powerful concept he introduced was that of partnership. In 1920 his staff became officially known as 'partners' – but not only in name, he also handed an interest in the company over to his employees by giving them shares. To this day the company is run on the principle of co-ownership and all Partners in the business also share in the decision-making process. An attempt to float the company in the mid-1990s was overwhelmingly rejected by Partners. Beverley comments on the advantages of a privately held company, "Not being publicly listed means that we can take a much longer view which is a huge advantage. For example, we are spending over £100 million on the refurbishment of Peter Jones. It is not likely that this would have gone past shareholders. Not having shareholders also enables us to take history and culture into account to a much higher degree. The notion of the partnership was born here at Peter Jones and it is seen to be very important to retain this site even though we would probably have been able to build a new department store for around £25 million. But it is quite unthinkable not to trade here any longer."

The Peter Jones department store in London goes back to 1871 when Peter Jones leased two adjoining shops in London. He moved to Sloane Square, in the affluent Chelsea district in 1877. A year after Peter Jones's death in 1905 the business was bought by John Lewis who handed it over to his son Spedan in 1914.

Peter Jones holds a special place within the John Lewis Partnership as it was here that Spedan first translated his vision into physical reality with a new building revealed to the public in 1936. It was to provide a pleasant and light environment for both shopper and staff. The building, which featured the first glass curtain wall in Europe, was highly acclaimed in the press but in the end did not provide the bright work environment Spedan had envisaged as shop fittings were put in front of the windows and he is quoted to have said, "It has the elegance of a hippopotamus where it should have been a Persian cat."

The redevelopment of the site had been under discussion for quite some time, not least because it consisted of a number of separate buildings and access between the parts was cumbersome and difficult – Spedan's original plans had been halted by the Second World War and the last phase was finished only in 1960. In Beverley's

words, "What we have inherited is a modernist architect's view of a modern building that did not quite get finished. In a way we are finishing what architects Crabtree and Riley started in the 30s." However, she also points out,

"If it had been a purely commercial decision we would probably have closed the building down." But closing down would have been completely against her principal purpose, which is " 'to secure the fairest possible sharing by all its members of the advantages of co-ownership, gain knowledge and power', that is to say, their happiness in the broadest sense . . .."

Normally a refurbishment project would have been taken on by John Lewis's in-house team. But getting planning permission for alterations to the grade II* listed building proved very difficult and the planning authorities had suggested that John Lewis commission a limited competition and bring in experts. Beverley commented on the appointment of McAslan & Partners, "We choose McAslan because of their track record in working with listed buildings and their experience in working with the local authority" and Peter Jeffree, the department store's Chief Architect commented, "John McAslan & Partners were approached in the spring of 1997, together with two other established practices. From the first telephone call John McAslan showed great interest in the proposed project. The interviewing team were impressed by his pragmatic approach to meeting our retailing needs. He appeared to offer a balance between the committed modernist and the reverent academic and I sensed that he understood our objectives. John has made a strong personal contribution and has very effectively managed his client."

Scott Lawrie, Lead Architect for John McAslan, comments on working with Peter Jones, "Whereas normally we would primarily be in contact with management of an organisation, here we get input from all levels of our client. This means we are getting direct feedback from the end user, how they would use the space, what they want, and so on. As everyone has his or her personal perspective on design issues this means that we get continually challenged." While there may be a danger of watering down a design

> The Royal Fine Art Commission strongly supports this proposal. It believes the John Lewis Partnership and the architects are to be congratulated for putting together a scheme which respects the integrity of the Peter Jones Building whilst adapting it so that it can trade more effectively as a department store.
>
> Royal Fine Art Commission letter, 3 August 1998
>
> English Heritage warmly supports the principle of refurbishing the listed building to ensure its continued life as a major department store.
>
> English Heritage letter, 13 August 1998
>
> The Twentieth Century Society does not object to the renovation and upgrading of the store, as its continued commercial success was considered to be paramount for protecting the long-term interests of this important listed building
>
> Twentieth Century Society letter, 3 August 1998

solution, Beverley comments, "Generally we are working together on finding a solution that is acceptable to everyone, but if it comes to something really important Scott is also known to dig in his heals – and rightly so." She also felt that that bringing in an outsider was beneficial in another way, "in the same way we often challenged their suggestions they also challenged what we did – and by doing so helped to create 20% more floor space".

While it was not possible to change too much on the outside inside they wanted their culture to be reflected as much as possible. They had started in 1995 with very broad design guidelines developed by the company's Chairman and design consultant Douglas Cooper and among the words they had come up with were 'elegant and self-effacing'. In 1999 they set about translating the vision into reality, developing guidelines for specific projects including: assortments, shop fittings, signage, corporate identity etc. For example, the guideline 'clean lines on interior' were reflected in the use of glass and brass rather than, say, wood. In a third step the guidelines were translated into drawings addressing each aspect of the interior, for example all doors were to be fully flush with the surface of the wall so they disappear rather than having architraves.

The Partners' needs were an important consideration from the outset. Beverley emphasises, "While the commercial side is always on my mind, I am here to make sure that the work environment is guided by the partnership concept and my principal objectives (i.e. ensuring the happiness of Partners and continuing to serve the community)." Many organisations write 'people are our most important asset' into their annual reports and value statements, but not many put

their money where their mouth is. Peter Jones does. Whereas you would normally expect about 80–90% of floor space in a department store to be dedicated to selling, in the new layout of Peter Jones they will have 50–60%, the rest will be dedicated to Partners. Beverley explains, "We will have light offices, rest rooms, dining facilities, an internet café – you have to keep up with times – a social club and a bar. The Partners' rest room will be on the seventh floor with two sides in glass, giving you fantastic views over London."

Questions

1.　Think about the work environment you are currently working in/last worked in. How would you describe it and what kind of behaviours and values does it support?

2.　If you are keen to develop a work environment that is supportive of innovation, what are the aspects you may want to include into the architect's brief?

APPENDIX 26.1: MAIN PLAYERS INVOLVED IN THE DESIGN AND BUILD OF YAPI KREDI BANK

Client	Yapi ve Kredi Bankasi AS
Architect	John McAslan & Partners
Associate architect	Metex Design Group, Istanbul
Engineering design	Arup Mühendislik ve Müsavirlik Ltd
Space design & office furniture	DEGW International Culsulting Ltd
Interior design	Tabanioglu Architects, Istanbul
Landscape advisor	Peter Walker, San Francisco

Electrical engineering advisor	Dr Turhut Tüfekci, Istanbul
Mechanical engineering advisor	Atakat Ltd, Istanbul
Security	Videf Security Management Ltd, Staffordshire
Catering	Deneyim Ltd, Istanbul
Main contractor	Baytur Constructing Inc, Istanbul

APPENDIX 26.2: DEVELOPMENT OF THE JOHN LEWIS PARTNERSHIP

1871

Peter Jones sets up his own business, eventually leasing two small stores in what is now Draycott Avenue.

1877-1884

The shop moves to Sloane Square, an affluent district of Chelsea, and turnover increases fourfold.

1900

Peter Jones is floated as a public company. Peter Jones himself is appointed chairman and his two sons become Board Directors.

1906

Self-made businessman John Lewis buys Peter Jones and becomes chairman. His son Spedan is appointed director at 21.

1914

John Lewis hands the business to Spedan. His approach heralds the birth of the John Lewis partnership.

1920

Staff at Peter Jones become known as "Partners" and the company as "The Partnership".

1936

The new look Peter Jones building is unveiled. It is the first London example of a "curtain wall" and is critically acclaimed by the architectural world.

1968

Peter Jones becomes one of the first 'modern' buildings to achieve listed status.

1985

Peter Jones extends its opening hours to six days a week.

1991

The first planning application is made to renovate Peter Jones.

1999

After a decade of planning applications, Peter Jones at last gets planning permission to renovate the grade II* listed building.

2000

Renovation work begins, PJ2 opened on May 2nd.

External walkways opened in August.

Centre of the shop completely closed from September.

27 Company culture and architecture

A major theme from my own work is that the daily environment provided by a firm is the single most important determinant of innovative thinking among its personnel. An effective intervention in that environment is far more productive than efforts to intervene in the individual manager's thinking.

Gerald Zaltman (quoted in Grant, 2000)

The McAslan case study has illustrated through three different stories about what managers might seek to achieve through the built work environment – such as helping to support the establishment of new working practices (Yapi Bank), creating a platform for unifying disparate companies and cultures (Max Mara) and preserving and enforcing a specific company culture (Peter Jones). However, this does unfortunately not mean that all building projects are informed by ambitions that go beyond the purely functional. Many organisations seem to focus on the functionality, neglecting additional benefits that can be gained by considering how the building should feel and what it should communicate. This chapter will explore how the physical work environment can support company culture and help facilitate a culture of creativity and innovation. We will also take a brief look at how the office environment is changing. As there has been very little research undertaken into the effect of the physical work environment, this chapter relies to a large extent on anecdotal evidence.

PUTTING YOUR WORK ENVIRONMENT TO WORK

Why, in the context of innovation, design and creativity, should we talk about the physical work environment? If you go to people's homes you will be able to find out what they value and like, and you will be able to deduce certain things about their behaviours. Someone who values good food, and good company, will probably have an open plan kitchen/living room area. In a friendly home where members of a family enjoy being together you will see open doors, and an emphasis on shared space. Walking into a company you can make similar observations. Closed doors, senior management on the top floor guarded by fierce personal assistants, send a message about the culture of the organisation. A common room that is in the corner of the basement sends a different message to one that occupies a light and airy space in the centre of the building, providing comfortable seating.

Architect Ralph Buschow[1] has identified another reason why the office and the office environment have become more important: companies seem to become more and more virtual which means that the office, the physical manifestation of the organisation, becomes the focal point for the organisation's culture. He states, "In a way, a virtual organisation needs a much stronger culture than a real organisation. The office can help people to identify with their organisation. It can show employees what the organisation stands for, what values it holds — and thereby it becomes the embodiment of that organisation's culture. And the architecture used to convey this culture should be implicit, not explicit — that's where post modernism got it wrong, they were trying to be too explicit and descriptive."

A recently conducted survey of over 1000 people in the UK (see Titteron, 2001) found that two-thirds of the British workforce believe that they would be more productive and would in fact work harder if their work environment was better — less crowded, better air conditioning, better lighting. But not only the physical conditions matter, respondents also commented on the importance of the degree of 'friendliness'. Titteron reported that "Having good people and good conversation around them was crucial to creating a positive atmosphere." A view shared by Lynn Frost, Vice-President of Product Innovation with FranklinCovey, who explains,[2] "To me environment is everything. I think people are more productive, more creative, when their environment is beautiful and relaxed. It opens up all those channels of the best ideas inside of them. I think every human being deserves to have the environmental support. It feeds the spiritual needs of the human; it feeds the mental needs, the emotional needs and it definitely comforts the physical needs."

We have already talked in Chapter 13 about the importance of internal collaboration for innovation. The work environment is something that can encourage and facilitate collaboration and exchange. Having areas where people 'bump into one another', where they can strike up conversations, or where they can exchange thoughts on the projects they are working on are areas in which seeds for innovation are planted.

Changing the work environment for the better has a positive impact on employee productivity for another reason. Titteron also quotes research from the US which found that *any* change in the work environment actually improves performance, because employees feel that managers care. However, there are a few more specific things that managers can do that will make a difference, particularly for innovation and creativity and we will come back to that later in this chapter.

In the context of innovation there are three things that your work environment can do for you:

- Send signals about a company's culture.
- Encourage certain behaviours.
- Help to communicate change.

Below we will take a look at the example of a company where management has used the physical work environment deliberately to communicate and reinforce its company culture.

---

[1] Interview conducted by Bettina von Stamm in April 1999 (von Stamm, 1999d).
[2] In an interview with G. Lynne Snead and Joyce Wycoff, published on the Innovation Network website (http://www.thinksmart.com/articles/collaboration_rooms.html).

SUPPORTING THE CREATION OF A CULTURE

You can use the environment to underline and accentuate certain behaviour, to underline values, to encourage and discourage certain behaviours.

David Magliano, Marketing Director, Go Fly[3]

When setting up business the low-cost airline Go Fly decided to take a very deliberate approach in the design of its office environment, making sure it would reflect characteristics and values of the new company's desired culture. In addition to being low cost, reflecting the company's positioning, Go Fly's Marketing Director David Magliano explained that they wanted to ensure that their work environment would reflect the company's key values which he described as:[4]

1.   Being open and honest – which refers primarily to the way we communicate.

2.   Being respectful – which involves being tolerant and accepting differences.

3.   Doing what you said you would do – honour your commitments.

4.   Being yourself, in the sense – for example, we encourage our cabin crew to be themselves on the plane, we do not have a clone model with a 'painted face', and we do not expect a standard set of behaviours.

5.   Being part of one team – we have a collaborative working environment.

6.   Getting involved – we want people to take responsibility for making a difference.

The Go Fly management believe in using the physical work environment to provide employees with cues that project and enact their values. David commented, "For example, low fares depend on low cost, so we need things to be low cost. If you have a look around you will find that the office looks a bit scruffy, a bit messy – informal. All sorts of notes are sellotaped to the doors – and I don't have a problem with that. That is a cue that we are low cost. We do not have expensive oak-framed notice boards, nor do things have to be high gloss and look like marble. We are just not that kind of company. I think it reflects that we are busy and democratic." He continues, "We use our environment to communicate values and culture."

It was also interesting to note that they lived in the office space before they started modifying it to meet their needs – and to support the culture they aimed to create. During this initial phase management identified needs and desired aspects of company culture. Before they changed the layout the space reflected a traditional office layout with straight corridors and small offices which made communication difficult and left people isolated. They took down the walls and opened the space up almost entirely and David commented on the change, "Now, because you can see what is going on, communication is much better. It is all much more informal and people just approach

---

[3] David Magliano in an interview conducted by Bettina von Stamm for the Innovation Exchange, May 1999.
[4] Go Fly is serious about its values and does not only have them written down, they are also part of the induction programme every employee goes through, and either David Magliano or CEO Barbara Cassani have a session with each new employee to make sure that the values are communicated and received appropriately.

someone they see walking past to have a chat or ask some questions – communications has become a sort of spontaneous byproduct."

However, Go Fly was a start-up situation and David admitted that deliberately creating a company culture is much harder for an established company to achieve the same. "We had an advantage because we were able to do three things. First, we talked about how we wanted to manage and how that should be reflected in all aspects, including our work environment. Second, we started with a blank piece of paper regarding the people and third, we were able to choose who we recruited. I also believe that it was also helped a lot by the fact that our core team had a clear and shared vision about the kind of company we wanted to create. I don't think there are many established companies that operate under such conditions. It is not that I think it is impossible for an established company to change but it is much harder, much more like trying to steer a super-tanker – whereas we can behave like a little yacht."

Many managers aim to make their organisations more innovative, and this tends to require a change in culture. Some aspects of change were discussed in Chapter 6, particularly relevant here is the fact that in most cases change will be resisted. There are several aspects where the physical work environment can support managers in their change efforts. First, making changes in the physical work environment indicates that this change initiative is serious and that management are putting their money where their mouth is. Second, the planning of changes in the built environment allows the involvement and engagement of employees in the change, increasing the likelihood of buy-in not only into the physical changes but also in the drivers of the change. Finally, the way office space is laid out can stimulate certain behaviours. If every employee has to enter the office through a wide open space with coffee tables, newspapers and ample seating the likelihood for chance encounters and informal networking are much higher than if you walk straight past a receptionist into the lift and along a narrow corridor into the office.

A space to think

The R&D Director of a former government agency wanted to do something with the work environment that would send the message: we want and support innovation. He thought about what kind of environment he associated with innovation – and found it was his garden shed: a place to think, to potter and to experiment. So, much to the initial horror of the company's health and safety people, he put a small garden shed into the open plan space. It is right next to a window, it has shelves full of books, magazines, as well as pens, white boards and other tools one might want when getting creative!

The message to people in the organisation was clear: we want you to be innovative; we acknowledge that one needs space to think in order to be innovative – so here is some space where you can go to think.

Of course senior management needs to lead the way in making sure people understand that having a chat with colleagues over a cup of coffee is accepted behaviour, and not seen as a waste of time. The CEO I interviewed mentioned that he was encouraging people to have lunch in the nearby park to refresh their minds. When asked whether he actually did so himself he commented, "No, I think that is a bit of a waste of time." Not surprising then that his employees did not go either. Most employees are too intelligent to fall for the 'do as I say don't do as I do'.

But besides providing employees with spaces that facilitate change encounters, there are more things managers can do to encourage and facilitate creativity and innovation through the work environment.

CHARACTERISTICS OF WORK ENVIRONMENTS THAT SUPPORT CREATIVITY AND INNOVATION

The following aspects associated with the work environment will help managers create an atmosphere where creativity and innovation flourish:

- Meeting and recreational spaces.
- A variety of different work spaces.
- Arrangement of departments.
- Space dedicated to project teams.
- Spaces dedicated to innovation and creativity.

Meeting and recreational spaces

David Magliano has already alluded to the value that lies in spontaneous encounters and informal networking. Both are important facilitators of innovation. So for managers who are seeking ways to improve the innovation performance of their company, providing space where people can casually meet and just 'bump into each other' is one possible lever.

Architect Ralph Buschow has observed a change in attitude towards spaces that in architectural speak used to be called 'functional areas' – kitchens, corridors, restrooms, etc. The aim used to be to keep such spaces to a minimum as they were seen as a necessary evil to allow people to get from A to B, or pick up a cup of coffee – in many organisations not something that managers wanted to encourage. However, this has changed. Ralph comments, "In the work environment the kitchen, for example, is a very important element. It used to be in the corner, in the basement – somewhere out of the way. Today we have come to change our view on this: the kitchen is a meeting point, people bump into each other, exchange ideas, this is where networking happens – this is where things generally just happen. Questions which in the old days may have been saved up for the weekly meeting are now discussed in the corridor, in between meetings. Views are collected and decisions are made on a much more continuous and spontaneous basis than before."

A variety of different work spaces

Up until fairly recently office space was either one or the other: open plan or separate offices. Ralph Buschow argues that this is no longer enough. "It is clear that there is no one right environment that suits everyone. It would be naïve to think that we are all the same and have the same needs. Even splitting people into extrovert and introvert is too simplistic. We all tend to be a bit of both. So you cannot say this person is introverted so he or she gets a separate office, and this person is extroverted so they will prefer an open plan situation with continuous stimulation. You have to offer both. The employee then decides what he or she needs, and when. Most are happy to use shared spaces, get away from their own little area – be right in the middle of things – at times. We believe that people should be allowed to make the choice which environment they prefer – not just once but basically every day."

Jon Leach, partner of the advertising company HHCL, agrees and believes in providing employees with a choice of working spaces and meeting rooms.[5] He commented, "We do have a certain number of different sized meeting rooms. They vary not only in terms of size but also in terms of their atmosphere, some have a very quiet ambience, there are some with nice views, others where you can't look out at all. These meeting rooms are scattered throughout the place – for private conversations, rooms without chairs for brief meetings, there is a café area, and so on. So we try to offer a variety of meeting spaces to cover all sorts of needs and different kinds of human interaction."

HHCL & Partners

(Howell Henry Chaldecott) has been in existence since 1987. Founded as an advertising agency, it was relaunched in 1994 as a Total Marketing Communications Company. Not only has HHCL been voted agency of the year twice – in 1989 and 1994 – in 1996 independent analysts also found that it was the most profitable UK marketing communications company.

Arrangement of departments

Another trick to encourage cross-departmental communication, which coincidentally also enhances mutual understanding and respect, which in turn makes collaboration easier, is to mix departments up, or arrange their locations in such a way that maximises traffic. David Magliano explained, "While we have avoided functional silos as such, there are certain more or less dedicated areas such as the rooms for the cabin crews to meet. On the other hand, we have deliberately put two groups

"Because these project teams expand and contract and interact with lots of other people throughout the course of a project, we have not isolated any of the support functions, such as finance. These are not located in some far away corner but scattered in between."

Jon Leach, HHCL

which have to talk to each other a lot in separate corners of the building so that there has to be a lot of traffic across the office space between those groups. So we try to force movement."

Space dedicated to project teams

Linking from the previous point is to provide dedicated space for project teams. Jon Leach commented, "Rather than having distinct departments we are organised around disciplines, and as a consequence there is no strong departmental ethos. By looking at job functions and sharing clients, the organising principle for us is the project team. This tends to be a 5–6 person unit, consisting of an account manager, a planner, a creative team, maybe a publicist, maybe a producer – whatever is needed on that particular project. So basically it means that a small team works together on the project from beginning to end. We find that this way of working produces better ideas and higher levels of customer as well as employee satisfaction, which, at least theoretically, also leads to higher profits. Our architecture is designed to support this particular structure, i.e. project teams, not departments; it is designed to support groups of people working together."

[5]Jon Leach was interviewed by Bettina von Stamm (1999c) for the Innovation Exchange, June 1999.

Additional benefits were highlighted by the innovation agency IDEO. During a workshop run for the Innovation Exchange a company representative explained that they dedicate space to project teams. Such space would be decorated with drawings, notes from brainstorming sessions, prototypes and other items. As such project space tends to be part of the open plan structure, it is easy for other members of the organisation to see what is going on, to drop in and thereby contribute to that particular project and provide their insight and expertise.

Additional stimuli

Not explicitly part of the physical work environment but somehow related is the benefit of providing a wide range of stimuli – be it in the office space itself, in meeting rooms, or other parts of the office. Such stimuli can be books, materials, prototypes, objects that people value or find particularly innovative, competitor products and so on. IDEO provide an additional source of inspiration: their materials library. In each of the eight offices around the world the company maintains a set of drawers full of interesting, curious and strange materials and products which are suggested by employees, and entered into a database. Into this database comments, benefits, problems, uses and application are entered providing a rich source of information.

Spaces dedicated to innovation and creativity

> **Axa's innovation corridor**
>
> Axa is the world's largest insurance company, headquartered in Paris. After acquiring an Irish-based insurance company making the organisation more innovative was one of the key objectives. One of the initiatives to ensure that all employees would be aware of the objective to "foster innovation as a means of achieving business results" was the establishment of what became known as the 'innovation corridor'. This (real) corridor was the one all employees passed through on their way to the company's restaurant. It became the company's 'large notice board' through which innovation was promoted, where employees were kept informed about innovation initiatives, and where innovation successes were exhibited.

Finally, many companies have come to provide their employees with dedicated innovation spaces. Such spaces are designed to encourage creativity, and take people away from their everyday job and everyday environment. Snead and Wycoff (1996) refer to such spaces as collaboration rooms and emphasise the need to distinguish them from meeting or conference rooms. They explain, "It's important to keep in mind that most meeting and conference rooms are designed for presentations, not collaboration. The standard conference room set-up is a long table surrounded by chairs, perhaps a small whiteboard at one end of the room, an overhead projector and a video system. These rooms are designed primarily for information presentation. One person sits or stands at the front of the room and presents information, using the whiteboard, the overhead projector or the video monitor. Participants are focused on the front of the room and the information being presented. Discussion may or may not be encouraged, but participants are seldom invited to take control of the pen or the overhead or video monitor. There is no real co-creation of understanding or plans. There is, however, order and control. Collaboration rooms are very different in that they invite a flow of ideas and energy with little concern for either order or control. Imagine a room surrounded with floor-to-ceiling whiteboards well stocked with coloured markers. There are moveable easel pads and an abundance of sticky notes of various colours. Tables and chairs are smaller . . . or non-existent, allowing more space to move around, cluster around engaging ideas, or back off for contemplation." The characteristics they believe innovation centres should have are listed in Box 27.1.

Box 27.1   Characteristics of innovation centres

Interaction – Collaborative spaces invite interaction and movement, allowing people to move around, grouping and regrouping as ideas and energies shift. Small tables for 4–5 people are generally better than large conference tables.

Visual thinking – Ideas and thoughts gather power and energy when they can be seen and interacted with. No collaboration room is complete without generous whiteboard space, large sheets of paper, boxes of coloured markers and a large supply of Post-it™ notes.

Beauty – Beauty operates at a deep level, opening up the imagination and the heart. Lynn Frost, Vice President of Product Innovation with FranklinCovey states, "I believe in Goethe's quote that every day you should read some poetry, see a beautiful picture, get into nature so that we don't lose the sense of the beautiful that's in all of us." You can make your space visually pleasing by using plants, water fountains, windows that let in natural light and beautiful scenes, colours, and a variety of textures.

Fun – Play is an important part of creativity and collaboration. Fun breaks down barriers and frees us from the inhibitions that keep us "in the box". Beanbag chairs, toys, bright graphics, crayons and silly hats all help create an atmosphere of fun.

Abundance – An atmosphere of abundance sets up a mindset of generosity and sharing which promote collaboration and idea generation. A feeling of abundance can be created by having large bowls of fruit, candy or snacks available (chocolate is always a winner), keeping a refrigerator well-stocked with bottled water and soft drinks, making sure there's always markers, writing pads and sticky notes available.

Tools – The purpose of collaboration rooms is to work together more effectively. It's very important to have the right tools immediately available in the room. This will vary for different organisations but generally includes a phone with a fast modem for connection to the Internet, a good computer system complete with mindmapping and project management software, a printer, an overhead projector and VCR.

Source: Snead, G.L. & Wycoff, J. (1996). To Do, Doing, Done! A Creative Approach to Managing Projects and Effectively Finishing What Matters Most. Simon & Schuster. Reproduced by permission of J. Wycoff

---

In my work I have come across a number of different innovation centres, with different characteristics and purposes. Some of these are listed in Table 27.1.

Some characteristics that innovation centres share

- **Different** – one fundamental aspect of innovation centres is that they try to create a different atmosphere, a different attitude and a different environment to what people are used to in other parts of the organisation.

- **Inspiration** – not only should innovation centres be different, they are also seen to be a source of inspiration. This can be just by being open, light and colourful, but it generally goes beyond; often you find additional

Table 27.1 Examples of innovation spaces (author's own observations)

Company	Space	Purpose
3M UK	Large room, space separated off in the centre with IT facilities and whiteboards at the centre; around it samples, pictures, explanations of 3M's technologies and products	• Showcase to inform and engage outsiders (customers, suppliers) • Stimulation of ideas • Facilitate collaboration
Post Office	Started off in a Portakabin; once concept was proven, moved into dedicated building. Entry to the space via lift-like room, simulating a journey in a space rocket; main part comprises a number of different rooms; some are kitted out to simulate a future state of an office, a living room, a kitchen etc.; there is much IT for generating, sharing and evaluating ideas; are also lots of toys and gadgets	• Inspiration, brainstorming and idea generation • Scenario planning
Nestlé	Some previously unused space, fitted out with nice eating facilities, comfortable chairs, football table – lots of space	• Encourage cross-functional relations • Encourage exchange and collaboration
Visteon	Space in an old house, part of a moated castle	• Facilitate collaboration between different disciplines • Allow involvement of customers • Provide a distinct and different environment
BMW	Munich is one of BMW's three innovation centres (California, Japan); purpose built to support innovation; described as, "divided into open modules the functional architecture allows employees short ways and greater closeness". Supports new organisational structures, teamwork and networks support the innovation capability and flexibility of the BMW group	• Collaborative development of new designs, concepts and products • Cross-disciplinary development
Smith & Nephew	Inspired by IDEO's deep dive process (which is about immersing yourself in the users' situation) S&N created a space dedicated to innovation, part of which is a room for idea generation which has windows like a submarine	• Demonstration of a cultural shift • Facility for brainstorming and idea generation • Space dedicated to innovation
Department for Trade & Industry	Dedicated innovation space made up of three different rooms: a theatre-style room for which there are some pre-made films available; these films/succession of slides are designed to provoke, challenge and bring people out of their current thinking and comfort zone. One room has a suite of computers for IT-facilitated idea generation, development and selection, the other is more open plan with whiteboards etc. for capture of brainstorming sessions etc.; facilitators are provided by the centre; they will be chosen based on the topic under discussion; available to internal as well as external parties	• Providing a space 'out of the usual' for brainstorming and idea generation

stimuli which can range from books and journals, to boxes of crayons, to music, paintings, exhibitions (of own and competitors' products); toys are also frequently found (Lego have developed a methodology around using their toys for encouraging creativity and brainstorming).

- **Encourage collaboration and cross-functional exchange** – the innovation space is also generally set out to attract people from different parts of the organisation; it should be easily accessible and open.

- **Provide dedicated space for high-level innovation projects** – often the innovation centres have space where teams working on high-profile innovation projects find some dedicated space to work together. Depending on the nature of the project this can be not only for meetings but also permanent for the duration of the project.

- **Attract and engage customers** – often these spaces are used for exchange and interaction with customers and suppliers.

CHANGES IN WORKING PRACTICES AND THE OFFICE ENVIRONMENT

This section could well have been called, 'New Ways of Working' or perhaps equally appropriate, 'How Information Technology Changes the Way We Work' as it is IT that has triggered significant changes in working practice. One change is the increasing number of people who are working from home. This has been facilitated by increasingly powerful computers, modems and mobile phones. What does working from home – or, for that matter, any place outside the office – mean? What are the implications for innovation, design management and product development?

> "According to the 1997 Olsten Forum on Managing Workplace Technology (http:www.olsten. com), 51% of North American companies now permit employees to telecommute through pilot and ongoing schemes, with 74% expecting their use of telecommuting to increase."
> Matathia & Salzman (1999)

IT has a fundamental impact on how we communicate. There used to be two constraints to communication: location and time. People had to be in the same place at the same time for communication to take place. Telephone has removed the first and now email and internet chat-

> In the UK 2.2 million people or 7.4% of the workforce work at home at least one day per week.
> Source: www.flexibility.co.uk, 9 August 2007

rooms have removed the latter. More and more people rely on email – rather than phone calls or face-to-face interaction to communicate with their colleagues. Several aspects about emails are worth noting. It takes no time at all to write and send an email – which on the one hand is a good thing: it speeds up communication, independent of the location of the sender and recipient. On the other hand, because it is so easy emails tend to be much more informal. The fact that emails are so easy to produce, and that it is so easy to copy as many people in as one likes, also means that people are getting inundated with emails. And finally, emails tend to be much more informal. They are written in a hurry, without greeting and closure, often in a language that is casual and likely to be less precise than language used in a memo or letter.

But what is the purpose of communication? It is to transfer information. If we are imprecise, the information might not be conveyed properly, if too many emails are received people get selective with the ones they read. This can lead to important information getting lost. In fact, some organisations have introduced rules that emails are not allowed if people work in the same building, people have to pick up the phone or go and seek a direct conversation with the person in question. There are several reasons why face-to-face communication is so important, particularly if a difficult or new subject is broached. In a face-to-face conversation we have the opportunity to see the person's reaction. We can read their body language and facial expression and we can hear their tone of voice. This gives us an idea whether or not the message has been received and at least an indication of whether it has been received correctly (one of the reasons that video conferencing has become so popular). Over the phone we have at least the voice to help. But when sending an email we do not have any opportunity to judge whether our message has been received correctly or not.

The American professor Albert Mehrabian[6] researched the effectiveness of the spoken word extensively. His widely used research indicates that only 7% of meaning is conveyed by the words, another 38% is communicated through the tone of voice, the rest – 55% – is conveyed through our facial expression and posture. An important argument against relying entirely on telecommunication.

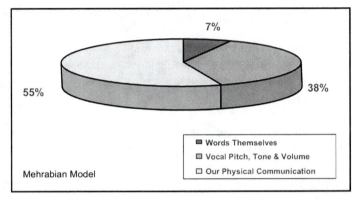

Mehrabian Model

Imprecise communication can cause problems for innovation and product development. Successful development of a new product depends on all members of the team sharing an understanding of what the aim of the project is and how they are going to achieve it. Without the possibility to ask and explain immediately, there is a greater risk of misunderstanding and misinterpretation. This does not mean that project teams should not communicate remotely, but it does mean that greater care has to be taken to ensure a shared understanding. By the way, the fact that different departments, let alone companies, tend to speak 'different languages' does not make this task any easier – see Figure 3.2 in Chapter 3.

On the other hand, IT enables sharing of information, irrespective of time and location, which can have great advantages for new product development. People working in different organisations, on different continents – where ever – can work on the same project either together at the same time or, if on different continents, during their respective working hours. Ford Motor Company is an example of a company where project teams in several different locations and time zones work together on one project, accelerating development time significantly.

Architect Ralph Buschow also commented on the changes in working practice he was observing during his work. He commented on the impact of information technology, "A number of things affect the way we work, technology being one. Not necessarily technology itself but the effects it has. Today's technology allows consideration of a subject while being physically removed. It also enables much faster decision making than ever before. Previously the boss in his (!) corner office used to sign off a number of letters or proposals at the end of the day. Today, with

---

[6]http://en.wikipedia.org/wiki/Albert_Mehrabian.

hierarchies much flatter, more people are involved in decision making, all over the organisation. This has increased complexity. Another contributor to complexity is the fact that companies tend to be involved in a wide range of activities. There are lots of specialists around – who cannot be managed top-down any more. Because of their special expertise they need to be involved in the decision-making process which means that decisions are often made by teams. Not that there weren't any specialists before, but they tended to write lengthy reports that were then used by their bosses as basis for decision making. In today's fast-moving environment this process is far too cumbersome and time consuming." As a consequence, he reasons, the previously static work environment has to become much more flexible and needs to offer both flexibility and continuity.

He reasons that spending money on the work environment makes sense. For most companies, particularly in the service industry, salaries are the largest expenditure. This naturally means that it should be in the interest of an organisation to get the best out of their people – and the best way to achieve that it to make them want to come to work, to make them happy at work. He comments, "A 1% increase in productivity will pay for all sorts of things!"

However, Ralph also points out that one cannot change a work environment for employees, one has to do it with them, "We generally start by looking at how people in the client organisation work, what they need, what their history is – in short, we undertake a cultural analysis to ensure that the solution we propose fits with their culture and ambition."

Jon Leach of HHCL agrees, "The important thing is not to get too hung up about the principle but to develop ways to tolerate different views and different needs. You have to watch that you develop things in a way that takes all – or at least most – people with it. I believe it worked for us because we had good communication throughout and good people working on it, rather than seeing it as a facilities exercise. We put together a team of people who could talk to architects and planners but also talked to people who were interested in the human psyche and human behaviour patterns. It had to be right for everyone and so we did not have that many casualties."

And in addition it is important to understand about the work environment – as with everything to do with innovation – that it is essential to remain open and to continue experimenting. To quote Jon Leach again, "It never finishes: But we also find that there are some parts of the blueprint we wrote 18 months ago where we ask ourselves today, why did we want one of those? For example, we have one room upstairs with very expensive revolving doors which no one really uses. Probably because it feels very unpleasant – but it still seems to have been too expensive to change. So we are continuously reviewing what we have and how we can improve it."

CHANGE THE WORK ENVIRONMENT – BUT FOR THE RIGHT REASONS

Design represents a minute proportion of the lifetime cost of a building – less than 1% – but done well it has a disproportionate impact on how well the building, and its surroundings, perform.
    Stuart Lipton, Chairman, Commission for Architecture and the Built Environment, *The Independent*, 8 February 2001

Finally, a comment on the motivation behind changes to the work environment. Managers in many companies are motivated to review the workspace arrangement out of financial and cost considerations. However, employees will be well aware as to whether changes in the work environment are suggested to save cost, or improve working conditions. Jon Leach comments, "One of the key aspects of our space planning is that it was not about 'how much can we save'. It so happened that our density has increased. It is about 70 square foot per person, which is pretty low – it was about 110 before. But increasing density was not where we were starting from, our starting point was, we are in the people communication business, which is to do with innovation and collaboration, how can we create an office space that encourages that? It was rather nice to discover that because of the way the people work, we did not need quite as much space as we did with the previous model but it was a side effect, not the reason for doing it."

READING SUGGESTIONS

Olmsted, B. & Smith, S. (1994). *Creating a Flexible Workplace*. AMACOM.

Comment: This book presents alternative work arrangements including flexitime, compressed workweek, flexplace and part-time alternatives such as regular part-time employment, job sharing, phased and partial retirement, voluntary reduced work time programmes, leave time and work sharing. For each option the authors explain the origins, who uses it, where it is appropriate, what the advantages and disadvantages are, whether it might be appropriate for your organisation, how to introduce the concept and special considerations for managers and supervisors.

Turner, G. & Myerson, J. (1998). *New Workspace New Culture – Office Design as a Catalyst for Change*. Gower Publishing.

Comment: This book provides insights into current working practices, what the barriers to change are, how these can be overcome, and possible future work scenarios.

SOME USEFUL WEBSITES

http://www.spaceforbiz.com

Comment: Lots of articles relevant to workplace issues are summarised or referenced; more recently also emphasis on innovation.

28 Outsourcing – designers in or out?

Although not directly addressed, the McAslan case study included some insights relevant to working with external designers, or to put it differently, to the outsourcing of design services. Architecture is probably one of the most likely candidates for outsourcing. However, there are many organisations that outsource all design activities as well as development activities. There are a number of issues to be considered in the outsourcing decision, and selection of the most appropriate designers, which we will investigate in this chapter, and which will be illustrated through the case study of the Skorpion, a motorbike designed by a British design consultancy for a former East German company. There is of course a wider debate on outsourcing in general and we will briefly review a few insights into outsourcing in general before focusing on the outsourcing of design services.

INS AND OUTS OF OUTSOURCING

In a way outsourcing is a variation on the theme of collaboration and some of the issues addressed in Chapter 13 are applicable to the outsourcing debate, such as:

- Doing it for the right reasons – e.g. a strategic need and not a short-term cost saving exercise.

- The need for a good fit of areas of expertise.

- Mutual respect and understanding of each other's needs and ways of operating.

In fact outsourcing is one end of a spectrum of possibilities of collaborating with other organisations. In their article on how to decide on whether to outsource or not Chesbrough and Teece (1996) provide a number of useful categorisations and guidelines. Their spectrum of possible forms of collaboration ranges from 'virtual company' (which I read to be 'outsourcing') to 'integrated corporation'. They argue that a fully integrated approach is advisable when there are no incentives to take risks. This is also the scenario under which there is the greatest ability to deal with conflicts and coordinate activities – see Figure 28.1

> "American firms have traditionally taken a piece-meal approach to outsourcing: in deciding what to contract out, they have tended to look at short-term savings in overheads, rather than at long-term strategy. By contrast, the Japanese companies, which pioneered outsourcing, use it to improve long-term quality and efficiency rather than to cut overheads. This, paradoxically, has resulted in bigger savings. Outsourcing now accounts for more than a third of Japanese companies' total manufacturing costs, and routinely reduces those costs by over 20%."
>
> *Economist*, 1995

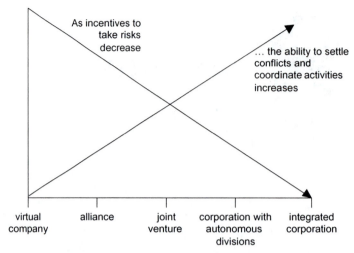

Figure 28.1   Finding the right degree of centralisation.
Source: Chesbrough, H.W. & Teece, D.J. (1996). When is virtual virtuous? Organizing for innovation. *Harvard Business Review*, Jan–Feb. Reprinted by permission of *Harvard Business Review*. Copyright © 1996 by the Harvard Business School Publishing Corporation; all rights reserved.

But principally their starting point is the suggestion that outsourcing is a potentially fast route to innovation. However, they warn that managers should consider carefully the kind of innovation they are engaged in before making the outsourcing decision. In order to facilitate such a decision they differentiate two different types of innovation:

- **Autonomous innovation** – something that can be developed independently of other parts or components that stands alone and does not affect/is not affected by other parts such as a turbocharger in an engine. They suggest that for such an innovation a virtual organisation would be suitable.

- **Systemic innovation** – something that makes sense only in conjunction with other innovations such as instant photography where both camera and film are needed. For such innovation an integrated corporation would be more suitable.

So the first three questions managers should ask are: (i) What is the possible pay-off (and hence the incentive to take risks)? (ii) How important is the ability to settle conflicts and coordinate activities; and (iii) What kind of innovation are we seeking? A fourth question is whether capabilities are readily available or whether they have to be developed. This is probably a tough question to answer at the outset of a development – not least habits and assumptions can get in the way of realistic assessment of a development task (see also Chapter 25). However, depending on what kind of innovation – autonomous or systemic – and availability of capabilities – existing or need to develop – the authors suggest choosing from a spectrum between going virtual or bringing everything in-house (see Figure 28.2).

According to the Outsourcing Institute in America managers have come to realise that outsourcing only adds value beyond the short term if a strategic approach is taken. In their *Fifth Annual Outsourcing Index*,[1] in which they report

---

[1] The *Index* is based on survey data collected from 1110 outsourcing buyers in 2002: 69% of responses came from US-based companies.

Type of innovation

		Autonomous	Systemic
Capabilities	**Exist outside**	Go virtual	Ally with caution
	Must be created	Ally or bring in-house	Bring in-house

Figure 28.2 Matching organisation to innovation.

Source: Chesbrough, H.W. & Teece, D.J. (1996). When is virtual virtuous? Organizing for innovation. *Harvard Business Review*, Jan–Feb. Reprinted by permission of *Harvard Business Review*. Copyright © 1996 by the Harvard Business School Publishing Corporation; all rights reserved.

the latest outsourcing trends and challenges, the Institute comments on "The diminishing role that cost saving plays when deciding to outsource. The majority of participants (55%) gave 'improving their company's focus' as their main reason for outsourcing with 'reducing and controlling operating costs' holding the second place (54%)." The numbers become more significant when realising that in the previous year's survey improving focus was identified by only 40% of participants as the main driver of outsourcing, whereas 48% declared the cost issue to be the main reason. The authors of the report consider this insight particularly relevant as they would not have expected focus to take precedence over cost in times of economic downturn. However, in my view conflicting with the above is the finding that 65% of participants determine whom they are outsourcing to based on price (65%) with quality taking only second place (51%).[2] However, this varied with size of company whereby larger companies placed almost equal value on quality. Still, it seems that intentions and knowing what it should be are ahead of reality.

A White Paper produced by the company Wind River considers the following to be strategic benefits of outsourcing:

- Time to profitability – outsourcing is seen to decrease time to market.

- Product robustness and reliability – due to brought-in expertise that may not all be available in-house.

- Product features set – linked to the above, the additional expertise is considered to lead to improved product features.

- Controlled costs – due to contractual agreements costs are agreed upfront, no need to train and invest in expertise, infrastructure and organisational structures.

- Optimal use of resources – only the people, technology, space required for the project are paid for; gives company optimum level of flexibility.

---

[2] The third most common reported factor in selecting an outsourcing vendor is flexible contract terms (39%), followed by reference/reputation (34%) and scope of resources (28%).

However, whether these benefits can always be realised is an entirely different matter. A recent survey of 420 business IT professionals revealed that only 50% consider their outsourcing efforts a success, about a third are neutral and as many as 17% of them call the outsourcing experience a disaster (McDougall, 2004). The main reasons named for failure were:

- Poor customer service, vendor responsiveness or flexibility.
- Hidden vendor costs.
- Insufficient up-front planning.

Other issues identified by Wind River for outsourcing failure are:

- Teaming up with the wrong partner, which is often due to insufficient care and time being spent during the selection process.

- Start looking too late in the process, companies might progress their products too far in-house before involving the outsourcing partner.

- Wrong expectations, generally due to unclear specifications of brief or changes in programme after the project has started.

- Treating a strategic partner like a 'body shop', problems can arise when the outsourcing company tries to interfere with the outsourcing partner's structures and systems.

- Poor supervision, a lack of monitoring and management of the relationship.

- Internal barriers, resentment and resistance in the outsourcing company.

- Poor contracts.

So not surprising, across different company sizes the three main factors seen to underlie a successful outsourcing relationship were:

- Finding the right vendor (63%).
- Managing the relationship (rated higher by larger companies than by small and medium sized ones).
- Structuring the contact properly (ranked number two for medium-sized companies – 500–999 employees).

These, interestingly, were seen to be more important than understanding the firm's goals and objectives.

To maximise chances of success Wind River recommends the following process:

1.   Identify your needs – what does success and failure mean in the context of your organisation (see also Chapter 25), what is it the company you are outsourcing to should deliver, how should the relationship be structured?

2. Develop a request for proposal – the authors suggest that whether you want to invite one or more companies to submit proposals will depend on how many companies could realistically provide the services you are seeking.

3. Evaluation process – ensure that you are only considering proposals that meet *all* your needs before you look at costs and make sure you evaluate against your success criteria.

4. Selection process – the authors suggest that you take the finalists through the 'best and final offer' process, ensuring that they have the skills and resources to deliver what you need. One interviewee suggested that cost/price should account for around 30% of the decision. However, it will also depend on the key success drivers and the authors give the example of selecting a neurosurgeon where you would want to go for the technically best rather than the cheapest, however much cheaper he or she might be.

5. Contract execution – signing the deal.

6. Administrative functions – this includes regular reporting, the authors suggest asking for reports on a monthly basis, to make sure the project says on track.

7. Close out – after completion of the contract a final report should be requested that provides a review of the contract and its fulfilment, any changes to the original plan and why they have occurred as well as measurement against the set success and performance criteria.

DESIGNERS – IN OR OUT?

After a more general view on outsourcing this section turns to the specific issue of outsourcing design. In 1997 about £10 billion or 2.6% of annual manufacturing turnover in the UK was spent on product development and design both in-house and bought in (Sentance & Clark, 1997).[3] The two critical questions managers should ask are: (a) Should we design in-house or should we buy-in outside expertise? and (b) If we decide to involve external designers, how should the relationship be structured? Interestingly, the trend towards outsourcing reported in the above-mentioned report by the Outsourcing Institute has been observed in the specific area of design and new product development (Cooper & Press, 1995; Anonymous, 1996). In the following we will take a look at the different options an organisation has regarding the location of design, as well as the advantages and disadvantages for each choice. The decision on whether designers are employed internally or not will also vary with the type of design in question (see Table B.1 in Appendix B).

Managers have three basic options when considering the location of design:

- Develop the design in-house.
- Employ an external designer or design consultancy to develop the design.
- Use a combination of in-house and external design.

[3]Much of this section is based on the article 'Whose design is it? The use of external designers' by von Stamm (1997).

If the in-house option is chosen there are several possible locations for design:

- With marketing – a choice quite popular with fast-moving consumer goods.

- Within the technical domain (either R&D or production) – most likely to be found in engineering or technology based organisations.

- An independent design department.

- A combination of the above.

- An organisation might decide not to have any explicit design expertise at all.

Not using designers, be they located in-house or externally, does by no means mean that companies do not undertake design. In their research Walsh et al. (1992) found that design activities are often undertaken by someone without any particular design-related qualification. Then there is also the issue of 'silent designers' (see also Chapter 1), that is people whose decisions have a critical impact on design and development of a product but who would not consider themselves designers or perceive themselves to be actually making design decisions.[4]

The importance of design for a company's competitive position and the MD's attitude towards design are company-specific factors that are likely to influence the treatment of design within an organisation, as will the level of design consciousness that prevails within an organisation (see Figure 1.3, Chapter 1). How frequently an organisation engages in the design and development of new products will also influence the decision. A company being continuously engaged in the design and development of new products is more likely to develop an in-house expertise than an organisation where development efforts are only undertaken sporadically.

A discussion with members of small and medium-sized organisations in the UK identified the following as factors that may influence the decision about the treatment of design.[5]

- Company size – a small company may not have the resources to entertain an in-house designer or design team.

- Radical or incremental – some companies might engage external designers to help develop radical new product concepts.

- Market segment – how important design is to the customer. If design is not considered to be important organisations might consider it unimportant, rightly or wrongly, to spend money on design.

- Innovator or a follower – participants felt that a company might be quite successful copying what other companies develop, without the help of any designer though I would argue this is in the long term not a sustainable position.

---

[4]For a discussion on 'silent design' please refer to Gorb and Dumas's (1987) article on this subject.
[5]The workshops took place at the Design Museum, London, in autumn 1993.

- Commodity or customised – several factors might influence the perspective on design such as:
  - Is the purchase a one-off or a repeat purchase?
  - Can specific features make a difference to the purchasing decision?
  - Does the purchase depend on reputation?
  - Is it the product or the packaging which distinguishes one product from the other?

The views brought forward by participants of the discussion allow two conclusions. First, many organisations, SMEs in particular, seem to hold the view that involving designers in the product development process is a luxury that 'one can get by without'. Second, the discussion with members of SMEs confirms views presented in the literature, for example Pilditch (1989) and Sparrow (1987), that the major driver behind the decision on whether or not to outsource design is the need for, and degree of, creativity and new ideas. Based on a study of the UK textile industry Coles et al. (1997) described the trade-off between internal and external design activities as one between greater control and design protection on the one hand versus access to a wider range of ideas on the other. Drawing on the insights from the discussion and the literature Table 28.1 lists the arguments for and against each choice.

As usual, there is no one right solution and as Sparrow (1987) points out, each company needs to make the decision about whether or not to outsource the design.

A study into the relationship between external designer and commissioning organisation, conducted on behalf of Business Link London City Partners in 1997 sheds some light on barriers to using external designers, the benefits of using external designers and how businesses tend to find designers.[6] Interestingly, half of the participating companies that had not used external designers declared having an in-house design team and about one-third declared that they did not have a need for design services.

The majority of organisations used external designers for their company logo (82% or 32 organisations) and company stationery (77% or 30 organisations). Table 28.3 lists for which tasks and how frequently external designers are used by business organisations.

The most frequently noted barrier to the use of external designers (about two-thirds) was the cost – reflecting the view that design is a luxury, followed by difficulties in finding the designer or design consultancy most appropriate for the company's need (see Table 28.4). There was generally a concern that design companies did not understand business concerns – a criticism that filters through to the debate on design education today and the call for increased commercial awareness and education of designers. The 'Media and Creative Industries Skills Dialogue' (DfES, 2002) reported that one of the concerns of business recruiting designers was their lack of business awareness.[7] The three barriers very much reflect the commonly held preconception about the design profession.

---

[6] The results are based on questionnaires returned by about 70 businesses and design consultancies. In each category 20 companies were interviewed either in person, or over the telephone. The questionnaires suggested possible answers, additional space was provided for respondent's personal comments. Focus group discussions were used to devise the suggested answers. The 70 participating business organisations came from five industries: printing/publishing, clothing, professional services, city/financial services and information technology; over 85% of the respondents had fewer than 50 employees.

[7] In Facts and Figures on Design in Britain 2002–03, a publication by the Design Council (www.designcouncil.org.uk).

Table 28.1 Advantages and disadvantages of internal and external design

Design route	Advantage	Disadvantage
In-house	• Cost efficiency • Accessibility • Easier coordination with other in-house departments • Company retains control • Designer develops intimate understanding of company	• Lack of creativity/new ideas • Keeping the design team busy, e.g. ongoing development work • Losing touch with external developments
External	• New inspiration • Access to specialists' expertise • Relieves work load • Accessibility of additional skills/staff • Speed • Options of changing and exploring different options	• Lack of understanding of company-specific issues • Problems of ready accessibility • Problems in the coordination with in house design and/or other departments • Potential lack of confidentiality • Company needs skills to evaluate the design work • Not-invented-here syndrome • Problems with industrialising the externally developed design • Loss of control • Credibility gap if design is too far removed from company's own style

Source: von Stamm, B. (1997). Whose design is it? The use of external designers. *Design Journal*, **1**, 41–53.

Table 28.2 Survey responses – industries

Area of business	% of respondents ($n = 51$)
Printing/publishing	8
Clothing industry	21
Professional services	6
City/financial services	21
IT companies	34
Other	10

Source: von Stamm, B. (1997). Whose design is it? The use of external designers. *Design Journal*, **1**, 41–53.

Table 28.3 Tasks for external designers

Project	% of respondents (n = 39)
Company logo	82
Company stationery	77
Company brochure	59
Product literature	33
Forms	23
Advertising	23
External signage	21
Exhibition design	21
Interior design	15
Packaging	13
Fashion design	13
Textile design	8
Industrial design	3
Work-flow design	3

Source: von Stamm, B. (1997). Whose design is it? The use of external designers. *Design Journal*, **1**, 41–53.

Table 28.4 Barriers to using external designers

Barrier	% of respondents (n = 52)
Too expensive	65
To difficult to identify the design organisation with the right skills	35
Might not understand business concerns	29
To difficult to know where to start looking for a design organisation	19
Would not understand specific needs	15
Problems with on-time delivery	13
We have all skills in-house	12

Source: von Stamm, B. (1997). Whose design is it? The use of external designers. *Design Journal*, **1**, 41–53.

The barriers identified in the Business Link research show some overlap with barriers identified by the Design Council (1998) – at least with the main obstacle to using external designers, finances. The three barriers identified by the Design Council are:

- The financial barrier – design is seen as cost rather than investment; there is also still a problem of acknowledging and evaluating the benefits of design from the investor side.

- The right barrier – it can be difficult, costly and time consuming to obtain and protect intellectual property rights.

●   The size barrier – particularly small businesses often do not have the time, experience or finance to employ the services of a designer.

By far the greatest benefit from using designers was seen to be an increase in the company's recognition. This was followed by increases in brand awareness and employee satisfaction. It is interesting to note that nearly 30% of organisations felt that as a consequence of using external designers their turnover had increased whereas only just over 10% felt that it had increased their profit. Table 28.5 lists the benefits suggested and the frequency with which business organisations agreed. Interestingly, those organisations that experienced benefits from using external designers saw more than one benefit, for example those that found that the use of external designers had increased turnover also felt that it had increased company recognition and employee satisfaction.

A survey conducted by the Design Council in 2002 shows a very different picture, though it has to be noted that the use of design – rather than external designers – had been the issue of concern. Depending on company size, up to 82% of respondents felt that the use of design had increased their competitiveness (see Table 28.6).

Table 28.5   Benefits from using external designers

Benefit	% of respondents ($n = 26$)
Increase in company recognition	88
Increase in brand awareness	46
Increase in employee satisfaction	38
Increase in turnover	35
Increase in customer satisfaction	27
Increase in market share	23
Increased efficiency (cost)	23
Increased press exposure	15
Increase in profit	12
Other – professionalism	8
Increase efficiency (materials)	4

Source: von Stamm, B. (1997). Whose design is it? The use of external designers. *Design Journal*, **1**, 41–53.

Table 28.6   Percentage of all companies (by employment size) saying design has contributed at least to some extent, to the following

	0–19	20–49	50–249	250+
Increased competitiveness	25	75	82	80
Increased profits	22	79	78	76
Better communications with customers	26	80	83	87
Reduced costs	6	62	64	54
Improved quality of products and services	26	69	87	78
Increased market share	16	70	83	83

Source: Design Council National Survey 2002. Reproduced by permission of the Design Council.

According to the Design Council survey, companies that experienced rapid growth in 2001/2002 were among those that said that design was an integral part or a significant part of their strategy (71%), as opposed to the overall national average of 41% and only 9% of rapidly growing companies declared that design had no part to play, compared with 42% of all participating companies. To top this, the Design Council also reports that UK companies recognised for their positive use of design, as indicated by design awareness, outperformed the stock market by 25%.

Once the decision to outsource design has been made managers need to address two questions. First how to find the most appropriate designer or design consultancy, and second, how to manage the relationship (Oakley, 1990). The second part of the study for the Business Link London research involved questioning design consultancies on their relationship with clients. Design consultancies reported that most frequently the contact had been initiated through a third-party recommendation, followed by repeat business (see Table 28.7). Considering that businesses mentioned difficulties in finding the most appropriate designer or design consultancies as one of the main barriers to using outside consultants it seems that there is a need to provide 'matchmaking' services, trusted by both designers and businesses, to bring companies and designers together. One attempt at filling this gap has been undertaken by the Design Council through setting up a website (www.designdirectory.org) which provides companies with some help on how to find the right designer/design consultancy and how to brief a designer.

The problems in finding the right partner might also suggest nurturing the relationship once it has been successfully established. In addition developing a long-term relationship can also help to overcome issues such as the perceived lack of understanding of business-specific issues or the 'not-invented-here' syndrome. However, research indicates that "In-house product development and design activities have a much more positive impact on business growth prospects than bought-in design" (Sentance & Clark, 1997) and that one reason underlying the failure of projects which involved external design consultants was the actual management of this relationship (Roy & Potter, 1990). Hence careful attention needs to be paid to the management of that relationship. This should lead managers to reconsider their position on the outsourcing of design.

The section above has contemplated theoretical issues around the location of design and selected aspects of the relationship between designer and business organisation. The following section provides a 'real-life' example of a cooperation between company and external designer.

Table 28.7 How do designers and business get together? (von Stamm, 1997)

Initiation of contact	% of respondents ($n = 244$)
Third-party recommendation	32
Existing client (repeat business)	20
Competitive and credentials pitch	11
Personal contact	10
Cold call and telesales	9
By client directly	6
Direct mail (by design consultancy)	6
Reputation	3
Roster	3
From a design directory/Yellow Pages	1

Source: von Stamm, B. (1997). Whose design is it? The use of external designers. *Design Journal*, **1**, 41–53.

THE CASE STUDY OF THE MUZ SKORPION[8]

The Skorpion is a motorbike produced by the former East German company MuZ. The motorbike, designed by a British design consultancy, was first presented to the public in December 1992 at a major motor show in the UK.

Background to the project

The commissioning company was a producer of motorbikes founded at the beginning of the twentieth century. Before the Second World War it was one of the leading manufacturers of motorbikes in the world, innovative and creative. Located in what was the Eastern Bloc and, hence, with company policy set by central government, the formerly innovative company lost its leading edge and became known for cheap, simple and badly designed, if robust, motorbikes. In Eastern Bloc countries the company continued to be a market leader, producing 80,000 motorbikes per year. To put this figure in perspective, total sales of motorbikes in the UK in 1988 was just under 62,000, in Germany about 93,000; while Japan produced 5.8 million bikes the same year.

Its success in the Eastern Bloc was due not least to the fact that people had to wait up to 16 years to get even the most basic car. A motorbike was *the* alternative means of transport. The company was neither aware of its actual cost structure nor did it have any responsibility for marketing its products or finding customers. A cost analysis undertaken by the government institution charged with privatising the state-owned enterprises after the collapse of communism, revealed a loss of an equivalent of £267 per bike.[9]

With the collapse of most communist regimes, caused not least by liquidity problems, the company's export markets in Eastern Europe folded and 2500 of the company's 3500 employees were made redundant. Finding investors proved difficult. In July 1992 the assets of the company were bought by private investors. Only in July 1993, having been threatened by closure several times, did the company finally manage to secure a government guarantee and with it access to new financial resources.[10] By this time total staff was down to about 200 employees.

When the new Managing Director – who had initially been brought in to help with privatising the company but then decided to buy the company himself – took over in June 1992 he continued what had been initiated by one of the company's European importers: the development of a new motorbike.

Development of the new bike

According to the Managing Director the selection of a foreign design consultancy was influenced by the consultancy's reputation in designing motorbikes and its in-depth knowledge of the motorbike market. The briefing for the new

---

[8] The data for the case study were collected by the author post-event, in three phases between autumn 1993 and spring 1997. Interviews were conducted with the senior management of the manufacturing company, the lead designer, as well as other organisations such as the government institution charged with the privatisation of the company, the lending bank and industry experts. The interviews were supplemented with documentation available in the public domain

[9] Calculated at exchange rate at the time.

[10] No bank would have been willing to lend capital to the company without a government guarantee underwriting it.

bike was simple, "Here is a four stroke engine, the one we use for all our other four-stroke models, develop a prototype that will help us to survive. There is hardly any money and the bike has to be ready for a big motor show in six months' time." For a similar job the design consultancy would normally have scheduled 18 months.

But the design consultancy was delighted to accept this job, as one of the partners put it, "This motorbike producer was the one company that all bike designers would want to work for and they approached us with the absolute dream brief, please help us, what should we do?" The concept was agreed upon later in July 1992 and it was not until 30 November 1992, with only a few hours to the opening of the Birmingham Motorshow, that the MD saw the new bike for the first time.

The working prototype of the motorbike had been developed almost exclusively by the design consultancy. For some critical technical issues industry specialists were involved, for example for the development of the frame for which the designer brought in a renowned bike specialist. He also knew that the well-informed motorbike market would know that when this person got involved, the result would be a light and therefore fast machine.

The outstanding success at the motor show came as a surprise and a journalist commented, "The idea that a new motorbike by this company could be the star of a major international motorcycle show in the 1990s might seem as unlikely as a Trabant outshining a Ferrari, but by common consensus the improbable became reality at this event."

The acclaimed design of the motorbike and the attention it had received at the show played an important part when the local government granted the company a guarantee which secured the company's medium-term financial survival.

The motorbike and its predecessors

The prototype of the new product was a major deviation from the motorbikes the company had produced previously:

- The frame was glued (not welded) together with adhesives normally used in the aircraft industry.
- Some parts of the bike had dual functions (structural and functional) such as:
  - the chassis which also contained the tank;
  - the battery box which structurally supported the steering head.
- It had some 30% fewer parts than conventional bikes.
- It weighed only 134 kg.[11]

Some of the changes were not only new to the company, but had not been generally used in the industry before.

The designer commented, "When the Japanese came on the motorcycle scene in the late 1960s they hijacked the concept of the motorcycle as a simple, economical form of transport and slowly turned it into the technically complex, expensive piece of leisure equipment we know today. This motorbike doesn't need a high-tech factory because it's simple to manufacture and assemble."

---

[11] A bike of comparable power, such as the Kawasaki 500cc bike, would weigh around 180 kg.

During the reorganisation of the company, and driven by the aims to reduce cost and control stock, it was decided to increase outsourcing from just under 5% under the communist regime to up to 85% under the new management.[12] In addition to the introduction of new products, new production processes and outsourcing, the organisation underwent several changes in management and organisational structure, while at the same time fighting for economic survival. The financial difficulties were also acting as a barrier to bringing in more highly qualified staff or developing staff dedicated to new product development internally.

The prototype

At the outset of the project, the design consultancy decided to base the new bike on what they perceived as the old values of the innovative and creative company of the early part of this century. Said the designer, "Our guiding principles in designing the bike as a focal point for the company's resurgence were the three qualities which the company have traditionally pursued – the three Ss, as we call them: simplicity, sustainability and (common) sense. By applying these principles, which governed the company's product development for decades, yet are an entirely appropriate proposition for the 1990s, it is possible to produce high-quality, low-cost motorcycles which represent an attractive alternative to the overcomplicated, overweight machines currently on offer elsewhere."

Even though the technologies used to assemble the bike were chosen for their simplicity and ease, the technological concepts which had worked well for the prototype and had helped to create a simple but elegant looking product, proved difficult in the production of the 'real' product, primarily because the necessary skills were not available in-house. Several changes to the specification were required which took time, increased cost and ultimately changed and diluted the original design concept.

Realisation of the design concept

Resistance, not to the externally developed bike itself but to the production methods, came from the workforce. There had been resistance to using an increasing number of parts from a Japanese motorbike manufacturer (with whom the design consultancy had a long-standing working relationship). The aim had been to position the company as a local producer, not least because of the high levels of unemployment in the area. Whereas the use of Japanese parts could not be avoided, the company's engineers succeeded in vetoing the manufacturing technique. Instead of using the novel, for the motorbike industry, gluing technique they reverted to traditional welding. This had the advantage that the workforce did not have to acquire new skills, while the disadvantages were that it was more expensive and time consuming to produce, and that it diluted the original design.

The reasons for changes were manifold:

- As stated above, due to company-internal objections the suggested manufacturing technique (gluing) had to make way for conventional welding.

- The exhaust needed to be changed to adjust to environmental regulations (noise emission).

---

[12]Up to 85% of the parts for the new motorbike were outsourced, around 60% for old models.

- A tank for the oil reserve had to be added as the original idea, to use the frame for the oil reserve, would only have worked in winter, i.e. there was a cooling problem.

- Despite objections by the company's marketers, who tried to establish the motorbike as a nationally-made motorbike, a Japanese engine was used (it was the only one that would fit into the constrained space available for the engine).[13]

All these changes led to over three months delay for the first delivery and to a much lower than anticipated production output. Industry experts felt that due to this delay the company lost out on the 'spring rush' characteristic of the motorbike industry. Exports to the US had to be delayed even further because additional adjustments were required to meet stricter US noise and emission standards.

Despite the bike's big success at the motor show and the fact that it had won several design awards in both the UK and the US, the company continued to struggle and filed for liquidation in July 1996.[14]

Lesson from the case study

This case study clearly represents an extreme situation and not a company's everyday experience of developing new products. Both parties acted under severe constraints: the design consultancy was given only six months to develop a working prototype and the MD of the commissioning organisation: (a) had to spend most of his time fighting for the financial survival of the company; (b) had not led a manufacturing organisation before; and (c) financial resources were extremely restricted. However, similar, if less drastic, problems can arise in any client–consultant relationship.

One of the major problems concerning the design of the new motorbike was that while industry specialists and journalists praised the simplicity of the bike – and the designer had emphasised that the bike was "simple to manufacture and assemble" – this was not how it presented itself to the manufacturing organisation. The motorbike required manufacturing techniques with which the company was not familiar. There was a significant mismatch between the company's capabilities and the manufacturing demands arising from the new motorbike.

Even if the end result was perceived to be simple: (a) the way to achieve the result may not be simple, particularly taking into account that the skills required to achieve the result were not readily available within the firm and (b) how complex a product is within a company's context depends on the degree of newness *to the company*, and only to a certain degree on the newness to the industry. In short, the manufacture of the motorbike was by no means simple for the people who had to actually do it.[15]

The development challenge and the scope of complexities of transferring the project back into the commissioning organisation need to be understood at the outset. Applying the Complexity Framework introduced in Chapter 25 would have helped identify the gaps between existing and the new motorbikes, and might have helped if not prevent

---

[13]This meant that the only specification given in the design brief was disregarded.
[14]In late spring 1997 the remains of the company were bought by an Asian conglomerate, which named the company's new product development capacity as a major motivator behind the purchase (Anonymous, 1997b).
[15]However, the gluing technique was also new to the industry.

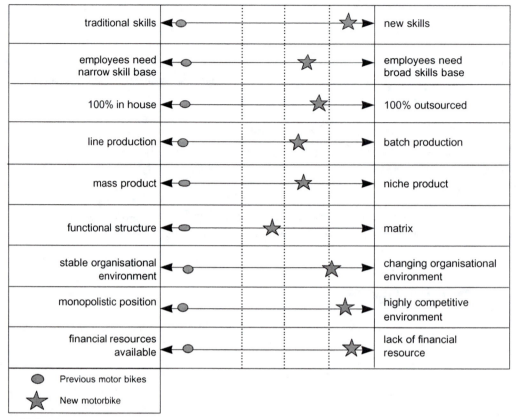

Figure 28.3 Development conditions new motorbike – predecessors.
Source: von Stamm, B. (1997). Whose design is it? The use of external designers. *Design Journal*, **1**, 41–53.

the problems to at least minimise their negative impact. Figure 28.3 summarises and compares the conditions under which previous products (●) and the new product (★) were developed and produced.

From this comparison it becomes clear that the conditions and demands of the new bike were significantly different. While it is not suggested that the required changes were impossible to achieve, the company would have needed to: (a) be aware of the differences; (b) take actions to initiate and facilitate the changes (training, acquisition of new skills, change in company culture); (c) provide sufficient resources (time and money); and (d) ensure close communication between designer and company to enable it. Instead, and as a consequence of the persistent financial constraints, compromises were made: the design was diluted and the market entry delayed. But rather than being an educated decision and conscious trade-off it was reactive fire fighting.

In-house versus external designer

The successful development of a new product was seen to be critical to repositioning the company and achieving a turnaround. Management was aware that the skills necessary to develop a radically new design were not available in-house and hence decided to use a design consultancy. In addition, even if a new product could have been developed in-house the company would have had difficulties convincing the motorbike community that this new product would be of higher quality than its predecessors. To employ a designer experienced in the industry – the design consultancy had worked with other motorbike manufacturers before – also had the advantage of bringing in market expertise and awareness of trends in consumer taste.

Authority of the designer

Because management was preoccupied with securing the financial survival of the firm – and trusted the designer explicitly – they did not get involved in the development of the new product, and nor did anyone else from the company. As the MD put it, "He is the designer, he knows what he is doing." The result of this development process was a product that attracted unexpected attention at an important international motor show and won several design awards, but which was also seen to be very different from everything else the company had developed before.

There were concerns whether the company might have overstretched its brand and there was a debate as to whether the bike would actually be associated with the company – or rather with the designer. This meant that the company had to convince dealers and bikers that it was capable of building the new product to the high standards set by the designers. The fact that the design was diluted and that the product reached the market with a significant delay did not help to defuse the concerns.

Communication and expectations

Many of the problems could have been avoided not only by an increased awareness of actual levels of complexity but also by better communication. Better communication and closer cooperation between designer and commissioning company could have highlighted potential problem areas in advance while time was still available for either training the workforce or adjusting the motorbike design to the skills available within the company.

Conclusions

It is not suggested that the company should not have taken on the new design or should have designed a motorbike entirely within its existing capabilities. However, it should have become clear during the design and development of the prototype that the product would be far beyond the company's capabilities and there are a number of lessons which can be learned from this experience.

1. Outsourcing decision

Given the starting point of the motorbike manufacturer, with a reputation for low-quality bikes, a workforce that was used to being punished for taking initiative, and the company's desperate need to come up with a new, creative and imaginative bike, the decision to employ an external designer was the only way forward. The choice of design consultancy, an organisation renowned for its knowledge of and expertise in the motorbike industry, was sensible and appropriate – as the success at the motor show proved. The decision promised all the benefits the employment of an external designer can bring: new inspiration, access to specialists' expertise and additional skills, and speed of development.

However, downsides of outsourcing, such as problems with the coordination of external designer and in-house team, the not-invented-here syndrome, problems with industrialising the externally developed design, and the credibility gap, meant that the commissioning organisation was unable to profit from the significant benefits the relationship could have offered.

2. Managing the relationship

The main problem lay in the management, not necessarily of the relationship between the designer and the MD, but the management of the transfer of the externally developed design into the manufacturing organisation. Both the designer and the MD should have been aware that this new bike needed special attention and preparation within the organisation to accommodate the unusual production methods, being so different not only from what the organisation had produced previously but also from the industry standard in general.

Actions would have been required to address the deficit in skills and to prepare the organisation for the manufacture of the new product. This should have taken place in parallel with the development of the prototype, not once full production was supposed to start. Instead of enabling staff to build this new bike through training or bringing in adequately skilled staff, the company chose to change the design to make it manufacturable with the skills readily available within the organisation. Had in-house staff been involved in the design and development of the new product it is likely that potential problems would have been noticed earlier and might have led to a more successful transition from prototype to manufactured product.

CONCLUDING REMARKS

The involvement of external designers is frequently motivated by a lack of the necessary expertise in house – be it creativity or any particular technical or other knowledge. However, involving external experts can only benefit a product's design and development process when these experts become an integral part of the development team and apply their expertise with an awareness of the organisation's context, its capabilities and constraints.

The bike was a huge success at the motor show in Birmingham – but many people felt that the bike would be associated with the design consultancy that had developed the bike, rather than the manufacturing company. Because the bike was sleek, exciting and well designed, people doubted that MuZ, known for its rather basic, out-of-date if cheap bikes, would be capable of producing the new bike to the quality and aesthetic standards required. The gap between the company's perceived capabilities and the positioning of the new bike caused dealers and end users to be cautious, resulting in slower than anticipated sales, which in turn contributed to the liquidity problems for the company, and eventually liquidation. Hence, a company should consider carefully whether by outsourcing new product development and design management activities it reduces its core capabilities, and with it what the company stands for.

Hence, when employing an external designer to develop a new product, it is important that in-house staff take part in the development – and the further the new design departs from existing products the more important close cooperation and integration become. Participation of and exchange with in-house staff are important not only to allow staff to 'own' the product once responsibility is passed over to the manufacturing organisation, but also to allow designer and commissioning company to notice – and address – constraints and problems as early as possible.

READING SUGGESTIONS

Greaver, M. (1999). *Strategic Outsourcing: Risk Management, Methods and Benefits*. Amacom.

Comment: An amazon.com reviewer wrote, Maurice Greaver has written a comprehensive and practical guide for any senior executive considering or currently undertaking an outsourcing initiative within their organization.

Heywood, J.B. (2001). *The Outsourcing Dilemma: the Search for Competitiveness*. Financial Times Prentice-Hall.

Comment: The book addresses questions such as: why outsource, what are the benefits of outsourcing, which functions should an organisation consider outsourcing, what are the alternatives to full outsourcing and how does an organisation choose an outsourcing service provider?

SOME USEFUL WEBSITES

http://www.outsourcing.com

Comment: The Outsourcing Institute (OI) is the only neutral professional association dedicated solely to outsourcing. Recognised worldwide for its intellectual capital, outsourcing practice expertise and unbiased thought leadership, OI tracks and forecasts the rapid evolution of outsourcing while providing new services and programmes to assist buyers of outsourcing services. To get access to most of their information you need to register – but it's free.

www.designdirectory.org

Comment: A website recently set up by the Design Council to help companies find and brief designers and design consultancies.

29 Putting all pieces into place

CASE STUDY 10: THE TECHNOLOGY PARTNERSHIP[1]

The Technology Partnership is infuriatingly difficult to define. At one level, it is a research organisation, with an almost academic interest in knowledge for its own sake; at another, it trades brains for cash, finding solutions to industrial problems.

Financial Times, 15 January 2001

A NEW DIRECTION?

Late 1999 Anne Miller went to Gerald Avison, Managing Director of TTP Group, to say she was ready for a change. Anne had a background in mechanical engineering and innovation with 30–40 patents under her belt. She had joined PA Technology in 1981 and left to become a founder member of TTP, a company set up under Gerald's direction in 1988. She explained, "In joining Gerald, I wanted to be part of the culture he creates which is participative, not dictatorial."

At TTP she had built up and led the Innovative Engineering Sector of TTP's business and had invented a diverse range of products, ranging from power tools for Bosch to the manufacturing system for the Femidom (the 'female' condom). In 1999 she knew that she wanted to explore new avenues, though initially not sure exactly what she wanted to do. Gerald suggested she go out and talk about innovation to people that TTP would not normally contact because "something interesting will come of it, and in any case it will be good PR". She soon realised that many companies were struggling with infusing innovation into their organisation, and were very interested in how TTP had come to be so successful at it. Training and coaching was not an area that TTP had yet had much involvement in, although innovation was something Anne and TTP knew something about: it was the lifeblood of everything they did. So Anne asked herself, "How are we doing it? Is there something in understanding the way we operate that would help other organisations to improve their own innovativeness?"

The seeds for a training arm of TTP were sown in Anne's mind – but how would the board react to such an idea that was far removed from the technology focus that had driven the company for 12 years?

---

[1] The case has been prepared by Dr Bettina von Stamm as a basis for class discussion rather than to illustrate either effective or ineffective handling of a management situation.

How it all started

The seeds for The Technology Partnership (TTP), or TTP Group as the company is known today, were sown over 40 years ago when a small group of academics left Cambridge University to form Cambridge Consulting.[2] Originally their aim was to provide technology development services to industry, which they did. They also developed their own products, the Cambridge Audio Amplifier being a technical success, albeit commercially suspect.

> The Cambridge Amplifier was very popular at the time. During its development the group learned a lot about manufacturing, not least because the Amplifier with its brushed aluminium front was expensive to manufacture and to maintain blemish free.

In 1969, seeking a fresh challenge, a group of about five people led by Gordon Edge approached PA Consulting, assuring them that PA desperately needed a technology business. PA bought into the idea and left it to Gordon and his team to set up and run what was then called Patscentre (short for, PA Technology and Science Centre) and which later became PA Technology. Under Gordon's leadership the division thrived and become a major contributor to PA's profitability. By 1986 PA Technology was a global business under Gordon's overall authority and had laboratory operations in Melbourn Cambridgeshire, Princeton NJ, Melbourne Australia and Brussels as well as Industrial Design Studios in London and Sydney. Overall the Group accounted for over 20% of PA's turnover and a rather higher proportion of the profit. The growth was entirely organic, with overseas operations being set up by a small team relocating from the UK and then recruiting locally.

In 1985 the arrival of a new CEO to the PA Consulting Group resulted in a structural reorganisation and a significant reduction in Gordon's sphere of influence. Not happy with how things were developing, Gordon made alternative plans, which eventually led, in autumn 1986 to him leaving with a number of other staff to form Scientific Generics (now the Generics Group). As a consequence the CEO of PA called a meeting of PA Technology's 15 most senior people declaring, "If any of you want to leave as Gordon did, just go, we are not standing in your way." Over the next six months about 15 PA Technology staff

> In September 1987 PA sued three people they regarded as the ring leaders for breach of contract; they also sued the Australian and the new company; PA Technology's remaining 22 people were sent off to gardening leave and forbidden to take up new work. Around January 1988 PA had to release all those who wanted to join TTP. The legal battle was finally settled out of court in February 1990.

joined The Generics Group. Three months after Gordon Edge left, the Melbourne Australia Laboratory of PA Technology, then employing about 65 staff, successfully negotiated with PA a management buyout of the company. The new company was called Invetech. A number of years later Invetech reversed into a quoted Australian company, Vision Systems.

Over the following nine months the changes being introduced by the new PA CEO gathered pace and many of the PA Technology staff felt that this was not the company that they had originally joined. In September 1987 this culminated in the simultaneous resignation of about 25 (85%) of the senior managers at the Melbourn Cambridge Laboratory and the formation of The Technology Partnership, with the financial support of Invetech and an Australian venture capitalist.

---

[2] Today Cambridge Consultants is owned by Arthur D. Little.

Company growth and development

To finance the new venture a mixture of internal and external investment was sought. Staff were – and still are – encouraged to own shares in the company. The company's management went to Lloyds and Barclays to negotiate preferable conditions for loans their employees could take out to buy a stake in the business. The arrangements eventually negotiated were that the banks would lend employees up to £25,000, with no security, at an interest rate of 2.5% over base, with a three-year repayment holiday, and 10-year payback.[3] By this means the founders raised over £700,000 of their own money to invest in the business. Staff, of whatever seniority, were allowed to invest as much or as little as they could afford. As a consequence the shareholding was very evenly spread, with no one individual holding more than 4%.

TTP is a private company operating an Employee Share Ownership Programme (ESOP)

TTP has set up a scheme under which shares are allocated to employees on a bi-annual basis, funded out of a share of the profits. Everybody gets the same allocation; no new shares are issued, and the pool is fed by shares bought by the ESOP in the internal market from former and existing employees. Shares allocated by the ESOP have to be A shares.

There are four classes of TTP shares

1.   A shares: may be held by anyone. If offered for sale they must be offered in turn to B, C and A holders and only then to anyone else. The price for A shares has to be approved by the directors. This type was held by the Australian venture capitalist and the Australian Lab.

2.   B shares: can only be bought and owned by current employees of TTP and its subsidiaries; by employees' spouses, adult children and family trusts; and by the ESOP. When B shares are sold it tends to be more like an auction.

3.   C shares: can only be held by the venture capitalist backer, originally CINVen, but now 3i. The price for C shares has to be approved by the directors.

4.   D shares are what B shares become when the employee leaves or retires and are non-voting. They can only be sold back into the company and become B shares again when bought.

Additional money came, as noted, from the backer of the Invetech management buy-out, and, eventually, CINVen, the venture capital arm of the Coal Board and British Rail Pension Fund.

CINVen had a mixture of ordinary shares and convertible, redeemable preference shares. The latter had a coupon of 7% and were redeemable over years three to five. A proportion of these could be converted into normal shares if the cumulative profit over the first three years was less than £1.89 million on a linear sliding scale down to £1.13 million. At £1.13 million profit, CINVen's share of the equity would be increased by 70% from about 13% to 22%. But, as Gerald Avison recalls, "In our third year we were firing on all eight cylinders, so our financial results were very good, and we made it."

---

[3] When employees approached their own banks, most were happy to match these conditions.

Part of the agreement with CINVen was that no dividends should be paid during the first five years, any profit was to be ploughed back into the business. After five years 50% of post tax profit was to be paid out as dividends. Future flotation was raised as a possibility though TTP's management, who privately agreed that they would rather keep the company private, made no firm commitment. In 1988 60% of the company shares were owned by TTP staff[4] and the remaining 40% by institutions (CINVen, Vision Systems, and the Australian venture capitalist).

The five units with which TTP started in 1988 were formed around the founding members' key skills and interests. The units, with 2–5 people each, were: Scientific Products, Product Engineering, Computers & Communications, Tactical Technology and Automation. In 1989, with a turnover of £4.5 million, the company grew to 50 people, including five more from PA who set up a Control Group, and a person from Deloittes who contacted the company after seeing a newspaper article and who joined to set up a strategy consulting arm. The following years saw continuous growth and expansion and by 1999 the turnover had grown to £41.1 million resulting in operating profits of £6.8 million (more details can be found in Appendix 29.3). Milestones in the company's development are shown in Box 29.1.

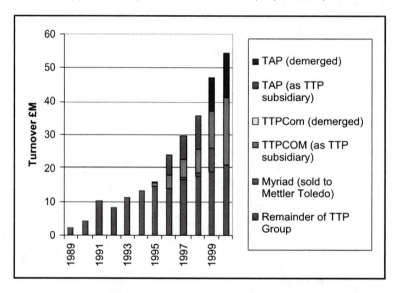

TTP clients

• BA	• Fuji	• Philips
• Bayer	• GlaxoWellcome	• Rhode & Schwarz
• Bosch	• ICI	• Smith & Nephew
• BOC	• Merck	• Sony
• Braun	• NEC	• Sulzer
• Burmah Castrol	• Norton	• Tetrapak
• Compaq	• NCR	• Zeneca
• Esselte		

---

[4]With no one individual owning more than about 4%.

Box 29.1   Milestones in TTP's development

1989   Consulting assignment for the Consortium that became Orange to help them secure a first generation digital communications spectrum licence. TTP's first involvement with GSM technology.

1990   Commence design of first GSM chip.
Australian VC sells his 15% stake, which are picked up by 3i (80%) and TTP employees (20%), including an ESOP set up to involve new employees in share ownership.

1991   Development of first pharmaceutical automation product.
Early studies of ink-jet printing market and first involvement with Research Labs of Australia (RLA).

1992   Undertake major automation supply contract for Merck in the US.

1993   Computers & Communications division starts partnership with Analog Devices Inc to make GSM chips.
Set up ToneJet, a 50/50 joint venture with RLA in non-contact digital printing.
Set up Wavedriver, a 50/50 joint venture with PowerGen on electric vehicle drives.

1994   Automation division takes on a pharmaceutical focus.
Tactical Technology division is renamed Manufacturing Technology. It has a mainly consulting function

1995   Acquired Signal Computing, a software company based in Guidford which had been working primarily for the defence sector, from ITN.
Set up Automation unit as a wholly owned subsidiary The Automation Partnership.

1996   Exit from Wavedriver, the joint venture with PowerGen, as timing for introduction of electric vehicles in California was delayed.
Established Silent Software division to provide complex software development service to the group.
Computers & Communications division achieves first type approval of a mobile phone containing its chip designs and GSM software.
CINVen sells its shares to: TTP for its ESOP (50%), Vision Systems (25%), and 3i (25%), changing the ownership structure to 75% TTP staff and 25% institutional. All shares except the ones purchase by 3i were converted from C to B shares.

1997   Change in group holding structure. TTP Group created as a holding company, with TTP, Signal Computing and The Automation Partnership as wholly owned subsidiaries.

1998   Full statutory de-merger of The Automation Partnership.
Sale of the rights to the Myriad product range of synthesisers for combinatorial chemistry, as well as the transfer of seven staff to Mettler-Toledo to form Mettler-Toledo Myriad.
Computers & Communications division set up as separate business called TTP Communications.
TTP Venture Managers set up as wholly owned subsidiary and TTP venture fund started.
TTP Group increased investment in life sciences.

1999	Set up Libris, a joint venture with Dextra Laboratories, to develop and sell carbohydrate compound libraries.
	Set up Apocyte, a joint venture with the University of Nottingham in the field of cell aptosis.
	Set up IP.Access to use and develop TTPCom's intellectual property to provide mobile phone network basestations.
2000	De-merged and floated TTP Communications (including IP.Access).
	Acquisition of Melbourn Science Park enabling continued joint location of TTP business.
	Set up Odem, a joint venture with Bespak (UK) and Pari (German) (1/3, 1/3, 1/3) for the development of drug inhaler products.
	Set up Ashes Investments, 50/50 joint venture with RLA for electrographic printing.
2001	Set up TTP Labtech (instrumentation) and Acumen Bioscience (high throughput screening) as wholly owned subsidiaries.

Gerald Avison is serious when he comments, "I would rather we made 200 people relatively well off than a handful of us very rich." Fifteen per cent of company profits are redistributed to employees through a bonus. Two-thirds of it is handed out as a percentage of salary whereby the percentage is the same for everyone, the other one-third is given in shares whereby each person receives the same number of shares. This is about to change as a consequence of the replacement of the old ESOP rules by the new SIP. The balance is likely to shift towards equality.

Salary distribution is one of Gerald's responsibilities. He agrees with the board how much the company can spend on salaries. After setting aside about 10% of the budgeted amount to retain some flexibility, he does a dummy run on who is getting how much. This is used as a basis for advising each head of department how much they have to spend and asking them how they wish to distribute this. Once they come back to him he looks at peer groups and makes sure that all is fair, part of which involves making suggestions for moving people up or down a bit and using the sum set aside earlier to balance where necessary. The ownership structure for 2000 is shown in Figure 29.1.

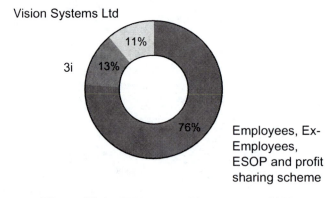

Figure 29.1   TTP ownership structure, 2000.

You are who you hire

As well as its work with mobile phones and industrial automation, the group is also involved in the printing and pharmaceutical sectors. It is currently investing in electrographic techniques, which could one day replace web offset printing. In pharmaceuticals it is working on ways to screen chemicals for biological activity, and for spotting cancer cells 'needle in a haystack' fashion.

Cambridge Evening News, 20 March 2001

Gerald Avison comments: "Since inception our purpose has been to innovate. Our core values are 'partnership', 'we deliver what we say we will' and 'have fun and make money'." The latter is certainly true considering that someone who had invested £1 in the company in 1987 would have seen it grow to £600 by the end of 2000. But the fun bit is taken seriously too. Again, Gerald says, "We do things because they look interesting and we don't do things if we think they are boring. When everyone jumped

> "While we enjoy joint ventures, growth through acquisition does somehow not feel right for TTP. Organic growth allows people to grow with the business. People get the chance to grow knowledge and responsibilities over time, within the business."
>
> Gerald Avison

onto the bandwagon of the Millennium Bug, where lots of money was to be made, we did not do it because we were just not interested. For us there has always to be the curiosity factor. For example, we floated TTPCom partly because we had not done that before – of course there were other reasons too but that was an important one. If someone says, things have to be done this way, we tend to do just the opposite – we very much avoid the message that there is a standard way of doing things." There are no fixed office hours, people can more or less come as they please, as long as they work the contractually agreed hours – and as most employees are enthusiastic about their work delivery of content has never been a problem, in fact they probably work between 45 and 50 hours on average.

From the outset management was aware that the kind of organisation they had in mind would only work with the right kind of people. Gerald commented, "During a conference I heard someone from an IT service business of about 2000 staff talk about the scientific approach they take to recruitment. He explained that they were using 50 criteria on which they assessed and selected their staff and

> "You need cultural fit at a personal level but not at the professional level. We go for individuals and move people between groups to ensure good cultural fit between individuals and groups."
>
> Gerald Avison

the speaker was very proud to announce that they had a staff turnover of only 20%. A second speaker of another company described a quite different approach, he just said, 'We hire nice people and are nice to them, and our staff turnover is 6%'." Staff turnover at TTP runs between 4 and 5%.

"We seek talented, experienced people who not only have bright ideas, but who can create innovative solutions to make their ideas work. We invest heavily in core technologies, facilities and training. I believe that we have established a working environment in which every individual has a voice and the chance to develop and grow. We know there's more to life than work, so we also try to make it fun!" So states Gerald Avison in TTP's recruitment brochure. Gerald explains that each successful candidate will be interviewed at least twice, the first time they will meet 2–3 people from their prospective peer group. After some consultation and comparing notes those who come the second time will meet the MD of the operating subsidiary and Gerald. The meeting with Gerald has three objectives: first, to ensure the applicant understands what the business as a whole is about; second, for TTP to find out about the applicants, what they are good at and what they are like as a person; and third, to give some space to ask any questions the applicant may not have had a chance to ask earlier. Every candidate is also encouraged to talk to anyone in the organisation and ask any questions they want, off the record.

Elaborating on the company's recruitment process Gerald explains, "Until I became Group MD and handed over recruitment recently to the MD of TTP, I made sure to meet every single person we recruited. I still try to do that but we make sure that, as a minimum, the MD of the operating subsidiary meets every person who will join their company. We believe strongly that business is about people and that it is therefore essential that the person running the business knows every person working for them." Heads of business units have the responsibility to make sure that there is a fit between the people and the

> After years of downsizing and concentrating on the short term, many companies have lost the ability to innovate and are asking TTP to carry out the whole product development process or to assist them in becoming more creative. But as one of the TTP founders Chas sims says, this is a lot easier to talk about than to achieve. Stressing that TTP tends to take on staff who have had some experience in the real world fo manufacturing, he says that the company succeeds because staff are given freedom and responsibility. The front end of product development "Is not about monkeys and typewriters," he adds. "It comes down to people, how you stimulate them and how you let them react to each other."
>
> Independent on Sunday, 27th July 1997

environment. In addition all prospects meet the top so they understand the tone and culture of the company as well as the wider picture of the organisation. "Our HR function is there to support recruitment, to run the salary system, benefits and keep records – the administrative side – but selection and management of people is the responsibility of management," Gerald emphasises. Once people have joined they attend an induction course that Gerald runs every six weeks. They are also encouraged to meet as many of their colleagues as possible. To quote Gerald again, "If you want to find out about who knows what you go and talk to people. We have a comprehensive intranet, but we do not have a database in which we store information about people – people should talk to each other. Face-to-face meetings are important – that's why we have lots of free drinks machines. We believe that if people want to find someone with a particular expertise they should find him or her within three conversations and about 10 minutes."

Personnel reviews are held by managers on an annual basis. But, as Gerald points out, "It is not an annual criticising event. I strongly believe that positive as well as negative feedback should be given right away and not be saved for an annual conversation. The reviews are about establishing development plans, where a person is going next, what the responsibilities are and should be, what training is required

> "I can meet people who are far more experienced than me. I'm surrounded by people who are incredibly intelligent, and I have the opportunity to pick their brains."
>
> From TTP's recruitment brochure

in the coming year and so on. A lot of the learning takes place on the job and through conversations." Preparation for management roles is part of the menu. Gerald, who keeps an eye on people's development, strongly believes that, "Professionals should be led by professionals and not by administrators. There is no one management style – but whoever is in a management role better make sure he or she is open and fair. And if something seems to go wrong the management team gets involved to help sort it out. For example, in the early 90s one group was disbanded and the staff distributed amongst other groups because of limitations in the manager's capability." He also points out that no one is forced into a management role. When he handed over responsibility for the Group's largest operating subsidiary to the then head of Scientific Products division, that division was split in two. One of the people who were approached was not too sure whether he really wanted to move into management. Conversations and discussions continued over two months and while management were very confident that he was the right person for the job they made sure not to push him. In the end he accepted the job, but there was no inducement or pressure.

Twice a year meetings are held to report the company's half-year and full-year results. In addition informal meetings with drinks and snacks are held late afternoon every Friday. The responsibility for organising these events, which last about one hour and to which 25–30% of employees turn up, rotates between the different groups of the organisation. During these sessions the director summarises important events and development of the week – and anything else that might be of interest to everyone in the organisation. In addition, the group arranging the event nominates one of their people to talk about a subject of their choice – and this does not have to be work-related. For example, past presentations included talks about Chinese cooking, scuba diving, radio telescopes and the activities of GCHQ in the last war. "Presenting in front of a bunch of bright and curious people can be quite a daunting prospect," Gerald acknowledges, "so to encourage less experienced speakers to get involved we have an agreement that questions should be aligned to the speaker's experience and confidence."

The paths we choose

Curiosity and people's personal interests play an important role in determining the areas in which the company operates. When the company started off business units were set up around people's expertise. Gerald describes their approach as 'planned opportunism' and uses the story of how they got involved in GSM technology as an example.

"Senior people do not have the copyright on ideas – or on benefits. All benefits – pension, health insurance etc. – are the same throughout the company, and we do not have a company car policy."

Gerald Avison

In 1990 Maggie Gray, wife of a TTP employee, and a man from British Aerospace (BAe) met over coffee while doing their part-time MBA at Cranfield. The BAe man was concerned about a recommendation that they had received from a consulting company regarding the communication standard that should be adopted for a satellite linked telephone system that BAe were planning to develop for deployment in underdeveloped locations. Maggie suggested that they should get a second opinion from TTP's Communications consultants. They commissioned a study, which recommended the newly emerging GSM standard, rather than the out-of-date CT2 standard proposed by the first report. BAe concurred with this and invited TTP to develop GSM technology for them. During the early stages of the development it became clear to TTP that not only was the GSM standard based on IP owned by companies such as Nokia, Motorola and Ericsson, but that these companies also had a monopoly on some of the silicon needed. Moreover, they were not interested in selling these components to potential competitors. By now hooked on the idea, this obstacle did not deter TTP and they decided to invest in creating their own intellectual property in GSM purchasing suitable computers and software and hiring a team of chip designers.

When BAe subsequently decided to dispose of their satellite communications business to the French company, Matra, the project was stopped. This decision naturally had an adverse effect on TTP's financial performance that year. However, management at TTP decided to keep the team together and when in the following year TTP met Analog Devices (AD) they entered into an agreement to design a new generation of GSM chipsets, which would be sold and

"Teamwork is essential, it is part of the development process; you are always likely to encounter problems that have been impossible to anticipate; you want people who are interested in sorting out problems, not allocating blame."

Gerald Avison

fabricated by AD, in return for royalties. This was the starting point for the TTP Communications plc. In the three and a half years following the agreement TTP invested 250 person-years in the development of the technology. It was mid-1996 before the first handset designed around TTP's IP gained type approval and six months after this that the royalty stream began to flow and TTP started to get a return on the investment.

Through normal prospection activity, which involves a lot of travelling and securing meetings with companies who have been chosen as potential customers or partners, TTP established contact with Hitachi in 1994. Hitachi was market leader in GSM radio frequency (RF) power amplifiers, had developed good silicon processing technology and was looking for a partner who could provide them with the technology for their next generation GSM RF chip. TTP's Computers & Communications division had extensive expertise in radio engineering and was looking for an opportunity to add an RF offering to the digital baseband GSM chip technology embodied in the AD agreement as well their own suite of software. This would mean they would be in a position to supply all the technology neces-

> Pure development projects are always risky and a key issue for TTP is how to manage this risk. Projects are structured in phases to ensure that risk is contained and TTP uses its experience in development to estimate the development costs. Inevitably some developments prove more difficult and more expensive than anticipated. Where the benefits to the customer are clearly substantial, the terms of business allow TTP to pass these costs on to the customer. In other cases TTP may absorb the overspend, particularly if it is judged that the problems should have been foreseen.

sary to make a GSM mobile phone. The two companies decided to collaborate on a development, which eventually led to a range of GSM radio chips which became known as the BRIGHT radio chips. Without countless lawyers being involved, it was agreed that the collaboration would be royalty based, that intellectual property would be owned jointly, and that rather that spelling out each party's tasks in detail, broad areas of responsibility would be allocated under which TTP Communications were responsible for the overall system architecture and design, and Hitachi were responsible for the detailed silicon circuit layout, fabrication, sales and distribution. To kick off the collaboration Hitachi engineers spent four weeks in the UK, working alongside their TTP counterparts. The relationships were sustained through six face-to-face meetings annually as well as frequent video conference calls.

Despite the fact that the first product gained limited acceptance in the market and was not commercially successful for either partner, the relationship continued. The partners were thus well positioned to take advantage of the shift towards dual band technology in 1997, which required a phone to operate either at a frequency of 900 MHz, as used in the UK or 1800 MHz as used in much of the rest of Europe. The second product achieved a significant success and the partners are now onto the development of the fourth generation triple band product, which will work also at the 1900 MHz frequency used in the USA.

By 1998, TTP's Computers & Communications division had developed considerable expertise in GSM software

> "The first of its [TTP's] offspring to make a stock market debut, TTP Communications, which designs the insides of mobile phones, was subscribed nine times when it went public four months ago. Its shares, although closing on Friday at 217.5 p below the 245 p offer price, have held up well compared with the devastation in the technology sector, suggesting TTP is in the business of producing golden eggs rather than the turkeys which resulted from dotcom mania."
>
> *Financial Times*, 15 January 2001

and associated chipsets, and the business around had grown sufficiently to make it appropriate to set it up as a separate wholly owned subsidiary business, called TTP Communications (TTPCom).[5] In 1999 when TTP Group and

---

[5] When the business was demerged and floated on the London Stock Exchange in 2000 it was valued at £540 million.

TTPCom established IP.Access, shares were offered to staff, who raised about £250,000, the equivalent of 12.5% of the equity.[6]

Lend a helping hand

It came to prominence last year as an incubator, an organisation which nurtures small companies with big ideas until they are ready for the stock market. Rather than fostering separate companies, however, TTP cultivates its own specialist divisions.

Financial Times, 15 January 2001

Many good ideas fail to gain the support of venture capitalists because the technologies involved are difficult to understand. TTP knows this. To quote the *Financial Times*, "What Mr Avison realises is that the market has difficulty understanding what TTP does – and might not like it if it did. 'We can do more while privately held than as a public company,' he says. 'Some of the risks we have taken would be hard to justify to institutional shareholders.' He points, for example, to the investment of 250 man-years of effort – equivalent, say, to £38m – in establishing TTPCom as a market leader in its field." Because it nurtures business ideas internally, by the time TTP's offspring are spun out they have customers, products, a management structure and an accounting system. But, as TTP knows, these things do not happen overnight.

Being aware that many good ideas die because they are not understood by the financial markets, a couple of people within TTP felt very strongly that TTP should set up its own venture capital fund. They felt that the edge they would have over other venture capital firms was that they had the technical knowledge necessary to assess proposals. David Connell TTP Ventures' Chief Executive declares. "Our ability to understand and add value to science and technology-based investment propositions is proving highly attractive to both entrepreneurs and investors. We are only interested in those technologies and industries we are able to assess." He lists telecoms, electronics and IT equipment, instrumentation, hi-tech engineering, medical equipment and drug discovery technology, materials and chemicals as potential investment targets and continues: "The businesses which we would be interested to invest in would have to have a highly differentiated offering, based on science or engineering. They would have to prove that they have a strong management team – or the potential to create one." So rather than investing exclusively in their own ideas, the venture fund allows investing in external ideas. Gerald comments, "You will generally find that the more mature the investment fund, the more protectionist and complicated the structures tend to get. People are always trying to insure against the exception rather than provide for the rule. Our fund on the other hand is rather straightforward – not least because the two people who set it up did not have any preconceptions of Venture Capital, but had a lot of experience of being close to and involved in growing business around technology!" The Fund, which was set up as a separate entity called TTP Ventures and had £35 million at its disposal, received much attention from the press when it was set up in 1998.[7] TTP's track record for technical expertise and profit attracted a number of high-profile backers including NPM Capital, the

---

[6]When TTPCom was demerged and floated on the London Stock Exchange in October 2000, it acquired IP.Access from TTP Group in return for shares in TTP Communications plc. Staff who had invested in IP.Access nine months previously secured a return of about a factor of about 15 on their money.

[7]See Appendix 29.4 for an article on the venture fund published in the *Financial News*, July 2000.

largest independent fund in the Netherlands, Boeing, Siemens, two undisclosed UK pension funds, and Abbey National.

The work environment

The physical work environment at TTP has received special attention too. As reported in the *Cambridge Evening News* of 5 September 2001, "TTP Group has bought the Melbourn Science Park for an undisclosed sum from AXA Sunlife Pensions. The park is over 17 acres." Gerald is quoted as saying: "Ownership of the park enables us to accommodate our continuing growth and allows us to maintain our commitment to being based in Melbourn and supporting the local community. One of the most attractive features of the park is the planning permission that already exists for further development. This will give us the flexibility we need to shape the future of our business."

But it is not only flexibility, it is also variety. Acknowledging different views and needs, TTP has taken this approach to its nine conference rooms. To achieve this, three interior designers with quite different styles were selected to design three rooms each. The aim was to create environments for meetings that did not intrude on the business of the day but were at the same time memorable.

Since its inception the company has received many awards. To name a few:

- 1994: National winner of the *Sunday Times* 'Quest for Growth' award, awarded to the company judged most likely to demonstrate sustained growth.

- Spring 2001: Business Investment Award, sponsored by Barclays.

- May 2000: nominated one of the UK's most successful companies in profits growth in the *Sunday Times* and PricewaterhouseCoopers' survey.

- February 2001: TTP listed in the Vision 100 index, which recognises organisations with unique and exceptional vision.

- 1999: TTP received Queen's Award for Technological Achievement.

Questions

1.   How and why is this organisation different? What are aspects of the company that encourage and foster innovation?

2.   Is the learning transferable to other organisations and if so how?

3.   If you were in the position of Gerald Avison and his board, would you give Anne Miller the go-ahead? Arguing from the company's perspective, why or why not?

APPENDIX 29.1: MAJOR DEVELOPMENTS IN THE TTP GROUP SINCE 1990

1990

- Settled dispute with PA

- Company grows to 100 staff

- Cooperation with British Aerospace on the development of GSM/satellite-based telephony

- Commence design of first GSM chip

1991

- Turnover dropped because of recession and investment in GSM (part way through the year the contract with BAe stopped; BAe sold the Space Systems division to Matra in France)

- Automation division started work on the first pharmaceutical automation product

- Researched and sold a market report on emerging technologies and developments in digital printing, including ink jet printing. The aim was as much to get into the market and network with companies, as to generate consultancy work

- Through the above study, first contact with the Research Labs of Australia (RLA) whose expertise was in toners (printers, copiers) and were behind Canon's move into electrographic printing

1992

- Work on electric drive for electric vehicles leading to joint venture with PowerGen, called Wavedriver

- Search for means of capitalising on GSM expertise, including unsuccessful discussions with venture capitalists about a new company to finish and commercialise the development half completed for BAe

- Period of general consolidation as the economic climate picked up

1993

- The Computers & Communications GSM team met Analog Devices in US who wished to make a first generation digital chipset for GSM; Analog Devices would fabricate and sell the chip while TTP undertook the chip development, receiving royalties in return

- Meetings with RLA led to the companies setting a 50/50 joint venture (ToneJet) in which TTP would develop printhead technology and RLA would provide toner and ink formulation

- A further joint venture called Wavedriver, this time with PowerGen, was set up to develop technology for electric cars. TTP provided the IP and PowerGen the money

- Total number of employees of the TTP Group is up to 160

- Turnover up again

1994

- The Automation division focuses on automation products for the pharmaceutical industry

- Tactical Technology (TT) division is renamed Manufacturing Technology (MT)

1995

- TTP acquires the software company Signal Computing. When Signal's parent ITN was seeking for a purchaser of the software company, Signal approached TTP. Initially TTP left the company, which had primarily dealt with the defence sector, to its own devices, but when the business did not show any signs of significant growth after several years, TTP brought in its own manager. An attempt to move the business into m-commerce in 2000 was unsuccessful and the business was closed in 2001

- The Automation division becomes The Automation Partnership (TAP), a wholly owned subsidiary of TTP, marking the completion of a four-year transition process to an accounting system and management structure appropriate for a manufacturing company

1996

- TTP establishes a software division to undertake complex software system developments in support of hardware across the entire group. This was particularly valuable for the ink jet printing development, automated equipment and instrumentation. The division was set up by a former colleague from PA. Because software could often not be seen but was essential to making much of the projects work the division was called Silent Software (SS) – an abbreviation that made the company's marketing man in Germany uneasy

- TTP sold its 50% stake in Wavedriver to PowerGen when it became clear that electric vehicles would not happen as quickly as originally anticipated – legislation in California had changed

- The first mobile phone handset incorporating the Analog Devices chipset and TTP Communications software secures type approval and goes on sale

1997

- TTP's new group structure:

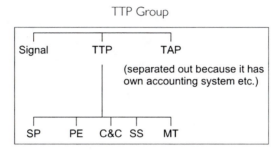

ToneJet is a separate business, which owns patents belonging to the joint venture but has no staff; the work is done by people in SP, SS, and RLA

1998

- The Computers & Communications division is set up as a separate, wholly owned business called TTP Communications (TTPCom)

- Full statutory demerger of TAP

- MT division is renamed to PID (Process & Instrumentation Division); because of the focus on life sciences it begins hiring chemists and biochemists

- Development of Myriad, a machine for synthesising new chemical entities, completed for consortium of seven pharmaceutical companies; TTP started selling the machine

- Swiss company Mettler-Toledo buys the rights to the Myriad product range and sets up a UK subsidiary, Mettler-Toledo Myriad under Richard Gray who transferred from TTP

- PID's ChemScan machine is awarded the status of a millennium product

- TTP Venture Managers is set up as a wholly owned subsidiary and the first TTP venture fund started

1999

- Libris, a joint venture for carbohydrate compound libraries, with Dextra Labs, a company specialising in carbohydrate chemistry (UK, Reading) is set up. The Myriad prototypes and the right to use them were kept and exploited through Libris. (Background: pharmaceuticals buy libraries of chemical compounds hoping that there is something in them they can use; Dextra Labs develop compounds, the Myriad machine is used to synthesise variations on these compounds to build large compound libraries. The compounds are sold to various pharmaceutical companies.)

- Apocyte, a joint venture with the University of Nottingham, is set up to work in the field of apoptosis (cell death) with the aim of discovering drug targets for a range of clinically important conditions such as cancer and wasting diseases

- IP.Access is formed from within TTPCom to exploit wireless GSM technology and the potential of the internet protocol to transport voice and data. IP.Access' mini basestations enable the use of mobile phones in areas of poor coverage as well extending their functionality so that they can be used as internal phones

- TTP Venture's first venture capital fund is closed at £35 million

2000

- TTPCom is separated through a partial statutory demerger floated on the London Stock Exchange (10% still held by TTP Group) with a market capitalisation of £540 million. TTPCom acquired IP.Access as part of the demerger. After flotation the company was 55% owned by staff and ex-staff; 45% owned by institutions (3i, RLA and new investors). In the flotation £30 million was raised by the selling shareholders and £40 million by TTP Communications.

- TTP Group has about 300 staff after the TTPCom demerger

- Odem, a joint venture with one-third each for TTP, Bespak and Pari (a private company based in Munich, Germany) is set up. TTP provided electronic aerosol technology, Pari provided high value nebulisers (about £30–£40/unit) used for respiratory conditions; Bespak provided high volume, low cost inhalers (£1–£2/unit, about 10 million units/year)

- Ashes Investments set up as a joint venture with RLA in electrographic printing (high speed and high quality web-based printing, for long and short print runs)

- Tagtec set up by a local entrepreneur with an idea for a radio tagging product. TTP developed technology and registered two patents in return for one-third of the equity. Now the company has secured external funding and TTP is working under contract to develop the product

- Melbourn Science Park Ltd is set up to run the newly acquired science park

2001

- Establish wholly owned high throughput screening subsidiary

- Establish wholly owned instrumentation development and manufacturing business

APPENDIX 29.2: TTP GROUP STRUCTURE

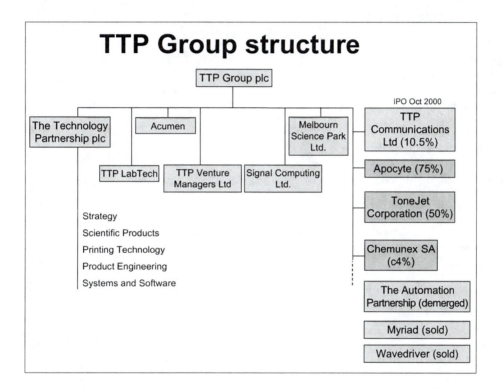

APPENDIX 29.3: FINANCIAL PERFORMANCE (FROM ANNUAL REPORT 2000)

Five year financial summary

Extracts from the consolidated profit and loss accounts of the group for the five years ended 31 March 2000 are set out below:

	1996 £000	1997 £000	1998 £000	1999 £000	2000 £000
Turnover	24,353	29,687	35,697	36,883	41,067
Cost of sales	(16,863)	(19,687)	(22,959)	(24,547)	(23,279)
Gross profit	7,490	10,000	12,738	12,336	17,788
Other operating expenses	(5,882)	(6,339)	(8,516)	(8,054)	(12,395)
Profit on sale of Myriad activities	–	–	–	5,581	–
Operating profit	1,608	3,661	4,222	9,863	5,393
(Provision for)/release of provision for investment in associates	(541)	541	–	–	–
Profits/(losses) from interests in joint ventures	(7)	(15)	36	(59)	9
Profits/(losses) from interests in associates	(4)	45	(61)	(4)	(6)
Profit on disposal of fixed asset investments	–	–	–	–	1,154
Income from investments	–	27	61	105	164
Interest receivable and similar income	118	154	296	342	266
Provision for reduction in value of investments	–	–	–	(427)	–
Interest payable and similar charges	(19)	(56)	(37)	(23)	(179)
Profit on ordinary activities before taxation	1,155	4,357	4,517	9,797	6,801
Tax on profit on ordinary activities	(380)	(1,318)	(1,461)	(1,775)	(1,943)
Minority interests	–	–	–	–	162
Dividends	(388)	(1,519)	(1,529)	(4,008)	(2,505)
Retained profit for the year	387	1,520	1,527	4,014	2,515
Statistics					
Earnings per share before exceptional items	£1.69	£2.16	£2.65	£2.46	£3.33
Earnings per share	£0.67	£2.63	£2.65	£7.06	£4.37
Diluted earnings per share before exceptional items	£1.69	£2.16	£2.65	£2.46	£3.25
Diluted earnings per share	£0.67	£2.63	£2.65	£7.05	£4.26
Dividends per ordinary share	£0.33	£1.29	£1.30	£3.40	£2.12
Group operating margin (%)	6.6	12.3	11.8	26.7	13.1

APPENDIX 29.4: THE VENTURE FUND – ARTICLE FROM *FINANCIAL NEWS*

Financial News, July 2000

Abbey pumps £5m into TTP, CAROLINE SWIFT

The well-documented profits growth of the TTP Group is enough of a pointer to see why Abbey National has just announced the commitment of £5m (€8m) to its early stage technology fund, TTP Venture Fund.

The £35m fund was launched by new venture capital firm TTP Ventures, a subsidiary of the technology development company which took the laurels as one of the UK's most successful companies in profits growth in the *Sunday Times* and PricewaterhouseCoopers' survey in May.

The fund is focused on early stage investments in technologies and industries in Western Europe in which its parent company has expertise. It is this ability to draw on TTP's skills, which has seen it acquire the backing of NPM Capital, the largest independent fund in the Netherlands as its cornerstone investor. Other investors include Boeing and Siemens and two undisclosed UK pension funds – a blue chip private sector pension fund and a local authority pension fund.

David Connell, TTP Ventures' chief executive, puts the ability to assess opportunities in science and technology as a key to investments, which so far have been made in three UK companies. "Our ability to understand and add value to science and technology-based investment propositions is proving highly attractive to both entrepreneurs and investors," he says.

The privately held TTP Group, formerly known as The Technology Partnership, a strong cash generator, has a non-discretionary co-investment in all investments. The 400-strong organisation is involved in product innovation with leading manufacturers such as Siemens, NCR, Hitachi, Gillette and GlaxoWellcome; in business strategy consulting with ICI, Shell, IBM and British Airways, and in product innovation and development contracts with companies ranging from Cadburys to Unilever.

"We are only interested in those technologies and industries we are able to assess," says Connell, who confines the fund to those with potential for superior financial returns He lists telecoms, electronics and IT equipment, instrumentation, hi-tech engineering, medical equipment and drug discovery technology, materials and chemicals.

"The businesses which we invest in must have a highly-differentiated offering, based on science or engineering. There must be a strong management team or the potential to create one," says Connell, who has no minimum investment policy.

Typical investments fall between £500,000 and £2.5m per company with initial shareholdings of 15% to 40%.

The funds chairman is serial entrepreneur Tony Davies, the chairman and managing director of Bowman Power. Other directors include Nigel Hamway, a director of Charterhouse Development Capital, John King, chairman of telecoms analysts Analysys, who is a former main board director of British Telecom, and Dr Gerald Avison, managing director of the TTP Group.

Investments by the 10-year limited-life fund include $1m invested as part of a $13m first funding round by Element-14, a business formed as a buy-out from Acorn Computers, the incubator of successful UK chip maker ARM, £500,000 in Visual Thinking International, a Glasgow-based supplier of decision management software, and the fund has led a small syndicate investing in Ashby BioSystems, a company based on patented "opencell" material for cell culture support, with applications in biotech processing and medical implants.

In the telecoms area, the venture fund draws on the expertise of TTP Communications, the telecoms subsidiary of the TTP Group and a leading provider of GSM technology to mobile phone manufacturers.

"For a fund of this kind we have to deliver very significant returns towards the top end of the VC spectrum," says Connell. "We look at highly differentiated business opportunities with the potential to deliver real value. What we have not done is limit ourselves to sectors that currently happen to be fashionable. We look at what a sector is going to deliver over the next few years and aim to beat that significantly. We are certainly looking for upper quartile performance."

30 The innovative organisation

Uncertainty and mystery are energies of life. Don't let them scare you unduly, for they keep boredom at bay and spark creativity.

R.I. Fitzhenry, Innovation Network, e-mail 11 November 2002

In the case study of the Technology Partnership almost all aspects of best practice for innovation, design and creativity are represented. Every aspect of the organisation is aligned to support the culture, to support the company's ambition. Systems, processes, leadership style and culture all enforce one another and we find illustrations of best practice discussed in previous chapters such as an emergent strategy, strong emphasis on internal and external collaboration, conscious use of the physical work environment and a learning culture.

Two aspects that have played their part in each of the 10 case studies and are paramount for creating a successful organisation but have not yet been discussed are the main subjects of this chapter: leadership style and culture.

LEADERSHIP – THE MOST CRITICAL INGREDIENT

Those who have changed the universe have never done it by changing officials, but always by inspiring the people.

Napoleon Bonaparte

If there is one single factor that is critical to innovation success it is committed and supportive leadership. In the literature there is far-reaching consensus about the importance of top management support in enabling successful new product development and innovation. Without clear senior management approval and encouragement innovation activities will lack a sense of importance and urgency – and as a consequence attention and commitment by participating individuals and functions; clear signals from the top are key. But there is also the issue of leadership which is different from senior management support.

Leadership can take place at any level within the organisation and whereas 'management' is about directing people, about efficiency, structuring and organising, leadership is about motivating people and about inspiring them to go the extra mile – something that is often required in innovative projects. "Leadership is about inspiring individuals to higher levels of performance", as Professor Rob Goffee, London Business School, puts it. In the Black & Decker case study it was the inspirational and supportive leadership from the top through Stephen Bird, Marketing Director Europe and Lawrie Cunningham, Director of Innovation, providing a balance between encouragement and freedom, which facilitated the creation of an innovative power tool. In the case study of Dumfries Recycling the licence to innovate and explore around the creation of products made from recycled material came from the very top of the organisation, from Cameron McLatchie, Chairman and CEO of BPI, the parent company. In a way, top management commitment is a qualifier, something that allows innovative projects to be initiated and developed, but what makes projects happen is generally the leadership at the project level. In fact, sometimes the leadership and determination at the project level can push projects through despite resistance at higher levels.[1] The BBC case study is an example of strong leadership at the project level. It was Tim's ability to enthuse his collaboration partners (Framestore), secure funding and manage the interface with senior management within the BBC thereby ensuring that the project team could get on with their work.

> The 3M Post-it notes happened despite having been rejected by senior management several times. Based on unofficial trials with secretaries in the organisation the project leader was convinced that there would be a market for his product. Using his 15% 'free time' he continued to develop and market test the product until its potential became undeniable.
>
> A lesson from this story is: ensure you embed innovation into your culture and systems, and it can thrive despite scepticism of senior managers (but, ultimately, senior management does have to believe in it).

Before going further into what makes for good leadership I would like to point out three fundamentals about leadership. First, leadership is non-hierarchical, meaning that it can happen at any level in the organisation. Second, leadership is relational, meaning that there is no leadership without followers; leadership is about the relationship between people. Third, leadership is contextual. What kind of leadership is most effective and how best to inspire people will depend on the context. Leading a bunch of academics is likely to require a different approach to leading a group of accountants or a battalion of soldiers.

Whatever the level, what makes good leadership? Research commissioned by the DTI and CBI in 1995 identified the following six traits as characteristics of good leaders:

- enthusiasm
- championing change
- communicating
- leading by example
- tolerating risk, and
- being open (approachable, willing to listen)

While it is not quite clear what 'good' meant in the context of the survey, it seems that a person with such characteristics would also make a good innovation champion. Findings from the Innovation Best Practice interviews certainly identified the ability to inspire people as one of the key characteristics of successful innovation leaders (von Stamm, 2001).

---

[1] For characteristics of successful project leaders see Chapter 3.

Insights into what it actually means to be an inspirational leader are provided by Goffee and Jones (2000). In their work they have identified four traits of inspirational leaders, all of which seem to be about being oneself, about empathy and sincerity, and about confidence:

- They selectively show their weaknesses. By exposing some vulnerability, they reveal their approachability and humanity.

- They rely heavily on intuition to gauge the appropriate timing and course of their actions. Their ability to collect and interpret soft data helps them to know just when and how to act.

- They manage employees with something we call tough empathy. Inspirational leaders empathise passionately – and realistically – with people, and they care intensely about the work employees do.

- They reveal their differences. They capitalise on what's unique about themselves.

I would like to explore each of the four characteristics in a little more detail.

Situation sensing[2]

Goffee and Jones's first characteristic of effective leaders is their ability to sense and understand situations. Considering that business, fundamentally, is about encounters and relationships. Connecting with people, understanding motivations and concerns, and being able to read situations is important for successful business transactions.

Without anyone having to spell it out, such leaders pick up signals that help them explain what is happening: they can sense tension, reservations, resistance and support. But not only that, they not only *read* the context they are also actively *influencing and shaping* it, often creating an alternative context. In short, they understand the limitations and opportunities of context. So, they do not take the existing context as an unchangeable given but shape the context they inherit in a way that helps them achieve their goal. The ability to understand situations also helps them to know where and when to make compromises, and when to stick to their guns.

But great leaders do not only rely on their intuition when reading situations. They do their homework and try to ensure they know as much as possible about the situation and people they are about to encounter. They often keep logs of their contacts, making sure they are aware of important personal information, insights and preferences. It is about building a complete picture of a person, not only the business persona visible in the office. But it is not about collecting information, such leaders have a real interest in people, they *want* to know. To achieve that they engage in two-way conversations, asking a lot of questions. Really getting to know a person tends to be easier in informal settings. And, by the way, helping people discover and develop their own talent is part of this process.

In the context of larger meetings it is also important to understand interactions between the individuals who are part of that group.

---

[2] The following section is based on the book as well as an in-depth interview conducted by the author with Rob Goffee, November 2006.

According to Goffee and Jones the ability to sense relies on three skill sets:

1.   Observational and cognitive skills (Knowing when to challenge, support, boost morale etc.; observing before taking action). Sensing is primarily based on observation.

2.   Behavioural and adaptive skills (knowing when and how to adjust own behaviour; looking for feedback and ensuring that the received feedback is honest). Participants pointed out that the ability to sense varies with context, i.e. at some times we are better able to sense than at others.

3.   Use own behaviour to change situation.

The rhythm of leaders is: observe – understand – adapt – rewrite. Goffee and Jones warn not to make the mistake of doing situation sensing only at the outset.

While some people are better at sensing than others, sensing skills can be improved. One key tool for this is to ask for feedback – and ensure that it is/can be honest. Another is to put yourself outside your comfort zone.

What can you do to improve conditions for sensing in your organisation? Encourage face-to-face meetings; make sure it is safe to venture personal and critical points of view. Make time for people to ask questions.

Tough empathy

Effective leaders evoke high levels of emotional response, loyalty and affection. They do that by being able to balance closeness and remoteness. Closeness evokes loyalty and commitment, and is about showing positive emotions. Truly caring leads to the ability to balance the respect for the individual and the need to achieve the task at hand/the shared higher purpose. Because followers feel a real and true interest in them as individuals, it is easier for them to accept tough decisions, particularly as these are generally made as a necessary part of the journey to achieve the desired goal. Take for example the story about Admiral Lord Nelson: Nelson had been wounded in battle and his aides were keen to get him to see the surgeon straight away whereupon he insisted, "I'll take my turn alongside my brave men." With this he showed the true respect and appreciation of his sailors. The 'empathy' bit implies a desire to help them improve and grow. In the end, as Rod Goffee put it, it is about giving people what they need rather than what they want.

In the interview Rob Goffee also pointed out that those at the top of an organisation are more likely to suffer from too much distance rather than too little. He advises to watch out for aspects that increase distance, such as separate parking or catering facilities for the top. However, remoteness is important when dealing with management performance, and is essential when having to make tough decisions if and when required. Distance is also essential when it is required to be able to see the bigger picture.

One potential issue is that for us as human beings it is easier to be close to those who are like us – but leaders cannot afford to be close only to those who are like them, they need to be able to engage with a wide range of different people. This is particularly important in the context of innovation. In homogeneous groups innovation is much less likely to happen than in highly diverse groups – though of course diverse groups are much harder to manage.

In terms of when to be close and when to be distant Goffee and Jones advise: "Be distant when telling *what* to do, be close when you talk about the *how*."

Revealing weaknesses

In the section above we emphasised that authenticity is essential. Part of being authentic means not only showing your strengths but also revealing your weaknesses. But of course the revealing of the weaknesses has to be done carefully. For example, each profession has some weaknesses that would be unacceptable and that would undermine the credibility of the leader: a skipper of a yacht declaring that he does not understand navigation would probably leave him without a crew. It is also advisable to establish credibility and strength first before revealing any weaknesses.

There are several reasons why revealing weaknesses has positive rather than negative consequences. First, pretending to be perfect and infallible only provokes others to seek the weak spot: in a way, denying weaknesses increases rather than decreases leaders' vulnerability. Admitting to a (non-critical) weakness makes leaders more human in the eyes of their followers. Another aspect of revealing a weakness is that it gives others an opportunity to help: people want real people not someone who is perfect. If the leader reveals enough of himself to show he is not perfect he also allows the followers to be less than perfect too. Think for example of Virgin's Richard Branson. He is such a successful business man and icon yet in front of the camera he seems insecure and nervous. Instead of engaging personal trainers and coaches to makes his public appearances smoother he does not seem to mind, he remains who he is. This enables others to think, if he does not worry about being nervous, it is OK for me to be nervous in public speaking situations too!

Points of caution on revealing weaknesses:

- Be careful not to serve up strength as weakness, e.g. 'I am too ambitious'.

- Don't cover up a real weakness with a fake one.

- Reveal your weaknesses – but do not let them rule you, e.g. BBC Director General Greg Dyke had a tendency to lose his temper and later apologise; he had to be careful not to do that too often.

Daring to be different

The last characteristic of effective leaders is that they dare to be different. Leaders are true to themselves, they do not conform to general expectations. But their difference is also important and meaningful to the followers. Think again of Richard Branson. The first thing that comes to mind about him is his casualness. It is possibly difficult to picture him in a suit and tie. He is different, he is casual, and through that communicates a lot about his attitude and outlook on life. He is liked by his 'followers' for defying the (business) system, and staying who he is. The casualness also says something about his past, where he came from; along similar lines leaders often reveal their past to 'explain' who they are and what they stand for. Good leaders know their differences and use them to their advantage. Personal story-telling ability is important, the way you reveal things about yourself and give people insights into what is really different about you (i.e. giving them a reason to follow *you* rather than someone else).

Some final thoughts about being yourself:

- We need to realise who we are before we understand better why we do certain things rather than others.

- We are mostly ourselves when what we enjoy is aligned with what we do – so be selective in career!

- We are ourselves most when we feel trusted and valued – an important message if you want to get the most out of your followers.

- If there is a difference between the you at home and the you at work you may want to ask yourself whether that can work long term.

- Be aware of a tendency of falling back into certain behaviours in certain context, e.g. being the youngest child rather than the experienced business person when you are back in your family context, or having difficulties being respected and accepted as a teacher in a place where you have been a student (by those who taught you).

- Many effective leaders use visual clues to signal their difference, e.g. Branson's casualness.

In a workshop on 'Leadership for Innovation' run by the Innovation Leadership Forum November 2006 participants agreed that all four characteristics of the Goffee–Jones framework were important to innovation. In addition innovation leaders were described as follows, "They have a strong future-oriented and external focus; they are by nature curious, have tenacity and a lot of passion for their cause which enables them (a) to tolerate failure and focus on the learning they can gain from it, and (b) to create a culture in which innovation can flourish."

In order for leaders to inspire people to innovate they themselves have to be open towards change and experimentation. Someone with a low score on Kirton's adaptor–innovator scale (see Chapter 10) might be a good leader, but not a great champion for innovation as his or her preference will be to improve things incrementally rather than encourage and implement step changes. A person who likes to drive change has a different profile from a person who is good at optimising things and making sure they run smoothly. While most senior managers nowadays seem to buy into the argument that innovation is important to their organisation's long-term success, their personal preference may be for incremental changes. In that case they will not be the most appropriate person to lead an organisation's change initiative or to improve innovation performance (see Figure 30.1). This may account for some of the discrepancies between what is said in annual reports and public statements – 'We believe that innovation is a major contributor to our organisation's growth' – and everyday reality where radical ideas are adjusted and changed until they seem less threatening and conform more with what is tried and tested. Kirton's questionnaire might be a good starting point for identifying people who would make good change and innovation leaders.

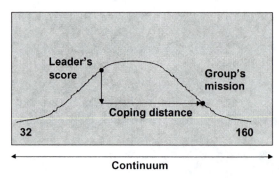

Figure 30.1   Finding the right leader.
Source: Reproduced from Prather, C.W. & Turrell, M.C. (2002). Involve everyone in the innovation process. *Research Technology Management*, 13–16.

There are also a number of checklists and list with suggestions on how to improve the climate for innovation within an organisation. In Box 30.1 you will find Thomas Kuczmarski's (1998) 20 questions for leaders who want to find out whether they are actually creating the right conditions for innovation to flourish.

Box 30.1   Questions for innovation leaders

Kuczmarski, 1998.

1. Do I currently incorporate innovation into our business plan as a strategic lever for increasing satisfaction with shareholders, employees, and customers?

2. Have I consciously used innovation and launched new products to help accelerate my company's stock price or increase my company's value?

3. Have I purposely developed a balanced portfolio of new product types with varying degrees of risk ranging from radically new-to-the-world to line extensions and repositionings?

4. Do I teach my management team to view innovation as an investment opportunity rather than as a cost center that negatively impacts quarterly earnings?

5. Do I have a commonly agreed-upon innovation strategy in place that links the role of innovation and new products to our business strategy?

6. Have I made innovation an attractive career path for employees to pursue?

7. Do I regularly celebrate, with all team members, new product failures with as much fervor as new product successes?

8. Do I uniformly communicate and act in ways that clearly convey trust in the cross-functional teams that are activating innovation?

9. Do I stimulate an entrepreneurial environment by having a performance-based compensation system in place for new product participants?

10. Do I measure and communicate throughout the organization the return on innovation for our company?

11. Do I really know how much innovation costs, and do I set realistic return expectations for innovation?

12. Do I provide 'ceilingless' and motivating compensation rewards to new-product participants and allow them to invest in the new products they are developing?

13. Do I select the best people within the company (for example, those I feel I can't afford to remove from the existing business) to activate the new-product process?

14. Do I make sure we conduct consumer research prior to idea generation to identify problems and needs?

15.   Do I ensure that idea generation is a problem-solving endeavor aimed at generating potential solutions to address consumer needs?

16.   Do I maintain funding and resource allocation for innovation at a consistent level rather than pulling the plug after a 'down' quarter?

17.   Do I truly accept that 40 to 50 percent of our future new-product launches will fail?

18.   Do all R&D people get at least 15 percent 'free time' (unassigned to any specific project) to give them room to breathe and freedom to explore their own ideas?

19.   Do I have a well-articulated technology strategy that defines technology platforms and areas of needed technical expertise to help support the innovation initiatives?

20.   Do I hear others throughout the organization talk about my positive, enthusiastic, supportive, and 'can-do' attitude toward innovation?

Source: Reproduced from Kuczmarski, 1998

The second is from Rosabeth Moss Kanter's (1983) book *The Change Masters*, first published over 20 years ago. She suggested five ways in which managers can improve an organisation's environment for innovation:

1.   **Encouragement of a culture of pride** – highlight the achievements of the company's own people through visible awards, through applying an innovation from one area to the problems of another, and letting the experienced innovators serve as 'consultants'.

2.   **Enlarge access to power tools for innovative problem solving** – provide vehicles (a council? An R&D committee? Direct access to the steering committees?) to support proposals for experiments and innovations – especially for those involving teams or collaborators across areas.

3.   **Improvement of lateral communications** – bring departments together; encourage cross-fertilisation through exchange of people, mobility across areas; create cross-functional links, and perhaps even overlaps; bring together teams of people from different areas who share responsibility for some aspects of the same end product.

4.   **Reduction of unnecessary layers of hierarchy** – eliminate barriers to resource access; make it possible for people to go directly after what they need; push decisional authority downward; create 'diagonal' slices cutting across the hierarchy to share information, provide quick intelligence about external and internal affairs.

5.   **Increased, and earlier, information about company plans** – where possible reduce secretiveness; avoid surprises; increase security by making future plans known in advance, making it possible, in turn, for those below to make their plans; give people at lower levels a chance to contribute to the shape of change before decisions are made at the top; empower and involve them at an earlier point, e.g. through task forces and problem-solving groups or through more open-ended, change-oriented assignments, with more room left for the person to define that approach.

Her list really summarises what still is the essence of innovation best practice, covering all aspects from leadership to strategy and vision, to the work environment and culture. Interestingly she does not mention processes as such. But the two lists above also reinforce that the single most influential factor in facilitating – or hindering – the right climate for innovation and design to flourish are the company's leaders. Aspects of a culture that support innovation, creativity and design, and other relevant issues around culture, will be explored further in the following section.

Before moving on to company culture I would like to introduce briefly the concept of 'Theory U' by academic Otto Scharmer (2007). The theory describes a process for leaders to achieve change and create a desired future. At the core of the process is 'presencing' whereby the term 'presencing' combines the words 'presence' and 'sensing'. It refers to a heightened state of attention "that allows individuals and groups to shift to an inner place from which they function". Scharmer continues, "When that shift happens, people begin to operate from a future space of possibility that they feel wants to emerge. Being able to facilitate that shift is the essence of leadership today."

The starting point for the concept was the observation that "successful leadership depends on the quality of attention that the leaders brings to any situation". The question then was, how can the quality of attention be improved? Scharmer's answer is Theory U, a process that, not surprisingly, describes a U curve – going down the curve: diving into a situation/problem to observe and understand; being at the bottom: reflecting and envisioning; going up the curve: developing a new, desired state of the future; hence the name 'Theory U'.

Scharmer describes five steps:

1.   Co-initiating – which involves the building of a common intent which in turn requires leaders to stop and listen to others and to what life calls them to do (see Box 30.2 for different types of listening).

2.   Co-sensing – which involves to observe, observe, observe: Scharmer advises to go to the places of most potential and listen with your mind and heart wide open.

3.   Presencing – which involves connecting to the source of inspiration, and will: it requires the leader to go to the 'place of silence' and allow the inner knowing to emerge.

4.   Co-creating – which involves prototyping the new, living examples to explore the future by doing.[3]

5.   Co-evolving – building on the learning from the prototyping, the new needs to be embodied in the ecosystems and consider the whole.

Being able to follow this process is not easy and Scharmer has identified barriers on the way down as well as on the way up. What prevents us from going down the U curve are the typical enemies of innovation: judgement, cynicism and fear. On the way up the enemies are: executing without improvisation and mindfulness (reactive action), endless reflection without a will to act (analysis paralysis), and talking without a connection to course and action (blah blah blah). In his words, "These prevent the balancing of head, heart and hand."

---

[3] Interestingly Scharmer also notes that current education is quite wrong for innovation, and that designers are the ones most likely to have the required skill set, not least because of their use of prototypes.

Box 30.2   Types of listening

Scharmer differentiates four different kinds of listening:

- **Downloading**: listening by reconfirming habitual judgements (past).

- **Factual listening**: paying attention to facts and to novel or disconfirming data (current it world).

- **Emphatic listening**: engaging in real dialogue and paying careful attention; seeing the world through someone else's eyes (open heart) (current you world).

- **Generative listening**: listening from the emerging field of future possibility (open heart and open will) (highest future possibility that is wanting to emerge).

Source: Based on Scharmer, 2007

THE ROLE OF COMPANY CULTURE

Culture consists of patterns, explicit and implicit of and for behaviour acquired and transmitted by symbols, constituting the distinctive achievement of human groups, including their embodiment in artefacts; the essential core of culture consists of traditional (i.e. historically derived and selected) ideas and especially their attached values; culture systems may, on the one hand, be considered as products of action, on the other, as conditioning elements of future action.

Kroeber and Kluckhohn (1952)

I would like to introduce a model for understanding company culture that, again, has been developed by Goffee and Jones (1998). The model of culture is based around the concepts of sociability and solidarity. Sociability is in essence friendliness. This suggests that people enjoy working together, they tend to have fun and they are generally more creative. It works because friendships are not based upon careful calculations of who has done what for who. Solidarity is a measure of how you get things done. So, comments like 'I don't like, Peter, but he is the best store manager' would be typical in an organisation with high solidarity. Such organisations have a real shared interest in what has to be done – focus and efficiency. Combining these two dimensions leads to four possible cultures:

- Networked cultures (high sociability, low solidarity) – unashamedly marvellously friendly. Go to such an organisation's training centre, it is likely to have a bar that's open 24/7. The main reason for people to go there is not to drink but to talk.

- Fragmented cultures (low sociability, low solidarity) – universities, running a university is like herding cats; all specialists who'd rather not talk to each other.

- Mercenary cultures (high solidarity, low sociability) – a company that's strongly driven by results. You might hear comments such as, 'We were all working very well together and then all of a sudden one of us just disappears!' Gone! They missed their quarterly targets.

- Communal cultures (high sociability, high solidarity) – companies that live their vision.

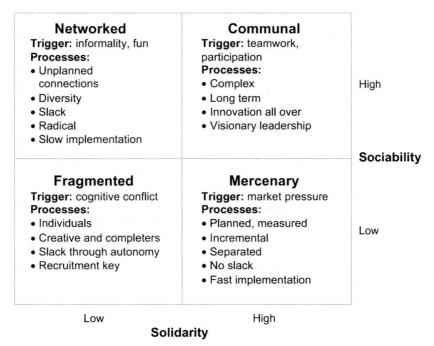

Figure 30.2 How innovation happens.
Source: Based on Goffee & Jones 1998 and presentation notes from Innovation Exchange conference, December 2001.

There is no right or wrong. Organisations of each culture can be successful or unsuccessful, and all four cultures have their 'dark side' where the benefits turn into disadvantages or negatives. In each of the four cultures innovation is likely to have different triggers, and innovation-related processes are likely to have different characteristics – see Figure 30.2. As a general rule, positive aspects of the cultures tend to support innovation and negative aspects tend to hinder innovation.

What are the key issues around creating a culture for design, creativity and innovation? First of all, we have just established that creating the right culture is key to innovation, and that the most influential person in establishing culture is a company's leader. Second, it is important to note that when trying to change a culture towards increased innovativeness many companies encounter resistance. There is a general reluctance to change that seems to be part of human nature as well as some specific reasons to object changes such as a loss of power or autonomy. As Italian political philosopher, musician and poet Niccolò Machiavelli said so fittingly almost 500 years ago, "There is nothing more difficult to take in hand, more perilous to conduct, or more uncertain in its success, than to take the lead in the introduction of a new order of things. Because the innovator has for enemies all those who have done well under the old conditions, and lukewarm (indifferent, uninterested) defenders in those who may do well under the new."

To expand on this, research by von Stamm (2001) indicates that many companies move towards stronger central-isation to coordination innovation activities and better harness the benefits (see also Chapter 4). However, as

> "I strongly believe that the person at the top is the person with the most influence on company culture."

many organisations used to have decentralised structures with far-reaching autonomy of the regions, the shift
towards centralisation means that they would have to give
up their power and coordinate stronger with the centre.

> "Our new CEO is single-handedly changing the culture."

Third, there may also be aspects of a company's heritage that go against the grain of what innovation is about. Again to give an example from the Innovation Best Practice research, a scientist-based company commented on the fact that collaboration – a central aspect of innovation – tends to be seen as a weakness by scientists. It is therefore important to uncover and understand any aspects of an organisation's cultural and heritage that might get in the way of changing towards greater innovativeness.

Finally there are certain characteristics that are typically found in an innovation culture – most of which are implicit in the two lists above. The arguably most important ones will be discussed briefly below.

Experimentation and termination

One of the key characteristics of innovative organisations is their willingness to *experiment*. Coming up with a range of feasible starting points for experimentation also includes the *challenging* of the status quo. One reason stated by Gerald Avison to float TTP Com was that they had not done this before. However, if you experiment and play around you cannot expect every attempt to succeed. For example, TTP did not hesitate to pull out of the Hydro Car venture when it turned out that legislation and resulting time frames would delay progress significantly.

Three further characteristics of an innovation culture follow from that. First, an essential part of the experimentation culture is the *acceptance of failure* – though, interestingly, innovative organisations tend not to speak of failure but of a 'learning experience'. Second, if you start with many different options, exploring a number of different avenues you also have to have the ability and willingness to terminate projects. The art lies in starting as broad as possible and narrowing down as quickly as feasible. Innovation Agency IDEO has the motto of 'failing often but failing early'. Finally, innovative companies are not only good at killing projects at an early stage, they are also good at analysing projects, particularly ones that have failed or been discontinued at a late stage, to see what can be learned from why and how they went wrong.

A further characteristic of an innovation culture related to the habit of experimentation is the 'can-do' approach. It is best encapsulated in the typical 3M line of 'it is better to ask for forgiveness than permission'. People in innovative organisations feel at liberty to try things out and experiment, often without asking explicit permission from anyone before doing so. The following example is from aforementioned IDEO. An employee, usually travelling to the office on his bicycle, never quite knew where to put it upon arrival. He started hoisting it up into the beams of the roof construction. No one complained, no one needed to be asked for permission, and soon others copied the idea.

This displays a degree of ownership and feeling at home that many organisations lack. If people feel comfortable to experiment and explore they are more likely to bring forward some 'ridiculous' idea they have – and of course there is the saying that if an idea does not seem ridiculous at first it is probably not worth pursuing. Another example of what can happen if people feel free to bring themselves to work is again described by Hargadon and Sutton (2000).

One of IDEO's designers, Dennis Boyle, was in the habit of brining samples of his vast collection of things – toy cars, robots, prototypes from previous projects and other assorted objects – to brainstorming sessions and other occasions in the office. He describes the items as "A congealed process-three-dimensional snapshots of the ideas from previous projects." It was his collector's habit that seeded the idea for the materials libraries, cabinets with over 400 materials and products, which can now be found in each of the eight IDEO offices around the world (also referred to in Chapter 27).

Collaboration and competition

The importance of collaboration to innovation has already been elaborated upon in Chapter 13. Innovative companies engage in collaboration, be it internally through cross-functional teams, or externally through joint ventures, alliances, or less structured forms of networking. But many innovative organisations also believe in the value of internal and external competition, though this does not tend to be cut-throat competition with high levels of secrecy or fierce and negative politics. It has more to do with setting up competing project teams that spur each other to higher performance where when the best teams wins, the 'losers' are happy to support the winners on their way forward. In a company with a positive competitive culture to lose is not equal to losing face or missing out on the next potential promotion. In companies that believe in collaboration people cannot help but to collaborate, as Hargadon and Sutton (2000) report from a visit at IDEO:

> IDEO's studios are also laid out so that everyone sees and hears everyone else's design problems. We witnessed hundreds of unplanned interactions in which designers overheard nearby conversations, realized that they could help, and stopped whatever they were doing to make suggestions. One day we were sitting with engineers Larry Shubert and Roby Stancel, who were designing a device for an electric razor that would vacuum up cut hair. We were meeting at a table in front of Rickson Sun's workstation. He soon shut his sliding door to muffle the noise from our meeting, but he could still hear us. He emerged a few minutes later to say he'd once worked on a similar design problem: a vacuum system for carrying away fumes from a hot scalpel that cauterized skin during surgery. Sun brought out samples of tubing that might be used in the new design and a report he had written about the kinds of plastic tubing available from vendors. The encounter shows how having the right attitude drives people to help each other solve problems. Shubert commented, "Once Rickson realized he could help us, he had to do it or he wouldn't be a good IDEO designer."

Fun and focus

A third trait is a combination of fun and focus. Fun, exploration and play are all aspects that prepare a fertile ground for innovation. A humorous atmosphere encourages ideas and suggestions, makes 'failure' more bearable and allows the exploration of seemingly silly ideas. But at the same time successful innovation cultures are result-oriented – as reflected in TTP's vision statement that reads 'Have fun and make money'.

It is actually a myth that innovation is strangled through focus or constraints. Max de Pree writes, "Creative persons, like the rest of us, need constraints. The famous industrial designer Charles Eames once called restraints 'liberating'.

And I doubt that Rembrandt ever began a painting on an unlimited canvas. One of the most striking characteristics of the creative persons I know is their ability to renew themselves through constraints." The widely held view that 3M allows its scientists 15% of their time to explore their own ideas means total and utter freedom is not quite true. Scientists at 3M are well aware of the core technologies and areas of business on which the company focuses and most of their innovations are within and between what the core of the company is about. Providing no framework at all for innovation can lead to the development of concepts and ideas that do not have anything whatsoever to do with the company, resulting in wastage of valuable company resources.

On the other hand innovative companies show a remarkable degree of flexibility as to their company's direction. 3M started as a mining company and has been involved in a number of different industries during its existence. Pearson is another example of a company that has morphed and changed throughout its existence. Having started out as a construction company in 1844 Pearson moved into media in 1920 and says about itself, "Today, Pearson is all about education. We help teachers teach, students learn, train professionals and enrich minds." So many innovative organisations are characterised by an ability to shift and change their focus, letting go of areas that used to be the core of their expertise. So it is 'letting go' of things not only at the project level as indicated above, it is also the ability to let go of 'projects' at the business level.

Alignment of systems and processes

A fourth characteristic of an innovative organisation is that all systems and processes, particularly concerning those related to human resource management are set out to support an innovation culture. The TTP case study provides some good examples hereof.

Human resource policy, including recruitment and remuneration, are particularly critical factors as they determine how things are done and what is valued within an organisation. They should reinforce company strategy and support the culture. If a culture of teamwork and cooperation is desired but rewards and remuneration of employees are based on their individual achievements, people will be reluctant to cooperate and share. If people are recruited based on their technical qualifications alone rather than being also assessed on their 'cultural' fit with the organisation managers will at best end up with the sum of the parts. The more important teamwork and cooperation are for a company's success, the more emphasis should be placed on the right 'soft' skills. It might also be worth considering what kind of person is required, no organisation can survive with 'innovators' or 'adaptors' alone, a good mix of different skills and strengths is required to come up with great ideas, *and* realise them in the marketplace.

It starts with their recruitment and the signals they are sending through their website to potential applicants (see Box 30.3 for the recruitment text from their website www.ttp.com). Once an applicant has entered the process he or she has the opportunity to talk to current employees, as well as to the CEO. All this also reflects the open and flat-hierarchy culture. Once an employee has joined he or she might even get the opportunity to influence company direction, as two people who suggested the setting up of an investment fund or Anne Miller, who suggested the establishment of a subsidiary to provide creativity and innovation training services. When she had the idea she did not spend days or weeks on developing elaborate business plans but took her idea straight to the CEO who, as she knew, would be open and willing to listen. Of course, once the idea was discussed a business plan was developed with all necessary details and diligence. The commitment to its employees is also reflected in a subsidised canteen and support of sports activities.

Box 30.3 Recruitment text from TTP's website

Mavericks. Non-conformists. Revolutionaries.

In other words, our kind of people.

TTP provides solutions to problems that in many cases the industry is not yet aware exist. We identify situations where new technology is able to satisfy a market need. We then develop the product.

Smart, fresh thinking is critical to our growth and on-going success. We recruit outstanding minds. We want to hear from enthusiastic, energetic people who can identify market opportunities and come up with fresh, effective, ingenious solutions to problems ahead of deadlines.

The facilities, core technologies and training are of a jaw-dropping quality at TTP. And not only is the work environment first class, but everybody has a voice in the way we conduct our business too.

We're here to have fun and make money. It's our mission statement. What's yours?

Communication processes also play an important part in TTP. The informal presentation meetings on Friday afternoons provide employees with a platform to test their presentation skills, allow them to bring themselves into the organisation, and foster informal networks between members from different parts of the organisation. Further ways of fostering informality, familiarity and networking are the policy of keeping individual business units below 200 people, working through multiple overlapping project teams and dynamic desks which mean that people get mixed up on a regular basis.

True to its mission of 'Having fun and making money' the company has also the tendency to devolve businesses. As Anne Miller commented in a presentation to members of the Innovation Exchange in May 2001, "We believe that continually devolving power and businesses supports innovation and growth and is good for our existing shareholders and employees. However, this strategy might not be right for everyone as it makes the business difficult to value, and it's bad for the MD's ego."

The human resource function can in itself become a source of innovation, as the example from an insurance company illustrates. There was an increasing concern that the senior management was too much out of touch with technology development, primarily the advance of the internet. A conversation between the manager of the e-commerce section and the HR people led to the development of a scheme through which board members would be matched up with young high flyers, familiar with the internet and world wide web.

Design awareness

To create a strong company culture, reflecting what the company stands for, the values and beliefs ought to be reflected in everything it does and produces. Management, leadership and the human resource function can establish the values and facilitate and encourage the right behaviours. Design and design management can facilitate the accurate visual representation of the beliefs and values and ensure consistency in the physical appearance and representation of the organisation, including products, any form of company literature and the physical work environment (see also Chapter 27). In companies such as BMW that have placed design at the core of their strategy, it is the role of design management at the strategic level to ensure visual consistency and the alignment of the company's interfaces (products, services, other forms of communication such as promotional literature, advertising, etc.) with company strategy and company culture. The role of a strategic design manager is also to ensure that an awareness for the value and contribution of design in the organisation is maintained, as Blaich and Blaich (1993) point out in their book *Product Design and Corporate Strategy*.

Commitment to innovation

Finally, innovative companies are committed to the course of innovation, they do not change policies, dissolve innovation teams or cancel projects because economic times are getting a bit more difficult. A survey conducted by the Innovation Exchange in spring 2002[4] revealed that companies that consider themselves to have a positive attitude towards innovation tend to spend more, not less, on innovation when times get difficult. And interestingly, but not surprisingly, those companies who indicated a positive attitude towards innovation in general seemed to have fared better than companies who cut back on innovation (see Box 30.4). This was reflected in increased market share and/or profitability in comparison with the industry, as well as increased profitability in the current year.

Box 30.4   Benefits from being an innovator

- Seventy per cent of organisations with a positive attitude towards innovation declared that they are outperforming their competitors (an additional 17% felt their performance was at least level with their competitors).

- Those companies that have seen an increase in profits over past years all possess a positive attitude towards innovation.

- These companies also tend to have larger market shares than their closest competitors.

Source: von Stamm, B. & Riley, D. (2002). Innovation in turbulent times. Unpublished Report to Members of the Innovation Exchange

---

According to the survey companies that subscribe to innovation are also more likely to engage in radical innovation, and are successful at it. Those organisations that were successful in the past indicated that in future they are planning: (a) innovation in additional areas, for example strategic, operational and/or organisational; and (b) more radical innovation than in the past. Success seems to increase companies' willingness to take risks, creating a positive momentum for innovation.

---

[4] The survey was conducted between April and May 2002 by Dr Bettina von Stamm for the Innovation Exchange, in collaboration with the InnovationNetwork (www.thinksmart.com) and the Design Management Institute (www.dmi.org).

I would like to finish with two quotes:

If most of us are ashamed of shabby clothes and shoddy furniture, let us be more ashamed of shabby ideas and shoddy philosophies.

Albert Einstein

Don't worry about people stealing an idea. If it's original, you will have to ram it down their throats.

Howard Aiken

READING SUGGESTIONS

Goffee, R. & Jones, G. (1998). *The Character of a Corporation: How Your Company's Culture Can Make or Break Your Business*. HarperCollins.

Comment: Building on their earlier Harvard Business Review article, they expand and develop their framework. Full of case studies and examples.

Goffee, R. & Jones, G. (2006). *Why Should Anyone be Led by You?* Harvard Business School Press.

Comment: This book too builds on an earlier *Harvard Business Review* article. Brought to life through many examples from their work with companies on both sides of the pond.

Clegg, B. (1999). *Creativity and Innovation for Managers*. Butterworth-Heinemann.

Comment: Useful and easy-to-read book on innovation; useful stuff including mechanisms for innovation, training, rewards and remuneration for innovation, etc.

Kuczmarski, T. (1996). *Innovation – Leadership Strategies for the Competitive Edge*. NTC Business Books.

Comment: This book, equally relevant for the Leadership section, provides some good insights about how to lead innovation from the top; it has a few checklists and questionnaires that might help determine how you or your CEO (as an innovation leaders) make do – Kuczmarski's questionnaire on the Innovation Mind Set can also be found on the Innovation Exchange website (library).

Changes in the world and innovation

Since the publication of the first edition of this book the world of innovation has evolved. Processes and tools have been developed to help organisations to become more adept at innovation. So while some parts of the world's map of innovation have been coloured in, new lands have emerged and new paths around the world of innovation are being explored.

We will start this chapter with a brief look at the next items on the innovation agenda. Some of the developments that have moved from the fringes closer to the centre of attention are discontinuous innovation, open innovation and user-led innovation. We have already discussed issues around open and user-led innovation in Chapter 13. This chapter will provide an overview of thinking around discontinuous innovation. I will draw on the work of Clayton Christensen who has brought the topic to the forefront of managers' attention with his book *Innovator's Dilemma* (1997) and subsequently by *Innovator's Solution* (2003) and *Seeing What's Next*. A second source I am drawing on for the subject of discontinuous innovation is a project to understand better how companies currently address the issue of discontinuous innovation, which was supported by the Advanced Institute of Management (www.aimresearch.org).[1] We will actually see that open innovation and user-led innovation have an important role to play in preparing for discontinuous innovation.

I will close this chapter by taking a look at developments in the wider economic and social environment that have implications for the way we do business.

THE NEXT INNOVATION CHALLENGES

Let us take a look at some of the next big challenges around innovation identified in the latest round of Innovation Best Practice research (for a more comprehensive list see Appendix B).

Encouraging a systemic view of innovation – in Chapter 21 we have already discussed the different approaches to infusing innovation used by organisations in the past, namely either a process- or a people-centred

---

[1] The programme started in spring 2006 and is based on collaboration between universities and groups of companies in Denmark, Germany and the UK (further countries such as Australia, France and Sweden have since joined the programme). The programme is structured around the three phases of the innovation process, search, selection and implementation. Activities involved a mixture of experience-sharing workshops (both in host countries and internationally) coupled with in-depth case research. The first report, on the search phase, has been published by AIM in autumn 2007.

approach. However, processes and structures alone are not enough and more and more organisations realise that innovation requires an approach that touches all the different aspects of an organisation and that creating an innovative organisation is, fundamentally, about a company's culture and leadership. While this realisation is becoming more widespread, the challenge remains how to translate the insight into company reality.

Creating effective idea management systems – despite the fact that there is a lot of knowledge and insight around idea management, there is still a large number of organisations that struggle with this aspect of the innovation agenda. Issues exist mainly around capturing and storing ideas in a meaningful way, finding ways to build on ideas, and getting a better understanding of how to select. Finding ways to identify which projects to take forward in particular remains an issue, especially for ideas at the radical or even discontinuous end of the innovation spectrum. Noticeable also is that interviewees spoke increasingly about the need to **focus on value creation**. Some felt that innovation had become an end in itself whereas, clearly, it ought to be a means to an end. The aim of innovation is to support a profitable, sustainable business. For that to happen, innovation needs to create value for multiple stakeholders. However, the value must not necessarily be monetary. Enhanced reputation, learning or breaking into a new market can be other 'values' created through innovation.

An issue indirectly related to that around ideas is on how best to share, communicate and develop innovations. Prototyping is emerging as a key tool for achieving this, yet companies still have to work out exactly what it means, and acquire the skills necessary to do it successfully. It is in this context that design, or rather **design thinking**, is being considered. Managers increasingly asked what lessons can be learned from designers, and how can design tools and design thinking be integrated with management tools and management thinking. I have already referred to the Rotman School of Management in Toronto where this is firmly on the agenda. Another example is the d.school at Stanford University (http://dschool.stanford.edu).

Also closely linked to the issue of idea development and selection is the continued challenge of finding **meaningful measures of innovation performance**. It does not help that many managers remain obsessed with hard financial data and short-term performance. *Direct* links between investment in innovation and financial performance are often difficult to establish – although there is evidence that long-term successful organisations place strong emphasis on innovation. Again I would not like to fail to point out that in order to be successful in the long term, organisations also need to be good at the 'operating' aspects. The need to balance and engage with both innovating and operating has been emphasised several times throughout this book and it cannot be emphasised enough. Problems arise when the same measures and key performance criteria are applied to different types of innovation. Measures for the operating versus innovating aspects/projects of the organisation need to differ to reflect the different conditions and contexts in which they thrive.

Having just mentioned the need to balance innovating and operating, the challenge companies are facing is how to **identify the right balance between innovating and operating**. What is the appropriate balance for any particular business in a particular context, and how to split the limited resources between the different innovation fields?

Then there is the issue of collaboration which we have discussed in more detail in Chapter 13. Again, awareness of the benefits of collaboration is on the increase; however, the question on how to **manage the boundaries** remains. Underlying this is the increased opening to the outside world and involvement of customers and other external constituencies in the development of new products and services. Having said that, it seems that **breaking down internal boundaries** can be a similar challenge. True cross-functional teams are difficult to run and tools are needed to help facilitate the process. Trust and understanding of different contributions and mindsets from those of different functional backgrounds is a particular issue here. There is often still a long way to go to create a feeling of 'oneness' for the entire organisation, particularly if it is made up of several business units.

Then there is the big question on whether and how to engage with **discontinuous innovation**, the kind of innovation that encroaches onto our territory but for which a different skill set (approaches, strategies etc.) is required. Insights, tools and process for how to deal with incremental innovation have increased many times over the recent years. It is still tricky to understand how to anticipate, recognise and deal with disruptive or discontinuous innovation. We will look at the topic of discontinuous innovation in more detail below.

Finally, changes caused by technology and globalisation, as well as environmental and social challenges facing the world, lead to the need to search for new ways to address these issues, one of which involves **rethinking the way business is done**. This will be the topic of the last section of this chapter.

DISCONTINUOUS INNOVATION

Let us start by taking a closer look at what discontinuous innovation actually is. You know when discontinuous innovation has hit you when 'the rug is being pulled out from under you': situations, when the rules of the industry are changing in a way that renders your current skill set obsolete. What you needed to succeed in the past will no longer help you to secure your future. For example, a radical new technology, such as digital photography, emerges and changes the underlying knowledge base on which incumbents operate. Or completely new markets emerge, such as MP3 players, which are initially at the edges of existing industries but over time become mainstream. When moving from the fringes new players upset the balance among existing players and often drive them out of business. Another level at which disruption can take place is at the business model level; think for example about computers being sold online, low-cost airlines or music downloads.

It is not that incumbent companies are daft, they are actually very good at what they are doing – just often far too focused on it to see what is happening at the fringes. This 'not seeing' – or even 'seeing and yet not seeing' is fundamental and we will take a look at what companies can actually do to stay alert to tangential developments a little later on.

Take the example of Polaroid. The company, which itself started with a discontinuous innovation, and has for a long time been a technically great company, is now in Chapter 11 bankruptcy. It is not that the company's managers did not see digital photography coming, they spotted it very early – but they then took then some wrong decisions. Because of their heritage and mindset they believed that photography would always be about high-quality pictures. But people were quite happy with poor resolution, primarily using the additional functionality of their mobile phones. Another problem was Polaroid's underlying business model. They made their money selling consumables, that is films, and did not make the switch to a business model based on selling hardware (Tripsas & Gavetti, 2000).

But we are getting ahead of ourselves; let's first take a closer look at definitions.[2] In addition to 'discontinuous innovation' there are also the terms 'radical innovation' and 'disruptive innovation'. In literature and practice these terms are often used interchangeably but slowly some distinct definitions emerge.

---

[2] You may also want to refer back to Boxes 1.2 and 1.3 in Chapter 1.

Let us start with **radical innovation** which Leifer *et al.* (2000) describe as having the potential, "to produce one or more of the following: an entirely new set of performance features, improvements in known performance features, improvements in known performance features of five times or greater, a significant (30% or greater) reduction in cost". So fundamentally we are still talking about the same thing.

Talking about disruptive or discontinuous innovation we are stepping up the level of differentness. Let's first have a look at the difference between **disruptive and discontinuous innovation**. Coming from a technology perspective Kassicieh *et al.* (2002) comment, "Disruptive technologies can be described as scientific discoveries that break through the usual product/technology capabilities and provide a basis for a new competitive paradigm. Discontinuous innovations can be considered as products/processes/services that provide exponential improvements in the value received by the customer." Adding to this, Linton and Walsh (2002) remark, "Disruptive technologies are discontinuous, but discontinuous technologies are not necessarily disruptive."

The fundamental differences to understand are the ones between innovation that build on what exists, and innovation that creates something entirely new.[3] You may want to call it 'steady-state innovation' versus 'discontinuous innovation' or, as Christensen (1997) does, 'sustaining innovation' versus 'disruptive innovation'. In the context of this book I will use the terms 'steady state' to refer to improvements, doing things better and exploitation; and 'discontinuous innovation' to refer to discontinuous and disruptive innovation, doing things differently, doing different things and exploration. But to do the differences justice I would like to spend a little more time exploring different definitions found in the literature.

Christensen defines sustaining and disruptive innovation as follows:

- **Sustaining innovation** – maintains a steady rate of product improvement (making the existing better).

- **Disruptive innovation** – has new attributes opening entirely new markets or revolutionising existing ones; in doing so, performance dimensions important for existing customers are often blurred.

It is essential to understand the differences between these two types, however you call them, as each thrives under very different conditions, and requires different tools and approaches. Some of the conditions and characteristics for each are listed in Table 31.1. Applying tools and measures that are appropriate to sustaining innovation to disruptive innovation will invariably lead to failure of the latter, and vice versa.

Christensen (1997) also described disruptive innovation as, "A technology, product or process that creeps up from below an existing business and threatens to displace it. Typically the disrupter offers lower performance and less functionality at a much lower price. The product or process is good enough for a meaningful number of customers – indeed, some don't need the older version's higher functionality and welcome the disruption's simplicity. And gradually, the new product or process improves to the point where it displaces the incumbent."

The point that the new entrant offers a product of seemingly inferior performance is an important one. It is because of this that incumbent players do not often take the 'new kid in town' seriously. Surely, an established player in the

---

[3]As early as 1942 Schumpeter (5th edition, 1976) made some observations regarding different types of innovation which he referred to as 'discontinuities'. The two types of discontinuity he identified are: first, a competence-destroying discontinuity which renders obsolete the expertise required to master the technology that it replaces; and second, a competence-enhancing discontinuity which builds on the existing know-how embodied in the technology that it replaces.

Table 31.1 Benefits and pitfalls of cross-industry collaboration

Type 1 innovation (Christensen's sustaining innovation)	Type 2 innovation (Christensen's disruptive innovation)
Operates within mental framework based on clear and accepted set of rules of the game	No clear rules – these emerge over time High tolerance for ambiguity
Strategies path dependent	Path independent, emergent, probe and learn
Clear selection environment	Fuzzy, emergent selection environment
Selection and resource allocation linked to clear trajectories and criteria for fit	Risk taking, multiple parallel bets, tolerance of (fast) failure
Operating routines refined and stable	Operating patterns emergent and fuzzy
Strong ties and knowledge flows along clear channels	Weak ties and peripheral vision important

Source: Bessant & von Stamm, 2007

high-end camera market does not have to take a mobile phone manufacturer, dabbling in low-quality digital cameras, seriously? This is why it is often said that disruptive innovation tends to sneak up on incumbents. Which bank or insurance company would have expected to have to compete against supermarkets?

While incumbents tend to focus on pushing existing products further and further up the performance curve – often far beyond the point the customer is interested in and willing to pay for – the disruptor offers a solution to the problem that offers less, but tends to be at a much lower price point (see Figure 31.1). Initially the innovator is not in direct competition with incumbents, and hence, does not show up on their radar screen. However, over time the quality and performance of the new technology improve, encroaching slowly but surely onto the incumbent's territory, ultimately replacing it. Being able to read the early warning signs, and being alert to possible implications of tangential developments is essential if incumbents want to prevent becoming victims of disruptive innovation. A bit further on we will take a look at what companies already do today to prevent this from happening.

The story of Dell

When Dell was launched in 1984 to sell computers via mail-order catalogue (and from 1994 also over the internet) existing competitors such as Compaq or IBM did not take the incomer seriously. Come to think of it, neither did Wall Street or financial analysts. To quote Rod Canio, a co-founder of Compaq Computer Corp, "We didn't worry about Dell and Gateway. For us, the distribution (reseller and retail) channel defined the market. Mail order was very limited. But over a period of nine or 10 years direct became the distribution channel of choice." In 2001, Dell became the biggest PC seller in the world, surpassing Compaq.

Interestingly, by pushing the price point down they also did what many disruptive innovations do, they grew the market for everybody.

Source: The above draws primarily on the article 'Dell changed industry with direct sales' in *The American Statesman* by John Pletz, 3 May 2004.

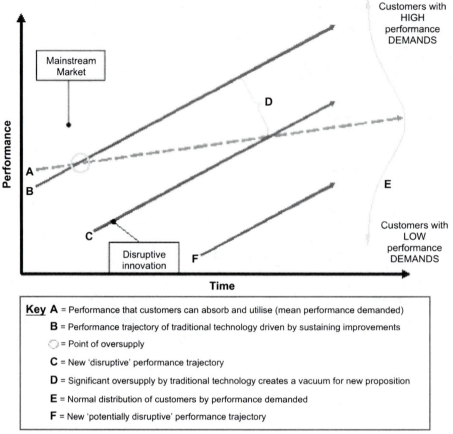

Figure 31.1   The Impact of Sustaining and Disruptive Technological Innovation.
Source: Christensen (1997).

While Christensen's 1997 definition talks about technological discontinuities, Veryzer (1998) adds 'commercial discontinuities' as second category, whereby he considers commercial and technological discontinuities to be a consequence of changes in the technological capability and perceived product capability. Examples of different types of discontinuities are shown in Figure 31.2.

For 'steady-state innovation' we know about tools to identify new opportunities, what criteria to apply to select which ideas to take forward, and what to do to implement them; many of them have been presented in this book. But how can organisations prepare for discontinuous innovation? Or even better, be the ones to identify such an opportunity? To investigate how to identify, select and implement discontinuous innovation opportunities was the aim of the aforementioned project supported by the Advanced Institute of Management. I would like to share briefly insights from the first phase of the project which was concerned with search strategies for discontinuous innovation.

The first phase of the project involved around 50 primarily large companies and eight universities from three countries: Denmark, Germany and the UK. The insights from the research (a survey, workshops and in-depth

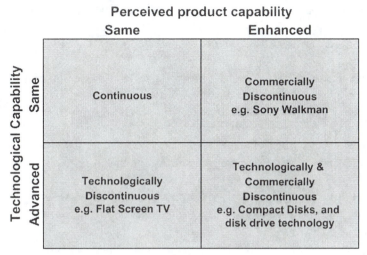

Figure 31.2 Types of discontinuous innovation performance.
Source: Adapted from Veryzer (1998) in Thomond *et al.* (2003).

Figure 31.3 The wheel of discontinuous innovation search strategies.
Source: Bessant & von Stamm, 2007.

interviews) were distilled into the 'wheel of search strategies', with 12 spokes, representing the 12 different search strategies that were identified (see Figure 31.3). It should be pointed out that in practice one or more of these strategies is often used in combination. However, to understand possible approaches they have been listed below in their 'pure' form.

All these strategies are designed to detect early signs of potential discontinuities, to put out some antennae into possible futures. In the following I will give a brief introduction to each of the 12 search strategies and provide some illustrating examples.

Sending out scouts – companies dispatch people, sometimes also referred to as 'idea hunters', to track down possible new innovation triggers. This can involve attending conferences, keeping in regular contact with people at universities, searching the net or networking, etc. Examples are:

• Thomas Swann: by reading newspapers and spending time roaming the corridors of universities where they have informal chats with researchers, Thomas Swann, a technically-oriented chemical company, has developed considerable skill in finding 'strange' early stage ideas and benefiting from them.

• O2 has a trend-scouting group of about 10 people who interpret externally identified trends into O2's specific business context. Once a year the group meets with the board to discuss and select ideas.

Exploring multiple futures – this basically refers to the use of scenario-planning techniques to investigate different possible futures; but it is not only about applying the traditional scenario-planning techniques pioneered by Shell, as the following examples show:

• BASF went through a multi-stage process, using the mega trend 'ageing population' as a starting point. The process began with a discussion of experts from a wide variety of professions (e.g. airport, newspaper, medical profession) about what life for the aged would be and feel like in 2020. Next, internal experts looked at the results of the discussion and related these results to BASF's industries. Further steps were verification of conclusions internally as well as externally. GSK Consumer Health used a similar process to strengthen their medium- to long-term pipeline.

• Ordnance Survey in the UK uses an annual conference to bring leading thinkers from related industries together and to discuss what the future might look like.

Using the web – involves harnessing the power of the internet to detect new trends, for example through online communities, and virtual worlds:

• Lego has set up the Lego Factory website where you can build your own model online and then have the ready-to-assemble set sent out to you (http://factory.lego.com/). This supports direct communication with users that can be difficult to identify otherwise, e.g. train enthusiasts. In this case LEGO can get feedback from the most advanced users and use this information in its mainstream products.

• BMW makes use of the web to enable a 'Virtual Innovation Agency' – a forum where suppliers from outside the normal range of BMW players can offer ideas which BMW may be able to use. These can be both product related and also process related, for example a recent suggestion was for carbon recycling from factory waste. Although this carries the risk that many 'cranks' will offer ideas, these may also provide stepping stones to new domains of interest.

Working with active users – companies team up with product and service users to see the ways in which they change and develop existing offerings. This has already been explored in Chapter 9. Additional examples are:

• **Coloplast**, a Danish medical devices firm, has made extensive use of user perspectives in its design of various medical devices. Working through panels of specialist nurses and other health professionals they have managed to gain deep insights into how their products are used and features which users would find valuable.

- **Webasto**, a supplier to the car industry, went through a systematic approach to understand what lead users are and how to identify them. Building on existing literature they identified four aspects that really drive people's propensity to innovate (cognitive complexity, team expertise, general knowledge, willingness to help). Based on those aspects they developed a questionnaire that they sent out, depending on the project in question, to up to 5000 people from their database. About 20% returned the questionnaires, there were several selection steps (e.g. age bracket, innovation potential) before they arrived at a lead user group of between 10 and 30. The lead users committed to come for an entire weekend, and without pay.

Deep diving – a term coined by innovation consultancy IDEO refers to studying the consumer through observation to elicit what people actually do – rather than what they say they do. As IDEO puts it so deftly, "you need to observe because:

- people do not always do what they say they do
- people do not always do what they think they do
- people do not always do what you think they do
- people cannot always tell you what they need."

Examples include:

- Towards the end of the last century **Unilever** felt that they had become too far removed from their consumers, particularly in less developed countries. So they decided to send their people out to spend some time where their customers were, even live in their homes. Such community-based observations led, for example, to the development of a reduced foam detergent for the Indian market where washing is mainly done by hand. This meant that less water was required to rinse clothes, saving up to two buckets of water per wash.

- When medical supplies company **Smith & Nephew** shut down most of its projects as a consequence of a major strategic review the people whose projects had been closed down were sent into the field to observe how their products were actually being used in the market. The ideas and insights they brought back into the organisation led to a number of exciting and radical new developments. Such was the success of the exercise that the company has established a programme under which anyone, and they really do mean anyone, in the organisation can spend a day in the field, everything being organised for them.

Probe and learn – this basically means, try things out with your customers (internally or externally) as early as possible; get their feedback and insights sooner rather than later, and do not try to get things perfect before sharing them with others. This is about prototyping ideas and services – not only products.

- The mobile phone industry does this a lot: new features are introduced, the reaction is gauged and then the feature is either made part of the base offering or rejected. Arvato described multiple probe and learn experiments around content, user segments and financial models, while O2 report similar activities.

- Bang & Olufsen has revitalised its prototyping department and made it refer directly to the innovation hub of the company. The prototyping department is engaged in new ideas as early as possible and the experiences are that this strongly supports the process.

Mobilise the mainstream – many organisations seem to forget that they already have some people out there, potentially observing the starting of a new discontinuous revolution. But not many organisations have formalised processes and structures that bring the knowledge 'from the front' back into the organisation. Even if frontline people are aware of an emerging trend, would they know whom to talk to, and would they be listened to? Examples of organisation that do this rather well are:

- **Reckitt Benckiser** has a network of 'internal correspondence' who feed what is happening in their market into a central team. They also tap into PAs who process a lot of the information anyway and tend to focus on 'hot spots' and/or certain industries. The role of a central team is to take the information provided by the people from the field and combine it with information gathered from other sources and into a bulletin that is published every 6–8 weeks. Unused material is stored and kept accessible and available for future reference. The bulletin is sent to select senior management. The process is outlined in Figure 31.4.

- **3M** – another firm with a strong innovation pedigree dating back over a century – puts much of its success down to making and managing connections. Larry Wendling, Vice President for Corporate Research talks of 3M's 'secret weapon' – the rich formal and informal networking which links the thousands of R&D and market-facing people across the organisation. Its long history of breakthrough innovations – from masking tape, through Scotchgard, Scotch tape, magnetic recording tape to Post-Its and their myriad derivatives – arise primarily out of people making connections.

Corporate venturing – this is about creating units with capital to invest in start up and promising ideas, mainly with the intention of having a stake in organisations, which may have implications for the main organisation at some point in the future. Most of these venture units have an external focus although some of them are also open to ideas from the organisation's employees (but would generally expect employees to exit the organisation to set up their own business).

- Nokia's Venturing Organisation is focused on corporate venturing activities that include identifying and developing new businesses, or as they put it "the renewal of Nokia". Nokia Venture Partners invests

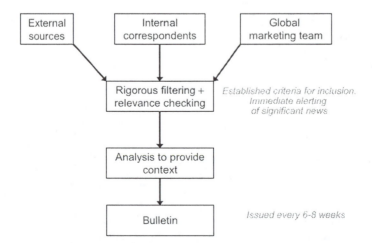

Figure 31.4 How Reckitt Benckiser mobilises its mainstream.

exclusively in mobile and internet protocol (I/P) related start-up businesses. They have a very interesting third group called Innocent that directly supports and nurtures nascent innovators with the hope of growing future opportunities for Nokia.

- SAP has set up a venture unit called SAP Inspire to fund start ups with interesting technologies. The mission of the group is to "be a world-class corporate venturing group that will contribute, through business and technical innovation, to SAP's long-term growth and leadership." It does so by:

    ○ seeking entrepreneurial talent within SAP and providing an environment where ideas are evaluated on an open and objective basis

    ○ actively soliciting and cultivating ideas from the SAP community as well as effectively managing the innovation process from idea generation to commercialisation

    ○ looking for growth opportunities that are beyond the existing portfolio but within SAP's overall vision and strategy.

Corporate entrepreneuring and intrapreneuring – as opposed to the previous search strategy, this one is about discovering and nurturing the entrepreneurial talent inside the organisation.

- 3M is well known for its 15% rule which says that every scientist can spend 15% of his or her time on a project of their choosing. That allows them to explore and develop their own ideas; they are also allowed to engage/persuade their colleagues to spend their 15% on the project. Some people are so good at it that they almost build up their own undercover R&D organisation within 3M.

- Within BMW there is a strong commitment to 'bootlegging' – encouraging people to try things out without necessarily asking for permission or establishing a formal project. This approach – in BMW these are called 'U-boot projects' – means that people deploy their natural entrepreneurial abilities and often come up with creative solutions. Importantly they also learn ways of getting the attention of the mainstream and managing changes in attitudes. A good example was the Series 3 Estate version which the mainstream company thought was not wanted and would conflict with the image of BMW as a high-quality, high-performance and somewhat 'sporty' car. A small group of staff worked on a U-boot project, even using parts cannibalised from other cars to make a prototype – and the model has gone on to be a great success and opened up new market space.

Use brokers and bridges – here the idea is to use the principles of bees: cross-fertilisation between different industries through agents such as designers or other forms of consultants. It builds on networks and 'people who know people who know people'. Examples are:

- The UK engineering services company **Arup** has done extensive work on mapping its social networks inside and outside the business to better exploit the connectivity. It has a map of the Arup 'brain' which indicates where connections are made and could be made and who could engineer such links.

- A number of organisations – **Coloplast**, **B&O**, **Grundfos** for example – hold regular events and conferences where the prime purpose is to bring people together and enable networking and potential brokering across what are otherwise diverse organisations.

Deliberate diversity – connecting previously unconnected bodies of knowledge leads to innovation. Companies have these different bodies of knowledge available to them in their different departments and business units – but often neglect to facilitate connections between them. Deliberately creating and nurturing diversity – especially across industry boundaries – is one means to come up with disruptive ideas, diverse teams and a diverse workforce.

- In her days as CEO at Hewlett Packard Carly Fiorina declared, "The value proposition for diversity is very clear: Diversity drives creativity. Creativity drives invention. Invention drives profitability and business success."

- Design and innovation consultancy IDEO hire people from backgrounds as diverse as medicine, engineering, anthropology and physics to create a team with a strong track record in coming up with groundbreaking new ideas.

Idea generators – refers primarily to employing tools, and often engaging external people, to generate ideas around specified concepts or scenarios, for example:

- **P&G Encore** uses retirees to help act as gatekeepers and spotters.

- **IBM** engages school children as trend spotters and information feeds to its pattern recognition toolkit.

Some of these strategies are more directed towards the generation of better, more focused ideas. Understanding developments at the fringes of one's industry and considering their implications are the best strategy to prevent unwelcome surprises – if organisations do not see relevant developments coming, or if they see them too late, they may find their skill set under threat before they know it. There is much evidence: established firms tend to do well under 'steady-state' conditions and badly when the rules of the game change.

However, whether the discontinuity is identified internally or externally, the next step is infinitely more difficult than the first one: it requires overcoming the corporate immune system which is triggered by the very skill sets that have served the organisation so well in the past coming under threat. Cutting off one limb in order to grow a new one is very painful, and requires a lot of courage, vision and determination.

THE BALANCING ACT

It seems that in the past organisations were focusing on one kind of innovation at a time, either steady state or discontinuous, with the latter more often than not being pursued by start ups. Established organisations might swing between the two extremes occasionally, but rarely doing both at the same time. In terms of the terminology used in Figure 31.5 (Boer & Gertsen, 2003) this would mean that these organisations are either 'singular organic' or 'singular mechanistic'. I would argue that those organisations that are pure 'reactors', that is neither explore nor exploit very much, cannot expect a long life in today's environment.

In today's fast-moving environment doing either/or this is no longer enough. The true mastery lies in the simultaneous pursuit of stability and change, of order and chaos, and renewal and renovation. In the past this was considered to be incompatible – today it has become almost a necessity. On Boer and Gertsen's graph it means that organisations have to be at least 'binary', ideally 'dual'.

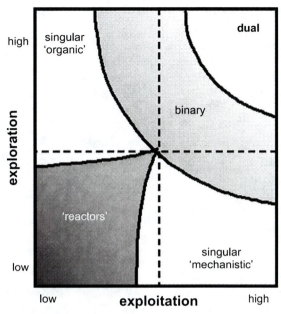

Figure 31.5 Balancing exploration and exploitation.
Source: Boer & Gertsen 2003.

Either/or is no longer good enough

A participant in the Innovation Best Practice interviews commented, "Our share price had gone down by nearly 60% – but this was not because of losing market share or being less profitable – that was just no longer seen to be enough." Clearly, focus on past and present is not enough.

However, too much focus on the future can be equally deadly: as Birkinshaw and Gibson (2004) point out, "communication technology company Ericsson led the way in the development of communication technologies. It has pumped money into R&D, at its peak it employed 30,000 people in some 100 technology centres. With such substantial investment in the future Ericsson was hit hard during the recent crash in the telecoms industry. Forced to concentrate on the present it closed many of its technology centres."

An organisation capable of mastering the balancing act is generally known as an 'ambidextrous organisation' (Tushman & O'Reilly III, 2004). In the past the view was that this was impossible and that organisations needed to set up separate structures, such as venture capital funds, to deal with discontinuous innovation (e.g. Birkinshaw & Gibson, 2004). However, the number of those who believe that organisations have to learn increasingly to deal with dualities, such as steady-state versus discontinuous, is on the increase.[4]

---

[4]For an introduction to the concept and an assessment tool you may want to download the AIM report 'The Ambidextrous Organisation' by Julian Birkinshaw and Christina Gibson. (http://www.aimresearch.org/publications/ambidexterousrpt.pdf)

Table 31.2   Structural ambidexterity versus contextual ambidexterity

	Structural ambidexterity	Contextual ambidexterity
How do we attain ambidexterity?	Through alignment and adaptability focused activities carried out in separate teams	Individuals divide their time between alignment and adaptability focused activities
What kind of skills do employees have?	Tend to be specialists	Tend to be generalists
Who makes the decisions about alignment and adaptability?	Senior management, line managers	Employees whether they are customer facing, office workers, plant workers etc.
What is senior management's role?	Defining structure, weighing up adaptability against alignment	Creating the organisational context within which employees operate
What is the nature of roles within the organisation?	Cleary defined	Flexible

Source: Adapted from Birkinshaw & Gibson, 2004
Note: For 'alignment' read 'steady state' and for 'adaptability' read 'discontinuous'.

Birkinshaw and Gibson (2004) propose that to achieve true ambidexterity organisations have to move away from a focus on structure and focus on contextual dexterity instead. They argue that contextual dexterity, which is linked to individuals rather than structures, provides the organisation with the necessary flexibility and agility that is needed to deal with both states of innovation simultaneously. Table 31.2 contrasts the two different approaches.

In their analysis of context for ambidexterity Birkinshaw and Gibson focus on two aspects: social support and performance management. They argue that the social support context is key if decisions about focus are to be made at the individual level. Without the provision of a supportive environment – in terms of resources as well as trust and encouragement – from senior management this is not possible. The second aspect, performance management, involves providing a context in which people are stimulated to deliver high-quality results while at the same time being held accountable. In order to create an ambidextrous organisation senior management needs to provide both. One without the other is not enough.

What the right balance between steady state and discontinuous is will depend very much on the industry as well as the organisational context. Highly technology focused companies are likely to require a stronger slant towards discontinuous whereas fast-moving consumer goods companies may require a stronger emphasis on steady state.

THE FUTURE OF BUSINESS – ALL CHANGE

Informal relations among employees – not who they answer to, but rather who they trust, who they rely on, who they discuss things with casually – are key to the operation of a firm.

Ronald Burt, University of Chicago, *Rotman Magazine*, winter 2007

This book has been dedicated to exploring all the different aspects that managers wanting their organisations to become more innovative have to understand and address. Becoming more innovative means becoming more flexible and responsive, thereby enhancing establishing the basis for an organisation's survival into the future. Becoming better at innovation does not mean giving up on cost focus on efficiencies. Organisations that outperform their competitors in the future will be able to hold dualities rather than choose between them. Achieving this requires a different mindset, and different ways of working from what we see today. Cultures that thrive on control and command will not have the flexibility to deal with today's challenges and opportunities. At the end of this chapter we will come back to what the mindsets of the future might look like.

The integrative thinker

"Integrative thinking can be defined as 'the ability to think and act responsibly and responsively in the face of multiple and possibly conflicting models of oneself, others and the world' ".

Roger Martin and Mihnea Moldeveanu, Designing the Thinker of the Future. *Rotman Magazine*, winter 2007.

There are also other factors that drive us to seek different approaches to the way businesses operate. One of them is a significant change in the way we work. Internet access and technological mobility mean that for many professions the locus of work does not matter any longer. But if I am no longer working 'on site' my manager can no longer control what I do; our relationship has to change. My side of the bargain is self-motivation and commitment to deliver, the manager's side of the bargain is to extend trust and delegate. This is a very different scenario from what we find in most organisations today. Particularly organisations with a strong paternalistic culture may find this quite difficult as employees are not used to making decisions and tend to expect to be told what to do, rather than taking initiative themselves, and managers in such organisations are more used to telling people what to do, to take care of them. However, there are organisations around that operate on the basis of self-motivation and trust, which, in fact, could not operate without it: voluntary organisations (at least until structure and bureaucracy take over).

I would like to bring forward one other argument to support my call for 'business – all change' and that is the issue of engagement. Engagement has two components: an emotional one, for example taking pride in working for a company (or team, or leader) and a rational one, for example understanding how your job fits into the bigger picture. If you have engaged people in the organisation you will find that they are willing to go the 'extra mile', that they feel they can contribute, and that attrition rates are likely to be low.

Over the past few decades most organisations, particularly commercial ones, have gone through round after round of downsizing and rehiring. This has sent a clear message to employees: you are but a number. As a consequence the psychological contract between employer and employee has been broken, and people no longer find a sense of belonging and identification with the organisations they are working for. In the past they might have done things 'for the company'. Today this is less and less likely.

A consequence of the disenchantment with corporations is an increased disengagement of employees. The following figures are taken from a survey conducted by Towers Perrin in 2005:[5]

---

[5] http://www.kathleenredmond.com/newsletter/60secondsOct06.html.

- Only 17% of the workforce are *Highly Engaged* which means that these people are freely putting in an extra effort at work.

- The large majority, 66%, were *Moderately Engaged* which means these people are open and evaluating.

- And a number equal to those engaged, i.e. 17%, are *Disengaged* which means they have mentally already 'checked out'.

Clearly, at least in my view, there are too many people who are at work 'in body' but not 'in mind'. As the Australian-born corporate culture specialist Keith Ayers put it, "Lack of employee engagement is like a cancer, eating away at an organisation's vital organs."[6] There is more evidence to support this:

- A survey by Gallup of the US workforce revealed that 55% of employees are not engaged, and an additional 16% are actively disengaged!

- Commenting on the study, Denny Macha of HPower & Associates, points out, "If you are an average company in terms of employee engagement, 70% of your employees are giving you back only 50% for what they are being paid. That means that 35% of your payroll is going down the drain. For a 100-person company, that works out to $1,750,000. And remember, we are assuming that the *Actively Disengaged* employees are giving you 50% of their capabilities and the *Engaged* employees 100%. The real figure could be substantially worse."

- Along similar lines consultant Tim Field calculated that, "The cost to UK plc of lost work days due to lack of engagement was estimated to be between £39–48 billion a year."[7]

- At the same time you have a large proportion of the workforce gladly giving their time for free (Dixon, 2005).

There is another reason why I believe engagement is critical, particularly in the context of innovation: you cannot really tell people to be more innovative! You have to inspire them, you have to paint a vision that they *want* to help achieve. You need people who are engaged and enthusiastic as pushing innovation through organisations is a tough job, and not for the faint hearted. This is where it links back to the discussion around leadership of the previous chapters; without inspiring leadership there is little hope of engaging employees, and without engaged employees the creation of an innovative organisation is impossible.

I would like to close this chapter by looking at five mindsets that, according to Howard Gardner (2007), are required in the business of the future, or as he puts it, the "five mindsets will lead the way in the uncertain world that is our future".

The first is the **disciplined mind**. Until the recent past the specialist was king. Having deep, detailed expertise was valued and respected in organisations. But as fields develop and morph there is no resting on one's laurels any more. Tomorrow's hero is required to continue learning and evolving, ideally becoming a master in more than one discipline. Not a mean feat considering that it takes about 10 years to become an expert in a discipline.

---

[6] See for example his book, *Engagement is Not Enough*, Advantage, 2006.
[7] http://samvak.tripod.com/pp114.html.

The second is the **synthesising mind**. A person with such a mind is able to scan a wide range of sources, realise what is important and should be considered, and then put it together in a way that is meaningful and make sense to others. Such a person is also able to focus on both the big picture and the small detail. Nobel Laureate and physicist Murray Gell-Mann is such a master of many disciplines, as was Einstein.

As mastering existing knowledge is not sufficient, the third mind that will be valued is the **creating mind**. Here Gardner suggests that personality and temperament are equally if not more important than 'talent'. Such a person must be happy to experiment and take changes and go 'where no one has dared to go before'.

The **respectful mind** is the fourth mind. This plays to the theme of diversity: a person with a respectful mindset is open and welcomes differing points of view and avoids prejudices. But more than that, such a person gives others the benefit of doubt.

And finally, there is the **ethical mind**. Gardner emphasises that this is a 'more sophisticated stance than respect'. Such a person is highly reflective of herself as well as the context and others. Such a person would ask what kind of person she ought to be, and what the world would be like if everyone behaved like her for such a person the 'do as I say don't do as I do' would be unacceptable. Gardner quotes the French playwright Jean-Baptiste Molière who said, "We are responsible not only for what we do but for what we don't do."

Gardner emphasises that these minds are not separate but also interconnected as, for example, synthesising without some deep knowledge is not possible, and creation often springs from the recombination of knowledge that originates from different domains.

These mindsets are very different from the profiles described in many job advertisements today. But a change in mindset, in attitude and behaviours is required if the flexible, innovative organisation is to become a reality.

The next two chapters offer two case studies that build on the insights in this chapter. The two case studies are: (a) from Unilever, a large, multinational company where senior management faces a decision about a product that would take them onto unfamiliar territory and which has high uncertainty about its market potential; and (b) from a small but fast-growing headhunting organisation that faces some challenges around its way of operating.

READING SUGGESTIONS

Wheatley, M. (1999). *Leadership and the New Science: Discovering Order in a Chaotic World.* Berrett-Koehler.

Comment: Wheatley draws on subjects as diverse as quantum physics, chaos theory and molecular biology and relates them to leadership and organisational performance.

Prahalad, C.K. (2004). *The Fortune at the Bottom of the Pyramid.* Prentice-Hall.

Comment: Prahalad suggests that if we stop thinking of the poor as victims or as a burden and start recognising them as resilient and creative entrepreneurs and value-conscious consumers, a whole new world of opportunity will open up.

Scharmer, O. (2007). *Theory U: Leading from the Future as it Emerges.* SoL, the Society for Organizational Learning.

Comment: An interesting and different approach, primarily directed at leaders, for achieving learning and changes that draws on involvement, active and prejudice-free listening and what might be described as meditation; it seems to suggest that if you can imagine the future you can create it.

SOME INTERESTING WEBSITES

http://www.elias-global.com/

Comment: The initiative, **Emerging Leaders For Innovation Across Sectors** (ELIAS), is a network and prototyping platform that links 20 leading global institutions across the three sectors of business, government and civil society in order to co-create and test profound system innovations for a more sustainable world.

http://www.london.edu/managementinnovationlab.html

Comment: Website of the **Management Innovation Lab**, an initiative led by Garry Hamel and Julian Birkinshaw, based at London Business School. On the website a management innovation is described as "a marked departure from traditional management principles, processes and practices or a departure from customary organisational forms that significantly alters the way the work of management is performed". The goal of the initiative is, "To dramatically accelerate the evolution of management processes and practices that will define competitive success in the 21st century."

www.unfrozenmind.com

Comment: Unfrozenmind is one of the emerging organisations that looks at individual transformation as the lever for better – and more innovative - future in business. One of its strap lines is: "putting the mind back into business".

32

Innovation beyond the comfort zone?

CASE STUDY 11: UNILEVER[1]

Can we spread this far?

"Spreads such as margarines are a major contributor to our turnover and profit but the market is shrinking by about 2% per year. We need something to get off that slippery slope."

Kevin Povey, Global Project Leader, Unilever

"I really believe we should push on with this, I am sure that there is a market." This was the view of a small but determined group within Unilever's 'yellow fat' business. Unilever had been working on developing a spread with serious cholesterol-reducing properties for some time but so far they had not been able to get the price point to a level that would convince senior management to commit the necessary resources. There had been development activities around a 'heart health' platform, and Unilever's existing product did already have some positive effect on cholesterol levels, but the desire was to develop a product that would have a significant impact on cholesterol – at the existing price point.

> **Unilever and margarine**
>
> The company, with such brands as Flora in the UK and I Can't Believe It's Not Butter in the US, is already the world's leading margarine manufacturer and it dominates the global margarine sector. "We practically invented margarine", said a Unilever spokesman. The Dutch companies that later formed Unilever, Jurgens and Van den Bergh, invented the commercial manufacturing of butter in Holland in 1872.

The fact that market research on whether or not the consumer would be willing to pay a price premium for such a product had come back negative did not exactly help either. Various avenues had been pursued to bring cost down – but so far no one had hit on the right solution: the price point remained at about three to four times of what was expected. Yet the team was convinced that with heart disease being the main cause of death in the developed world there should be a market.

But costs were not the only grounds for objection within the company. Unilever was very good at incremental improvements and constantly upgrading its products but was not quite as comfortable with breaking new ground.

---

[1] The case has been prepared by Dr Bettina von Stamm as a basis for class discussion rather than to illustrate either effective or ineffective handling of a management situation.

Getting involved in developing foods with stronger functional properties, such as cholesterol-reducing spreads, would be a significant departure from the way things were currently done within Unilever, this much had become clear during the many discussions that had taken place.

There was a whole raft of issues around health and safety considerations. For example, could they produce a good tasting product, and one that would truly be effective in lowering cholesterol? Proving the effectiveness would require a level of clinical testing that Unilever had not done on this scale before. And if they could prove it was effective, the next step would be to demonstrate that the product would be safe, which would require extensive testing, which would be costly as well as time consuming.

Possible cholesterol-reducing ingredients
1.   Sterol esters
2.   Rice bran oil sterols (a relatively cheap source)
3.   Shea sterols (some safety data readily available)
4.   Stanol esters (used in Raisio)

As the spread would have 'functional properties' it would have to get regulatory approval – in fact there were regulations that said that, if you are selling food, you could not make medical claims. So, if Unilever had a product with positive health implications but could not publicly make a statement of that nature, how could they communicate the benefits to the consumer? Of course, the regulatory approval process would again be time consuming.

Then there were those who would not fail to point out that, while there was clearly a growing trend towards functional foods, many companies had tried their hand at it but for most it had gone not quite as well as hoped. Among those who had pioneered in this field, companies such as Kellogg, Novartis and even M&S had got into trouble with their functional foods. So was this really the way to go for a traditional foods company?

Not to forget that there were some new rules on EU safety assessment due in November 1997. It transpired that regulatory and safety requirements could potentially delay the project by up to two years. Should they decided to go ahead, should they try to get something through the system before the new regulations kicked in or follow the new process which would definitely mean a delay in getting the product to market? However, it seemed clear that they would not be able to comply fully to the internal safety programme by then.

Then there was the question of whether or not Unilever would have credibility with the consumers. There were several aspects to this. Would consumers trust Unilever to offer a product with health properties, and would they trust it to be effective and safe? The next point was hugely important from Unilever's perspective: would the new product cannibalise the existing product range that was an important cash cow for the business? After all, spreads contributed around 10% to Unilever's business. Or even worse, would the new product turn one of Unilever's most important mainstream products into a niche market? Given the price point, it was considered unlikely that the new spread would ever be more than a niche product. The question was, should Unilever go there, being as it was about big brands and large production runs? And finally, if they decided to go ahead, how would the product be marketed? Would it go as an extension of one of Unilever's main brands? What if it failed and negative consequences for the established brand followed? On the other hand, creating a new brand would be extremely costly and, again, time consuming.

On the other hand if the product proved to be as successful, would they be able to secure access to sufficient quantities of plant sterols, the key ingredient of the product? Would they be able to produce sufficient quantities on a global scale? Securing supply was considered to be critical to a successful introduction of the product.

While these questions were pondered within Unilever their Finnish company reported the launch of a cholesterol-reducing spread by a small local company called Raisio (late 1996). The product promised a cholesterol reduction of about 12% and was selling at a significant price premium; in fact it cost six times as much as ordinary margarine.[2] Raisio too had had negative feedback from market research about the pricing but as they had already invested heavily they felt that there was not really a choice but to move ahead. Unilever's Finnish team asked whether Unilever was planning anything in reaction to the launch. Raisio's launch was considered interesting news but did not really change senior management's position of the project. It was felt that Raisio, a conglomerate with an offering ranging from margarine to animal food and chemicals, was pretty much a local player with little international ambition and hence did not pose any threat.

Raisio's story

From the beginning Raisio had focused on stanol esters from wood pulp; they had also gone straight to the European Commission in Brussels to get confirmation that they had grandfathered the product, i.e. it was not novel, and then patented it. Interestingly Raisio had got approval to put stanol esters into oil (not spreads) but they argued that that's what they did – then they just used that oil in the production of spreads.

They were also very public about announcing the superior performance of the ingredient. Raisio argued that the advantage of stanol esters was that you needed less – something Johnson & Johnson emphasised heavily. However, an independent study commissioned by Unilever revealed that there was actually little difference between the two ingredients: both the claim of lower quantities and the claim of better performance could be refuted. The message seemed clear: "We have superior performance, and we have a patent, so you might as well give up now."

Raisio anticipated a large market, especially in the US. Partly in response to the better than anticipated initial sales and partly in anticipation of a large global market Raisio decided that existing capacity would not be sufficient and that they would need to build a new plant – which had to be recouped through increases in per-unit prices for the consumer.

Unilever on the other hand used sterol ester which was based on sterol, a byproduct from the production of vitamin E.

However, the next bit of news caused a bit more of a stir: news got around that Johnson & Johnson were interested in the new product. They were planning to acquire the licence rights to Raisio's spread, access to Raisio's raw material sourcing, and the use of the brand. While Johnson & Johnson were not really considered to be a direct competitor in this particular market the fact that they would probably be interested in pushing the product globally reopened the discussion on what to do about 'project cholesterol'.

So, in addition to the aforementioned concerns that prevented a green light for the project there was now an additional one, namely: could the Unilever team come up with a product that was safe, effective and at the right cost point *quickly enough* to satisfy impatient internal stakeholders who would rather see an instant response to

---

[2] *Source:* http://www.retailmerchandising.net/candy/SpecialSection/margarine.htm.

the competitor threat? And given the time constraints, on which of the possible raw materials should they place their bet?

In short, the questions Unilever needed to answer – sooner rather than later – should they step up R&D and try to launch their product as quickly as possible? Bearing in mind the facts that they did not have the marketing budget and that the market was shrinking by 2% every year, should they try to buy Raisio? Should they try to challenge the claims Raisio made? Should they challenge the lack of safety data on the Raisio product? Should they just wait to see what would happen?

A little more on the project's background

Margarine had always been core to Unilever and a strong contributor to its overall business; in fact, spreads were the single biggest contributor for Unilever. However, in the mid to late 1990s it was noticed that while the main brand was still performing strongly, its sales were decreasing by about 2% per year. Early in 1996 this got the attention of Niall Fitzgerald, Unilever's Chairman at the time, who challenged the margarine and spreads team to come up with something soon.

Of course the R&D department had not been standing still and had for some time been looking into possibilities of giving a new edge to a very mature product. They had been looking at adding Omega 3 to spreads – but the idea of using oils from fish did not go down too well with test groups. Insights into the effects of cholesterol-reducing ingredients had been around since the 1950s and Unilever had done significant amounts of research around it. They had been working on cholesterol-lowering spreads, which were based on polyunsaturated fats; however, these were more targeted at prevention/general health than outright cholesterol lowering.

Unilever had even done some clinical trials with a number of possible ingredients that had cholesterol-reducing properties such as shea nut oil, rice bran and sterol ester – each with different benefits and downsides. For example, sterol esters were already naturally present in oils and spread but would normally be consumed in tiny quantities of about 0.3 g per day. For the spread to be effective it would require amounts that would be over five times that; in fact 1.62 g per day would be required. In addition to having been used in foods before another benefit of sterol ester was that there was already a body of literature available on it. However, once the necessary quantities had been identified Unilever's internal safety position was clear: we cannot do this without fully evaluating safety.

In 1993 Unilever dispatched someone to India to see whether rice bran oil could be collected and used instead. The conclusion was that this could be a much cheaper source of sterols but it would need quite a lot of infrastructure development to collect it. In addition there were some questions over the slightly different molecular structures of sterols from rice bran oil and whether they would work in the same way as sterols from other sources.

It was also in 1993 that it was finally decreed that background R&D in this area should be stopped. After which very limited work around small-scale experiments on making sterol ester and literature searches took place.

Questions

1.   What are the different options open to Unilever? Which one would you have chosen and why?

2.   What are the best and worst case scenarios should Unilever give the project the go ahead?

3.   Assume you had decided to go ahead, what are the challenges and how would you have progressed the project?

4.   In large organisations, what are ways to mitigate risk associated with radical and discontinuous innovation?

33 Management without control?

CASE STUDY 12: SAM HEADHUNTING [1]

Trust is OK – is control better?

I do not believe in control, hierarchy and rigid structure; such things might make people feel that they are in control – but in reality they are not.

Niels Schreiner Andersen, Senior Partner, SAM Headhunting

Figure 33.1

"This is the third time since headhunting has become our main area of activity that people have abused the system, don't you think it is time we did something about it?" This was a question senior partners in SAM Headhunting were facing late 2006 when a partner in one of their European organisations had borrowed rather heavily from the company without declaring it. Admittedly, it had not been to fund a glamorous lifestyle but to finance some medical treatment for his wife – but still, it was a misappropriation of company money and needed to be dealt with. When exposed the person had argued that, being the managing director, it was legal in his country to borrow money from the company. But he was not able to provide evidence of that; in addition the level of borrowing was such that payback seemed rather unrealistic.

A few of the eight senior partners felt quite strongly that this required a review of company policies. They felt that stricter controls needed to be in place to ensure that similar incidences would not happen in future. On the other hand, the principle of founder Niels Schreiner Andersen, and hence the company, had always been, "Delegate and trust." Despite geographical dispersion there had always been a minimum of controls and procedures.

---

[1] The case has been prepared by Dr Bettina von Stamm as a basis for class discussion rather than to illustrate either effective or ineffective handling of a management situation.

Those in favour of stricter control brought up the two other occasions up where the system had been abused. The first case had actually been in Denmark itself where different parts operate as separate entities. At the time they were not double-checking accounts of partners; but in 2001 they felt that receipts from a particular region were not what they should have been. When they arranged for the accounts to be checked they found that about DKr 200,000 (ca £20,000) had been misappropriated over four years. When ask to put the money back the partner in question refused.

Even though it was against the grain of the organisational culture, the person was expelled – whereupon he sued SAM, arguing that SAM's management had had all the necessary information but had failed to spot the discrepancy earlier. As a response SAM had counter-sued him. In the first instance the court agreed with the partner that SAM's management was partly to blame. This had not been acceptable to Niels and SAM put in an appeal. The second court completely rejected the claim of joint responsibility and in the end the partner not only had to pay the money back but also pay for all costs associated with proceedings. Niels had hoped that this would send a strong signal throughout the organisation that even though you did not have any controls and constant checks, this did not mean that SAM could be cheated in any way without defending itself.

Of course there had then been discussion of whether to introduce more controls, but Niels had pointed out that this would have meant more rules to follow for *everyone*. After some debate it was decided that SAM should continue as before except that it was decided to ensure that all accounts in the group would be double-checked on a regular basis.

The second incidence had been in one of the Benelux countries. The person had recently started in the company and proved to be a very good headhunter. The company developed rapidly. Contact between him and headquarters became less and less frequent, and he proved difficult to get hold off. Initially it had been attributed to the success of his business, but when, on top of that, money coming from him started to get scarce, suspicions arose. SAM management realised that he was actually taking money out of the company – and in this case it was because he was a big spender. Proving that something was wrong was not easy as the country manager was the only one with access to the bank statements and accounts. Niels realised that headquarters had to act.

As it was clear that it would be difficult to get the money back by going to court it was decided instead that all licence rights would go back to SAM, so that the fraudster would have to take over the company but change the company name. In addition he had to pay back the money he had appropriated. In the end they lost some money but not much. As Niels pointed out, it was also quite a difficult thing to do as the fraudster was a very likeable and charming person.

Needless to say that the beast of control had raised its head again and yet the overriding response had been: delegate and trust. But, as in the first instance, they took some learning from the situation. The first was to ensure

---

Shareholding structure

All the operating units in the Group are owned partly by SAM A/S (or by another company in the SAM Group) and partly by one or more partners being operative in this unit.

SAM A/S directly or indirectly always has a controlling shareholding of all operating units.

SAM companies established after 1 January 2004 have one leading partner with a shareholding of approximately 25 points and a number of partners sharing the remaining 24 points.

---

that in future there would be double access to national bank accounts; and second, they realised that staying in constant contact was really important.

Background to the company

The fundamental principle on which SAM is built is: delegate and trust. This means that we have a minimum of controls and procedures in place. When looking for new people, particularly partners, the acceptance and buy-in into this principle is essential.

Niels Schreiner Andersen

The SAM Group originates from 1993 when Schreiner Andersen Management was established as a private company owned by Niels Schreiner Andersen with 100%. With a background in engineering Niels had moved up in management: only six years after graduation he took on his first director role. While he enjoyed working in industry it had always been his plan to eventually set up his own company. He had even set himself a date: his fiftieth birthday. True to his word, he resigned from the Danish company Wittenborg, leading manufacturer of food vending machines with effect of 31 December 1993.

> ### Niels Schreiner Andersen's background
>
> 1986–93 Managing Director of Wittenborg A/S, Europe's leading manufacturer of food vending machines. 1980–6 Managing Director of Damixa A/S, one of Europe's leading manufacturers of fittings, part of the American MASCO group. 1978–80 Director of Thrige-Titan A/S. 1965–78 A/S Regnecentralen (as Director from 1973 onwards).
>
> Examiner at the Faculty of Business Economics, Odense University and the Copenhagen School of Economics and Business Administration.

Building on insights gained from his career he had developed strong views of what his company would look like. Having had plenty opportunity to observe boards and their issues and problems he had thought about partnerships for a long time. For example, having seen what can happen if such a thing is not in place, an exit strategy was particularly important to him. Unlike situations he had observed he would not want the family to suffer when the breadwinner was made redundant, left the company or died.

Niels and his wife Helle had discussed at length what the company should be about and in the end they decided that Niels should offer his skills as a problem solver to management teams in crisis, which would allow an incumbent team to focus on their core business. It went fantastically well and soon Niels asked the technical manager from his previous company to join him. Whereas Niels could see problems and issues related to administration and management immediately, his former colleague Henning Back could do the same for the factory.

So, where does headhunting come into this? As Niels explains with a smile, "The move into headhunting was quite coincidental; it was all about being prepared to grasp the opportunity." It all started with a call from Henning Stoutaard, a former colleague, in August 1995. Henning said, "You know so many people, can you find me an export manager, he would have to relocate to the plant?" Niels agreed knowing that his network was sure to provide some suitable candidates. Sure enough, there was the wife of a friend who was from the town in question and who wanted to move back in order to be closer to her daughter. Within two weeks he had found three suitable people. His search proved almost too successful: Henning took not only one but two out of the three proposed candidates! So he got two for the price of one. How did Niels find the people?

Word soon got around and they increasingly got enquiries whether they might now be in the business of finding people. After having achieved their first three jobs in headhunting they asked themselves, do we have a product here? Early 1996 they answered that question with 'yes', thinking that this would be an ideal door opener to allow them to sell their real expertise, crisis management, into organisations. That's also when the third partner, Per Krenk, joined Niels and Henning.

By the end of that year they realised that headhunting made up 50% of their income. A decision was made that headhunting should be kept at around 50% – but the next time they looked it was at about 70%! So they sat back and said, "Hang on a second, what are we doing? What would we recommend if we were one of our clients?"

On 1 January 1997 Niels Schreiner Andersen, Henning Bach and Per Krenk established a new company taking over the name Schreiner Andersen Management A/S as well as all management consultancy activities from the existing company. The new company, Schreiner Andersen Holding A/S, held a 50% share of Schreiner Andersen Management A/S. Henning Bach and Per Krenk each acquired 25% of the new Schreiner Andersen Management A/S.

The headhunting activities were growing rapidly, and during 1999 it was decided to concentrate all future activities on two product areas:

- headhunting (today more than 90% of total turnover)

- business broking (mergers and acquisitions – M&A)

Global expansion started in 2000, and today the company has over 100 employees in 16 European countries as well as China. Therefore the position as majority shareholder is a key element in the group structure: Schreiner Andersen Management A/S controls a majority of the shares directly or indirectly in all new SAM international companies.

> **SAM Business Broker A/S**
>
> In January 2001 the M&A activities formed the basis for establishing SAM Business Broker A/S (SAM BB).
>
> Schreiner Andersen Management A/S is a 70-point shareholder in SAM Business Broker A/S, and Preben Holmboe holds the remaining 30 points.
>
> SAM BB concentrates its activities in the Danish market combined with cooperation partners internationally.

SAM Headhunting–Going international			
Denmark	1993	Netherlands	2004
Germany	2000	Belgium	2004
Sweden	2001	Luxembourg	2004
Switzerland	2001	Slovakia	2005
Norway	2001	Italy	2005
UK	2003	Spain	2006
Finland	2003	Ireland	2006
Poland	2004	France	2007
China	2004		

Growth over recent years has been tremendous: increase in turnover in the group was 50% in 2005 and 40% in 2006 resulting in a group turnover of near to €10 million in 2006. The budget for 2007 is again showing more than 30% increase in turnover.

SAM's approach to headhunting

To Niels SAM's approach to headhunting is described easily: "Go and talk to people! The important thing is to be able to get along with people." He continues, "Even if the person you contact is not the right person he or she might be able to point you into the right direction."

Whereas traditional headhunting firms use their junior researchers to identify a 'long list' of potential candidates, having had an initial discussion with an HR person as to what the requirements are and where in a company the required person might be located, SAM looks for people who know where to look. One way to do this is to approach someone who is overqualified for the job and then ask him/her whether they might know someone, not quite as good as themselves, who might be interested in the job. This way they get a list of names that are most likely to be the best suited for the job – not the names of all the other people that could have been mentioned. As Niels points out, "De facto these initial contacts do a pre-selection for you." He continues, "We get a lot of referrals from people who have been part of the process (even if they did not get the job)."

Another thing that sets them apart is that, working back from when the person is needed, a delivery date is agreed upon acceptance of contract: the day they take on the job a date is made to review the candidates with the decision makers. From initial contact to presentation of suitable candidates using the SAM approach takes about 3–5 weeks.

By operating as one company, rather than a network of local, often internationally competing organisations, SAM can take a lot off a company's shoulders. As Niels points out, "If a company from Germany wants to find someone in Sweden all they need to do is to get in touch with their local contact in Germany and the rest is sorted out for them." But working across Europe SAM also knows just how important local knowledge is and actively collects country-specific information, which is made available to everyone in the organisation through the intranet that was established in 1999. For example, in Sweden a successful sales manager will be driving a Volvo – not the VW perhaps prescribed by the German parent company. Another example of national difference is that a company recruiting in Germany has to pay for the travel of the candidate, which needs to be taken into account when agreeing the cost structure of a contract.

Company philosophy

From the day SAM was established, the basic idea has been to seek organisational structures offering the highest possible degree of flexibility. The virtual organisation is seen as one of the keys to ensure flexibility, which is why SAM headhunters, consultants and partners work out of offices in their homes. Concept development, administration and support to each of the SAM Headhunting companies are services offered by SAM A/S in Denmark. This has the advantage that the entire organisation is supported by only eight administrative staff who are paid out of the centre. Niels emphasises, "Our admin staff love everything they do – which is everything a headhunter would hate to do." Another job of the admin people is to make sure there is a consistent picture of the outside world.

Another way of ensuring that the outside gets a consistent view of the virtual organisation is shared processes. Here the need to leave some freedom and flexibility is recognised: about 80% of processes and procedures are standard, the rest is customised to address company/country specific issues.

Extranet and intranet systems are vital in tying the virtual organisation together by offering effective communication and cooperation internally in the organisation as well as in connection to the relationships with customers and candidates. The intranet is a very important tool for every headhunter in the SAM organisation both in his/her own work as well as in communication with colleges and administration.

SAM's intranet, which is constantly being improved, offers the following:

- CV database with around 15,000 CVs (by law they have to remove people from their database after six months – unless they agree to be kept on)

- SAM CRM System

- Best Practice

- Internal SAM Bulletin

- A number of administrative tools

With 1.5 million unique visitors per year viewing the SAM positions on these portals the extranet works as SAM's main marketing tool: it has an additional 20–25 visitors on other portals. As Niels puts it, "Being out there and being nice to people is our main approach to marketing." However, as they are not really on the radar screen of their major competitor, despite being the largest headhunter (by placements) in Denmark, they decided to run some advertising in autumn 2007.

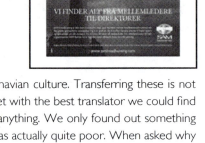

The two fundamental principles on which the company runs are:

- partnership
- learning

As Niels explains, "Both principles are very much embedded in the Scandinavian culture. Transferring these is not always easy. For example, we had written a brochure for the German market with the best translator we could find in Denmark; the Germans seemed to like it – or, at least, they did not say anything. We only found out something was not quite right when our Swiss partner pointed out that the German was actually quite poor. When asked why they had not said anything the German partner admitted that they had not said anything because they felt they could not criticise the 'authority'."

Working in partnership and working virtually, as well as SAM's approach to headhunting make it critical that partners are good networkers, which is why 'The Power of Networking' was introduced as one of SAM's mantras in 2006. That is why SAM uses its database also to build networks, rather than only to identify potential candidates.

Reporting is based on a 'need to have' basis; for example, the internet system works in a way that a headhunter cannot proceed with a job until he or she has provided a minimum of relevant information, for example company name, VAT number, etc. In other words, they need to create a client and job specification before they can proceed.

There is also a certain amount of information that needs to be provided before an invoice can be raised. By the way, all headhunters and consultants in the Group are remunerated purely on commission, with all payments being a percentage of the net income related to the headhunter or consultant.

Questions

1. Given the company's history and philosophy, what would your response to the call for more control be and why?

2. Is the fundamentally Scandinavian model transferable to other cultural regions?

3. In recruiting for SAM, what would be the main characteristics of your candidates and what would you do to ensure a thorough understanding of the company's culture and values?

4. Compare SAM's approach to headhunting to that of a traditional company – what are up- and downsides of each?

'The Power of Networking'

In SAM we are thinking and working in networks. In our daily work we have four basic networks:

- Local personal networks in every SAM Headhunting company.

- The SAM internet network constantly communicating and branding.

- The international SAM network offering interesting cross-border business opportunities.

- The SAM A/S support organisation.

The local network has to be the main avenue to business success, but in a start-up period we do experience that the internet and cross-border business can bring the first success.

APPENDIX 33.1: SAM HEADHUNTING – MISSION AND VALUES

The SAM Mission

The SAM Mission describes the business and concept as well as the response and characteristics for which we want to be known.

We want to be known as a reliable supplier of headhunter and management consultative services in our operating markets. Our customers are private and public companies. Our most important assignment is to contribute to the development of the companies which are our customers.

We make an effort to be on the edge with new market demands to ensure the highest level of customer satisfaction. Our consultative services are supported by the technology that ensures effectiveness and that makes us a preferred supplier.

Our partners and employees should be known for their experience and reliability as well as their ability to put themselves in the customer's place. We want to attract and maintain the best employees.

We aim to be the best within our main business area to obtain growth and increased values for SAM, our employees, and partners.

The SAM Values

The SAM Values describes the principles of management, competences, and basic values, being the precondition for achieving the goals.

This means that the SAM Values are principles controlling our effort and the standards we wish to enhance as we believe they create the best long-term results.

Each partner and employee must do his/her best to live by these values in their everyday activities, and ensure that decisions are followed into action.

To ensure a mutual reinforcing effort, there should be accordance between the following:

Basic approach

- We aim to be the best in all matters

- We are willing to change

- We have high morals and are reliable

- We are engaged and consistent

Strategy

Our strategies must ensure:

- That our partners – customers, collaborators, employees, and partners are content

- That SAM obtains profitable growth

- The development of new products and markets, while ensuring sufficient resources for the existing business

- Well-considered decisions based on clear risk-evaluations

Organisation

Our organisation supports our strategy by being:

- Clear and understandable for all employees

- Task oriented

- Virtual and geographically spread with consequent customer vicinity and flexibility

- Built with few organisational levels with a high degree of delegation, concurrent with the possibilities of a knowledge-based organisation

- Variable to the highest extent in its cost structure

Management

To obtain the goals, management must:

- Be sensitive and encouraging

- Distribute tasks and responsibility and fight bureaucracy

- Support personal and educational development

- Be fair and show respect

Employees

The employees of SAM must:

- Be customer oriented

- Create and conquer work challenges

- Show leadership and guts to act

- Be willing to learn

Skills

To claim priority to the competition each employee must:

- Be willing to change

- Work to win

- Be innovative

- Take initiatives instead of letting others do it

- Be responsible for getting relevant information

Processes

Our internal management processes must be clear and aimed towards:

- Measuring performances regarding customers, employees, and the fiscal result

- Fulfilling strategy and goals through suitable estimation of fiscal and non-fiscal results

- Fulfilling the demands of our customers

- Making everybody work from the same preconditions

APPENDIX 33.2: THE BUSINESS OF HEADHUNTING

Headhunting is principally about identifying the best people for a particular job who are at that time not really looking for it. It started in the United States where the first companies began in the 1950s, opening their first dependences in London a decade later. European companies also started in the 1960s. Most headhunters would not take any jobs below a certain salary level – generally around £35,000 per annum. Without quite realising it SAM had brought headhunting into areas where it had not previously been used. With increasing globalisation, headhunting, particularly for senior positions, seems to become increasingly important. According to a recent publication by *The Economist* (Jenn, 2005), "By 2004 Europe had become the most important market for headhunting; the top 20 in Europe accounted for 49% of total worldwide revenue; 37% US, 11% Pacific Asia."

The forefathers of headhunting

Four main players emanating from the US:

- Heidrick & Struggles (1953) 1968 in London; Spencer Stuart (1956) 1961 in London; Russel Reynolds (1969) 1971 in London; Kom/Ferry (1969) 1973 in London

Europe grown headhunting firms:

- Egon Zehnder (1964, Zurich); Alexander Hughes (1965, London); Goddard Kay Rogers (1970, London); Whitehead Mann (1976, London); Norman Broadbent (1983, London); Saxton Bampfylde (1986, London)

In terms of organisational structure there are two basic forms, wholly-owed, e.g. Egon Zehnder or networked, e.g. the Global Search Group. As ever there is also a combination of the two, e.g. the Amrop Hever Group.

From the client perspective there are two distinct approaches:

- 'Retained organisations' – a particular headhunting firm is chosen to find a particular candidate; fee generally 33% of recruited candidate's salary; the search takes place after a contract has been signed.

- 'Contingent headhunters' – the client organisation hires based on a short-list provided by the headhunter; in this scenario the search takes place before the contract is signed; this is more typical for non-executive vacancies.

The generic headhunting process has five main stages:

- Tender – several firms are pitching for a job; selling takes place based on competencies, knowledgeable employees and past expertise.

- Definition – headhunter and client work together to define what's required of the candidate in terms of professional skills but also what the company culture is like to ensure fit.

- Development of short-list; in database on consultants' networks; search generally undertaken by researchers, creating a 'long-list' which is then reviewed and sorted through by a partner; short-listed candidates are discreetly contacted by consultant before being finalised and passed on to client.

- Client reviews short-list and meetings with selected candidates are agreed; confidentiality and discretion are key here.

- Consultant is involved in negotiations, salary etc.

An assignment is generally considered to be unsuccessful if the candidate leaves, for whatever reason, within the first year.

Appendix A How to use the case studies

MBA

The cases can be used individually in traditional MBA courses (see Table A.1), to infuse innovation into traditional subjects; or as a set, forming the foundation for a course dedicated to innovation, as has been done at the London Business School. The latter might challenge current business school and university structures as it is not likely to fit neatly into any existing department. As creating an innovative organisation is heavily dependent on leadership, and is about creating an appropriate culture, organisational behaviour departments might be best suited to accommodate such a course. While it is strongly recommended that the overall coordination of the course remains with one or maximum two people to assure consistency and continuity, the course would benefit tremendously if additional expertise from other faculty areas, as well as from 'the real world' could be integrated.

Table A.2 shows in which traditional faculty areas the case studies might be used.

Table A.1 By discipline

	BBC	ihavemoved	Black & Decker	Lotus Elise	Dumfries	Roche	GKN	Bank of Scotland	John McAslan & Partners	TTP Group	Unilever	SAM
Strategic management		X		X	X	X	X	X	X	X	X	X
Operations management/ Manufacturing			X	X	X	X	X					
Marketing incl. branding & market research	X	X	X	X	X			X			X	
Organisational behaviour	X		X	X		X	X			X		X
Finance/ Entrepreneurship		X		X	X		X	X		X		
Economics					X	X						

The following cases have a Part B: ihavemoved, Black & Decker, Roche; they are available on the instructor's website (http://www.wiley.co.uk/vonstamm).

Table A.2   Exploring issues relevant to innovation

	BBC *Walking with Dinosaurs*	ihavemoved	Black & Decker Quattro	Lotus Elise	Dumfries Recycling	Roche Saquinavir	GKN	Bank of Scotland	John McAslan & Partners	TTP Group	Unilever	SAM
Wider context					X	X	X	X				X
Timing		X			X		X	X			X	
Green issues				(X)	X		(X)			(X)		
Patenting			X			X	(X)					
Strategy – Internet		X										X
Strategy – Flexibility		X		X		X						X
Globalisation	X											X
Internal investment	X			X	X		X	X		X	X	
External investment	X	X					X	X		X		
Levels of innovation							X				X	
Def. of success & failure					X			X				
Innovation culture			X	X				X		X	X	
The role of individuals	X	X	X	X	X		X	X		X		X
Project leader	X	X	X	X			X	X		X		
Company leader		X	X	X	X			X		X		X
Commercial awareness	X	X	X	X						X	X	
Passion/Commitment/Determination	X	X	X	X		X	X	X		X		
Communication		X	X	X		X	X			X		X
Personal relationships	X	X	X	X		X	X	X	X	X	X	X
Defiance		X	X	X	X		X					
Internal networks	X		X	X		X	X	X	X	X		X
External collaboration		X	X					X	X	X		
Designers' involvement		X	X									
Team spirit	X		X	X		X				X		X
Early involvement			X	X								
Role of market research			X					X			X	
Prototypes	X		X	X								

Appendix B Innovation – achievements, realisations and next challenges

Below are insights from the *Third Innovation Best Practice and Future Challenges Report* (von Stamm, 2006) on what companies on their innovation journey have achieved to date, some realisations and what the next challenges for innovators are.

Achievements and realisations

- **Innovation is firmly on the agenda** – the Boston Consulting Group found that 87% of senior executives that participated in their 2005 survey believe innovation essential to success, and 74% report increased spending on innovation (that 51% are dissatisfied with innovation results is another matter).

- **Establishing an innovation strategy** – most participating organisations have embraced the necessity of developing an innovation strategy to guide their organisation's innovation activities; however, there is still widespread uncertainty of what exactly an innovation strategy is and looks like.

- **Overall realisation of the importance of leadership** – together with the realisation that innovation needs a holistic, culture-based approach goes the increasing awareness that the right kind of leadership is absolutely paramount to creating an innovative organisation (again, emphasised in the 2006 IMB CEO study).

- **Heavyweights lead the way** – whereas a few years ago the task of investigating what is required to become more innovative would have been given to a fairly junior person, it is now firmly in the hands of experienced, respected and multifaceted senior people.

- **Processes have been established** – stage-gate processes are now commonplace, and most organisations have some system or process to collect and manage ideas (for information on the stage gate process see www.stage-gate.com); although companies are also starting to realise that traditional stage-gate does not work for radical or discontinuous innovation.

- **Insights rather than market research** – organisations have realised that in order to find starting points for innovation, traditional market research is not providing the necessary insights; instead organisations tend to focus more on observation-based methodologies (previously primarily used by designers).

- **Recognition is more important than (financial) rewards** – whereas a few years back there was still a lot of faith in encouraging innovation through financial rewards, this has given way to the realisation that recognition is much more powerful.

- **Making most of the physical assets** – many organisations have started to consciously use the physical work environment to create spaces dedicated to innovation, or designed the workspace layout to encourage behaviours that are supportive of innovation.

Next challenges

- **Encouraging a systemic view of innovation** – innovation requires that a company-wide perspective is taken, and one that takes the interaction between different forces into account.

- **Creating effective idea management systems** – despite the fact that there is a lot of knowledge and insight around idea management, there are still a large number of organisations that struggle with this aspect of the innovation agenda.

- **Which horse to back?** – finding ways to identify which projects to take forward remains an issue – particularly if they are towards the radical or even discontinuous end of the innovation spectrum.

- **Managing boundaries** – with the increased opening to the outside world and involvement of customers and other external constituencies in the development of new products and services, issues of intellectual property need to be addressed.

- **Break down internal boundaries** – while the use of teams in general and cross-functional teams in particular has already contributed significantly to the breaking down of silos in organisations, there is often still a long way to go to create a feeling of 'oneness' for the entire organisation, particularly if it is made up of several business units.

- **Focus on value creation** – it sometimes seems that innovation has become an end in itself whereas, clearly, it ought to be a means to an end, ultimately to create a profitable, sustainable business (which means that the value for the organisation might be an enhanced reputation, learning or breaking into a new market).

- **Identifying the right balance between innovating and operating** – while it is understood that there needs to be a balance between innovating and operating, most organisations still have to work out what the appropriate balance for their particular business is; how to split the limited resources between the different innovation fields, and why.

- **Avoid 'second-class citizens'** – whereas a few years ago it was more difficult to attract the better people to innovation, there now seems to be a shift the other way; the challenge seems to have become: how to avoid those who are not involved directly with innovative projects feeling left out.

- **Meaningful measures of innovation performance** – this was one of the main challenges identified in the previous report and seems to remain a concern; however, innovation leaders seem to be less obsessed with hard financial data and tend to take a longer term perspective; having said that, having 'hard' data would make it easier for those driving innovation to gain wider buy-in within their organisations.

- **Move away from a paternalistic culture** – organisations with a paternalistic culture may find that this is holding back their innovation capability: employees are not used to making decisions and tend to expect to be told what to do, rather than taking the initiative themselves.

- **Dealing with discontinuous innovation** – knowledge about how to manage innovation (incremental and radical) has increased many times over the recent years. However, what is still tricky is, how to anticipate, recognise and deal with disruptive or discontinuous innovation; the kind of innovation that encroaches onto our territory but for which a different skill set (approaches, strategies etc.) is required.

Appendix C   Categories of design

Here we will consider the different categories of design projects one might encounter.[1] Some references to additional reading as well as case studies are provided. Some aspects of the design process may vary with project type and I aim to point this out where appropriate. Before we take a look at individual types of design, a brief discourse into the history of the development of 'design' is given below.

HISTORY OF 'DESIGN'

In the traditional understanding, 'design' is often associated with a person who is involved in both the design and production of an object. This concept began to change with the outset of the Industrial Revolution, which initiated the division of work and the need for specialisation. Resulting from this, two strands of design evolved: 'design as art' and 'design as engineering', each with a different meaning and different emphasis in education. Part and consequence of the development into specialisation was the separation of industrial and engineering design about which Ivor Owen (1990), a former director of the Design Council, says, "I strongly believe that the schism between engineering design and industrial design has been one of the most damaging issues in manufacturing industry imaginable." Sir William Barlow (1988), a former chairman of the Design Council, asserts this by pointing out that almost every product requires an appropriate balance of both. A similar view is presented in the earlier Corfield Report (1979), which states that product design includes both industrial and engineering design. While the Bauhaus attempted to reconcile these two strands, with Gropius promoting the 'marriage between design and machine', the split between the two aspects of design remained. In recent years the shift towards working in multidisciplinary teams has brought the different strands back together, if not in one person at least in a closely operating team.

The closer cooperation between different functions has also brought out cultural and language differences between departments and highlighted the need to develop tools and methods to overcome these differences and allow the development of a shared understanding. Here metaphors, suggested by, for example, Black (1962), Kendall and Kendall (1994), McWilliam and Dumas (1995) and Walsham (1991), and prototypes, suggested by Leonard-Barton (1991) or Rettig (1994), are frequently mentioned as tools that can help to achieve this aim (see also Chapter 12). The further specialisation went, the wider the range of activities that were associated with the term 'design'. Walker (1989) devised what he calls the 'Design Family Tree' (see Figure C.1), which shows the different types of specialisation associated with design while at the same time giving a feeling for their historical development. There does seem to be some overlap between categories, whichever way one tries to cut them, i.e. each category of design project is likely to involve a range of different types of design activity. Table C.1 links Walker's five categories with the categories suggested here.

Any one project is likely to involve a range of different types of design and for each project the skills mix required will be different. However, the mix will not only vary by product but is also likely to differ at different stages of that

---

[1] This is but one way design categories may be cut differently and other categories added.

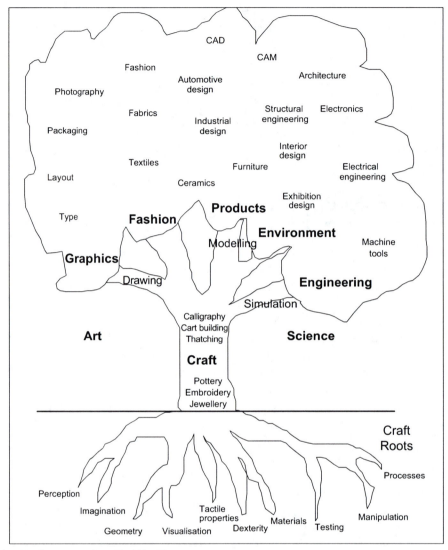

Figure C.1   Walker's Design Family Tree.
Source: Walker (1989)

product's life cycle. Remember the Sony Walkman. Focus on miniaturisation of the technology in the early phases, then modifying to serve the needs of different customer segments. Each of these changes required a different set of design skills: engineering design for the former; industrial and packaging design for the latter. One implication is that if a second generation of a product is developed, an organisation should think carefully whether the original team is the best solution or whether different skills are required. Another is that constraints are likely to vary.

When thinking about different types of design projects, it might also be worth thinking about the time horizon and the number of 'units' produced. Some categories are, by nature, one-off, whereas others are repeated frequently. For example, architectural and town planning projects tend to be one-off, whereas graphic design projects, such as

Table C.1 Types of design

	Environment	Product	Graphic	Fashion	Engineering
Town planning & urban design	X	X	X		
Architecture & interior design	X	X	X		X
Garden & landscape design	X	X	X		
Exhibition design	X	X	X		X
Product design	X	X			X
Packaging design		X	X		
Graphic design		X	X		
Corporate identity	X	X	X	X	
Brands		X	X		
IT design & multimedia	(X – virtual!)		X		
Service design			X		
Textile design	X	X		X	

annual reports or stationery, happen quite frequently. Corporate identity projects are somewhere in the middle. While I am not suggesting that it does not matter if a graphic design project does not meet customer requirements, particular care should go into one-off projects to ensure that it meets customer needs. After all, the cost and effort involved into printing new stationery is quite different from attempting to rectify than an architectural project.[2]

The design process will vary slightly for different types of design projects and the following publications prepared by the Design Business Association for the DTI, also referred to in the relevant categories, might be useful:

- Managing corporate identity programmes (1992)
- Managing interior design projects (1992)
- Managing packaging design projects (1992)
- Managing product design projects (1992)

TOWN PLANNING AND URBAN DESIGN

Town planning and urban design projects tend to be of a large scale and, more often than not, initiated by the public rather than the private sector. They also tend to be long term in nature and can require a lengthy negotiation process involving citizens, politicians and special interest groups. Hence, the involvement of stakeholders and the incorporation of their concerns is a major part of the development process. It can have a critical influence, particularly on the timing of the execution.

With increasing population and ever-growing demand for new dwellings, environmental concerns and environmental impact analysis are becoming increasingly important. Just recently it was announced that over 900,000 new homes should be built in the South of England over a 10-year period – one wonders whether there will be any countryside left. But at the same time the demand opens up new opportunities: disused land, empty dwellings, sites left unused

---

[2] Having said that, even buildings that are dysfunctional are being pulled down (many of which were built in the 1960s and 1970s).

by dying industries in the centres and around the edges of towns are all calling out for imaginative reuse of what is called 'brown fields'.

ARCHITECTURE AND INTERIOR DESIGN

Much of research into the design process and decision making in design has taken place in the field of architecture – for many it is still closely associated with 'design as art'. More than most other types of design projects, architecture and interior design projects are centred around an individual – rather than a group or a company name. Many of the big architectural practices are known by their founders' name(s), and their personality is often the main selling point.

But it is also the architects you probably find wandering into 'foreign' territory most frequently. Think of Le Corbusier, Mies van der Rohe, or Behrens who has not only designed the buildings for AEG but also their logo and other products (electric irons, heaters, kettles, fans, etc.). Even though it might not have been called that at the time, the AEG story is an early example of a holistic approach to corporate identity. It seems to me that today organisations are becoming more aware of the importance of architecture and interior design in supporting and shaping a company's image. I believe the importance will continue to increase, not least because of an increasing need for organisations to have a strong culture. Why? Because in a time where people work away from the office and outside the cultural atmosphere of the organisation more and more, the organisation needs to take greater care in communicating its culture, and the work environment is one way this can be done. So, the built environment can support an organisation's culture – or work against it.

Thinking about retailing, interior design is probably even more closely associated with branding and image. Particularly with franchised businesses the 'product concept' and design language are essential.

Architecture is also a field where environmental considerations can have a significant impact: on heating, 'green' climate control, reuse of water, use of environmentally friendly/recycled building material, and so on. It is a field where much is possible – but little is done at present.

Garden and landscape design

This is a type of design project where planning and execution are often undertaken by the same person. It is probably also a category of design that does not come immediately to mind when talking about 'design' in the context of this course – and it is an area where designers from other areas hardly ever venture. It is also an area where you are less likely to find a formalised design process and the team that develops and executes the design is generally quite small. As design manager you are probably most likely to come across it as part of larger architectural projects.

EXHIBITION DESIGN

Exhibition design is an interesting one: it is extremely short term in two ways: (a) it is generally only for the duration of the exhibition; and (b) developed and delivered in quite a short time span. It is generally offered by highly specialised companies. I believe it basically breaks down into two markets: one is for standardised exhibition products such as poster stands etc.; the other is for specialist, custom-made solutions. Think about the big motor shows where car manufacturers tend to invest heavily in spectacular stands.

While the past has seen exhibition design that was, more often than not, removed from the company's identity, I believe that in future companies should use their exhibition stands to make a statement about their organisation, about their personality. They should use the opportunity to communicate their values and what they stand for. I have recently come across a manufacturer who can offer bespoke solutions at mass-production prices.

PRODUCT DESIGN

This category is what probably comes to mind first when talking about design in the business context. While all products are designed – if design (as activity) is defined as 'generating information from which a required product can become reality' – by no means all products are developed with the involvement of an industrial designer. It seems that product design may be undertaken by engineers, marketers, other technical staff, the manager – just about everyone. As we know, these designing 'non-designers' are called 'silent designers' (Gorb & Dumas, 1987). In many cases the industrial design is used only for the 'styling', and only at the end of the development process. In my view this is a big mistake as design can contribute significantly beyond the aesthetic aspects of a product.

Whether a design consultant or internal resources are used varies from company to company (see Chapter 28 for a discussion of advantages and disadvantages of each option). But I believe that there are also trends at industry and country level. For example, hi-fi products are more likely to be developed with the involvement of designers than, say, microwaves and washing machines. I also believe that there are some differences at national level. For example, in Germany companies are more likely to have in-house design facilities than in the UK. However, I think that this type of design is generally the one most likely to be undertaken in-house. Most of the literature on the design process concerns this category.[3]

PACKAGING DESIGN

Packaging design is probably most important for FMCGs (fast-moving consumer goods). Repackaging has sometimes brought a brand back into customers' favour and it is here that communicating the right values messages is very important. Think about all the fancy water bottles you can get today – sold at a premium. Generally, with food products packaging is particularly important as it often contains important information about use and preparation – and is a major factor of differentiation. But increasingly packaging design goes beyond the 'around the product', becomes part of the product itself and is often source for innovation. Think about aerosol cans, 'blown-up' packaging for crisps, elaborate perfume bottles, and so on. On the other hand, for electronic consumer goods, being displayed without packaging, the packaging is less important. This is a category where companies tend to rely on external rather than internal designers.

---

[3] And to be even more specific, a lot of it originates from research into the automotive industry.

Graphic design

Graphic design can play a part in many other design projects such as exhibition design, product design, packaging design, and of course corporate identity projects. Typeface, layout, colour and language all carry a message and need to be selected carefully. Some typefaces convey traditional values, some look modern, elegant, technical and so forth. Colours have messages too – red for danger, green for environment, blue is generally perceived as cool – but beware, the meaning of colours can vary from country to country. Graphic design is of particular importance for the front end of service products, where visual clarity and ease of access are critical.

CORPORATE IDENTITY

For me corporate identity encompasses everything an organisation stands for and this should be reflected in every encounter with the organisation be it with a person or product, reception, shop floor, cloak room, or director's office. Designers are responsible for translating what a company stands for into a visual image, into the appropriate symbols, colours and typefaces. BP and Shell are examples of corporate identities that have been changed and adapted over time. The core ingredients are still the same but the visualisation has been updated in keeping with the time.

Managing the corporate identity is often the main task for a company-internal design manager. While many companies restrict the responsibility to managing company literature and logo, I believe that it should go further and include products – tangible and intangible, and environments.

Visual representation is more powerful than many people realise. I always liked an exercise used by Dr Angela Dumas to illustrate this: she shows pictures of three abstract paintings (the ones shown in Box C.1 are not exactly the ones she has used but I hope close enough to make her point).

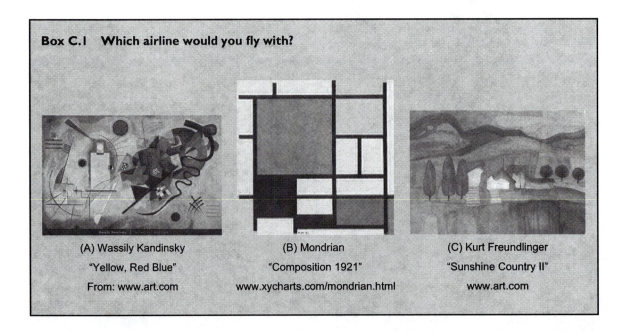

Box C.1   Which airline would you fly with?

(A) Wassily Kandinsky	(B) Mondrian	(C) Kurt Freundlinger
"Yellow, Red Blue"	"Composition 1921"	"Sunshine Country II"
From: www.art.com	www.xycharts.com/mondrian.html	www.art.com

She then asks two questions: the first is, if these paintings represented organisations, which one would you like to work for? The answer depends on preferences for structure and freedom and so on. She then asks, and if these paintings represented airlines, which one would you like to fly with? She generally does not need to say any more to convince people of the power of visual images. It is interesting though that the answers shift over time – since Virgin Airlines have entered the market people are not quite as worried any more about flying with 'A'. There are also cultural differences. I found it interesting that most Westerners assumed that Japanese would prefer to work organisation B – but in fact, the fast majority of Japanese see themselves working for a company A. So visual metaphors and tools can also be extremely helpful in uncovering hidden assumptions.

BRANDS

Brand design and corporate identity are closely related, both are concerned with communicating a certain set of values and both have a stronger strategic component than other categories of design. One could say that corporate identity deals with branding issues at the company level, brand issues concern the product level.

IT AND MULTIMEDIA DESIGN

IT and multimedia design is probably the youngest member in the design category family. And, particularly for web design, this is a field where technical and design skills have to be matched. Technical possibilities are probably ahead of customer requirements and conscious needs and development cycles are often extremely short. Developments in IT have changed the way we work, where we work and how we interact. Whether an interaction is a pleasurable or unpleasurable experience depends very much on user-friendliness and design.

TEXTILE AND FASHION DESIGN

Textile design is another category of design you are probably less likely to encounter, unless of course you work in the fashion or textile industry. Branding plays an important role, certainly at the top end of the market, fashion is certainly one area where people are paying a premium to be associated with a certain brand, and the lifestyle associated with it. While custom-made cloths have been a privilege of the rich and famous, mass customisation techniques allow more and more people to walk into a shop and have their, for example, jeans made to order to their particular shape and figure. Interior design is probably the other design field most likely to incorporate some aspects of textile design.

FURNITURE DESIGN

Finally, there is furniture design. As above, it tends to happen in dedicated companies, though many architects also try their hand in furniture design. It seems that furniture design seems to take on more and more characteristics of fashion design, with parallels in custom-made items and mass-produced goods.

SUMMARY

Table C.2 summarises some aspects for the different design categories, it does not aim to be comprehensive but provides some food for thought.

Table C.2 Different Types of Design

	Link with other design activities	Time horizon/ 'life expectancy'	Frequency	Tends to be associated with:	More likely to be located
Town & Urban	Graphic	Long term	One-off	Organisation	External
Architecture & Interior	Graphic Textile Landscape Furniture	Long term Medium term	One-off Sporadic	Individual/ organisation	External External
Garden & Landscape	Architecture	Medium term	Sporadic	Organisation	External
Exhibition	Graphic Interior Architecture IT and multimedia	Short term Medium term	Sporadic/regular	Organisation	External
Product (Industrial & Engineering)	Packaging Graphic Branding	Depending on product, short to long term	Depending on product, sporadic to ongoing	Organisation/ individual	Internal
Packaging	Graphic Product Brands	Medium term	Sporadic	Organisation	External
Graphic	Most other categories	Short to medium term	Sporadic	Organisation	External
Corporate identity	Architecture Interior Branding, Graphic IT and multimedia	Should be long term	Sporadic	Organisation	External
Brands	Product Graphic Packaging	Should be long term	Sporadic	Organisation	Internal
IT & Multimedia	Graphic Product	Short to medium term	Sporadic	Organisation	External
Service	Graphic Architecture Interior IT and multimedia	Medium term	Depending on product, sporadic to ongoing	Organisation	Internal
Textile & Fashion	Branding Graphic	Seasonal	Depending on product, sporadic to ongoing	Individual/ organisation	Internal/ external
Furniture	Textile	Medium	Sporadic/ ongoing	Individual/ organisation	

READING SUGGESTIONS

Buying into Design (1998). London: The Design Council.

Comment: Booklet with case studies illustrating how to purchase design, as well as the positive implications from using design.

Managing . . . series (1992), prepared by the Design Business Association for the DTI.

Comment: Useful booklets on process and management of a number of different design projects including corporate identity, interior design, packaging design, product design.

Thackara, J. (1997). *European Design Prize Winners! How Today's Successful Companies Innovate by Design*. Aldershot, UK: Gower.

Comment: The book not only presents case studies of the winners of the European Design Prize 1997 but also provides much useful information, statistics and trends that are relevant to design and innovation.

Olins, W. (1996). *The Guide to Identity: How to Create and Sustain Change Through Managing Identity*. Aldershot, UK: Gower.

Comment: Wally Olins, co-founder of probably the first corporate identity consultancy to take the subject to a strategic level, provides a comprehensive guide to corporate identity, explaining what it is and how it can be used to full effect.

Mackenzie, D. (1991). *Green Design: Design for the Environment*. London: Laurence King.

Comment: Offers an environmental perspective on different types of design, providing a number of case studies.

Lyle, J.T. (1999). *Designs for Human Ecosystems, Landscape, Land Use, and Natural Resources*. New York: Island Press.

Comment: Providing a number of examples and case studies the author explores methods of designing landscapes which function like natural ecosystems.

Allinson, K. (1995). *The Wild Card of Design – A Perspective on Architecture in a Project Management Environment*. Oxford: Butterworth Heinemann.

Comment: This book provides an architectural perspective on the design process.

Some useful websites

www.ArchitectsWorldwide.com
The portal site for international architects websites.

http://www.riba.org
The website of the Royal Institute of British Architects.

http://store.yahoo.com/riba-links
This site provides more than 500 architecture related websites.

www.aiaonline.com
The website of the American Institute of Architecture.

www.BuildItWorldwide.com
The portal site for international construction websites.

www.DesignersWorldwide.com
The portal site for international designer websites

www.EngineersWorldwide.com
The portal site for international engineering web sites

www.cfsd.org.uk
Centre for Sustainable Design. A European centre of excellence focusing on the implications of sustainable on the design of products. Facilitates discussion and research about the effects of the 'triple bottom line' on design: environmental, social and economic needs.

http://www.csfi.org.co
Website of the Centre for the Study of Financial Innovation; the CSFI is an independent London-based think tank, funded by the world's top banks. It explores the future of the financial services industry. They have an active agenda of meetings, seminars and research projects which are of wide interest to all who work in, or use, the financial markets. 18 Curzon Street, London W1Y 7AD, UK, Tel: +44 (0)171 493 0173, Fax: +44 (0)171 493 0190.

http://members.optusnet.com.au/~charles57/Creative/index2.html
Charles Cave's extensive collection of creativity information.

http://www.edwdebono.com
Edward de Bono's website – an extensive catalogue of items related to Edward de Bono from around the world, including training centres, seminar schedules, books, and games.

http://www.micaworld.com
MICA Management. A Toronto-based training and consulting organisation, specialising in creativity and innovation, leadership development, and personal and organisational effectiveness. MICA distributes the Serious Creativity CD in Canada and North America.

http://www.creativesparks.org
NCCI (National Center for Creativity). A non-profit organisation established to help facilitate the growing interest in the field of creativity and innovation. NCCI provides educational opportunities through seminars, training courses and a specialty bookstore, the NCCI Resource Mart.

References

Aaker, D. (1991). *Managing Brand Equity: Capitalising on the Value of a Brand Name*. New York: Free Press.

Abernathy, W.J. & Clark, K.B. (1985). Innovation: mapping the winds of creative destruction. *Research Policy*, **14**, 3–22.

Adler, N. (1986). *International Dimensions of Organizational Behavior*. Boston, MA: PWS-Kent.

Adler, P.S. (1992). Managing DFM: learning to co-ordinate product and process design. In G.I. Susman (ed.), *Integrating Design and Manufacturing for Competitive Advantage*. New York: Oxford University Press.

Allen, D. (2000). Living the brand. *Design Management Journal*, 35–40.

Allinson, K. (1995). *The Wild Card of Design – A Perspective on Architecture in a Project Management Environment*. Oxford: Butterworth-Heinemann.

Amabile, T.M. (1988). A model of creativity and innovation in organizations. In B.M. Staw & L.P. Cummings (eds), *Research in Organizational Behavior* (pp. 123–67). Greenwich, CT: JAI Press.

Amabile, T.M. (1989). How to kill creativity. *Harvard Business Review*, 77–87.

Amabile, T.M., Conti, R., Coon, H., Lazenby, J. & Herron, M. (1996). Assessing the work environment for creativity. *Academy of Management Journal*, **39**, 1154–84.

Ambler, T. (1997). Do brands benefit consumers? *International Journal of Advertising*, **16**, 167–97.

Ambler, T. (2002). Brand and innovation. Presentation given at the London Business School as part of the course 'Managing Innovation Design & Creativity'.

Ancona, D.G. & Caldwell, D. (1990). Improving the performance of new product teams. *Research-Technology Management*, **33**, 25–9.

Anonymous (1996). Outsourcing product development. *Supervision*, **57**, 10–12.

Anonymous (1997a). Sharing knowledge through BP's virtual team network. *Harvard Business Review*, **75**, 152–3.

Anonymous (1997b). *Bei MuZ brummt der Motor wieder*. Kiel, Germany: Kieler Nachrichten.

Anonymous (2001). *A Question of Culture? Collaborative Innovation in UK Business*. London: CBI.

Anonymous (2002). Consumer products – Branding. http://www.sgs.co.uk/consulting/industries/consumer/branding.htm.

Anonymous (2003). A question of risk. *Growth Strategies*, May, 2–4.

Anonymous (2004). Why Whirlpool is cleaning up. *Business Week*, 8 February.

Baker, B.N. & Wilemon, D.L. (1977). Managing complex programs: a review of major research findings. *R&D Management*, **8**, 23–8.

Balachandra, R. & Friar, J.H. (1997). Factors for success in R&D projects and new product innovation: a contextual framework. *IEEE Transactions on Engineering Management*, **44**, 276–87.

Balmer, J. (1999). Increasing sensitivity to corporate branding and identity. Speech given by Professor John Balmer, Director of International Corporate Branding at the 1st summer symposium for the ICCIS.

Barclay, I. (1992). The new product development process: past evidence and future practical application, Part 1. *R&D Management*, **22**, 255–63.

Barclay, I. & Lunt, P.J. (1987). Successful management of the introduction of new technology. In R. Rothwell & J. Bessant (ed.), *Innovation, Adaptation and Growth* (pp. 81–91). Amsterdam: Elsevier.

Barkan, P. & Iansiti, M. (1993). Prototyping: a tool for rapid learning in product development. *Concurrent Engineering Research and Applications*, **1**, 125–34.

Barkema, H.J., Bell, J. & Pennings, J. (1996). Foreign entry, cultural barriers, and learning. *Strategic Management Journal*, **17**, 151–66.

Barlow, W. (1988). The importance of design. In P. Gorb (ed.), *Design Talks!* London: The Design Council.

Barnholt, E.W. (1997). Fostering business growth with breakthrough innovation. *Research Technology Management*, **40**, 12.

Barnholt, E. (2002). Risk management. *Vital Speeches of the Day*, **68**, 525–9.

Baxter, M. (1995). *Product Design – Practical Methods for the Systematic Development of New Products*. London: Chapman & Hall.

Belbin, M. (1991). Design innovation and the team. *Design Management Journal*, 38–42.

Berner, K.M. (1997). Is your prototype yours? *Design News*, **52**, 200.

Bernstein, D. (1986). *Company Image and Reality*. Eastbourne: Holt, Rinehard & Winston.

Bernstein, P. (1998). *Against the Gods: The Remarkable Story of Risk*. Chichester, UK: John Wiley & Sons, Ltd.

Bessant, J. & von Stamm, B. (2007). Twelve search strategies that could save your organisation. Advanced Institute of Management Executive Briefing.

Birkinshaw, J. & Gibson, C. (2005). *The Ambidextrous Organisation*. AIM Executive Briefing.

Birkinshaw, J. (2001). Managing internal R&D networks in global firms – what sort of knowledge is involved? *Long Range Planning*, **35**(3), 245–67.

Black, A. (1990). 32 traits of creative people. http://www.cre8ng.com/newsletter/news02.html.

Black, M. (1962). *Models and Metaphors, Studies in Language and Philosophy*. Ithaca, NY: Cornell University Press.

Blaich, R. & Blaich, J. (1993). *Product Design and Corporate Strategy – Managing the Connection for Competitive Advantage*. New York: McGraw-Hill.

Blumberg, D. (1987). Developing service as a line of business. *Management Review*, **76**, 58.

Bobrow, E.E. (1997). *The Complete Idiot's Guide to New Product Development*. New York: Alpha Books.

Boer, H. & Gertsen, F. (2003). From continuous improvement to continuous innovation: a (retro) (per)spective. *International Journal of Technology Management*, **26**, 805–27.

Bohm, D. & Peat, F.D. (1991). Science, order and creativity. In J.V. Henry (ed.), *Creative Management*, volume 1 (pp. 24–33). London: Sage.

Boisot, M., von Stamm, B. & Griffiths, D. (1995). Integrating design and organisation: a research proposal. Submitted to the Design Council.

Booz Allen Hamilton (1982). *New Product Development in the 1980s*. New York: Booz Allen Hamilton.

Bower, J.L. & Hout, T.M. (1988). Fast-cycle capability for competitive power. *Harvard Business Review*, 110–18.

Boze, B.V. & Patton, C.R. (1995). The future of consumer branding as seen from the picture today. *Journal of Consumer Marketing*, **12**.

Branscomb, L.M., Florida, R., Hart, D., Keller, J. & Boville, D. (1999). *Investing in Innovation*. Boston, MA: MIT Press.

Breen, Bill (2004). The six myths of creativity. *Fast Company*, **89**, December.

Brenner, M.S. (1994). Practical R&D project prioritization. *Research Technology Management*, **37**, 38–42.

Brezet, H. & van Hemel, C. (1997). Ecodesign. A promising approach to sustainable production and consumption. United Nations Environment Programme (UNEP).

British Brands Group (2003). *A Guide to Brands X*. London: British Brands Group.

Brown, J.L. & Agnew, N.M. (1982). The balance of power in matrix structure. *Business Horizon*, **25**(6), 52–4.

Bruce, M. & Biemans, W.G. (1995). *Product Development: Meeting the Challenge of the Design–Marketing Interface*. Chichester, UK: John Wiley & Sons, Ltd.

Bruce, M. & Cooper, R. (1997). *Marketing and Design Management*. London: International Thomson Business Press.

Bruce, M. & Morris, B. (1995). Approaches to design management in the product development process. In M. Bruce & W.G. Biemans (eds), *Product Development: Meeting the Challenge of the Design–Marketing Interface* (pp. 99–116). Chichester, UK: John Wiley & Sons, Ltd.

Bryan, L., Fraser, J., Oppenheim, J. & Rall, W. (1999). *Race for the World*. Boston, MA: Harvard Business School Press.

Buchanan, L. (2003). How to take risks in a time of anxiety. *Inc.com* (online magazine), May.

Bullmore, J. (2002). *Posh Spice & Persil: the Brands Lecture 2001*. London: The British Brands Group.

Burall, P. (1992). How to be green. *Design*, August.

Burall, P. (1996). *Product Development and the Environment*. Aldershot, UK: Gower.

Burt, R. (2007). Questions for Ronald Burt. *Rotman Magazine*, winter.

Calantone, R.J., Schmidt, J.B. & Di Benedetto, C.A. (1997). New product activities and performance: the moderating role of environmental hostility. *Journal of Product Innovation Management*, **14**, 179–89.

Carter, C.F. & Williams, B.R. (1957). *Industrial and Technical Progress*. Oxford: Oxford University Press.

Chesbrough, H. (2003). *Open Innovation: The New Imperative for Creating and Profiting from Technology*. Boston, MA: Harvard Business School Press.

Chesbrough, H.W. & Teece, D.J. (1996). When is virtual virtuous? Organizing for innovation. *Harvard Business Review*, 67–73.

Chiesa, V. (1996). Strategies for global R&D. *Research Technology Management*, **39**, 19ff.

Christensen, C. (1997). *Innovator's Dilemma: When New Technologies Cause Great Firms to Fail*. Boston, MA: Harvard Business School Press.

Christensen, C. (2003). *The Innovator's Solution: Creating and Sustaining Successful Growth*. Boston, MA: Harvard Business School Press.

Christensen, C., Roth, E.A. & Anthony, S.D. (2004). *Seeing What's Next: Using Theories of Innovation to Predict Industry Change*. Boston, MA: Harvard Business School Press.

Chryssochoidi, G.M. & Wong, V. (2000). Service innovation multi-country launch: causes of delays. *European Journal of Innovation Management*, **3**, 35.

Clark, K.B. & Wheelwright, S.C. (1993). *Managing New Product and Process Development: Text and Cases.* New York: Free Press.

Claxton, G. (1997). *Hare Brain, Tortoise Mind: Why Intelligence Increases When You Think Less.* London: Fourth Estate.

Cleland, R.S. (2000). Building successful brands on the internet. MBA Dissertation at the Judge Institute of Management Studies, Cambridge University, UK.

Cohen, M.A., Eliashberg, J. & Ho, T.-H. (1996). New product development: the performance and time-to-market tradeoffs. *Management Science*, 173–86.

Cohen, S.H. (1996). Tools for quantitative market research. In M.D.J. Rosenau, A. Griffin, G. Castellion & N. Anschuetz (eds), *The PDMA Handbook of New Product Development*, volume 1 (pp. 253–67). New York: John Wiley & Sons, Inc.

Coles, A.M., Dickson, K. & Woods, A. (1997). Not designed here? Decision making over design sources of UK textile firms. Academy of Management Annual Conference.

Cooper, R.G. & Kleinschmidt, E.J. (1996). Winning business in product development: the critical success factors. *Research Technology Management*, **39**, 18–29.

Cooper, R.G. & Kleinschmidt, E.J. (2001). Stage-gate process for new product success. *Innovation Management* (http://www.u3.dk/).

Cooper, R.G. & Press, M. (1995). *The Design Agenda: A Guide to Successful Design Management.* Chichester, UK: John Wiley & Sons, Ltd.

Cooper, R.G. (1986). *Winning at New Products.* London: Kogan Page.

Cooper, R.G. (1988). The new product process: a decision guide for management. *Journal of Marketing Management*, **3**, 238–55.

Cooper, R.G. (1994). Third-generation new product processes. *Journal of Product Innovation Management*, **11**, 3–14.

Corfield, K.G. (1979). *Product Design.* London: National Economic Development Office.

Craig, A. & Hart, S. (1992). Where to now in new product development research. *European Journal of Marketing*, **26**, 1–49.

Crawford, C.M. (1994). *New Product Management.* Reading, MA: Addison-Wesley.

Cross, N. (1993). Science and design methodology: a review. *Research in Engineering Design*, **5**, 63–9.

Davies, H. & Hom, H. (1993). The impact of competitive structure and technological environment on design management: a case study of the UK touring caravan industry. *Design Studies*, **14**, 365–78.

Davis, R.E. (1993). From experience: the role of market research in the development of new consumer products. *Journal of Product Innovation Management*, **10**, 309–17.

Davis, R.E. (1996). Market analysis and segmentation issues for new consumer products. In M.D.J. Rosenau, A. Griffin, G. Castellion & N. Anschuetz (eds), *The PDMA Handbook of New Product Development* (pp. 35–49). New York: John Wiley & Sons, Inc.

Davis, S. & Lawrence, P.R. (1977). *Matrix*. Reading, MA: Addison-Wesley.

de Brentani, U. (1989). Success and failure in new industrial services. *Journal of Product Innovation Management*, **6**, 239–58.

de Brentani, U. (1996). Success factors in developing new business services. In S. Hart (ed.), *New Product Development: A Reader* (pp. 401–27). London: The Dryden Press.

de Brentani, U. & Kleinschmidt, E. (1999). Achieving new product success in highly innovative versus incremental new industrial services. Paper presented at the 28th European Marketing Association Conference, Humboldt University, Berlin.

de Meyer, A. & Mizushima, A. (1989). Global R&D management, *R&D Management*, **19**, 135ff.

de Pree, M. (2001). Creative leadership. *Leader to Leader*, spring.

Dermody, J. & Hammer-Lloyd, S. (1995). Developing environmentally responsible new products: the challenge for the 1990s. In M. Bruce & W.G. Biemans (eds), *Product Development: Meeting the Challenge of the Design–Marketing Interface*. Chichester, UK: John Wiley & Sons Ltd.

Design Council (1998) *Design in Britain 1998–9: Facts, Figures and Quotable Quotes*. London: Design Council.

Design Council (2002). *Facts and Figures on Design in Britain 2002–3*. London: Design Council.

Dixon, J.R. & Duffey, M.R. (1990). The neglect of engineering design. *California Management Review*, **32**, 9–22.

Dixon, P. (2005). *Building a Better Business*. London: Profile Business

Dollinger, M.J. (1998). *Entrepreneurship Strategy and Resources*. Hemel Hempstead: Prentice-Hall.

Donnellan, E. (1995). Changing perspectives on research methodology in marketing. *Irish Marketing Review*, **8**, 81–90.

Dorfman, M.S. (2004). *Introduction to Risk Management and Insurance*, 8th edition. Hemel Hempstead: Prentice-Hall.

Dormer, P. (1993). *Design since 1945*. London: Thames and Hudson.

Dougherty, D. & Bowman, E. (1995). The effects of organizational downsizing on product innovation. *California Management Review*, **37**, 28–44.

Driscoll, M. (2003). Whirlpool: innovation and organizational learning, March; http://www.clomedia.com/content/templates/clo_inpractice.asp?articleid=135&zoneid=88.

Dumas, A. (1994). Building totems: metaphor-making in product development. *Design Management Journal*, 71–82.

Dumas, A. & Mintzberg, H. (1991). Managing the form, function, and fit of design. *Design Management Journal*, **2**, 26–31.

Earle, V.N. (1973). Once upon a matrix: a hindsight on participation. *Optimum*, **4**(2), 28–36.

Ehrlich, P.R. & Ehrlich, A. (1990). *The Population Explosion*. New York: Simon and Schuster.

Elkington, J. & Burke, T. (1989). *The Green Capitalists*. London: Gollancz.

Espey, J. (1991). When global markets get tough. *Chief Executive*, 48ff.

Evamy, M. (1994). The train that lost its way. *Design*, 16–19.

Fairhead, J. (1988). *Design for Corporate Culture: How to Build a Design and Innovation Culture*. National Economic Development Office.

Fairtlough, G. (1994). *Creative Compartments: A Design for Future Organizations*. London: Adamantine Press.

Faust, W. (1993). Cross-functional teams in design: a case study of the Thermos thermal electric grill. *Design Management Journal*, 28–33.

France, G., Kohen, S. & Mahieddine, Y. (2001). *Pulling Together: Making Alliances Work*. New York: Ernst & Young.

Frances, H. (2003). No risk, no innovation: does innovation happen because of HR's systems or in spite of them? *Canadian HR Reporter*, **16**, 26.

Franke, N. & von Hippel, E. (2003). Finding commercially attractive user innovations: an exploration and test of the lead user theory. Center for eBusiness @ MIT, paper 183.

Friedman, T.L. (2000). *The Lexus and the Olive Tree*. New York: Anchor Books/Doubleday.

Fujimoto, T. (1991). Product integrity and the role of designer-as-integrator. *Design Management Journal*, 29–34.

Fujimoto, T., Iansiti, M. & Clark, K.B. (1991). *External Integration in Product Development*. Boston, MA: Harvard Business School Press.

Gaddis, P.O. (1959). The project manager. *Harvard Business Review*, 89–97.

Gadrey, J.F., Gallouj, S.L. & Weinstein, O. (1994). Innovation et R-D dans les services: des modalites originales, qui peuvent enrichir les conceptions industrielles. *Management of Services: A Multidisciplinary Approach*.

Gardner, H. (2007). The five minds of the future. *Rotman Magazine*, winter.

Gause, D.C. & Weinberg, G.M. (1989). *Exploring Requirements: Quality before Design*. New York: Dorset House.

Goel, V. & Pirolli, P. (1992). The structure of design problem spaces, *Cognitive Science*, **16**, 395–429.

Goffee, R. (1996). What holds the modern company together? *Harvard Business Review*, 133–48.

Goffee, R. & Jones, G. (1998). *The Character of a Corporation. How Your Company's Culture Can Make or Break Your Business*. New York: HarperCollins.

Goffee, R. & Jones, G. (2000). Why should anyone be led by you? *Harvard Business Review*, 62–70.

Goffee, R. & Jones, G. (2006). *Why Should Anyone Be Led By You?* Boston, MA: Harvard Business School Press.

Gorb, P. & Dumas, A. (1987). Silent design. *Design Studies*, **8**, 150–6.

Government Office (2006). *Innovation and risk management – a recipe for performance*. National School of Government (Cabinet Office), Crown Copyright, April.

Grant, J. (2000). Goodbye, pork-pie hat. *Financial Times Weekend Magazine*, 38–41.

Grant, R.M. (1991). *Contemporary Strategy Analysis: Concepts, Techniques, Applications*. Cambridge, MA: Basil Blackwell.

Gray, R. (2001). Modifying NPD for a shrinking world. *Marketing*, 39–40.

Green, A., Karan, S. & Rasmussen, B. (2004). Factors indicating first-mover advantages and second-mover advantages. Bachelor Dissertation, Kristianstad University College.

Greiner, L.E. & Schein, V.E. (1981). The paradox of managing a project-oriented matrix: establishing coherence within chaos. *Sloan Management Review*, **22**(2), 17–22.

Griffin, A. & Hauser, J.R. (1996). Integrating R&D and marketing: a review and analysis of the literature. *Journal of Product Innovation Management*, **13**, 191–215.

Gurteen, D. (1998). Knowledge, creativity and innovation. *Journal of Knowledge Management*, **2**, 5–13.

Haigh, D. (1996). *A Review of Current Practice in Brand Valuation*. London: Institute of Practitioners in Advertising.

Hales, C. (1986). *Analysis of the Engineering Design Process in an Industrial Context*. Cambridge: University of Cambridge Press.

Hall, D. (2001). *Jump Start Your Business Brain – Win More, Lose Less and Make Money*. Cincinnati, OH: Brain Brew Books.

Hargadon, A. & Sutton, R.I. (2000). Building an innovation factory. *Harvard Business Review*, **78**, 157–66.

Hart, S.J. & Service, L.M. (1988). The effects of managerial attitudes to design on company performance. *Journal of Marketing Management*, **4**, 217–29.

Hart, S.J., Service, L.M. & Baker, M.J. (1989). Design orientation and market success. *Design Studies*, **10**, 103–11.

Hatch, M.J. (1993). The dynamics of organizational culture. *Academy of Management Review*, **18**, 657.

Hatch, M.J. (1997). *Organization Theory, Modern Symbolic and Postmodern Perspectives*. Oxford: Oxford University Press.

Hay, M. & Williamson, P. (1991). Strategic staircase: planning the capabilities required for success. *Long Range Planning*, **24**, 36.

Hay, M. & Williamson, P. (1997). Good strategy: the view from below. *Long Range Planning*, **30**, 651–64.

Heany, D.F. (1983). Degrees of product innovation. *Journal of Business Strategy*, 3–14.

Heiss, B. & Fraser, E. (2000). Is your company ready to go global? *Communication World*, **17**, 29–32.

Hem, L., de Chernatony, L. & Iversen, N.M. (2001). Factors influencing successful brand extension. Unpublished paper can be viewed on www.interbrand.com.

Henke, J.W., Krachenberg, A.R. & Lyons, T.F. (1993). Cross-functional teams: good concept, poor implementation! *Journal of Product Innovation Management*, **10**, 216–29.

Henry, J. (1991). Making sense of creativity. In J.V. Henry (ed.), *Creative Management*, volume 1 (pp. 3–11). London: Sage

Higgins, J.M. (1996). A plan for innovation. *R&D Innovator*, **5**.

Hipple, J., Harde, D., Wilson, S.A. & Michalski, J. (2001). Can corporate innovation champions survive? *Chemical Innovation*, 14–22.

Hodgson, C.A. (1999). Create an experts database. *EContent*, October/November.

Hofstede, G. (1980). *Culture's Consequences: International Differences in Work Related Values*. New York: Sage.

Hofstede, G. (1991). *Cultures and Organizations: The Software of the Mind*. New York: McGraw-Hill.

Hollins, G. & Hollins, B. (1991). *Total Design: Managing the Design Process in the Service Sector*. London: Pitman.

Holt, K. (1987). *Innovation: a Challenge to the Engineer*, 2nd edition. Amsterdam: Elsevier.

Hultink, E.J. & Robben, H.S.J. (1996). Measuring product development success and failure. In M.D.J. Rosenau, A. Griffin, G. Castellion & N. Anschuetz (eds), *The PDMA Handbook of New Product Development*, volume 1 (pp. 455–61). New York: John Wiley & Sons, Inc.

Idenburg, P.J. (1993). Four styles of strategy development. *Long Range Planning*, **26**, 123.

Johne, A. & Storey, C. (1998). New service development: a review of the literature and annotated bibliography. *European Journal of Marketing*, **32**, 184–251.

Johne, F.A. & Harborne, P. (1985). How large commercial banks manage product innovation. *International Journal of Bank Marketing*, **3**, 54–70.

Jones, T. (1997). *New Product Development, an Introduction to a Multifunctional Process*. Oxford: Butterworth Heinemann.

Judge, P. (2001). In my opinion. *Management Today*, **8**, 14.

Justice, L. (2001). Predicting the success of your web site. *Design Management Journal*, 63–9.

Kalmbach Jr, C. & Roussel, C. (1999). Dispelling the myths of alliances. *Outlook Special Edition*, October.

Kapferer, J.-N. (1997). *Strategic Brand Management*. London: Kogan Page.

Kaplan, R.S. & Norton, D.P. (1992). The balanced scorecard: measures that drive performance. *Harvard Business Review*, **70**, 71–9.

Kaplan, S.M. (1999). Discontinuous innovation and the growth paradox. *Strategy & Leadership*, **27**, 16–21.

Karger, D. (1960). *The New Product*. New York: The Industrial Press.

Kassicieh, S.K., Walsh, S.T., Cummings, J.C., McWhorter, P.J., Romig, A.D. & Williams, W.D. (2002). Factors differentiating the commercialization of disruptive and sustaining technologies. *IEEE Transactions on Engineering Management*, **494**, 375–87.

Katzenbach, J.R. & Smith, D.K. (1993). *The Wisdom of Teams*. Boston, MA: Harvard Business School Press.

Kelley, T. (2001). Prototyping is the shorthand of innovation. *Design Management Journal*, 35–42.

Kemp, R. (1993). *The European High Speed Rail Network*. Manchester: GEC Alsthom Transport.

Kendall, J.E. & Kendall, K.E. (1994). Metaphors and their meaning for information systems development. *European Journal of Information Systems*, **3**, 37–47.

Kennedy, M. (2001). Building a service innovation engine. *Telecommunications Americas*, **35**, 24.

Khurana, A. & Rosenthal, S.R. (1997). Integrating the fuzzy front end of new product development. *Sloan Management Review*, 103–20.

Khurana. A. (2006). Strategies for global R&D. *Research Technology Management*, **49**, 48–57.

Kim, C.W. & Mauborgne, R. (2000). Knowing a winning business idea when you see one. *Harvard Business Review*, Sept–Oct, 129–37.

Kingdon, D.R. (1973). *Matrix Organizations*. London: Tavistock.

Kirton, M.J. (1980). The way people approach problems. *Planned Innovation*, **3**, 51–4.

Klein, N. (2001). *No Logo*. London: Flamingo.

Kleinschmidt, E.J. & Cooper, R.G. (1988). The performance impact of an international orientation on product innovation. *European Journal of Marketing*, **22**, 56ff.

Knight, F.H. (1921). Risk, uncertainty and profit. Dissertation.

Kolodny, H.F. (1979). Evolution of an organisation. *Academy of Management Review*, **4**(4), 543–53.

Kolodny, H.F. (1980). Matrix organization designs and new product success. *Research Management*, **23**, 29–33.

Kotler, P. & Rath, A. (1984). Design: a powerful but neglected strategic tool. *Journal of Business Strategy*, **5**, 16–21.

Kotter, J.P. & Cohen, D.S. (2002). *The Heart of Change: Real-Life Stories of How People Change their Organizations*. Boston, MA: Harvard Business School Press.

Kroeber, A.L. & Kluckhohn, F. (1952). Culture: a critical review of concepts and definitions. *Peabody Museum Papers*, **47**, 181.

Kuczmarski & Associates Inc (1995). *Winning New Products and Services for the 1990s*. Chicago: Kuczmarski & Associates Inc.

Kuczmarski, T.D. (1988). *Managing New Products*. Hemel Hempstead: Prentice-Hall.

Kuczmarski, T.D. (1998). Tools@work: the CEO innovation mindset test. *Journal for Quality and Participation*, **21**, 48–9.

Kuczmarski, T.D. (2000). Measuring your return on innovation. *Marketing Management*, **9**, 24.

Kuczmarski, T.D. (2001). Five fatal flaws of innovation metrics. *Marketing Management*, **10**, 34–9.

Lamming, R. (1993). *Beyond Partnership: Strategies for Innovation and Lean Supply*. Hemel Hempstead: Prentice Hall.

Lane Keller, K., Sternthal, B. & Tybout, A. (2002). Three questions you need to ask about your brand. *Harvard Business Review*, 3–8.

Leifer, R., McDermott, C.M., Colarelli O'Conner, G., Peters, L.S., Rice, M. & Veryzer, R.W. (2000). *Radical Innovation – How Mature Companies Can Outsmart Upstarts*. Boston, MA: Harvard Business School Press.

Leonard, D. & Rayport, J.F. (1997). Spark innovation through empathic design. *Harvard Business Review*, **75**, 102–8.

Leonard-Barton, D. (1991). Inanimate integrators: a block of wood speaks. *Design Management Journal*, 61–7.

Leonard-Barton, D. (1992). Core capabilities and core rigidities: a paradox in managing new product development. *Strategic Management Journal*, **13**, 111–25.

Lewis, H., Gertsakis, J., Grant, T., Morelli, N. & Sweatman, A. (2001). *Design + Environment – A Global Guide to Designing Greener Goods*. Sheffield, UK: Greenleaf.

Liebermann, M.B. & Montgomery, D.B. (1998). First mover (dis-)advantages: retrospective and link with the resource-based view. *Strategic Management Journal*, **19**, 1111–25.

Linton, J.D. & Walsh, S.T. (2002). Forecasting the market diffusion of disruptive and discontinuous innovation. *IEEE Transactions on Engineering Management*, **494**, 365–74.

Littler, D., Leverick, F. & Bruce, M. (1995). Factors affecting the process of collaborative product development: a study of UK manufacturers of information and communications technology products. *Journal of Product Innovation Management*, **12**.

Lockwood, T. (2000). Designing automobiles for global value: ten market trends. *Design Management Journal*, **12**(4).

Lord, M.D., Mandel, S.W. & Wager, J.D. (2002). Spinning out a star. *Harvard Business Review*, Jan, 5–11.

Lorenz, C. (1990). *The Design Dimension*. Oxford: Basil Blackwell.

Lovins, A.B., Lovins, L.T. & Hawken, P. (2001). A road map for natural capitalism. In J. Henry (ed.), *Creative Management*, volume 2. London: Sage.

Machlis, S. (1996). Rapid prototyping weeds out bad designs early. *Design News*, 70–4.

Mackenzie, D. (1997). *Green Design: Design for the Environment*. London: Laurence King.

MacKenzie, G. (1996). *Orbiting the Giant Hairball*. New York: OpusPocus Publishing.

Mahajan, V. & Wind, J. (1992). New product models: practice, shortcomings and desired improvements. *Journal of Product Innovation Management*, **9**, 128–39.

Mainemelis, C. (2001). When the muse takes it all: a model for the experience of timelessness in organizations. *Academy of Management Review*, **26**, 548–65.

Majchrzak, A. & Wang, O. (1996). Breaking the functional mind-set in process organizations. *Harvard Business Review*, **74**, 93–9.

March, J.G. (1991). Exploration and exploitation in organisational learning. *Organisational Science*, **2**, 71–87.

Markides, C. (1999). *All the Right Moves*. Boston, MA: Harvard Business School Press.

Markides, C. & Geroski, P. (2004). *Fast Second: How Smart Companies Bypass Radical Innovation to Enter and Dominate New Markets*. San Francisco, CA: Jossey Bass.

Martin, C.R.J. & Horne, D.A. (1995). Level of success inputs for service innovations in the same firm. *International Journal of Service Industry Management*, **6**.

Martin, J. (1995). Ignore your customers. *Fortune*, 83–9.

Martin, R. & Moldeveanu, M. (2007). Designing the thinker of the future. *Rotman Magazine*, winter.

Matathia, I. & Salzman, M. (1999). *Next? A Vision of Our Lives in the Future*. London: HarperCollins.

Maylor, H. (1996). *Project Management*. London: Pitman.

McDougall, P. (2004). There's no stopping the offshore-outsourcing train. *Information Week*, **990**, 18.

McGrath, M.E. (1996). *Setting the PACE in Product Development*. Newton, MA: Butterworth-Heinemann.

McWilliam, G. & Dumas, A. (1995). Using metaphors in new brand design. Working Paper, London Business School.

Meltmuka, K. (2004). Innovation democracy. *Computerworld*, 16 February.

Mintzberg, H. (1990). The design school: reconsidering the basic premises of strategic management. *Strategic Management Journal*, **11**, 171–95.

Monge, P. & Fulk, J. (1999). Communication technology for global network organizations. In G. DeSanctis & J. Fulk (eds), *Shaping Organization Form: Communication, Connection, and Community* (pp. 71–100). London: Sage.

Morley, I.E. & S. Pugh (1987). The organization of design: an interdisciplinary approach to the study of people, process and contexts. Paper presented at the International Conference on Engineering Design 17–20 August.

Morris, P.W.G. (1994). *The Management of Projects*. London: Thomas Telford.

Moss Kanter, R. (1985). *The Change Masters*. New York: Touchstone Books.

Moss Kanter, R. (1989). *When Giants Learn to Dance*. New York: Simon & Schuster.

Nadler, G. (1991). Design teams: breakthrough for effectiveness. *Design Management Journal*, 10–19.

Nahapiet, J., Lynda, G. & O'Rocha, H. (2005). Knowledge and relationships: when cooperation is the norm. *European Management Review*, **2**, 3–14.

Naslund, B. (1986). Financial innovations. A comparison with R&D in physical products. EFI Research Paper/Report, Stockholm.

Nonaka, I. (1991). The knowledge-creating company. *Harvard Business Review*, **69**, 96–1044.

Norman, D.A. (1988). *The Psychology of Everyday Things*. New York: Basic Books.

Oakley, M. (1984). *Managing Product Design*. London: Weidenfeld and Nicolson.

Oakley, M. (1990a). Assembling and managing a design team. In M. Oakley (ed.), *Design Management, a Handbook of Issues and Methods*. Oxford: Blackwell.

Oakley, M. (1990b). Policies, objectives and standards. In M. Oakley (ed.), *Design Management, a Handbook of Issues and Methods*. Oxford: Blackwell.

Ogawa, S. & Piller, F.T. (2006). Reducing the risk of new product development. *Sloan Management Review*, **47**, 2.

Ohno, T. (1988). *Toyota Production System: Beyond Large-Scale Production*. Portland: Productivity Press.

Olson, E.M., Cooper, R. & Slater, S.F. (1998). Design strategy and competitive advantage. *Business Horizons*, **41**, 55–61.

Olson, E., Slater, S. & Cooper, R. (2000). Managing design for competitive advantage: a process approach. *Design Management Journal*, **11**, 10–17.

Olson, E.M., Walker, O.C. & Ruekert, R.W. (1995). Organizing for effective new product development: the moderating role of product innovativeness. *Journal of Marketing*, **59**, 48–62.

Owen, I. (1990). Industry and design. In P. Gorb. *Design Management*. London: Architectural Design and Technology Press.

Papanek, V. (1991). *Design for the Real World*. London: Thames & Hudson.

Patterson, F. & Silvester, J. (1998). Counter measures. *People Management*, **4**, 46–8.

Pavitt, J.E. (2000). *brand.new*. London: V&A Publishing.

Perry, T.S. (1995). Designing a culture for creativity. *Research Technology Management*, 14–16.

Peters, T. & Waterman, R.H. (1982). *In Search of Excellence*. New York: Harper & Row.

Peters, T. (1995). Design is . . . . *Design Management Journal*, 29–33.

Petroski, H. (1997). Designed to fail. *American Scientist*, **85**, 412–16.

Phillips, W.E. & Nokes, H. (2003). Discontinuous innovation. Literature review for the DIF Project.

Pilditch, J. (1987). What makes a winning company? In D. Walker & J. Henry (eds), *Managing Innovation*. London: Sage.

Pilditch, J. (1989). *Winning Ways*. London: Mercury Business Books.

Plant, R. (2000). *E-Commerce: Formulation of Strategy*. London: Financial Times/Prentice Hall.

Pletz, J. (2004). Dell changed industry with direct sales. *American Statesman*, 3 May.

Plsek, P.E. (1996). The creativity process. From http://www.directedcreativity.com/pages/WPModels.html.

Polanyi, M. (1983). *The Tacit Dimension*. Gloucester, MA: Peter Smith.

Pomeroy, A. (2004). Cooking up innovation: when it comes to helping employees create new products and services, HR's efforts are a key ingredient. *HR Magazine*, November.

Porter, M.E. (1980). *Competitive Strategy: Techniques for Analyzing Industries and Competitors*. New York: Free Press.

Prather, C.W. & Gundry, L.K. (1995). *Blueprints for Innovation*. New York: American Management Association.

Prather, C.W. & Turrell, M.C. (2002). Involve everyone in the innovation process. *Research Technology Management*, 13–16.

Pringle, H. & Thompson, M. (1999). *Brand Spirit: How Cause Related Marketing Builds Brands*. Chichester, UK: John Wiley & Sons, Ltd.

Prokesch, S.E. (1997). Unleashing the power of learning: an interview with British Petroleum's John Browne. *Harvard Business Review*, **75**, 146–68.

Purcell, J. Raising finance. *Innovation Business*, Issue 28 of a publication by the NatWest & The Royal Scottish Bank.

Quinn, J.B. (1980). *Strategies for Change, Logical Incrementalism*. Richard D. Irwin.

Quintas, P., Lefrere, P. & Jones, G. (1997). Knowledge management: a strategic agenda. *Long Range Planning*, **30**, 385–91.

Reingold, J. (2005). What P&G knows about the power of design. Fast Company, Issue 95, 56.

Reingold, J. (2005b). The interpreter. *Fast Company*, June, Issue 95, 58.

Repenning, N.P. (2002). A simulation-based approach to understanding the dynamics of innovation implementation. *Organization Science*, **13**, 109–27.

Rettig, M. (1994). Prototyping for tiny fingers. *Communications of the ACM*, **37**, 21–7.

Robinson, A.G. & Stern, S. (1997). *Corporate Creativity – How Innovation and Improvement Actually Happen*. San Francisco, CA: Berrett-Koehler.

Rock, A. (1992). Strategies versus tactics from a venture capitalist. In W.A. Schulman & H.P. Stevenson (eds), *The Entrepreneurial Venture* (pp. 215–21). Boston, MA: Harvard Business School Press.

Roellig, L. (2001). Designing global brands: critical lessons. *Design Management Journal*, **12**, 40–5.

Ross Ashby, W. (1964). *An Introduction to Cybernetics*. London: Chapman & Hall.

Rothaermel, F.T. (2002). *Technological discontinuities and interfirm cooperation: what determines a startup's attractiveness as alliance partner? IEEE Transactions on Engineering Management*, 494.

Rothwell, R. (1992). Successful industrial innovation: critical factors for the 1990s. *R&D Management*, **22**, 221–39.

Rowen, T.D., Howell, C.D. & Gugliotti, J.A. (1981). The pros and cons of matrix management. *Administrative Management*, **41**(12), 22–4, 50–9.

Roy, R. & Potter, S. (1990). *Design and the Economy*. London: Design Council.

Rugman, A. & Hodgetts, R. (2001). The end of global strategy. *European Management Journal*, **19**, 333–4.

Rugman, A. (2000). *The End of Globalization*. London: Random House.

Rumizen, M.C. (1998). Report on the Second Comparative Study of Knowledge Creation Conference. *Journal of Knowledge Management*, **2**, 77–81.

Sanchez, R. & Sudharshan, D. (1993). Real-time market research. *Marketing Intelligence & Planning*, **11**, 29–38.

Sayles, L.R. (1976). Matrix management, the structure with a future. *Organisational Dynamics*, **5**(2), 2–17.

Scharmer, O. (2007). *Theory U: Leading from the Future as it Emerges*. SoL, the Society for Organizational Learning.

Schein, E.H. (1992). *Organisational Culture and Leadership*. San Francisco, CA: Jossey-Bass.

Schrage, M. (1993). The culture(s) of prototyping. *Design Management Journal*, 55–65.

Schrage, M. (2000). *Serious Play – How the World's Best Companies Simulate to Innovate*. Boston, MA: Harvard Business School Press.

Schumpeter, J.A. (1976). *Capitalism, Socialism, and Democracy*, 5th edition. London: Routledge.

Seltzer, K. & Bentley, T. (1999). *The Creative Age*. London: Demos.

Sentance, A. & Clark, J. (1997). *The Contribution of Design to the UK Economy*. London: The Design Council.

Simon, H.A. (1992). *Sciences of the Artificial*. Cambridge, MA: MIT Press.

Sisodia, R. (1992). Competitive advantage through design. *Journal of Business Strategy*, **13**, 33–40.

Slevin, D.P. & Covin, J.G. (1997). Strategy formation patterns, performance, and the significance of context. *Journal of Management*, **23**, 189–209.

Sloan, A.P. (1963). *My Years with General Motors*. London: Sedgwick and Jackson.

Slusher, A.E. & Ebert, R.J. (1992). Prototyping for managing engineering design processes. In A.E. Susman (ed.), *Integrating design and manufacturing for competitive advantage* (pp. 123–39). New York: Oxford University Press.

Smith, M. (2001). Sorry, that's too interesting for us. *Financial Times*, 15.

Smith, P.G. & Reinertsen, D.G. (1995). *Developing Products in Half the Time*. New York: Van Nostrand Reinhold.

Snead, G.L. & Wycoff, J. (1997). *To Do, Doing, Done! A Creative Approach to Managing Projects and Effectively Finishing What Matters Most*. New York: Simon & Schuster.

Snyder, N. & Duarte, D.L. (2004). *Strategic Innovation*. Chichester, UK: John Wiley & Sons, Ltd.

Sowrey, T. (1987). *The Generation of Ideas for New Products*. London: Kogan Page.

Sparrow, S. (1987). Design: in-house or agency. *Industrial Marketing Digest*, **12**, 35–9.

Storey, C. & Kelly, D. (2001). Measuring the performance of new service development activities. *The Service Industries Journal*.

Sundbo, J. (1997). Management of innovation in services. *The Service Industries Journal*, **17**, 432–55.

Takeuchi, H. & Nonaka, I. (1986). The new product development game. *Harvard Business Review*, 137–46.

Temple, P. & von Stamm, B. (1996). *Design and ISO 9000*. Report to the British Design Council.

Terrill, C.A. & Middlebrooks, A.G. (1996). Service development. In M.D.J. Rosenau, A. Griffin, G. Castellion & N. Anschuetz (eds), *The PDMA Handbook of New Product Development*, volume 1 (pp. 313–31). New York: John Wiley & Sons, Inc.

Tether, C.S. (2002). Who co-operates for innovation, and why – an empirical analysis. *Research Policy*, **31**, 947–67.

Thackara, J. (1997). *European Design Prize Winners! How Today's Successful Companies Innovate by Design*. Aldershot, UK: Gower.

Thomond, P., Herzgergh, T. & Lettice, F. (2003). Disruptive innovation: removing the innovator's dilemma. Paper published in British Academy of Management 2003 Conference Proceedings.

Tidd, J. (1993). Technological innovation, organizational linkages and strategic degrees of freedom. *Technology Analysis & Strategic Management*, **5**, 273–83.

Tidd, J., Bessant, J. & Pavitt, K. (2001). *Managing Innovation; Integrating Technological, Market and Organisational Change.* Chichester, UK: John Wiley & Sons, Ltd.

Titteron, D. (2001). Spotlight on workplace atmosphere. Sunday Times Enterprise Network (STEN) website (www.sunday-times.co.uk/enterprisenetwork).

Tripsas, M. & Gavetti, G. (2000). Capabilities, cognition and inertia: evidence from digital imaging. *Strategic Management Journal*, **21**, 1147–61.

Tripsas, M. (1997). Unravelling the process of creative destruction: complementary assets and incumbent survival in the typesetter industry. *Strategic Management Journal*, **18**, 119–42.

Turner, R. (2000). Design and business: who calls the shots? *Design Management Journal*, 42–7.

Turrell, M. (2004). Idea management – an introduction. www.imaginatik.com/research.

Tushman, M.L. & Anderson, P. (1986). Technological discontinuities and organisational environments. *Administrative Science Quarterly*, **31**, 439–65.

Tushman, M.L. & O'Reilly, C.A. III (1997). *Winning through Innovation.* Boston, MA: Harvard Business School Press.

Tushman M.L. & O'Reilly, C.A. III (2004). The ambidextrous organization. *Harvard Business Review*, April.

Ulijn, J.O.D., Weggeman, M., Ledlow, G. & Hall, H.T. (2000). Innovation, corporate strategy, and cultural context: what is the mission for international business communication? *Journal of Business Communication*, **37**, 293–316.

Ulrich, K.T. & Eppinger, S.D. (1995). *Product Design and Development.* Singapore: McGraw-Hill.

Ulrich, P. & Fluri, E. (1988). *Management.* Bern: Verlag Paul Haupt.

Upshaw, L.B. & Taylor, E. (2000). *The Masterbrand Mandate.* Chichester, UK: John Wiley & Sons Ltd.

Upshaw, L.B. (2001). Building a brand.com. *Design Management Journal*, 34–9.

Urban, G.L. & Hauser, J.R. (1993). *Design and Marketing of New Products.* USA: Prentice-Hall.

Utterback, J.M. (1994). *Mastering the Dynamics of Innovation: How Companies can Seize Opportunities in the Face of Technological Change.* Boston, MA: Harvard Business School Press.

Vasconcellos, E. (1979). A model for a better understanding of the matrix structure. *IEEE Transactions on Engineering Management*, **25**(3), 56–64.

Veryzer, R.W. (1998). Discontinuous innovation and the new product development process. *Journal of Product Innovation Management*, **15**, 304–21.

Vishwanath, V. & Mark, J. (1997). Your brand's best strategy. *Harvard Business Review*, 123–9.

von Hippel, E. (1994). *The Sources of Innovation*. New York: Oxford University Press.

von Hippel, E. (2005). *Democratising Innovation*. Boston, MA: MIT Press.

von Stamm, B. (1997). Whose design is it? The use of external designers. *Design Journal*, **1**, 41–53.

von Stamm, B. (1999a). The effects of context and complexity in new product development. Doctoral thesis, London Business School.

von Stamm, B. (1999b). Creativity is an individual act. Interview with John Hunt: conducted for the Innovation Exchange, London Business School.

von Stamm, B. (1999c). Interview with Jon Leach: conducted for the Innovation Exchange, London Business School.

von Stamm, B. (1999d). Interview with Ralph Buschow: conducted for the Innovation Exchange, London Business School.

von Stamm, B. (2001). *Innovation Best Practice and Future Challenges: A Study into Innovation Best Practice in Innovation Exchange Member Companies and the Literature*. London: Innovation Exchange, London Business School.

von Stamm, B. (2002). *Innovation in Turbulent Times*. London: Innovation Exchange, London Business School.

von Stamm, B. (2003). *Second Innovation Best Practice and Future Challenges: A Study into Innovation Best Practice in Innovation Exchange Member Companies and the Literature*. London: Innovation Exchange, London Business School.

von Stamm, B. (2006). *Third Innovation Best Practice and Future Challenges: A Study into Innovation Best Practice in Innovation Exchange Member Companies and the Literature*. London: Innovation Exchange, London Business School.

von Stamm, B. & Riley, D. (2002). Innovation in turbulent times. Unpublished Report to Members of the Innovation Exchange.

Voss, C., Johnston, R.J., Silvestro, R., Fitzgerald, L. & Brignall, T. (1992). Measurement of innovation and design performance in services. *Design Management Journal*, 40–6.

Walker, D. (1989). *Managing Design: Overview: Issues*. Milton Keynes: Open University Press.

Walker, D. (1990). Managers and designers: two tribes at war? In M. Oakley (ed.), *Design Management: A Handbook of Issues and Methods*. Oxford: Blackwell.

Wallas, G. (1926). *The Art of Thought*. New York: Harcourt Brace Jovanovich.

Walsh, S. & Kirchhoff, B. (2002). Disruptive technologies: innovators' problems and entrepreneurs' opportunity. *IEEE Transactions on Engineering Management*, **494**, 365–8.

Walsh, V., Roy, R., Bruce, M. & Potter, S. (1992). *Winning by Design, Technology, Product Design and International Competitiveness*. Oxford: Blackwell.

Walsham, G. (1991). Organizational metaphors and information system research. *European Journal of Information Systems*, **1**, 83–94.

Warner, F. (2001). Recipe for growth. *Fast Company*, Issue 51, October.

Weick, K.E. (1979). *The Social Psychology of Organizing*. Reading, MA: Adison-Wesley.

Weisburg, R.W. (1986). *Creativity, Genius and Other Myths*. New York: Freeman.

Wheatley, M. (1999). *Leadership and the New Science: Discovering Order in a Chaotic World*. San Francisco, CA: Berrett-Koehler.

Wheelwright, S.C. & Clark, K.B. (1992) *Revolutionizing Product Development: Quantum Leaps in Speed, Efficiency and Quality*. New York: Free Press.

Wheelwright, S.C. & Clark, K.B. (1995). *Leading Product Development: The Senior Manager's Guide to Creating and Shaping the Enterprise*. New York: Free Press.

Willcocks, L.P. & Plant, R. (1999). E-branding: leadership strategies. *Mastering Management Review*, 34–7.

Williams, G. (2000). *Branded? Products and their Personalities*. London: V&A Publications.

Williamson, M. (1994). Becoming a world power. *CIO*, **7**, 40ff.

Wood, B.D. (2000). The globalization question. (Delegation of the European Commission) *Europe*, 12–14.

Wright, I. (1998). *Design Methods in Engineering and Product Design*. London: McGraw-Hill.

Wylie, I. (2001). Failure is Glorious. *Fast Company*, Issue 51, 35.

Zien, K.A. & Buckler, S.A. (1997). From experience: dreams to market: crafting a culture of innovation. *Journal of Product Innovation Management*, **14**, 274–87.

Zuckerman, A. (2001). Managing global logistics operations, *Transportation & Distribution*, **42**, GL4–GL9.

Index

CPSIA information can be obtained at www.ICGtesting.com
Printed in the USA
BVOW07s0001210515

401265BV00004B/30/P